T0235672

Jaap van den Herik · Ana Paula Rocha ·
Luc Steels (Eds.)

Agents and Artificial Intelligence

11th International Conference, ICAART 2019
Prague, Czech Republic, February 19–21, 2019
Revised Selected Papers

 Springer

Editors
Jaap van den Herik
Leiden University
Leiden, The Netherlands

Ana Paula Rocha
LIACC, University of Porto
Porto, Portugal

Luc Steels
ICREA, Institute of Evolutionary Biology
Barcelona, Spain

ISSN 0302-9743   ISSN 1611-3349   (electronic)
Lecture Notes in Artificial Intelligence
ISBN 978-3-030-37493-8   ISBN 978-3-030-37494-5   (eBook)
https://doi.org/10.1007/978-3-030-37494-5

LNCS Sublibrary: SL7 – Artificial Intelligence

This Springer imprint is published by the registered company Springer Nature Switzerland AG
The registered company address is: Gewerbestrasse 11, 6330 Cham, Switzerland

Preface

The present book includes extended and revised versions of a set of selected papers from the 11th International Conference on Agents and Artificial Intelligence (ICAART 2019), held in Prague, Czech Republic, during February 19–21, 2019.

ICAART 2019 received 202 paper submissions from 43 countries, of which 8,4% were included in this book. The selection procedure was as follows. First, the papers were selected by the event chairs. Their selection was based on a number of criteria that include (1) the classifications and comments provided by the Program Committee members, (2) the session chairs' assessments, and (3) the program chairs' global view of all papers presented in the technical program. Then the authors of the selected papers were invited to submit a revised and extended version of their papers having at least 30% innovative material. Finally, the remaining submissions were thoroughly reviewed, leading to the publication of 17 submissions.

The purpose of the ICAART is to bring together researchers, engineers, and practitioners interested in the theory and applications in the areas of Agents and Artificial Intelligence (AI). Two simultaneous related tracks have been held, covering both applications and current research work. One track focused on Agents, Multi-Agent Systems and Software Platforms, Distributed Problem Solving, and Distributed AI in general. The other track focused mainly on AI, Knowledge Representation, Planning, Learning, Scheduling, Perception, Reactive AI Systems, Evolutionary Computing, and other topics related to Intelligent Systems and Computational Intelligence.

The book opens with a publication on Natural Language Processing (NLP), titled "The Dynamics of Semantic Change." This is then followed by 12 publications on AI. The topics, vast and interesting, range from wide and deep reinforcement learning via Neural Hidden Markov Model to the Social Golfer Problem Revisited. Thereafter, the book includes four publications on Agents, ranging from inspiring the multi-agent cooperation to the application of conversational agents. Here the books shows four interesting topics to the ICAART community.

Finally, we would like to thank all the authors for their contributions and the reviewers who have helped us ensure the quality of this publication.

February 2019

Jaap van den Herik
Ana Paula Rocha
Luc Steels

Organization

Conference Chair

Jaap van den Herik   Leiden University, The Netherlands

Program Co-chairs

Ana Rocha   LIACC - FEUP, Portugal
Luc Steels   ICREA and Institute of Evolutionary Biology
     (UPF-CSIC), Spain

Program Committee

Jose Gonzalez	University of Seville, Spain
Sahar Abbaspour	Volvo Car Group, Sweden
Maysam Abbod	Brunel University, UK
Thomas Ågotnes	University of Bergen, Norway
Shamim Akhter	International University of Business Agriculture and Technology (IUBAT), Bangladesh
Varol Akman	Bilkent University, Turkey
Isabel Alexandre	Instituto Universitário de Lisboa (ISCTE-IUL) and Instituto de Telecomunicações, Portugal
Vicki Allan	Utah State University, USA
Klaus-Dieter Althoff	German Research Center for Artificial Intelligence and University of Hildesheim, Germany
Frédéric Amblard	IRIT - Université Toulouse 1 Capitole, France
Alla Anohina-Naumeca	Riga Technical University, Latvia
Antonio Arauzo-Azofra	Universidad de Córdoba, Spain
Marcelo Armentano	ISISTAN Research Institute (CONICET- UNICEN), Argentina
Jean-Michel Auberlet	IFSTTAR (French Institute of Science and Technology for Transport, Development and Networks), France
Reyhan Aydogan	Ozyegin University, Turkey
Irene Barba Rodriguez	Universidad de Sevilla, Spain
Federico Barber	Universidad Politécnica de Valencia, Spain
Roman Barták	Charles University, Czech Republic
Montserrat Batet	Universitat Rovira i Virgili, Spain
Nabil Belacel	National Research Council of Canada, Canada
Salem Benferhat	CRIL, France
Carole Bernon	University of Toulouse III, France
Daniel Berrar	Tokyo Institute of Technology, Japan
Carlos Bobed	everis - NTT Data and University of Zaragoza, Spain

Rafael Bordini	PUCRS, Brazil
Marco Botta	Università degli Studi di Torino, Italy
Lars Braubach	Universität Hamburg, Germany
Joerg Bremer	University of Oldenburg, Germany
Ramon Brena	Tecnologico De Monterrey, Mexico
Paolo Bresciani	Fondazione Bruno Kessler, Italy
Aleksander Byrski	AGH University of Science and Technology, Poland
Giacomo Cabri	Università di Modena e Reggio Emilia, Italy
Patrice Caire	University of Luxembourg, Luxembourg
Silvia Calegari	Universita' Degli studi di Milano Bicocca, Italy
Valérie Camps	IRIT - Université Paul Sabatier, France
Javier Carbó Rubiera	Universidad Carlos III de Madrid, Spain
John Cartlidge	University of Bristol, UK
Matteo Casadei	Università Di Bologna, Italy
Ana Casali	Universidad Nacional de Rosario (UNR) and CIFASIS, Argentina
Christine Chan	University of Regina, Canada
Wen-Chung Chang	National Taipei University of Technology, Taiwan
François Charpillet	Loria - Inria Lorraine, France
Mu-Song Chen	Da-Yeh University, Taiwan
Rung-Ching Chen	Chao-Yang University of Technology, Taiwan
Marco Chiarandini	University of Southern Denmark, Denmark
Davide Ciucci	Universita' degli Studi di Milano Bicocca, Italy
Flavio Correa da Silva	University of São Paulo, Brazil
Gabriella Cortellessa	ISTC-CNR, Italy
Paulo Cortez	University of Minho, Portugal
Anna Costa	Universidade de São Paulo, Brazil
Fernando da Souza	Universidade Federal de Pernambuco, Brazil
Dipankar Das	Jadavpur University, India
Patrick De Causmaecker	Katholieke Universiteit Leuven, Belgium
Daniele De Martini	University of Oxford, UK
Andreas Dengel	German Research Center for Artificial Intelligence (DFKI GmbH), Germany
Enrico Denti	Università di Bologna, Italy
Sebastien Destercke	CNRS - Université de Technologie de Compiègne, France
Nicola Di Mauro	Università di Bari, Italy
Bruno Di Stefano	Nuptek Systems Ltd., Canada
Dragan Doder	Université Paul Sabatier, France
Michel Dojat	Université Grenoble Alpes, France
Francisco Domínguez Mayo	University of Seville, Spain
Ruggero Donida Labati	Università degli Studi di Milano, Italy
Julie Dugdale	Laboratoire d'Informatique de Grenoble, France
Thomas Eiter	Technische Universität Wien, Austria
El-Sayed El-Alfy	King Fahd University of Petroleum and Minerals, Saudi Arabia

Fabrício Enembreck	Pontifical Catholic University of Paraná, Brazil
Savo Fabio	Università degli Studi di Bergamo, Italy
Xenofon Fafoutis	DTU Compute, Denmark
Christophe Feltus	Luxembourg Institute of Science and Technology, Luxembourg
Edilson Ferneda	Catholic University of Brasília, Brazil
Vladimir Filipovic	Belgrade University, Serbia
Klaus Fischer	German Research Center for Artificial Intelligence DFKI GmbH, Germany
Roberto Flores	Christopher Newport University, USA
Claude Frasson	University of Montreal, Canada
Raquel Fuentetaja	Universidad Carlos III De Madrid, Spain
Katsuhide Fujita	Tokyo University of Agriculture and Technology, Japan
Naoki Fukuta	Shizuoka University, Japan
Salvatore Gaglio	University of Palermo, Italy
Jesus Garcia	Universidad Carlos III, Spain
Leonardo Garrido	Tecnológico de Monterrey, Mexico
Benoit Gaudou	University Toulouse 1 Capitole, France
Andrey Gavrilov	Novosibirsk State Technical University, Russia
Franck Gechter	University of Technology of Belfort-Montbiliard, France
Herman Gomes	Universidade Federal de Campina Grande, Brazil
Jorge Gomez Sanz	Universidad Complutense de Madrid, Spain
Francisco Gómez Vela	Pablo de Olavide University, Spain
Madhu Goyal	University of Technology Sydney, Australia
Emmanuelle Grislin-Le Strugeon	LAMIH, Université de Valenciennes, France
Perry Groot	Radboud University Nijmegen, The Netherlands
Luciano H. Tamargo	Universidad Nacional del Sur, Argentina
James Harland	RMIT University, Australia
William Harrison	Cognition and Collaboration Group in the Intelligent Systems Division of the U. S. National Institute of Standards and Technology, USA
Hisashi Hayashi	Advanced Institute of Industrial Technology, Japan
Emma Hayes	University of the Pacific, USA
Samedi Heng	Université de Liège, Belgium
Pedro Henriques	University of Minho, Portugal
Vincent Hilaire	UTBM, France
Hanno Hildmann	TNO, The Netherlands
Koen Hindriks	Vrije Universiteit Amsterdam, The Netherlands
Rolf Hoffmann	Darmstadt University of Technology, Germany
Sviatlana Höhn	University of Luxembourg, Luxembourg
Wladyslaw Homenda	Warsaw University of Technology, Poland
Wei-Chiang Hong	Jiangsu Normal University, China
Mark Hoogendoorn	Vrije Universiteit Amsterdam, The Netherlands

Ales Horak	Masaryk University, Czech Republic
Marc-Philippe Huget	University of Savoie Mont-Blanc, France
Luke Hunsberger	Vassar College, USA
Dieter Hutter	German Research Centre for Artificial Intelligence, Germany
Carlos Iglesias	Universidad Politécnica de Madrid, Spain
Hiroyuki Iida	JAIST, Japan
Thomas Ioerger	Texas A&M University, USA
Luis Iribarne	University of Almería, Spain
Agnieszka Jastrzebska	Warsaw University of Technology, Poland
Michael Jenkin	York University, Canada
Luis Jiménez Linares	University of de Castilla-La Mancha, Spain
Yasushi Kambayashi	Nippon Institute of Technology, Japan
Norihiro Kamide	Teikyo University, Japan
Geylani Kardas	Ege University International Computer Institute, Turkey
Petros Kefalas	CITY College, International Faculty of the University of Sheffield, Greece
Gabriele Kern-isberner	TU Dortmund University, Germany
Sung-Dong Kim	Hansung University, South Korea
Matthias Klusch	German Research Center for Artificial Intelligence (DFKI GmbH), Germany
Mare Koit	University of Tartu, Estonia
Martin Kollingbaum	University of Aberdeen, UK
Ah-Lian Kor	Leeds Beckett University, UK
John Korah	Illinois Institute of Technology, USA
Jaroslaw Kozlak	AGH University of Science and Technology, Poland
Pavel Kral	University of West Bohemia, Czech Republic
Amruth Kumar	Ramapo College of New Jersey, USA
Yau-Hwang Kuo	National Cheng Kung University, Taiwan
Setsuya Kurahashi	University of Tsukuba, Japan
Cat Kutay	University of Technology Sydney, Australia
Divesh Lala	Kyoto University, Japan
Ramoni Lasisi	Virginia Military Institute, USA
Egons Lavendelis	Riga Technical University, Latvia
Marc Le Goc	Polytech'Marseille, France
Agapito Ledezma	Carlos III University of Madrid, Spain
Ladislav Lenc	University of West Bohemia, Czech Republic
Letizia Leonardi	Università di Modena e Reggio Emilia, Italy
Ho-fung Leung	The Chinese University of Hong Kong, Hong Kong, China
Renato Levy	Intelligent Automation, Inc., USA
Jingpeng Li	University of Stirling, UK
Churn-Jung Liau	Academia Sinica, Taiwan
Francesca Lisi	Università degli Studi di Bari Aldo Moro, Italy
Jonah Lissner	ATINER, USA

Juan Liu	Wuhan University, China
Stephane Loiseau	LERIA, University of Angers, France
António Lopes	ISCTE - Instituto Universitário de Lisboa, Portugal
Henrique Lopes Cardoso	Faculdade de Engenharia da Universidade do Porto, Portugal
Daniela Lopéz De Luise	CIIS Lab, Argentina
Bernd Ludwig	University Regensburg, Germany
Audrone Lupeikiene	VU Institute of Data Science and Digital Technologies, Lithuania
Luis Macedo	University of Coimbra, Portugal
Lorenzo Magnani	University of Pavia, Italy
Lyuba Mancheva	Université Grenoble Alpes, France
Letizia Marchegiani	Aalborg University, Denmark
Jerusa Marchi	Universidade Federal de Santa Catarina, Brazil
Goreti Marreiros	Polytechnic Institute of Porto, Portugal
Mourad Mars	Umm Al-Qura University, Saudi Arabia
Philippe Mathieu	University of Lille, France
Eric Matson	Purdue University, USA
Toshihiro Matsui	Nagoya Institute of Technology, Japan
Fiona McNeill	Heriot-Watt University, UK
Paola Mello	Università di Bologna, Italy
Eduardo Mena	University of Zaragoza, Spain
Benito Mendoza	CUNY - New York City College of Technology, USA
Daniel Merkle	University of Southern Denmark, Denmark
Marjan Mernik	University of Maribor, Slovenia
Elena Messina	National Institute of Standards and Technology, USA
Tamás Mészáros	Budapest University of Technology and Economics, Hungary
Sabine Moisan	Inria - StarsProject, France
Raul Monroy	Tec de Monterrey in Mexico, Mexico
Manuela Montangero	Università di Modena e Reggio Emilia, Italy
Monica Mordonini	University of Parma, Italy
José Moreira	Universidade de Aveiro, Portugal
Pedro Moreira	Instituto Politécnico de Viana do Castelo, Portugal
Maxime Morge	Université de Lille, France
Andrea Morichetta	Unicam, Italy
Gildas Morvan	Université d'Artois, France
Bernard Moulin	Université Laval, Canada
Haralambos Mouratidis	University of Brighton, UK
Ahmed Mousatafa	Nagoya Institute of Technology, Japan
Muhammad Marwan Muhammad Fuad	Coventry University, UK
Luis Nardin	Brandenburg University of Technology, Germany
Viorel Negru	West University of Timisoara, Romania
Juan Carlos Nieves	Umeå Universitet, Sweden

Jens Nimis	Hochschule Karlsruhe - Technik und Wirtschaft, Germany
Paulo Novais	Universidade do Minho, Portugal
Michel Occello	Université Grenoble Alpes, France
Akihiko Ohsuga	The University of Electro-Communications (UEC), Japan
Haldur Õim	University of Tartu, Estonia
Andrei Olaru	University Politehnica of Bucharest, Romania
Joanna Isabelle Olszewska	University of West Scotland, UK
Stanislaw Osowski	Warsaw University of Technology, Poland
Hong-Seok Park	University of Ulsan, South Korea
Andrew Parkes	University of Nottingham, UK
Krzysztof Patan	University of Zielona Gora, Poland
Manuel G. Penedo	Investigation Center CITIC, University of A Coruña, Spain
Célia Pereira	Université de Nice Sophia Antipolis, France
Smiljana Petrovic	Iona College, USA
Danilo Pianini	Università di Bologna, Italy
Sébastien Picault	INRA, France
Marcin Pietron	University of Science and Technology in Cracow, Poland
Anitha Pillai	Hindustan Institute of Technology and Science, India
Agostino Poggi	University of Parma, Italy
Ramalingam Ponnusamy	CVR College of Engineering, India
Enrico Pontelli	New Mexico State University, USA
Filipe Portela	Centro ALGORITMI, University of Minho, Portugal
Roberto Posenato	Università degli Studi di Verona, Italy
Juan Carlos Preciado	University of Extremadura, Spain
Mariachiara Puviani	Università di Modena e Reggio Emilia, Italy
David Pynadath	University of Southern California, USA
Riccardo Rasconi	National Research Council of Italy, Italy
Barbara Re	University of Camerino, Italy
Marek Reformat	University of Alberta, Canada
Lluís Ribas-Xirgo	Universitat Autònoma de Barcelona, Spain
Patrizia Ribino	ICAR-CNR, Italy
Fátima Rodrigues	Instituto Superior de Engenharia do Porto (ISEP/IPP), Portugal
Juha Röning	University of Oulu, Finland
Silvia Rossi	Università degli Studi di Napoli Federico II, Italy
Ruben Ruiz	Universidad Politécnica de Valencia, Spain
Luca Sabatucci	ICAR-CNR, Italy
Fariba Sadri	Imperial College London, UK
Lorenza Saitta	Università degli Studi del Piemonte Orientale Amedeo Avogadro, Italy
Francesco Santini	Università di Perugia, Italy
Manuel Santos	Centro ALGORITMI, University of Minho, Portugal

Fabio Sartori	University of Milano-Bicocca, Italy
Jurek Sasiadek	Carleton University, Canada
Stefan Schiffer	Knowledge-Based Systems Group, RWTH Aachen University, Germany
Christoph Schommer	University of Luxembourg, Luxembourg
Stefan Schulz	Medical University of Graz, Austria
Frank Schweitzer	ETH Zurich, Switzerland
Ted Scully	Cork Institute of Technology, Ireland
Valeria Seidita	University of Palermo, Italy
Emilio Serrano	Universidad Politécnica de Madrid, Spain
Huma Shah	Coventry University, UK
Denis Shikhalev	The State Fire Academy of EMERCOM of Russia, Russia
Jaime Sichman	University of São Paulo, Brazil
Gheorghe Silaghi	Babes-Bolyai University, Romania
Marius Silaghi	Florida Institute of Technology, USA
Giovanni Sileno	University of Amsterdam, The Netherlands
Ricardo Silveira	Universidade Federal de Santa Catarina, Brazil
Gerardo Simari	Universidad Nacional del Sur, Argentina
Guillermo Simari	Universidad Nacional del Sur in Bahia Blanca, Argentina
David Sislak	Czech Technical University in Prague, Czech Republic
Alexander Smirnov	SPIIRAS, Russia
Armando Sousa	Inesc Tec and FEUP, Portugal
Gerasimos Spanakis	Maastricht University, The Netherlands
Ioanna Stamatopoulou	CITY College, International Faculty of the University of Sheffield, Greece
Bernd Steinbach	Freiberg University of Mining and Technology, Germany
Daniel Stormont	The PineApple Project, USA
Thomas Stützle	Université Libre de Bruxelles, Belgium
Toshiharu Sugawara	Waseda University, Japan
Zhaohao Sun	PNG University of Technology, Papua New Guinea, and Federation University Australia, Australia
Thepchai Supnithi	NECTEC, Thailand
Yasuhiro Suzuki	Nagoya University, Japan
Karim Tabia	CRIL (Centre de Recherche en Informatique de Lens - CNRS UMR 8188) Lab, France
Ryszard Tadeusiewicz	AGH University of Science and Technology, Poland
Nick Taylor	Heriot-Watt University, UK
Mark Terwilliger	University of North Alabama, USA
Satoshi Tojo	Japan Advanced Institute of Science and Technology, Japan
Michele Tomaiuolo	University of Parma, Italy
José Torres	Universidade Fernando Pessoa, Portugal
Viviane Torres da Silva	IBM Research, Brazil

Franco Turini   KDD Lab, University of Pisa, Italy
Paulo Urbano   Faculdade de Ciências da Universidade de Lisboa,
                                 Portugal
Marina V. Sokolova   Orel State University named after Turgenev, Russia
Egon L. van den Broek   Utrecht University, The Netherlands
Srdjan Vesic   CNRS, France
Jørgen Villadsen   Technical University of Denmark, Denmark
Emilio Vivancos   Universitat Politecnica de Valencia, Spain
Marin Vlada   University of Bucharest, Romania
Wojciech Waloszek   Gdansk University of Technology, Poland
Yves Wautelet   KU Leuven, Belgium
Rosina Weber   Drexel University, USA
Gerhard Weiss   Maastricht University, The Netherlands
Mark Winands   Maastricht University, The Netherlands
Bozena Wozna-Szczesniak   Jan Dlugosz University in Czestochowa, Poland
Kristina Yordanova   University of Rostock, Germany
Neil Yorke-Smith   TU Delft, The Netherlands
Jing Zhao   ECNU, China
Haibin Zhu   Nipissing University, Canada

Additional Reviewers

Ilze Andersone   Riga Technical University, Latvia
Hércules Antônio do Prado   Universidade Católica de Brasília, Brazil
Giovanna Castellano   University of Bari Aldo Moro, Italy
Riccardo De Benedictis   CNR, Italy
Alessandra De Paola   University of Palermo, Italy
Viktor Eisenstadt   University of Hildesheim, Germany
Sarah Elkasrawi   DFKI, Germany
Shuyue Hu   The Chinese University of Hong Kong, Hong Kong,
                                 China
Valentin Montmirail   I3S - Côte d'Azur University, France
Giovanni Pilato   ICAR-CNR, Italy
Pablo Pilotti   Cifasis, Argentina
Alvaro E. Prieto   Univesity of Extremadura, Spain
Syed Tahseen Raza Rizvi   German Research Center for Artificial Intelligence
                                 (DFKI), Germany
Jakob Schoenborn   University of Hildesheim and Competence Center
                                 Case-Based Reasoning, German Research Center
                                 for Artificial Intelligence, Germany
Yuichi Sei   University of Electro-Communications, Japan
Ana Paula Silva   UCB, Brazil
Jose Simmonds Sheppard   Universidad de Panamá, Panama

Invited Speakers

Penousal Machado	University of Coimbra, Portugal
Carla Gomes	Cornell University, USA
Michal Pechoucek	Czech Technical University in Prague, Czech Republic
Lambert Schomaker	University of Groningen, The Netherlands

Contents

The Dynamics of Semantic Change:
A Corpus-Based Analysis

Mohamed Amine Boukhaled[(⊠)], Benjamin Fagard, and Thierry Poibeau

Laboratoire Langues, Textes, Traitements Informatique, Cognition,
LATTICE, CNRS, ENS & Université Paris 3; PSL & USPC, Paris, France
{amine.boukhaled,benjamin.fagard,thierry.poibeau}@ens.fr

Abstract. In this contribution, we report on a computational corpus-based study to analyse the semantic evolution of words over time. Though semantic change is complex and not well suited to analytical manipulation, we believe that computational modelling is a crucial tool to study this phenomenon. This study consists of two parts. In the first one, our aim is to capture the systemic change of word meanings in an empirical model that is also predictive, making it falsifiable. In order to illustrate the significance of this kind of empirical model, we then conducted an experimental evaluation using the Google Books N-Gram corpus. The results show that the model is effective in capturing semantic change and can achieve a high degree of accuracy on predicting words' distributional semantics. In the second part, we look at the degree to which the S-curve model, which is generally used to describe the quantitative property associated with linguistic changes, applies in the case of lexical semantic change. We use an automatic procedure to empirically extract words that have known the biggest semantic shifts in the past two centuries from the Google Books N-gram corpus. Then, we investigate the significance of the S-curve pattern in their frequency evolution. The results suggest that the S-curve pattern has indeed some generic character, especially in the case of frequency rises related to semantic expansions.

Keywords: Semantic change · Diachronic word embedding · Recurrent neural networks · Computational semantics · S-curve model

1 Introduction

The availability of very large textual corpora spanning several centuries has recently made it possible to observe empirically the evolution of language over time. This observation can be targeted toward a few isolated words or a specific linguistic phenomenon, but it can also be interesting to combine these specific studies with the search for more general laws of language change and evolution. Semantic change, on which we shall focus in this contribution, includes all changes affecting the meaning of lexical items over time. For example, the word *awful* has drastically changed in meaning, moving away from a rather positive connotation, as an equivalent of *impressive* or *majestic*, at the beginning of the nineteenth century, and toward a negative one, as an equivalent of *disgusting* and *messy* nowadays [1]. It has been established that there are some systemic

© Springer Nature Switzerland AG 2019
J. van den Herik et al. (Eds.): ICAART 2019, LNAI 11978, pp. 1–15, 2019.
https://doi.org/10.1007/978-3-030-37494-5_1

regularities that direct the semantic shifts of words meanings. Not all words exhibit the same degree and speed of semantic change. Some words (or word categories) might be more resistant than others to the phenomenon of semantic change, as proposed by Dubossarsky et al. [2]. Various hypotheses have been proposed in the literature to explain such regularities in semantic change from a linguistic point of view [3].

One of the main challenges facing researchers studying the phenomenon of semantic change is its formidable complexity. It seems impossible to grasp all details and factors involved in this type of change, its abstract nature making it analytically intractable. However, computational models have no difficulties in handling complexity, and can therefore be used as means to make the study of semantic changes more accessible. Computational modelling of language change is a relatively new discipline, which includes early works that aimed at characterising the evolution through statistical and mathematical modelling [4, 5] and more recent and advanced works involving artificial intelligence, robotics and large-scale computer simulations [6].

In this context, the computational study of text temporality in general and semantic change in particular has become an active research topic, especially with the emergence of new and more effective methods of numerical word representations. The interest of taking into account the temporal dimension and the diachronic nature of meaning change as a research direction has been effectively demonstrated in several studies. It makes it possible to model the dynamics of semantic change [7], to analyse trajectories of meaning change for an entire lexicon [8], to model temporal word analogy or relatedness [9, 10], to capture the dynamics of semantic relations [11], and even to spell out specific laws of semantic change, among which:

- The Law of Conformity, according to which frequency is negatively correlated with semantic change [12].
- The Law of Innovation, according to which polysemy is positively correlated with semantic change [12].
- The Law of Prototypicality, according to which prototypicality is negatively correlated with semantic change [2].

In other studies on language change, researchers have been more interested in analysing the quantitative patterns associated with the propagation of changes. It has been shown that the diffusion of linguistic changes over time can be commonly presented as a sigmoidal curve (slow start/latency, accelerating period followed by a slow end/saturation) [13]. In this matter, the so-called S-curve model is generally used to describe the quantitative properties of frequency profiles. However, there have been only few computational studies in the literature to attest this quantitative pattern, and to the best of our knowledge, this claim is yet to be supported by case studies in the case of lexical semantic change as well.

In this work, we address the question of semantic change from a computational point of view. We conduct a computational corpus-based study that consists of two parts. In the first part, our aim is to capture the systemic change of word meanings in an empirical model that is also predictive, contrary to most previous approaches that meant to reproduce empirical observations. In the second part, we try to analyse the degree to which the S-curve model applies in the case of phenomena of lexical semantic change.

Both parts of our study were conducted using a large-scale diachronic corpus, namely the Google Books N-gram corpus.

The rest of the chapter is organised as follows: Sect. 2 presents the concept of diachronic word embedding and describes how this technique can be used to empirically quantify the degree of semantic change. Section 3 presents the first part of our study consisting of modelling and predicting semantic change using diachronic word embedding. In Sect. 4, we report on the second part of our contribution concerned with analysing the quantitative behaviour of some cases of semantic change. Finally, Sect. 5 concludes the chapter.

2 Empirical Assessment of the Semantic Change Using Diachronic Word Embedding

2.1 Diachronic Word Embedding

To represent computationally the meaning of words over time-periods, it is necessary first to extract the embedded projections of these words in a continuous vector space according to their contextual relationships [14]. Various methods can be used to obtain such vectors, such as Latent Semantic Analysis [15] and Latent Direchlet Allocation [16]. However, more recent and advanced techniques such as word2vec [17] and GloVe [18], known commonly as word embedding techniques, seem capable of better representing the semantic properties and the contextual meaning of words compared to traditional methods. Indeed, word embedding techniques have established themselves as an important step in the processing pipeline of natural languages.

The word2vec algorithm is one of the most frequently used techniques to construct word embeddings, with a huge impact in the field. It consists in training a simple neural network with a single hidden layer to perform a certain task (see Fig. 1). Training is achieved through stochastic gradient descent and back-propagation.

In the case of the skip-gram with negative sampling (SGNS) variant of the algorithm [17], the learning task is as follows: Given a specific word in the middle of a sentence, the model uses this current word to predict the surrounding window of context words. The words are in fact projected from a discrete space of V dimensions (where V is the vocabulary size) onto a lower dimensional vector space using the neural network. The goal is not to use the network afterward. Instead, it is just to learn the weights of the hidden layer. These weights constitute actually the word embedding vectors. Despite its simplicity, the word2vec algorithm, given an appropriate amount of training text, is highly effective in capturing the contextual semantics of words.

Such word embedding techniques can be tweaked to work in a diachronic perspective. The method consists first in training and constructing embeddings for each time-period, then in aligning them temporally, so as to finally use them as a means to track semantic change over time and thus to identify the words that have known the biggest semantic change in the corpus.

In our case, we used pre-trained diachronic word embeddings constructed on the basis of time-periods measured in decades from 1800 to 1990 [12]. The training text used to produce these word embeddings is derived from the Google Books N-gram

Input Word   Word Embedding   Output Word

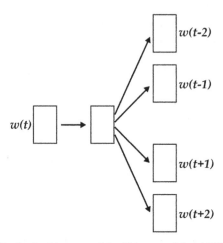

Fig. 1. Architecture of the Skip-gram Model [17].

datasets [19] which contain large amounts of historical texts in many languages (N-Grams from approximately 8 million books, roughly 6% of all books published at that time). Each word in the corpus appearing from 1800 to 1999 is represented by a set of twenty continuous 300-th dimensional vectors; one vector for each decade.

2.2 Quantifying the Degree of Semantic Change

From a technical point of view, the degree of semantic change can be computationally examined with the help of mainly two different measures using diachronic word embeddings. The first one, known as the global measure, simply consists in computing the cosine distance between a given word's vectors from two consecutive decades t and $t + 1$. The bigger the distance, the higher the semantic change [8]. The second measure, which we chose to use in our work, is known as the local neighbourhood measure, recommended by Hamilton et al. [20]. It consists in evaluating the amount of semantic change of a word based on how much its corresponding semantic neighbours have changed between two consecutive decades, as illustrated in Fig. 2. To do so, we first extract for each word x_i, with its corresponding embedding vector w_i, the set of k nearest neighbours, denoted by $N_k(x_i)$, according to cosine-similarity for both consecutive decades t and $t+1$. Then, in order to measure the change which took place between these two decades, we compute a second-order similarity vector for $x_i^{(t)}$ from these neighbour sets. This second-order vector, denoted by $s_i^{(t)}$, contains the cosine similarity of w_i and the vectors of all x_i's nearest semantic neighbours in the time-periods t and $t + 1$, with entries defined as:

$$S^{(t)}(j) = cosine\_sim\left(w_i^{(t)}, w_j^{(t)}\right) \forall x_j \in N_k\left(x_i^{(t)}\right) \cup N_k(x_i^{(t+1)}) \tag{1}$$

An analogous vector for $x_i^{(t+1)}$ is similarly computed as well.

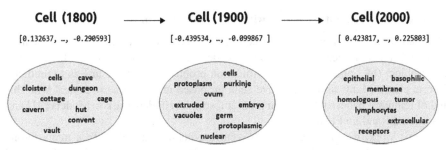

Fig. 2. Visualisation of the semantic change in the English word *"cell"* using diachronic word embedding. In the early 19th century the word *cell* was typically used to refer to a prison cell, hence the frequency of *cage* and *dungeon* in the context of *cell* in 1800, whereas in the late 19th century its meaning changed as it came to be frequently used in a scientific context, referring to a microscopic part of a living being (see *protoplasm, ovum,* etc. in the 1900 context).

Finally, we compute the local neighbourhood distance that measures the extent to which x_i's similarity with its nearest neighbours has changed as:

$$d(x_i^{(t)}, x_i^{(t+1)}) = cosine\_dist\left(s_i^{(t)}, s_i^{(t+1)}\right) \qquad (2)$$

Hamilton et al. [20] have found that the local neighbourhood measure is more effective in capturing specific cultural and semantic shifts than the global measure, while being less sensitive to other types of change such as grammaticalization.

3 Modelling the Semantic Change Dynamics Using Diachronic Word Embedding

In this first part of our study, we aim to capture the systemic change of words meanings in an empirical model that can also predict such changes, making it falsifiable. Our goal is thus to define a model capable of learning how the meanings of words have changed over time, and then use this model to predict how these meanings may evolve. This can then be checked against the actual meaning change which can be assessed with the same corpus. We propose a model that consists of two components:

1. *Diachronic word embeddings* to represent the meanings of words over time as the data component of the model as described in the previous section.
2. *A recurrent neural network* to learn and predict the temporal evolution patterns of these data.

The idea behind our model is to train Long Short Term Memory units (LSTMs) Recurrent Neural Network (RNN) on word embeddings corresponding to given time-periods (measured in decades) and try to predict the word embeddings of the following decade. We then evaluate the model using the diachronic embeddings derived from the English Google Books N-Gram corpus. The next two subsections describe more thoroughly the architecture of the recurrent neural network used in our work and the experimental evaluation respectively.

3.1 Predicting Semantic Change with Recurrent Neural Networks

As we are interested in predicting a continuous vector of d dimensions representing a word's contextual meaning in a given decade, this task is considered to be a regression problem (by opposition to a classification problem, where the task is to predict a discrete class). Many algorithms have been proposed in the literature to deal with this kind of temporal pattern recognition problem, such as Hidden Markov Models [21] and Conditional Random Fields [22].

In this work, we propose to use a recurrent neural network with a many-to-one LSTMs architecture to address this problem. RNNs are a powerful class of artificial neural networks designed to recognise dynamic temporal behaviour in sequences of data such as textual data [23]. RNNs are distinguished from feed-forward networks by the feedback loop connected to their past states. In this feedback loop, the hidden state h_t at time step t is a function F of the input at the same time step x_t modified by a weight matrix W, added to the hidden state of the previous time step h_{t-1} multiplied by its own transition matrix U as in Eq. (3):

$$h_t = F(Wx_t + Uh_{t-1}) \tag{3}$$

More specifically, we used a LSTMs architecture [24] (see Fig. 3) which is a variety of RNNs designed to deal effectively with the problem of vanishing gradient that RNNs suffer from while training [25].

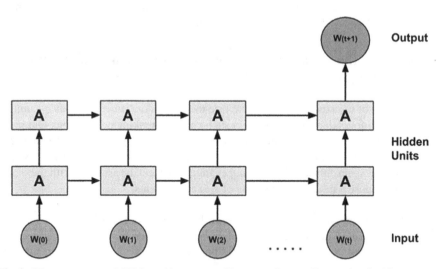

Fig. 3. The many-to-one LSTMs architecture used in our work to predict word embedding vectors. For each word in the vocabulary, the network is trained on diachronic word embedding vectors of time-periods $(1, \ldots, t)$ as input and tries to predict the embedding vector for time $t + 1$ as output [7].

Problem Formulation. In this contribution, we use the same mathematical formulation used in [7]. Let us consider a vocabulary V_n consisting in the top-n most frequent words of the corpus and $W(t) \in R^{d*n}$ to be the matrix of word embeddings at time step t.

The LSTMs network is trained on word embeddings over time-period $(1, \ldots, t)$ as input and asked to predict word embeddings $\widehat{W}(t + 1)$ of time $t + 1$ as output. The predicted embedding $\widehat{W}(t + 1)$ is then compared to the ground truth word embedding $W(t + 1)$ in order to assess the prediction accuracy. Predicting a continuous 300-th dimensional vector representing a word's contextual meaning is thus, as indicated above, formulated as a regression problem. Traditionally, researchers use mean-squared-error or mean absolute-error cost functions to assess the performance of regression algorithms. However, in our case, such cost functions would not be adapted, as they provide us with an overview (i.e., numerical value) of how the model is performing but little detail on its prediction accuracy. To have a more precise assessment of the prediction accuracy, we need to be able to say whether the prediction, for each word taken individually, is correct or not. Overall prediction accuracy is then computed. To do so, we proceed as follows:

Given the vocabulary V_n constituted from the top-n most frequent words and the matrix $W(t)$ of word embeddings at decade t, let us consider a word $x_i \in V_n$ and $\widehat{w}_i(t+1)$ its predicted word-embedding at decade t + 1. Though it is virtually impossible to predict exactly the same ground truth vector $w_i(t + 1)$ for this decade, as we are working on a continuous 300-th dimensional space, the accuracy of the predicted vector $\widehat{w}_i(t + 1)$ can be assessed by extracting the words that are closest semantically, based on cosine-similarity measure. If the word x_i is actually the nearest semantic neighbour to the predicted vector $\widehat{w}_i(t + 1)$, then it is considered to be a correct prediction. Otherwise, it is considered to be a false prediction.

3.2 Experimental Evaluation

In our experiment, we used word embeddings of all decades from 1800 to 1990 as input for the network, and we trained it to predict the embeddings of the 1990–1999 decade as output. We then conducted two types of evaluations. The first one consisted in reconstructing the overall large-scale evolution of the prediction accuracy on most frequents words from the corpus. The second one consisted in evaluating the prediction accuracy for a handful of word forms that have known considerable semantic shifts in the past two centuries. In what follows, we describe the experimental protocol and the results for both evaluations.

Overall Evaluation. In this first part of the evaluation, we experimented with different vocabulary sizes (top-1,000, 5,000, 10,000 and 20,000 words respectively, consisting of the most frequent words as computed from their average frequency over the entire historical time-periods). The experimental settings can help us evaluate the effect of a word's frequency on the degree of semantic change, and hence on prediction accuracy. For each experiment, and in order to get a reasonable estimate of the expected prediction performance, we used a 10-fold cross-validation method. Each time, we used 90% of the words for training the model, and the remaining 10% for testing its prediction accuracy. The training and testing process was repeated 10 times. The overall prediction accuracy is taken as the average performance over these 10 runs.

The results of measuring the prediction accuracy in our experimental evaluation are summarised in Table 1. They show that the model can be highly effective in capturing semantic change and can achieve a high accuracy when predicting words' distributional semantics. For example, the model was able to achieve 71% accuracy trained and tested exclusively on embeddings coming from the 10,000 most frequent words of the corpus.

Table 1. Results of prediction accuracy measured for different vocabulary sizes [7].

Vocabulary size	Acc.
1,000	91.7%
5,000	86.1%
10,000	71.4%
20,000	52.2%

The results also show a better performance when using a smaller vocabulary size, containing only the most frequent words. This is due to the fact that frequent words are repeated a sufficient number of times for the embedding algorithm to represent them accurately, and therefore to have a better distinction of the semantic change pattern which those embeddings may contain, which in turn can lead the RNN model to better capture this semantic change pattern and yield a more accurate prediction. Indeed, having a large corpus is essential to enable the models to learn a better word representation. These results are also in line with previous works claiming that frequency plays an important role in the semantic change process. For instance, Hamilton et al. [12] have shown that frequent words tend to be more resistant to semantic change (statistical Law of Conformity).

Table 2. Neighbouring words according to cosine similarity (based on word2vec embeddings) for sample words that have known important semantic shifts in the past two centuries [7].

Word	Neighbours in 1800s	Neighbours in 1990s
Circuit	Habitable, district, lanes, range, area, outer, globe, traverse	Circuits, appeals, amplifier, voltage, transistor, capacitor, appellate, court, resistor, district
Signal	Commodore, hoisted, victory, tack, admiral, commemoration, victories, chace, flag, announce	Signals, modulated, amplitude, input, noise, modulation, transmitter, analog, waveform, transduction
Array	Banners, spears, shields, ensigns, ranged, pikes, trumpets, banner, standards	Arrays, variety, range, integers, integer, byte, wide, pointer, formats, pointers
Mail	Waistcoat, boots, shirt, gloves, breeches, velvet, pistols, shoe, helmet, spurs	Mailing, email, send, internet, telephone, sending, fax, messages, mails, postage

Case Studies. We further examined the prediction accuracy on a handful of words. Based on the automatic procedure to assess the degree of semantic change as described in Sect. 2, we automatically extracted from the Google Books N-Gram Corpus the top-100 words that have known the most important semantic shifts in the past two centuries. We noticed that these words correspond mostly to cases that are correlated with important cultural shifts, which makes them a harder challenge for the prediction model compared to datasets used earlier in the overall evaluation. Table 2 presents sample words that gained new meanings due to their evolution towards uses in scientific and technological contexts. The model was able to correctly predict the semantic evolution of 41% of the studied cases, including words that have known an important and attested semantic change in the last two centuries such as the word *cell*. Moreover, a large portion of the false predictions corresponds to borderline cases for which the model has a tendency to predict vectors that are closer to much more frequent words, occurring in the same semantic context in the corpus, such as predicting a vector closer to the (emerging but more frequent) word *optimistic* for the (declining) word *sanguine*. The word *sanguine* comes from Old French *sanguin* (itself from Latin *sanguineus*, on *sanguis* 'blood'). It originally means 'blood-red' (14th c., Merriam-Webster's), and by extension 'hopeful, optimistic' (15th c., ibid.). In our corpus examples from the early 18th c., it is already used with the meaning 'optimistic', as in "My lords, I am sanguine enough to believe that this country has in a great measure got over its difficulties" (*Speech of the Earl of Liverpool*, 1820: 31) and "she is sanguine enough to expect that her various Novelties will meet the approbation of all Ladies of taste" (*La belle assemblee*, vol. XV, April 1st, 1817). But Fig. 4 shows that its frequency in the 19th and 20th c. has dropped steadily, while *optimistic* has seen its frequency rise sharply. Thus, the pair *sanguine/optimistic* seems to be a good example of lexical replacement, which explains our model's prediction.

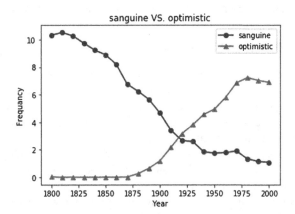

Fig. 4. Frequency profiles of *sanguine* and *optimistic* in Google Books N-Gram Corpus measured in millions [7].

Thus, among other benefits for historical linguists, our method makes it possible to identify the semantic replacement of one word by another in a specific context.

Despite being effective in predicting the semantic evolution of words, some difficulties remain regarding our method. For instance, our model works best for the most frequent words, i.e., according to the Law of Conformity, those with the least semantic evolution. One could thus wonder whether the words for which the model correctly predicts the semantic are not simply those which display little or no semantic change. The examples given in these case studies show that this is at least not always the case, but a more systematic investigation of individual cases is needed in order to get a clear picture. Another way to answer this question would be to explore more finely the effect that both polysemy and word frequency may have on our results, especially on the word representation part of our model. These two factors have been shown to play an important role in the semantic change, and their effects need to be studied and formalized more explicitly. Exploring more advanced and semantic-oriented word embedding techniques, referred to as sense embeddings, such as SENSEMBED [26], could help make the model less sensitive to those factors. In the next section describing the second part of our contribution, we will take a closer look at the frequency aspect of that matter by investigating the frequency pattern associated with lexical semantic change.

4 Investigating the Frequency Pattern Associated with Lexical Semantic Change

In this second part of our study, our aim is to analyse the degree to which the S-curve model applies in the case of phenomena of lexical semantic change. We investigate the significance of this pattern through an empirical observation using the same large-scale diachronic corpus as before, namely Google Books N-gram corpus. The rest of the section is organized as follows: Subsect. 4.1 presents a brief review of the S-curve pattern in linguistics. Subsect. 4.2 describes how to automatically extract it from corpus data. In Subsect. 4.3, we describe our experimental settings and present the results.

4.1 The S-curve Pattern in Linguistics

S-curved functions have been used to analyse the diffusion of changes and innovations in various scientific domains [27]. They describe change as resulting from the fact that different parts of a given population successively adopt a new variant, which increases its frequency of use over time. This frequency subsequently reaches a saturation point at which the adoption of the variant stagnates.

The S-curve has been used starting from the early 1950s to model phenomena of language change [28]. It supposes that language change occurs commonly according to an S-curve, which means that the frequency rise associated with the new change variant should obey a sigmoid function, or any similar function which has approximately the same shape. The main reference in the literature on such matter is the work of Kroch [5]. Several other works follow [29–31]. Blythe and Croft [32] have performed a detailed survey on S-shaped patterns in linguistics totalising about 40 cases of changes. Feltgen et al. [33] have provided a statistical survey on frequency patterns associated with about 400 cases of functional semantic change (grammaticalization) in French. This investigation has shown that 70% of the studied cases display at least one S-curve increase of frequency in the course of their adoption. Apart from these studies and despite having an important part to play in the understanding of the underlying mechanisms of language evolution, it appears that large-scale quantitative studies of the statistical properties of language change were left aside, limited mostly by both the quantity and the quality of the available historical linguistic data.

In semantic change, and more precisely in the case of semantic expansion, it is expected to observe an increase in frequency for the word whose meaning changes. In such cases, the generic character of the S-curve as a pattern associated with meaning change can be described by the following three steps:

1. The first occurrences of the word linked to the new meaning start to appear in the corpus and the frequency slightly increases to a certain low value. The word linked to the same new meaning continues to show in the corpus, but not so much as to reach a momentum. The frequency may thus remain constant for a certain period of time.
2. Following its adoption, the word carrying the new meaning is used in a broader number of contexts by an increasing portion of the population. The frequency rises rapidly.
3. At a certain point, the rise in frequency reaches a saturation point. Saturation occurs either because there is a limited number of new 'adopters' or because there is a limited number of compatible linguistic contexts in which the new meaning can be used [33].

In the following subsection, we describe how this pattern can be mathematically extracted from diachronic textual data.

4.2   Extraction of S-curve Patterns from a Diachronic Corpus

In order to identify and extract S-curve patterns in diachronic data, we used a similar procedure to the one described in [13]. The process is as follows:

1. For each word in the investigation dataset, we first extract its frequency x_i in each time period i of the diachronic corpus (in our case, we consider each year as one time period). These frequencies are smoothed by computing a moving average over the past five years.
2. For each frequency profile, we identify the two years i_{start} and i_{end} marking respectively the beginning and the end of the time-range of a frequency rise, and we note their corresponding frequencies x_{min} and x_{max} respectively.
3. We apply the logit transformation to the frequency points between x_{min} and x_{max}:

$$y_i = log\left(\frac{x_i - x_{min}}{x_{max} - x_i}\right). \tag{4}$$

4. If the data actually follows a sigmoid function $\tilde{x}_i$ of the form:

$$\tilde{x}_i = x_{min} + \frac{x_{max} - x_{min}}{1 + e^{-hi-b}}, \tag{5}$$

then the logit transformation of this sigmoid function fits a linear function of the form:

$$\tilde{y}_i = hi + b, \tag{6}$$

which gives us the slope h, the intercept b and the residual r^2 quantifying the linear quality of the fit. Figure 6 provides an illustration of an extracted S-curve pattern of frequency rise and its corresponding logit transform.

4.3 Experimentation

Experimental Settings. We investigated the presence of S-curve patterns on a handful of words. We used the same 100 words that we have considered for the case studies of the first part of our study (See Table 2 for examples). We then used the mathematical procedure described in the previous subsection to look for S-curve patterns in the frequency profile of these words over time. We have decided to keep the investigation dataset small in order to facilitate the subsequent qualitative analysis.

Results. In our study, we wanted to select only S-curves of highly satisfying quality. We set the residual r^2 quantifying the quality of the logit fit, as explained in Subsect. 4.2, to a high value (98%) in order to ensure the S-shape quality of the extracted curves. Moreover, we restricted the extraction to S-curves that cover at least one decade in length. Still, our method enabled us to find at least one S-curve (and up to four in some cases) in the frequency evolution for 46% of the studied. A lower threshold for r^2 would have yielded many more. The word *Array*, as we have seen in Table 2 above, is a good example of semantic change, having shifted from the idea of order of battle (Webster, 1828, s.v. *array*, first entry: "Order; disposition in regular lines; as an army in battle array. Hence a posture of defense") to that of imposing numbers (Merriam-Webster, online edition, s.v. *array*, first entry: "an imposing group: large number") [34]. Figure 5 illustrates the frequency profile of this word in the past two centuries, while Fig. 6 shows the S-curve pattern of frequency rise period extracted from its profile.

Theoretically speaking, semantic change can occur in two cases: because a word gains new meanings (semantic expansion), or because it loses some (semantic reduction). Since only the former case is associated with a frequency rise, we decided to focus the extraction on words having a growing frequency trend over time (instances of semantic expansion). This brings up the percentage of S-curve pattern presence to 75%. These results suggest that the S-curve does indeed seem to be, to some extent, a generic pattern of lexical semantic change, and especially of semantic expansion. However, when questioning the universality of the S-curve pattern, the results show that it is actually not so pervasive as to be qualified as universal, at least on the basis of our investigation dataset based on frequencies extracted from the Google Books N-gram corpus. A more systematic investigation into bigger datasets, along with individual case studies, is in order if we want to get a full picture.

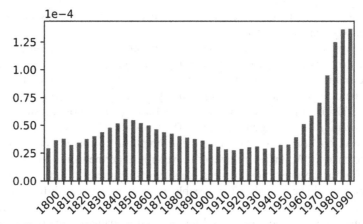

Fig. 5. Overall evolution of the relative smoothed frequency of use of the form *array* in the corpus.

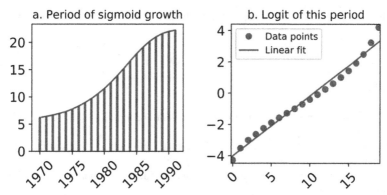

Fig. 6. Extracted S-curve pattern of frequency rise period for the form *array* (left) and its corresponding logit transform (right).

5   Conclusions

In conclusion, we presented a computational corpus-based study to analyse the semantic evolution of words over time. First, we tried to capture the systemic change of word meanings in an empirical model that is also predictive, making it falsifiable. In order to illustrate the significance of this kind of empirical model, we conducted an experimental evaluation using the Google Books N-Gram corpus. The results show that the model is partly successful in capturing the semantic change and can achieve a high degree of accuracy on predicting words' distributional semantics.

We then proposed to investigate the pervasive nature of the S-curve pattern in the case of semantic change. To do so, we used an automated procedure both to empirically extract the words that have known biggest semantic shifts in the past two centuries, and to extract S-curve patterns from their frequency profiles. Performing a statistical observation over 100 cases of semantic change from the Google Books N-gram corpus, we established the generic character of the S-curve, especially in the case of frequency rises related to semantic expansion.

Although our experiments described in this study are still in their preliminary stages, we believe that this approach can provide linguists with a refreshing perspective on language evolution by making it possible to observe large-scale evolution in general and semantic change in particular. It thus nicely complements existing methods and reinforces a falsifiability approach to linguistics. Based on the current results, we have identified several future research directions. The RNN model that we propose to use in the first part of our study is rather standard and simplistic compared to the complexity of semantic change. We therefore intend to explore deeper networks and to put more time and effort in the fine tuning process of its hyper-parameters. On the other hand, a good question would be to analyse the possible interactions between different linguistic properties of the word such as its actual degree of semantic change and the degree of its polysemy in the time period covered by the S-curve pattern. This is only a broad perspective of research, which we shall explore more thoroughly in future works.

Acknowledgements. This work is supported by the project 2016-147 ANR OPLADYN TAP-DD2016.

References

1. Simpson, J.A., Weiner, E.S.C.: The Oxford English Dictionary. Oxford University Press, Oxford (1989)
2. Dubossarsky, H., Tsvetkov, Y., Dyer, C., Grossman, E.: A bottom up approach to category mapping and meaning change. In: NetWordS, pp. 66–70 (2015)
3. Traugott, E.C., Dasher, R.B.: Regularity in Semantic Change. Cambridge University Press, Cambridge (2001)
4. Bailey, C.-J.N.: Variation and linguistic theory (1973)
5. Kroch, A.S.: Reflexes of grammar in patterns of language change. Lang. Var. Change. **1**, 199–244 (1989)
6. Steels, L.: Modeling the cultural evolution of language. Phys. Life Rev. **8**, 339–356 (2011)
7. Boukhaled, M., Fagard, B., Poibeau, T.: Modelling the semantic change dynamics using diachronic word embedding. In: Proceedings of the 11th International Conference on Agents and Artificial Intelligenc, ICAART 2019. Prague, Czech Republic (2019)
8. Kim, Y., Chiu, Y.-I., Hanaki, K., Hegde, D., Petrov, S.: Temporal analysis of language through neural language models. arXiv Preprint. arXiv:1405.3515 (2014)
9. Rosin, G.D., Radinsky, K., Adar, E.: Learning Word Relatedness over Time. arXiv Preprint arXiv:1707.08081 (2017)
10. Szymanski, T.: Temporal word analogies: identifying lexical replacement with diachronic word embeddings. In: Proceedings of the 55th Annual Meeting of the Association for Computational Linguistics (Volume 2: Short Papers), pp. 448–453 (2017)
11. Kutuzov, A., Velldal, E., Øvrelid, L.: Temporal dynamics of semantic relations in word embeddings: an application to predicting armed conflict participants. arXiv Preprint arXiv:1707.08660 (2017)
12. Hamilton, W.L., Leskovec, J., Jurafsky, D.: Diachronic word embeddings reveal statistical laws of semantic change. arXiv Preprint arXiv:1605.09096 (2016)

13. Feltgen, Q., Fagard, B., Nadal, J.-P.: Frequency patterns of semantic change: corpus-based evidence of a near-critical dynamics in language change. R. Soc. Open Sci. **4**, 170830 (2017)
14. Turney, P.D., Pantel, P.: From frequency to meaning: vector space models of semantics. J. Artif. Intell. Res. **37**, 141–188 (2010)
15. Deerwester, S., Dumais, S.T., Furnas, G.W., Landauer, T.K., Harshman, R.: Indexing by latent semantic analysis. J. Am. Soc. Inf. Sci. **41**, 391–407 (1990)
16. Blei, D.M., Ng, A.Y., Jordan, M.I.: Latent dirichlet allocation. J. Mach. Learn. Res. **3**, 993–1022 (2003)
17. Mikolov, T., Chen, K., Corrado, G., Dean, J.: Efficient estimation of word representations in vector space. arXiv Preprint arXiv:1301.3781 (2013)
18. Pennington, J., Socher, R., Manning, C.: Glove: global vectors for word representation. In: Proceedings of the 2014 Conference on Empirical Methods in Natural Language Processing (EMNLP), pp. 1532–1543 (2014)
19. Lin, Y., Michel, J.-B., Aiden, E.L., Orwant, J., Brockman, W., Petrov, S.: Syntactic annotations for the Google books ngram corpus. In: Proceedings of the ACL 2012 System Demonstrations, pp. 169–174 (2012)
20. Hamilton, W.L., Leskovec, J., Jurafsky, D.: Cultural shift or linguistic drift? comparing two computational measures of semantic change. In: Proceedings of the Conference on Empirical Methods in Natural Language Processing, p. 2116 (2016)
21. Bengio, Y.: Markovian models for sequential data. Neural Comput. Surv. **2**, 129–162 (1999)
22. Lafferty, J., McCallum, A., Pereira, F.C.N.: Conditional random fields: Probabilistic models for segmenting and labeling sequence data (2001)
23. Medsker, L.R., Jain, L.C.: Recurrent neural networks. Des. Appl. **5** (2001)
24. Hochreiter, S., Schmidhuber, J.: Long short-term memory. Neural Comput. **9**, 1735–1780 (1997)
25. Pascanu, R., Mikolov, T., Bengio, Y.: On the difficulty of training recurrent neural networks. In: International Conference on Machine Learning, pp. 1310–1318 (2013)
26. Iacobacci, I., Pilehvar, M.T., Navigli, R.: Sensembed: learning sense embeddings for word and relational similarity. In: Proceedings of the 53rd Annual Meeting of the Association for Computational Linguistics and the 7th International Joint Conference on Natural Language Processing (Volume 1: Long Papers), pp. 95–105 (2015)
27. Rogers, E.M.: Diffusion of Innovations. Simon and Schuster, New York (2010)
28. Denison, D.: Logistic and simplistic S-curves. Motiv. Lang. Chang. **54**, 70 (2003)
29. Labov, W.: Principles of Linguistic Change, Volume 3: Cognitive and Cultural Factors. Wiley, Oxford (1994)
30. Ghanbarnejad, F., Gerlach, M., Miotto, J.M., Altmann, E.G.: Extracting information from S-curves of language change. J. R. Soc. Interface **11**, 20141044 (2014)
31. Nevalainen, T.: Descriptive adequacy of the S-curve model in diachronic studies of language change. In: Can We Predict Linguistic Change? (2015)
32. Blythe, R.A., Croft, W.: S-curves and the mechanisms of propagation in language change. Language (Baltim) **88**, 269–304 (2012)
33. Feltgen, Q.: Statistical physics of language evolution: the grammaticalization phenomenon (2017)
34. Webster, N.: Noah Webster's first edition of an American dictionary of the English language. Foundation for Amer Christian (1828)

Reinforcement Learning Method for Ad Networks Ordering in Real-Time Bidding

Reza Refaei Afshar$^{(\boxtimes)}$ ⓘ, Yingqian Zhang$^{(\boxtimes)}$ ⓘ, Murat Firat$^{(\boxtimes)}$ ⓘ,
and Uzay Kaymak$^{(\boxtimes)}$ ⓘ

Eindhoven University of Technology, 5600 MB Eindhoven, The Netherlands
{r.refaei.afshar,yqzhang,m.firat,u.kaymak}@tue.nl

Abstract. High turnover of online advertising and especially real time bidding makes this ad market very attractive to beneficiary stakeholders. For publishers, it is as easy as placing some slots in their webpages and sell these slots in the available online auctions. It is important to determine which online auction market to send their slots to. Based on the traditional Waterfall Strategy, publishers have a fixed ordering of preferred online auction markets, and sell the ad slots by trying these markets sequentially. This fixed-order strategy replies heavily on the experience of publishers, and often it does not provide highest revenue. In this paper, we propose a method for dynamically deciding on the ordering of auction markets for each available ad slot. This method is based on reinforcement learning (RL) and learns the state-action through a tabular method. Since the state-action space is sparse, a prediction model is used to solve this sparsity. We analyze a real-time bidding dataset, and then show that the proposed RL method on this dataset leads to higher revenues. In addition, a sensitivity analysis is performed on the parameters of the method.

Keywords: Reinforcement learning · Real time bidding · Waterfall strategy

1 Introduction

Online advertising is a growing industry in recent years. Many companies choose this market to advertise their services or products because of its popularity and visibility. For owners of websites, or *publishers*, participating in online advertising is as easy as placing some blocks, called *ad slot*, and selling them to advertisers. Advertisers aim to find publishers who match best with their objectives. For example, producers of sport shoes want to target athletes and therefore, a sport news website could be an ideal publisher. The objective of online publishers is to sell their ad slots as high as possible to increase their revenue.

When a user open a website containing ad slots, an *impression* is generated. This impression brings the opportunity of being viewed by end users. The traditional means of selling impressions is offline, i.e. publishers contact directly to advertisers to negotiate and agree on a contract. *Real Time Bidding (RTB)* and generally the *Programmatic Advertising* are developed to automate the process of online buying and selling the

© Springer Nature Switzerland AG 2019
J. van den Herik et al. (Eds.): ICAART 2019, LNAI 11978, pp. 16–36, 2019.
https://doi.org/10.1007/978-3-030-37494-5_2

impressions. Based on RTB, *ad networks* are placed between publishers and advertisers to help them connect efficiently. Ad networks receive the impressions as goods and the willingness to pay of advertisers as bids and run auctions to sell the impressions to the holder of the maximum bid. These auctions are performed in real time and should not take more than few milliseconds which is the loading time of a webpage. To make things easier for publishers and advertisers, *Supply Side Platform (SSP)* and *Demand Side Platform* come to play. SSPs help publishers in participating to the auction and send the ad requests to the ad networks. DSPs are advertiser assistants and help them manage their campaigns and determine their bids. We will focus on the environment from publisher's side. In this structure, an SSP on behalf of a publisher initializes and sends the *ad requests* to the online auctions.

When a webpage containing ad slots starts to load, an ad request to fill the ad slot is generated and sent to the ad networks. Ad networks receive the impression and run auctions to find a buyer. The publishers determine a minimum price, called reserve, for the impression, which eliminates all bids that are lower than the reserve price.

Different ad networks are available for a publisher to send the ad requests. A common way of participating in auctions is the so called *Waterfall Strategy* [8]. In this strategy, a publisher sends the ad requests to the ad networks sequentially until finding a bid value. The first request is sent to the first ad network. If there is no winner in the auction of this ad network, the second ad network is determined and a new request is sent. This process continues until finding a bidder or attempting all of the ad networks. For all impressions, the ad networks are used in a fixed ordering. However, the fixed ordering is not optimal and the best ad networks varies from one impression to another.

In our preliminary works [1,2], we developed a method to derive the best ordering of ad networks dynamically for each impression. The ad network selection problem is a sequential decision making problem. At each step, the decision maker decides an ad network to send the ad request. Then, a reward is received and the next state is determined accordingly. The method is based on *reinforcement learning (RL)* and model the RTB environment as a reinforcement learning problem. In [2] the basic method consists of a prediction model and a reinforcement learning step is presented. We used a prediction model to find initial state-action values and updated these initial values using a real time bidding dataset provided by our industrial partner. We considered the sequences of requests for filling an ad slot as episodes and we used the Monte Carlo algorithm to learn the state-action values based on averaging sample returns [19]. In [1] we showed that the prediction model is not enough for ad networks ordering and the revenue is lower than following the complete method.

In this paper, we analyze the sensitivity of the method to some of the parameter values. In the prediction model, 5-fold cross validation was used for training. Here, the sensitivity to the number of folds is discussed. Furthermore, we show that the reward function control the trade-off between loading time and the revenue. The sensitivity of the method to the reward or unsuccessful attempts is also discussed in this paper. We show that the higher penalty results in higher revenue. We also explain where does the states definition come from. In fact, the states are the combination of the most important features.

This paper is structured as follows. Section 2 presents a brief literature review. In Sect. 3 the proposed method is discussed. The real-time bidding data is discussed in Sect. 4. The experimentation and the sensitivity analysis are presented in Sect. 5. Finally, we make our concluding remarks and discuss future work.

2 Related Works

In recent years, real time bidding is a very hot topic for researchers because of its importance for both publishers and advertisers. From the publisher's point of view, problems like dynamic pricing are popular. However, assisting the publishers in participating to the auction is the subject that gain less attention though its importance. In this section, some of related works and our contribution are presented.

The process of programmatic advertising is defined as "the automated serving of digital ads in real time based on individual ad impression opportunities" [5]. Programmatic advertising helps publishers and advertisers to reach their goals and increase the efficiency of online advertising. The programmatic buying and selling of ad slots prepares new environment for publishers and advertisers to better communicate with each other. Publishers may easily find suitable advertisements for their ad slots while advertisers may target suitable users, thus increasing potential product sales and brand visibility [21].

An important factor in determining a publisher's revenue is the *reserve price*. Reserve price or floor price is the minimum price that a publisher expects to obtain by selling the ad slots [27]. If it is too high and no advertiser wants to pay it, the advertisement slot will not be sold, whereas if this price is set too low the publisher's profit is affected. For this reason, specifying that price is important and adjustments in reserve price may lead to increase in publisher's revenue. The adjustment of the reserve price is not a trivial issue and has motivated a lot of research.

In [3], the reserve price is expressed as the weighted sum of features and the weight values are found to maximize the price. In this study, the main task is learning weights of features for which gradient descent is used. The inner product of these two vectors computes the value of the reserve price. The limitation of this paper is that they adjust an optimized floor price for all auctions regardless of the properties of auctions like time, user characteristics, etc. The output floor price of their method is fixed for all future bidding auctions. Xie et al. introduce a method to set the floor price dynamically [24]. The assumption is that there is no information about the bids. Based on this method, first the top bid is predicted using a family of classifiers. Because those higher top bids are more important in case of revenue, the authors discretized the values of top bids and predict the high bids with binary classifiers. In the next step they use the idea of cascading [14] and try to reduce the false positive rate of the prediction algorithm by combining the series of classifiers obtained before. They inspire [11] who follow the same basic idea with their own feature and classification models. Then, the difference between the top and the second bid is predicted by another set of binary classifiers. These classifiers determine whether the difference is high or not by comparing with a threshold. Finally the reserve price is set for high top bids that their difference with the second bid is also high. In a recent work [12], the authors try to set the floor price in multi channels. The online channel is the real time auction and the offline channel is the direct link with the advertisers. Separate mathematical models are developed for setting floor price in offline and online settings. Then a parametric formulation for the expected revenue of a publisher from both online and offline channel is defined. The floor price is determined by another equation containing two functions. These two functions are obtained by differentiation of the total expected revenue. The methods introduced in [15–17], are useful in non-stationary environments. The price setting is based on considering the gap between top bid and second bid in second price auction. Other research such as [25] and [23] propose methods for price setting by modeling the real time bidding environment as a dynamic game and considering censored bid data respectively.

Wu et al. utilize a censor regression model to fit the censor bidding data that a DSP suffers from these censored information especially for lost bids [23]. Because the assumption of censored regression does not hold on the real time bidding data, they proposed a mixture model namely a combination of linear regression for observed data and censored regression for censored data, so as to predict the winning price.

The other research area that is the main topic of this paper, is to choose proper ad networks in the waterfall strategy. Selecting the most profitable ordering of ad networks in waterfall strategy is a research topic which has gained less attention in recent years in comparison to reserve price optimization. However, it is an important topic because unsuccessful attempts to find ads increases the response and loading time of the webpage containing the ad slot. This decreases the performance of the website. A potential method to find the best ordering is to model the publisher as an agent and using reinforcement learning. Our preliminary works to solve this problem are published [1,2]. In this paper, we follow the same methodology and perform sensitivity analysis. We present the sensitivity of our method to the parameters like penalty value and the number of folds in k-fold clustering.

Sometimes there is a contract between a publisher and an ad network. There should be a balance between selecting this ad network and other ad networks that may achieve higher revenue [13]. According to [9], when the number of ad networks increases, the most important factor in selection policy is the expected revenue. However, sometimes the better ad network may not fill the ad slot and the publisher should try other ad networks. This latency in filling ad slots may have bad effects on the performance of publisher's website. In [4], the authors optimize the trade-off between the short-term revenue from ad exchange and the long-term benefits of delivering good spots to the reservation ads. They formalize this combined optimization problem as a multi-objective stochastic control problem. In [18], the authors study a variant of the ad allocation problem to help online publisher to decide which subset of advertisement slots should be used in order to fulfill guaranteed contracts and which subset should be sold on SSPs in order to maximize the expected revenue. They propose a two-stage stochastic programming approach to formulate and solve the display-ad allocation problem.

Reinforcement Learning (RL) in real-time bidding is also one of the hot topics during the last few years. Basically in RL, the agent observes the current state of the environment and decides which action to take [19]. Using reinforcement learning in the context of real time bidding has gained remarkable attention in recent years. However, the modeling of the RTB environment is mainly from the bidder side in previous research. In [20] a reinforcement learning method is proposed to help sellers in dynamic pricing. In this method a learning algorithm tunes the parameters of a seller's dynamic pricing policy. This method is general and is not specifically for RTB. In [6] a reinforcement learning modeling of RTB is introduced to help advertisers in setting their bid price. In a recent work [22], the authors formulate the budget constraint bidding as a Markov Decision Process and propose a model free reinforcement learning framework to derive the optimal bidding strategy for the advertisers. We will focus on the publishers in our study and develop the decision support system centered by them.

3   Methodology

The method for deriving the best ordering of ad networks is presented in this chapter. This method serves as a decision support tool for online ad publishers to maximize their revenue. Since the problem is a sequential decision making problem, we model that as a reinforcement learning problem and the publisher learns the optimal policy by interacting with the environment.

In reinforcement learning, an agent learns through interaction with the environment and estimates the value of each action in each state. Basically the agent observes the current state of the environment and decides which action to take. We assume that accessing to the RTB environment and exploration is not possible and the historical data is the only available source. This limitation is common in RTB research. States, actions and responses are determined from the data and state transitions are deterministic based on what is available in the data. In other words, the exploration is confined to the observed actions that are selected for each state. Therefore, the state-action space might be sparse because the action selection policy is based on a predefined and fixed ordering. A prediction model solves this sparsity and is explained shortly. Sequences of ad requests to sell a certain impression are episodes in our modeling. Hence, the problem is an episodic problem. Monte Carlo algorithm is opted for learning state-action values. In order to model the problem as a reinforcement learning problem, we need to define states, actions, reward function, algorithms for learning state-action values and action selection policy [19].

3.1   States

Features in ad requests influence on the bidding process and also on an advertiser's intention about buying the impression. Therefore, states should be related to the ad requests. One approach to define a state is to consider each unique ad request as an individual state. There are huge number of ad requests in each day and assigning a state to each ad request creates an extremely large state space. This large state space is not manageable and helpful because new states are adding to the space continuously and the data is not sufficient for learning. Conversely, mapping a single state to a large number of unique ad requests is the concept of predefined ordering. Conclusively, there is a trade-off in defining the states. On one hand, if the states are more specific, there is not enough ad requests in the RTB data obtained from a predefined ordering of ad networks. On the other hand, if each state contains large number of ad requests, the approach is similar to the predefined ordering because the method selects the same action for large number of ad requests.

In order to solve this problem, we select some of the features and partition their values into intervals to define the states. Through developing a classifier for predicting whether an ad request is successful or not, we derived the importance of the features. This classifier is also used in solving the sparsity and is explained in Sect. 3.4. The *ad tag id*, *floor price* and *request order* are the most important features and make a balance between the number of states and the number of observed ad networks for each state. We also set two thresholds named t_{fp} for floor price and t_{ro} for request order to group ad requests based on these thresholds. In the new states, values of floor price are divided into two categories: below t_{fp} and over t_{fp}. The same approach has been followed for request order: below t_{ro} and over t_{ro}. This definition reduced the number of states from one million to around $3,000$. Equation (1) defines the states in our model.

$$s(x_i) = \{id(x_i), F(x_i), R(x_i)\},$$
$$x_i \in D \; : \; i^{th} ad\ request,$$
(1)

$$F(x_i) = \begin{cases} 0 & if\ floor\_price(x_i) \in [0, t_{fp}) \\ 1 & if\ floor\_price(x_i) \in [t_{fp}, m_f] \end{cases}$$
(2)

$$R(x_i) = \begin{cases} 0 & if\ request\_order(x_i) \in [0, t_{ro}) \\ 1 & if\ request\_order(x_i) \in [t_{ro}, m_r] \end{cases}$$
(3)

$$m_r = \max_{x_i \in D}(request\_order(x_i))$$
(4)

$$m_f = \max_{x_i \in D}(floor\_price(x_i))$$
(5)

where m_f and m_r indicate the maximum values for floor price and request order in the RTB data. D contains all of the ad requests that we use for our method.

3.2 Actions

The action is the decision that a publisher makes at each decision moment. Hence, in the reinforcement learning modeling of real time bidding problem, the actions stand for selections of ad networks. In each state, the model decides which ad network makes the most revenue. There are N possible ad networks and each ad request could be sent to any one of them. Based on Waterfall Strategy, ad networks are selected in a predefined and fixed ordering. The episodes come from the historical data. Thereby, the number of samples for each state-action pairs is different. In sum, the actions are ad networks and there are at most N possible actions in each state.

The definition of the possible actions in each state is shown in (6). Because some combinations of states and actions do not exist in the historical data, the actions set of each state is a subset of all actions.

$$a(x_i) \in \{a_1, a_2, ..., a_N\}$$
(6)

In this formulation $a_1, ..., a_N$ are ad networks. Based on the definitions of states and actions, there are more than one action for each state in historical data. Therefore, the

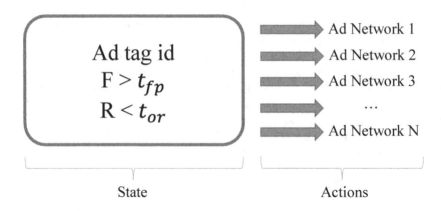

Fig. 1. State and actions [2].

problem is the ordering of these actions. Figure 1 illustrates the formation of a sample state and actions.

Equation (7) defines the ad requests for each state-action pair. In this equation, $D(s, a)$ is the list of ad requests that their corresponding state and action are (s, a).

$$D(s,a) = \{x_i \in D | (s(x_i), a(x_i)) = (s, a)\} \tag{7}$$

3.3   Reward Function

Increasing the revenue is the main objective of an ad publisher and the responses from the environment determine the value function as well as the policy. In addition, the publisher needs to receive the ads as fast as possible to load its webpage quickly. Thus, the reward function should incorporate the preferences of the publisher. The publisher should select an action that has the most success probability and highest expected revenue. The floor price is the lower bound of revenue for an impression (ad request with event state = 1) and is the only available information regarding to selling impression in the auction and the actual revenue is not observable[1]. We assign the value of floor price as the reward of successful ad requests. Conversely, unsuccessful attempts are penalized by the value -1. This forces the agent (SSP) to find the advertisement in the shortest time possible. Equation (8) defines the reward function of our model. In Sect. 5.4 the sensitivity to the penalty is discussed.

$$Reward^{x_i}(s,a) = \begin{cases} -1 & if\ event\_state(x_i) = 0 \\ floor\_price(x_i) & if\ event\_state(x_i) = 1 \end{cases} \tag{8}$$
$$x_i \in D(s,a)$$

where $floor\_price$ and $event\_state$ come from the ad request x_i.

---

[1] This is the case for online publishers who rely on SSPs to sell their impressions.

Table 1. Top most important features.

Rank	Feature	Importance
1	$Floor Price$	0.303459
2	$AdNetwork$	0.200992
3	$RequestOrder$	0.184083
4	URL	0.060835
5	$AdTagId$	0.052920
6	$PageDomain$	0.036096
7	$Timestamp$	0.027170
8	$OpportunityOrder$	0.021922
9	$OperatingSystem$	0.018707
10	$DeviceName$	0.018375
11	$Browser$	0.016962

3.4 Finding Initial Values for Reinforcement Learning Algorithm

As mentioned before, there are not enough data to estimate all state-action values and the state-action table is sparse. For this reason we build a prediction model to estimate an initial value for all state-action values. This prediction model helps in providing an estimated revenue for all entries of state-action table regardless of whether they are observed in the data or not.

In order to find initial state-action values, we first find the success probability of sending requests to a certain ad network. We use supervised learning methods. The feature vector contains information related to the ad request and the target value is whether selecting an ad network will provide an advertisement or not.

The dataset is provided by our industrial partner, which contains ad requests. Ad requests are the information of interactions between a publisher and ad networks to sell ad impressions. The publisher is an entertainment company website, using ad networks such as Google ad exchange, AOL and SpotX to sell their ad slots. Each webpage of this website has some advertising slots which should be filled with ads provided from the real time auction. There are many ad request per day and they are divided into two groups. The majority are unsuccessful attempts in finding an advertisement and the rest are impressions. The features in ad requests are the same with what are introduced in [1].

Our feature vector is a selected subset of the features discussed in [2] , which has shown to provide the best success prediction. The most promising combination of features contains floor price, time, ad tag id, request order, ad networks, page domain, device name, operating system, opportunity order, browser name and URL. From the time feature, we consider the hour of a day. The importance of the features are illustrated in Table 1. As mentioned in Sect. 3.1 the first and the third features plus the ad tag id are chosen to shape the states. The ad network is the action.

The prediction model is applied on a subset of the dataset. This subset contains only those samples that are in a sequence which the event state of its last ad request is one.

Since there is no information in the datasets about these sequences, we followed the algorithm in [2] to obtain the sequence of ad requests for a certain impression.

The prediction task is to classify each ad request into one of two classes: 0 for unsuccessful and 1 for successful. In other words, the target is the value of the event state and the objective of the prediction model is to predict this value.

Event state is a binary variable. The classifier receives an ad request and return its success probability. Hence, for each ad request containing an ad network id, we obtain a probability which determines the likelihood of filling the ad slot. The multiplication of this probability to the floor price of the current ad request yields the expected lower bound for the revenue of the ad request. Equation (9) shows this expected lower bound of revenue.

$$E[\underline{R}(x_i, a(x_i))] = P(event\_state(x_i) = 1|x_i, a(x_i)) \times floor\_price(x_i) \quad (9)$$

In this equation x_i is an ad request, $a(x_i)$ is the ad network id of x_i and $event\_state(x_i)$ determines whether x_i is successful or not. $P(event\_state(x_i) = 1)$ is the success probability acquired from the prediction model, $floor\_price(x_i)$ is the floor price of x_i, and $E[\underline{R}]$ is the expected lower bound of the revenue when ad request x_i is successful. Because the revenue is zero for $event\_state = 0$, it is not written in the equation. Through this formula we can find an initial value for state-action pairs.

A simple ordering method is to select ad networks based on the output of the prediction model. However, this is shown that this ordering strategy does not provide the maximum revenue [1]. In addition, the initial values are not sufficient for decision making because there is no information about the long term revenue in these values. These values are just useful to find the ad network that will provide the advertisements in the shortest time. For instance, if the success probability of an ad network is 0.9, the floor price is 0.5 and the request order is 1, this method does not care about the revenue that another ad networks may make when this request fails [1]. To consider long term revenue as well as time, we model the problem as a reinforcement learning problem. For this reason we merely use them as initial values in the reinforcement learning process. Then, the reinforcement learning process takes the long term revenue into consideration when selecting ad networks.

The revenue obtained from (9) is used for learning state-action values. As we said before, these values are helpful in dealing with sparsity.

3.5 Learning State-Action Values

SSPs or ad networks are the agents. They observe the current user and impression properties and select one of the ad networks to send the ad request. Upon the response is received, the reward is determined which might be −1 or the value of floor price. The problem is episodic where, as explained in Sect. 3.4, each episode consists of a sequence of ad requests. We use Monte Carlo method to learn state action values. In the Monte Carlo algorithm, for each state s and action a, $Q(s, a)$ is obtained through averaging over all returns starting from s until end of episode. Since in each episode there is at most one occurrence of a certain state-action pair, the first visit Monte Carlo can do well [19].

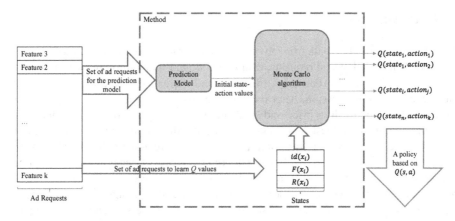

Fig. 2. Proposed method for learning the expected revenue of selecting each ad network in each state. First, some of ad requests are used by the prediction model to find an expected lower bound of the revenue. Then, we use these expected values and new ad requests to find state-action values through Monte Carlo algorithm. Finally, greedy action selection policy will select the best action in each state [2].

The typical Monte Carlo starts with initializing all Q values with zero or arbitrary values. We change this version to be fit with our purposes. In our approach, the values acquired from (9) are considered as initial Q values and they are updated incrementally. The number of data samples used for prediction model is used as a weight for the initial values. The Monte Carlo algorithm yields the value of each state-action pair. The modified updating rule of the Monte Carlo algorithm is defined in (10).

$$Q(s,a) = \frac{\sum_{j=1}^{n_1(s,a)} Reward_j^{x_i}(s,a) + E[\underline{R}(s,a)] \times n_2(s,a)}{n_1(s,a) + n_2(s,a)} \tag{10}$$

$$s.t. \ \ x_i \in D(s,a)$$

where $n_1(s,a)$ is the number of $s(x_i)$ and $a(x_i)$ pair in the data samples observed so far, and $n_2(s,a)$ is the number of $s(x_i)$ in the dataset used for initialization when its ad network id is $a(x_i)$. In other words, $n_1(s,a)$ is the length of $D(s,a)$. Before computing the average and updating $Q(s,a)$, the current ad request should be added to $D(s,a)$. $E[\underline{R}(s,a)]$ is the average of the expected revenue of all ad requests that their corresponding state is s.

The final output of this method is the state-action values. The publisher can decide which ad networks to send the ad requests to achieve the maximum expected revenue in the shortest time. In the next section, we discuss the results and evaluate our method by comparing the expected rewards using our method to actual revenues obtained in the dataset. Figure 2 provides an overview of our proposed method.

4   Data Analysis

We use real-time bidding data from an online publisher to test our method. Each dataset corresponds to one day's ad requests, containing around one million records. For each impression, the request order starts from one and increases after each unsuccessful attempt to sell that impression. After receiving an unsuccessful response, the publisher decreases the value of floor price and sends the new ad request to a new ad network. Thus, increasing the request order and changing the floor price are the properties of the environment in each state transition. In other words, we assume that the pattern for changing the floor price is fixed. In order to know the rate of changing the floor price and the request order, we consider all sequences of a certain day and plot the average of the floor prices for each request order. Figure 3 illustrates the average of the floor prices per request orders for successful, unsuccessful and all of the sequences. This figure shows how the environment changes after each attempt.

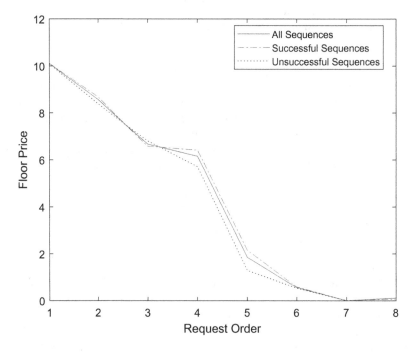

Fig. 3. The changing in the value of floor price after unsuccessful attempts.

Figure 3 also shows that there is no huge difference between the distribution of the floor prices in successful and unsuccessful sequences. It is possible that setting floor price dynamically will increase the revenue but we leave this problem as a future work and focus on the role of the ad networks. Based on this figure, the decreasing rate for different request orders are different. For instance, the slope of the line between request order 3 and 4 are lower than others. The reason behind this observation comes from

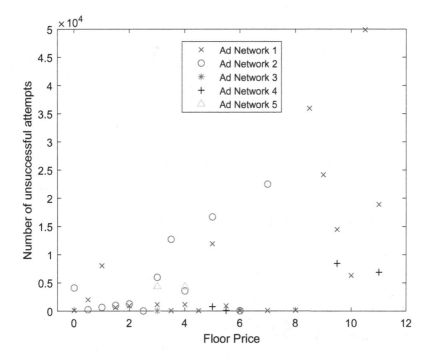

Fig. 4. The number of unsuccessful attempts for each floor price and ad network.

the fixed changing pattern of floor price. As we observed from the data, in some of the sequences, the floor price increases between these two request orders. It is not a problem because we assume the changing pattern as a property of the environment and the publisher as an agent cannot alter that.

Figure 4 shows the number of unsuccessful attempts per floor price for each ad network. A sequential numbering started from one is used for the name of ad networks. As it is concluded from this figure, ad network 1 is the first ad network in the predefined ordering and in many cases it cannot sell the impression with the highest price. However, ad network 4 has lower number of failures than ad network 1 for the high prices. Conversely, for the lower prices ad network 1 is more successful. This is a good motivation for finding a dynamic ordering of ad networks instead of predefined and fixed one.

Different ad networks have different success rate. Based on the values of floor price and request order, success rate varies. As it is shown in Table 1, these two values are important in predicting success probability. Figures 5a and b show the effects of floor price and request order on the success rate of each ad network. These figures shows that the success rate changes for different values of floor price and request order and this observation supports the definition of the states which is based on floor price and request order.

As mentioned before, the time feature is not involved in the state definition. Although it seems that it is necessary to consider the time in decision making, this

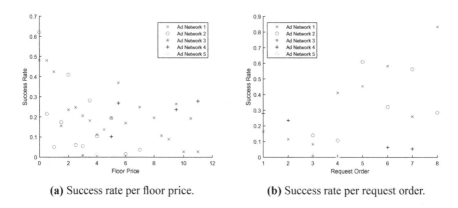

(a) Success rate per floor price.   **(b)** Success rate per request order.

Fig. 5. The success rate per floor price and request order for each ad network.

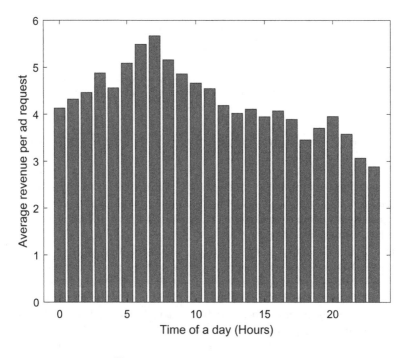

Fig. 6. The average revenue per hour.

feature is not as important as request order and floor price. We have seen that the importance of this feature based on the prediction model is lower than the selected features. As another convincing explanation, Fig. 6 shows the average revenue per hours of a day. In fact, this revenue is the total revenue divided by the number of ad requests. Therefore, each bar in Fig. 6 shows the revenue per ad request. Based on this figure, the average revenue does not vary too much during a day. Thus, a proper decision support tool for selecting ad networks will increase the revenue regardless of the time of ad requests.

5   Experiments and Results

The ordering method is developed to increase the revenue of ad publishers. This section evaluates the method. The evaluation is based on testing on real time bidding data. The method requires initial state-action values and uses the ad requests to learn final Q values. For the evaluation of the initial values obtained from the prediction model, we use binary classification performance measures. Since it is not feasible to test our method in the real environment, we compare the expected revenue of selecting the action corresponding to the highest Q value with the actual revenue obtained from the historical data. We consider the floor price as a lower bound of revenue for impressions.

The dataset D contains the ad requests of one week (20–26 November 2017) for users in the Netherlands. We use some part of this dataset for finding the initial state-action values and the rest for the Monte Carlo algorithm. The attributes of our dataset are introduced in [2].

Table 2. Performance measures for prediction model.

Event state = 1	Nov 20	Nov 21	Nov 22	Nov 23	Nov 24	Nov 25	Nov 26
Precision	0.7388	0.7668	0.7468	0.7382	0.7816	0.7991	0.8012
Recall	0.7165	0.7291	0.6781	0.6967	0.7486	0.7598	0.7662
F1	0.7275	0.7475	0.7108	0.7168	0.7647	0.7790	0.7833
Accuracy	0.7314	0.7549	0.7240	0.7261	0.7700	0.7844	0.7879
Kappa	0.4628	0.5098	0.4480	0.4521	0.5400	0.5689	0.5758

5.1   Initial Values Evaluation

In this section we discuss the result of event state prediction on the refined dataset. The new dataset only contains successful sequences. As mentioned before, incomplete sequences are removed because there is no information about the reason and distribution. This section shows that if we assume that all ad slots will finally be sold in the auction, we can predict whether an ad network could find a proper bidder or not with an acceptable performance. This assumption does not restrict the problem because when the price of an ad slot is zero, it will definitely be sold. The reduction in floor price is observed in the historical data and it is involved in state transitions.

There are seven available datasets that each one corresponds to a day of week in the period of 20th to 26th of November 2017. Briefly speaking, the prediction model is a classifier that labels each data sample with 0 or 1. A zero value denotes that this attempt to get an advertisement from specified ad network will not be successful. Conversely, if the prediction result is one, then the request to this ad network will result in filling the ad slot. Our classifier is evaluated for this task using standard classification performance measures, namely precision, recall, F1 score, kappa and ROC curve.

After data preprocessing that is explained in Sect. 3.4, the feature vector consists of 673 features. We tested different classification methods such as Bayesian classifier,

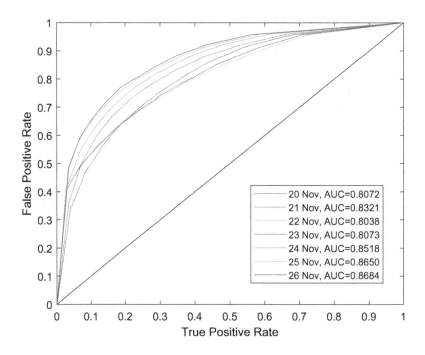

Fig. 7. ROC curve for 7 datasets.

Support Vector Machine and Random Forest classifier. We finally opted for the random forest classifier as it has shown to achieve the best performance on our data.

Each sequence contains one to eight ad requests and only the last one is successful. Therefore, the number of successful requests is far lower than the number of unsuccessful ones and balancing is necessary. Undersampling and oversampling are the two possible approaches. The SMOTE NC is reported to be a good method for oversampling [7]. However, this method does not consider the dependencies between features. For instance, if the browser of all ad requests from a given user is Chrome but the prevalent browser of the nearest neighbors is Firefox, then sampling using SMOTE NC would result in an incorrect sample combining this user characteristics to Firefox. Because the number of samples per day are too high (about 1 million), oversampling makes the dataset very large and loading the data for the classifier is not practical. The samples with event state 1 are more important in our prediction model because they provide the initial state-action values for our method. For this reason, we opted for the random undersampling method for balancing the dataset [10]. Using this sampling method prevents information loss, because these values are initial state-action values and the rest of data samples containing incomplete sequences will be used in the Monte Carlo algorithm.

Table 2 contains the performance measures of the prediction model. We applied the classifier separately on each day. For each day, we implemented a 5-fold cross validation method and computed the average performance over all folds. In Sect. 5.2 the sensitivity of the performance to the number of folds is experimented. As illustrated in Table 2, if there is not any incomplete sequences we can predict whether an ad request will provide an advertisement or not with a good F1 score (above 0.7). Figure 7 shows the ROC curves of predicting success probability for seven consecutive days. The average value of AUC for these seven dataset is 0.74.

The success probabilities for each ad network may be obtained with a good precision when there is not any incomplete sequences. Through multiplying the probability of $event\_state = 1$ for each ad request and ad network to the value of $floor\_price$ of that ad request, a lower bound of revenue is obtained.

5.2 Sensitivity to the Number of Folds

As it is mentioned earlier, 5-fold cross validation is used to train the classifier. In this section we try to realize the sensitivity of our prediction model to the number of folds. For this purpose, we develop three different models that are trained based on 5-fold, 10-fold and 20-fold cross validation. In this structure, two k-fold selection procedures are followed. In the first one, the folds are selected uniformly based on a static ordering of ad request. In other words, there is no shuffling in the ad requests. The second one selects fold after shuffling the ad requests. Generally, the shuffling increases the average performance of the prediction. Table 3 contains the average F-score of each k-fold cross validation and Fig. 8 illustrates the ROC curves of these approaches. Based on this result, we infer that the best k-fold method is to first shuffle the dataset and then divide it into five part and follow 5-fold cross validation approach.

Table 3. Performance measures for prediction model.

K-fold	5-fold	10-fold	20-fold
F-Score of shuffled dataset	0.7848	0.7847	0.7846
F-Score without shuffling	0.6547	0.7038	0.7507

5.3 State-Action Values Evaluation

Evaluation of the Q values is based on the total reward that is obtained by following the greedy policy. There are about 1 million ad requests per day and all of them are used in learning. The reinforcement learning requires merely one observation of the environment at a time, there is no need to load all the data entirely. This property provides the possibility of processing a large number of ad requests.

The episodes used in the Monte Carlo algorithm are obtained by considering the chronological ordering of ad requests. We used the ad requests of 20th of November for the initialization and found initial state-action values. Then, we used the data samples of the next five days in the Monte Carlo algorithm. Finally, we compared the real revenue (based on sum of the values of floor prices for ad requests with $eventstate = 1$ as a lower bound for revenue) with the expected revenue that is based on a greedy policy with respect to the state-action values.

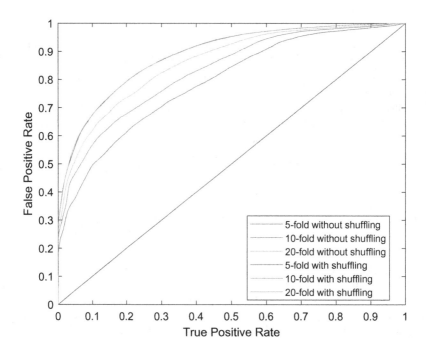

Fig. 8. ROC curves for 6 k-fold clustering.

To determine the threshold values t_{fp} and t_{ro}, we tested different values and found that medians of the values of floor price and request order make the best balance between the number of states and the number of observed actions for each state. Figure 9 illustrates the cumulative revenue prediction for the test dataset (red curve) compared to the real revenue earned (blue curve). The ad requests of November 26 were used for testing the method. As you can see in the figure, there is noticeable difference between the two curves. For each episode, we considered only the first ad request, because the state-action value of each state-action pair is the expected revenue of a sequence starting from that state. Therefore, if a SSP acts greedily with respect to the state-action values and selects the ad network with the highest value, the resulting revenue would be far more than following the predefined ordering approach.

Theoretically there are huge differences between these two values which indicate the potential of our proposed method. In the future we will test it on the real platform and compare the theoretical results with the observed ones.

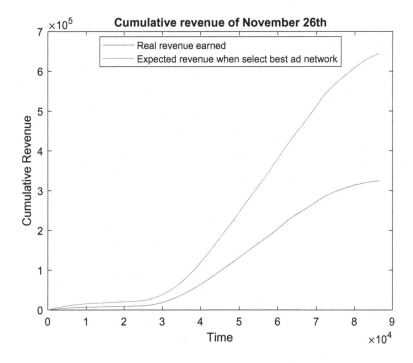

Fig. 9. Expected revenue vs. real revenue. (Color figure online)

5.4 Sensitivity to the Penalty Value

Current structure is based on setting a -1 for the reward of unsuccessful attempts. This penalty value is responsible to find the advertisements as soon as possible. By altering the penalty, we actually alter the priority of time in our model. If the minus value of the penalty is too large, the publisher's policy is too find the advertisements in the shortest time regardless of the revenue. For example, when the penalty is -10, being unsuccessful in the first attempt add a large minus value to the Q values. The publisher tries to take the action corresponding to the maximum Q value. This action is the one that provides the advertisement faster than the others. Obviously, the revenue is affected based on this policy. The penalty value deals with the trade-off between time and revenue. Figure 10 shows the comparison between the total revenue of setting different penalty values.

Based on Fig. 10, the lower penalty entails decreasing in the amount of revenue. This makes sense because when the penalty is very low (the minus value of penalty is high), the policy is mainly to acquire advertisements as soon as possible. Therefore, selling the ad slot to the lower bid in the first attempt, is preferred to the optimal bid that may be received in the next attempts. In sum, the penalty value determines the preference of a publisher. The publisher can set it dynamically to keep a balance between response time and revenue.

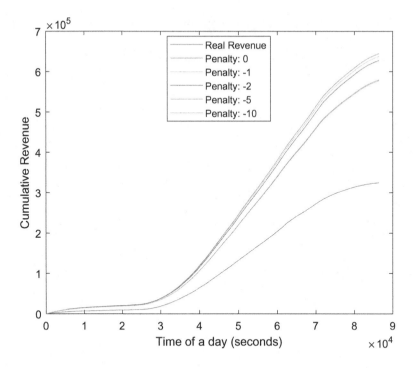

Fig. 10. Impact of different penalty values on the policy and total reward.

6   Conclusions

This paper proposed a reinforcement learning based decision support tool for online ad publishers to help them finding an ordering of ad networks through that the maximum revenue can be earned. The revenue is obtained by selling ad impressions in real time auctions. Different ad networks for running auctions are available for a publisher. Our method helps publishers to decide the best ad network at each step. The method models the problem as a reinforcement learning problem by defining a set of ad requests as states and the ad networks as actions. Then, it assigns a Q value for each state-action pair. A prediction model initializes these Q values and the modified Monte Carlo algorithm updates them continuously until convergence. Since, the number of episodes is limited, batch updating is followed.

The method is suitable for publishers that participate in the real time bidding via waterfall strategy. The response of sending ad requests are either a bid value or a message showing that no bid could be found. During the procedure of selling a certain impression, the ad networks are selected sequentially until finding proper bid. At each trial, our method determines the best ad network and following the method results in increasing the revenue.

Advertising is an important way of making money for website owners. Although real time bidding and programmatic advertising make the connection between publishers and advertisers much easier, the publishers should take care of the way of participating to the auction. Waterfall strategy and Header Bidding are the two ways [26]. Our proposed method increases the revenue in waterfall strategy by dynamically determining the best ad network. This method is very helpful for publishers and they no longer need to define a fixed ordering.

This ordering approach is also applicable for the header bidding. In header bidding, connecting with ad networks is not sequentially anymore. A publisher sends separate ad requests to all ad networks at the same time. Then, the highest bid is selected for selling the impression. This strategy guarantees that the maximum possible bid would not be missed. However, a challenging issue is the loading time of the webpage. Although all of the ad requests are sent simultaneously, the publisher should wait until receiving the responses from all of ad networks. Sometimes, the maximum bid is received very fast and it is not necessary to wait for all responses. Nonetheless, the publisher is not aware of the other bids and the maximum is determined only after receiving all bids. In the future we will adapt our method with the header bidding. Instead of deriving an ordering of ad networks, we will find a subset of ad networks for each impression to optimize the response time and the revenue. In other word, the goal is to solve the trade-off between time and revenue in header bidding which is discussed in Sect. 5.4.

Instead of developing a prediction model to solve the sparsity, we plan to use function approximation as future work. Even though the prediction model could be counted as an approximation method, it is separated from the RL step and is learned offline. We will assign a parametric function instead of the tabular one to replace the offline learning part. Through this modification, the algorithm can learn without any initial values and the sparsity is solved by using a continuous function.

Acknowledgment. This work was supported by EU EUROSTARS (Project E! 11582).

References

1. Afshar, R.R., Zhang, Y., Firat, M., Kaymak, U.: A decision support method to increase the revenue of ad publishers in waterfall strategy. In: IEEE Conference on Computational Intelligence for Financial Engineering and Economics (CIFEr) (2019)
2. Afshar, R.R., Zhang, Y., Firat, M., Kaymak, U.: A reinforcement learning method to select ad networks in waterfall strategy. In: Proceedings of the 11th International Conference on Agents and Artificial Intelligence, vol. 2, pp. 256–265. SCITEPRESS-Science and Technology Publications (2019)
3. Austin, D., Seljan, S., Monello, J., Tzeng, S.: Reserve price optimization at scale. In: 2016 IEEE 3rd International Conference on Data Science and Advanced Analytics (DSAA), pp. 528–536. IEEE (2016)
4. Balseiro, S.R., Feldman, J., Mirrokni, V., Muthukrishnan, S.: Yield optimization of display advertising with ad exchange. Manag. Sci. **60**(12), 2886–2907 (2014)
5. Busch, O.: The programmatic advertising principle. In: Busch, O. (ed.) Programmatic Advertising. MP, pp. 3–15. Springer, Cham (2016). https://doi.org/10.1007/978-3-319-25023-6_1
6. Cai, H., et al.: Real-time bidding by reinforcement learning in display advertising. In: Proceedings of the Tenth ACM International Conference on Web Search and Data Mining, pp. 661–670. ACM (2017)
7. Chawla, N.V., Bowyer, K.W., Hall, L.O., Kegelmeyer, W.P.: Smote: synthetic minority oversampling technique. J. Artif. Intell. Res. **16**, 321–357 (2002)

8. Dinodia, P.: Header bidding vs waterfall: how the two revenue optimisation hacks differ (2017). https://www.adpushup.com/blog/header-bidding-vs-waterfall/

9. Ghosh, A., McAfee, P., Papineni, K., Vassilvitskii, S.: Bidding for representative allocations for display advertising. In: Leonardi, S. (ed.) WINE 2009. LNCS, vol. 5929, pp. 208–219. Springer, Heidelberg (2009). https://doi.org/10.1007/978-3-642-10841-9_20

10. Japkowicz, N., et al.: Learning from imbalanced data sets: a comparison of various strategies. In: AAAI Workshop on Learning from Imbalanced Data Sets, Menlo Park, CA, vol. 68, pp. 10–15 (2000)

11. Jones, M.J., Viola, P.: Robust real-time object detection. In: Workshop on Statistical and Computational Theories of Vision, vol. 266, p. 56 (2001)

12. Li, J., Ni, X., Yuan, Y.: The reserve price of ad impressions in multi-channel real-time bidding markets. IEEE Trans. Comput. Soc. Syst. **5**(2), 583–592 (2018)

13. Muthukrishnan, S.: Ad exchanges: research issues. In: Leonardi, S. (ed.) WINE 2009. LNCS, vol. 5929, pp. 1–12. Springer, Heidelberg (2009). https://doi.org/10.1007/978-3-642-10841-9_1

14. Quinlan, J.R.: Induction of decision trees. Mach. Learn. **1**(1), 81–106 (1986)

15. Rhuggenaath, J., Akcay, A., Zhang, Y., Kaymak, U.: Fuzzy logic based pricing combined with adaptive search for reserve price optimization in online ad auctions. In: IEEE International Conference on Fuzzy Systems (FUZZ-IEEE) (2019)

16. Rhuggenaath, J., Akcay, A., Zhang, Y., Kaymak, U.: Optimizing reserve prices for publishers in online ad auctions. In: IEEE Conference on Computational Intelligence for Financial Engineering and Economics (CIFEr) (2019)

17. Rhuggenaath, J., Akcay, A., Zhang, Y., Kaymak, U.: A PSO-based algorithm for reserve price optimization in online ad auctions. In: 2019 IEEE Congress on Evolutionary Computation (CEC) (2019)

18. Rhuggenaath, J., Zhang, Y., Akcay, A., Kaymak, U.: Optimal display-ad allocation with guaranteed contracts and supply side platforms, working paper (2018)

19. Sutton, R.S., Barto, A.G., et al.: Reinforcement Learning: An Introduction. MIT Press, Cambridge (1998)

20. Vengerov, D.: A gradient-based reinforcement learning approach to dynamic pricing in partially-observable environments. Future Gene. Comput. Syst. **24**(7), 687–693 (2008)

21. Wang, J., Zhang, W., Yuan, S., et al.: Display advertising with real-time bidding (RTB) and behavioural targeting. Found. Trends® Inf. Retrieval **11**(4–5), 297–435 (2017)

22. Wu, D., et al.: Budget constrained bidding by model-free reinforcement learning in display advertising. In: Proceedings of the 27th ACM International Conference on Information and Knowledge Management, pp. 1443–1451. ACM (2018)

23. Wu, W.C.H., Yeh, M.Y., Chen, M.S.: Predicting winning price in real time bidding with censored data. In: Proceedings of the 21st ACM SIGKDD International Conference on Knowledge Discovery and Data Mining, pp. 1305–1314. ACM (2015)

24. Xie, Z., Lee, K.C., Wang, L.: Optimal reserve price for online ads trading based on inventory identification. In: Proceedings of the ADKDD 2017, p. 6. ACM (2017)

25. Yuan, S., Wang, J., Chen, B., Mason, P., Seljan, S.: An empirical study of reserve price optimisation in real-time bidding. In: Proceedings of the 20th ACM SIGKDD International Conference on Knowledge Discovery and Data Mining, pp. 1897–1906. ACM (2014)

26. Zawadziński, M.: What's the difference between waterfall auctions & header bidding? (2016). http://bit.ly/2KpT5Po

27. Zhang, W., Yuan, S., Wang, J.: Optimal real-time bidding for display advertising. In: Proceedings of the 20th ACM SIGKDD International Conference on Knowledge Discovery and Data Mining, pp. 1077–1086. ACM (2014)

Neural Hidden Markov Model

Zuoquan Lin[✉] and Jiehu Song

Department of Information Science, School of Mathematical Sciences,
Peking University, Beijing 100871, China
{linzuoquan,songjh}@pku.edu.cn

Abstract. Hidden Markov models are tractable to capture long-term dependencies but intractable to compute the transition probabilities of higher-order process. We propose a neural hidden Markov models to compute the transition probabilities of higher-order hidden Markov model by a neural network and reduce the cost of computation. It is applied for time-aware recommender systems to show the benefits from the hybrid of combining neural network and hidden Markov model. We implement the recommender system and experiment on real datasets to demonstrate better performances over the existing recommender systems.

Keywords: Hidden Markov model · Neural network · Recommender system · Collaborative filtering

1 Introduction

Hidden Markov models (HMMs) have been widely applied to many real-world applications. Usually HMMs only deal with first-order transition probability distribution among the hidden states. Due to their very nature higher-order HMMs are suitable to capture longer range sequential dependencies.

Higher-order HMMs are extremely complicated due to their large number of states that require estimation of the joint probabilities of the previous states. Classical algorithms, such as the Baum-Welch reestimation equations, can either be generalized to higher-order cases, or reduced to lower-order (e.g., first-order) equivalents for training. Unfortunately, the number of transition probabilities in higher-order HMMs grows with the power of the order of the model. Conventional training procedures rapidly become computationally intractable due to their space and runtime requirements.

In the previous work [9], we proposed the neural HMMs (NHMMs) that replace the computation of the transition probabilities of higher-order HMMs by neural networks (NNs). NHMMs reduce the time and space cost of higher-order HMMs due to computational ability of deep learning. In this paper, we extend NHMMs to applications that encompass sequential or temporal data with long-term dependencies and apply NHMMs for recommender systems to illustrate.

The recommendation predicts a user's behavior from historical data. Higher-order HMMs are well suited for modeling the recommendation problem. Time-aware recommender systems (TARS) exploit time information and track the

© Springer Nature Switzerland AG 2019
J. van den Herik et al. (Eds.): ICAART 2019, LNAI 11978, pp. 37–54, 2019.
https://doi.org/10.1007/978-3-030-37494-5_3

evolution of users and items that are important for giving satisfactory recommendations [5]. HMMs and NNs are two common models for TARS. HMMs use the hidden states to describe dynamic of users and items [25], but most of them are simple first-order HMMs. NNs have been well applied for recommender systems in recent years [37]. Recurrent neural networks (RNNs) are suitable for sequential data with long-term dependencies [8,10,11,17,18,20,27,33]. However, RNNs have some shortages compared with HMMs for recommender systems: (1) RNNs use the order of the users' behaviors, but neglect the time span between the behaviors; (2) There is not an overall time axis in RNNs to indicate actual time points of each behavior; (3) RNNs can not represent temporal relationship among the behaviors from multiple users, and hence lack of personalization for each user. HMMs can provide meaning of the hidden states for the analysis of the properties of both users and items where RNNs can not.

We implement the time-aware recommender system based on NHMMs with the algorithm in both batch-learning and online-updating situations. It is beneficial from the hybrid of combining higher-order HMMs and NNs. We experiment on real datasets to demonstrate better performances over the state-of-the-art recommender systems.

In the next section, we discuss the related works. In Sect. 3, we present the NHMM. In Sect. 4, we apply NHMM in recommender systems. In Sect. 5, we experiment on real datasets to show the improvement performances of our algorithm. Finally, we make concluding remarks.

2 Related Works

First-order HMMs were first introduced for recommender systems [1,2,25]. These models can capture the duration that a user stays in a state. The hidden semi-Markov models were applied for recommender systems [35,36], which extended first-order HMMs on the dependency length from one time point to one staying state. These models can not describe long-term affects in which the user changes the states. Another kind of HMMs that were applied to recommender systems is the Kalman Filter [6,14,22,23,28,29]. This approach has continuous state space and continuous time axis. The dependency length in these models is extended to the last time point that the user has ratings. But it has the same problem about the long-term dependencies that is changed by the states.

In recent years, NNs have been applied for recommender systems, such as autoencoder [21,32], RBM [26], MLP [16,34], CNN [12]. In particular, RNNs are used for TARS. The sequential models apply the RNNs to model the history of the users' behavior as a sequence [10,11,27]. This approach uses the sequential order of the behavior generated by the users, but neglect the time span of the data. The session-based models make recommendation on the session data generated by users [8,17,18,20]. Similar to the sequential models, they use the order of the users' behavior sequence to make recommendation. Because there is no overall time axis in these approaches, they can not find temporal relationship between different users and describe the changes of multiple users at the same time. In [32], the model applied two separate RNNs for users and items for TARS. Because the RNNs do not provide the meaning of the hidden states, it is difficult to choose the function for interaction between users and items. Thus the two RNNs model have to add some stationary components, e.g., an additional matrix factorization model, to undertake the recommendation task.

There is literature of combining HMMs and NNs in other research fields. In speech recognition, the hybrid model of combining HMM and NN in [4] applied an NN to improve the discriminating power of HMM, in which the NN was considered as a general form of Markov model and used to capture contextual information. In molecular biology, the hybrid model in [3] applied an NN to reduce the number of parameters of HMM. These hybrid models deal with the problem of large number of the hidden states in HMM and use an NN to reduce the parameter size. They discussed long-term dependencies, but chose multiple first-order HMMs rather than a higher-order HMM. These models are totally different from the NHMM.

3 NHMM

In this section, we present the NHMM, including the inference and learning algorithm.

Let X_t be temporal state variable and E_t temporal evidence variable, whose possible values are in $\{1, \ldots, N\}$ and $\{1, \ldots, K\}$ respectively, and follow higher-order hidden Markov assumptions:

$$
\begin{aligned}
&P(X_t|X_{t-1}, X_{t-2}, \ldots, E_{t-1}, E_{t-2}, \ldots) \\
&= P(X_t|X_{t-1}, X_{t-2}, \ldots, X_{t-L}) \\
&= P(X_0|X_{-1}, X_{-2}, \ldots, X_{-L}),
\end{aligned}
\tag{1}
$$

$$
\begin{aligned}
&P(E_t|X_t, X_{t-1}, X_{t-2}, \ldots, E_{t-1}, E_{t-2}, \ldots) \\
&= P(E_t|X_t) \\
&= P(E_0|X_0),
\end{aligned}
\tag{2}
$$

where L is the order and N, K, L are integers. In higher-order HMMs, a matrix of transition probabilities with N^L rows is needed to describe $P(X_t|X_{t-1}, X_{t-2}, \ldots, X_{t-L})$ in (1) for the N^L value combinations of X_{t-1}, $X_{t-2}, \ldots, X_{t-L}$. The number of transition probabilities grows with the power of the order of the model and rapidly become computationally intractable. We use an NN to replace it to reduce the cost of computation.

Let $\phi(\cdot)$ and $\psi(\cdot)$ be NNs with parameters. Given the marginal distribution of X at the previous L time points,

$$
P(X_{t-i}) = \overrightarrow{x_{t-i}}, \quad i = 1, 2, \ldots, L.
\tag{3}
$$

Then $P(X_t)$ is defined as follows:

$$
P(X_t) = \phi(\overrightarrow{x_{t-1}}, \overrightarrow{x_{t-2}}, \ldots, \overrightarrow{x_{t-L}}),
\tag{4}
$$

where the input and output of $\phi(\cdot)$ are vectors with the dimensions LN and N respectively. The output satisfies $0 \leq \phi_j \leq 1$ and $\sum_{j=1}^{N} \phi_j = 1$. Note that $\phi(\cdot)$ may be any NN, such as feed-forward networks, RNNs or any NN that deals with such input and output. In this paper, we take $\phi(\cdot)$ as LSTM [19], which is formulated as follows:

$$
\begin{aligned}
C_{t-L} &= \mathrm{LSTM}(\overrightarrow{x_{t-L}}, \overrightarrow{0}, \overrightarrow{0}), \\
h_{t-L} &= \mathrm{LSTM}(\overrightarrow{x_{t-L}}, \overrightarrow{0}, C_{t-L}), \\
C_i &= \mathrm{LSTM}(\overrightarrow{x_i}, h_{i-1}, C_{i-1}), \quad t - L < i \leq t, \\
h_i &= \mathrm{LSTM}(\overrightarrow{x_i}, h_{i-1}, C_i), \quad t - L < i \leq t, \\
\phi &= \mathrm{softmax}(\overrightarrow{h_t}),
\end{aligned}
\tag{5}
$$

where for every i satisfying $t - L \leq i \leq t$, C_i is the cell state at time i while h_i is the output at time i.

The observation and initial state of NHMM are defined with a matrix and a vector just like standard HMM:

$$
P(E_t = k | X_t = j) = B_{j,k},
\tag{6}
$$

$$
P(X_t = i) = \pi_i, \quad -L \leq t < 0.
\tag{7}
$$

The inference of NHMM finds the conditional distribution $P(X_t | E_{0:T-1} = \overrightarrow{e})$, given an evidence sequence $\overrightarrow{e} = [e_0, e_1, \ldots, e_{T-1}]$. To do this, we present the neural network approximated forward-backward algorithm. It imitates the procedure of the forward-backward algorithm of HMM [24], and calculates an approximation $\gamma(t) = P(X_t | E_{0:T-1} = \overrightarrow{e})$.

The forward steps are in the following:

$$
\alpha(t) = \begin{cases} \pi, & -L \leq t < 0, \\ \phi(\alpha'(t-1), \ldots, \alpha'(t-L)), & 0 \leq t, \end{cases}
\tag{8}
$$

where

$$
\alpha'(t) = normalize(\alpha(t) \odot B_{:,e_t}),
\tag{9}
$$

and $\odot$ means element-wise product of two vectors. $B_{:,e_t}$ means the e_t column of the matrix B. If there is not evidence at t (for $t < 0$ or $t \geq T$), $B_{:,e_t}$ is $normalize(\overrightarrow{1})$. The function $normalize(\cdot)$ is defined as follows:

$$
normalize(\overrightarrow{v}) = \frac{\overrightarrow{v}}{\sum_{j=1}^{N} |v_j|}.
\tag{10}
$$

The backward steps are in the following:

$$
\beta(t) = \begin{cases} normalize(\overrightarrow{1}), & T \leq t < T + L, \\ \psi(\beta'(t+1), \ldots, \beta'(t+L)), & t < T, \end{cases}
\tag{11}
$$

where

$$
\beta'(t) = normalize(\beta(t) \odot B_{:,e_t}).
\tag{12}
$$

Where $\psi(\cdot)$ is another NN, whose lengths of the input and the output are the same as the ones of $\phi(\cdot)$. Note that $\psi(\cdot)$ may be any NN, here we taken as LSTM. $\psi(\cdot)$ is said the reverse sequence network of $\phi(\cdot)$. If ϕ is the function $(\overrightarrow{v_L}, \overrightarrow{v_{L-1}}, \ldots, \overrightarrow{v_1}) \to \overrightarrow{v_{L+1}}$, ψ is the function $(\overrightarrow{v_2}, \overrightarrow{v_3}, \ldots, \overrightarrow{v_{L+1}}) \to \overrightarrow{v_1}$.

Thus, we can find γ by the following:

$$\gamma(t) = normalize(\alpha'(t) \odot \beta(t)). \tag{13}$$

Another inference task of NHMM is to find the distribution at the next time point as follow:

$$\gamma(T) = P(X_T | E_{0:T-1} = \overrightarrow{e}) = \phi(\gamma(T-1), \ldots, \gamma(T-L)), \tag{14}$$

from which we find $\gamma(T+1)$ with $\gamma(T), \ldots, \gamma(T-L+1)$, and any $\gamma(t)$ for $t > T$.

The learning algorithm of NHMM is described as follows: Suppose that we have some evidence sequences $ES = \{\overrightarrow{e}^{(1)}, \overrightarrow{e}^{(2)}, \ldots, \overrightarrow{e}^{(R)}\}$, where $\overrightarrow{e}^{(r)} = [e_0^{(r)}, e_1^{(r)}, \ldots, e_{T^{(r)}-1}^{(r)}]$. We need to learn the set of parameters $\theta = \{\phi, \psi, \pi, B\}$, where we simply write ϕ and ψ for the parameters of $\phi(\cdot)$ and $\psi(\cdot)$ respectively.

The learning algorithm works by inference-updating iterations similar to EM algorithm. We firstly use some initial parameters θ in the inference steps and calculate $z = \{\alpha, \alpha', \beta, \beta', \gamma\}$ for every evidence sequence. We then use z in updating steps to find a better θ^*. Finally we use θ^* in inference steps and carry on until finding satisfactory parameters.

The updating steps of π and B follow the Baum-Welch algorithm of HMM [24] as follows:

$$\pi^* = normalize(\sum_{r=1}^{R} \sum_{t=-L}^{-1} \gamma^{(r)}(t)), \tag{15}$$

$$B_{j,k}^* = \frac{\sum_{r=1}^{R} \sum_{t=0}^{T^{(r)}-1} 1_{e_t^{(r)}=k} \gamma_j^{(r)}(t)}{\sum_{r=1}^{R} \sum_{t=0}^{T^{(r)}-1} \gamma_j^{(r)}(t)}, \tag{16}$$

where

$$1_{e_t^{(r)}=k} = \begin{cases} 1, & e_t^{(r)} = k, \\ 0, & \text{else.} \end{cases} \tag{17}$$

To update the NNs $\phi(\cdot)$ and $\psi(\cdot)$, we need to build training sets for them. The sampling method is as follows: we firstly select a random $\overrightarrow{e}^{(r)} \in ES$, then select a random t such that $0 \le t < T^{(r)}$. According to the inputs and expected outputs of $\phi(\cdot)$ and $\psi(\cdot)$, we add the following two examples to the training set respectively:

$$(\alpha'^{(r)}(t-1), \alpha'^{(r)}(t-2), \ldots, \alpha'^{(r)}(t-L)) \to \gamma^{(r)}(t), \tag{18}$$

$$(\beta'^{(r)}(t+1), \beta'^{(r)}(t+2), \ldots, \beta'^{(r)}(t+L)) \to \gamma^{(r)}(t). \tag{19}$$

By the training sets, we use standard training algorithm of the NNs (taken as LSTM) to train.

4   Recommendation

In this section, we apply the NHMM to provide the model of TARS and the algorithm for recommendation.

Let $RS = <User, Item, Time, Level, Rating>$ be a recommender system, where

- $User$ is the set of users, and $user$ (or u) $\in User$ is a user.
- $Item$ is the set of items, and $item$ (or i) $\in Item$ is an item.
- $Time = \mathbb{Z}$ is the set of time points, where $\mathbb{Z}$ is the set of integers.
- $Level = \{1, 2, \ldots, N\}$ is the set of rating levels, where N is a given integer.
- $Rating$ is the set of ratings. $rating = (user, item, time, level)$ (or $r = (u, i, t, l)$) $\in Rating$ is a rating. It means $user$ gives $item$ rating $level$ at $time$.

We make collaborative filtering recommendation by analyzing the similarity of both users and items.

We introduce two hidden variables for the user type and the item type to describe the common properties of users and items. Intuitively, the users with the same type have similar properties. Any user (or item) has a type at a specific time. Because users and items change, their types change as well.

Let $X_{user,t}$ and $Y_{item,t}$ be state variables, which describe the user type and the item type at time t respectively. For ratings, we define a variable $R_{user,item,t}$ for each triplet $(user, item, t)$. In addition, RS has the following:

- $UserType = \{1, 2, \ldots, J\}$ is the set of user types, where J is a given integer.
- $ItemType = \{1, 2, \ldots, K\}$ is the set of item types, where K is a given integer.
- $X_{user,t} \in UserType$ is the variable for $user$'s type at t.
- $Y_{item,t} \in ItemType$ is the variable for $item$'s type at t.
- $R_{user,item,t} \in Level$ is the variable for the rating $user$ gives $item$ at t.

By some known ratings, $R_{user,item,t}$ are (partially) observed, while $X_{user,t}$ and $Y_{item,t}$ are hidden states.

For example, consider a recommender system where $User = \{u_1, u_2, u_3\}$, $Item = \{i_1, i_2\}$, $N = 5$, $Rating = \{ (u_1, i_1, 1, 5), (u_2, i_2, 3, 3), (u_1, i_2, 5, 1), (u_3, i_1, 6, 4) \}$, and set $J = 2$, $K = 3$. There are three user variables $X_{u_1,t}$, $X_{u_2,t}$ and $X_{u_3,t}$ whose possible values are in $UserType = \{1, 2\}$. The two item random variables $Y_{i_1,t}$, $Y_{i_2,t}$ have possible values in $ItemType = \{1, 2, 3\}$. There are four observed rating variables $R_{u_1,i_1,1} = 5$, $R_{u_2,i_2,3} = 3$, $R_{u_1,i_2,5} = 1$, and $R_{u_3,i_1,6} = 4$.

We consider that the users and the items generate ratings. When a user with the j-th type meets an item with the k-th type, the probability that the user likes the item is $p_{j,k}$. We use the binomial distribution $B(N-1, p_{j,k})$ to convert $p_{j,k}$ into discrete ratings as follows:

$$
\begin{aligned}
&P(R_{u,i,t} = n \mid X_{u,t} = j, Y_{i,t} = k) \\
&= \Pr(n - 1; N - 1, p_{j,k}) \\
&= \binom{N-1}{n-1} (p_{j,k})^{n-1} (1 - p_{j,k})^{N-n}.
\end{aligned}
\tag{20}
$$

The transitions of $X_{u,t}$ and $Y_{i,t}$ are described with two L-order NHMMs, whose parameters are $\theta = \{\phi, \psi, \pi\}$ and $\widetilde{\theta} = \{\widetilde{\phi}, \widetilde{\psi}, \widetilde{\pi}\}$ respectively. θ is shared by all the users and $\widetilde{\theta}$ is shared by all the items. There is no matrix B in θ because $p_{j,k}$ plays the role of generating evidences.

For the users, assume a user u has ratings at $M(u)$ time points $t_1 < t_2 < \ldots < t_{M(u)}$. For $1 \leq m \leq M(u)$, if we know $P(X_{u,t_{m-l}}) = \overrightarrow{x}_{u,t_{m-l}}$, $l = 1, 2, \ldots, L$, then $P(X_{u,t_m})$ is as follows:

$$P(X_{u,t_m}) = \phi(t_m - t_{m-1}, \overrightarrow{x}_{u,t_{m-1}}, t_m - t_{m-2}, \overrightarrow{x}_{u,t_{m-2}}, \ldots, t_m - t_{m-L}, \overrightarrow{x}_{u,t_{m-L}}). \tag{21}$$

Compared with (4), we make an adjustment here. We only consider the time points that the user has ratings, for there are a lot of time points that a user has no ratings in recommender systems. To indicate the actual time length between t_m and t_{m-l}, we add L dimensions in the input of $\phi(\cdot)$. For t_l with index $l \leq 0$, we set $t_l = t_1 - \tau$ and $\overrightarrow{x}_{u,t_l} = \pi$, where τ is a given small time span.

Similarly, for the items, if item i is rated at $M(i)$ time points $t_1 < t_2 < \ldots < t_{M(i)}$ and we know $P(Y_{i,t_{m-l}}) = \overrightarrow{y}_{i,t_{m-l}}$, $l = 1, 2, \ldots, L$ for $1 \leq m \leq M(i)$, then $P(Y_{i,t_m})$ is as follows:

$$P(Y_{i,t_m}) = \widetilde{\phi}(t_m - t_{m-1}, \overrightarrow{y}_{i,t_{m-1}}, t_m - t_{m-2}, \overrightarrow{y}_{i,t_{m-2}}, \ldots, t_m - t_{m-L}, \overrightarrow{y}_{i,t_{m-L}}). \tag{22}$$

Now we consider the inference tasks of RS. Consider a user u who has ratings at $M(u)$ time points $t_1 < t_2 < \ldots < t_{M(u)}$. At time points t_m, the user gives $S(u,t_m)$ ratings. These ratings are given to the items $i_1, i_2, \ldots i_{S(u,t_m)}$ and the levels are $n_1, n_2, \ldots, n_{S(u,t_m)}$.

We first calculate the conditional probability that a type-j user gives these $S(u,t_m)$ ratings at t_m, denoted as $b_{u,t_m,j}$. From (20) we have:

$$\begin{aligned}
b_{u,t_m,j} &= P(R_{u,i_1,t_m} = n_1, \ldots, R_{u,i_{S(u,t_m)},t_m} = n_{S(u,t_m)} \mid X_{u,t_m} = j) \\
&= \prod_{s=1}^{S(u,t_m)} P(R_{u,i_s,t_m} = n_s \mid X_{u,t_m} = j) \\
&= \prod_{s=1}^{S(u,t_m)} \sum_{k=1}^{K} \Pr(n_s - 1; N - 1, p_{j,k}) P(Y_{i_s,t_m} = k).
\end{aligned} \tag{23}$$

The vector $b_{u,t_m,:} = (b_{u,t_m,1}, \ldots, b_{u,t_m,J})$ shows the probability that the user generates these ratings at t_m with each type. It plays the role of $B_{:,e_t}$ in Sect. 3.

The Algorithm 1 is the forward-backward algorithm for users. When we refer to t_l with index $l < 1$, we set $t_l = t_1 - \tau$ and $\alpha'_u(t_l) = \pi$. For t_l with index $l > M(u)$, we set $t_l = t_{M(u)} + \tau$ and $\beta'_u(t_l) = normalize(\overrightarrow{1})$. For convenience, we abbreviate the procedure of getting $\alpha_u(t_m)$ and $\beta_u(t_m)$ as $\phi(t_m - t_{m-1}, \alpha'_u(t_{m-1}), \ldots, t_m - t_{m-L}, \alpha'_u(t_{m-L}))$ and $\psi(t_{m+1} - t_m, \beta'_u(t_{m+1}), \ldots, t_{m+L} - t_m, \beta'_u(t_{m+L}))$, respectively.

Algorithm 1. Forward-backward algorithm for users.

1: **function** INFERENCE_USER(u)
2:    **for** $m = 1$ to $M(u)$ **do**
3:        $C_{m-L} \leftarrow \text{LSTM}([t_m - t_{m-L}, \alpha'_u(t_{m-L})], \vec{0}, \vec{0})$
4:        $h_{m-L} \leftarrow \text{LSTM}([t_m - t_{m-L}, \alpha'_u(t_{m-L})], \vec{0}, C_{m-L})$
5:        **for** $i = L - 1$ to 1 **do**
6:            $C_{m-i} \leftarrow \text{LSTM}([t_m - t_{m-i}, \alpha'_u(t_{m-i})], h_{m-i-1}, C_{m-i-1})$
7:            $h_{m-i} \leftarrow \text{LSTM}([t_m - t_{m-i}, \alpha'_u(t_{m-i})], h_{m-i-1}, C_{m-i})$
8:        $\alpha_u(t_m) \leftarrow \text{softmax}(h_{m-1})$
9:        $\alpha'_u(t_m) \leftarrow normalize(\alpha_u(t_m) \odot b_{u,t_m,:})$
10:    **for** $m = M(u)$ to 1 **do**
11:        $C_{m+L} \leftarrow \text{LSTM}([t_{m+L} - t_m, \beta'_u(t_{m+L})], \vec{0}, \vec{0})$
12:        $h_{m+L} \leftarrow \text{LSTM}([t_{m+L} - t_m, \beta'_u(t_{m+L})], \vec{0}, C_{m+L})$
13:        **for** $i = L - 1$ to 1 **do**
14:            $C_{m+i} \leftarrow \text{LSTM}([t_{m+i} - t_m, \beta'_u(t_{m+i})], h_{m+i+1}, C_{m+i+1})$
15:            $h_{m+i} \leftarrow \text{LSTM}([t_{m+i} - t_m, \beta'_u(t_{m+i})], h_{m+i+1}, C_{m+i})$
16:        $\beta_u(t_m) \leftarrow \text{softmax}(h_{m+1})$
17:        $\beta'_u(t_m) \leftarrow normalize(\beta_u(t_m) \odot b_{u,t_m,:})$
18:    **for** $m = 1$ to $M(u)$ **do**
19:        $\gamma_u(t_m) \leftarrow normalize(\alpha'_u(t_m) \odot \beta_u(t_m))$

The inference steps for items are similar to the one for users. Consider an item i that is rated at $M(i)$ time points and has $S(i, t_m)$ rating at t_m. These ratings are from $u_1, \ldots, u_{S(i,t_m)}$ and the levels are $n_1, \ldots n_{S(i,t_m)}$. Then

$$b_{i,t_m,k} = \prod_{s=1}^{S(i,t_m)} \sum_{j=1}^{J} \Pr(n_s - 1; N - 1, p_{j,k}) P(X_{u_s,t_m} = j). \qquad (24)$$

The forward-backward algorithm Inference_Item(i) is similar to Algorithm 1 except for the function name, the function input and the indexes.

The inference steps are taken separately for each user and each item. When we do it for user u, we assume that the probability $P(Y_{i_s,t_m} = k)$ in (23) is known. Similarly, $P(X_{u_s,t_m} = j)$ in (24) is assumed to be known for inference steps of item i. In practical, we use $P(X_{u,t} = j) = (\gamma_u(t))_j$ and $P(Y_{i,t} = k) = (\gamma_i(t))_k$. The symbol $(\cdot)_j$ means the j-th element of the vector. We first initialize γ_u and γ_i, then take inference steps for u and i alternately to update them.

Finally, we present the learning algorithm for RS as follows. We update the parameters $\theta = \{\phi, \psi, \pi\}$, $\widetilde{\theta} = \{\widetilde{\phi}, \widetilde{\psi}, \widetilde{\pi}\}$, and $p_{j,k}$ with α, β and γ that we calculate in the inference steps. $p_{j,k}$ is updated according to the parameter estimation of binomial distribution as follows:

$$p^*_{j,k} = \frac{\sum_{(u,i,t,l)\in Rating}(l-1)\gamma_u(t)\gamma_i(t)}{\sum_{(u,i,t,l)\in Rating}(N-1)\gamma_u(t)\gamma_i(t)}. \qquad (25)$$

The prior π is updated as a sum of all the users' distribution of $t_{-L+1}, \ldots, t_0$. To find $\gamma(t_l)$ with $l \leq 0$, we take backward steps several times to find β and then γ.

In practical, a fixed $\pi = normalize(\overrightarrow{1})$ often has good performance because $\phi(\cdot)$ can generate the first L value of $\alpha(t_l)$ for $l > 0$ from those $normalize(\overrightarrow{1})$. We have

$$\pi^* = \text{normalize}(\sum_{u \in User} \sum_{l=-L+1}^{0} \gamma_u(t_l)). \qquad (26)$$

The $\phi(\cdot)$ and $\psi(\cdot)$ are trained with standard training algorithm of the NN taken as LSTM. We only need to build the training sets for them. To sample examples, we first select a random user $u \in User$, then select a random t_m from $M(u)$ time points when the user generates ratings. The following two examples are added to the training sets of ϕ and ψ respectively:

$$(\alpha'_u(t_{m-1}), \ldots, \alpha'_u(t_{m-L})) \rightarrow \gamma_u(t_m), \qquad (27)$$

$$(\beta'_u(t_{m+1}), \ldots, \beta'_u(t_{m+L})) \rightarrow \gamma_u(t_m). \qquad (28)$$

The updating of $\widetilde{\pi}$ and the training example sampling steps of $\widetilde{\phi}$ and $\widetilde{\psi}$ are the same as those of π, ϕ and ψ except for the indexes.

We present the algorithms for the routines of the NHMM for RS, including batch learning, online updating and prediction.

The batch learning algorithm learns the model from a set of training ratings. It firstly initializes the θ, $\widetilde{\theta}$, $p_{j,k}$, $\gamma_u(t)$, $\gamma_i(t)$ and empty training sets for each LSTM. Then it takes inference-learning iterations for a given loop number. In the inference steps, we randomly select a $u \in User$ or an $i \in Item$, call the Inference_User or Inference_Item functions to update γ. In the learning steps, we calculate $p_{j,k}, \pi, \widetilde{\pi}$, build the training sets for each LSTM and train them in standard way.

The online updating algorithm updates the model when receiving a rating $r = (u, i, t, l)$. We only take inference steps for both user and item that are related to this rating. Then we update $p_{j,k}, \pi, \widetilde{\pi}$ by (25) and (26). The first equation is a fraction of two sums in $Rating$, and the second equation is a sum in $User$ (or $Item$). We only need to subtract the previous contribution of the updated rating, user or item in these sums, and add their new contributions. We do not need to calculate the whole sums again. For the LSTMs, we sample some examples from u and i, and update the $\phi, \psi, \widetilde{\phi}, \widetilde{\psi}$ with these examples, i.e., only run several steps of the training algorithm of LSTM on them.

The prediction algorithm gives the prediction about the rating that a user u would give to an item i at time t. We firstly calculate $\gamma_u(t)$ and $\gamma_i(t)$ with the γ in the model:

$$\gamma_u(t) = \phi(t - t_{M(u)}, \gamma_u(t - t_{M(u)}), \ldots, t - t_{M(u)-L+1}, \gamma_u(t - t_{M(u)-L+1})), \quad (29)$$

$$\gamma_i(t) = \widetilde{\phi}(t - t_{M(i)}, \gamma_i(t - t_{M(i)}), \ldots, t - t_{M(i)-L+1}, \gamma_i(t - t_{M(i)-L+1})). \quad (30)$$

Then we use $\gamma_u(t)$ and $\gamma_i(t)$ to calculate the model predicted $P(R_{u,i,t} = n)$, denoted as $q_{u,i,t,n}$. The algorithm returns the vector $q_{u,i,t,:} = (q_{u,i,t,1}, \ldots, q_{u,i,t,N})$:

$$q_{u,i,t,n} = \sum_{j=1}^{J} \sum_{k=1}^{K} (\gamma_u(t))_j (\gamma_i(t))_k \Pr(n-1; N-1, p_{j,k}). \tag{31}$$

5 Experiments

The experiments adopt four datasets with different sizes as illustrated in Table 1.

Table 1. Datasets.

Dataset	User	Item	Rating	Density
MovieLens100k	944	1,683	100,000	6.29%
MovieLens1M	6,040	3,706	1,000,209	4.47%
Epinions	2,874	2,624	122,361	1.62%
Epinions Extended	11,201	109,520	5,449,415	0.44%

MovieLens100k (MLK) and **MovieLens1M (MLM)** [15] are two movie datasets scratched through the web site MovieLens. The **MovieLens100k** dataset consists of $100,000$ ratings from levels 1 to 5 which contain 943 users and $1,682$ movies. The **MovieLens1M** is comprised of $1,000,209$ ratings from levels 1 to 5 including $6,040$ users and $3,900$ movies. Two datasets own well-defined data of cleaning up by the providers, where the number of movies that every user rates is at least 20 movies.

Epinions (Ep) [30,31] and **Epinions (EpEx)** [30,31] are two e-commerce dataset collected through the web site Epinions. The **Epinions (Ep)** has data span from 1999 to 2011. It contains 27 categories of items rated into levels 1 to 5. We first make a clean-up preprocess to produce a 20-core dataset (every user rates at least 20 items and every item is rated by at least 20 users), which has $2,874$ users, $2,624$ items and $122,361$ ratings. The additional information in this dataset, like the categories of items and the trust relationships of users, are not adopted by our experiments. The **Epinions Extended (EpEx)** is about the reviews. A rating is between 1–5 levels to denote whether the review is considered to be helpful or not. We make a clean-up preprocess to produce a 20-core dataset. After doing that, there are $5,449,415$ ratings from $11,201$ users and $109,520$ items. It is a sparse dataset whose density (the number of ratings divided by the number of users and the number of items) is only 0.44%.

We make three kinds of experiments to test the performance of the algorithms in different environments.

- **Classical Experiment.** The ratings in the datasets are randomly divided into training set (80%) and test set (20%). The algorithms are trained by the training set to provide predictions about the ratings in the test set.

- **Time-order Experiment.** The ratings in the datasets are reordered according to the time they are generated. We take the former 80% as training set and the latter 20% as test set. This is a reasonable setup for TARS for it ensures that the algorithms predict the future by the past.
- **Time-order Online Experiment (TOO).** The ratings in the datasets are reordered according to the time they are generated and imported one by one to the algorithms. For every rating, the algorithms are first required to give their predicted rating, and then updated their parameters every time they receive new coming rating. This method simulates the situation of real-world online recommendation applications and is suitable to evaluate time-aware and online algorithms.

The test ratings related to the users and the items that have no ratings in the training set are not counted in the evaluation scores. In this case, the parameters of some algorithms for the related users or items are not defined, or just initialized by small random values. So the algorithms can not provide reasonable ratings. For the same reason, in time-order online experiments, the very first ratings for every user and item (i.e., the cold-start in the sense the user or item has not appeared before) are not counted in the scores.

The algorithms are evaluated by RMSE, MAE, MRR and NDCG. RMSE (Root Mean Square Error) and MAE (Mean Absolute Error) are two common metrics in recommender systems:

$$RMSE = \sqrt{\frac{\sum_{(u,i,t)\in R_{test}}(R_{u,i,t} - \hat{R}_{u,i,t})^2}{|R_{test}|}}, \tag{32}$$

$$MAE = \frac{\sum_{(u,i,t)\in R_{test}}|R_{u,i,t} - \hat{R}_{u,i,t}|}{|R_{test}|}, \tag{33}$$

where R_{test} denotes the test sets, $R_{u,i,t}$ is the real rating level , in which user u gives item i at time t and $\hat{R}_{u,i,t}$ represents the corresponding predicted rating level. The smaller value RMSE or MAE is, the better performance is. In addition, we refer to two other metrics MRR and NDCG. MRR (Mean Reciprocal Rank) equals to the average value of those reciprocal ranks. For user u, the reciprocal rank is the multiplicative inverse of $rank_u$ denoting the position of the first positive item in recommendation list of user u:

$$MRR = \frac{1}{|User|} \sum_{u=1}^{|User|} \frac{1}{rank_u}. \tag{34}$$

NDCG (Normalized Discounted cumulative gain) is the average of the $NDCG_u$ for all users. For user u, $NDCG_u$ is normalized DCG_u (Discounted Cumulative Gain) via being divided by the maximum possible gain $IDCG_u$. DCG_u is defined by the following:

$$DCG_u = \sum_{i=1}^{2} Rel_i + \sum_{i=3}^{N} \frac{Rel_i}{\log_2 i}, \tag{35}$$

where Rel_i denotes the relevancy of the i-th item and N is equal to the length of recommendation list of user u. For simplicity, we directly take levels 1-5 as relevancy.

We compare our algorithm NHMM-RS with several representative algorithms as follows.

- **Time Weight Collaborative Filtering (TWCF)** [13] is time-related item-based neighborhood method. It uses Pearson correlation coefficient to calculate the similarity of items, and then an exponential time weight function and the item similarity to make predictions. Similar to other neighborhood methods, the algorithm is able to run in online experiments.
- **Collaborative Kalman Filter (CKF)** [14] is a HMM that uses the Kalman Filter to make recommendation. The model has continuous time axis and continuous variables for users, items and ratings. It has an online updating algorithm and each update step only uses the most recent rating.
- **Recurrent Recommender Networks (RRN)** [33] is a time-aware model by the RNN. It uses an LSTM to capture dynamics of users and items in addition to a traditional low-rank factorization to describe the stationary components.
- **Streaming Recommender Systems (SRec)** [7] is a time-aware probabilistic model for recommender systems. It handles data as streams for effective recommendation, and uses a continuous-time random process to capture dynamics of users and items. It provides an online algorithm for real-time updating and making recommendation.

The hyperparameters of the tested algorithms are decided by grid search. Each hyperparameter is selected from a set of candidates to produce the best performance. In detail, the learning rate and regularization coefficient of RRN, NHMM-RS and the decay rate λ of TWCF are selected from $\{1, 0.1, 0.01, 0.001, 0.0001\}$. Because the CKF used a hyperparameter $\sigma = 1.76$, we select σ from $\{0.5, 0.6, 0.7, \ldots, 2.5\}$ for CKF. We use LSTM to implement the NNs in RRN and NHMM-RS. Another hyperparameter is latent vector length (for CKF, RRN and NHMM-RS). Because it is directly related to the time and space cost, we set it 10 for each algorithm for the sake of fairness.

Tables 2 and 3 summary the experiment results about RMSE and MAE. The results show that NHMM-RS has best performances on most experiments (19 of 24 scores). In other scores, it also has competitive performance in the nearly second place. Especially on the MovieLens1M, it achieves the best place on 5 scores. In time-order online experiments, it outperforms the existing algorithms, which shows that our model makes use of the time information in a proper way.

Tables 4 and 5 summary the experiment results about MRR and NDCG. On the MRR metric, NHMM-RS gains 8 No. 1 rankings among 12 lists. CKF owns 2 best results on Movielens1M in classical and time-order setup. RRN achieves the first place on 3 experiments. SRec also shows best performance on Epinions in classical setup. On the NDCG metric, NHMM-RS shows best performance on 9 experiments. Besides, CKF performs best on 3 experiments which all are on

Table 2. RMSE.

Setting	Datasets	TWCF	CKF	RRN	SRec	NHMM-RS
Classical	MLK	0.959	0.959	0.924	1.165	**0.923**
	MLM	1.044	**0.882**	0.895	1.399	0.900
	EP	1.219	1.075	1.107	1.097	**1.037**
	EPEX	0.460	0.404	0.445	1.002	**0.349**
Time-order	MLK	1.141	1.115	1.021	1.644	**1.008**
	MLM	1.622	**0.907**	1.034	1.395	0.932
	EP	1.324	1.167	1.123	1.175	**1.065**
	EPEX	0.513	0.879	0.479	1.118	**0.420**
Time-order online	MLK	1.004	1.062	1.090	1.467	**0.948**
	MLM	0.998	0.924	1.040	1.457	**0.913**
	EP	1.312	1.296	1.199	1.367	**1.065**
	EPEX	0.458	0.499	0.468	0.783	**0.358**

Movielens1M, and RRN shows best results on 1 experiments, and SRec performs best on 1 experiments.

We conduct experiments to analyze the convergency of the algorithms. The experiments are carried out on Movielens100K and Epinions datasets in time-order-online environment. As far as the size of dataset is concerned, an algorithm which can converge on small-size datasets further shows its excellent capacity. It is the reason why we choose those two small-scale datasets. To do that, we select two metrics RMSE and MAE. Then, for every algorithm, RMSE and MAE values are dynamically calculated and outputted with new 10% data as input.

Table 3. MAE.

Setting	Datasets	TWCF	CKF	RRN	SRec	NHMM-RS
Classical	MLK	0.756	0.749	0.936	0.912	**0.728**
	MLM	0.790	**0.694**	0.712	1.092	0.711
	EP	0.958	0.911	0.862	0.873	**0.803**
	EPEX	0.256	0.228	0.247	0.799	**0.169**
Time-order	MLK	0.891	0.842	0.829	1.284	**0.793**
	MLM	1.137	**0.709**	0.845	1.059	0.733
	EP	1.004	0.895	0.848	0.900	**0.812**
	EPEX	0.336	0.527	0.379	0.836	**0.318**
Time-order online	MLK	0.789	0.823	0.857	1.110	**0.756**
	MLM	0.788	0.724	0.812	1.111	**0.723**
	EP	1.010	0.995	0.929	1.049	**0.823**
	EPEX	0.234	0.293	0.327	0.404	**0.193**

Table 4. MRR.

Setting	Datasets	TWCF	CKF	RRN	SRec	NHMM-RS
Classical	MLK	0.784	0.800	0.772	0.733	**0.807**
	MLM	0.798	**0.870**	0.608	0.780	0.836
	EP	0.764	0.882	0.830	**0.896**	**0.896**
	EPEX	0.967	0.971	0.967	0.965	**0.973**
Time-order	MLK	0.673	0.727	**0.729**	0.692	**0.729**
	MLM	0.764	**0.841**	0.805	0.794	0.783
	EP	0.754	0.818	0.738	0.769	**0.819**
	EPEX	0.958	0.955	0.953	0.959	**0.984**
Time-order online	MLK	0.632	0.795	**0.803**	0.715	0.741
	MLM	0.654	0.862	**0.867**	0.722	0.718
	EP	0.748	0.861	0.842	0.824	**0.900**
	EPEX	0.964	0.956	0.950	0.958	**0.966**

Table 5. NDCG.

Setting	Datasets	TWCF	CKF	RRN	SRec	NHMM-RS
Classical	MLK	0.950	0.952	0.951	0.940	**0.953**
	MLM	0.951	**0.960**	0.919	0.946	0.955
	EP	0.942	0.968	0.956	**0.969**	**0.969**
	EPEX	0.995	0.991	0.989	0.988	**0.997**
Time-order	MLK	0.958	0.963	0.967	0.963	**0.967**
	MLM	0.954	**0.962**	0.956	0.957	0.958
	EP	0.969	0.978	0.966	0.974	**0.979**
	EPEX	0.997	0.990	0.989	0.990	**0.998**
Time-order online	MLK	0.928	0.945	0.946	0.930	**0.947**
	MLM	0.930	**0.959**	**0.959**	0.939	0.950
	EP	0.918	0.951	0.945	0.943	**0.960**
	EPEX	0.991	0.989	0.983	0.990	**0.992**

Figure 1 shows the final comparison results. As we can see in every experiment, the line of NHMM-RS is smoother than other algorithms, which reflects the fact that NHMM-RS achieves convergency faster.

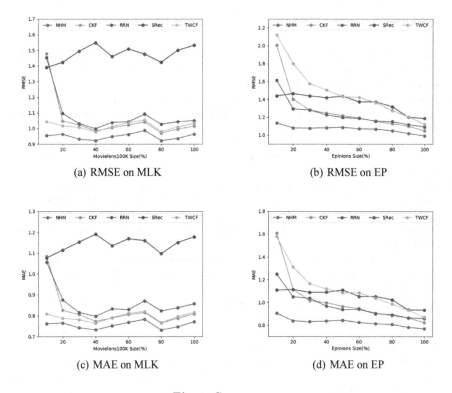

(a) RMSE on MLK   (b) RMSE on EP

(c) MAE on MLK   (d) MAE on EP

Fig. 1. Convergency.

6 Concluding Remarks

We proposed the neural hidden Markov model and apply it to time-aware recommender systems. It is well suitable for long-term dependencies and explainable for the interactions between users and items. We provided both offline batch-learning algorithm and efficient online updating algorithm. The experiments on real datasets demonstrate that our algorithm has better performance than the existing recommender systems.

We do not specify the neural networks in our models for the sake of generality. We can select the state-of-the-art NNs to implement our model to arrive at the best performance. If we adapt RNNs implementation in our model to deal with unfixed length input sequences, our model can be extended to unfixed order hidden Markov models, that is, we do not need to fix the order of hidden Markov models.

Many applications can use higher-order Markov models in a natural way, such as natural language precessing and reinforcement learning and so on, where the neural hidden Markov models can be applied.

Acknowledgements. This work is supported by Natural Science Fund of China under numbers 61672049/61732001.

References

1. Alanazi, A., Bain, M.: A people-to-people content-based reciprocal recommender using hidden Markov models. In: Proceedings of the 7th ACM Conference on Recommender Systems, pp. 303–306 (2013)
2. Alanazi, A., Bain, M.: A scalable people-to-people hybrid reciprocal recommender using hidden Markov models. In: The 2nd International Workshop on Machine Learning Methods for Recommender Systems (2016)
3. Baldi, P., Chauvin, Y.: Protein modeling with hybrid hidden Markov model/neural network architectures. In: International Conference on Intelligent Systems for Molecular Biology (1995)
4. Bourlard, H., Wellekens, C.J.: Links between Markov models and multilayer perceptrons. IEEE Trans. Pattern Anal. Mach. Intell. **12**(12), 1167–1178 (1990)
5. Campos, P.G., Díez, F., Cantador, I.: Time-aware recommender systems: a comprehensive survey and analysis of existing evaluation protocols. User Model. User Adap. Inter. **24**(1–2), 67–119 (2014)
6. Chang, S., Yin, D., Chang, Y., Hasegawa-johnson, M., Huang, T.S.: Streaming recommender systems. In: International Conference on World Wide Web, pp. 381–389 (2017)
7. Chang, S., et al.: Streaming recommender systems. In: Proceedings of the 26th International Conference on World Wide Web, WWW 2017, International World Wide Web Conferences Steering Committee, Republic and Canton of Geneva, Switzerland, pp. 381–389 (2017). https://doi.org/10.1145/3038912.3052627
8. Chatzis, S., Christodoulou, P., Andreou, A.S.: Recurrent latent variable networks for session-based recommendation. In: The 2nd Workshop on Deep Learning for Recommender Systems (2017)
9. Chen, H., Lin, Z.: A hybrid neural network and hidden Markov model for time-aware recommender systems. In: Proceedings of the 11th International Conference on Agents and Artificial Intelligence, vol. 2, pp. 204–213 (2019)
10. Chen, X., et al.: Sequential recommendation with user memory networks. In: ACM International Conference on Web Search and Data Mining, pp. 108–116 (2018)
11. Devooght, R., Bersini, H.: Collaborative filtering with recurrent neural networks (2016)
12. Ding, D., Zhang, M., Li, S.Y., Tang, J., Chen, X., Zhou, Z.H.: BayDNN: friend recommendation with Bayesian personalized ranking deep neural network. In: Conference on Information and Knowledge Management, pp. 1479–1488 (2017)
13. Ding, Y., Li, X.: Time weight collaborative filtering. In: Proceedings of the ACM International Conference on Information and Knowledge Management, pp. 485–492 (2005)
14. Gultekin, S., Paisley, J.: A collaborative Kalman filter for time-evolving dyadic processes. In: IEEE International Conference on Data Mining (2014)
15. Harper, F.M., Konstan, J.A.: The movielens datasets: history and context. ACM Trans. Interact. Intell. Syst. (2015)
16. He, X., Liao, L., Zhang, H., Nie, L., Hu, X., Chua, T.S.: Neural collaborative filtering. In: Proceedings of the 26th International Conference on World Wide Web (2017)
17. Hidasi, B., Karatzoglou, A., Baltrunas, L., Tikk, D.: Session-based recommendations with recurrent neural networks. In: The International Conference on Learning Representations (2016)

18. Hidasi, B., Quadrana, M., Karatzoglou, A., Tikk, D.: Parallel recurrent neural network architectures for feature-rich session-based recommendations. In: ACM Conference on Recommender Systems, pp. 241–248 (2016)
19. Hochreiter, S., Schmidhuber, J.: Long short-term memory. Neural Comput. **9**(8), 1735–1780 (1997). https://doi.org/10.1162/neco.1997.9.8.1735
20. Jannach, D., Ludewig, M.: When recurrent neural networks meet the neighborhood for session-based recommendation. In: ACM Conference on Recommender Systems, pp. 306–310 (2017)
21. Liang, H., Baldwin, T.: A probabilistic rating auto-encoder for personalized recommender systems. In: ACM International on Conference on Information and Knowledge Management, pp. 1863–1866 (2015)
22. Lu, Z., Agarwal, D., Dhillon, I.S.: A spatio-temporal approach to collaborative filtering. In: Proceedings of the 3rd ACM Conference on Recommender Systems, pp. 13–20 (2009)
23. Paisley, J., Gerrish, S., Blei, D.: Dynamic modeling with the collaborative Kalman filter. In: NYAS 5th Annual Machine Learning Symposium (2010)
24. Rabiner, L.R.: A tutorial on hidden Markov models and selected applications in speech recognition. In: Readings in Speech Recognition, pp. 267–296 (1989)
25. Sahoo, N., Singh, P.V., Mukhopadhyay, T.: A hidden Markov model for collaborative filtering. MIS Q. **36**(4), 1329–1356 (2012)
26. Salakhutdinov, R., Mnih, A., Hinton, G.: Restricted Boltzmann machines for collaborative filtering. In: International Conference on Machine Learning, pp. 791–798 (2007)
27. Soh, H., Sanner, S., White, M., Jamieson, G.: Deep sequential recommendation for personalized adaptive user interfaces. In: International Conference on Intelligent User Interfaces (2017)
28. Sun, J.Z., Parthasarathy, D., Varshney, K.R.: Collaborative Kalman filtering for dynamic matrix factorization. IEEE Trans. Sign. Process. (2014)
29. Sun, J.Z., Varshney, K.R., Subbian, K.: Dynamic matrix factorization: a state space approach. In: IEEE International Conference on Acoustics, Speech and Signal Processing (2012)
30. Tang, J., Gao, H., Liu, H.: mTrust: discerning multi-faceted trust in a connected world. In: Proceedings of the 5th ACM International Conference on Web Search and Data Mining, pp. 93–102. ACM (2012)
31. Tang, J., Liu, H., Gao, H., Das Sarmas, A.: eTrust: understanding trust evolution in an online world. In: Proceedings of the 18th ACM SIGKDD International Conference on Knowledge Discovery and Data Mining, pp. 253–261. ACM (2012)
32. Wang, H., Wang, N., Yeung, D.Y.: Collaborative deep learning for recommender systems. In: ACM SIGKDD International Conference on Knowledge Discovery and Data Mining, pp. 1235–1244 (2015)
33. Wu, C.Y., Ahmed, A., Beutel, A., Smola, A.J., Jing, H.: Recurrent recommender networks, pp. 495–503 (2017)
34. Xue, H.J., Dai, X.Y., Zhang, J., Huang, S., Chen, J.: Deep matrix factorization models for recommender systems. In: International Joint Conference on Artificial Intelligence, pp. 3203–3209 (2017)
35. Zhang, H., Ni, W., Li, X., Yang, Y.: A hidden semi-Markov approach for time-dependent recommendation. In: Pacific Asia Conference on Information Systems (2016)

36. Zhang, H., Ni, W., Li, X., Yang, Y.: Modeling the heterogeneous duration of user interest in time-dependent recommendation: a hidden semi-Markov approach. IEEE Trans. Syst. Man Cybernet. Syst. **48**(2), 2168–2216 (2016)
37. Zhang, S., Yao, L., Sun, A.: Deep learning based recommender system: a survey and new perspectives. ArXiv e-prints (2017)

A General Approach to Distributed and Privacy-Preserving Heuristic Computation

Michal Štolba[(✉)], Michaela Urbanovská, Daniel Fišer, and Antonín Komenda

Department of Computer Science, Faculty of Electrical Engineering,
Czech Technical University in Prague, Prague, Czech Republic
{stolba,fiser,komenda}@agents.fel.cvut.cz, urbanm30@fel.cvut.cz

Abstract. Multi-agent planning (MAP) has recently gained traction in both planning and multi-agent system communities, especially with the focus on privacy-preserving multi-agent planning, where multiple agents plan for a common goal but with private information they do not want to disclose. Heuristic search is the dominant technique used in MAP and therefore it is not surprising that a significant attention has been paid to distributed heuristic computation, either with or without the concern for privacy. Nevertheless, most of the distributed heuristic computation approaches published so far are ad-hoc algorithms tailored for the particular heuristic. In this work we present a general, privacy-preserving, and admissible approach to distributed heuristic computation. Our approach is based on an adaptation of the technique of cost partitioning which has been successfully applied in optimal classical planning. We present the general approach, a particular implementation, and an experimental evaluation showing that the presented approach is competitive with the state of the art while having the additional benefits of generality and privacy preservation.

1 Introduction

Automated planning is an established field of classical artificial intelligence studying the representation and algorithms necessary to find solutions of problems which can be described in the form of state transition systems. In the presence of multiple interacting entities, or agents, we consider multi-agent planning. If the agents are cooperative, that is, share a common goal or utility function, but each agent might have some knowledge it considers private, the relevant field of study is privacy-preserving multi-agent planning. Examples of such situations range from coalition mission planning to planning business operations for a consortium of companies.

In recent years, a number of privacy preserving multi-agent planners have been developed and published [10,13,22,24]. The most common paradigm used in multi-agent planners is, similarly to classical planning, heuristically guided (distributed) state-space search, first proposed as MAD-A* in [12]. MAD-A* is

© Springer Nature Switzerland AG 2019
J. van den Herik et al. (Eds.): ICAART 2019, LNAI 11978, pp. 55–71, 2019.
https://doi.org/10.1007/978-3-030-37494-5_4

also the only optimal distributed planning algorithm which considers privacy. As such it has been re-implemented also in other planning systems, e.g., MAPlan [3], which we use for implementation in this work. The recent work in multi-agent (and especially privacy-preserving) planning is summarized in the survey [23].

Heuristic search requires good heuristic to be efficient and admissible heuristic to be optimal. The same holds for multi-agent and distributed heuristic search. The agent can compute a heuristic estimate from its view of the global problem, i.e., its projection. Such projection also contains a view of other agents' public operators, which allows for a heuristic estimate of the entire problem, but such estimate may be significantly misguided as shown in [17]. The reason is that the projection does not take into account the parts of the problem private to other agents. Moreover in some problems, the optimal heuristic estimate may be arbitrarily lower for the projection than for the global problem. This has lead to the development of various distributed heuristics, but only few consider privacy properly. An example of such privacy-preserving distributed heuristic is the multi-agent potential heuristic [18].

In general, proper treatment of privacy has long been neglected. The first serious consideration for privacy in multi-agent planning was Brafman's Secure-MAFS [1] which is privacy-preserving for a certain class of problems, but (i) does not provide optimal solution (ii) does not consider privacy preservation of the used heuristic. Basically, the heuristic has to be computed only on the public projection of the problem for the proposed statements to hold.

Most of the distributed heuristics published up-to-date present ad-hoc techniques to distribute each particular heuristic. Typically, the distributed computation of heuristic estimate requires the cooperation of all (or at least most of) the agents and incurs a substantial amount of communication. In many scenarios, the communication may be very costly (multi-robot systems) or prohibited (military) and even on high-speed networks, communication takes significant time compared to local computation. In such cases, it may pay off to use the projected heuristic instead of its better-informed counterpart.

In [21] the authors present an idea of using the idea of cost-partitioning [7] in multi-agent planning as a general approach to distribute multi-agent heuristics in an additive way. In this work we take this approach even further by considering privacy rigorously. We extend the previous work in the following points:

- We analyze the privacy leakage of a general additive multi-agent heuristic.
- We analyze the privacy leakage of multi-agent cost-partitioning based on [18], first proposed in [21].
- We propose a general approach to secure additive heuristic computation using secure-sum algorithm [16].
- We apply the secure-sum computation on cost-partitioning based additive heuristic and evaluate the influence it has on the planning system.

The use of secure computation primitives such as secure LP computation [11] or secure sum computation [16] to improve the preservation of privacy in the distributed heuristic computation.

1.1   Privacy

An important aspect of MAP is privacy. In [13], the authors have defined the notions of weak and strong privacy, where strong privacy coincides with the definition used in Secure Multiparty Computation (MPC) [27]. Whereas most planners aim only for weak privacy, which is disputable as it gives no guarantees on the private information the adversary can learn, the authors in [1] have proposed a variant of the MAFS planner which is strong privacy preserving for a restricted set of problems. Nevertheless, the authors in [25] have shown that it is not possible to construct a complete, efficient, and strong privacy preserving multi-agent planner based on heuristic search (e.g., MAFS).

A more practical question is then what and how much private information leaks from the distributed computation. In the context of MAP, techniques for privacy leakage quantification have been presented in [20,26], both as theoretical frameworks, the only practical and usable implementation is [19]. In the latter, the amount of private information leaked due to the public information exchanged by the agents is quantified based on the number of possible transition systems of the agent according to the communicated information.

In MPC, assumptions are typically placed on the agents, computation power, and communication channels. Here, to assess the worst-case leakage, we assume that there is a single agent hiding its private information and all other agents collude to gain as much information as possible. We assume semi-honest agents, that is, agents which do not alter the communication protocol (and the distributed algorithm) but attempt to deduce as much private information as possible. We assume unlimited computational power of the adversaries (that is, we aim for unconditional security) and FIFO loss-less communication channels.

2   Formalism

In this section we define the formal definitions used throughout the paper.

2.1   Multi-Valued Planning Task

Let us first define a classical single-agent planning task in the form of Multi-Valued Planning Task (MPT). The MPT is a tuple

$$\Pi = \langle \mathcal{V}, \mathcal{O}, s_I, s_\star, \mathsf{cost} \rangle$$

where

- $\mathcal{V}$ is a finite set of finite-domain variables, each V in the finite set of variables $\mathcal{V}$ has a finite domain of values $\mathsf{dom}(V)$,
- $\mathcal{O}$ is a finite set of operators,
- s_I is the initial state,
- $s_\star$ is the goal condition and
- $\mathsf{cost} : \mathcal{O} \mapsto \mathbb{R}_0^+$ is a cost function.

Moreover, a *fact* $\langle V, v \rangle$ is a pair of a variable V and one of the values v from its domain (i.e., an assignment).

Let p be a partial variable assignment over some set of variables $\mathcal{V}$. We use

- $\mathsf{vars}(p) \subseteq \mathcal{V}$ to denote a subset of $\mathcal{V}$ on which p is defined and
- $p[V]$ to denote the value of V assigned by p.

Alternatively, p can be seen as a set of facts $\{\langle V, p[V] \rangle \,|\, V \in \mathsf{vars}(p)\}$ corresponding to that partial variable assignment. A complete assignment over $\mathcal{V}$ is a *state* over $\mathcal{V}$. A (partial) assignment p is *consistent* with an assignment p' iff $p[V] = p'[V]$ for all $V \in \mathsf{vars}(p)$.

An *operator* o from the finite set $\mathcal{O}$ has

- a precondition $\mathsf{pre}(o)$ and
- an effect $\mathsf{eff}(o)$ which are both partial variable assignments.

An operator o is applicable in a state s if $\mathsf{pre}(o)$ is consistent with s. Application of operator o in a state s results in a state s' such that all variables in $\mathsf{eff}(o)$ are assigned to the values in $\mathsf{eff}(o)$ and all other variables retain the values from s, formally $s' = o \circ s$.

A solution to MPT Π is a sequence $\pi = (o_1, ..., o_k)$ of operators from $\mathcal{O}$ (a plan), such that o_1 is applicable in $s_I = s_0$, for each $1 \leq l \leq k$, o_l is applicable in s_{l-1} and $s_l = o_l \circ s_{l-1}$ and s_k is a goal state (i.e., $s_\star$ is consistent with s_k).

2.2   Multi-Agent Multi-Valued Planning Task

MA-MPT is a multi-agent extension of the Multi-Valued Planning Task. For n agents, the MA-MPT problem $\mathcal{M} = \{\Pi^i\}_{i=1}^n$ consists of a set of n MPTs. Each MPT for an agent $\alpha_i \in \mathcal{A}$ is a tuple

$$\Pi^i = \left\langle \mathcal{V}^i = \mathcal{V}^{\mathsf{pub}} \cup \mathcal{V}^{\mathsf{priv}_i}, \mathcal{O}^i = \mathcal{O}^{\mathsf{pub}_i} \cup \mathcal{O}^{\mathsf{priv}_i}, s_I^{\triangleright i}, s_\star^{\triangleright i}, \mathsf{cost}^i \right\rangle$$

where

- $\mathcal{V}^{\mathsf{priv}_i}$ is a set of private variables,
- $\mathcal{V}^{\mathsf{pub}}$ is a set of public variables shared among all agents $\mathcal{V}^{\mathsf{pub}} \cup \mathcal{V}^{\mathsf{priv}_i} = \emptyset$ and
- for each $i \neq j$, $\mathcal{V}^{\mathsf{priv}_i} \cap \mathcal{V}^{\mathsf{priv}_j} = \emptyset$ and $\mathcal{O}^i \cap \mathcal{O}^j = \emptyset$.

All variables in $\mathcal{V}^{\mathsf{pub}}$ and all values in their respective domain are public, that is known to all agents. All variables in $\mathcal{V}^{\mathsf{priv}_i}$ and all values in their respective domains are private to agent α_i which is the only agent aware of such V and allowed to modify its value.

A *global state* is a state over $\mathcal{V}^{\mathsf{G}} = \bigcup_{i \in 1..n} \mathcal{V}^i$. A global state represents the true state of the world, but no agent may be able to observe it as a whole. Instead, each agent works with an *i-projected state* which is a state over $\mathcal{V}^i$ such that all variables in $\mathcal{V}^{\mathsf{G}} \cap \mathcal{V}^i$ are equal in both assignments (the assignments are consistent).

The set $\mathcal{O}^i$ of operators of agent α_i consists of private and public operators such that $\mathcal{O}^{\mathsf{pub}_i} \cap \mathcal{O}^{\mathsf{priv}_i} = \emptyset$. The precondition $\mathsf{pre}(o)$ and effect $\mathsf{eff}(o)$ of private operators $o \in \mathcal{O}^{\mathsf{priv}_i}$, are partial assignments over $\mathcal{V}^{\mathsf{priv}_i}$, whereas in the case of public operators $o \in \mathcal{O}^{\mathsf{pub}_i}$ the assignment is over $\mathcal{V}^i$ and either $\mathsf{pre}(o)$ or $\mathsf{eff}(o)$ assigns a value to at least one public variable from $\mathcal{V}^{\mathsf{pub}}$. Because $\mathcal{V}^{\mathsf{pub}}$ is shared, public operators can influence (or be influenced by) other agents. The function $\mathsf{cost}^i : \mathcal{O}^i \mapsto \mathbb{R}_0^+$ assigns a cost to each operator of agent α_i. The initial state s_I and the partial goal state $s_\star$ (partial variable assignment over $\mathcal{V}^{\mathsf{G}}$) are in each agent's problem represented only as i-projected (partial) states.

We define a *global problem* (MPT) as a union of the agent problems, that is

$$\Pi^{\mathsf{G}} = \left\langle \bigcup_{i \in 1..n} \mathcal{V}^i, \mathcal{O}^{\mathsf{G}} = \bigcup_{i \in 1..n} \mathcal{O}^i, s_I, s_\star, \mathsf{cost}^{\mathsf{G}} \right\rangle$$

where $\mathsf{cost}^{\mathsf{G}}$ is a union of the cost functions cost^i. The global problem is the actual problem the agents are solving.

An *i-projected problem* is a complete view of agent α_i on the global problem Π^{G}. The i-projected problem of agent α_i contains i-projections of all operators of all agents. Formally, an i-projection $o^{\triangleright i}$ of $o \in \mathcal{O}^i$ is o. For a public operator $o' \in \mathcal{O}^{\mathsf{pub}_j}$ of some agent α_j s.t. $j \neq i$, an i-projected operator $o'^{\triangleright i}$ is o' with precondition and effect restricted to the variables of $\mathcal{V}^i$, that is $\mathsf{pre}(o'^{\triangleright i})$ is a partial variable assignment over $\mathcal{V}^i$ consistent with $\mathsf{pre}(o')$ ($\mathsf{eff}(o')$ treated analogously). An i-projection of a private operator $o'' \in \mathcal{O}^{\mathsf{priv}_j}$ s.t. $j \neq i$ is $o''^{\triangleright i} = \epsilon$, that is a no-op operator with $\mathsf{cost}^{\triangleright i}(o''^{\triangleright i}) = \mathsf{cost}^i(\epsilon) = 0$. The cost of i-projection of $o'' \in \mathcal{O}^{\mathsf{pub}_j}$ is preserved, formally $\mathsf{cost}^{\triangleright i}(o^{\triangleright i}) = \mathsf{cost}^j(o)$.

The set of i-projected operators is

$$\mathcal{O}^{\triangleright i} = \{o^{\triangleright i} | o \in \bigcup_{j \in 1...n} \mathcal{O}^j\}$$

and an *i-projected problem* is

$$\Pi^{\triangleright i} = \left\langle \mathcal{V}^i, \mathcal{O}^{\triangleright i}, s_I^{\triangleright i}, s_\star^{\triangleright i}, \mathsf{cost}^{\triangleright i} \right\rangle$$

The set of all i-projected problems is then $\mathcal{M}^{\triangleright} = \{\Pi^{\triangleright i}\}_{i=1}^n$. The set $\mathcal{M}^{\triangleright}$ of all i-projected problems can be seen as a set of abstractions of the global problem Π^{G}. A *public projection* $\Pi^{\triangleright}$ of Π^i is defined analogously with all states, partial states, and operators restricted only to public variables $\mathcal{V}^{\mathsf{pub}}$.

Let us define the transition system of an MPT problem Π. A transition system of a planning task Π is a tuple $\mathcal{T}(\Pi) = \langle S, L, T, s_I, S_\star \rangle$, where $S = \prod_{V \in \mathcal{V}} \mathsf{dom}(V)$ is a set of states, L is a set of transition labels corresponding to the operators in $\mathcal{O}$ and $T \subseteq S \times L \times S$ is a transition relation of Π s.t. $\langle s, o, s' \rangle \in T$ if $o \in \mathcal{O}$ s.t. o is applicable in s and $s' = o \circ s$. A state-changing transition is $\langle s, o, s' \rangle \in T$ such that $s \neq s'$. The state $s_I \in S$ is the initial state and $S_\star$ is the set of all goal states (that is all states s s.t. $s_\star$ is consistent with s). The cost of a transition $\langle s, o, s' \rangle \in T$ is $\mathsf{cost}(o)$.

Formally, the private information of agent α_i is the set of private variables $\mathcal{V}^{\mathsf{priv}_i}$, the set of private operators $\mathcal{O}^{\mathsf{priv}_i}$, and the private preconditions and effects of the public operators in $\mathcal{O}^{\mathsf{pub}_i}$. According to [20], the private information agent α_i is hiding from other (adversary) agents is the isomorphic image of the transition system $\mathcal{T}(\Pi^i)$, whereas the transition system $\mathcal{T}(\Pi^{\triangleright})$ and a projection $\pi^{\triangleright}$ of the final plan π are public information. Privacy leakage can be quantified as the difference in the uncertainty of the actual transition system $\mathcal{T}(\Pi^i)$ taking into account only the apriori information ($\mathcal{T}(\Pi^{\triangleright})$ and $\pi^{\triangleright}$) and taking into account all information obtained throughout the planning process (or heuristic computation in our case), e.g., all the exchanged messages.

3   Multi-agent Cost Partitioning

In this section, we briefly describe the idea of cost partitioning as used in classical planning [7] and define multi-agent cost partitioning as presented in [21].

Definition 1. *(Cost partitioning). Let Π be a planning task with operators $\mathcal{O}$ and cost function* cost. *A cost partitioning for Π is a tuple* $\mathsf{cp} = \langle \mathsf{cp}_1, ..., \mathsf{cp}_k \rangle$ *where* $\mathsf{cp}_l : \mathcal{O} \to \mathbb{R}_0^+$ *for $1 \leq l \leq k$ and $\sum_{l=1}^{k} \mathsf{cp}_l(o) \leq \mathsf{cost}(o)$ for all $o \in \mathcal{O}$.*

As shown in [7], a sum of admissible heuristics computed on the cost partitioned problem is also admissible, formally

Theorem 1. *(Katz and Domshlak 2010). Let Π be a planning task, let $h_1, ..., h_k$ be admissible heuristics for Π, and let* $\mathsf{cp} = \langle \mathsf{cp}_1, ..., \mathsf{cp}_k \rangle$ *be a cost partitioning for Π. Then $h_{\mathsf{cp}} = \sum_{l=1}^{k} h_l(s)$ where each h_l is computed with cp_l is an admissible heuristic estimate for a state s.*

Based on the particular cost partitioning cp, the heuristic estimate can have varying quality. By optimal cost partitioning (OCP) we mean a cost partitioning which maximizes h_{cp}. Finding an OCP can be cast as an optimization problem and is typically computed using a linear program (LP) formulations. Such formulations are known for OCP based on landmarks [5] and abstractions [7]. Now we proceed with the definition of a the multi-agent variant of cost partitioning, which differs in that the partitions are defined apriori by the set of the i-projected problems.

Definition 2. *(Multi-agent cost partitioning). Let $\mathcal{M}^{\triangleright} = \{\Pi^{\triangleright i}\}_{i=1}^{n}$ be the set of all i-projected problems with respective cost functions $\mathsf{cost}^{\triangleright i}$. A multi-agent cost partitioning for $\mathcal{M}^{\triangleright}$ is a tuple of functions* $\mathsf{cp} = \langle \mathsf{cp}_1, ..., \mathsf{cp}_n \rangle$ *where* $\mathsf{cp}_i : \mathcal{O}^{\triangleright i} \to \mathbb{R}_0^+$. *For $1 \leq i \leq n$ and for each $o \in \mathcal{O}^{\mathsf{G}}$ holds $\sum_{i=1}^{n} \mathsf{cp}_i(o^{\triangleright i}) \leq \mathsf{cost}^j(o)$ where α_j is the owner of o, that is, $o \in \mathcal{O}^j$.*

Theorem 2. *Let $\mathcal{M}^{\triangleright} = \{\Pi^{\triangleright i}\}_{i=1}^{n}$ be the set of all i-projected problems, Π^{G} the global problem respective to $\mathcal{M}$ and cp a multi-agent cost partitioning for $\mathcal{M}^{\triangleright}$. Then cp is a cost partitioning for Π^{G}.*

Proof. The theorem follows from Definition 1, Definition 2 for all public operators and from setting $o^{\triangleright i} = \epsilon$ for all $o \in \mathcal{O}^{\mathsf{priv}_j}$ s.t. $j \neq i$. As $\mathsf{cost}^{\triangleright i}(o^{\triangleright i}) = \mathsf{cost}^{\triangleright i}(\epsilon) = 0$ and $\mathsf{cost}^{\triangleright j}(o^{\triangleright j}) = \mathsf{cost}^j(o)$, the cost partitioning property $\sum_{i=1}^{n} \mathsf{cp}_i(o^{\triangleright i}) \leq \mathsf{cost}^j(o)$ holds also for private operators.

Thanks to Theorem 2 we can apply the Proposition 1 also in the multi-agent setting using a multi-agent cost partitioning. Thus, each agent α_i can compute its part of the heuristic locally on $\Pi^{\triangleright i}$ using cp_i instead of cost^i as the cost function. To obtain the global heuristic, the individual parts can be simply summed

$$h_{\mathsf{cp}}(s) = \sum_{i=1}^{n} h_{\mathsf{cp}_i}^{\triangleright i}(s^{\triangleright i}) \qquad (1)$$

where $h_{\mathsf{cp}_i}^{\triangleright i}$ is an i-projected heuristic computed on $\Pi^{\triangleright i}$ using cp_i.

Note that in multi-agent cost partitioning, private operators are partitioned implicitly as only their respective owners are aware of them, formally for $o \in \mathcal{O}^{\mathsf{priv}_i}$:

$$\mathsf{cp}_j(o^{\triangleright j}) = \begin{cases} \mathsf{cost}^i(o) & \text{if } i = j \\ 0 & \text{else} \end{cases}$$

In classical planning, the cost partitioning is typically computed for each state evaluated during the planning process. In privacy-preserving MAP, such approach does not make much sense as we want to avoid the distributed computation as much as possible. Thus, the envisioned use of such cost partitioning is to compute it once at the beginning of the planning process (as discussed in [6]), use the cost partitioned problems to evaluate heuristics locally and sum the local heuristics to obtain a global estimate.

3.1   Planning with Multi-agent Cost-Partitioning

In order for the reader to understand the consequences of communicating private information during the planning process, we describe how the multi-agent cost-partitioning is used throughout the distributed search (MAD-A*), similarly as was already proposed in [21]. In classical planning, the (optimal) cost partitioning computation is typically used as a means of computing heuristic value for each state, even though there are alternative approaches where the cost partitioning is not computed for every state [6,8,15]. As this work is the first to explore the benefits of cost partitioning in multi-agent planning we adopt the simplest approach based on [8].

The particular cost-partitioning is also often coupled with a particular heuristic (for which it is optimal), e.g., cost partitioning based on landmarks is coupled with the landmark heuristic (in fact, the objective value of the LP is the heuristic value). Here we aim for a somewhat more general and decoupled approach, that is, to provide a general technique for additive heuristic computation in multi-agent planning. By additive we mean that each part of the heuristic can be computed by each respective agent separately an then added together. As defined in [18]:

Definition 3. *(Agent-additive heuristic) A global heuristic h estimating the global problem Π^{G} is agent-additive iff for any agent $\alpha_i \in \mathcal{A}$ it can be represented as*

$$h(s) = h^{\mathsf{pub}}(s^{\triangleright}) + \sum_{\alpha_j \in \mathcal{A}} h^j(s^{\triangleright j})$$

where h^{pub} is a heuristic computed on the public projection problem $\Pi^{\triangleright}$ and h^j is a heuristic computed on the j-projected problem $\Pi^{\triangleright j}$.

Clearly, a heuristic is agent-additive even without the public part, that is, if $h^{\mathsf{pub}}(s^{\triangleright}) = 0$ for all states, which is the case of the heuristic computed on multi-agent cost partitioning defined in Eq. 1. In the rest of this section, we show how the agent-additive property can be utilized in the search.

The principle of the multi-agent heuristic search presented here is based on the MAD-A* algorithm (Multi-Agent Distributed A*) [12]. We first briefly summarize the main principles. The MAD-A* algorithm is a simple extension of classical A*. The agents search in parallel, possibly in a distributed setting (i.e., communicating over a network). Each agent $\alpha_i \in \mathcal{A}$ searches using its operators from $\mathcal{O}^i$ and if a state s is expanded using a public operator $o \in \mathcal{O}^{\mathsf{pub}_i}$, the resulting state s' is sent to other agents (the agents may be filtered in order to send the state only to the relevant ones). When some other agent α_j receives the state s', s' is added to the OPEN list of α_j and expanded normally when due. The original MAD-A* uses only projected heuristics computed on $\Pi^{\triangleright i}$. Each state sent by α_i is also accompanied with its i-projected heuristic estimate and when received, the receiving agent α_j computes the j-projected heuristic estimate of the received state s' and takes $h(s) = \max(h^{\triangleright i}(s^{\triangleright i}), h^{\triangleright j}(s^{\triangleright j}))$.

Let us now consider how can the agent-additive heuristic be utilized in the search to reduce heuristic computation and communication. In order to do so, we first state the following two propositions.

Proposition 1. Let $\mathcal{M} = \{\Pi^i\}_{i=1}^n$ be a multi-agent problem and let $h(s) = h^{\mathsf{pub}}(s^{\triangleright}) + \sum_{\alpha_i \in \mathcal{A}} h^i(s^{\triangleright i})$ be an agent-additive heuristic. Let s and s' be two states where s' is created from s by the application of a private operator $o \in \mathcal{O}^{\mathsf{priv}_j}$ of some agent j. Then for all h^j such that $j \neq i$ holds $h^j(s^{\triangleright j}) = h^j(s'^{\triangleright j})$ and

$$h(s') = h(s) - h^{\mathsf{pub}}(s^{\triangleright}) - h^i(s^{\triangleright i}) + h^{\mathsf{pub}}(s'^{\triangleright}) + h^i(s'^{\triangleright i}) \qquad (2)$$

Proof. As $o \in \mathcal{O}^{\mathsf{priv}_i}$ the states s, s' differ only in variables private to agent i and thus $s^{\triangleright j} = s'^{\triangleright j}$ and consequently $h^j(s^{\triangleright j}) = h^j(s'^{\triangleright j})$ for all $j \neq i$. Equation 2 follows directly from the fact that from the point of view of the agent i, the value of the private parts of the agent-additive heuristic of all other agents can be expressed as $\sum_{\alpha_j \in \mathcal{A} \setminus \{\alpha_i\}} h^j(s^{\triangleright j}) = h(s) - h^{\mathsf{pub}}(s^{\triangleright}) - h^i(s^{\triangleright i})$.

This means, that heuristic estimate of a state s' can be easily determined from the heuristic estimate of its predecessor s if s' was obtained from s by the application of a private operator. When a state is received from some other agent j, it is accompanied with its global heuristic estimate computed by agent j. When a state s is expanded by agent i with a private operator, the heuristic estimate of its successor s' can be computed using Eq. 2.

Proposition 2. Let $\mathcal{M} = \{\Pi^i\}_{i=1}^n$ be a multi-agent problem and let $h(s) = h^{\mathsf{pub}}(s^{\triangleright}) + \sum_{\alpha_i \in \mathcal{A}} h^i(s^{\triangleright i})$ be an agent-additive heuristic. Let s and s' be two states such that for some agent j holds $s^{\triangleright j} = s'^{\triangleright j}$. Then $h^j(s^{\triangleright j}) = h^j(s'^{\triangleright j})$.

Proposition 2 holds trivially. Of course, if the state s is expanded using a public operator, the heuristic estimate has to be computed as a sum of the particular projected heuristics over the cost-partitioned problems (as in Eq. 1). In this context, the multi-agent cost partitioning acts as a means of making any admissible classical heuristic (i) agent-additive, (ii) distributed, and (iii) privacy-preserving. How to achieve the third property (and to what degree) is discussed in the next section.

4   Privacy-Preserving Multi-agent Cost Partitioning

·In order to preserve privacy, we need to focus on the following aspects of the multi-agent cost partitioning:

- the computation of the cost partitioning,
- the computation of the heuristic value, and
- the cost-partitioned values themselves.

Clearly, additional private information can leak from the resulting heuristic value, especially in combination with the underlying planning algorithm, but we ignore this aspect here as it is out of the scope of this work.

4.1   Privacy-Preserving Additive Heuristic

In general we can assume that the computation of the individual components of an additive heuristic is already privacy preserving. Then the sum of the individual heuristics can be computed using a privacy-preserving sum algorithm such as [16]. In Sect. 5 we evaluate the effect of using secure sum algorithm (which is quadratic in the number of agents) on the computation of the heuristic for each public state.

To be able to compute sum of values of various parties without actually revealing the values, we implemented the dk-Secure-Sum protocol as described in [16]. The protocol works as follows.

1. There are k cooperative parties which are arranged in a ring for computational purposes according to their ID.
2. Each party breaks their value into k segments,
   (a) keeps one segment,
   (b) randomly assigns each of the remaining segments to one other party, so that exactly one segment is sent to one party,
   (c) distributes the randomized segments among all the other parties, sending one segment to each party.
3. At the end of this distribution process, each party has k segments from which only one is an original segment.

One of the parties is always the initiator of the whole protocol. After all segments are distributed, the initiator sends the first segment to the neighbor party in the formed ring. Party which receives a value adds its own segment to it and sends the result to the neighbor in the formed ring. This procedure continues until every party runs out of segments. In that case the initiating party receives the final sum of all the values which can be further distributed amongst all the parties, without knowing the original value of any of the parties.

In our implementation, the number of sent messages is slightly higher than in the protocol proposed in [16] but the overall communication complexity remains the same. Higher number of messages we use is caused by the need to confirm received messages in order to be sure that all parties are aware of the current algorithm stage and are synchronized.

Another question is what private information actually leaks if the sum is computed plainly and whether the performance decrease is compensated by the increase in preserved privacy. Based on [19], one important privacy breach is the ability to discerns states which are equal in their public projection. The access to the individual components of the additive heuristic may increase the ability of the adversary to detect such distinct states, formally:

Proposition 3. *Let s, s' be two states such that $s^\triangleright = s'^\triangleright$ and $h^i(s^{\triangleright i}) \neq h^i(s'^{\triangleright i})$ for any $\alpha_i \in \mathcal{A}$. Then agents $\alpha_j \in \mathcal{A}$ other than α_i learn that $s^{\triangleright i} \neq s'^{\triangleright i}$.*

In other words, the agents learn that two states which differ in the heuristic of agent α_i differ in the private part (private variables) of the agent α_i. This could influence the leakage computation and result in a higher privacy leakage.

4.2   Privacy-Preserving Cost Partitioning Computation

Let us now focus on how to compute a multi-agent cost partitioning in a privacy-preserving way. The very baseline in cost partitioning computation presented in [21] is the uniform cost partitioning, where

$$\mathsf{cp}_j(o^{\triangleright j}) = \frac{\mathsf{cost}^i(o^{\triangleright i})}{n} \tag{3}$$

for each operator $o \in \mathcal{O}^{\mathsf{pub}_i}$ and each agent $\alpha_j \in \mathcal{A}$. Unlike the uniform cost partitioning defined in used in classical planning, we cannot focus only on the partitions where the operator has effect on the heuristic value as (a) we do not assume any particular heuristic and (b) doing so would leak private information. This most simple variant does not leak any private information as there is no communication of private nor public parts of the agent's problems and the CP is computed independently by each agent.

The commonly used LPs for OCP computation are based on landmarks [5] and abstractions [8]. Nevertheless, the landmark-based OCP computation requires the use of global landmarks. Global landmarks can be found using the distributed LM-Cut heuristic [17] which is not privacy preserving and therefore private information would leak even before the OCP LP was even constructed.

The abstraction-based OCP is computed by expressing the transition system of each abstraction as a shortest-path computation LP where the LP variables represent the distance from a state to the goal and the constraints in the form of

$$\bar{s}' \leq \bar{s} + \bar{o} \text{ for all } \langle s, o, s'' \rangle \in T \tag{4}$$

represent the cost of the transition from s to s' via operator a. In the case of MACP, the abstractions (and thus the transition systems) are given up front by the agent problems, which can be in the worst case as big as the global problems (if all variables and all operators are public). This means that the transition systems would be too big to be represented in a LP. Of course this can be avoided by constructing a set of smaller abstractions for each agent problem and computing the OCP over such larger set of smaller abstractions.

The OCPs are typically computed using a linear program (LP). Secure LP computation techniques such as [2,11] can be used to compute the LP objective function and values without revealing the private parts of the LP. Such secure LP computation has already been used in PP-MAP to compute securely the potential heuristic [18], thus the secure LP computation tools are readily available in the MAPlan planner[1] [3].

An adaptation of the potential heuristic LP to cost-partitioning computation was proposed already in [21]. Here we briefly describe the components of the potential heuristic LP as described in [14] and its adaptation to cost-partitioning computation so that in the following section, we can analyze the privacy leakage of such cost-partitioning.

The objective function of the LP is simply the sum of potentials for a state (or average for a set of states). The simplest variant is to use the initial state s_I as the optimization target. For a partial variable assignment p, let $\mathsf{maxpot}(V, p)$ denote the maximal potential that a state consistent with p can have for variable V, formally:

$$\mathsf{maxpot}(V, p) = \begin{cases} \mathsf{pot}(\langle V, p[V] \rangle) & \text{if } V \in \mathsf{vars}(p) \\ \max_{v \in \mathsf{dom}(V)} \mathsf{pot}(\langle V, v \rangle) & \text{otherwise} \end{cases}$$

The LP contains a potential LP-variable $\mathsf{pot}(\langle V, v \rangle)$ for each fact (that is each possible assignment to each variable) and a maximum potential LP-variable maxpot_V for each variable in $\mathcal{V}$. The constraints ensuring the maximum potential property are simply

$$\mathsf{pot}(\langle V, v \rangle) \leq \mathsf{maxpot}_V$$

for all variables V and their values $v \in \mathsf{dom}(V)$. To ensure goal-awareness of the heuristic, i.e., $h_{\mathsf{pot}}(s) \leq 0$ for all goal states s, we add the following constraint

$$\sum_{V \in \mathcal{V}} \mathsf{maxpot}(V, s_\star) \leq 0$$

---

[1] https://github.com/danfis/maplan.

restricting the heuristic of any goal state to be less or equal to 0. The final set of constraints ensures consistency. For each operator o in a set of operators $\mathcal{O}$ we add the following constraint

$$\sum_{V \in \mathsf{vars}(\mathsf{eff}(o))} (\mathsf{maxpot}(V, \mathsf{pre}(o)) - \mathsf{pot}(\langle V, \mathsf{eff}(o)[V]\rangle)) \leq \mathsf{cost}(o) \tag{5}$$

The optimization function of the LP can be set to the sum of potentials in the initial state. A solution of the LP yields the values for potentials which are then used in the heuristic computation.

We obtain a cost partitioning LP by replacing the operator costs with variables, concatenating the respective LPs for each of the agent problems and adding the cost partitioning constraints. The LP contains separate LP variables for each potential and maxpot of public variables for each of the agents. Let $o \in \mathcal{O}^{\mathsf{pub}_i}$ be a public operator of α_i, the consistency constraints from Eq. 5 for operator o are re-formulated as

$$\sum_{V \in \mathsf{vars}(\mathsf{eff}(o))} (\mathsf{maxpot}(V, \mathsf{pre}(o))^{\triangleright i} -$$

$$\mathsf{pot}(\langle V, \mathsf{eff}(o)[V]\rangle)^{\triangleright i}) \leq \bar{o}^{\triangleright i} \tag{6}$$

$$\sum_{V \in \mathsf{vars}(\mathsf{eff}(o^{\triangleright j}))} (\mathsf{maxpot}(V, \mathsf{pre}(o^{\triangleright j}))^{\triangleright j} -$$

$$\mathsf{pot}(\langle V, \mathsf{eff}(o^{\triangleright j})[V]\rangle)^{\triangleright j}) \leq \bar{o}^{\triangleright j} \qquad \forall j \neq i \tag{7}$$

$$\sum_{k=1}^{n} \bar{o}^{\triangleright k} \leq \mathsf{cost}^i(o) \tag{8}$$

where $\mathsf{maxpot}(V, v)^{\triangleright k}$ and $\mathsf{pot}(\langle V, v\rangle)^{\triangleright k}$ represent the LP variables respective to agent α_k. Note that in the case of projected operators $o^{\triangleright j}$, the set $\mathsf{vars}(\mathsf{eff}(o^{\triangleright j}))$ contains only public variables. All other constraints are treated similarly.

The cost partitioning LP can also be seen as a set of n individual potential heuristic LPs which are interconnected only by the cost partitioning variables $\bar{o}^{\triangleright k}$ and the respective CP constraint. The optimization function is constructed simply as a sum of the individual optimization functions.

4.3 Privacy Leakage of the Partitioned Costs

The only aspect of the additive heuristic based on multi-agent cost partitioning which cannot be handled by a privacy-preserving algorithm is the actual partitioning of the operator costs. Clearly, the way how the cost of an operator $o \in \mathcal{O}^i$ is partitioned among other agents $j \neq i$ gives away some information about the structure of the problem Π^i of agent i. The question is, what is this information and how can it be reflected in the existing privacy leakage quantification schemes such as [19].

As already described in the introduction, we assume that there is a single agent $\alpha_l \in \mathcal{A}$ and all other agents collude to gain as much information as possible.

One technique the adversary agents can use is to compare the cost partitioning obtained from the global computation over the MAP $\mathcal{M}^{\triangleright} = \{\Pi^{\triangleright i}\}_{i \in \mathcal{A}}$ with a cost partitioning obtained from a MAP problem $\mathcal{M}'^{\triangleright} = \{\Pi^{\triangleright i}\}_{i \in \mathcal{A} \setminus \alpha_l} \cup \{\Pi^{\triangleright}\}$ where the problem Π^l of the agent α_l is replaced by its public projection $\Pi^{\triangleright}$. Let $\mathsf{cp} = \langle \mathsf{cp}_1, ..., \mathsf{cp}_n \rangle$ be a multi-agent cost partitioning computed over $\mathcal{M}^{\triangleright}$ and $\mathsf{cp}' = \langle \mathsf{cp}'_1, ..., \mathsf{cp}'_n \rangle$ computed over $\mathcal{M}'^{\triangleright}$. Any difference in the values of cp and cp' indicates an influence of the private parts of the agent's problem Π^l.

In particular in the context of the CP based on the potential heuristic LP, the main difference lies in the Eq. 8 where for operator $o \in \mathcal{O}^l$ the difference in $\mathsf{cp}_j(o)$ and $\mathsf{cp}'_j(o)$ for some $\alpha_j \neq \alpha_l$ indicates that

$$\sum_{V \in \mathsf{vars}(\mathsf{eff}(o))} (\mathsf{maxpot}(V, \mathsf{pre}(o))^{\triangleright l} - \mathsf{pot}(\langle V, \mathsf{eff}(o)[V] \rangle)^{\triangleright l}) \neq$$

$$\sum_{V \in \mathsf{vars}(\mathsf{eff}(o^{\triangleright}))} (\mathsf{maxpot}(V, \mathsf{pre}(o^{\triangleright}))^{\triangleright l} - \mathsf{pot}(\langle V, \mathsf{eff}(o^{\triangleright})[V] \rangle)^{\triangleright l}) \quad (9)$$

which can be caused either by different values of potentials (or maximum potentials) of the public variables in both $\mathsf{eff}(o^{\triangleright})$ and $\mathsf{eff}(o)$ or by additional private variables in $\mathsf{eff}(o)$. Since all the potentials (and their respective LP variables) are known only to the agent α_l, the adversaries cannot distinguish which of the reasons caused the inequality.

Even though some private information clearly leaks from the values of the cost partitioning, it is not clear how to map such information on the privacy leakage quantification schemes. In [19] the leakage is computed based on the private preconditions and effects of operators (and their consequent applicability). As it is not possible to determine whether the cause of inequality in Eq. 9 is the presence of private preconditions and effects, such information does not influence the considered leakage quantification. In [26] the leakage quantification is based on the possible plans which, again, is not influenced by Eq. 9 and its consequences.

In the case of uniform cost-partitioning, the question of privacy leakage based on the partitioned cost is clearly irrelevant. As the cost-partitioning is computed regardless the private problems and thus without any knowledge of the private problems, no private information can be deduced from the partitioned costs. This makes uniform cost-partitioning strongly secure, similarly to the projected heuristic. Moreover, in contrast to the projected heuristic which can be used to discern equivalent states as described in [19], uniform cost-partitioning with secure sum algorithm does not allow for such inference. This makes it a perfect general approach to distributed heuristic computation with respect to privacy.

5   Evaluation

We have evaluated the proposed approach on the benchmark set of the CoDMAP'15 [9] competition. In the evaluation we focus on two key metrics:

- The number of problems solved in time limit of 30 min (coverage).
- The time needed to find the solution (capped by the 30 min limit).

The proposed methods were implemented in the MAPlan planner [3] and evaluated on the LM-Cut heuristic [4]. The configurations we have evaluated are the following:

proj is the classical projected heuristic computed by each agent on its respective projected problem.

uni is the uniform baseline cost partitioning (Eq. 3).

uni-sec-sum is the uniform baseline cost partitioning (Eq. 3) with the secure sum computation.

pot is the potential-based cost partitioning computed using the LP in Eq. 8. The implementation is based on the distributed potential heuristic LP computation [18].

pot-sec-sum is the potential-based cost partitioning as in pot together with the secure sum computation.

ma-lm-cut is the state-of-the-art distributed variant of the LM-Cut heuristic [17].

5.1   Coverage

In this section, we focus on the actual performance of the MAD-A* algorithm together with the proposed heuristics and the search improvements described in this work. The main question is, whether the use of the secure-sum algorithm has significant negative effect of the planner performance in terms of the coverage.

In order to perform this evaluation, we have replicated the configuration of the distributed track of the CoDMAP'15 [9] competition, where each agent runs on a dedicated machine with 4 cores (with multi-threading) on 3.8 GHz and 32GB RAM. The agents communicated over TCP-IP on a local area network (Table 1).

The results show that the proposed cost-partitioning methods without the secure sum algorithm are on par with the ad-hoc multi-agent variant of the LM-Cut heuristic, albeit being more general. Nevertheless, the secure variants pay their price of decreased coverage, although the negative effect is not as bad as could be expected and the heuristics are still competitive. Overall, the best performance is provided by the projected heuristic. This is not surprising but the effect is amplified by the use of more RAM in the experiments than is typical in the literature. This allows for the less-informed but faster projected heuristic to dominate the results. As shown in [19], projected heuristic causes more privacy leakage in the overall search evaluation.

5.2   Speed

In this experiment we present the comparison of both uniform and potential-based cost-partitionings either using or not using the secure-sum algorithm with respect to the speed of finding the solution. The setting of the experiment is the same as in the previous case.

Table 1. Numbers of problems solved (coverage).

Domain	proj	uni		pot		ma-lm-cut
		add	sec-sum	add	sec-sum	
blocksworld	**2**	2	2	2	2	2
depot	6	0	0	0	0	2
driverlog	**15**	14	13	13	12	10
elevators	0	0	0	0	0	0
logistics	5	4	2	4	3	7
rovers	1	0	0	0	0	1
satellites	2	1	0	1	0	**4**
sokoban	13	8	3	8	5	1
taxi	20	20	7	0	15	15
wireless	0	0	0	0	0	0
woodwork.	0	0	0	0	0	0
zenotravel	6	6	6	6	6	**8**
$\sum$	71	55	43	34	28	50

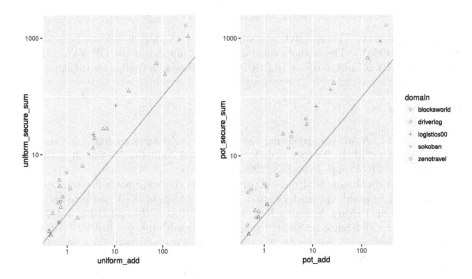

Fig. 1. Planning speed comparison. Time in seconds, logarithmic scale.

The Fig. 1 shows a comparison of planning speed of the cost partitioning approaches using plain addition and using the secure sum algorithm. We can see, that even though the difference in coverage is not that dramatic, the difference in speed is in the order of magnitude. This is clearly due to the quadratic communication complexity of the secure sum algorithm.

6 Conclusion and Future Work

In this work, we have extended the recently published multi-agent cost-partitioning towards privacy. We have theoretically analyzed the possible sources of leakage in multi-agent planning with such cost-partitioning and proposed a technique to prevent privacy leakage from one of such sources–the additive heuristic computation. We have used an existing secure sum algorithm to do so. We have shown, that uniform cost partitioning with the secure sum algorithm is a general strong privacy-preserving approach to distributed heuristic computation. Finally, we have evaluated the newly proposed secure variants of the cost partitioning in comparison with the original versions and baseline projection and distributed heuristics. We have shown that the use of secure-sum algorithm has negative effect on the metrics of coverage and planning speed, but the negative effect can be outweighed by the gain in privacy preservation.

As future work directions we see firstly the application of the secure multi-agent computations also on other methods of cost-partitioning. The cost-partitioning can also be applied on other heuristics than just LM-Cut as it is fully general. Secondly, it would be interesting to evaluate secure cost-partitioning in a quantitative evaluation of the privacy leakage in context of the whole search algorithm.

Acknowledgments. This research was supported by the Czech Science Foundation (grant no. 18-24965Y). The authors acknowledge the support of the OP VVV MEYS funded project CZ.02.1.01/0.0/0.0/16_019/0000765 "Research Center for Informatics".

References

1. Brafman, R.I.: A privacy preserving algorithm for multi-agent planning and search. In: Proceedings of the Twenty-Fourth International Joint Conference on Artificial Intelligence, IJCAI, pp. 1530–1536 (2015)
2. Dreier, J., Kerschbaum, F.: Practical privacy-preserving multiparty linear programming based on problem transformation. In: Proceedings of IEEE 3rd International Conference on Privacy, Security, Risk and Trust (PASSAT) and IEEE 3rd Third Inernational Conference on Social Computing (SocialCom), pp. 916–924 (2011)
3. Fišer, D., Štolba, M., Komenda, A.: MAPlan. In: Proceedings of the Competition of Distributed and Multi-Agent Planners (CoDMAP-2015), pp. 8–10 (2015)
4. Helmert, M., Domshlak, C.: Landmarks, critical paths and abstractions: what's the difference anyway? In: Proceedings of the 19th International Conference on Automated Planning and Scheduling (ICAPS), pp. 162–169 (2009)
5. Karpas, E., Domshlak, C.: Cost-optimal planning with landmarks. In: IJCAI, pp. 1728–1733 (2009)
6. Karpas, E., Katz, M., Markovitch, S.: When optimal is just not good enough: learning fast informative action cost partitionings. In: ICAPS (2011)
7. Katz, M., Domshlak, C.: Implicit abstraction heuristics. J. Artif. Intell. Res. **39**, 51–126 (2010)
8. Katz, M., Domshlak, C.: Optimal admissible composition of abstraction heuristics. Artif. Intell. **174**(12–13), 767–798 (2010)

9. Komenda, A., Stolba, M., Kovacs, D.L.: The international competition of distributed and multiagent planners (CoDMAP). AI Mag. **37**(3), 109–115 (2016)
10. Maliah, S., Brafman, R.I., Shani, G.: Privacy preserving LAMA. In: Proceedings of the 4th Workshop on Distributed and Multi-Agent Planning, DMAP-ICAPS 2016, pp. 1–5 (2016)
11. Mangasarian, O.L.: Privacy-preserving linear programming. Opt. Lett. **5**(1), 165–172 (2011)
12. Nissim, R., Brafman, R.I.: Multi-agent A* for parallel and distributed systems. In: Proceedings of the 11th International Conference on Autonomous Agents and Multiagent Systems (AAMAS 2012), pp. 1265–1266 (2012)
13. Nissim, R., Brafman, R.I.: Distributed heuristic forward search for multi-agent planning. J. Artif. Intell. Res. **51**, 293–332 (2014)
14. Pommerening, F., Helmert, M., Röger, G., Seipp, J.: From non-negative to general operator cost partitioning: Proof details. Technical Report CS-2014-005, University of Basel, Department of Mathematics and Computer Science (2014)
15. Seipp, J., Keller, T., Helmert, M.: A comparison of cost partitioning algorithms for optimal classical planning (2017)
16. Sheikh, R., Kumar, B., Mishra, D.K.: A distributed k-secure sum protocol for secure multi-party computations. arXiv preprint arXiv:1003.4071 (2010)
17. Štolba, M., Fišer, D., Komenda, A.: Admissible landmark heuristic for multi-agent planning. In: Proceedings of the 25th International Conference on Automated Planning and Scheduling (ICAPS), pp. 211–219 (2015)
18. Štolba, M., Fišer, D., Komenda, A.: Potential heuristics for multi-agent planning. In: Proceedings of the 26th International Conference on Automated Planning and Scheduling, ICAPS 2016, pp. 308–316 (2016)
19. Štolba, M., Fišer, D., Komenda, A.: Privacy leakage of search-based multi-agent planning algorithms. In: Proceedings of the 29th International Conference on Automated Planning and Scheduling, ICAPS 2019 (2019)
20. Štolba, M., Tožička, J., Komenda, A.: Quantifying privacy leakage in multi-agent planning. ACM Trans. Internet Technol. (TOIT) **18**, 28 (2017)
21. Štolba, M., Urbanovská, M., Fišer, D., Komenda, A.: Cost partitioning for multi-agent planning. In: Proceedings of the 11th International Conference on Agents and Artificial Intelligence, ICAART (2019)
22. Torreño, A., Onaindia, E., Sapena, O.: FMAP: distributed cooperative multi-agent planning. Appl. Intell. **41**(2), 606–626 (2014)
23. Torreño, A., Onaindia, E., Komenda, A., Štolba, M.: Cooperative multi-agent planning: a survey. ACM Comput. Surv. (CSUR) **50**(6), 84 (2017)
24. Tožička, J., Jakubuv, J., Komenda, A.: Generating multi-agent plans by distributed intersection of Finite State Machines. In: Proceedings of the 21st European Conference on Artificial Intelligence (ECAI 2014), pp. 1111–1112 (2014)
25. Tožička, J., Štolba, M., Komenda, A.: The limits of strong privacy preserving multi-agent planning. In: Proceedings of the 27th International Conference on Automated Planning and Scheduling, ICAPS 2017 (2017)
26. Van Der Krogt, R.: Quantifying privacy in multiagent planning. Multiagent Grid Syst. **5**(4), 451–469 (2009)
27. Yao, A.C.: Protocols for secure computations. In: Proceedings of the 23rd Annual Symposium on Foundations of Computer Science, SFCS, pp. 160–164 (1982)

Social Golfer Problem Revisited

Ke Liu$^{(\boxtimes)}$ ⓘ, Sven Löffler, and Petra Hofstedt

Department of Mathematics and Computer Science (MINT),
Brandenburg University of Technology Cottbus-Senftenberg,
Konrad-Wachsmann-Allee 5, 03044 Cottbus, Germany
{liuke,sven.loeffler,hofstedt}@b-tu.de

Abstract. In a golf club, $n = g * s$ golfers want to play in g groups of s golfers for w weeks. Does there exist a schedule for each golfer to play no more than once with any other golfer? This simple but overwhelmingly challenging problem, which is called social golfer problem (SGP), has received considerable attention in constraint satisfaction problem (CSP) research as a standard benchmark for symmetry breaking. However, constraint satisfaction approach for solving the SGP has stagnated in terms of larger instance over the last decade. In this article, we improve the existing model of the SGP by introducing more constraints that effectively reduce the search space, particularly for the instances of the specific form. And on this basis, we also provide a search space splitting method to solve the SGP in parallel via data-level parallelism. Our implementation of the presented techniques allows us to attain the solutions for eight instances with maximal number of weeks, in which six of them were open instances for constraint satisfaction approach, and two of them are computed for the first time, and super-linear speedups are observed for all the instances solved in parallel. Besides, we survey the extensive literature on solving the SGP, including the best results they have achieved, and analyse the cause of difficulties in solving the SGP.

Keywords: Constraint programming · Parallel constraint solving · Resolvable steiner systems · Combinatorial optimization · Design theory · Mutually Orthogonal Latin Squares · Affine plane

1 Introduction

The *social golfer problem* (SGP), i.e., 010 problem in CSPLib [13], is a typical combinatorial optimization problem that has attracted significant attention from the constraints community because of its highly symmetrical and combinatorial nature. The original SGP, which was posted to sci.op-research in May 1998 [13,38], can be stated as follows: In a golf club, 32 golfers wish to play in foursomes for 10 weeks. Is it possible to find a schedule for maximum socialization; that is, each golfer can only meet any other no more than once? In fact, the SGP dates back to Thomas Penyngton Kirkman's 1850 query [16] in which the number of golfers and the size of a group are 15 and 3 respectively.

© Springer Nature Switzerland AG 2019
J. van den Herik et al. (Eds.): ICAART 2019, LNAI 11978, pp. 72–99, 2019.
https://doi.org/10.1007/978-3-030-37494-5_5

Hence, we can readily generalize the SGP to the following: The SGP consists of scheduling $n = g * s$ players into g groups of s players for w weeks so that any two players are assigned to the same group at most once in w weeks. According to the constraints community's convention on this problem, an instance of the SGP is denoted by a triple g-s-w, where g is the number of groups, s is the number of players within a group, and w is the number of weeks in the schedule. In addition, we can also regard the SGP as a discrete optimization problem that maximizes the number of weeks w^* for a given g and s, where $w^* \leq \frac{g*s-1}{s-1}$. Clearly, a solution for an instance g-s-w^* indicates itself as the solution for all instances g-s-w with $0 < w < w^*$. In practice, the computational difficulty of solving the g-s-w^* and g-s-w instance is often not in the same order of magnitude due to the huge difference in the solution density of two instances. For example, the 8-4-9 instance can be solved in a second on a state-of-the-art constraint solver. The 8-4-10 instance, by contrast, is still unsolvable for constraint approach at the time of writing, although at least three non-isomorphic solutions are known to exist. In light of this, this research concentrates on solving the g-s-w^* instances with maximal number of weeks, which we call *the full instance*. For instance, Table 1 depicts one solution for the full instance 7-3-10.

Table 1. A solution for 7-3-10 (transformed from the solution depicted in Table 2) The text in bold indicates that the values have been initialized before search. (Table reproduced from [20]).

Week \ Group	1			2			3			4			5			6			7		
1	**1**	**2**	**3**	**4**	**5**	**6**	**7**	**8**	**9**	**10**	**11**	**12**	**13**	**14**	**15**	**16**	**17**	**18**	**19**	**20**	**21**
2	**1**	4	7	**2**	10	13	**3**	16	19	5	8	17	6	11	14	9	12	20	15	18	21
3	**1**	10	14	**2**	4	17	**3**	9	11	5	7	21	6	12	16	8	15	19	13	18	20
4	**1**	17	21	**2**	6	19	**3**	4	12	5	10	20	7	15	16	8	11	13	9	14	18
5	**1**	8	12	**2**	5	16	**3**	7	13	4	14	21	6	9	15	11	17	20	10	18	19
6	**1**	9	16	**2**	11	15	**3**	10	21	4	8	20	5	14	19	6	13	17	7	12	18
7	**1**	13	19	**2**	9	21	**3**	6	20	4	11	18	5	12	15	8	10	16	7	14	17
8	**1**	5	11	**2**	8	18	**3**	15	17	4	9	19	6	7	10	14	16	20	12	13	21
9	**1**	6	18	**2**	7	20	**3**	8	14	4	10	15	5	9	13	11	16	21	12	17	19
10	**1**	15	20	**2**	12	14	**3**	5	18	4	13	16	6	8	21	9	10	17	7	11	19

The research on the SGP is not only meaningful to itself, but also for other Constraint Satisfaction Problems (CSPs) that exhibit symmetrical and combinatorial nature. For example, balanced incomplete block design (BIBD), problem 28 in CSPLib [26], is a standard combinatorial problem from design theory and also a test bed for symmetry breaking methods. Moreover, steel mill slab design [23], which is a real industry problem, can also benefit from the SGP. The reason is that we are likely to face the same difficulties as the SGP when solving other CSPs through the constraint satisfaction approach.

This article is an extended and revised version of our previous work [20]. In this version, the formulations of the constraints in the models have been improved. Besides, we have added a new section which explains the difficulties of the SGP and presents the background constraint programming. We also present additional experimental results for the solved instances in Appendix A. We make the following contributions: (1) The improvement of existing constraint model on the SGP enables constraint approach to solve larger instances. (2) We discover some patterns in the solutions of particular forms of the instances. (3) We show that the two-stage models with static partitioning are well-suited for solving the SGP in parallel since the instances which are unsolvable for a single model can be solved in parallel.

The remainder of this article is organized as follows. Section 2 analyses the causes of the difficulties of solving the SGP in the context of the CSP and introduces the constraints required to encode the model. A modeling approach improved on the model proposed by [3] are described in Sect. 3, and some instance-specific constraints are presented in Sect. 4. In addition, we elaborate on how to employ Embarrassingly Parallel Search (EPS) [30] to solve the SGP in Sect. 5. We then present the experimental results in Sect. 6. In Sect. 7, we classify the researches on the SGP and also survey the studies relevant to the SGP outside the context of the CSP. We finally conclude in Sect. 8.

2   Background

In this section, we first explain why it is challenging to solve the SGP in the context of the CSP. Then we review the definition of the CSP and the constraints relevant to our model of the SGP.

2.1   The Difficulties of Solving the SGP

At first sight, the SGP is a simple-sounding question. And indeed, one can model the problem by using several frequently-used constraints derived from the problem definition. The constraint satisfaction approach, however, still has enormous difficulties in obtaining the solution even for some small instances (e.g. 7-4-9, 8-4-10, etc.). We believe that the following two reasons result in the difficulties of the SGP:

The First Difficulty. The inherent highly symmetrical nature of the SGP cannot be entirely known before solving process. There exist four types of symmetries: (1) We can permute the w weeks, that is, arbitrarily ordered weeks ($w!$ symmetries). (2) Within each week, we can (separately) permute the g groups, that is, interchangeable groups inside weeks ($g!$ symmetries). (3) Within each group, we can permute the s players, that is, interchangeable players inside groups ($s!$ symmetries). (4) Finally, we can also permute the n players ($n!$ symmetries), which can also be viewed by renumbering n golfers. The first three types of symmetries can be relatively easy to remove through model reformulation or static symmetry breaking constraints. Nevertheless, it is difficult to eliminate all the symmetries among players caused by the fourth type of symmetry.

For example, if players $[16, 17, 18, 19, 20, 21]$ in Table 1 replace with $[19, 20, 21, 16, 17, 18]$ in turn, an isomorphism of the solution depicted in Table 1 will be generated even if the first row of the solution is fixed with $[1, \ldots, 21]$. Apparently, we are unable to foresee this symmetry before search. Consequently, the unnecessary symmetrical search space is explored redundantly.

The Second Difficulty. It is common to observe that some unfortunate choices of variables early on are to blame for a long-running search process [12]. The SGP has also been experienced such phenomena. More precisely, invalid partial assignments lead to the backtrack search to trap in a barren part of the search space since no consistent assignment can be found. More importantly, it is often hard to determine the usefulness of a partial assignment until almost all variables are instantiated; and these invalid partial assignments predominate in the overall search space.

2.2 The Global Constraints

The constraint programming (CP) is a powerful technique to tackle combinatorial problems, generally NP-complete or NP-hard. The idea behind the CP is that the user states the problem by using constraints and a general purpose constraint solver is used to solve the problem. The classic definition of a constraint satisfaction problem (CSP) is as follows. A CSP P is a triple $\langle X, D, C \rangle$, where $X = \{x_0, \ldots, x_n\}$ is a set of decision variables, $D = \{D_{(x_0)}, \ldots, D_{(x_n)}\}$ contains associated finite domains for each variable in X, and $C = \{c_0, \ldots, c_t\}$ is a collection of constraints. Each constraint $c_i \in C$ is a relation defined over a subset of X, and restricts the values that can be simultaneously assigned to these variables. A solution of a CSP P is a complete instantiation satisfying all constraints of the CSP P.

The *allDifferent*[1] constraint is the most influential global constraint in constraint programming and widely implemented in almost every constraint solver, such as Choco solver [27] and Gecode [34]. Formally, let X_a denote a subset of variables of X, the *alldifferent*(X_a) constraint can be defined as:

$$\forall x_i \in X_a \forall x_j \in X_a (x_i \neq x_j)$$

The *global cardinality constraint* $GCC(X_g, V, O)$ is defined using two lists of variables X_g and O, and an array of integer values V, where $X_g = \{x_l, \ldots, x_m\} \subseteq X$ and O is a list of variables not defined in X and predefines the range of the number of occurrences for each value in V. The GCC constraint restricts that each value V_i appearing exactly O_{i_j} times in X_g, where O_{i_j} is in the domain of O_i. More formally:

$$\{(d_l, \ldots, d_m) \mid d_l \in D_{(x_l)}, \ldots, d_m \in D_{(x_m)} \wedge$$
$$\forall i \forall O_{i_j} \in O_i (occur(V_i, (d_l, \ldots, d_m)) = O_{i_j})\}$$

where *occur* counts the number of occurrences of V_i in $(d_l, \ldots, d_m)$.

---

[1] This article follows the naming convention and order of the arguments of constraints in Choco solver.

The *count* constraint is similar to the *GCC*, but with the restriction for only one value. More precisely, the $count(v, X_c, occ)$ constraint only restricts the number of occurrences of value v for the list of variables $X_c = \{x_l, \ldots, x_m\}$, given by:

$$\{(d_l, \ldots, d_m) | \ d_l \in D_{(x_l)}, \ldots, d_m \in D_{(x_m)} \wedge$$
$$\forall O_j \in occ(occur(v, (d_l, \ldots, d_m)) = O_j)\}$$

The *table* constraint is another one of the most frequently-used constraints in practice. For an ordered subset of variables $X_o = \{x_i, \ldots, x_j\} \subseteq X$, a positive (negative) *table* constraint defines that any solution of the CSP P must (not) be explicitly assigned to a tuple in the tuples that consists of the allowed (disallowed) combinations of values for X_o. For a given list of tuples T, we can state the positive *table* constraint as:

$$\left\{(d_i, \ldots, d_j) \mid d_i \in D_{(x_i)}, \ldots, d_j \in D_{(x_j)}\right\} \subseteq T$$

Finally, the *arithm* constraint is used to enforce relations between integer variables or between integer variables and integer values. For example, an integer value can be assigned to an integer variable by using the *arithm* constraint. We refer to [6, 19, 33] for more comprehensive and profound introduction to the CP.

3   The Basic Model

There are various ways of modeling the SGP as a CSP proposed in the literature, which is one of the reasons why the problem is so compelling. In this article, we use a model improved on the model presented in [3] due to its untapped potential. Specifically, we can add more constraints into the model to tackle larger instances piece by piece.

The decision variables of our model is a $w \times n$ matrix G in which each element $G_{i,j}$ of the matrix G represents that player j is assigned to group $G_{i,j}$ in week i. Hence, the domain of decision variable $G_{i,j}$ is a set of integers $\{1 \ldots g\}$, where $0 \leq i < w$, $0 \leq j < n$.[2] The major advantage of the decision variables defined in this model is that the range of the variables are reduced from $\{1 \ldots n\}$ to $\{1 \ldots g\}$ while keeping an unchanged number of variables, compared with the naive model.

We mentioned, in Sect. 2.1, that symmetries among players are difficult to handle and only dynamic checks can remove them completely. However, we can partially eliminate the symmetries among players by fixing the first week (cf. Tables 1 and 2), i.e. the first row of the matrix G, which can be expressed as:

$$\forall j \in J(G_{0,j} = j/s + 1), J = \{j \in \mathbb{Z} | \ 0 \leq j \leq n\} \tag{1}$$

where the operator "/" denotes integer division. Equation (1) produces a sequence of integers from 1 to g in non-descending order, and every integer continuously repeats itself exactly s times. Moreover, we can also freeze the first

---

[2] In this article, we follow the Zero-based index.

s columns by assigning the first s players to the first s groups after the first week (cf. Table 2), given by:

$$\forall i \in I \forall j \in J (G_{i,j} = j + 1)$$
$$I = \{i \in \mathbb{Z} | \, 0 < i < w\}, J = \{j \in \mathbb{Z} | \, 0 \leq j < s\}$$

(2)

By applying Eq. (2) to the model, we can significantly reduce the search space. Note that, in the implementation, we can realize Eqs. (1) and (2) by either restricting the domain of the variables or using the *arithm* constraint. Therefore, we use the term Equation instead of Constraint.

Table 2. A solution is obtained by our model for 7-3-10 instance, and it is equivalent to the solution depicted in Table 1. The text in bold indicates that the values have been initialized before search. (Table reproduced from [20]).

Week \ Player	1	2	3	4	5	6	7	8	9	10	11	12	13	14	15	16	17	18	19	20	21
1	**1**	**1**	**1**	**2**	**2**	**2**	**3**	**3**	**3**	**4**	**4**	**4**	**5**	**5**	**5**	**6**	**6**	**6**	**7**	**7**	**7**
2	**1**	**2**	**3**	1	4	5	1	4	6	2	5	6	2	5	7	3	4	7	3	6	7
3	**1**	**2**	**3**	2	4	5	4	6	3	1	3	5	7	1	6	5	2	7	6	7	4
4	**1**	**2**	**3**	3	4	2	5	6	7	4	6	3	6	7	5	5	1	7	2	4	1
5	**1**	**2**	**3**	4	2	5	3	1	5	7	6	1	3	4	5	2	6	7	7	6	4
6	**1**	**2**	**3**	4	5	6	7	4	1	3	2	7	6	5	2	1	6	7	5	4	3
7	**1**	**2**	**3**	4	5	3	7	6	2	6	4	5	1	7	5	6	7	4	1	3	2
8	**1**	**2**	**3**	4	1	5	5	2	4	5	1	7	7	6	3	6	3	2	4	6	7
9	**1**	**2**	**3**	4	5	1	2	3	5	4	6	7	5	3	4	6	7	1	7	2	6
10	**1**	**2**	**3**	4	3	5	7	5	6	6	7	2	4	2	1	4	6	3	7	1	5

By the definition of the SGP, n different players are divided into g groups, which implies that each group includes exactly s players. Hence, the constraint required by this property, which are imposed on the rows of the matrix G, can be stated as:

$$\forall i \in I (GCC(G_{i,*}, V, O))$$
$$I = \{i \in \mathbb{Z} | \, 0 < i < w\}$$
$$V = \{v \in \mathbb{Z} | \, 1 \leq v \leq g\}$$
$$O = [s \ldots s]$$

(3)

where the length of O is g. The constraints (3) ensure that every value in the set of integers $\{1 \ldots g\}$ must occur exactly s times in all the rows of the matrix G (cf. Table 2).

The restriction, which no player meets any other player more than once, can be interpreted as saying that no two columns of the matrix G have the same value at the same row more than once, given by:

$$\sum_{0 \le i < w} |\ G_{i,j_1} - G_{i,j_2} = 0\ | \le 1 \tag{4}$$
$$j_1 \in \mathbb{Z},\ j_2 \in \mathbb{Z}\ , 0 \le j_1 < j_2 < n$$

Constraints (3) and (4) are the only two constraints presented in [3]. In particular, unlike [3], we implement Constraint (4) in a different way to avoid using the *reified* constraints because these constraints often slow the resolution speed down in solvers like Choco [21,27]. Specifically, the need for the *reified* constraints can be bypassed by introducing a $w \times m$ matrix C, where $m = \binom{n}{2}$. We then subtract every column from all other columns in the matrix G and the differences between two columns of the matrix G are assigned to a column of another matrix C. Simply put, the two matrices G and C are linked by the equations expressed by the *arithm* constraints, given by:

$$\forall i \in I \forall j_1 \in J_1 \forall j_2 \in J_2 (G_{i,j_1} - G_{i,j_2} = C_{i,j_3})$$
$$(j_1 < j_2) \wedge (0 \le j_3 < m) \wedge (j_3 \in \mathbb{Z})$$
$$I = \{i \in \mathbb{Z}|\ 0 \le i < w\} \tag{5}$$
$$J_1 = \{j_1 \in \mathbb{Z}|\ 0 \le j_1 < n\}$$
$$J_2 = \{j_2 \in \mathbb{Z}|\ 0 \le j_2 < n\}$$

Next, we impose the *count* constraint on every column of the matrix C so that the number of occurrences of value 0 on each column is no more than once. So the constraint are defined by:

$$\forall j \in J(count(0, C_{*,j}, occ))$$
$$J = \{j \in \mathbb{Z}|\ 0 \le j < m\} \tag{6}$$
$$occ \in \{0,1\}$$

where occ is an integer variable whose domain is $\{0,1\}$. Thus, the conjunction of Constraints (5) and (6) can logically realize the restriction required from Constraint (4).

So far, all the constraints as mentioned earlier have fully satisfied all the restrictions defined by the definition of the SGP and can be used to solve some small instances (e.g., 3-3-4, 5-3-7). However, we can further shrink the search space by placing *implied constraints*, which do not change the set of solutions, and hence are logically redundant [36].

Equation (1) has already fixed the first row of the matrix G, which implies that those players who have met in the first week cannot play in the same group in the subsequent weeks. Therefore, the *allDifferent* constraint can be used to enforce the groups of these players are pairwise distinct after the first week, and we express these *allDifferent* constraints by:

$$\forall i \forall j \ne j' \wedge j/s = j'/s(G_{i,j} \ne G_{i,j'})$$
$$i \in \{i \in \mathbb{Z}|\ 0 \le i < w\} \tag{7}$$
$$j, j' \in \{x \in \mathbb{Z}|\ 0 \le x < n\}$$

In summary, the basic model comprises Eqs. (1), (2), and Constraints (3), (5), (6), and (7). Nevertheless, the problem-solving ability of this model can be greatly improved by the introduction of additional constraints, such as static symmetry breaking constraints, and the constraints derived by instance-specific pattern. In the subsequent sections, we will present the additional constraints dedicated to different types of instances based on this model and discuss how to solve the instances, which cannot be solved sequentially, in parallel.

4   Instances Solved Sequentially

For a given number of groups g and a group size s, our goal is to compute a first solution for a full instance g-s-w^*, where w^* represents the maximum number of weeks. In this section, we consider a particular type of instance s-s-$(s+1)$, which means that the number of groups in each week is the same as the number of players in the groups within each week, and the number of weeks is equal to the number of groups within each week plus one. Moreover, the number of weeks is maximized because $\frac{s*s-1}{s-1} = s + 1$. The specific properties of the instances of the form s-s-$(s+1)$ enable us to discover the instance-specific constraints. Furthermore, we utilize the observed pattern from the relatively small instances to deduce more instance-specific constraints for the instances of the form *odd-odd-(odd+1)* (o-o-$(o + 1)$), especially for the form *prime-prime-(prime + 1)* (p-p-$(p + 1)$), and the form *even-even-(even + 1)* (e-e-$(e + 1)$).

Before introducing the constraints, we first define the submatrix GS of the decision variables matrix G. In the present paper, a submatrix GS of G is a $(w - 1) \times s$ matrix formed by removing the first row of G and selecting columns $[j \ldots (j + s - 1)]$, where j must be divisible by s, i.e. $j\%s = 0.$[3] Thus, G has exactly s such submatrices, each of which has $w - 1$ rows and s columns. The i-th submatrix of G is denoted by GS_i, where $0 \le i \le s - 1$ (Table 3).

Table 3. A solution of 5-5-6 expressed by groups. It can be converted to the solution expressed by the number of golfers easily. The submatrices GS_1 and GS_2 are surrounded in the dotted line. (Table reproduced from [20]).

Player Week	1	2	3	4	5	6	7	8	9	10	11	12	13	14	15	16	17	18	19	20	21	22	23	24	25
1	1	1	1	1	1	2	2	2	2	2	3	3	3	3	3	4	4	4	4	4	5	5	5	5	5
2	1	2	3	4	5	1	2	3	4	5	1	2	3	4	5	1	2	3	4	5	1	2	3	4	5
3	1	2	3	4	5	2	5	1	3	4	3	1	4	5	2	4	3	5	2	1	5	4	2	1	3
4	1	2	3	4	5	3	1	4	5	2	2	5	1	3	4	5	4	2	1	3	4	3	5	2	1
5	1	2	3	4	5	4	3	5	2	1	5	4	2	1	3	3	1	4	5	2	2	5	1	3	4
6	1	2	3	4	5	5	4	2	1	3	4	3	5	2	1	2	5	1	3	4	3	1	4	5	2

---

[3] The % (modulo) operator yields the remainder from the division of the first operand by the second.

4.1   7-7-8

For the instances of the form s-s-$(s+1)$, every player must play with every other exactly once since $s*s-1$ is divisible by $s-1$. Thus, players whose number is greater than s must meet every player whose number is less than or equal to s exactly once in every week except the first week since the first row and the first s columns of the matrix G are frozen by Eqs. (1) and (2). To put it another way, since the first s players, in turn, are assigned to the first s groups after the first week and there are only s groups within each week, all the rest of $n-s$ players have to be assigned to these s groups to avoid meeting the first s players more than once. Based on this analysis, we place the following constraints on the columns of the matrix G:

$$\forall i \in I \wedge i' \in I \wedge i \neq i' \forall j \in J(\ G_{i,j} \neq G_{i',j})$$
$$I = \{x \in \mathbb{Z} |\ 0 < x < w\} \tag{8}$$
$$J = \{x \in \mathbb{Z} |\ s \leq x < n\}$$

Constraint (8) states that starting with submatrix GS_1 of the matrix G, every column in the matrix GS_i $(i \geq 1)$ must be pairwise distinct, which can be implemented by the *allDifferent* constraint (cf. Table 3). Therefore, all the possible values of columns (column space) of the matrix GS_i $(i \geq 1)$ is reduced from s^s to $s!$ by introducing the Constraint 8, which is a significant search space reduction.

In Sect. 3, we have presented Eq. (1) to fix the first row of the matrix G. We can also fix the second row of the instances of the form s-s-$(s+1)$ for the following reason. In Constraint (7), we have explained that s players assigned in the same group in the first week cannot meet again in the subsequent weeks. Besides, for the form s-s-$(s+1)$, there are only s different groups, which implies that the possible groups assigned to these s players must be a permutation of the set of integers $\{1 \ldots s\}$. Thus, every row of the submatrix GS_i $(i \geq 1)$ is a permutation of the set of integers $\{1 \ldots s\}$. Moreover, arbitrary swapping two columns in the submatrix GS_i $(i \geq 1)$ leads to an isomorphism even when the first row of the matrix G is fixed by Eq. (1). Therefore, for the instances of the form s-s-$(s+1)$, we fix all the first rows of the submatrix GS_i $(i \geq 1)$ with the array $[1 \ldots s]$ (cf. the second row of Table 3), which can be expressed as:

$$\forall j \in J(G_{1,j} = j\%s + 1)$$
$$J = \{x \in \mathbb{Z} |\ s \leq x < n\} \tag{9}$$

Thus, the symmetries caused by renumbering players in the second row can be eliminated by imposing Constraint (9).

In summary, the model used to tackle 5-5-6, 6-6-7, and 7-7-8 consists of the constraints of the basic model and the additional constraints including Constraints (8) and (9).

4.2   9-9-10

The additional constraints for 7-7-8 are insufficient to solve 9-9-10 in an appropriate time since the size of the problem grows significantly. One possible way to tackle the larger instance is to shrink the overall search space by imposing more instance-specific constraints.

We observe the solutions of the 4-4-5, 5-5-6, and 7-7-8 instances; and discover that GS_1 can always be a symmetric matrix, namely $GS_1 = GS_1^T$. Hence, we conjecture that 9-9-10 can also have a symmetric submatrix and then impose the following constraints on the decision variables G:

$$\forall i \in I \forall j \in J(G_{i,j} = G_{(j-s),(i+s)})$$
$$I = \{x \in \mathbb{Z} |\ 0 \le x < w\} \tag{10}$$
$$J = \{x \in \mathbb{Z} |\ s \le x < 2 * s\}$$

Constraint (10) states that the entries of GS_1 are symmetric with respect to the main diagonal. Besides, the main diagonal of the submatrix GS_1 is pairwise distinct for 5-5-6 and 7-7-8, given by:

$$\forall i \in I \forall j \in J(G_{i,j} \ne G_{(i+1),(j+1)})$$
$$I = \{x \in \mathbb{Z} |\ 0 \le x < w\} \tag{11}$$
$$J = \{x \in \mathbb{Z} |\ s \le x < 2 * s\}$$

Apart from the fixed pattern of GS_1, there is also a fixed pattern among the submatrices of G. Because the second row has already been fixed by Constraint (9), we can impose the *allDifferent* constraints on the subsequent rows for those players who have played together in the second week since any two columns of G can only have identical values in exactly one row (e.g. *allDifferent*$(G_{3,5}, G_{3,10}, G_{3,15}, G_{3,20})$ in Table 3). These constraints are implied constraints and can be expressed as:

$$\forall i \in I \forall j \in J \wedge j' \in J \wedge j\%s = j'\%s \wedge j \ne j'(G_{i,j} \ne G_{i,j'})$$
$$I = \{x \in \mathbb{Z} |\ 1 \le x < w\} \tag{12}$$
$$J = \{x \in \mathbb{Z} |\ s \le x < n\}$$

We also notice that for 5-5-6 and 7-7-8, there is always a type solution in which the second row of GS_1 is fixed by the array $[2, s, 1, 3, 4, \ldots, s-1]$ (cf. the second row of GS_1 Table 3). We therefore assume that 9-9-10 also exists such solution, and solve 9-9-10 by fixing the second row of GS_1 with $[2, 9, 1, 3, 4, 5, 6, 7, 8]$.

In conclusion, we solve 9-9-10 by adding Constraints (10), (11), and (12) to the model of 7-7-8, as well as the fixed values for the second row of GS_1.

4.3   13-13-14 etc.

We have discovered some common features of the instances of the form s-s-$(s + 1)$, particularly for the instances of the form o-o-$(o + 1)$ when expressing a solution by groups; and these common features are mostly focused on the second submatrix GS_1 of G. It is also interesting to observe that the submatrix GS_i, $1 < i < s$, consists of s s-tuples that are derived from the second submatrix GS_1 on the 5-5-6 and 7-7-9 but 9-9-10 (cf. Table 3). Simply put, the rest of submatrices can be obtained by interchanging rows of GS_1 on these instances. Thus, we can solve larger instances of the form p-p-$(p + 1)$ by restricting row space of the submatrix GS_i $(1 < i < s)$ to the rows of the submatrix GS_1. Formally:

$$PT = \{(G_{i,j}, G_{i,j+1}, ..., G_{i,j+s-1})|$$
$$s \leq j < 2 * s \ \wedge \ 2 \leq i < w \ \wedge \ i,j \in \mathbb{Z}\} \tag{13}$$
$$(G_{i,j}, G_{i,j+1}, ..., G_{i,j+s-1}) \in PT,$$
$$2 \leq i < w, \ 2 * s \leq j < n, \ j\%s = 0, \ i,j \in \mathbb{Z} \tag{14}$$

where Constraint (13) defines the potential combination of values of columns of GS_1 as PT. Then we can limit the row space of the submatrices except GS_0 and GS_1 to PT by Constraint 14, which can be implemented by the *table* constraint. So the question then is, how to find the submatrix GS_1 that can lead to a solution of the instance.

To find the correct GS_1, we create a separate model defined on a $s \times s$ matrix (s must be a prime number), which comprises Constraints (10) and (11), and the *alldifferent* constraint imposing on each row and each column of the matrix. We also fix the first row and the second row with $[1 \ldots s]$ and $[2, s, 1, 3, 4, \ldots, s-1]$ respectively, as we did for the 9-9-10 instance. Incidentally, GS_1 is a *Latin square* since it is a $s \times s$ matrix filled with s distinct numbers and every row and column of the matrix is all different. Moreover, for the last row $(i = s - 1)$ of GS_1, starting with the third element $(j = 2)$ to the last element is fixed with the array $[2, 1, 3, 4, 5, \ldots, s - 2]$. Along with decrementing the row $(i --)$, the element at the tail of the array is removed and the starting position of the first element of the array incrementing $(j++)$ until the array is reduced to containing exactly one element $\{2\}$, as illustrated in Table 4.

Table 4. The second matrix GS_1 for the instance 13-13-14 (Table reproduced from [20]).

1	2	3	4	5	6	7	8	9	10	11	12	13
2	13	1	3	4	5	6	7	8	9	10	11	12
3	1	4	5	6	7	8	9	10	11	12	13	2
4	3	5	6	7	8	9	10	11	12	13	2	1
5	4	6	7	8	9	10	11	12	13	2	1	3
6	5	7	8	9	10	11	12	13	2	1	3	4
7	6	8	9	10	11	12	13	2	1	3	4	5
8	7	9	10	11	12	13	2	1	3	4	5	6
9	8	10	11	12	13	2	1	3	4	5	6	7
10	9	11	12	13	2	1	3	4	5	6	7	8
11	10	12	13	2	1	3	4	5	6	7	8	9
12	11	13	2	1	3	4	5	6	7	8	9	10
13	12	2	1	3	4	5	6	7	8	9	10	11

Having this observed pattern and aforementioned separated model, we can obtain exactly one GS_1 for the instance of the form p-p-$(p+1)$, and then utilize it as an input for Constraint (14) with the model of 7-7-8 to solve 11-11-12 and 13-13-14. Note that since GS_1 has already initialized before solving process, we do not use the model of 9-9-10 because it is redundant to impose Constraints (10), (11), and (12) on the model.

4.4   8-8-9

So far, all the instances we have discussed conform to the form of o-o-$(o+1)$. We now consider the form of instances $even$-$even$-$(even + 1)$. The 8-8-9 is solved by the following conjectures derived from 4-4-5 with the model for 7-7-8:

$$\forall i \in I(G_{i,(i+s-1)} = 1)$$
$$I = \{x \in \mathbb{Z} \mid 0 < x < w\} \tag{15}$$
$$\forall j \neq j' \wedge i \neq i' \wedge j/s = j'/s \wedge j\%s + 1 = i \wedge j'\%s + 1 = i'$$
$$(G_{i,j} \neq G_{i',j'})$$
$$i, i' \in \{x \in \mathbb{Z} \mid 0 < x < w\}$$
$$j, j' \in \{x \in \mathbb{Z} \mid 2 * s < x < n\} \tag{16}$$

Constraint (15) states that the main diagonal of the matrix GS_1 consists of the fixed values $[1,1,\dots,1]$; and the rest of submatrices have the main diagonal whose values must be pairwise distinct (Constraint (16)).

Table 5. The second matrix GS_1 for a solution 8-8-9 (Table reproduced from [20]).

1	2	3	4	5	6	7	8
2	1	4	3	6	5	8	7
3	4	1	2	7	8	5	6
4	3	2	1	8	7	6	5
5	6	7	8	1	2	3	4
6	5	8	7	2	1	4	3
7	8	5	6	3	4	1	2
8	7	6	5	4	3	2	1

Table 5 depicts the submatrix GS_1 of the solution of 8-8-9 we solved. It is interesting to observe that the GS_1 matrix of 4-4-5 and 8-8-9 are composed of four symmetric matrices. Moreover, we discover that their solutions also satisfy the Constraints (13) and (14), and it is still unclear whether or not the 16-16-17 instance shares these common features with 4-4-5 and 8-8-9.

5   Instances Solved in Parallel

In the previous section, we have presented the instances that can be solved sequentially via our modeling approach. We now turn to more difficult instances that must deal with by way of parallel processing to obtain one solution. The difficult instances refer to no fixed pattern discovered so far, which implies no instance-specific constraints to shrink search space for these instances and hence there are large search spaces even for relatively small size.

Our idea is to partition the search tree of the SGP into independent subtrees; then each worker that is associated with a thread works on distinct subtrees using the same CP model. Thus, this approach can be classified as *data-level parallelism* based on the taxonomy for parallelism in applications from [15]. Furthermore, since no communication is required during the solving process, to some extent, our parallel approach can also be seen as Embarrassingly Parallel Search (EPS) [31]. The EPS is defined as decomposing the problem in many sub-problems and assigning the sub-problems to workers dynamically [24]. By contrast, our parallel approach differs from the EPS due to the use of a separate model that is used to generate the sub-problems instead of Depth-bounded Depth First Search [31]. The generic procedure can be summarized as follows:

1. A subset of the decision variables of the model is selected.
2. A separate model generates all the partial assignments over selected variables in the subset before the search process.
3. The partial assignments are mapped to the workers so that each worker can work on its own independent search space by using its constraint solver.
4. Once a solution is found, the worker that finds the solution notifies other workers to stop.

Step 1 is crucial to the search space splitting because it determines the subtrees explored by each worker. The selection of the subset of the decision variables adhere to the following rules: First, they should be easy to generate by a separate model. Second, each worker should not be assigned too many partial assignments because one partial assignment might take a long time to evaluate for a large instance. Because of the usage of the separate model, the partial assignments are consistent with the propagation (i.e., running the propagation mechanism on them does not detect any inconsistency). Besides, the number of solutions of the separate model can help us decide the workload of each worker and workload distribution. In the following sections, we will gradually describe CP models for generating partial assignments for search-space splitting and the constraints imposed on the basic model for the 6-3-8, 6-4-7, and 7-3-10 instances in detail.

5.1   6-3-8

The 6-3-8 instance is a representative example to illustrate the effectiveness of our parallel approach for the SGP since the instances smaller than it can be solved quickly and the instances bigger than it are difficult to be solved sequentially by constraint solving. When switching the target instance from 5-3-7 to 6-3-8, the number of decision variables grows from $5*3*7 = 105$ to $6*3*8 = 144$, and the domain size of each variable is incremented by one for our modeling approach, which indicates the overall underlying search space significantly increased from 5^{105} to 6^{144} if we do not take account of the search space pruned by constraint propagation.

The idea behind the parallel approach is to freeze a part of the decision variables so that the size of the sub-problem is shrunk to solvable, thereby solving the original problem. For the 6-3-8 instance, we select the second row of the matrix G for the search space splitting since the first row of the matrix G is fixed by Constraint (1). A separate model is used to generate the solutions for the second row of the matrix G as the partial assignments for the search space splitting, which is composed of the following constraints:

$$J = \{x \in \mathbb{Z}| \ 0 \leq x < s\}$$

$$\forall j \in J(F_j = j + 1) \tag{17}$$

$$GCC(F, V, O), V = \{1 \ldots g\}, \ O = [s \ldots s] \tag{18}$$

$$\forall j \neq j' \wedge j/s = j'/s(F_j \neq F_{j'})$$

$$j' \in J \tag{19}$$

$$\forall j\%s = 0(F_j \leq F_{(j+s)}) \tag{20}$$

$$\forall j/s = (j+1)/s(F_j < F_{(j+1)}) \tag{21}$$

where F is an array of decision variables for the separate model, and the domain of each vairbales is also $\{1 \ldots g\}$. Constraints (17), (18), and (19) are identical to Constraints (1), (3), and (7) stated in the basic model (see Sect. 3) respectively. Constraints (20) and (21), which are not included in the basic model, are static symmetry breaking constraints. Constraint (20) removes the symmetries caused by interchangeable submatrices GS_i, $0 < i < s$. We eliminate these symmetries by arranging the values assigned to the first column of the first row of all the submatrices GS_i in non-decreasing order. (Please refer to the numbers with

Table 6. A solution of 6-3-8 expressed by groups.

Week \ Player	1	2	3	4	5	6	7	8	9	10	11	12	13	14	15	16	17	18
1	1	1	1	2	2	2	3	3	3	4	4	4	5	5	5	6	6	6
2	1[a]	2	3	1[a]	4	5	1[a]	3	6	2[a]	5	6	2[a]	4	5	3[a]	4	6
3	1	2	3	2[a]	1	3	3	4	6	5	6	4	6	2	5	1	4	5
4	1	2	3	3[a]	2	1	5	6	3	1	6	4	5	6	4	4	5	2
5	1	2	3	4[a]	3	5	6	5	2	6	3	1	1	6	4	2	4	5
6	1	2	3	4[a]	5	2	6	4	5	3	6	2	4	1	5	6	3	1
7	1	2	3	4[a]	5	6	2	5	1	5	4	3	6	3	2	6	1	4
8	1	2	3	4[a]	5	6	5	1	6	4	2	5	3	6	1	4	2	3

superscript a in the second row of Table 6.) Additionally, interchanging any two columns of a submatrix GS_i generates a solution symmetrical with the original one, which entails Constraint (21) to remove these symmetries. Because of Constraint (21), the players played together in the first week must be in ascending order of groups in the second week (cf. the second row of Table 6).

In addition to the constraints of the separate model, we also place the constraints to break the symmetries caused by interchangeable weeks partially. The idea is to restrict the groups of the 4th player in non-decreasing order from week two, given by:

$$\forall i \in I(G_{i,s} \leq G_{(i+1),s})$$
$$I = \{x \in \mathbb{Z} \mid 0 < x < w - 1\} \tag{22}$$

Please note that Constraint (22) cannot fully remove the symmetries among weeks because there are still symmetries whenever $G_{i,s} = G_{(i+1),s}$. For example in Table 6, interchanging the 7th week with 8th week results in a symmetrical solution.

Finally, the results of the above model are equally distributed to each worker that runs the basic model.

5.2   6-4-7

The separate model for 6-3-8 produces 424 solutions for the second row, while it produces 351 for the second row of 6-4-7. However, because of the increasing difficulty, we add the following constraints based on the separate model for 6-3-8 to produce less number of solutions for the second row of 6-4-7:

$$J = \{j \in \mathbb{Z} \mid 0 \leq j < n - s \wedge j\%s = 0 \wedge j = (s-1)*s \Rightarrow j + s \neq s^2\}$$
$$\forall j \in J(F_{j+1} \leq F_{j+s+1}) \tag{23}$$
$$\forall j \in J(F_{j+1} = F_{j+s+1} \Rightarrow F_{j+2} \leq F_{j+s+2}) \tag{24}$$
$$\forall j \in J(F_{j+1} = F_{j+s+1} \wedge F_{j+2} = F_{j+s+2} \Rightarrow F_{j+3} \leq F_{j+s+3}) \tag{25}$$

Table 7. A solution of 6-4-7. The numbers with the same superscript are in non-decreasing order in the second row. (Table reproduced from [20]).

Week \ Player	1	2	3	4	5	6	7	8	9	10	11	12	13	14	15	16	17	18	19	20	21	22	23	24
1	1	1	1	1	2	2	2	2	3	3	3	3	4	4	4	4	5	5	5	5	6	6	6	6
2	1^a	2^b	3^c	4^d	1^a	2^b	3^c	4^d	1^a	4^b	5^c	6^d	1^a	4^b	5^c	6^d	2^e	3^f	5^g	6^h	2^e	3^f	5^g	6^h
3	1	2	3	4	2	4	6	5	5	3	6	1	6	2	4	5	3	4	1	2	5	1	3	6
4	1	2	3	4	3	6	4	5	4	2	1	3	6	1	5	2	5	1	2	6	3	6	4	5
5	1	2	3	4	4	6	1	2	3	5	2	6	5	6	3	1	1	5	4	3	5	2	6	4
6	1	2	3	4	6	3	5	1	2	6	3	4	4	5	6	3	4	2	5	1	5	6	1	2
7	1	2	3	4	6	1	2	3	5	1	4	2	3	5	2	6	5	6	3	4	4	5	6	1

In short, Constraints (23)–(25) ensure that the values occupying the same positions in the first row of the first s submatrices (GS_0, GS_1, GS_2, GS_3) and the last two submatrices (GS_4, GS_5) are in non-decreasing order respectively (see Table 7). The reason why the submatrices are divided into two groups is that numeral 1 always takes up the first row of the first column in the first s submatrices due to the restrictions from Constraint (20) and (21). Thus, if a constraint enforces $G_{1,13} \leq G_{1,17}$, the solution shown in Table 7 will not be obtained. These additional constraints also reduce search space by removing symmetries. For example, if we do not impose Constraint (23) on the separate model, a second row such like [1 2 3 4 1 4 5 6 1 2 3 4 1 4 5 6 2 3 5 6 2 3 5 6] will be generated. In that case, we will require more workers to work on these symmetrical search spaces.

As with the 6-3-8 instance, we map the solutions of the separate model to different workers before the solving process. Then, to solve the 6-4-7 instance, we further reduce the search space by adding the following constraints onto the basic model:

$$\forall j \in J(GCC(G_{*,j}, V, O))$$
$$J = \{j \in \mathbb{Z}|\ s \leq j < 3s\} \tag{26}$$
$$V = \{1 \ldots s\},\ O = \{1 \ldots 1\},\ 0 < * < w$$

where $G_{*,j}$ denotes the columns from the sth column to the $(3s - 1)^{th}$ column of the matrix G with removed first element. More particularly, every value in the set $\{1, 2, 3, 4\}$ can appear only once in all the columns of the submatrices GS_1 and GS_2. We impose Constraint (26) on only the columns of GS_1 and GS_2 because each player only plays with other 21 players since $(24 - 1)\%(4 - 1) = 2$; thus not every column contains the set $\{1, 2, 3, 4\}$. Though Constraint (26) does not enforce all columns containing the values $\{1, 2, 3, 4\}$, it reduces much search space; our experiments show that we cannot solve 6-4-7 without these constraints.

5.3   7-3-10

The problem size of 7-3-10 is much larger than 6-4-7 and 6-3-8, we must harness more instance-specific constraints, which are given by:

$$\forall i \in I(G_{i,s} = i + 1), I = \{i \in \mathbb{Z}|\ 0 < i \leq s\} \tag{27}$$
$$\forall i \in I'(G_{i,s} = s + 1), I' = \{i \in \mathbb{Z}|\ s + 1 < i < 2\} \tag{28}$$
$$GCC(G_{*,(s+1)}, V, O),\ V = \{1, 2, 3, 6, 7\}$$
$$0 < * < w,\ O = [1, 1, 1, 0, 0] \tag{29}$$
$$GCC(G_{*,(s+2)}, V', O'),\ V' = \{1, 2, 3, 6\}$$
$$O' = [1, 1, 1, 0] \tag{30}$$
$$\forall s + s \leq j < n(GCC(G_{*,j}, V'', O''))$$
$$V'' = \{1 \ldots s\},\ O'' = [1 \ldots 1] \tag{31}$$

We strictly limit the positions of player 4 so that he/she will never be assigned to groups 5, 6, and 7. The reason is that player 4 must meet players 1, 2, and 3, and the groups of the first three (s) players are frozen by Eq. 2 after the first week, which implies that player 4 must stay in the first three groups from week 2 to week 4. Hence, player 4 can only play in the groups that are greater than or equal to 4 (s + 1) from week 5. Moreover, player 4 is always the smallest player starting from the 9th column of a solution (cf. Table 1). Therefore, player 4 cannot appear in groups 5, 6, and 7, and only stay in group 4 from week 5. Consequently, the 4th column of Table 2 is the result by imposing Constraint (27) and (28). These two constraints not only shrink the search space but also remove the symmetries caused by swapping the group containing player 4 with other groups after week 4.

Since player 4 can only play in group 4 after week 4, player 5 is impossible to stay in groups 6 and 7, because then there will be no player assigned in group 5. Similarly, player 6 cannot appear in group 7 and can only appear in group 6 once. Thus, we use Constraints (29) and (30) to limit the number of occurrences of the values 6 and 7.

Furthermore, because $(21 - 1)\%(3 - 1) = 0$, each player must play with other players exactly once. Hence, we guarantee the first s players must meet the rest of players once, which are ensured by Constraints (29), (30), and (31). Incidentally, Constraint (31) can be applied to any full instance that satisfies $(n - 1)\%(s - 1) = 0$ in our modeling approach (e.g. 7-4-9).

In the implementation of parallelism for 7-3-10, we also use the same separate model as the model for 6-4-7 to generate solutions of the second row and distribute them to the workers.

6   Experiments

In this section, we report the experimental results on instances discussed in Sects. 4 and 5 separately since different hardware and methods were used.

6.1   Experimental Results on Instance Solved Sequentially

To confirm our theoretical discussion and the conjecture for the instances discussed in Sect. 4, we implemented the basic model as described in Sect. 3 and the instance-specific constraints in Sect. 4 via the Choco Solver 4.0.6 [27] with JDK version 10.0.1. All experiments were performed on a laptop with an Intel i7-3720QM CPU, 2.60 GHz with 4 physical and 8 logical cores, and 8 GB DDR3 memory running Linux Mint 18.3.

Table 8 summarizes the experimental results on the instances solved sequentially, including the total CPU time, the number of visited nodes, backtracks, and fails. It also provides search strategies we used. By using our approach, we were able to prove the nonexistence of the solution of 6-6-7 and solved six open instances for constraint satisfaction approach but not for metaheuristic approach [7].

Table 8. Results on the s-s-$(s + 1)$ Instances. A superscript "c" means that the instance was open for constraint satisfaction approach; "dom" and "min" denote the predefined search strategies domOverWDegSearch and minDomLBSearch in Choco Solver, respectively. (Table reproduced from [20]).

Instance	Time(s)	Nodes	Backtracks	Fails	Strategy
5-3-7	0.095	111	179	94	dom
5-5-6	0.069	7	1	0	min
6-6-7^c	25	1.38e5	2.77e5	1.38e5	min
7-7-8^c	111	3.62e5	723e5	3.62e5	min
8-8-9^c	12	15,370	30,680	15,350	min
9-9-10^c	2559	2.08e6	4.16e6	2.08e6	min
11-11-12^c	62	3,150	6,279	3,144	min
13-13-14^c	2563	5.80e4	1.16e5	5.79e4	min

6.2   Experimental Results on Instance Solved in Parallel

To validate our parallel approach for the SGP, we switch to a computer with 250 GB DDR3 1066 memory and 4 Intel Xeon CPU E7-4830 2.13 GHz processors running on Linux CentOS 6.5, where each processor has 8 physical cores. The versions of Choco Solver and the JDK are unchanged. Table 9 reports the experimental results for comparing parallel and sequential execution when using the same model to solve the same instance. For parallel execution, the number of workers we used varies from instance to instance. For 6-3-8, we specified 8, 16 and 32 workers to execute in parallel, but super-liner speedup was only observed when using 8 workers, because the partial assignment that can lead to a solution does not happen to be evaluated first.

Table 9. Results on the Instances solved in parallel. A superscript "f" means that the instance is solved by computer for the first time. A "-" sign means the program was still running after a period which is equal to the number of workers multiplied by the execution time in parallel. (Table reproduced from [20]).

Instance	Workers	Time(s)	Nodes	Backtracks	Fails	Strategy
6-3-8^c	1	2.95e4	2.91e8	5.83e8	2.91e8	min
	8	50.2	2.09e5	4.18e5	2.09e5	min
	16	2.62e4	2.50e8	5.13e8	2.31e8	min
6-4-7^f	1	-	-	-	-	min
	48	8.59e3	1.66e7	3.32e7	1.66e7	min
7-3-10^f	1	-	-	-	-	dom
	32	7.61e4	1.86e8	3.73e8	1.86e8	dom

Then, for 6-4-7, we used 48 workers because there are only 48 solutions generated by the separate model. Finally, the result of 7-3-8 is given by selecting the first 8 solutions of the separate model, and every solution is allocated to 4 different workers, each of which employs their respective search strategies that are predefined in Choco Solver, including *minDomUBSearch*, *minDomLBSearch*, *defaultSearch* and *domOverWDegSearch*. Besides, we also performed three more experiments in which the separate model was specified with above mentioned search strategies. As a consequence, the first 8 solutions are different from the first experiment, and we obtained three more non-isomorphic solutions for the 7-3-10 instance. The solutions of the instances in Table 9, which are not given in the main body of this article, are provided in Appendix A.

6.3   Discussion

It is interesting to observe the results for the instances of the form s-s-$(s + 1)$ ($s = \{5, 7, 8, 11, 13\}$) consisting of s–1 mutually orthogonal $s \times s$ latin squares[4] (cf. GS_1, GS_2, GS_3, and GS_4 of Table 3). The results of these instances are consistent with the basic correspondence of *affine planes* and Latin squares, which proves that there exist n–1 Mutually Orthogonal Latin Squares (MOLS) of order n iff there exists an affine plane of order n [2,25], i.e., there are affine planes of order 5, 7, 8, 11, and 13. It is also not difficult to relate no solution for 6-6-7 to no MOLS of order 6 [4]. And we argue that the solution of 10-10-11 is nonexistent because there is no set of 7 MOLS of order 10 [22] and thereby no affine plane of order 10 [17]. More generally, we speculate that the solutions for the form np-np-$(np+1)$ (e.g., $np = 14, 21, 22, 30, 33$) do not exist because of the nonexistence of *projective planes*[5] for them according to the *Bruck-Ryser-Chowla theorem* [2], where $np \equiv 1 \ or \ 2 \pmod 4$ and the square-free part of np contain at least one prime $p \equiv 3 \pmod 4$.[6] Moreover, the 12-12-13 instance is hard for the CP approach, which corresponds to searching an affine plane of order 12—an unsettled case.

In addition to the results of the instances, we also show that more instance-specific constraints can shorten the execution time even if the size of instances increases. For example, 11-11-12 took much less time than 9-9-10 since more constraints are posted. The experimental results also show that parallel constraint solving through search space splitting is a very effective means to prevent backtrack search from getting stuck into a fruitless search area. Without surprise, the super-linear speedup was observed since only one invalid partial assignment is enough to cause instances such as 6-4-7 to be unsolvable for sequential solving and one valid partial solution can easily lead to backtrack search into a search area with a solution. Note that observed super-linear speedups are not in

---

[4] Two Latin squares are mutually orthogonal if, they have the same order n and when superimposed, each of the possible n^2 ordered pairs occur exactly once.

[5] An affine plane of order n exists iff a projective plane of order n exists.

[6] For instance, $14 = 2 * 7 \equiv 2 \pmod 4$, and the primes in the square-free part are 2 and 7.

contradiction with Amdahl's law since our goal is to obtain a first solution instead of all solutions.

7 Related Work

There is a substantial body of work available on symmetry breaking for the SGP from the constraints community, including model reformulation, static symmetry breaking constraints, and dynamic symmetry breaking.

7.1 Methods from the CSP Literature

Smith [37] presented the integer set model with extra auxiliary variables that automatically eliminates the symmetries inside of groups, which is probably one of the first works that break the symmetry of the SGP via model reformulation. Besides, Symmetry Breaking During Search (SBDS) with symmetry breaking constraints is employed to break renumbering symmetry but not entirely, where SBDS is essentially a search space reduction technique that adds constraints to remove symmetrical search space during search. Law and Lee [18] developed the *Precedence* constraint to break the symmetries of groups inside of weeks for the integer model and the symmetries caused by renumbering players for the set model. Symmetry Breaking via Dominance Detection (SBDD), another dynamic symmetry breaking technique, was developed separately by Focaci and Milano [10] and by Fahle *et al.* [9, 11]. The main idea of SBDD is to utilize no-good learning to avoid exploring search space that is symmetrical of previously explored nodes recorded on the no-goods. By using SBDD, Fahle and Milano discovered seven non-symmetric solutions for the 5-3-7 instance in less than two hours on a computer with an UltraSparc-II 400 MHz processor.

Barnier and Brisset [3] proposed SBDD+ for the SGP, which computes isomorphism not only for leaves of the search tree but also on current non-leaves node. The experimental results showed that SBDD+ only took around eight seconds to compute all the seven non-symmetric solutions for 5-3-7, which is a significant improvement compared with [9]. However, they also pointed out that SBDD+ has to tackle the explosion of node store and the time overhead due to nodes dominance checking for a larger instance. Puget [28] combined SBDD with Symmetry Breaking Using Stabilizers (STAB) to obtain a solution of 5-5-6 in 38 s on a laptop with a Pentium M 1.4 GHz processor, where STAB is a variant of SBDS that adds symmetry breaking constraints without changing specified partial assignment.

All of the above mentioned works aim at eliminating the symmetries of the SGP, which is the first difficulty mentioned in Sect. 2.1. To tackle the second difficulty, Sellmann and Harvey [35] developed the vertical constraints and horizontal constraints for propagation, which can check whether a given partial assignment is extensible to a solution. They obtained all unique solutions of the 5-3-7 instance in 393.96 s on a computer with Pentium III 933 MHz processor by using the dedicated constraints. However, the dedicated constraints are developed for the original naive model, and no efficient algorithm for finding the players who have conflicting residual graphs is given.

7.2 Methods from the Metaheuristic Literature

Despite having elegant and sophisticated search space reduction techniques such as SBDS, SBDD, etc., the constraint satisfaction approach, a systematic search method, cannot compete with the metaheuristic approaches on the SGP when the goal is to obtain one solution instead of all non-symmetric solutions. Dotú and Van Hentenryck [7] employed tabu search with a constructive seeding heuristic and good starting points to achieve significant results on the instances of the form *prime-prime-(prime + 1)* (e.g. 43-43-44, 47-47-48). Dotú and Van Hentenryck also solved 9-9-10 and 6-3-8 by using tabu search with a good starting point in 0.01 s and 51.93 s on a computer with Pentium IV 3.06 GHz processor [8]. Besides, the 6-3-8 instance was also solved by the evolutionary approach on a Pentium IV 3.06 GHz processor [5]. Unfortunately, the total CPU time is not reported in [8].

Triska and Musliu [38] are the first to solve the 8-4-10 instance reported in the literature, although one solution of 8-4-10 had already been published before [1] but without any explanation. The idea behind their metaheuristic approach is to employ a greedy heuristic for tabu search with the well-designed greedy initial configuration. The first solution of 8-4-10 instance was obtained in 11 min on a computer with an Intel Core 2 Duo 2.16 processor. Moreover, after varying the randomization factor of the greedy heuristic, they obtained two new non-isomorphic solutions for 8-4-10. In addition to the metaheuristic approach, they also explored a SAT encoding for the SGP [39]. Unfortunately, their SAT encoding is not competitive with other approaches.

Generally, solving the *q-q-(w + 2)* instance of the SGP amounts to finding *w* Mutually Orthogonal Latin Squares (MOLS). Thus, in addition to these approaches mentioned above which address the SGP head-on, Harvey and Winterer [14] exploited MOLS (in practice, MOLR) solutions found to construct solutions to the SGP. The most notable instance they solved is 20-16-6, which indicates that this is probably the most efficient method so far. However, no full instance *g-s-w** was resolved since this method heavily relies on the construction of MOLR.

7.3 Summary

Most of the research from the constraints community focus on search space reduction techniques, mainly dynamic symmetry breaking. The metaheuristic approach, by contrast, aims at finding a first solution as quickly as possible. For example, the 6-3-8 instance could be solved within reasonable time via the metaheuristic approach but not the constraint satisfaction approach. Note that the problem grows much faster even from 5-3-7 to 6-3-8 than the performance boost out of the processors. Table 10 summarizes the main accomplishments in the SPG from the computer-science community, including both the constraints and metaheuristics communities.

Table 10. The summary of the most significant results on the SGP from the computer-science community.

Instance	Year	Authors	Method	Description
4-3-4	2001	Smith [37]	SBDS	42 solutions found
5-3-7	2001	Fahle and Milnano [9]	SBDD	7 unique solutions in 2 h
5-3-7	2001	Barnier and Brisset [3]	SBDD+	7 unique solutions in 8 s
5-3-7	2002	Sellmann and Harvey [35]	Specific Constraints	7 unique solutions in 394 s
5-5-6	2005	Puget [28]	SBDD and STAB	A solution in 38 s
20-16-6	2005	Harvey and Winterer [14]	MOLR	Tabu search for MOLR
47-47-48	2005	Dotú *et al.* [7]	Tabu-search	Efficient for p-p-$(p+1)$
6-3-8	2007	Dotú *et al.* [8]	Tabu-search	A solution in 52 s
8-4-10	2011	Triska and Musliu [38]	Tabu-search	2 new unique solutions found

Finally, some instances which have not been solved by computer at present have already been constructed by combinatorics (e.g., 7-4-9, 9-3-13). For a detailed introduction, please refer to [29, 32].

8 Conclusion

In this paper, we have presented a combination of techniques which allows us to find solutions for eight open instances, where six of these instances are solved sequentially, and three of these instances are solved in parallel. In particular, we have shown the constraints derived from the relatively small instances can be used to solve larger instances that are in the same form as the smaller ones. In other words, we explore the properties of the instances of the form s-s-$(s+1)$ from the perspective of constraint programming. Besides, we have also shown that it is not uncommon for solving the SGP in parallel via search space splitting or with portfolio to gain super-linear speedups and parallel solving the SGP can be an effective method to address the instances that cannot be solved sequentially. The results show that our method is much more successful, even if we consider that the computers used for the other methods are up to 10 times slower than ours.

Unlike the earlier researches on the SGP which mainly focus on dynamic symmetry breaking, we attribute the success of our approach to the effectiveness of the instance-specific constraints and parallelism due to mitigating the two problems of solving the SGP mentioned in Sect. 2.1. Specifically, the instance-specific constraints imposed on the second submatrix of the decision variables matrix prune a large number of the sub-search trees near the root, including some symmetries. And since many partial assignments are extended simultaneously, fruitless partial assignments have no impact on overall execution time.

Not only that, but search space splitting can result in the partial assignments that can lead to a solution to be proceeded much earlier than the sequential search, which is the reason for super-linear speedup. Furthermore, we can conclude that early diversity brought by search space splitting before search can effectively alleviate the strong commitment due to the early decisions made by search strategy. Besides, we also remove the symmetries of the second row in the decision variables matrix when generating the partial assignments, which is helpful because nodes near the root contain much more symmetries than the nodes near the leaves of the search tree [28]. Therefore, with mainstream computers turning into parallel architectures, we believe that parallel constraint solving through search space splitting is a promising approach to solving more significant instances of the SGP.

Indeed, there is still a lot of potential to improve the performance of our approach. In particular, Constraints (22) is unable to eliminate the symmetries among weeks after week s when solving 6-3-8, 6-4-7, and 7-3-10. In fact, we have resolved it by enforcing the indices of the second "1" of all the weeks in ascending order, which means that the second golfers assigned in the first group are in ascending order. Unfortunately the performance is not satisfactory. As future work, we want to know whether the performance degradation is due to the use of the *IfThen* constraints or removal of symmetries that also simultaneously removes solutions. Besides, despite better than the *Reified* constraints, Constraints (5) and (6) introduce too many auxiliary variables that inevitably slow down the resolution process; thus, we have also implemented a specialized constraint to replace them. However, our constraint increases the difficulty of variable-selection since the constraint requires an additional variable to record the equality relationship among rows of the matrix G. To solve larger instances, in addition to using more processors and discovering more instance-specific constraints, we would like to consider combining the dynamic symmetry breaking and parallel constraint solving for the SGP.

In the end, we must regretfully admit that even if we have made some progress, some interesting instances are still open (e.g. 7-4-9, 8-3-11, and 9-3-13); notably, the original SGP 8-4-10 [13] is still unsolved for the CP approach, despite many efforts from the constraint programming community. Constraint technology should solve these instances to demonstrate itself as the first choice for solving combinatorial problems.

A   Appendix

The Solutions

See Tables 11, 12, 13, 14, 15, 16 and 17.

Table 11. The solution for 6-3-8 transformed from the solution shown in Table 6.

Week \ Group	1			2			3			4			5			6		
1	1	2	3	4	5	6	7	8	9	10	11	12	13	14	15	16	17	18
2	1	4	7	2	10	13	3	8	16	5	14	17	6	11	15	9	12	18
3	1	5	16	2	4	14	3	6	7	8	12	17	9	11	13	10	15	18
4	1	6	10	2	5	18	3	4	9	7	13	17	8	11	14	12	15	16
5	1	8	15	2	11	17	3	13	18	4	10	16	5	7	12	6	9	14
6	1	9	17	2	7	15	3	12	14	4	11	18	5	8	10	6	13	16
7	1	12	13	2	9	16	3	5	11	4	15	17	6	8	18	7	10	14
8	1	14	18	2	6	12	3	10	17	4	8	13	5	9	15	7	11	16

Table 12. A new non-isomorphic solution for the 6-3-8 instance.

Week \ Group	1			2			3			4			5			6		
1	1	2	3	4	5	6	7	8	9	10	11	12	13	14	15	16	17	18
2	1	4	7	2	5	8	3	6	10	9	13	16	11	14	17	12	15	18
3	1	5	16	2	4	15	3	7	12	6	8	14	9	10	17	11	13	18
4	1	6	9	2	10	18	3	4	11	5	12	13	7	14	16	8	15	17
5	1	8	18	2	12	16	3	9	15	4	13	17	5	10	14	6	7	11
6	1	10	13	2	7	17	3	14	18	4	8	12	5	9	11	6	15	16
7	1	11	15	2	9	14	3	8	13	4	10	16	5	7	18	6	12	17
8	1	12	14	2	6	13	3	5	17	4	9	18	7	10	15	8	11	16

Table 13. The solution for 6-4-7 transformed from the solution shown in Table 7.

Week \ Group	1				2				3				4				5				6			
1	1	2	3	4	5	6	7	8	9	10	11	12	13	14	15	16	17	18	19	20	21	22	23	24
2	1	5	9	13	2	6	17	21	3	7	18	22	4	8	10	14	11	15	19	23	12	16	20	24
3	1	6	10	24	2	7	12	15	3	8	13	19	4	11	20	21	5	16	18	23	9	14	17	22
4	1	7	16	17	2	8	11	22	3	9	15	20	4	5	19	24	6	12	14	23	10	13	18	21
5	1	8	20	23	2	9	18	24	3	6	11	16	4	12	13	17	5	10	15	22	7	14	19	21
6	1	11	14	18	2	10	16	19	3	5	12	21	4	7	9	23	6	13	20	22	8	15	17	24
7	1	12	19	22	2	5	14	20	3	10	17	23	4	6	15	18	7	11	13	24	8	9	16	21

Table 14. A new non-isomorphic solution for the 7-3-10 instance.

Week \ Group	1			2			3			4			5			6			7		
1	1	2	3	4	5	6	7	8	9	10	11	12	13	14	15	16	17	18	19	20	21
2	1	4	7	2	5	10	3	8	11	6	13	16	9	14	19	12	17	20	15	18	21
3	1	5	18	2	8	15	3	17	19	4	14	20	6	9	11	7	12	13	10	16	21
4	1	6	19	2	7	16	3	5	12	4	13	17	8	14	21	9	10	18	11	15	20
5	1	8	17	2	4	11	3	9	16	5	13	21	6	14	18	7	10	20	12	15	19
6	1	9	15	2	13	19	3	4	21	5	8	20	6	10	17	7	11	18	12	14	16
7	1	10	14	2	12	18	3	6	15	4	8	16	5	7	19	9	13	20	11	17	21
8	1	11	13	2	14	17	3	18	20	4	9	12	5	15	16	6	7	21	8	10	19
9	1	12	21	2	6	20	3	7	14	4	10	15	5	9	17	8	13	18	11	16	19
10	1	16	20	2	9	21	3	10	13	4	18	19	5	11	14	6	8	12	7	15	17

Table 15. A new non-isomorphic solution for the 7-3-10 instance.

Week \ Group	1			2			3			4			5			6			7		
1	1	2	3	4	5	6	7	8	9	10	11	12	13	14	15	16	17	18	19	20	21
2	1	4	7	2	10	13	3	16	19	5	8	20	6	11	14	9	12	17	15	18	21
3	1	5	11	2	8	21	3	15	20	4	9	16	6	7	10	12	13	18	14	17	19
4	1	6	21	2	7	17	3	8	14	4	10	15	5	9	13	11	18	19	12	16	20
5	1	8	12	2	5	19	3	7	13	4	14	18	6	9	15	10	16	21	11	17	20
6	1	9	19	2	11	15	3	10	18	4	8	17	5	14	16	6	13	20	7	12	21
7	1	10	14	2	4	20	3	9	11	5	7	18	6	12	19	8	15	16	13	17	21
8	1	13	16	2	9	18	3	6	17	4	11	21	5	12	15	7	14	20	8	10	19
9	1	15	17	2	12	14	3	5	21	4	13	19	6	8	18	7	11	16	9	10	20
10	1	18	20	2	6	16	3	4	12	5	10	17	7	15	19	8	11	13	9	14	21

Table 16. A new non-isomorphic solution for the 7-3-10 instance.

Week \ Group	1			2			3			4			5			6			7		
1	1	2	3	4	5	6	7	8	9	10	11	12	13	14	15	16	17	18	19	20	21
2	1	4	7	2	5	10	3	6	11	8	12	13	9	16	19	14	17	20	15	18	21
3	1	5	19	2	13	16	3	10	15	4	18	20	6	8	14	7	11	17	9	12	21
4	1	6	18	2	9	11	3	8	21	4	10	14	5	13	20	7	15	16	12	17	19
5	1	8	15	2	6	17	3	9	18	4	13	19	5	11	21	7	10	20	12	14	16
6	1	9	17	2	15	20	3	4	12	5	8	16	6	10	19	7	14	21	11	13	18
7	1	10	16	2	4	21	3	13	17	5	9	14	6	12	15	7	18	19	8	11	20
8	1	11	14	2	8	19	3	16	20	4	9	15	5	12	18	6	7	13	10	17	21
9	1	12	20	2	14	18	3	5	7	4	8	17	6	16	21	9	10	13	11	15	19
10	1	13	21	2	7	12	3	14	19	4	11	16	5	15	17	6	9	20	8	10	18

Table 17. A solution of 8-8-9 expressed by groups.

Week \ Player	1	2	3	4	5	6	7	8	9	10	11	12	13	14	15	16	17	18	19	20	21	22	23	24
1	1	1	1	1	1	1	1	1	2	2	2	2	2	2	2	2	3	3	3	3	3	3	3	3
2	1	2	3	4	5	6	7	8	1	2	3	4	5	6	7	8	1	2	3	4	5	6	7	8
3	1	2	3	4	5	6	7	8	2	1	4	3	6	5	8	7	3	4	1	2	7	8	5	6
4	1	2	3	4	5	6	7	8	3	4	1	2	7	8	5	6	6	5	8	7	2	1	4	3
5	1	2	3	4	5	6	7	8	4	3	2	1	8	7	6	5	8	7	6	5	4	3	2	1
6	1	2	3	4	5	6	7	8	5	6	7	8	1	2	3	4	2	1	4	3	6	5	8	7
7	1	2	3	4	5	6	7	8	6	5	8	7	2	1	4	3	4	3	2	1	8	7	6	5
8	1	2	3	4	5	6	7	8	7	8	5	6	3	4	1	2	5	6	7	8	1	2	3	4
9	1	2	3	4	5	6	7	8	8	7	6	5	4	3	2	1	7	8	5	6	3	4	1	2

Week \ Player	25	26	27	28	29	30	31	32	33	34	35	36	37	38	39	40	41	42	43	44	45	46	47	48
1	4	4	4	4	4	4	4	4	5	5	5	5	5	5	5	5	6	6	6	6	6	6	6	6
2	1	2	3	4	5	6	7	8	1	2	3	4	5	6	7	8	1	2	3	4	5	6	7	8
3	4	3	2	1	8	7	6	5	5	6	7	8	1	2	3	4	6	5	8	7	2	1	4	3
4	8	7	6	5	4	3	2	1	2	1	4	3	6	5	8	7	4	3	2	1	8	7	6	5
5	5	6	7	8	1	2	3	4	6	5	8	7	2	1	4	3	7	8	5	6	3	4	1	2
6	6	5	8	7	2	1	4	3	7	8	5	6	3	4	1	2	3	4	1	2	7	8	5	6
7	7	8	5	6	3	4	1	2	3	4	1	2	7	8	5	6	8	7	6	5	4	3	2	1
8	3	4	1	2	7	8	5	6	8	7	6	5	4	3	2	1	2	1	4	3	6	5	8	7
9	2	1	4	3	6	5	8	7	4	3	2	1	8	7	6	5	5	6	7	8	1	2	3	4

Week \ Player	49	50	51	52	53	54	55	56	57	58	59	60	61	62	63	64
1	7	7	7	7	7	7	7	7	8	8	8	8	8	8	8	8
2	1	2	3	4	5	6	7	8	1	2	3	4	5	6	7	8
3	7	8	5	6	3	4	1	2	8	7	6	5	4	3	2	1
4	5	6	7	8	1	2	3	4	7	8	5	6	3	4	1	2
5	3	4	1	2	7	8	5	6	2	1	4	3	6	5	8	7
6	8	7	6	5	4	3	2	1	4	3	2	1	8	7	6	5
7	2	1	4	3	6	5	8	7	5	6	7	8	1	2	3	4
8	4	3	2	1	8	7	6	5	6	5	8	7	2	1	4	3
9	6	5	8	7	2	1	4	3	3	4	1	2	7	8	5	6

References

1. Aguado, A.: A 10 days solution to the social golfer problem. Math games: Social Golfer problem. MAA Online (2004)
2. Ball, S.: Finite Geometry and Combinatorial Applications, vol. 82. Cambridge University Press, Cambridge (2015)
3. Barnier, N., Brisset, P.: Solving the Kirkman's schoolgirl problem in a few seconds. In: Principles and Practice of Constraint Programming - CP 2002, 8th International Conference, CP 2002, Proceedings, Ithaca, NY, USA, 9–13 September 2002, pp. 477–491 (2002). https://doi.org/10.1007/3-540-46135-3_32
4. Benadé, J., Burger, A., van Vuuren, J.: The enumeration of k-sets of mutually orthogonal latin squares. In: Proceedings of the 42th Conference of the Operations Research Society of South Africa, Stellenbosch, pp. 40–49 (2013)
5. Cotta, C., Dotú, I., Fernández, A.J., Hentenryck, P.V.: Scheduling social golfers with memetic evolutionary programming. In: Hybrid Metaheuristics, Third International Workshop, HM 2006, Proceedings, Gran Canaria, Spain, 13–15 October 2006, pp. 150–161 (2006). https://doi.org/10.1007/11890584_12
6. Dechter, R.: Constraint Processing. Elsevier Morgan Kaufmann (2003). http://www.elsevier.com/wps/find/bookdescription.agents/678024/description

7. Dotú, I., Hentenryck, P.V.: Scheduling social golfers locally. In: Integration of AI and OR Techniques in Constraint Programming for Combinatorial Optimization Problems, Second International Conference, CPAIOR 2005, Proceedings, Prague, Czech Republic, 30 May–1 June, 2005, pp. 155–167 (2005). https://doi.org/10.1007/11493853_13

8. Dotú, I., Hentenryck, P.V.: Scheduling social tournaments locally. AI Commun. **20**(3), 151–162 (2007). http://content.iospress.com/articles/ai-communications/aic402

9. Fahle, T., Schamberger, S., Sellmann, M.: Symmetry breaking. In: Principles and Practice of Constraint Programming - CP 2001, 7th International Conference, CP 2001, Proceedings, Paphos, Cyprus, 26 November–1 December 2001, pp. 93–107 (2001). https://doi.org/10.1007/3-540-45578-7_7

10. Focacci, F., Milano, M.: Global cut framework for removing symmetries. In: Principles and Practice of Constraint Programming - CP 2001, 7th International Conference, CP 2001, Proceedings, Paphos, Cyprus, 26 November–1 December, 2001, pp. 77–92 (2001). https://doi.org/10.1007/3-540-45578-7_6

11. Gent, I.P., Petrie, K.E., Puget, J.: Symmetry in constraint programming. In: Rossi, F., van Beek, P., Walsh, T. (eds.) Handbook of Constraint Programming, chap. 10, pp. 329–376. Elsevier (2006). https://doi.org/10.1016/S1574-6526(06)80014-3

12. Gomes, C.P., Selman, B., Crato, N., Kautz, H.A.: Heavy-tailed phenomena insatisfiability and constraint satisfaction problems. J. Autom. Reasoning **24**(1/2), 67–100 (2000). https://doi.org/10.1023/A:1006314320276

13. Harvey, W.: CSPLib problem 010: Social golfers problem (2002). http://www.csplib.org/Problems/prob010. Accessed 28 Apr 2019

14. Harvey, W., Winterer, T.J.: Solving the MOLR and social golfers problems. In: Principles and Practice of Constraint Programming - CP 2005, 11th International Conference, CP 2005, Proceedings, Sitges, Spain, 1–5 October 2005, pp. 286–300 (2005). https://doi.org/10.1007/11564751_23

15. Hennessy, J.L., Patterson, D.A.: Computer Architecture - A Quantitative Approach, 5th edn. Morgan Kaufmann, Burlington (2012)

16. Kirkman, T.P.: Note on an unanswered prize question. Cambridge Dublin Math. J. **5**, 255–262 (1850)

17. Lam, C.W., Thiel, L., Swiercz, S.: The non-existence of finite projective planes of order 10. Can. J. Math. **41**(6), 1117–1123 (1989)

18. Law, Y.C., Lee, J.H.: Global constraints for integer and set value precedence. In: Principles and Practice of Constraint Programming - CP 2004, 10th International Conference, CP 2004, Proceedings, Toronto, Canada, 27 September–1 October 2004, pp. 362–376 (2004). https://doi.org/10.1007/978-3-540-30201-8_28

19. Lecoutre, C.: Constraint Networks: Techniques and Algorithms. Wiley, Hoboken (2009)

20. Liu., K., Löffler., S., Hofstedt., P.: Solving the social golfers problems by constraint programming in sequential and parallel. In: Proceedings of the 11th International Conference on Agents and Artificial Intelligence - Volume 2: ICAART, pp. 29–39. INSTICC, SciTePress (2019). https://doi.org/10.5220/0007252300290039

21. Liu, K., Löffler, S., Hofstedt, P.: Solving the traveling tournament problem with predefined venues by parallel constraint programming. In: Mining Intelligence and Knowledge Exploration - 6th International Conference, MIKE 2018, Proceedings, Cluj-Napoca, Romania, 20–22 December 2018, pp. 64–79 (2018). https://doi.org/10.1007/978-3-030-05918-7_7

22. McKay, B.D., Meynert, A., Myrvold, W.: Small latin squares, quasigroups, and loops. J. Comb. Des. **15**(2), 98–119 (2007)

23. Miguel, I.: CSPLib problem 038: steel mill slab design (2012). http://www.csplib. org/Problems/prob010. Accessed 28 Apr 2019

24. Palmieri, A., Régin, J., Schaus, P.: Parallel strategies selection. In: Principles and Practice of Constraint Programming - 22nd International Conference, CP 2016, Proceedings, Toulouse, France, 5–9 September 2016, pp. 388–404 (2016). https:// doi.org/10.1007/978-3-319-44953-1_25

25. Parker, E.T.: Construction of some sets of mutually orthogonal latin squares. Proc. Am. Math. Soc. **10**(6), 946–949 (1959)

26. Prestwich, S.: CSPLib problem 028: balanced incomplete block designs (2001). http://www.csplib.org/Problems/prob010. Accessed 28 Apr 2019

27. Prud'homme, C., Fages, J.G., Lorca, X.: Choco Documentation. TASC - LS2N CNRS UMR 6241, COSLING S.A.S. (2017). http://www.choco-solver.org

28. Puget, J.: Symmetry breaking revisited. Constraints **10**(1), 23–46 (2005). https:// doi.org/10.1007/s10601-004-5306-8

29. Rees, R.S., Wallis, W.D.: Kirkman triple systems and their generalizations: a survey. In: Wallis, W.D. (ed.) Designs 2002. MIA, vol. 563, pp. 317–368. Springer, Boston, MA (2003). https://doi.org/10.1007/978-1-4613-0245-2_13

30. Régin, J.-C., Rezgui, M., Malapert, A.: Embarrassingly parallel search. In: Schulte, C. (ed.) CP 2013. LNCS, vol. 8124, pp. 596–610. Springer, Heidelberg (2013). https://doi.org/10.1007/978-3-642-40627-0_45

31. Régin, J., Rezgui, M., Malapert, A.: Embarrassingly parallel search. In: Principles and Practice of Constraint Programming - 19th International Conference, CP 2013, Proceedings, Uppsala, Sweden, 16–20 September 2013, pp. 596–610 (2013). https:// doi.org/10.1007/978-3-642-40627-0_45

32. de Resmini, M.J.: There exist at least three non-isomorphic s (2, 4, 28)'s. J. Geom. **16**(1), 148–151 (1981)

33. Rossi, F., van Beek, P., Walsh, T. (eds.): Handbook of Constraint Programming, Foundations of Artificial Intelligence, vol. 2. Elsevier (2006). http://www. sciencedirect.com/science/bookseries/15746526/2

34. Schulte, C., Tack, G., Lagerkvist, M.Z.: Modeling and programming with gecode. Gecode Team (2017). https://www.gecode.org/

35. Sellmann, M., Harvey, W.: Heuristic constraint propagation-using local search for incomplete pruning and domain filtering of redundant constraints for the social golfer problem. In: CPAIOR 2002, Citeseer (2002)

36. Smith, B.M.: Modelling. In: Rossi, F., van Beek, P., Walsh, T. (eds.) Handbook of Constraint Programming, chap. 11, pp. 377–406. Elsevier (2006). https://doi.org/ 10.1016/S1574-6526(06)80015-5

37. Smith, B.M.: Reducing symmetry in a combinatorial design problem. In: CPAIOR 2001, pp. 351–359, April 2001. http://www.icparc.ic.ac.uk/cpAIOR01

38. Triska, M., Musliu, N.: An effective greedy heuristic for the social golfer problem. Ann. Oper. Res. **194**(1), 413–425 (2012). https://doi.org/10.1007/s10479-011-0866-7

39. Triska, M., Musliu, N.: An improved SAT formulation for the social golferproblem. Ann. Oper. Res. **194**(1), 427–438 (2012). https://doi.org/10.1007/s10479-010-0702-5

Weighted Personalized Factorizations for Network Classification with Approximated Relation Weights

Ahmed Rashed$^{(\boxtimes)}$, Josif Grabocka, and Lars Schmidt-Thieme

Information Systems and Machine Learning Lab, University of Hildesheim,
Hildesheim, Germany
{ahmedrashed,josif,schmidt-thieme}@ismll.uni-hildesheim.de

Abstract. Classifying Multi-Label nodes in networks is a well-known and widely used task in different domains. Current classification models rely on mining the network structure either by random walks or through approximating the laplacian of the network graph which gives insight about the nodes' neighborhood. In implicit feedback relations, these models assume all relation edges to be equally strong and important. However, in real life, this is not necessarily the case as some edges might have different semantic weights such as friendship relation. To tackle this limitation we propose in this paper a weighted two-stage multi-relational matrix factorization model with Bayesian personalized ranking loss for network classification that utilizes different weighting functions for approximating the implicit feedback relation weights. Experiments on four real-world datasets show that the proposed model significantly outperforms the state-of-art models. Results also show that selecting the right weighting functions for approximating relation weights significantly improves classification accuracy.

Keywords: Multi-relational learning · Network representations
Multi-label classification · Recommender systems · Document
classification

1 Introduction

Multi-label node classification is a widely used in network analysis for predicting users interests [5,8,12,13], document classification [13,19] and in protein labeling in protein-protein interaction graphs [5,13].

Earlier approaches of node classification relied on extracting a set of informative features from each node and train a classification model on them. This typical way of feature processing has two main significant drawbacks. First, prior expert domain knowledge is needed to extract and preprocess such features. Second, to extract useful features, a decent amount of raw information should be embedded with each node such as profile details in social networks or document

© Springer Nature Switzerland AG 2019
J. van den Herik et al. (Eds.): ICAART 2019, LNAI 11978, pp. 100–117, 2019.
https://doi.org/10.1007/978-3-030-37494-5_6

title and body in citation networks. This kind of information, however, might not always be available or accessible due to privacy settings.

On the other hand, recent approaches focused on learning latent features for each node by mining the network structure instead of relying on node information. These approaches also optimize an objective function that aims to minimize the classification error of nodes labeling [4,13]. Multi-relation matrix factorization [7,8,17] is one example that follows this approach. This model represents every network relation as a matrix, and it aims to factorize the target relation matrix into two smaller matrices that represent the latent features of the interacting nodes. The main advantage of these recent approaches is that they can be better generalized to almost all node classification tasks without any need for feature engineering or expert domain knowledge. However, they face significant challenges with very sparse networks and especially if these networks have implicit feedback relations. These implicit relations are dominantly very sparse, and relation edges are either observed or unobserved without explicit weights which means that all edges will be treated equally by these models. In various real-world scenarios, those implicit relations have hidden semantic weights [9] which are not directly quantifiable but can be approximated using different weighting functions such as similarity measures. A famous example of such relations is the friendship relation in social networks. This relation is a type of implicit feedback relations that models the interaction between nodes that have the same types, and it is expressed as sparsely observed edges connecting those nodes. This kind of friendship relations frequently occurs in multi-relational settings and it is not only for representing a relation between users, but it can also represent a relation between any same type nodes [13]. In networks data, all of the friendship observed edges would have the same importance weight while in real-life, some friendship relations are stronger than others. The real-life weights of such relations can be approximated by measuring the similarity between every two interacting nodes which can be calculated using information from network structure only such as nodes degrees without the need of any complex side information.

In our previous work, we introduced a similarity based personalized two-stage multi-relation matrix factorization model (Two-Stage-MR-BPR) for multi-label network classification and ranking [13]. It utilizes the basic transitive node similarity for weighting implicit friendship relations and a two-stage training protocol to optimize the Bayesian personalized ranking loss. By optimizing the BPR loss, the model will output a ranked list of labels instead of only one label for any target node which means it will be suitable for recommender system problems and node classification problems. The weighted Two-Stage-MR-BPR can differentiate between observed and unobserved relations along with learning the different strength weights of the observed relations.

In this work, we present an extended version of the Two-Stage-MR-BPR paper [13] by applying a more in depths analysis and comparison between different weighting functions and their effect on the classification accuracy. We also conduct a sensitivity analysis on the regularization weights of the proposed model.

Our contributions can be summarized as follows:

- We conduct a comparative study between different weighting functions that can be used with the Two-Stage-MR-BPR model to approximate the semantic weights of all implicit relations that have interacting nodes of the same type. This allows the model to differentiate between weak and strong relations.
- We conduct multiple experiments on four real-world datasets. The results show that the proposed weighted Two-Stage-MR-BPR outperform the MR-BPR and current state-of-art models in multi-label and single-label classification problems. Results also show that the basic transitive friend similarity is a good weighting function across datasets from different domains.

The rest of the paper is organized as follows. In Sect. 2, we summarize the related work. We discuss the problem formulation of the multi-label classification task in Sect. 3. In Sect. 4, we present and discuss the technical details of the Two-Stage-MR-BPR model. We present the experiential results in Sect. 5. Finally, we conclude with discussing possible future work in Sect. 6.

2   Related Work

Current approaches for multi-label node classification automate the process of features extraction and engineering by directly learning latent features for each node. These latent features are mainly generated based on the global network structure and the connectivity layout of each node. In earlier approaches such as [20,21], they produce k latent features for each node by utilizing either the first k eigenvectors of a generated modularity matrix for the friendship relation [20] or a sparse k-means clustering of friendship edges [21]. These k features are fed into an SVM for labels predictions.

Recently, semi-supervised [22] and unsupervised approaches [5,12,24] have been proposed to extract latent node representations in networks data. These models are inspired by the novel approaches for learning latent representations of words such as the convolutional neural networks and the Skip-gram models [11] in the domain of natural language processing. They formulate the network classification problem as discrete words classification problem by representing the network as a document and all nodes as a sequence of words. The Skip-gram can then be used to predict the most likely labels for each node based on the assumption that similar nodes will have same labels.

In [8], MR-BPR was proposed as learning to rank approach for tackling the multi-label classification problem by extending the BPR [15] model for multi-relational settings. This approach expresses the problem as a multi-relational matrix factorization trained to optimize the AUC measure using BPR loss. Each network relation is represented by a sparse matrix and the relation between nodes and labels will be the target being predicted. Because of the BPR loss, this model is considered suitable for sparse networks with implicit feedback relations; however, since all implicit feedback connections are only observed or unobserved, the MR-BPR fail to realize that some implicit links are stronger than others in real-life. To solve this drawback in the original single relation BPR model, [9] proposed BPR++ an extended version of the BPR model for user-item rating prediction. They utilized multiple weighting functions to approximate the logical weights between users and items. Those functions relied on the frequency of interaction and timestamps to weight each edge. In the training phase, they randomly alternate between learning to distinguish observed and unobserved relations and learning to rank weighted observed relations. This learning approach expands the BPR capacity to differentiate between strong and weak connections.

Finally, the proposed Two-Stage-MR-BPR model [13] follow a similar intuition to that of BPR++ and it considers the more general multi-relational settings which allow it to be used for any multi-label and single-label network classification problems. The proposed model also can utilize different node similarity functions to approximate the weights of implicit relations that have interacting nodes of the same type. In this work, we also presenet MR-BPR++ [13] which is the extend an extended version of BPR++ for multi-relational settings. The learning algorithm for Two-stage-MR-BPR is different from MR-BPR++; it relies on two consecutive non-overlapping learning stages instead of random alternation. In the first stage, it allows the model to sufficiently learns to differentiate between strong and weak relations and in the second stage, it allows it to learns to differentiate between observed and unobserved relations.

3   Problem Definition

The problem can be formulated similarly to [8,13] as a relational learning setting on network data. Let $G = (V, E)$ be a network where V is a set of heterogeneous nodes, and E is the set of edges. Each node can be seen as an entity and each edge represents a relation between two entities. Let $\mathcal{N} := \{N_1, N_2, ..., N_{|\mathcal{N}|}\}$ be a set of node types and each type has a set of nodes as instances $N_i := \{n_i^{(1)}, n_i^{(2)}, ..., n_i^{(|N_i|)}\}$. Let $\mathcal{R} := \{R_1, R_2, ..., R_{|\mathcal{R}|}\}$ be a set of relations and each relation represents interactions between two specific node types N_{1R} and N_{2R} such that $R \subseteq N_{1R} \times N_{2R}$.

Our primary task in this paper is to predict missing edges in a primary target relation Y, and all other relations will be considered auxiliary relations that can be used to improve the prediction accuracy. In multi-label network classification, the relation Y represents the relation between a set of nodes and labels $Y \subseteq N_{Target} \times N_{Label}$, such as the relationship between multiple interests and users in social networks or document-labels and documents in citation networks. Examples of auxiliary relations are the friendship relation in social networks or citation links in citation networks.

The task of predicting missing edges in the target relation can be formulated as a ranking problem where we try to drive a ranked list of labels that represent the likelihood that a specific node belongs to each of them.

In case of sparse auxiliary relations with implicit edges, the current multi-relational matrix factorization model with BPR loss [8] does not exploit the full potential of the BPR loss because it only distinguishes between observed and unobserved edges without considering the edges weights [9].

Our proposed approach addresses the shortcomings of the current multi-relational matrix factorization model by firstly using a similarity function for weighting the implicit auxiliary relations and using a Two-Stage-MR-BPR learning algorithm that can rank observed edges and distinguish between observed and unobserved edges. The proposed approach is also suitable for cold-start scenarios where only the auxiliary relations information are available for the target nodes.

4   Proposed Model

The proposed model can be formulated as a two-stage multi-relational matrix factorization using node similarity for weighting implicit relations. Initially, the node similarity is used to weight all observed edges in any implicit auxiliary relations that has interacting nodes of the same type. In the first stage of learning, the model is trained to rank edges based on their weights. In the second stage, the model is trained to differentiate between observed and unobserved edges. Figure 1 illustrates the workflow of the Two-Stage-MR-BPR model with basic transitive node similarity as weighting function and each step will be discussed in details in the following subsections.

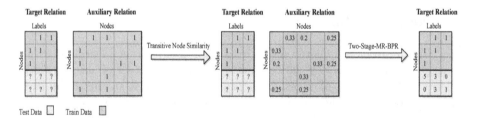

Fig. 1. Two-Stage-MR-BPR workflow. Initially, the transitive node similarity is used to weight all implicit relations with same type interacting nodes followed by learning a two stage multi-relational matrix factorization on all relations using the BPR loss to rank all labels with respect to each test node [13].

4.1   Basic Transitive Node Similarity for Implicit Feedback Relations

In the relational learning setting, in order to apply the two-stage MR-BPR learning technique we need first to convert all possible implicit feedback relations into weighted relations. To convert implicit relations into weighted relations, one needs a suitable weighting function that approximate relation weights by utilizing the available embedded information in each relation such as frequency or timestamps of interactions in user-item relations, or similarity measures in friendship relations. In the most basic case where there is no available embedded information, an implicit relation can be considered a relation that was weighted by a constant weighting function which outputs only one value if it encounters an observed edge.

Friendship relations are one of the prominent types of implicit relations in networks data. It can represent any relation between nodes of the same type such as users friendships in social networks or web links between web pages or citation links between documents. For weighting edges in general friendship relations, the similarity measures such as Adamic/Adar [1], common neighbors, Jaccard index [6] and friend transitive node similarity FriendTNS [18] are considered the best candidates to act as weighting functions [10,18].

$$\text{FTNS}(n_i, n_j) := \begin{cases} \frac{1}{deg(n_i)+deg(n_j)-1}, & \text{if } (n_i, n_j) \in R \\ 0, & \text{if } (n_i, n_j) \notin R \end{cases} \tag{1}$$

$$\text{Adamic/Adar}(n_i, n_j) = \sum_{u \in Neighbors(n_i) \cap Neighbors(n_j)} \frac{1}{\log |Neighbors(u)|} \tag{2}$$

$$\text{Jaccard}(n_i, n_j) = \frac{|Neighbors(n_i) \cap Neighbors(n_j)|}{|Neighbors(n_i) \cup Neighbors(n_j)|} \tag{3}$$

$$\text{Common Neighbors}(n_i, n_j) = |Neighbors(n_i) \cap Neighbors(n_j)| \tag{4}$$

where $deg(n_i)$ and $deg(n_j)$ is the degree of nodes n_i and n_j respectively. In case of directed graphs, we used the summation of the node's in-degree and out-degree as the total degree.

In our proposed approach we used the FriendTNS function because it showed a superior accuracy over other similarity functions in the experimental results which is inline with the earlier research findings [2,18] in link prediction tasks. Comparison between the different weighting functions is discussed in details in Sect. 5.6.

FriendTNS was used for weighting all the observed edges in all available implicit friendship relations and it was calculated only for observed edges because it is computationally expensive to calculate weights for all possible node pairs in very sparse networks. The FriendTNS similarity between two nodes can be calculated using Eq. (1).

4.2 Multi-relational Matrix Factorization with Basic Transitive Node Similarity

To formulate the problem as a multi-relational matrix factorization, each node type N_i can be represented by a matrix $E_i \in \mathbb{R}^{|N_i| \times k}$ where the rows are the latent feature vectors for all instances in the node type, and k represents the number of latent factors defined in the model. Similarly, each implicit relation R can be represented by a matrix $R \in \mathbb{R}^{|N_{1R}| \times |N_{2R}|}$ where N_{1R} and N_{2R} are the two types of the interacting nodes inside relation R. Each entry in the relation matrix is given by

$$R(n_{1R}^{(i)}, n_{2R}^{(j)}) := \begin{cases} Weight(n_{1R}^{(i)}, n_{2R}^{(j)}), & \text{if}(n_{1R}^{(i)}, n_{2R}^{(j)}) \in R \\ \\ unobserved, & \text{if}(n_{1R}^{(i)}, n_{2R}^{(j)}) \notin R \end{cases} \tag{5}$$

where $Weight(n_{1R}^{(i)}, n_{2R}^{(j)})$ is the weighting function used to approximate the weights of implicit relation between any two nodes such as similarity functions in case of friendship relations or frequency of interaction in case of user-item relations. If no available embedded information can be used to weight relations, a constant weighting function is assumed.

Finally, each relation R can be approximated by multiplying the latent matrices of the two relation node types E_{1R} and E_{2R} such that $R \approx E_{1R} \times E_{2R}^T$. For simplicity, we define a set of all the model parameters $\Theta := \{E_1, E_2, ..., E_{|\mathcal{N}|}\}$ which contain the matrices of all nodes types and our general objective will be to find the set of matrices Θ that minimize the sum of losses over all relations.

4.3   Two-Stage MR-BPR

The original BPR model [15] assumes that for a given user u, any item i this user interacted with should be ranked higher than any item j he did not interact with. In order to do so, the BPR model learns to maximize the difference $\hat{x}_{u,i,j}^R$ between the predicted rating $\hat{r}(u, i)$ for an observed item i and the rating $\hat{r}(u, j)$ for an unobserved item j.

To follow the same notation in a multi-relational setting, for any given relation R, the user u will represent a node of type N_{1R}, while i and j will represents two nodes of type N_{2R}. For each relation R the baseline MR-BPR model samples a set of triples D_R which is defined as follows:

$$D_R := \{(u, i, j) | (u, i) \in R \wedge (u, j) \notin R\}$$

The sampling is done using bootstrap sampling with replacement. The model is then trained to maximize the difference between the predicted ratings of the observed edges and unobserved edges for all relation using Eqs. (2) and (3).

$$\text{BPR-Opt}(R, E_{1R}E_{2R}^T) = \sum_{(u,i,j) \in R} ln\sigma(\hat{x}_{u,i,j}^R) \tag{6}$$

$$\text{MR-BPR}(R, \Theta) = \sum_{R \in \mathcal{R}} \alpha_R \text{BPR-Opt}(R, E_{1R}E_{2R}^T) + \sum_{E \in \Theta} \lambda_E ||E||^2 \tag{7}$$

where σ is the sigmoid logistic function and α_R is the loss weight for relation R. By following this learning approach, the MR-BPR model learns to distinguish between observed edges and unobserved edges over iterations. This approach is not optimal as it fails to realize the different semantic weights of the implicit relations. In [9] they proposed a new learning technique for the original BPR model called BPR++ which extend the BPR to learn weighted relations. There proposed extension allow the BPR model to provide better rankings for item ratings by utilizing the timestamps and frequency of user interactions to weight user-item edges. BPR++ is randomly alternating between learning to rank observed weighted edges and learning to distinguish between observed and unobserved edges. Instead of using such random alternation between the two learning tasks for multi-relational settings, we propose a two-stage learning approach that decouple the two learning tasks and learn them sequentially to avoid information overwrites across iterations. When applied to multi-relational settings, the proposed two-stage learning protocol and BPR++ will utilize a separate set of triples D_R^{++} beside the original set D_R. This new set contains observed weighted edges sampled using bootstrap sampling with replacement for each available weighted relation as follows:

$$D_R^{++} := \{(u, i, j) | Weight(u, i) > Weight(u, j) \wedge (u, i) \in R \wedge (u, j) \in R\}$$

The main difference between the proposed two-stage learning protocol and BPR++ is that the later will rely on random alternating sampling from D_R and D_R^{++} which introduce the risk of having information loss as some iterations might overwrite the previously learned information, e.g. if an node was selected first as an observed item from D_R and in the next iteration it was selected as the lower weighted item from D_R^{++}, the second iteration will overwrite the information gained in the first iteration as it will decrease the score of the item after it has been increased. On the other hand, Two-Stage-MR-BPR overcome such problem by learning to rank all weighted edges first then it learns to distinguish observed and unobserved edges afterward with no overlap between the two stages in each epoch. This means that the second stage will shift the learned

```
 1: procedure TWO-STAGE-MR-BPR(𝒟, ℛ, Θ)
 2:     Initialize All E ∈ Θ
 3:     repeat
 4:         for R ∈ ℛ do
 5:             // (Stage One)
 6:             if D_R^{++}\D_R ≠ ϕ then
 7:                 for ObsEdges_R times do
 8:                     draw (u,i,j) from D_R^{++}
 9:                     Θ ← Θ + μ ∂(MR-BPR(R,Θ))/∂Θ
10:                 end for
11:             end if
12:             // (Stage Two)
13:             for ObsEdges_R times do
14:                 draw (u,i,j) from D_R
15:                 Θ ← Θ + μ ∂(MR-BPR(R,Θ))/∂Θ
16:             end for
17:         end for
18:     until convergence
19: return Θ
20: end procedure
```

Fig. 2. Two-Stage-MR-BPR algorithm with learning rate μ and L2 regularization λ_Θ [13].

```
1: procedure MR-BPR++(𝒟, ℛ, Θ)
2:     Initialize All E ∈ Θ
3:     repeat
4:         for R ∈ ℛ do
5:             r = random(0, 1)
6:             if r ≤ β ∧ D_R^{++} \ D_R ≠ ϕ then
7:                 draw (u,i,j) from D_R^{++}
8:             else
9:                 draw (u,i,j) from D_R
10:            end if
11:            Θ ← Θ + μ ∂(MR-BPR(R,Θ))/∂Θ
12:        end for
13:    until convergence
14: return Θ
15: end procedure
```

Fig. 3. MR-BPR++ algorithm with learning rate μ, probability threshold β and L2 regularization λ_Θ [13].

scores of the observed edges away from the unobserved ones while maintaining the learned rankings between the weighted observed edges.

In our experiments, we applied both learning protocols on the MR-BPR model for performance comparison and we used the basic FriendTNS similarity as weighting function for all implicit relations where the participating nodes have the same type. In each learning epoch during the training phase, the number of sampling steps for D_R^{++} and D_R is equal to the number of observed edges $ObsEdges_R$ in R, similar to the original BPR [15] and MR-BPR [8] models. The generalized algorithms for training the Two-Stage-MR-BPR and MR-BPR++ are described in Figs. 2 and 3.

In the experiments section, we compared the two models against each other and the original MR-BPR model. The results showed that the proposed two-stage model provides better accuracy for multi-relational settings where we have multiple sparse relations without timestamps or frequency of interactions that can be used to weight relations.

Table 1. Datasets statistics [13].

	Type	Nodes	Labels	Edges	Features	Sparsity
BlogCatalog	Undirected	10312	39	667966	–	99.37%
PPI	Undirected	3890	50	76584	–	99.49%
Wiki	Directed	2405	19	17981	–	99.68%
Cora	Directed	2708	7	5429	1433	99.92%

5 Experiments

5.1 Datasets

We applied the Two-Stage MR-BPR and MR-BPR++ on four network classification datasets from four different domains. The first three datasets contain two relations while the fourth dataset is a citation network where nodes have an embedded feature vector that can be considered as third relations.

- BlogCatalog [25]: This dataset represents a large social network from the BlogCatalog website. It has two relations, a target relation which represents the relation between groups and users, and an auxiliary relation representing the friendship between users.
- Wiki [23]: This dataset represents a network of Wikipedia web pages. It also has two relations, a target relation which represents the categories of the web pages, and an auxiliary relation that represents links between the web pages.
- Protein-Protein Interactions (PPI) [3]: This dataset is a network of protein-protein interactions for homo sapiens. It has two relations, a target one which represents the relation between protein-labels and proteins, and an auxiliary relation that represents the interactions between proteins and other proteins. This dataset was used to check how well our proposed model performs in non-web-based domains.
- Cora [16]: This dataset represents a citation network where each document has 1433 binary feature vector representing words occurrence. This dataset can be considered as having three relations, a target relation which represents the class label of a document, an auxiliary relation that represents citation links between documents and a final auxiliary relation that represents a relation between a document and words that exist in this document.

Table 1 shows the detailed statistics of the datasets.

5.2 Baselines

- MR-BPR [8]: The original MR-BPR model that utilizes implicit auxiliary relations for ranking node labels. This model does not utilize transitive node similarities.
- DeepWalk [12]: One of the well-known models for multi-label network classification. This model learns node latent representations by utilizing uniform random walks in the network.
- Node2Vec [5]: This is one of the state-of-art models for multi-label network classification and can be seen as a generalized version of DeepWalk with two guiding parameters p and q for the random walks.
- GCN [22]: This model is one of the state-of-art models for document classification in citation networks. It relies on multi-layered graph convolutional neural network for learning network representation with text features.
- TADW [24]: This model is also one of the state-of-art models for document classification in citation networks. It is an extended version of the original Deep Walk model for learning network representation with text features.

On Cora dataset, our proposed model was compared only against GCN and TADW because they require nodes with embedded textual features which is missing in the first three datasets. On the other hand DeepWalk and Node2Vec where not used on Cora dataset because they can't represent nodes with embedded features.

Table 2. Mutli-lable classification results on BlogCatalog dataset [13].

	%Lable nodes	10%	20%	30%	40%	50%	60%	70%	80%	90%
Micro-F1(%)	DeepWalk	33.71	36.67	38.22	39.20	39.37	40.01	40.64	41.04	41.11
	Node2Vec	33.72	36.91	38.33	39.42	39.98	40.52	40.75	41.82	42.16
	MR-BPR	36.16	37.75	39.24	40.07	40.68	40.29	40.39	41.24	40.64
	MR-BPR++	35.47	38.00	39.49	40.22	40.84	40.83	40.99	41.92	41.14
	Two-Stage-MR-BPR	**37.27****	**39.30****	**40.49****	**41.52***	**42.22****	**41.76****	**42.03****	**42.83****	**42.51***
Macro-F1(%)	DeepWalk	18.19	22.18	23.61	24.63	25.32	26.24	27.20	27.21	27.84
	Node2Vec	19.24	23.13	24.70	25.64	26.80	27.81	27.80	28.75	29.15
	MR-BPR	22.21	24.74	26.20	27.59	27.95	28.26	28.49	29.33	29.13
	MR-BPR++	22.03	25.21	26.55	27.89	28.19	28.65	29.12	29.53	29.62
	Two-Stage-MR-BPR	**23.18****	**25.66****	**26.91****	**28.16****	**28.69****	28.76	**29.54****	29.85	**30.55***

Significantly outperforms MR-BPR at the: **0.01 and *0.05 levels.

Table 3. Mutli-lable classification results on PPI dataset [13].

	%Lable nodes	10%	20%	30%	40%	50%	60%	70%	80%	90%
Micro-F1(%)	DeepWalk	15.89	17.77	18.68	19.39	20.85	21.75	22.35	22.70	24.11
	Node2Vec	15.09	16.89	17.52	19.00	20.38	21.43	22.02	22.25	22.65
	MR-BPR	17.11	19.68	20.87	21.87	22.61	22.73	23.55	23.08	23.44
	MR-BPR++	16.97	19.46	20.62	21.90	22.46	23.14	23.33	23.28	23.56
	Two-Stage-MR-BPR	**18.21****	**20.45****	**21.88****	**22.63****	**23.31****	**23.70****	**24.78****	**24.48****	**25.38****
Macro-F1(%)	DeepWalk	12.73	14.20	15.41	17.06	18.50	18.84	18.49	18.49	19.15
	Node2Vec	12.17	13.47	14.51	16.72	18.01	18.62	18.89	18.45	18.76
	MR-BPR	12.88	15.56	16.83	18.09	18.81	18.98	19.54	19.16	19.48
	MR-BPR++	12.71	15.40	16.58	18.00	18.66	19.37	19.54	19.46	19.66
	Two-Stage-MR-BPR	**13.96****	**16.31****	**17.96****	**18.75****	**19.43****	**19.99****	**20.72****	**20.51****	**21.41****

Significantly outperforms MR-BPR at the: **0.01 and *0.05 levels.

5.3   Experimental Protocol and Evaluation

We followed the same experimental protocol in [5,8,12,13]. We used 10-fold cross-validation experiments on each target relation. These experiments were applied using different percentages of labeled nodes ranging from 10% to 90%. In each experiment, we only used the defined percentage of labeled nodes for training along with all the auxiliary relations, while the remaining percent of nodes were used for testing. We used Micro-F1 and Macro-F1 measures for performance evaluation on Blog Catalog, PPI and Wiki Dataset, and Accuracy on Cora Dataset.

We used the same hyper-parameters that were used in the original baselines' papers, and grid-search was used to find the best hyper-parameters if none were mentioned for the target dataset.

5.4 Results

The experimental results on the four datasets are shown in Tables 2, 3, 4, 5, and Fig. 4. The results shows that Two-Stage-MR-BPR with transitive node similarity outperformed the original MR-BRP model in all train-splits. In comparison with other well-known models for multi-label network classification, the Two-Stage-MR-BPR model outperformed the state-of-art Node2Vec over all trains-splits on BlogCatalog, PPI and Wiki datasets. It is worthy to note that all improvements over Node2Vec are statistically significant with a p-value less than 0.01 using paired t-test. Two-Stage-MR-BPR also outperformed Deep-Walk over all trains-splits on BlogCatalog and PPI, while on Wiki, DeepWalk only achieved better Macro-F1 scores on the 20%, 30%, and 40% trains-splits. The results also show that Two-Stage-MR-BPR outperformed all other models in terms of Micro-F1 with 40% less data using the 50% train-split on the Blog-Catalog dataset. On PPI, It outperformed all other models in terms of Micro-F1 and Macro-F1 with 30% less data using the 60% train-split. On the other hand, the document classification results on the Cora datasets show that Two-Stage-MR-BPR outperformed the state-of-art models on 10% and 90% splits, while it achieves comparable results on the 50% train-splits.

Table 4. Mutli-lable classification results on Wiki dataset [13].

	%Lable nodes	10%	20%	30%	40%	50%	60%	70%	80%	90%
Micro-F1(%)	DeepWalk	56.04	60.60	63.52	64.13	65.03	65.29	66.73	67.64	66.27
	Node2Vec	57.24	60.85	61.40	62.13	62.45	62.08	63.76	63.72	62.61
	MR-BPR	58.10	62.71	65.54	66.94	68.66	69.44	70.24	70.79	71.71
	MR-BPR++	59.56	63.26	65.61	67.26	68.56	69.31	69.99	70.48	70.34
	Two-Stage-MR-BPR	**60.40****	**64.42****	66.16	**67.99****	69.21	70.01	71.18	71.74	72.84
Macro-F1(%)	DeepWalk	44.33	**53.55**	**57.16**	57.42	56.21	56.93	58.71	60.50	61.20
	Node2Vec	42.95	48.88	51.96	53.34	52.25	50.88	53.25	52.57	55.04
	MR-BPR	44.41	49.32	53.23	55.32	57.50	58.88	59.17	59.76	63.99
	MR-BPR++	46.58	50.27	54.01	55.45	57.62	59.57	59.29	59.42	62.79
	Two-Stage-MR-BPR	**47.35****	51.12**	54.41*	57.20*	**58.33**	**60.21**	**60.32**	**61.27**	65.16

Significantly outperforms MR-BPR at the: **0.01 and *0.05 levels.

In comparison with Two-Stage-MR-BPR, MR-BRP++ also outperformed MR-BRP on BlogCatalog over most of the train splits, but it had minimal performance gains in some train-splits on PPI, Wiki and Cora. These results demonstrate the importance of using transitive node similarity to weight implicit relations, and they show that using two sequential non-overlapping stages to train the BPR loss is better than randomly alternating between ranking observed edges and distinguishing them from unobserved edges.

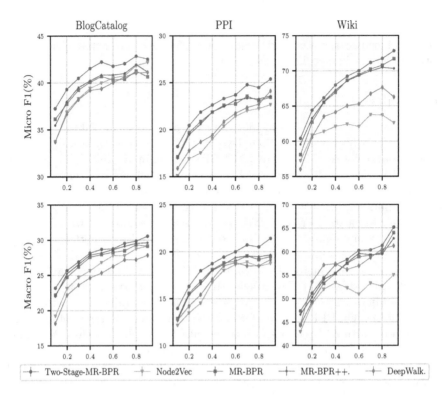

Fig. 4. Evaluation of the Two-Stage-MR-BPR model against other baseline models. The x axis denotes the percent of labeled nodes used in the training phase, while the y axis denotes the Micro-F1 and Macro-F1 scores [13].

Table 5. Document classification results on Cora dataset [13].

	%Lable Nodes	10%	50%	90%
Accuracy(%)	GCN	78.37	**86.53**	86.39
	TADW	75.24	85.99	85.60
	MR-BPR	75.03	78.76	81.66
	MR-BPR++	76.24	78.10	81.10
	Two-Stage-MR-BPR	**79.30****	84.20	**86.86**

Significantly outperforms GCN at the: **0.01 and *0.05 levels.

5.5 Parameters Sensitivity

In this section, we study the sensitivity of the Two-Stage-MR-BPR regularization parameters. To do so we compared their different values using the 10% data split with the best found number of dimensions on BlogCatalog, Wiki and PPI datasets. We used weights of [0.1, 0.05, 0.02, 0.0125, 0.01, 0.005] for the node's regularization parameter λ_1 and weights of [0.01, 0.005, 0.001, 0.0005, 0.0001] for the regularization parameter of labels λ_2.

Results in Fig. 5 show that the node's regularization parameter λ_1 is more sensitive than the regularization parameter of labels λ_2 across all three datasets and no significant correlation is observed between the two values. Results also show a similar smooth pattern in all three datasets which indicate that it is easy to find the best hyper-parameter configuration for the Two-Stage-MR-BPR across different datasets.

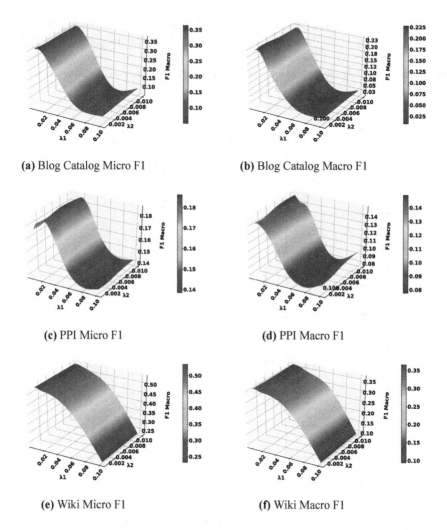

(a) Blog Catalog Micro F1   **(b)** Blog Catalog Macro F1

(c) PPI Micro F1   **(d)** PPI Macro F1

(e) Wiki Micro F1   **(f)** Wiki Macro F1

Fig. 5. Sensitivity analysis on the regularization parameters of nodes (λ_1) and labels (λ_2).

5.6   Comparison Between Different Weighting Functions

In this section, we compare the effect of different weighting functions on the accuracy of the Two-Stage-MR-BPR model, specifically the FriendTNS [18], Adamic/Adar [1], Jaccard index [6] and the number of common neighbors. To do so we applied each weighting function separately using the best-found Two-Stage-MR-BPR configuration on BlogCatalog, Wiki and PPI datasets using the 10% data split.

Results in Fig. 6 show that the FriendTNS has the highest positive effect on the accuracy across all datasets and it is followed by the Jaccard index. These results also prove that weighting the implicit relation has a diverse effect on the multi-relational classification task and a careful selection is required for the weighting function.

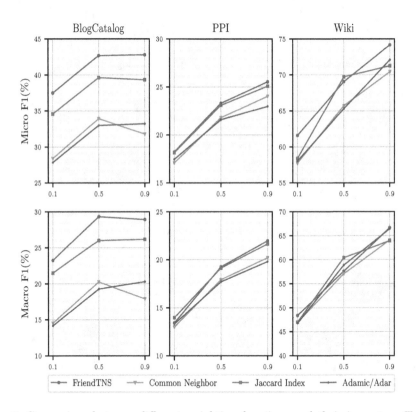

Fig. 6. Comparison between different weighting functions and their impact on Two-Stage-MR-BPR performance.

5.7   Reproducibility of the Experiments

For each model we used the following hyper-parameters during in experiments similar to the original paper [13].

- MR-BPR: The hyper-parameters are $k = 500$, $\mu = 0.02$, $\lambda_{user} = 0.0125$, $\lambda_{item} = 0.0005$, 300 iterations and $\alpha = 0.5$ for BlogCatalog; $k = 500$, $\mu = 0.01$, $\lambda_{protein} = 0.0125$, $\lambda_{label} = 0.0005$, 400 iterations and $\alpha = 0.5$ for PPI; $k = 600$, $\mu = 0.02$, $\lambda_{page} = 0.0125$, $\lambda_{label} = 0.0005$, 1000 iterations and $\alpha = 0.5$ for Wiki; and $k = 900$, $\mu = 0.03$, $\lambda_{document} = 0.005$, $\lambda_{label} = 0.0001$, $\lambda_{words} = 0.0001$, 1400 iterations and $\alpha = 0.33$ for Cora.
- MR-BPR++: The hyper-parameters are $\beta = 0.75$, $k = 500$, $\mu = 0.02$, $\lambda_{user} = 0.0125$, $\lambda_{item} = 0.0005$, 300 iterations and $\alpha = 0.5$ for BlogCatalog; $\beta = 0.75$, $k = 500$, $\mu = 0.01$, $\lambda_{protein} = 0.0125$, $\lambda_{label} = 0.0005$, 400 iterations and $\alpha = 0.5$ for PPI; $\beta = 0.75$, $k = 600$, $\mu = 0.02$, $\lambda_{page} = 0.0125$, $\lambda_{label} = 0.0005$, 1000 iterations and $\alpha = 0.5$ for Wiki; and $k = 900$, $\mu = 0.03$, $\lambda_{document} = 0.005$, $\lambda_{label} = 0.0001$, $\lambda_{words} = 0.0001$, 1400 iterations and $\alpha = 0.33$ for Cora.
- Two-Stage-MR-BPR: We used the same hyper-parameters of MR-BPR
- DeepWalk: The hyper-parameters are $d = 128$, $r = 10$, $l = 80$ and $k = 10$ for all datasets.
- Node2Vec: The hyper-parameters are $d = 128$, $r = 10$, $l = 80$, $k = 10$, $p = 0.25$ and $q = 0.25$ for BlogCatalog; $d = 128$, $r = 10$, $l = 80$, $k = 10$, $p = 4$ and $q = 1$ for PPI and Wiki.
- GCN: We used the same hyper-parameters from the original paper. Dropout rate $= 0.5$, L2 regularization $= 5.10^{-4}$ and 16 (number of hidden units)
- TADW: We used the same default hyper-parameters from the original papers which are $k = 80$ and $\lambda = 0.2$.

6 Conclusions

In this paper, we extended the original Two-Stage-MR-BPR paper by utilizing and comparing four different similarity weighting functions for the implicit feedback relations. The weighting functions are utilized by the Two-Stage-MR-BPR model to convert all implicit relation edges into weighted ones which allow the model to learn edge rankings based on their approximated weights. Experiments on well-known four real-world datasets showed that selecting the right weighting function is crucial for improving the classification accuracy. Results also show that with the basic transitive node similarity as a weighting function, Two-Stage-MR-BPR outperformed the original MR-BPR and other state-of-art models in the task of multi-label network classification and document classification. [14].

Acknowledgements. The authors gratefully acknowledge the funding of their work through the ÜberDax project (https://www.ismll.uni-hildesheim.de/projekte/ UberDax.html) which is sponsored by the Bundesministerium für Bildung und Forschung (BMBF) under the grant agreement no. 01IS17053.

References

1. Adamic, L.A., Adar, E.: Friends and neighbors on the web. Soc. Netw. **25**(3), 211–230 (2003)
2. Ahmed, C., ElKorany, A., Bahgat, R.: A supervised learning approach to link prediction in twitter. Soc. Netw. Anal. Min. **6**(1), 24 (2016)
3. Breitkreutz, B.J., et al.: The biogrid interaction database: 2008 update. Nucleic Acids Res. **36**(suppl_1), D637–D640 (2007)
4. Cai, H., Zheng, V.W., Chang, K.: A comprehensive survey of graph embedding: problems, techniques and applications. IEEE Trans. Knowl. Data Eng. **30**, 1616–1637 (2018)
5. Grover, A., Leskovec, J.: node2vec: Scalable feature learning for networks. In: Proceedings of the 22nd ACM SIGKDD International Conference on Knowledge Discovery and Data Mining, pp. 855–864. ACM (2016)
6. Jaccard, P.: Lois de distribution florale dans la zone alpine. Bull. Soc. Vaudoise Sci. Nat. **38**, 69–130 (1902)
7. Jamali, M., Ester, M.: A matrix factorization technique with trust propagation for recommendation in social networks. In: Proceedings of the Fourth ACM Conference on Recommender Systems, pp. 135–142. ACM (2010)
8. Krohn-Grimberghe, A., Drumond, L., Freudenthaler, C., Schmidt-Thieme, L.: Multi-relational matrix factorization using Bayesian personalized ranking for social network data. In: Proceedings of the Fifth ACM International Conference on Web Search and Data Mining, pp. 173–182. ACM (2012)
9. Lerche, L., Jannach, D.: Using graded implicit feedback for Bayesian personalized ranking. In: Proceedings of the 8th ACM Conference on Recommender Systems, pp. 353–356. ACM (2014)
10. Liben-Nowell, D., Kleinberg, J.: The link-prediction problem for social networks. J. Assoc. Inf. Sci. Technol. **58**(7), 1019–1031 (2007)
11. Mikolov, T., Chen, K., Corrado, G., Dean, J.: Efficient estimation of word representations in vector space. arXiv preprint arXiv:1301.3781 (2013)
12. Perozzi, B., Al-Rfou, R., Skiena, S.: Deepwalk: online learning of social representations. In: Proceedings of the 20th ACM SIGKDD International Conference on Knowledge Discovery and Data Mining, pp. 701–710. ACM (2014)
13. Rashed, A., Grabocka, J., Schmidt-Thieme, L.: Multi-label network classification via weighted personalized factorizations. In: Proceedings of the 11th International Conference on Agents and Artificial Intelligence, pp. 357–366. SCITEPRESS-Science and Technology Publications, Lda (2019)
14. Rendle, S., Freudenthaler, C.: Improving pairwise learning for item recommendation from implicit feedback. In: Proceedings of the 7th ACM International Conference on Web Search and Data Mining, pp. 273–282. ACM (2014)
15. Rendle, S., Freudenthaler, C., Gantner, Z., Schmidt-Thieme, L.: BPR: Bayesian personalized ranking from implicit feedback. In: Proceedings of the Twenty-Fifth Conference on Uncertainty in Artificial Intelligence, pp. 452–461. AUAI Press (2009)
16. Sen, P., Namata, G., Bilgic, M., Getoor, L., Galligher, B., Eliassi-Rad, T.: Collective classification in network data. AI Mag. **29**(3), 93 (2008)
17. Singh, A.P., Gordon, G.J.: Relational learning via collective matrix factorization. In: Proceedings of the 14th ACM SIGKDD International Conference on Knowledge Discovery and Data Mining, pp. 650–658. ACM (2008)

18. Symeonidis, P., Tiakas, E., Manolopoulos, Y.: Transitive node similarity for link prediction in social networks with positive and negative links. In: Proceedings of the Fourth ACM Conference on Recommender Systems, pp. 183–190. ACM (2010)
19. Tang, J., Qu, M., Wang, M., Zhang, M., Yan, J., Mei, Q.: Line: large-scale information network embedding. In: Proceedings of the 24th International Conference on World Wide Web, pp. 1067–1077. International World Wide Web Conferences Steering Committee (2015)
20. Tang, L., Liu, H.: Relational learning via latent social dimensions. In: Proceedings of the 15th ACM SIGKDD International Conference on Knowledge Discovery and Data Mining, pp. 817–826. ACM (2009)
21. Tang, L., Liu, H.: Scalable learning of collective behavior based on sparse social dimensions. In: Proceedings of the 18th ACM Conference on Information and Knowledge Management, pp. 1107–1116. ACM (2009)
22. Thomas, N.K., Welling, M.: Semi-supervised classification with graph convolutional networks. arxiv preprint. arXiv preprint arXiv:1609.02907 103 (2016)
23. Tu, C., Zhang, W., Liu, Z., Sun, M.: Max-margin DeepWalk: discriminative learning of network representation. In: IJCAI (2016)
24. Yang, C., Liu, Z., Zhao, D., Sun, M., Chang, E.Y.: Network representation learning with rich text information. In: IJCAI, pp. 2111–2117 (2015)
25. Zafarani, R., Liu, H.: Social computing data repository at ASU (2009)

Multi-agent Path Finding
with Generalized Conflicts:
An Experimental Study

Pavel Surynek[(✉)] [ID]

Faculty of Information Technology, Czech Technical University in Prague,
Thákurova 9, 160 00 Praha 6, Czech Republic
`pavel.surynek@fit.cvut.cz`

Abstract. This paper gives an overview of conflict reasoning in generalizations of multi-agent path finding (MAPF). MAPF and derived variants assume items placed in vertices of an undirected graph with at most
one item per vertex. Items can be relocated across edges while various
constraints depending on the concrete type of relocation problem must
be satisfied. We recall a general problem formulation that encompasses
known types of item relocation problems such as multi-agent path finding (MAPF), token swapping (TSWAP), token rotation (TROT), and
token permutation (TPERM). We then focused on three existing optimal algorithms for MAPF: search-based CBS, and propositional satisfiability (SAT) - based MDD-SAT and SMT-CBS. These algorithms were
modified to tackle various types of conflicts. The major contribution of
this paper is a thorough experimental evaluation of CBS, MDD-SAT,
and SMT-CBS on various types of relocation problems.

Keywords: Conflicts · MAPF · Token swapping · Token rotation ·
Token permutation · SMT · SAT

1 Introduction

Item relocation problems in graphs such as *token swapping* (TSWAP) [7,13],
multi-agent path finding (MAPF) [22,28,53], or pebble motion on graphs (PMG)
[15,47] represent important combinatorial problems in artificial intelligence with
specific applications in coordination of multiple robots and other areas such as
quantum circuit compilation [8]. Graphs in item relocation problems may be
directly derived from the physical environment where items move but can be
also represented by abstract spaces like *configuration spaces* in robotics [52].

Distinguishable items placed in vertices of an undirected graph such that at
most one item is placed in each vertex. Items can be moved across edges while
problem specific rules must be observed. For example, PMG and MAPF usually

This work has been supported by GAČR - the Czech Science Foundation, grant regis-
tration number 19-17966S.

assume that items (pebbles/agents) are moved to unoccupied neighbors only. TSWAP on the other hand permits only swaps of pairs of tokens along edges while more complex movements involving more than two tokens are forbidden. The task in item relocation problems is to reach a given goal configuration from a given starting configuration.

We focus here on the optimal solving of item relocation problems with respect to common objectives. Two cumulative objective functions are used in MAPF and TSWAP - *sum-of-costs* [19,25] and *makespan* [35,55]. The sum-of-costs corresponds to the total cost of all movements performed. The makespan corresponds to the total number of time-steps until the goal is reached. We trying to minimize the objective in both cases.

Many practical problems from robotics involving multiple robots can be interpreted as an item relocation problems. Examples include discrete multi-robot navigation and coordination [18], item rearrangement in automated warehouses [4], ship collision avoidance [14], or formation maintenance and maneuvering of aerial vehicles [57]. Examples not only include problems concerning physical items but problems occurring in virtual spaces of simulations [12], computer games [45], or quantum systems [8].

The contribution of this paper consists in an experimental evaluation of a general framework for defining and solving item relocation problems based on *satisfiability modulo theories* (SMT) [6,40] and *conflict-based search* (CBS) [24].

The framework has been used to define two problems derived from TSWAP: *token rotation* (TROT) and *token permutation* (TPERM) where instead of swapping pairs of tokens, rotations along non-trivial cycles and arbitrary permutations of tokens respectively are permitted. We show how to modify existing algorithms for various variants of item relocation problems. We will adapt the standard *conflict-based search* (CBS) but also propositional satisfiability (SAT) - based MDD-SAT [42] and recent SMT-based SMT-CBS [40].

This work originally appeared as a conference paper [41]. In this revised version we provide more thorough experimental study of concepts presented in the original conference paper. We first introduce TSWAP and MAPF. Then prerequisites for conflict handling formulated in the SMT framework are recalled. On top of this, the combination of CBS and MDD-SAT is developed - the SMT-CBS algorithm. Finally, a thorough experimental evaluation of CBS, MDD-SAT, and SMT-CBS on various benchmarks including both small and large instances is presented.

2   Background

Multi-agent path finding (MAPF) problem [23,27] consists of an undirected graph $G = (V, E)$ and a set of agents $A = \{a_1, a_2, ..., a_k\}$ such that $|A| < |V|$. Each agent is placed in a vertex so that at most one agent resides in each vertex. The placement of agents is denoted $\alpha : A \rightarrow V$. Next we are given nitial configuration of agents α_0 and goal configuration α_+.

At each time step an agent can either *move* to an adjacent location or *wait* in its current location. The task is to find a sequence of move/wait actions for each agent a_i, moving it from $\alpha_0(a_i)$ to $\alpha_+(a_i)$ such that agents do not *conflict*, i.e., do not occupy the same location at the same time. Typically, an agent can move into adjacent unoccupied vertex provided no other agent enters the same target vertex but other rules for movements are used as well.

The following definition formalizes the commonly used *move-to-unoccupied* movement rule in MAPF.

Definition 1 Movement in MAPF. *Configuration α' results from α if and only if the following conditions hold: (i) $\alpha(a) = \alpha'(a)$ or $\{\alpha(a), \alpha'(a)\} \in E$ for all $a \in A$ (agents wait or move along edges); (ii) for all $a \in A$ it holds that if $\alpha(a) \neq \alpha'(a) \Rightarrow \alpha'(a) \neq \alpha(a')$ for all $a' \in A$ (target vertex must be empty); and (iii) for all $a, a' \in A$ it holds that if $a \neq a' \Rightarrow \alpha'(a) \neq \alpha'(a')$ (no two agents enter the same target vertex).*

Solving the MAPF instance is to search for a sequence of configurations $[\alpha_0, \alpha_1, ..., \alpha_\mu]$ such that α_{i+1} results using valid movements from α_i for $i = 1, 2, ..., \mu - 1$, and $\alpha_\mu = \alpha_+$.

In many aspects, a *token swapping problem (TSWAP)* (also known as *sorting on graphs*) [49] is similar to MAPF. It represents a generalization of sorting problems [44]. While in the classical sorting problem we need to obtain linearly ordered sequence of elements by swapping any pair of elements, in the TSWAP problem we are allowed to swap elements at selected pairs of positions only.

Using a modified notation from [50] the TSWAP each vertex in G is assigned a color in $C = \{c_1, c_2, ..., c_h\}$ via $\tau_+ : V \to C$. A token of a color in C is placed in each vertex. The task is to transform a current token placement into the one such that colors of tokens and respective vertices of their placement agree. Desirable token placement can be obtained by swapping tokens on adjacent vertices in G.

We denote by $\tau : V \to C$ colors of tokens placed in vertices of G. That is, $\tau(v)$ for $v \in V$ is a color of a token placed in v. Starting placement of tokens is denoted as τ_0; the goal token placement corresponds to τ_+. Transformation of one placement to another is captured by the concept of *adjacency* defined as follows [48,50]:

Definition 2 Adjacency in TSWAP. *Token placements τ and τ' are said to be adjacent if there exists a subset of non-adjacent edges $F \subseteq E$ such that $\tau(v) = \tau'(u)$ and $\tau(u) = \tau'(v)$ for each $\{u, v\} \in F$ and for all other vertices $w \in V \setminus \bigcup_{\{u,v\} \in F} \{u, v\}$ it holds that $\tau(w) = \tau'(w)$.*[1]

The task in TSWAP is to find a swapping sequence of token placements $[\tau_0, \tau_1, ..., \tau_m]$ such that $\tau_m = \tau_+$ and τ_i and τ_{i+1} are adjacent for all $i = 0, 1, ..., m - 1$. It has been shown that for any initial and goal placement of tokens τ_0 and τ_+ respectively there is a swapping sequence transforming τ_0 and τ_+ containing $\mathcal{O}(|V|^2)$ swaps [51]. The proof is based on swapping tokens on a spanning tree of G. Let us note that the above bound is tight as there are

---

[1] The presented version of adjacency is sometimes called *parallel* while a term adjacency is reserved for the case with $|F| = 1$.

instances consuming $\Omega(|V|^2)$ swaps. It is also known that finding a swapping sequence that has as few swaps as possible is an NP-hard problem.

If each token has a different color we do not distinguish between tokens and their colors c_i; that is, we will refer to a token c_i.

3 Related Work

Although many works sudying TSWAP from the theoretical point of view exist [7,19,51] practical solving of the problem started only lately. In [39] optimal solving of TSWAP by adapted algorithms from MAPF has been suggested. Namely *conflict-based search* (CBS) [24,26] and *propositional satisfiability-based* (SAT) [5] MDD-SAT [42,43] originally developed for MAPF have been modified for TSWAP.

3.1 Search for Optimal Solutions

We will commonly use the *sum-of-costs* objective funtion in all problems studied in this paper. The following definition introduces the sum-of-costs objective in MAPF.

Definition 3. Sum-of-costs *(denoted ξ) is the summation, over all agents, of the number of time steps required to reach the goal vertex [10,24,25,28]. Formally, $\xi = \sum_{i=1}^{k} \xi(path(a_i))$, where $\xi(path(a_i))$ is an individual path cost of agent a_i connecting $\alpha_0(a_i)$ calculated as the number of edge traversals and wait actions.[2]*

Observe that in the sum-of-costs we accumulate the cost of wait actions for items not yet reaching their goal vertices. Also observe that one swap in the TSWAP problem yields the cost of 2 as two tokens traverses single edge.

A feasible solution of a solvable MAPF instance can be found in polynomial time [15,47]; precisely the worst case time complexity of most practical algorithms for finding feasible solutions is $\mathcal{O}(|V|^3)$ (asymptotic size of the solution is also $\mathcal{O}(|V|^3)$) [16,17,31,32,37,46]. This is also asymptotically best possible as there are MAPF instances requiring $\Omega(|V|^2)$ moves. As with TSWAP, finding optimal MAPF solutions with respect to various cummulative objectives is NP-hard [21,33,54].

3.2 Conflict-Based Search

CBS uses the idea of resolving conflicts lazily; that is, a solution is searched against an incomplete set of movement constraints hoping a valid solution can be found before all constraints are added.

---

[2] The notation $path(a_i)$ refers to path in the form of a seqeunce of vertices and edges connecting $\alpha_0(a_i)$ and $\alpha_+(a_i)$ while ξ assigns the cost to a given path.

The high level of CBS searches a *constraint tree* (CT) using a priority queue in breadth first manner. CT is a binary tree where each node N contains a set of collision avoidance constraints $N.constraints$ - a set of triples (a_i, v, t) forbidding occurrence of agent a_i in vertex v at time step t, a solution $N.paths$ - a set of k paths for individual agents, and the total cost $N.\xi$ of the current solution.

The low level process in CBS associated with node N searches paths for individual agents with respect to set of constraints $N.constraints$. For a given agent a_i, this is a standard single source shortest path search from $\alpha_0(a_i)$ to $\alpha_+(a_i)$ that avoids a set of vertices $\{v \in V | (a_i, v, t) \in N.constraints\}$ whenever working at time step t. For details see [24].

Algorithm 1. Basic CBS algorithm for MAPF solving [41].

```
1  CBS (G = (V, E), A, α₀, α₊)
2      R.constraints ← ∅
3      R.paths ← {shortest path from α₀(aᵢ) to α₊(aᵢ)|i = 1, 2, ..., k}
4      R.ξ ← ∑ᵏᵢ₌₁ ξ(N.paths(aᵢ))
5      insert R into OPEN
6      while OPEN ≠ ∅ do
7          N ← min(OPEN)
8          remove-Min(OPEN)
9          collisions ← validate(N.paths)
10         if collisions = ∅ then
11             return N.paths
12         let (aᵢ, aⱼ, v, t) ∈ collisions
13         for each a ∈ {aᵢ, aⱼ} do
14             N'.constraints ← N.constraints ∪ {(a, v, t)}
15             N'.paths ← N.paths
16             update(a, N'.paths, N'.conflicts)
17             N'.ξ ← ∑ᵏᵢ₌₁ ξ(N'.paths(aᵢ))
18             insert N' into OPEN
```

CBS stores nodes of CT into priority queue OPEN sorted according to ascending costs of solutions. At each step CBS takes node N with lowest cost from OPEN and checks if $N.paths$ represents paths that are valid with respect to movements rules in MAPF. That is, if there are any collisions between agents in $N.paths$. If there is no collision, the algorithms returns valid MAPF solution $N.paths$. Otherwise the search branches by creating a new pair of nodes in CT - successors of N. Assume that a collision occurred between agents a_i and a_j in vertex v at time step t. This collision can be avoided if either agent a_i or agent a_j does not reside in v at timestep t. These two options correspond to new successor nodes of N - N_1 and N_2 that inherits set of conflicts from N as follows: $N_1.conflicts = N.conflicts \cup \{(a_i, v, t)\}$ and $N_2.conflicts = N.conflicts \cup \{(a_j, v, t)\}$. $N_1.paths$

and $N_1.paths$ inherit path from $N.paths$ except those for agent a_i and a_j respectively. Paths for a_i and a_j are recalculated with respect to extended sets of conflicts $N_1.conflicts$ and $N_2.conflicts$ respectively and new costs for both agents $N_1.\xi$ and $N_2.\xi$ are determined. After this N_1 and N_2 are inserted into the priority queue OPEN.

The pseudo-code of CBS is listed as Algorithm 1. One of crucial steps occurs at line 16 where a new path for colliding agents a_i and a_j is constructed with respect to an extended set of conflicts. Notation $N.paths(a)$ refers to the path of agent a.

3.3 SAT-Based Approach

An alternative approach to optimal MAPF solving is represented by the reduction of MAPF to propositional satisfiability (SAT) [30,34]. The idea is to construct a propositional formula such $\mathcal{F}(\xi)$ such that it is satisfiable if and only if a solution of a given MAPF of sum-of-costs ξ exists.

Being able to construct such formula $\mathcal{F}$ one can obtain optimal MAPF solution by checking satisfiability of $\mathcal{F}(0), \mathcal{F}(1), \mathcal{F}(2),...$ until the first satisfiable $\mathcal{F}(\xi)$ is met. This is possible due to monotonicity of MAPF solvability with respect to increasing values of common cummulative objectives such as the sum-of-costs. The framework of SAT-based solving is shown in pseudo-code in Algorithm 2.

Algorithm 2. Framework of SAT-based MAPF solving [41].

---

1 **SAT-Based** $(G = (V, E), A, \alpha_0, \alpha_+)$
2      $paths \leftarrow \{$shortest path from $\alpha_0(a_i)$ to $\alpha_+(a_i)|i = 1, 2, ..., k\}$
3      $\xi \leftarrow \sum_{i=1}^{k} \xi(N.paths(a_i))$
4   **while** $True$ **do**
5          $\mathcal{F}(\xi) \leftarrow$ encode$(\xi, G, A, \alpha_0, \alpha_+)$
6          $assignment \leftarrow$ consult-SAT-Solver$(\mathcal{F}(\xi))$
7   **if** $assignment \neq UNSAT$ **then**
8              $paths \leftarrow$ extract-Solution$(assignment)$
9   **return** $paths$
10         $\xi \leftarrow \xi + 1$

The advantage of the SAT-based approach is that state-of-the-art SAT solvers can be used for determinig satisfiability of $\mathcal{F}(\xi)$ [1].

Construction of $\mathcal{F}(\xi)$ relies on time expansion of underlying graph G [38]. Having ξ, the basic variant of time expansion determines the maximum number of time steps μ (also refered to as a *makespan*) such that every possible solution of the given MAPF with the sum-of-costs less than or equal to ξ fits within μ timestep (that is, no agent is outside its goal vertex after μ timestep if the sum-of-costs ξ is not to be exceeded).

Time expansion itself makes copies of vertices V for each timestep $t = 0, 1, 2, ..., \mu$. That is, we have vertices v^t for each $v \in V$ time step t. Edges from G are converted to directed edges interconnecting timesteps in time expansion. Directed edges (u^t, v^{t+1}) are introduced for $t = 1, 2, ..., \mu - 1$ whenever there is $\{u, v\} \in E$. Wait actions are modeled by introducing edges (u^t, t^{t+1}). A directed path in time expansion corresponds to trajectory of an agent in time. Hence the modeling task now consists in construction of a formula in which satisfying assignments correspond to directed paths from $\alpha_0^0(a_i)$ to $\alpha_+^\mu(a_i)$.

Assume that we have time expansion $TEG_i = (V_i, E_i)$ for agent a_i. Propositional variable $\mathcal{X}_v^t(a_j)$ is introduced for every vertex v^t in V_i. The semantics of $\mathcal{X}_v^t(a_i)$ is that it is $True$ if and only if agent a_i resides in v at time step t. Similarly we introduce $\mathcal{E}_{u,v^{t+1}}(a_i)$ for every directed edge (u^t, v^{t+1}) in E_i. Analogously the meaning of $\mathcal{E}_{u,v}^t(a_i)$ is that is $True$ if and only if agent a_i traverses edge $\{u, v\}$ between time steps t and $t + 1$.

Finally constraints are added so that truth assignment are restricted to those that correspond to valid solutions of a given MAPF. The detailed list of constraints is given in [42]. We here just illustrate the modeling by showing few representative constraints. For example there is a constraint stating that if agent a_i appears in vertex u at time step t then it has to leave through exactly one edge (u^t, v^{t+1}). This can be established by following constraints [41]:

$$\mathcal{X}_u^t(a_i) \Rightarrow \bigvee_{(u^t, v^{t+1}) \in E_i} \mathcal{E}_{u,v}^t(a_i), \tag{1}$$

$$\sum_{v^{t+1} | (u^t, v^{t+1}) \in E_i} \mathcal{E}_{u,v}^t(a_i) \leq 1 \tag{2}$$

Similarly, the target vertex of any movement except wait action must be empty. This is ensured by the following constraint for every $(u^t, v^{t+1}) \in E_i$ [41]:

$$\mathcal{E}_{u,v}^t(a_i) \Rightarrow \bigwedge_{a_j \in A \wedge a_j \neq a_i \wedge v^t \in V_j} \neg \mathcal{X}_v^t(a_j) \tag{3}$$

Other constraints ensure that truth assignments to variables per individual agents form paths. That is if agent a_i enters an edge it must leave the edge at the next time step [41]:

$$\mathcal{E}_{u,v}^t(a_i) \Rightarrow \mathcal{X}_u^t(a_i) \wedge \mathcal{X}_v^{t+1}(a_i) \tag{4}$$

Agents do not collide with each other; the following constraint is introduced for every $v \in V$ and timestep t [41]:

$$\sum_{i=1,2,...,k | v^t \in V_i} \mathcal{X}_v^t(a_i) \tag{5}$$

A common measure how to reduce the number of decision variables derived from the time expansion is the use of *multi-value decision diagrams* (MDDs) [25]. The basic observation that holds for MAPF and other item relocation problems is that a token/agent can reach vertices in the distance d (distance of a vertex is measured as the length of the shortest path) from the current position of the agent/token no earlier than in the d-th time step.

Above observations can be utilized when making the time expansion of G. For a given agent or token, we do not need to consider all vertices at time step t but only those that are reachable in t timesteps from the initial position and that ensure that the goal can be reached in the remaining $\sigma - t$ timesteps.

The combination of SAT-based approach and MDD time expansion led to the MDD-SAT algorithm described in [42] that currently represent state-of-the-art in SAT-based MAPF solving.

4   Generalizations of Item Relocation

We define two problems derived from MAPF and TSWAP: *token rotation* (TROT) and *token permutation* (TPERM)[3].

4.1   Token Rotation and Token Permutation

A swap of pair of tokens can be interpreted as a rotation along a trivial cycle consisting of single edge. We can generalize this towards longer cycles. The TROT problem permits rotations along longer cycles but forbids trivial cycles; that is, rotations along triples, quadruples, ... of vertices is allowed but swap along edges are forbidden.

Definition 4 Adjacency in TROT. *Token placements τ and τ' are said to be adjacent in TROT if there exists a subset of edges $F \subseteq E$ such that components $C_1, C_2, ..., C_p$ of induced sub-graph $G[F]$ satisfy following conditions:*

(i) *$C_j = (V_j^C, E_j^C)$ such that $V_j^C = w_1^j, w_2^j, ..., w_{n_j}^j$ with $n_j \leq 3$ and*
    $E_j^C = \{\{w_1^j, w_2^j\}; \{w_2^j, w_3^j\}; ...; \{w_{n_j}^j, w_1^j\}\}$
    (components are cycles of length at least 3)
(ii) *$\tau(w_1^j) = \tau'(w_2^j), \tau(w_3^j) = \tau'(w_3^j), ..., \tau(w_{n_j}^j) = \tau'(w_1^j)$*
    (colors are rotated in the cycle one position forward/backward)

The rest of the definition of a TROT instance is analogous to TSWAP.

Similarly we can define TPERM by permitting all lengths of cycles. The formal definition of *adjacency* in TPERM is almost the same as in TROT except relaxing the constraint on cycle lenght, $n_j \leq 2$.as

We omit here complexity considerations for TROT and TPERM for the sake of brevity. Again it holds that a feasible solution can be found in polynomial time but the optimal cases remain intractable in general.

---

[3] These problems have been considered in the literature in different contexts already (for example in [56]). But not from the practical solving perspective focused on finding optimal solutions.

Both approaches - SAT-based MDD-SAT as well as CBS - can be adapted for solving TROT and TPERM without modifying their top level design. Only local modification of how movement rules of each problem are reflected in algorithms is necessary. In case of CBS, we need to define what does it mean a conflict in TROT and TPERM. In MDD-SAT different movement constraints can be encoded directly.

Motivation for studying these item relocation problems is the same as for MAPF. In many real-life scenarios it happens that items or agents enters positions being simultaneously vacated by other items (for example mobile robots often). This is exactly the property captured formally in above definitions.

4.2   Adapting CBS and MDD-SAT

Both CBS and MDD-SAT can be modified for optimal solving of TSWAP, TROT, and TPERM (with respect to sum-of-costs but other cumulative objectives are possible as well). Different movement rules can be reflected in CBS and MDD-SAT algorithms without modifying their high level framework.

Different Conflicts in CBS. In CBS, we need to modify the understanding of conflict between agents/tokens. In contrast to the original CBS we need to introduce edge conflicts to be able to handle conflicts properly in TSWAP and TROT.

Edge conflicts have been introduced to tackle conflicting situations in TSWAP and TROT properly within CBS and SMT-CBS. An edge conflict is triple $(c_i, (u, v), t)$ with $c_i \in C$, $u, v \in V$ and timestep t. The interpretation of $(c_i, (u, v), t)$ is that token c_i cannot move across $\{u, v\}$ from u to v between timesteps t and $t + 1$.

Conflict reasoning in individual item relocation problems follows.

TPERM: The easiest case is TPERM as it is least restrictive. We merely forbid simultaneous occurrence of multiple tokens in a vertex - this situation is understood as a collision in TPERM and conflicts are derived from it. If a collision (c_i, c_j, v, t) between tokens c_i and c_j occurs in v at time step t then we introduce conflicts (c_i, v, t) and (c_j, v, t) for c_i and c_j respectively.[4]

TSWAP: This problem takes conflicts from TPERM but adds new conflicts that arise from doing something else than swapping [39]. Each time edge $\{u, v\}$ is being traversed by token c_i between time steps t and $t + 1$, a token residing in v at time step t, that is $\tau_t(v)$, must go in the opposite direction from v to u. If this is not the case, then a so called *edge collision* involving edge $\{u, v\}$ occurs and corresponding *edge conflicts* $(c_i, (u, v), t)$ and $(\tau_t(v), (v, u), t)$ are introduced for agents c_i and $\tau_t(v)$ respectively.

---

[4] Formally this is the same as in MAPF, but in addition to this MAPF checks vacancy of the target vertex which may cause more colliding situations.

Edge conflicts must be treated at the low level of CBS. Hence in addition to forbidden vertices at given time-steps we have forbidden edges between given time-steps.

TROT: The treatment of conflicts will be complementary to TSWAP in TROT. Each time edge $\{u, v\}$ is being traversed by token c_i between time steps t and $t+1$, a token residing in v at time step t, that is $\tau_t(v)$, must go anywhere else but not to u. If this is not the case, then we again have edge collision $(c_i, \tau_t(v), \{u,v\}, t)$ which is treated in the same way as above.

Encoding Changes in MDD-SAT. In MDD-SAT, we need to modify encoding of movement rules in the propositional formula $\mathcal{F}(\xi)$. Again, proofs of soundness of the following changes are omitted.

TPERM: This is the easiest case for MDD-SAT too. We merely remove all constrains requiring tokens to move into vacant vertices only. That is we remove clauses (3).

TSWAP: It inherits changes from TPERM but in addition to that we need to carry out swaps properly. For this edge variables $\mathcal{E}_{u,v}^t(c_i)$ will be utilized. Following constraint will be introduced for every $\{u^t, v^{t+1}\} \in E_i$ (intuitively, if token c_i traverses $\{u, v\}$ some other token c_j traverses $\{u, v\}$ in the opposite direction) [41]:

$$\mathcal{E}_{u,v}^t(c_i) \Rightarrow \bigvee_{j=1,2,\ldots,k|j\neq i\wedge(u^t,v^{t+1})\in E_j} \mathcal{E}_{v,u}^t(c_j) \qquad (6)$$

TROT: TROT is treated in a complementary way to TSWAP. Instead of adding constraints (6) we add constraints forbidding simultaneous traversal in the opposite direction as follows [41]:

$$\mathcal{E}_{u,v}^t(c_i) \Rightarrow \bigwedge_{j=1,2,\ldots,k|j\neq i\wedge(u^t,v^{t+1})\in E_j} \neg\mathcal{E}_{v,u}^t(c_j) \qquad (7)$$

5 Combining the SAT-Based Approach and CBS

A close look at CBS reveals that it works similarly as problem solving in *satisfiability modulo theories* (SMT) [6,20]. SMT divides satisfiability problem in some complex theory T into an abstract propositional part that keeps the Boolean structure of the problem and simplified decision procedure $DECIDE_T$ that decides only conjunctive formulae over T. A general T-formula is transformed to *propositional skeleton* by replacing atoms with propositional variables. The SAT-solving procedure then decides what variables should be assigned $TRUE$ in order to satisfy the skeleton - these variables tells what atoms holds in T. $DECIDE_T$ checks if the conjunction of selected (satisfied) atoms is satisfiable. If so then solution is returned. Otherwise a conflict from $DECIDE_T$ is reported back and the skeleton is extended with a constraint that eliminates the conflict.

Following the above observation we rephrased CBS in the SMT manner. The abstract propositional part working with the skeleton was taken from MDD-SAT except that only constraints ensuring that assignments form valid paths interconnecting starting positions with goals will be preserved. Other constraints, namely those ensuring collision avoidance between items will be omitted initially. Paths validation procedure will act as $DECIDE_T$ and will report back a set of conflicts found in the current solution (here is a difference from the SMT-style solving that reports only one conflict while here we take all conflicts). We call the new algorithm SMT-CBS and it is shown in pseudo-code as Algorithm 3 (it is formulated for MAPF; but is applicable for TSWAP, TPERM, and TROT after replacing conflict resolution part).

Algorithm 3. SMT-CBS algorithm for solving MAPF [41].

---

1 **SMT-CBS** $(\Sigma = (G = (V, E), A, \alpha_0, \alpha_+))$
2      $conflicts \leftarrow \emptyset$
3      $paths \leftarrow \{\text{shortest path from } \alpha_0(a_i) \text{ to } \alpha_+(a_i) | i = 1, 2, ..., k\}$
4      $\xi \leftarrow \sum_{i=1}^{k} \xi(paths(a_i))$
5   **while** $True$ **do**
6          $(paths, conflicts) \leftarrow \text{SMT-CBS-Fixed}(conflicts, \xi, \Sigma)$
7   **if** $paths \neq UNSAT$ **then**
8   **return** $paths$
9          $\xi \leftarrow \xi + 1$

10 **SMT-CBS-Fixed**$(conflicts, \xi, \Sigma)$
11      $\mathcal{F}(\xi)) \leftarrow \text{encode-Basic}(conflicts, \xi, \Sigma)$
12   **while** $True$ **do**
13          $assignment \leftarrow \text{consult-SAT-Solver}(\mathcal{F}(\xi))$
14   **if** $assignment \neq UNSAT$ **then**
15              $paths \leftarrow \text{extract-Solution}(assignment)$
16              $collisions \leftarrow \text{validate}(paths)$
17   **if** $collisions = \emptyset$ **then**
18   **return** $(paths, conflicts)$
19   **for** each $(a_i, a_j, v, t) \in collisions$ **do**
20                  $\mathcal{F}(\xi) \leftarrow \neg \mathcal{X}_v^t(a_i) \vee \neg \mathcal{X}_v^t(a_j)$
21                  $conflicts \leftarrow conflicts \cup \{[(a_i, v, t), (a_j, v, t)]\}$

22   **return** $(UNSAT, conflicts)$

The algorithm is divided into two procedures: SMT-CBS representing the main loop and SMT-CBS-Fixed solving the input MAPF for a fixed cost ξ. The major difference from the standard CBS is that there is no branching at the high level. The high level SMT-CBS roughly corresponds to the main loop of MDD-SAT. The set of conflicts is iteratively collected during entire execution of the algorithm. Procedure $encode$ from MDD-SAT is replaced with $encode\text{-}Basic$

that produces encoding that ignores specific movement rules (collisions between agents) but on the other hand encodes collected conflicts into $\mathcal{F}(\xi)$.

The conflict resolution in the standard CBS implemented as high-level branching is here represented by refinement of $\mathcal{F}(\xi)$ with a disjunction (line 20). Branching is thus deferred into the SAT solver. The advantage of SMT-CBS is that it builds the formula lazily; that is, it adds constraints on demand after a conflict occurs. Such approach may save resources as solution may be found earlier than all constraints are added. In contrast to this, the eager approach of MDD-SAT first adds all constraints and then solves the complete formula.

6   Experimental Evaluation

To evaluate how different conflicts affect the performance of solving algorithms we performed an extensive evaluation of all presented algorithms on both standard synthetic benchmarks [9,25] and large maps from games [29]. A representative part of results is presented in this section.

Fig. 1. Example of *4-connected grid, star, path,* and *clique* [41].

6.1   Benchmarks and Setup

We implemented the SMT-CBS algorithm in C++ on top of the Glucose 4 SAT solver [1,2]. The choice of Glucose 4 is given by the fact that it ranks among the best SAT solvers according to recent SAT solver competitions [3]. The standard CBS has been re-implemented from scratch since the original implementation written in Java does support only grids but not general graphs [24] that we need in our tests.

Regarding MDD-SAT we used an existing implementation in C++ [42]. The original MDD-SAT has been developed for MAPF but versions applicable on TSWAP, TROT, and TPERM are implemented in the existing package as well. All experiments were run on a Ryzen 7 CPU 3.0 Ghz under Kubuntu linux 16 with 16 GB RAM[5].

Our experimental evaluation is divided in three parts. The first part of experimental evaluation has been done on diverse instances consisting of **small** graphs: *random graphs* containing 20% of random edges, *star* graphs, *paths*, and *cliques*

---

[5] To enable reproducibility of results presented in this paper we provide complete source codes and experimental data on author's web page: http://users.fit.cvut.cz/surynpav/research/icaart2019revised.

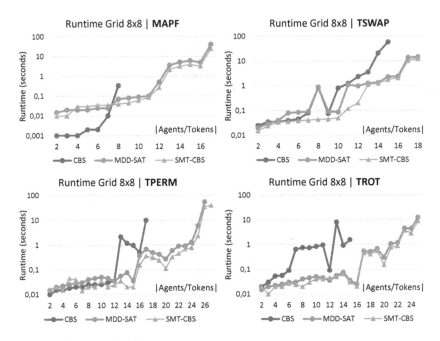

Fig. 2. Runtime comparison of CBS, MDD-SAT, and SMT-CBS algorithms solving MAPF, TSWAP, TPERM, and TROT on 8×8 *grid* [41].

(see Fig. 1). The initial and the goal configuration of tokens/agents was set at random in all tests. The size of the set of vertices of clique, random graph, path, and star graphs was 16. Small graphs were densely populated with tokes/agents. Instances containing up to 40 tokens/agents in grids of size 8×8 and up to 64 tokens/agents in grids of size 16×16 were generated. All generated instances were solvable but not all of them could be solved under the given timeout.

The second part of experiments has been done on medium-sized graphs - *4-connected open grids* of size 8×8 and 16×16. This is the standard benchmark being used for evaluation of MAPF algorithms [11].

And finally the third part of experimental evaluation took place on large 4-connected maps taken from *Dragon Age* [24, 29] - three maps we used in our experiments are shown in Fig. 3. These are structurally different maps focusing on various aspects such as narrow corridors, large almost isolated rooms, or topologically complex open space. In contrast to small instances, these were only sparsely populated with items. Initial and goal configuration were generated at random again.

We varied the number of items in relocation instances to obtain instances of various difficulties; that is, the underlying graph was not fully occupied - which in MAPF has natural meaning while in token problems we use one special color $\perp \in C$ that stands for any empty vertex (that is, we understand v as empty if and only if $\tau(v) = \perp$). For each number of items in the relocation instance we

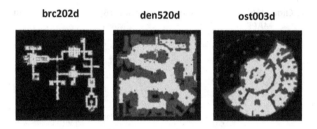

Fig. 3. Three structurally diverse `Dragon-Age` maps used in the experimental evaluation. This selection includes: narrow corridors in `brc202d`, large topologically complex
space in `den520d`, and open space with large almost isolated rooms in `ost003d` [41].

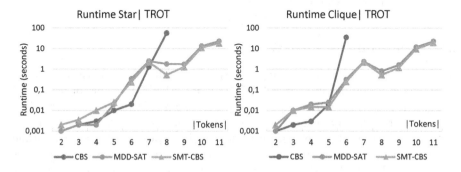

Fig. 4. Comparison of TROT solving by CBS, MDD-SAT, and SMT-CBS on a *star*
and *clique* graphs consisting of 16 vertices [41].

Number of generated clauses

|Agents|	4	8	12	16	20
MDD-SAT	556	56 652	1 347 469	3 087 838	2 124 941
SMT-CBS	468	31 973	598 241	1 256 757	803 671

Fig. 5. Comparison of the size of encodings generated by MDD-SAT and SMT-CBS
(number of clauses is shown) on MAPF instances [41].

generated 10 random instances. For example, a *clique* consisting of 16 vertices
gives 160 instances in total.

The timeout was set to 60 s in the series of tests comparing the performance of
CBS, MDD-SAT, and, SMT-CBS with respect to the growing number of items.
The next series of large scale tests comparing the performance of CBS and
SMT-CBS with respect to the growing difficulty of instances used the timeout
of 1000 s (sorted runtimes are compared). All presented results were obtained
from instances finished under the given timeout.

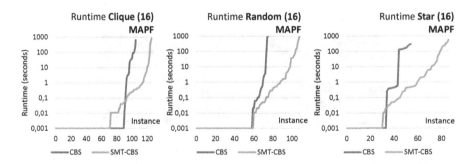

Fig. 6. Sorted runtimes of CBS and SMT-CBS solving MAPF on *clique, random,* and *star* graphs consisting of 16 vertices.

6.2   Comparison on Small Graphs

Tests on small graphs were focused on the runtime comparison and the evaluation of the size of encodings in case of MDD-SAT and SMT-CBS. Part of results we obtained is presented in Figs. 2, 4, and 5. The mean runtime out of 10 random instances is reported per each number of items. Surprisingly we can see in Fig. 4 that instances are relatively hard even for small graphs. For CBS the runtime quickly grows with the increasing number of items. The runtime growth is slower in case of MDD-SAT and SMT-CBS but even these algorithms are not fast enough to solve all instances under the given timeout (only instances with up to 11 items were solved).

In all tests CBS turned out to be uncompetitive against MDD-SAT and SMT-CBS on instances containing more agents. This is an expectable result as it is known that performance of CBS degrades quickly on densely occupied instances [43].

If we focus on the number of clauses generated by SAT-based solvers MDD-SAT and SMT-CBS we can see that MAPF, TSWAP and TROT have more clauses in their eagerly-generated encodings by MDD-SAT than TPERM hence SMT-CBS has greater room for reducing the size of the encoding by constructing it lazily in these types of relocation problems.

Experiments indicate that using SMT-CBS generally leads to reduction of the size of encoding to less than half of the original size generated by MDD-SAT in case of MAPF, TSWAP, and TROT. Results concerning this claim for MAPF are shown in Fig. 5. The number of clauses for 4-connected grids are analyzed in the next section.

In the rest of runtime experiments that are focused on large scale evaluation we omitted MDD-SAT.

Figures 6, 7, 8, and 9 show sorted runtimes of CBS and SMT-CBS solving MAPF, TSWAP, TROT, and TPERM on all types of small graphs: *clique, path, random graph,* a *star* all consisting of 16 vertices (some combinations were not applicable: MAPF is typically unsolvable on *path*; TROT is trivial on *clique* but unsolvable on *path*; and TPERM is also trivial on *clique*).

The general trend is that CBS clearly dominates in easier instances but its performance degrades faster as instances gets harder where SMT-CBS tends to dominate. Eventually SMT-CBS solved more out of 160 instances per test than CBS under the given timeout of 1000 s.

Some cases are particularly interesting as they point to the role of the structure of the underlying graph in the difficulty of instance. CBS significantly outperforms SMT-CBS on easy instances over *cliques* (and generally highly connected graphs). Instances over *paths* seem to yield biggest difference in performance of CBS and SMT-CBS, CBS looses very quickly here.

Interesting results can be seen on *star* graphs. The growth of the runtime across sorted instances looks step-wise here (especially in TPERM - Fig. 9). The interpretation is that adding an item into the graph causes sharp increase in the runtime (a step consists of 10 instances of roughly similar difficulty).

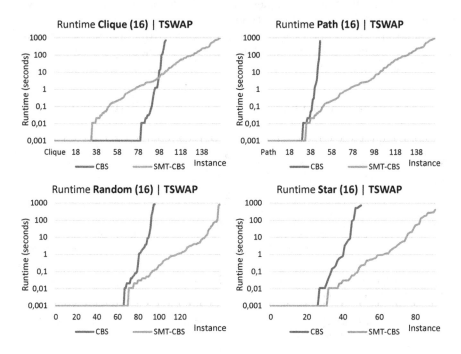

Fig. 7. Sorted runtimes of CBS and SMT-CBS solving TSWAP on *clique, path, random,* and *star* graphs consisting of 16 vertices.

SMT-CBS turned out to be fastest in performed tests on small graphs. SMT-CBS reduces the runtime by about 30% to 50% relatively to MDD-SAT. More significant benefit of SMT-CBS was observed in MAPF and TSWAP while in TROT and TPERM the improvement was less significant.

6.3   Comparison on 4-Connected Grids

Solving of all types of relocation problems on girds - the 8×8 grid and the 16×16 grid - is shown in Figs. 10 and 11. A different pattern can be observed in these results, SMT-CBS dominates across all difficulties of instances over CBS.

The 8×8 grid contained up to 40 items, so having 10 random instances per number of agents, we had 400 instances in total, but only about 300 were solvable under 1000 s in the case of TPERM problem using SMT-CBS. In the 16×16 grid we had up to 64 items yielding to 640 instances in total. Almost all were solvable in the case of TPERM by SMT-CBS.

On the 16×16 grid the dominance of SMT-CBS seems to be pronounced. The general observation from this trend is that the difficulty on instances for CBS grows faster with every new item on larger maps than in smaller maps (disregarding the region where the performance of CBS and SMT-CBS is roughly the same). This observation complements results for large maps where we will see even bigger difference in difficulty growth.

In addition to runtime experiments we measured the number of generated clauses for instances on the 8×8 grid and the 16×16 grid. Results are presented in Figs. 12 and 13.

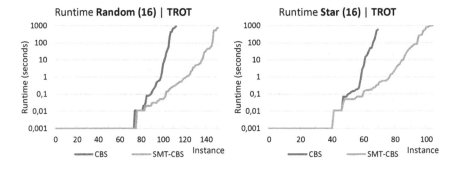

Fig. 8. Sorted runtimes of CBS and SMT-CBS solving TROT on *random* and *star* graphs consisting of 16 vertices.

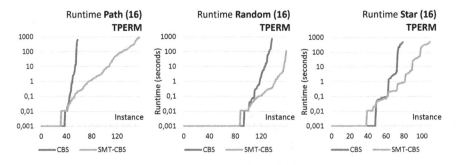

Fig. 9. Sorted runtimes of CBS and SMT-CBS solving TPERM on *random* and *star* graphs consisting of 16 vertices.

We can observe that there is a small difference in the number of generated clauses between MDD-SAT and SMT-CBS on the TPERM problem. This can be attributed to the fact that TPERM is the least constrained version of relocation problems hence conflicts here arise less frequently and are simpler to express than in other more constrained versions. In other words, an encoding forbidding no conflict is of similar size as that eagerly forbidding all conflicts.

In MAPF, TSWAP, and TROT we can observe on both the 8×8 grid and the 16×16 grid that the difference in the size of eagerly generated encoding and lazily generated encoding grows in instances containing more agents. The reduction to about half of the size of the encoding generated by MDD-SAT can be achieved by SMT-CBS in sparsely occupied instances. But the difference is up to the factor of 10 in densely occupied instances.

6.4   Evaluation on Large Maps

The final category of tests was focused on the performance of CBS and SMT-CBS on large maps (experimenting with MDD-SAT was omitted here). In the three structurally different maps, up to 64 items were placed randomly. Again we had 10 random instances per each number of items.

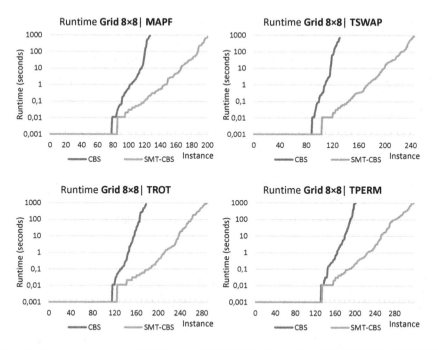

Fig. 10. Sorted runtimes of CBS and SMT-CBS solving MAPF, TSWAP, TPERM, and TROT on the 8×8 *grid* [41].

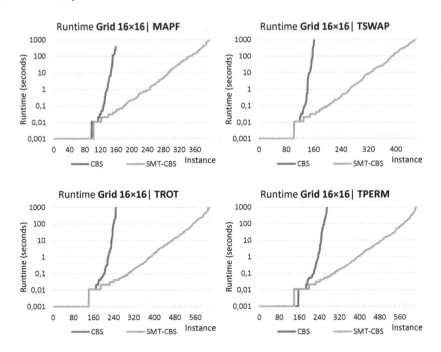

Fig. 11. Sorted runtimes of CBS and SMT-CBS solving MAPF, TSWAP, TPERM, and TROT on the 16×16 *grid*.

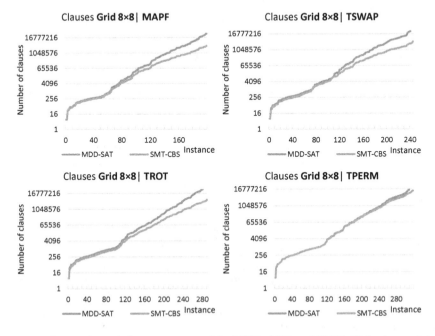

Fig. 12. The number of clauses generated by MDD-SAT and SMT-CBS when solving MAPF, TSWAP, TPERM, and TROT on the 8×8 *grid*.

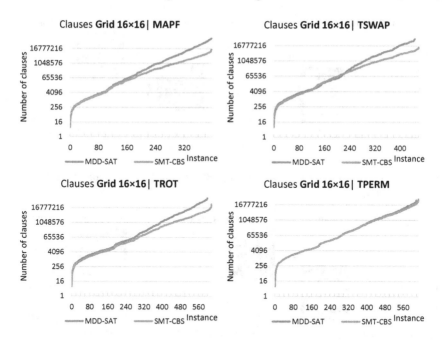

Fig. 13. The number of clauses generated by MDD-SAT and SMT-CBS when solving MAPF, TSWAP, TPERM, and TROT on the 16×16 *grid*.

Sorted runtimes are reported for each individual map and each version of relocation problem in Figs. 14, 15, 16, and 17. Somewhat different picture can be seen here in comparison with experiments on small graphs. We attribute the different picture to the fact that we observe the problem in a different scale.

CBS shows its advantage over SMT-CBS across large set of easier instances where these correspond to instances containing fewer items. Eventually however SMT-CBS wins since the runtime of SMT-CBS goes quickly up when instances get more difficult. This is quite expectable from the theoretical properties of CBS and SMT-CBS. In instances with few items, CBS mostly searches for single source shortest paths while not needing to handle conflicts frequently. This is easier than building a SAT instance for the same problem. The situation changes when CBS must handle frequent conflicts between items in more densely occupied instances. Here viewing the problem as SAT and handling many conflicts in SAT as done by SMT-CBS seems to be more efficient than handling conflicts via branching the search at the high level in CBS.

MAPF and TSWAP are relatively more constrained than TROT and TPERM while TPERM is the least constrained version of item relocation. This property is clearly reflected in the line with the above observation in experiments. We can see that in less constrained cases CBS performs better than SMT-CBS for larger set of instances. Especially it is observable in TROT and TPERM solving on the brc202d map.

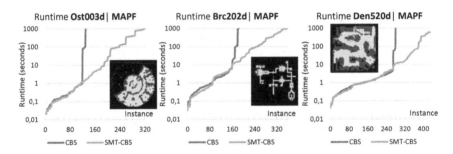

Fig. 14. Sorted runtimes of CBS and SMT-CBS solving MAPF on ost003d, brc202d, and den520d maps.

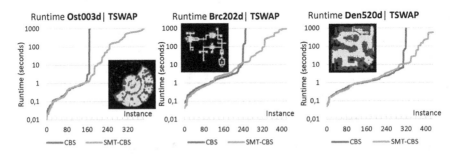

Fig. 15. Sorted runtimes of CBS and SMT-CBS solving TSWAP on ost003d, brc202d, and den520d maps.

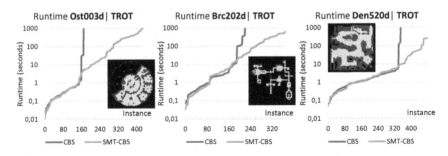

Fig. 16. Sorted runtimes of CBS and SMT-CBS solving TROT on ost003d, brc202d, and 2den520d maps.

The overall analysis of runtimes can be summarized into the observation that whenever CBS has a chance to search for a long conflict free path it can outperform SMT-CBS. On the other hand if conflict handling due to intensive interaction among items prevails then SMT-CBS tends to dominate.

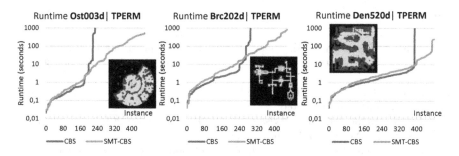

Fig. 17. Sorted runtimes of CBS and SMT-CBS solving TPERM on ost003d, brc202d, and den520d maps.

7   Conclusions

This paper summarizes a general framework for reasoning about conflicts in item relocation problems in graphs based on concepts from the CBS algorithm. Different types of conflicts in four versions of relocation problems derived from multi-agent path finding (MAPF) are studied. In addition to two well studied problems MAPF and TSWAP, we also cover two derived variants TROT and TPERM. We presented thorough experimental evaluation of conflict handling in CBS, MDD-SAT and novel algorithm SMT-CBS that combines CBS and SAT-based reasoning from MDD-SAT. The experimental evaluation has been focused on runtime comparison as well as on the size of generated SAT encodings.

Experiments with CBS, MDD-SAT, and SMT-CBS showed that SMT-CBS outperforms both CBS and MDD-SAT on harder instances in all types of graphs. The most significant benefit of SMT-CBS can be observed on highly constrained MAPF and TSWAP instances where disjunctive conflict elimination is intensively used. The CBS algorithm on the other hand suffers from steep growth of the runtime in instances containing more items because it has to eliminate many conflicts through branching at the high level. This observation can be made across all individual types of relocation problem. The search for long paths with few conflicts is, on the other hand, the performance bottleneck of SMT-CBS. Hence in easier instances CBS is usually the fastest option.

MDD-SAT placed in the middle between CBS and SMT-CBS. The performance of MDD-SAT almost copies that of SMT-CBS though it is worse approximately by a factor of 2.0.

For the future work we plan to revise SAT encodings used in SMT-CBS and perform relevant experiments. Variables $\mathcal{E}_u, v^t(a_i)$ are auxiliary in fact as they can be derived from $\mathcal{X}_v^t(a_i)$. Hence we plan to make experiments with modified encodings where $\mathcal{E}_u, v^t(a_i)$ variables will not be used. This attempt is inspired by the DIRECT encoding [36] that was the first MAPF encoding relying on only $\mathcal{X}_v^t(a_i)$ variables.

References

1. Audemard, G., Lagniez, J., Simon, L.: Improving glucose for incremental SAT solving with assumptions: application to MUS extraction. In: SAT, pp. 309–317 (2013)
2. Audemard, G., Simon, L.: Predicting learnt clauses quality in modern SAT solvers. In: IJCAI, pp. 399–404 (2009)
3. Balyo, T., Heule, M.J.H., Järvisalo, M.: SAT competition 2016: recent developments. In: AAAI, pp. 5061–5063 (2017)
4. Basile, F., Chiacchio, P., Coppola, J.: A hybrid model of complex automated warehouse systems - part I: modeling and simulation. IEEE Trans. Autom. Sci. Eng. **9**(4), 640–653 (2012)
5. Biere, A., Biere, A., Heule, M., van Maaren, H., Walsh, T.: Handbook of Satisfiability: Volume 185 Frontiers in Artificial Intelligence and Applications. IOS Press, Amsterdam (2009)
6. Bofill, M., Palahí, M., Suy, J., Villaret, M.: Solving constraint satisfaction problems with SAT modulo theories. Constraints **17**(3), 273–303 (2012)
7. Bonnet, É., Miltzow, T., Rzazewski, P.: Complexity of token swapping and its variants. In: STACS 2017. LIPIcs, vol. 66, pp. 16:1–16:14. Schloss Dagstuhl (2017)
8. Botea, A., Kishimoto, A., Marinescu, R.: On the complexity of quantum circuit compilation. In: Bulitko, V., Storandt, S. (eds.) Proceedings of the Eleventh International Symposium on Combinatorial Search, SOCS 2018, Stockholm, Sweden - 14–15 July 2018, pp. 138–142. AAAI Press (2018)
9. Boyarski, E., et al.: ICBS: improved conflict-based search algorithm for multi-agent pathfinding. In: IJCAI, pp. 740–746 (2015)
10. Dresner, K., Stone, P.: A multiagent approach to autonomous intersection management. JAIR **31**, 591–656 (2008)
11. Felner, A., et al.: Search-based optimal solvers for the multi-agent pathfinding problem: Summary and challenges. In: Proceedings of the Tenth International Symposium on Combinatorial Search, SOCS 2017, pp. 29–37. AAAI Press (2017)
12. Kapadia, M., Ninomiya, K., Shoulson, A., Garcia, F.M., Badler, N.I.: Constraint-aware navigation in dynamic environments. In: Motion in Games, MIG 2013, Dublin, Ireland, 6–8 November 2013, pp. 111–120. ACM (2013)
13. Kawahara, J., Saitoh, T., Yoshinaka, R.: The time complexity of the token swapping problem and its parallel variants. In: Poon, S.-H., Rahman, M.S., Yen, H.-C. (eds.) WALCOM 2017. LNCS, vol. 10167, pp. 448–459. Springer, Cham (2017). https://doi.org/10.1007/978-3-319-53925-6_35
14. Kim, D.G., Hirayama, K., Park, G.K.: Collision avoidance in multiple-ship situations by distributed local search. J. Adv. Comput. Intell. Intell. Inform. **18**, 839–848 (2014)
15. Kornhauser, D., Miller, G.L., Spirakis, P.G.: Coordinating pebble motion on graphs, the diameter of permutation groups, and applications. FOCS **1984**, 241–250 (1984)
16. Luna, R., Bekris, K.E.: Push and swap: fast cooperative path-finding with completeness guarantees. In: IJCAI, pp. 294–300 (2011)
17. Luna, R., Bekris, K.: Efficient and complete centralized multi-robot path planning. In: IROS, pp. 3268–3275 (2011)
18. Luna, R., Bekris, K.E.: Network-guided multi-robot path planning in discrete representations. In: IROS, pp. 4596–4602 (2010)

19. Miltzow, T., Narins, L., Okamoto, Y., Rote, G., Thomas, A., Uno, T.: Approxima-
    tion and hardness of token swapping. In: ESA 2016. LIPIcs, vol. 57, pp. 66:1–66:15.
    Schloss Dagstuhl (2016)
20. Nieuwenhuis, R., Oliveras, A., Tinelli, C.: Solving SAT and SAT modulo theories:
    from an abstract davis-putnam-logemann-loveland procedure to dpll(T). J. ACM
    53(6), 937–977 (2006)
21. Ratner, D., Warmuth, M.K.: Finding a shortest solution for the N x N extension
    of the 15-puzzle is intractable. In: AAAI, pp. 168–172 (1986)
22. Ryan, M.R.K.: Graph decomposition for efficient multi-robot path planning. In:
    IJCAI 2007, Proceedings of the 20th International Joint Conference on Artificial
    Intelligence, pp. 2003–2008 (2007)
23. Ryan, M.R.K.: Exploiting subgraph structure in multi-robot path planning. J.
    Artif. Intell. Res. (JAIR) **31**, 497–542 (2008)
24. Sharon, G., Stern, R., Felner, A., Sturtevant, N.: Conflict-based search for optimal
    multi-agent pathfinding. Artif. Intell. **219**, 40–66 (2015)
25. Sharon, G., Stern, R., Goldenberg, M., Felner, A.: The increasing cost tree search
    for optimal multi-agent pathfinding. Artif. Intell. **195**, 470–495 (2013)
26. Sharon, G., Stern, R., Felner, A., Sturtevant, N.R.: Conflict-based search for opti-
    mal multi-agent path finding. In: AAAI (2012)
27. Silver, D.: Cooperative pathfinding. In: AIIDE, pp. 117–122 (2005)
28. Standley, T.: Finding optimal solutions to cooperative pathfinding problems. In:
    AAAI, pp. 173–178 (2010)
29. Sturtevant, N.R.: Benchmarks for grid-based pathfinding. Comput. Intell. AI
    Games **4**(2), 144–148 (2012)
30. Surynek, P.: Towards optimal cooperative path planning in hard setups through
    satisfiability solving. In: Anthony, P., Ishizuka, M., Lukose, D. (eds.) PRICAI 2012.
    LNCS (LNAI), vol. 7458, pp. 564–576. Springer, Heidelberg (2012). https://doi.
    org/10.1007/978-3-642-32695-0_50
31. Surynek, P.: An application of pebble motion on graphs to abstract multi-robot
    path planning. ICTAI **2009**, 151–158 (2009)
32. Surynek, P.: A novel approach to path planning for multiple robots in bi-connected
    graphs. ICRA **2009**, 3613–3619 (2009)
33. Surynek, P.: An optimization variant of multi-robot path planning is intractable.
    In: AAAI 2010. AAAI Press (2010)
34. Surynek, P.: On propositional encodings of cooperative path-finding. In: ICTAI
    2012, pp. 524–531. IEEE Computer Society (2012)
35. Surynek, P.: Compact representations of cooperative path-finding as SAT based
    on matchings in bipartite graphs. In: ICTAI, pp. 875–882 (2014)
36. Surynek, P.: Simple direct propositional encoding of cooperative path finding sim-
    plified yet more. In: Gelbukh, A., Espinoza, F.C., Galicia-Haro, S.N. (eds.) MICAI
    2014. LNCS (LNAI), vol. 8857, pp. 410–425. Springer, Cham (2014). https://doi.
    org/10.1007/978-3-319-13650-9_36
37. Surynek, P.: Solving abstract cooperative path-finding in densely populated envi-
    ronments. Comput. Intell. **30**(2), 402–450 (2014)
38. Surynek, P.: Time-expanded graph-based propositional encodings for makespan-
    optimal solving of cooperative path finding problems. Ann. Math. Artif. Intell.
    81(3–4), 329–375 (2017)
39. Surynek, P.: Finding optimal solutions to token swapping by conflict-based search
    and reduction to SAT. In: IEEE 30th International Conference on Tools with Arti-
    ficial Intelligence, ICTAI 2018, pp. 592–599. IEEE (2018)

40. Surynek, P.: Lazy modeling of variants of token swapping problem and multi-agent path finding through combination of satisfiability modulo theories and conflict-based search. CoRR abs/1809.05959 (2018). http://arxiv.org/abs/1809.05959

41. Surynek, P.: Conflict handling framework in generalized multi-agent path finding: advantages and shortcomings of satisfiability modulo approach. In: Proceedings of the 11th International Conference on Agents and Artificial Intelligence, ICAART 2019, vol. 2, pp. 192–203. SciTePress (2019)

42. Surynek, P., Felner, A., Stern, R., Boyarski, E.: Efficient SAT approach to multi-agent path finding under the sum of costs objective. In: ECAI, pp. 810–818 (2016)

43. Surynek, P., Felner, A., Stern, R., Boyarski, E.: An empirical comparison of the hardness of multi-agent path finding under the makespan and the sum of costs objectives. In: Symposium on Combinatorial Search (SoCS) (2016)

44. Thorup, M.: Randomized sorting in O(n log log n) time and linear space using addition, shift, and bit-wise boolean operations. J. Algorithms **42**(2), 205–230 (2002)

45. Wender, S., Watson, I.: Combining case-based reasoning and reinforcement learning for unit navigation in real-time strategy game AI. In: Lamontagne, L., Plaza, E. (eds.) ICCBR 2014. LNCS (LNAI), vol. 8765, pp. 511–525. Springer, Cham (2014). https://doi.org/10.1007/978-3-319-11209-1_36

46. de Wilde, B., ter Mors, A., Witteveen, C.: Push and rotate: a complete multi-agent pathfinding algorithm. JAIR **51**, 443–492 (2014)

47. Wilson, R.M.: Graph puzzles, homotopy, and the alternating group. J. Comb. Theory Ser. B **16**(1), 86–96 (1974)

48. Yamanaka, K., et al.: Sequentially swapping colored tokens on graphs. In: Poon, S.-H., Rahman, M.S., Yen, H.-C. (eds.) WALCOM 2017. LNCS, vol. 10167, pp. 435–447. Springer, Cham (2017). https://doi.org/10.1007/978-3-319-53925-6_34

49. Yamanaka, K., et al.: Swapping labeled tokens on graphs. In: Ferro, A., Luccio, F., Widmayer, P. (eds.) FUN 2014 Proceedings. LNCS, vol. 8496, pp. 364–375. Springer, Heidelberg (2014)

50. Yamanaka, K., et al.: Swapping labeled tokens on graphs. Theor. Comput. Sci. **586**, 81–94 (2015)

51. Yamanaka, K., et al.: Computational complexity of colored token swapping problem. In: IPSJ SIG Technical Report, vol. 156 (2016)

52. Yershova, A., LaValle, S.M.: Improving motion-planning algorithms by efficient nearest-neighbor searching. IEEE Trans. Robot. **23**(1), 151–157 (2007)

53. Yu, J., LaValle, S.M.: Planning optimal paths for multiple robots on graphs. ICRA **2013**, 3612–3617 (2013)

54. Yu, J., LaValle, S.M.: Optimal multi-robot path planning on graphs: structure and computational complexity. CoRR abs/1507.03289 (2015)

55. Yu, J., LaValle, S.M.: Optimal multirobot path planning on graphs: complete algorithms and effective heuristics. IEEE Trans. Robot. **32**(5), 1163–1177 (2016)

56. Yu, J., Rus, D.: Pebble motion on graphs with rotations: efficient feasibility tests and planning algorithms. In: Eleventh Workshop on the Algorithmic Foundations of Robotics (2014)

57. Zhou, D., Schwager, M.: Virtual rigid bodies for coordinated agile maneuvering of teams of micro aerial vehicles. ICRA **2015**, 1737–1742 (2015)

Dynamics of Narrow-Minded Belief and Its Cut-Free Sequent Calculus

Shoshin Nomura[1(✉)], Norihiro Arai[2], and Satoshi Tojo[2]

[1] National Institute of Informatics, Tokyo, Japan
nomura@nii.ac.jp
[2] Japan Advanced Institute of Science and Technology, Ishikawa, Japan
tojo@jaist.ac.jp

Abstract. The purpose of this paper is to consider and formalize an important factor of human intelligence, belief affected by passion, which we call narrow-minded belief. Based on Public Announcement Logic, we define our logic, Logic Of Narrow-minded belief (LON), as that which includes such belief. Semantics for LON is provided by the Kripke-style semantics, and using this semantics, we formally analyze the mental state of the hero of Shakespeare's tragedy *Othello* as an example of narrow-minded belief and its formalization. A proof system for it is given by a Hilbert-style proof system. In addition to that, we provide a complete labelled sequent calculus for LON based on the Hilbert-style proof system, and it syntactic cut elimination theorem is shown.

Keywords: Dynamic epistemic logic · Labelled sequent calculus · Doxastic logic · Othello

1 Introduction

Love is blind, and hatred is also blind. To generalize these phrases, we may say that passion causes narrow-mindedness. It is not unusual that people cannot emotionally stop believing what they do not want to believe without any specific reason to believe so. The hero of William Shakespeare's play, *Othello*, is involved in a pitiful but possible situation where he wants to believe his wife's chastity but he cannot since he heard a bad rumor about her. It may be difficult to answer whether or not he believes that his wife is a betrayer of their marriage given that he has heard this rumor. In this situation, Othello has at least two different types of belief and/or knowledge. One is *passionate* or *narrow-minded belief*, which he is willing to believe or cannot stop believing emotionally. The other is belief, which is more rational (less passionate) or, without considering any philosophical discussions regarding the relationship between knowledge and belief, it may even be said, is *knowledge* whereby he judges something based on information attained via rational inferences. The latter type of knowledge or belief is treated by a standard epistemic (or doxastic) logic and the current

© Springer Nature Switzerland AG 2019
J. van den Herik et al. (Eds.): ICAART 2019, LNAI 11978, pp. 143–165, 2019.
https://doi.org/10.1007/978-3-030-37494-5_8

researchers would like to introduce the former belief, passionate belief or narrow-minded belief.

In fact, the notion of passion has a philosophically and psychologically profound meaning in terms of belief, and it is highly possible that such emotional belief plays a significant role in rationality. In *A Treatise of Human Nature*, Hume famously (or even notoriously) wrote the following quotation.

> [T]he principle, which opposes our passion, cannot be the same with reason, and is only called so in an improper sense. We speak not strictly and philosophically when we talk of the combat of passion and of reason. Reason is, and ought only to be the slave of the passions [...]. [13, Book II, Sec. 3, Part 3].

Here, Hume says not only that passion has the same significance as rationality, but also that reason is a subordinate of passion. We introduce one more quotation from modern literature, Damasio's *Descartes' error*, to support the importance of consideration on the relationship between passion and rationality.

> [T]here may be a connecting trail, in anatomical and functional terms, from reason to feelings to body. It is as if we are possessed by a passion for reason [...]. Reason, from the practical to the theoretical, is probably constructed on this inherent drive by a process which resembles the mastering of a skill or craft. Remove the drive, and you will not acquire the mastery. But having the drive does not automatically make you a master. [7, Part III, Chap. 11].

By referring neurological evidence, Damasio argues that feeling (or passion) and rationality are strongly connected with other, and they cannot be separated as Descartes thought. The current researchers would like to take a similar stance to that of Damasio, where passion and rationality (in our term, narrow-minded belief and knowledge) are related to one another in a formal language of epistemic logic.

In this paper, we treat such a paradigm of agent communication that each agent changes his/her belief, after receiving messages from others, to strengthen/weaken his/her tolerance. Towards this motivation, we present a logic that adequately reflects human minds which tends to be biased by certain kinds of information. Additionally, we define a sequent calculus for a logic of narrow-minded belief and show its syntactic cut-elimination theorem.

The outline of the paper is as follows. In Sect. 2, we introduce logic of narrow-minded belief (LON) which is based on Public Announcement Logic by Plaza [19] and refers to the ideas of explicit and implicit belief in dynamic epistemic awareness logic by van Benthem and Velázquez-Quesada [6]. Its semantics are given by an expansion of the Kripke-style semantics. In Sect. 3, we attempt to investigate and formalize a person's belief and emotion through focusing on a literary work, *Othello* since this is a story of delicate transition of the hero's narrow-minded belief towards his wife. In Sect. 4, we introduce a Hilbert-style proof system H_{LON} of LON, and show some proof theoretic properties, and its completeness theorem. (Theorem 3) through the innermost strategy for reducing a formula for

LON into a formula without announcement operators. In Sect. 5, we introduce our labelled sequent system for LON and its cut-elimination theorem by a syntactic procedure (Theorem 5). In Sect. 6, we introduce related epistemic/doxastic logics to the present work.

We also note that this paper is an extended version of our conference paper [16]. To be specified, main points of modification are adding Sect. 5 of a labelled sequent calculus, and modifying LON from single-agent to multi-agent framework.

2 Language and Semantics of LON

2.1 Language

First of all, we address the syntax of LON. Let $\mathbb{P} = \{p, q, \ldots\}$ be a non-empty set of atomic propositions and $\mathbb{A} = \{a, b, \ldots\}$ be a countable set of agents. Then, formula φ of the language $\mathcal{L}_{(\mathsf{K}_a \mathsf{N}_a \sharp b!)}$ is inductively defined as follows ($p \in \mathbb{P}, a \in \mathbb{A}$):

$$\varphi ::= p \mid \neg\varphi \mid (\varphi \to \varphi) \mid \mathsf{K}_a\varphi \mid \mathsf{N}_a\varphi \mid [\sharp\varphi]\varphi \mid [\flat\varphi]\varphi \mid [!\varphi]\varphi.$$

We define other Boolean connectives such as $\varphi \wedge \chi$, $\varphi \vee \chi$, $\varphi \leftrightarrow \chi$ and $\bot$ in a usual manner. We call operators $[\flat\varphi]$, $[\sharp\varphi]$ and $[!\varphi]$ *announcement operators*. Besides, $\widehat{\mathsf{K}}_a$ is defined by $\neg\mathsf{K}_a\neg$ and $\widehat{\mathsf{N}}_a$ is defined by $\neg\mathsf{N}_a\neg$. Note that K_a and N_a can be considered as the box operator $\Box$ in modal logic, and $\widehat{\mathsf{K}}_a$ and $\widehat{\mathsf{N}}_a$ can be considered as the diamond operator $\Diamond$.

- $\mathsf{K}_a\varphi$ reads 'the agent a knows that φ',
- $\mathsf{N}_a\varphi$ reads 'the agent a narrow-mindedly believes that φ',
- $[\sharp\varphi]\chi$ reads 'after obtaining information φ which may *strengthen* the agent's narrow-mindedness, χ holds',
- $[\flat\varphi]\chi$ reads 'after obtaining information φ which may *weaken* the agent's narrow-mindedness, χ holds,' and
- $[!\varphi]\chi$ reads 'after obtaining truthful information (announcement) φ, χ holds'.

2.2 Semantics of LON

We call the tuple $(S, (\mathcal{R}_a)_{a \in \mathbb{A}}, V)$ an *epistemic model* if the domain S is a nonempty countable set of states, each accessibility relation $\mathcal{R}_a$ in the list $(\mathcal{R}_a)_{a \in \mathbb{A}}$ is an equivalence relation on S and $V : \mathbb{P} \to \mathcal{P}(S)$ is a valuation function. The set S is called domain of $\mathcal{M}$ and may be denoted by $\mathcal{D}(\mathcal{M})$. Subsequently, we define an *epistemic narrow-doxastic model* (or simply *en-model*) $\mathcal{M} = (S, (\mathcal{R}_a)_{a \in \mathbb{A}}, (\mathcal{Q}_a)_{a \in \mathbb{A}}, V)$ where the components of S, $\mathcal{R}_a$ and V are the same as that of the epistemic model, and each $\mathcal{Q}_a$ is a binary relation on S such that $\mathcal{Q}_a \subseteq \mathcal{R}_a$ ($a \in \mathbb{A}$). Intuitively, $\mathcal{R}_a$ is a relation of all possibilities that an agent can imagine. In other words, the agent never imagine a state x from s if $(s, x) \notin \mathcal{R}_a$. This is why $\mathcal{Q}_a \subseteq \mathcal{R}_a$; narrow-minded condition does not allow an agent to imagine possibilities which exceeds the agent's knowledge states.

Definition 1 (Satisfaction Relation). *Given an en-model $\mathcal{M}$, a state $s \in \mathcal{D}(\mathcal{M})$, and a formula $\varphi \in \mathcal{L}_{(K_a N_a \sharp b!)}$, we inductively define the satisfaction relation $\mathcal{M}, s \models \varphi$ as follows:*

$$
\begin{aligned}
\mathcal{M}, s &\models p & &\text{iff } s \in V(p), \\
\mathcal{M}, s &\models \neg\varphi & &\text{iff } \mathcal{M}, s \not\models \varphi, \\
\mathcal{M}, s &\models \varphi \to \chi & &\text{iff } \mathcal{M}, s \models \varphi \text{ implies } \mathcal{M}, s \models \chi, \\
\mathcal{M}, s &\models K_a\varphi & &\text{iff for all } x \in S : s\mathcal{R}_a x \text{ implies } \mathcal{M}, x \models \varphi, \\
\mathcal{M}, s &\models N_a\varphi & &\text{iff for all } x \in S : s\mathcal{Q}_a x \text{ implies } \mathcal{M}, x \models \varphi, \\
\mathcal{M}, s &\models [\sharp\varphi]\chi & &\text{iff } \mathcal{M}^{\sharp\varphi}, s \models \chi, \\
\mathcal{M}, s &\models [b\varphi]\chi & &\text{iff } \mathcal{M}^{b\varphi}, s \models \chi, \\
\mathcal{M}, s &\models [!\varphi]\chi & &\text{iff } \mathcal{M}, s \models \varphi \text{ implies } \mathcal{M}^{!\varphi}, s \models \chi,
\end{aligned}
$$

where the notations $\mathcal{M}^{\sharp\varphi}$, $\mathcal{M}^{b\varphi}$ and $\mathcal{M}^{!\varphi}$ above respectively indicate the en-models defined by $\mathcal{M}^{\sharp\varphi} = (S, (\mathcal{R}_a)_{a\in\mathbb{A}}, (\mathcal{Q}_a^{\sharp\varphi})_{a\in\mathbb{A}}, V)$, $\mathcal{M}^{b\varphi} = (S, (\mathcal{R}_a)_{a\in\mathbb{A}}, (\mathcal{Q}_a^{b\varphi})_{a\in\mathbb{A}}, V)$ and $\mathcal{M}^{!\varphi} = (\llbracket\varphi\rrbracket_\mathcal{M}, (\mathcal{R}_a^{!\varphi})_{a\in\mathbb{A}}, (\mathcal{Q}_a^{!\varphi})_{a\in\mathbb{A}}, V^{!\varphi})$ with

$$
\begin{aligned}
\llbracket\varphi\rrbracket_\mathcal{M} &:= \{x \in S \mid \mathcal{M}, x \models \varphi\} & \mathcal{Q}_a^{\sharp\varphi} &:= \mathcal{Q}_a \cup \{(s,t) \in \mathcal{R}_a \mid t \in \llbracket\varphi\rrbracket_\mathcal{M}\} \\
\mathcal{R}_a^{!\varphi} &:= \mathcal{R}_a \cap \llbracket\varphi\rrbracket_\mathcal{M} \times \llbracket\varphi\rrbracket_\mathcal{M} & \mathcal{Q}_a^{!\varphi} &:= \mathcal{Q}_a \cap \llbracket\varphi\rrbracket_\mathcal{M} \times \llbracket\varphi\rrbracket_\mathcal{M} \\
V^{!\varphi}(p) &:= V \cap \llbracket\varphi\rrbracket_\mathcal{M} & \mathcal{Q}_a^{b\varphi} &:= \mathcal{Q}_a \cap S \times \llbracket\varphi\rrbracket_\mathcal{M}
\end{aligned}
$$

where $p \in \mathbb{P}$ and $a \in \mathbb{A}$.

The intuitive meaning of dynamic operators are as follows: the *strengthening* operator $[\sharp]$ makes the agent come to notice states which are put out of the agent's mind; the *weakening* operator $[b]$ makes the agent to refuse to face some states (at the unconscious level); and the *truthful* operator $[!]$ correct the agent's knowledge (a well-known operator in DEL). It should be noted that we do not think of a mechanism which guides the selection of an announcement operator, according to which a transition of person's mental states would be triggered. As a practical matter, it is beyond a person's character and standings, and thus this should be defined outer framework which utilize this logic.

Now, we define the validity of a formula in a usual way.

Definition 2 (Validity). *A formula φ is valid at $\mathcal{M}$ if $\mathcal{M}, s \models \varphi$ for any $s \in \mathcal{D}(\mathcal{M})$, and we write $\mathcal{M} \models \varphi$. A formula φ is valid if $\mathcal{M} \models \varphi$, for any en-model $\mathcal{M}$, and we write $\models \varphi$.*

We confirm that an en-model, which is modified by announcement operators $[b\varphi]$, $[\sharp\varphi]$ and $[!\varphi]$, preserves frame properties, i.e., $\mathcal{R}_a$ is an equivalence relation and the subset relation $\mathcal{Q}_a \subseteq \mathcal{R}_a$.

Proposition 1 (Preserving Frame Properties). *Let $\varphi \in \mathcal{L}_{(K_a N_a \sharp b!)}$ be any formula. If $\mathcal{M} = (S, (\mathcal{R}_a)_{a\in\mathbb{A}}, (\mathcal{Q}_a)_{a\in\mathbb{A}}, V)$ is an en-model, then $\mathcal{M}^{\sharp\varphi} = (S, (\mathcal{R}_a)_{a\in\mathbb{A}}, (\mathcal{Q}_a^{\sharp\varphi})_{a\in\mathbb{A}}, V)$, $\mathcal{M}^{b\varphi} = (S, (\mathcal{R}_a)_{a\in\mathbb{A}}, (\mathcal{Q}_a^{b\varphi})_{a\in\mathbb{A}}, V)$ and $\mathcal{M}^{!\varphi} = (\llbracket\varphi\rrbracket_\mathcal{M}, (\mathcal{R}_a^{!\varphi})_{a\in\mathbb{A}}, (\mathcal{Q}_a^{!\varphi})_{a\in\mathbb{A}}, V^{!\varphi})$ are also en-models.*

Proof. Consider an arbitrary agent $a \in \mathbb{A}$. What we wish to show is that (1) $\mathcal{R}_a^{!\varphi}$ is an equivalence relation (i.e., it satisfies reflexivity, Euclidicity), and (2) the subset relation $\mathcal{Q}_a^{!\varphi} \subseteq \mathcal{R}_a^{!\varphi}$, (3) the subset relation $\mathcal{Q}_a^{\sharp\varphi} \subseteq \mathcal{R}_a$ and (4) the subset relation $\mathcal{Q}_a^{b\varphi} \subseteq \mathcal{R}_a$. We only treat one of (1) in the following.

(1)-2 $\mathcal{R}_a^{!\varphi}$ satisfies Euclidicity. Fix any $x, y, z \in [\![\varphi]\!]_{\mathcal{M}}$. Suppose $x \mathcal{R}_a^{!\varphi} y$ and $x \mathcal{R}_a^{!\varphi} z$, and show $y \mathcal{R}_a^{!\varphi} z$. Since $\mathcal{R}_a$ is Euclidean i.e., $x \mathcal{R}_a y$ and $x \mathcal{R}_a z$ jointly imply $y \mathcal{R}_a z$ for all $x, y, z \in S$. By the assumption $x, y, z \in [\![\varphi]\!]_{\mathcal{M}} \subseteq S$, we have $x, y, z \in S$ and $y \mathcal{R}_a z$. So we get the goal $\mathcal{R}_a^{!\varphi}$ is also Euclidean with $y, z \in X$.

□

3 Examples of Formalization of Narrow-Minded Belief

3.1 Comments on Knowledge and Narrow-Minded Belief Operators

Before moving on the topic of narrow-minded belief, we add some comments on the general features of knowledge operator K_a and accessibility relation $\mathcal{R}_a$ in epistemic logics. Let $\mathbb{A} = \{a\}$ us look at the epistemic model $(S, \mathcal{R}_a, V) = (\{w, v\}, S^2, V)$ where $V(p) = \{v\}$ (that can be regarded as an en-model $\mathcal{M} = (\{w, v\}, S^2, \varnothing, V))$, and the graphic form of this model is as follows.

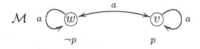

In this model, at world w, the agent is ignorant about p's truth-value. This is because the formula $\widehat{\mathsf{K}}_a p \wedge \widehat{\mathsf{K}}_a \neg p$, which intuitively means that the agent does not know whether p, is true at w. As it implies, in epistemic logic, an arrow between states has a negative meaning in general. In other words, van Ditmarsch et al. state that "the more worlds an agent considers possible, the less he believes, and vice versa." [10, p. 55]. The operator $\widehat{\mathsf{K}}_a$ represents at least one arrow in an epistemic model. The narrow-minded belief operator $\widehat{\mathsf{N}}_a$ basically preserves these features; nevertheless, we cannot say that 'the more worlds an agent considers possible, the less he believes, and vice versa' in case of the operator N_a since the narrow-mind belief is affected by uncertain information or even the agent's imagination and may be wrong. In other words, to express such capricious belief, we introduce the operator N_a.

Additionally, we note on the frame property of $\mathcal{R}_a$ and $\mathcal{Q}_a$. The accessibility relation $\mathcal{R}_a$ represents the accessibility relation for knowledge, and so we assume that the agent is an introspective agent, i.e., $\mathcal{R}_a$ is an equivalence relation. Moreover, the formulas of $\mathsf{K}_a\varphi \to \varphi$, $\mathsf{K}_a\varphi \to \mathsf{K}_a\mathsf{K}_a\varphi$ (positive introspection) and $\neg\mathsf{K}_a\varphi \to \mathsf{K}_a\neg\mathsf{K}_a\varphi$ (negative introspection) are valid at $\mathcal{M}$ where its accessibility relation is equivalence relation. However, since $\mathcal{Q}_a$ represents a narrow-minded belief, we do not assume the agent is introspective since introspectiveness is based on some kind of rationality, which is the exact opposite of narrow-mindedness. That is why $\mathcal{Q}_a$ does not have any frame property. By distinguishing these two accessibility relations, we formally express the distinction between knowledge and narrow-minded belief.

3.2   Formalizing Othello's Narrow-Minded Belief

As mentioned in the introduction, our target, which we consider and formalize, is Shakespeare's *Othello* as it depicts a typical case of the change in a person's delicate mental state. Its story depicts how the lives of the four main characters (Othello, Desdemona, Iago and Cassio) are woven together and driven by passion. The following is the short summary of the play:

> General in the Venetian military Othello was recently married to a rich senator's daughter Desdemona. Although there is a great disparity of age between the two, they build a good relationship of trust, and Othello and Desdemona love and believe each other from their hearts. However, Othello's trusted subordinate Iago who secretly holds a deep grudge against Othello tells him a rumor that Desdemona is having an affair with a young handsome soldier named Cassio. This causes Othello to feel uncertain towards his wife's innocence. Deepening Othello's doubt against his wife, Iago steals Desdemona's handkerchief, a present from Othello, and leads Cassio up to find it. Using the handkerchief as proof, Iago succeeds in convincing Othello that Desdemona has engaged in an immoral relationship with Cassio. Finally, Othello narrow-mindedly believes what Iago has told him and he feels great jealousy and anger towards his wife. Even though Desdemona protests her innocence, Othello, who is now mad with jealousy, kills his wife in a fit of passion. Following her death, Desdemona's servant confesses that her mistress was innocent and that Iago fabricated the story, which resulted in such a tragedy. Othello comes to his senses and realizes his mistake, at which point he loses hope and takes his own life.

Of course, this summary is extremely simplified and actual tale is more intricately woven. There are at least four main scenes in the story, which highlight Othello's narrow-minded belief, and we would like to focus on these in this paper. The four main points are as follows:

1. Othello believes Desdemona from the heart.
2. Iago spreads a bad rumor about Desdemona, which causes doubt about her innocence in Othello's mind.
3. Iago uses fake evidence (a handkerchief) to convince Othello of Desdemona's immoral actions and he narrow-mindedly believes it.
4. A servant truthfully informs Othello that Desdemona is innocent.

Othello's mind, including narrow-minded belief in each of the four scenes, may be semantically modeled as follows. We note that, in the graphic form of en-models, the double circle indicates the actual state. In addition, arrows of the straight line represent the line of $\mathcal{R}_a$ and arrows of the dotted line represent that of $\mathcal{Q}_a$. Moreover, let an atomic proposition p to read 'Desdemona is having an affair,' and $\mathbb{P} = \{p\}$, and let $\mathbb{A}$ be the singleton set $\{a\}$ and a represents Othello (Fig. 1).

$\neg p$ p

Fig. 1. $\mathcal{M}$.

(1) Othello Deeply Believes His Wife. In the initial stage, Othello, who was recently married, believes his wife from the depth of his heart and does not doubt her immorality. However, Othello does not have any specific evidence that Desdemona is having an affair and he does not actually know if she is innocent or not at this stage. Therefore, the initial stage already includes some contradiction in his mind, i.e., he does not explicitly know if she is innocent, but he narrow-mindedly believes her. Thus, the mental state of Othello at the opening of the play may formally be expressed by en-model $\mathcal{M} = (S, \mathcal{R}_a, \mathcal{Q}_a, V) = (\{s, t\}, S^2, \{(t, s), (s, s)\}, \{p \mapsto \{t\}\})$. Therefore, we may say that, at this stage, formulas $\widehat{\mathsf{K}}_a p \wedge \widehat{\mathsf{K}}_a \neg p$ and $\mathsf{N}_a \neg p$ are valid at $\mathcal{M}$ (Fig. 2).

$\neg p$ p

Fig. 2. $\mathcal{M}^{\sharp p}$.

(2) Iago Spreads a Bad Rumor about Desdemona, Which Leads to Doubts in Othello's Mind. After Iago tells Othello a bad rumor ($[\sharp p]$) about Desdemona, he begins to doubt his wife. In other words, he is now unsure about her constancy and does not know if she is innocent or not. Separately from Othello's narrow-minded belief, his state of knowledge remains unchanged since he has not obtained any new truthful information and can only go by Iago's story in which his wife is accused of infidelity. Then the mental state of Othello at the second stage of the play may formally be expressed by en-model $\mathcal{M}^{\sharp p} = (S, \mathcal{R}_a, \mathcal{Q}_a^{\sharp p}, V) = (\{s, t\}, S^2, S^2, \{p \mapsto \{t\}\})$, where the formula $\widehat{\mathsf{N}}_a p \wedge \widehat{\mathsf{N}}_a \neg p$ is now valid at this en-model. This formula represents a confusion in his mind about his wife's innocence (Fig. 3).

Fig. 3. $\mathcal{M}^{\sharp p \flat p}$.

(3) Iago uses Fake Evidence to Convince Othello of Desdemona's Immorality. At this stage of the play, Iago attempts to deceive his superior, Othello, by using fake evidence (Desdemona's handkerchief) to pretend she spent her time with Cassio, and Othello is completely taken in. Consequently, Othello completely loses his self-control, and strongly and narrow-mindedly believes that his wife is having an affair with Cassio. This is also represented by en-model $\mathcal{M}^{\sharp p \flat p} = (S, \mathcal{R}_a, \mathcal{Q}_a^{\sharp p \flat p}, V) = (\{s, t\}, S^2, \{(t, t), (s, t)\}, \{p \mapsto \{t\}\})$. Formally, in his mind, the formula $\widehat{\mathsf{N}}_a p$ is valid at this en-model, but $\widehat{\mathsf{N}}_a \neg p$ is not anymore. Let us remind the reader that in the case of the operator $\widehat{\mathsf{N}}_a$, it does *not* mean that if the number of arrows is reduced, then the agent's ignorance is reduced (Fig. 4).

Fig. 4. $\mathcal{M}^{\sharp p \flat p! \neg p}$.

(4) A Servant Truthfully Informs that Desdemona is Innocent. In the last scene of the play, Desdemona's faithful servant truthfully tells the fact that Desdemona is innocent, implying that Othello's narrow-minded belief regarding his wife is completely erroneous. Othello faces such a surprising fact and he is heart-broken by the confession. This is represented by en-model $\mathcal{M}^{\sharp p \flat p! \neg p} = ([\![\neg p]\!]_{\mathcal{M}^{\sharp p \flat p}}, \mathcal{R}_a^{!\neg p}, \mathcal{Q}_a^{\sharp p \flat p! \neg p}, V^{!\neg p}) = (\{s\}, \{(s, s)\}, \varnothing, \varnothing\})$. Formally, by the truthful information of $\neg p$, a state t where p holds is eliminated, and as a result, while the agent (Othello) knows $\neg p$ (his wife is innocent), the arrow of narrow-minded belief is empty. This means that he narrow-mindedly believes everything even if it is a contradiction $\mathcal{M}^{\sharp p \flat p! \neg p} \models \bot$, i.e., he is going crazy. As a result, the tragedy ends with the suicide of Othello in the final scene.

4   Hilbert-System for LON

We move on the topic of a proof theory for LON. Hilbert-system for LON ($\mathsf{H}_{\mathrm{LON}}$), is defined in Table 1. In (RE) of the rule, the substitution for formula $\varphi(\frac{\psi}{\chi})$ means ψ appearing in a formula φ is replaced by χ. Axioms (4) and (5) indicate what we call positive introspection and negative introspection, respectively. Axiom $(\mathsf{K}_a \& \mathsf{N}_a)$ indicates a relation of knowledge and narrow-mined belief, in which if the agent knows something, he/she also narrow-mindedly believes. This implies that narrow-minded belief is one of the bases of our knowledge, and this view of belief and knowledge can be supported by philosophers and/or psychologists like Hume and Damasio, as discussed in the introduction. Axioms $(RA*)$ are called *reduction axioms*. Through the reduction axioms and rules, each theorem of H_{LON} may be reduced into a theorem of the language $\mathcal{L}_{(K_a N_a)}$ which will be shown in Sect. 4.1.

Table 1. Hilbert-system for LON : H_{LON}.

Axioms for K_a and N_a		**Reduction Axioms for [!]**
(taut)	all instantiations of	$(RA!1)$ $[!\psi]p \leftrightarrow (\psi \to p)$
	propositional tautologies	$(RA!2)$ $[!\psi]\neg\varphi \leftrightarrow (\psi \to \neg[!\psi]\varphi)$
(K_{K_a})	$K_a(\varphi \to \chi) \to (K_a\varphi \to K_a\chi)$	$(RA!3)$ $[!\psi](\varphi \to \chi) \leftrightarrow ([!\psi]\varphi \to [!\psi]\chi)$
(K_{N_a})	$N_a(\varphi \to \chi) \to (N_a\varphi \to N_a\chi)$	$(RA!4)$ $[!\psi]K_a\varphi \leftrightarrow (\psi \to K_a[!\psi]\varphi)$
(T)	$K_a\varphi \to \varphi$	$(RA!5)$ $[!\psi]N_a\varphi \leftrightarrow (\psi \to N_a[!\psi]\varphi)$
(5)	$\neg K_a\varphi \to K_a\neg K_a\varphi$	
$(K_a \& N_a)$	$K_a\varphi \to N_a\varphi$	**Reduction Axioms for $[\flat]$**
		$(RA\flat1)$ $[\flat\psi]p \leftrightarrow p$
Inference Rules		$(RA\flat2)$ $[\flat\psi]\neg\varphi \leftrightarrow \neg[\flat\psi]\varphi$
(MP)	*From φ and $\varphi \to \chi$, infer χ*	$(RA\flat3)$ $[\flat\psi](\varphi \to \chi) \leftrightarrow ([\flat\psi]\varphi \to [\flat\psi]\chi)$
$(NecK_a)$	*From φ, infer $K_a\varphi$*	$(RA\flat4)$ $[\flat\psi]K_a\varphi \leftrightarrow K_a[\flat\psi]\varphi$
$(NecN_a)$	*From φ, infer $N_a\varphi$*	$(RA\flat5)$ $[\flat\psi]N_a\varphi \leftrightarrow N_a(\psi \to [\flat\psi]\varphi)$
$(Nec[*])$	*From φ, infer $[*\chi]\varphi$*	
	where $* \in \{\sharp, \flat, !\}$	**Reduction Axioms for $[\sharp]$**
(RE)	*From $\varphi \leftrightarrow \chi$,*	$(RA\sharp1)$ $[\sharp\psi]p \leftrightarrow p$
	infer $\psi \leftrightarrow \psi\binom{\varphi}{\chi}$	$(RA\sharp2)$ $[\sharp\psi]\neg\varphi \leftrightarrow \neg[\sharp\psi]\varphi$
		$(RA\sharp3)$ $[\sharp\psi](\varphi \to \chi) \leftrightarrow ([\sharp\psi]\varphi \to [\sharp\psi]\chi)$
		$(RA\sharp4)$ $[\sharp\psi]K_a\varphi \leftrightarrow K_a[\sharp\psi]\varphi$
		$(RA\sharp5)$ $[\sharp\psi]N_a\varphi \leftrightarrow N_a[\sharp\psi]\varphi \wedge K_a(\psi \to [\sharp\psi]\varphi)$

We provide some basic definitions and properties for proofs in the next section.

Definition 3 (Derivable).
A derivation in H_{LON} consists of a sequence of formulas of $\mathcal{L}_{(K_a N_a \sharp\flat!)}$ each of which is an instance of an axiom or is the result of applying an inference rule to formula(s) that occur earlier. If φ is the last formula in a derivation in H_{LON}, then φ is derivable in H_{LON}, and we write $\vdash_{H_{LON}} \varphi$.

4.1   Completeness of H'_{LON}

Let us move onto a proof of the completeness theorem of H_{LON} with a similar argument in [10, Section 5].

Let *the language* $\mathcal{L}_{(K_a N_a)}$ be our formal language $\mathcal{L}_{(K_a N_a \sharp\flat!)}$ without announcement operators ($[\sharp], [\flat]$ and $[!]$). For an en-model $\mathcal{M}$ and $s \in \mathcal{D}(\mathcal{M})$ and $\varphi \in \mathcal{L}_{(K_a N_a)}$, the satisfaction relation $\mathcal{M}, s \models \varphi$ is naturally defined by following the definition in Sect. 2. Additionally, *Hilbert-system* H'_{LON} is also generated by removing the reduction axioms and inference rules of $(Nec[\sharp])$, $(Nec\flat)$ and $(Nec[!])$ in Table 1. Note that definitions of the derivation and derivability of H'_{LON} are given in the same manner as that of H_{LON} in Definition 3.

Theorem 1 (Soundness and Completeness of H'_{LON}). *For any formula* $\varphi \in \mathcal{L}_{(K_aN_a)}$,

$$\vdash_{H'_{LON}} \varphi \text{ if and only if } \models \varphi.$$

Proof. **only-if-part (Soundness).** Fix any $\varphi \in \mathcal{L}_{(K_aN_a)}$ such that φ is derivable in H'_{LON}. We show that φ is valid by induction on the height of the derivation. In the base case, the derivation height is 0 i.e., it consists of only an axiom. Therefore, we show the validity of each axiom of H_{LON}. We only confirm the following case.

   Case of $(K_a\&N_a)$**.** We show that $\models K_a\varphi \rightarrow N_a\varphi$. Fix any en-model $\mathcal{M} = (S, (\mathcal{R}_a)_{a\in\mathbb{A}}, (\mathcal{Q}_a)_{a\in\mathbb{A}}, V)$ and $s \in S$, and suppose $\mathcal{M}, s \models K_a\varphi$. What we show is $\mathcal{M}, s \models N_a\varphi$ i.e., for all $t \in S, s\mathcal{Q}_a t$ implies $\mathcal{M}, t \models \varphi$. So that, fix any $t \in S$ such that $s\mathcal{Q}_a t$ and show $\mathcal{M}, t \models \varphi$. Since $\mathcal{Q}_a \subseteq \mathcal{R}_a$, we obtain $s\mathcal{R}_a t$. Therefore, together with $\mathcal{M}, s \models K_a\varphi$, we obtain the goal as desired.

if-part (Completeness). A direct proof of the completeness theorem of H'_{LON} can be shown in a usual manner with Lindenbaum's lemma.

$\square$

4.2   Completeness of H_{LON}

Based on the completeness theorem of H'_{LON}, we expand the discussion to the completeness of H_{LON}. A proof of the completeness theorem of H_{LON} is given in this section by the reduction method whose basic idea was introduced in the previous work [19, Theorem 2.7]. The essential idea of this method is based on the fact that every formula in $\mathcal{L}_{(K_aN_a\sharp\flat!)}$ is reducible into a formula in $\mathcal{L}_{(K_aN_a)}$ which will be shown in Lemma 2.

Remark 1. We note that reduction axioms for sequential announcement operators e.g.,

$$(RA!6) \quad [!\chi][!\psi]\varphi \leftrightarrow [!(\chi \wedge [!\chi]\psi)]\varphi$$

are not included since, without them, any formula with announcement operators can be reducible. It is known that there are at least two strategies to reduce a formula with announcement operators into a formula without any such operator. Let us consider the formula $[!p][!q]r - (i)$. One approach, we may call it 'outermost strategy', focuses on the outermost occurrence of announcement operator, for example $[!p]$ of the above formula (i). Following this strategy, an axiom like $(RA!6)$ is required for reducing the formula. By using $(RA!6)$, we may obtain $[!(p \wedge [!p]q)]r$. Then $(RA!1)$ becomes applicable, and so we obtain the formula which does not include any announcement operator but is equivalent to the initial formula. This approach is introduced by [10]. The other strategy may be called 'innermost strategy' and focuses on the innermost occurrence of announcement operator, for example $[!q]$ of (i). Thus, by applying $(RA!1)$ to the innermost occurrence i.e., $[!q]r$, we obtain $[!p](q \rightarrow r)$. After that, $(RA!3)$ and $(RA!1)$ are subsequently applicable, and so we obtain the formula without any announcement operator but equivalent to the initial formula of (i). The latter strategy does not require reduction axioms for reducing sequential announcement operators into a single. Therefore, we employ this strategy to avoid introducing many and messy axioms.[1] The idea of this innermost strategy was introduced by [5], and [4, p. 54]. Furthermore, an attentive proof for reducibility of a formula of Dynamic logic into a formula of standard modal logic by using the innermost strategy is given in [2, Proposition 3.3.5].[2]

At first, we treat the soundness theorem of it.

Theorem 2 (Soundness of H_{LON}). *For any formula $\varphi \in \mathcal{L}_{(K_a N_a \sharp \flat !)}$,*

$$\vdash_{H_{LON}} \varphi \text{ implies } \models \varphi.$$

Proof. We prove the soundness theorem of H_{LON} by induction on the height of the derivation of H_{LON}, and it suffices to show the validity of reduction axioms of H'_{LON} and additional inference rules $(Nec[\sharp]), (Nec[\flat])$ and $(Nec[!])$. The validity of additional rules and axioms are also easily shown by following semantics of H_{LON}. We confirm the base cases of $(RA\sharp 5)$ and $(RA\flat 5)$.

Case of $(RA\sharp 5)$. We show that $\models [\sharp\psi]N_a\varphi \leftrightarrow N_a[\sharp\psi]\varphi \wedge K_a(\psi \rightarrow [\sharp\psi]\varphi)$. Therefore, fix any $\mathcal{M} = (S, (\mathcal{R}_a)_{a\in\mathbb{A}}, (\mathcal{Q}_a)_{a\in\mathbb{A}}, V)$ and $s \in S$. The following equivalent relation holds as below.

$$\mathcal{M}, s \models [\sharp\psi]N_a\varphi$$
$$\Longleftrightarrow \forall x \in S : sQ_a^{\sharp\psi}x \Longrightarrow \mathcal{M}, x \models [\sharp\psi]\varphi$$
$$\Longleftrightarrow \forall x \in S : sQ_a x \text{ or } (s\mathcal{R}_a x \text{ and } x \in \llbracket\psi\rrbracket_\mathcal{M}) \Longrightarrow \mathcal{M}, x \models [\sharp\psi]\varphi$$
$$\Longleftrightarrow \forall x \in S : (sQ_a x \Longrightarrow \mathcal{M}, x \models [\sharp\psi]\varphi)$$
$$\text{and } (s\mathcal{R}_a x \text{ and } x \in \llbracket\psi\rrbracket_\mathcal{M} \Longrightarrow \mathcal{M}, x \models [\sharp\psi]\varphi)$$
$$\Longleftrightarrow \mathcal{M}, s \models N_a[\sharp\psi]\varphi \wedge K_a(\psi \rightarrow [\sharp\psi]\varphi)$$

Case of $(RA\flat 5)$. We show that $\models [\flat\psi]N_a\varphi \leftrightarrow N_a(\psi \rightarrow [\flat\psi]\varphi)$. Therefore, fix any $\mathcal{M} = (S, (\mathcal{R}_a)_{a\in\mathbb{A}}, (\mathcal{Q}_a)_{a\in\mathbb{A}}, V)$ and $s \in S$. Then we show the the following equivalence relation.

---

[1] If we follow the outermost strategy, six additional axioms (e.g, axioms for reducing combination of $[\flat A][\sharp B]$ and $[!A][\flat B]$ etc.) are required.

[2] We add one more comment for a technical difference between the two strategies. In the outermost strategy of public announcement logic, we need to include axiom like $(RA!6)$ to reduce sequential announcement operators into a single, but the inference rule of $(Nec[!])$ is derivable. On the other hand, the rule is indispensable in the case of the innermost strategy, instead of economizing the number of axioms.

$$\mathcal{M}, s \models [\flat\psi]\mathsf{N}_a\varphi$$
$$\Longleftrightarrow \forall x \in S : (s, x) \in \mathcal{Q}_a \cap S \times [\![\psi]\!]_{\mathcal{M}} \Longrightarrow \mathcal{M}, x \models [\flat\psi]\varphi$$
$$\Longleftrightarrow \forall x \in S : ((s, x) \in \mathcal{Q}_a \text{ and } x \in [\![\psi]\!]_{\mathcal{M}}) \Longrightarrow \mathcal{M}, x \models [\flat\psi]\varphi$$
$$\Longleftrightarrow \mathcal{M}, s \models \mathsf{N}_a(\psi \to [\flat\psi]\varphi)$$

For induction steps, we require to show the additional cases of $(Nec[\sharp])$, $(Nec[\flat])$ and $(Nec[!])$ to Theorem 1.

Case Where the Last Applied Rule is $(Nec[\sharp])$. In this case, we obtain the part of derivation as follows.

$$\vdots$$
$$\frac{\vdash_{\text{H}_{\text{LON}}} \varphi}{\vdash_{\text{H}_{\text{LON}}} [\sharp\chi]\varphi} \ (Nec[\sharp])$$

And we show $[\sharp\chi]\varphi$ is valid. So, fix any $\mathcal{M}$ and $s \in \mathcal{D}(\mathcal{M})$. Then we show $\mathcal{M}^{\sharp\chi}, s \models \varphi$. Therefore, we have that φ is valid by induction hypothesis. Then, we obtain $\mathcal{M}^{\sharp\chi}, s \models \varphi$.

$\square$

Next, we give some definitions and lemmas for proof of the completeness.

Definition 4 (Length). *The length function* $\ell : \mathcal{L}_{(\mathsf{K}_a\mathsf{N}_a\sharp\flat!)} \to \mathbb{N}$ *is inductively defined as follows:*

$$\ell(p) := 1, \qquad\qquad\qquad \ell(\mathsf{N}_a\varphi) := 1 + \ell(\varphi),$$
$$\ell(\neg\varphi) := 1 + \ell(\varphi), \qquad\quad \ell([\flat\varphi]\chi) := (4 + \ell(\varphi))^{\ell(\chi)},$$
$$\ell(\varphi \to \chi) := 1 + \ell(\varphi) + \ell(\chi), \ \ell([\sharp\varphi]\chi) := (4 + \ell(\varphi))^{\ell(\chi)},$$
$$\ell(\mathsf{K}_a\varphi) := 1 + \ell(\varphi), \qquad\quad \ell([!\varphi]\chi) := (4 + \ell(\varphi))^{\ell(\chi)}.$$

With these settings, we may show the following lemma.

Lemma 1. *Let* $*$ *be* $\flat, \sharp$ *or* $!$. *Then for all reduction axioms* $[*\varphi]\chi \leftrightarrow \psi$, $\ell([*\varphi]\chi) > \ell(\psi)$ *holds.*

Proof. We only confirm the following case.

Case of $(RA\sharp5)$. The less-than relation $\ell(\mathsf{N}_a[\sharp\psi]\varphi \wedge \mathsf{K}_a(\psi \to [\sharp\psi]\varphi)) < \ell([\sharp\psi]\mathsf{N}_a\varphi)$ holds as follows. Let $k := 4 + \ell(\psi)$ (hence, $k \geq 5$) and $n := \ell(\varphi)$. So, by Definition 4, $\ell(\mathsf{N}_a[\sharp\psi]\varphi \wedge \mathsf{K}_a(\psi \to [\sharp\psi]\varphi)) = k + 2 \cdot k^n$ and $\ell([\sharp\psi]\mathsf{N}_a\varphi) = k^{1+n}$. Then, it obviously holds that if $k > 3$, then $k^{1+n} > k + 2 \cdot k^n$ for any fixed $n \geq 1$.

$\square$

Definition 5. $\ell' : \mathcal{L}_{(\mathsf{K}_a \mathsf{N}_a \sharp \flat !)} \to \mathbb{N}$ *is defined as follows.*

$$\ell'(\varphi) := \begin{cases} 0 & if \varphi \in \mathcal{L}_{(\mathsf{K}_a \mathsf{N}_a)} \\ \ell(\varphi) & otherwise \end{cases}$$

Lemma 2 (Reduction lemma). *For any* $\varphi \in \mathcal{L}_{(\mathsf{K}_a \mathsf{N}_a \sharp \flat !)}$, *there exists* $\psi \in \mathcal{L}_{(\mathsf{K}_a \mathsf{N}_a)}$ *such that* $\vdash_{\mathsf{H_{LON}}} \varphi \leftrightarrow \psi$.

Proof. By induction on $\ell'(\varphi)$. We only treat the following case.

Case: $\ell'(\varphi) > 0$. In this case, $\varphi \in \mathcal{L}_{(\mathsf{K}_a \mathsf{N}_a \sharp \flat !)}$ includes at least one subformula which is of the form $[*\chi_1]\chi_2$ (where $* \in \{\flat, \sharp, !\}$ and $\chi_1 \in \mathcal{L}_{(\mathsf{K}_a \mathsf{N}_a \sharp \flat !)}, \chi_2 \in \mathcal{L}_{(\mathsf{K}_a \mathsf{N}_a)}$). On the other hand, there is a reduction axiom which has the form of $[*\chi_1]\chi_2 \leftrightarrow \chi_3$, and let this reduction axiom be $(RA*)$. Then we may obtain the following derivation.

1. $\vdash_{\mathsf{H_{LON}}} [*\chi_1]\chi_2 \leftrightarrow \chi_3$ $(RA*)$
2. $\vdash_{\mathsf{H_{LON}}} \varphi \leftrightarrow \varphi\binom{[*\chi_1]\chi_2}{\chi_3}$ 1 and (RE)
3. $\vdash_{\mathsf{H_{LON}}} \varphi\binom{[*\chi_1]\chi_2}{\chi_3} \leftrightarrow \psi$ Induction hypothesis
4. $\vdash_{\mathsf{H_{LON}}} (X \leftrightarrow Y) \to ((Y \leftrightarrow Z) \to (X \leftrightarrow Z))$
           for any $X, Y, Z \in \mathcal{L}_{(\mathsf{K}_a \mathsf{N}_a \sharp \flat !)}$ (taut)
5. $\vdash_{\mathsf{H_{LON}}} \varphi \leftrightarrow \psi$ 2, 3 and 4 with (MP)

Induction hypothesis at the third line is applicable, since the less-than relation $\ell'(\varphi\binom{[*\chi_1]\chi_2}{\chi_3})) < \ell'(\varphi)$ holds by Lemma 1.

□

Actually, Lemma 2 is the core of the proof of the completeness theorem. Through this, we may straightforwardly show the theorem as follows.

Theorem 3 (Completeness of $\mathsf{H_{LON}}$ w.r.t. the semantics of $\mathcal{L}_{(\mathsf{K}_a \mathsf{N}_a \sharp \flat !)}$). *For any formula* $\varphi \in \mathcal{L}_{(\mathsf{K}_a \mathsf{N}_a \sharp \flat !)}$, *the following holds:*

$$\models \varphi \text{ implies } \vdash_{\mathsf{H_{LON}}} \varphi.$$

Proof. Fix any $\varphi \in \mathcal{L}_{(\mathsf{K}_a \mathsf{N}_a \sharp \flat !)}$ such that $\models \varphi$. By Lemma 2, we obtain $\vdash_{\mathsf{H_{LON}}} \varphi \leftrightarrow \chi$ for some $\chi \in \mathcal{L}_{(\mathsf{K}_a \mathsf{N}_a)}$. Then consider such $\chi \in \mathcal{L}_{(\mathsf{K}_a \mathsf{N}_a)}$. By Theorem 2 (the soundness of $\mathsf{H_{LON}}$), we obtain $\models \varphi \leftrightarrow \chi$. With the assumption $\models \varphi$, we have $\models \chi$. Next, by Theorem 1 (the completeness of $\mathsf{H'_{LON}}$), we obtain $\vdash_{\mathsf{H'_{LON}}} \chi$, and so $\vdash_{\mathsf{H_{LON}}} \chi$ trivially holds; therefore, we obtain $\vdash_{\mathsf{H_{LON}}} \varphi$ with $\vdash_{\mathsf{H_{LON}}} \varphi \leftrightarrow \chi$ again. That is what we desired. □

5   Labelled Sequent Calculus for LON

We, in this section, introduce a cut-free sequent calculus $\mathsf{G_{LON}}$ for LON. which is based on the sequent calculus **GPAL** for public announcement logic given in [17]. Let $\mathsf{Var} = \{x, y, z, ...\}$ be a countably infinite set of variables. Then, given any

$x, y \in \mathsf{Var}$, any list α of formulas and any formula φ, we say $x{:}^{\alpha}\varphi$ is a *labelled formula* and, for any agent $a \in \mathbb{A}$, $x\mathsf{R}_a^{\alpha}y$ and $x\mathsf{Q}_a^{\alpha}y$ are *relational atoms*. We use ε for the empty list, and write $x{:}^{\varepsilon}\varphi$ by $x{:}\varphi$ if it is clear from the context. We also use the term, *labelled expressions* to indicate that they are either labelled formulas or relational atoms and we denote by $\mathfrak{A}, \mathfrak{B}$, etc. labelled expressions. A *sequent* is a pair of finite multi-sets of labelled expressions Γ and Δ, and we denote the pair by $\Gamma \Rightarrow \Delta$. The set of inference rules of $\mathsf{G_{LON}}$ is defined in Table 2. Hereinafter, for any sequent s, if s is derivable in $\mathsf{G_{LON}}$, we write $\vdash_{\mathsf{G_{LON}}} s$.

Moreover, $\mathsf{G_{LON}^+}$ is $\mathsf{G_{LON}}$ with the following rule (Cut):

$$\frac{\Gamma \Rightarrow \Delta, \mathfrak{A} \quad \mathfrak{A}, \Gamma' \Rightarrow \Delta'}{\Gamma, \Gamma' \Rightarrow \Delta, \Delta'} \ (Cut),$$

where $\mathfrak{A}$ in (Cut) is called a *cut expression*. We use the term *principal expression* of an inference rule of $\mathsf{G_{LON}^+}$ if a labelled expression is newly introduced on the left uppersequent or the right uppersequent by the rule of $\mathsf{G_{LON}^+}$.

Because, for any labelled expression $\mathfrak{A}$ and arbitrary finite multi-sets Γ and Δ of labelled expressions, $\mathfrak{A}, \Gamma \Rightarrow \Delta, \mathfrak{A}$ is provable in $\mathsf{G_{LON}}$ by the straightforward induction on the height of the derivation, we also treat this sequent as an initial sequent.

5.1   Every Provable Formula in $\mathsf{H_{LON}}$ is also Provable in $\mathsf{G_{LON}^+}$

Let us define the length of a labelled expression $\mathfrak{A}$ for a preparation of the following theorem.

Definition 6. *For any labelled expression $\mathfrak{A}$, $\ell^*(\mathfrak{A})$ is defined as follows. Note that the length function for a formula $\ell(\varphi)$ is already defined in Definition 4.*

$$\ell^*(\alpha) = \begin{cases} 0 & \text{if } \alpha = \varepsilon \\ \ell^*(\beta) + \ell(\varphi) & \text{if } \alpha = \beta, \circ\varphi \end{cases} \qquad \ell^*(\mathfrak{A}) = \begin{cases} \ell^*(\alpha) + \ell(\varphi) & \text{if } \mathfrak{A} = x{:}^{\alpha}\varphi \\ \ell^*(\alpha) + 1 & \text{if } \mathfrak{A} = x\mathsf{R}_a^{\alpha}y \text{ or } x\mathsf{Q}_a^{\alpha}y \end{cases}$$

where $\circ \in \{!, \sharp, \flat\}$. We define the notion of substitution of variables in labelled expressions.

Definition 7. *Let $\mathfrak{A}$ be any labelled expression. Then the substitution of x for y in $\mathfrak{A}$, denoted by $\mathfrak{A}[x/y]$, is defined by*

$$
\begin{aligned}
z[x/y] &:= z \quad (\text{if } y \neq z) & (z\mathsf{R}_a^{\alpha}w)[x/y] &:= (z[x/y])\mathsf{R}_a^{\alpha}(w[x/y]) \\
z[x/y] &:= x \quad (\text{if } y = z) & (z\mathsf{Q}_a^{\alpha}w)[x/y] &:= (z[x/y])\mathsf{Q}_a^{\alpha}(w[x/y]) \\
(z{:}^{\alpha}\varphi)[x/y] &:= (z[x/y]){:}^{\alpha}\varphi
\end{aligned}
$$

Substitution $[x/y]$ to a multi-set Γ of labelled expressions is defined by $\Gamma[x/y] := \{\mathfrak{A}[x/y] \mid \mathfrak{A} \in \Gamma\}$. For a preparation of Theorem 4, we show the next lemma.

Lemma 3. (i) $\vdash_{\mathsf{G_{LON}}} \Gamma \Rightarrow \Delta$ *implies* $\vdash_{\mathsf{G_{LON}}} \Gamma[x/y] \Rightarrow \Delta[x/y]$ *for any* $x, y \in \mathsf{Var}$.
(ii) $\vdash_{\mathsf{G_{LON}^+}} \Gamma \Rightarrow \Delta$ *implies* $\vdash_{\mathsf{G_{LON}^+}} \Gamma[x/y] \Rightarrow \Delta[x/y]$ *for any* $x, y \in \mathsf{Var}$.

Table 2. Labelled Sequent Calculus for LON :$\mathcal{G}_{\text{LON}}$.

(Initial Sequents)

$$\mathfrak{A} \Rightarrow \mathfrak{A}$$

(Structural Rules)

$$\frac{\Gamma \Rightarrow \Delta}{\mathfrak{A}, \Gamma \Rightarrow \Delta} \ (Lw) \quad \frac{\Gamma \Rightarrow \Delta}{\Gamma \Rightarrow \Delta, \mathfrak{A}} \ (Rw) \quad \frac{\mathfrak{A}, \mathfrak{A}, \Gamma \Rightarrow \Delta}{\mathfrak{A}, \Gamma \Rightarrow \Delta} \ (Lc) \quad \frac{\Gamma \Rightarrow \Delta, \mathfrak{A}, \mathfrak{A}}{\Gamma \Rightarrow \Delta, \mathfrak{A}} \ (Rc)$$

(Rules for propositional connectives)

$$\frac{\Gamma \Rightarrow \Delta, x:^{\alpha}\varphi}{x:^{\alpha}\neg\varphi, \Gamma \Rightarrow \Delta} \ (L\neg) \quad \frac{x:^{\alpha}\varphi, \Gamma \Rightarrow \Delta}{\Gamma \Rightarrow \Delta, x:^{\alpha}\neg\varphi} \ (R\neg)$$

$$\frac{x:^{\alpha}\varphi, x:^{\alpha}\chi, \Gamma \Rightarrow \Delta}{x:^{\alpha}\varphi \wedge \chi, \Gamma \Rightarrow \Delta} \ (L\wedge) \quad \frac{\Gamma \Rightarrow \Delta, x:^{\alpha}\varphi \quad \Gamma \Rightarrow \Delta, x:^{\alpha}\chi}{\Gamma \Rightarrow \Delta, x:^{\alpha}\varphi \wedge \chi} \ (R\wedge)$$

(Rules for knowledge and narrow-minded belief operators)

$$\frac{\Gamma \Rightarrow x\mathsf{R}_a^{\alpha}y \quad y:^{\alpha}\varphi, \Gamma \Rightarrow \Delta}{x:^{\alpha}\mathsf{K}_a\varphi, \Gamma \Rightarrow \Delta} \ (LK_a) \quad \frac{x\mathsf{R}_a^{\alpha}y, \Gamma \Rightarrow \Delta, y:^{\alpha}\varphi}{\Gamma \Rightarrow \Delta, x:^{\alpha}\mathsf{K}_a\varphi} \ (RK_a)\dagger$$

$$\frac{\Gamma \Rightarrow x\mathsf{Q}_a^{\alpha}y \quad y:^{\alpha}\varphi, \Gamma \Rightarrow \Delta}{x:^{\alpha}\mathsf{N}_a\varphi, \Gamma \Rightarrow \Delta} \ (LN_a) \quad \frac{x\mathsf{Q}_a^{\alpha}y, \Gamma \Rightarrow \Delta, y:^{\alpha}\varphi}{\Gamma \Rightarrow \Delta, x:^{\alpha}\mathsf{N}_a\varphi} \ (RN_a)\dagger$$

$\dagger$ y does not appear in the lowersequent.

(Rules for announcement operators)

$$\frac{x:^{\alpha}p, \Gamma \Rightarrow \Delta}{x:^{\alpha,*\varphi}p, \Gamma \Rightarrow \Delta} \ (Lat*) \quad \frac{\Gamma \Rightarrow \Delta, x:^{\alpha}p}{\Gamma \Rightarrow \Delta, x:^{\alpha,*\varphi}p} \ (Rat*)$$

where $* \in \{!, \flat, \sharp\}$

$$\frac{\Gamma \Rightarrow x:^{\alpha}\varphi \quad x:^{\alpha,!\varphi}\chi, \Gamma \Rightarrow \Delta}{x:^{\alpha}[!\varphi]\chi, \Gamma \Rightarrow \Delta} \ (L[!]) \quad \frac{x:^{\alpha}\varphi, \Gamma \Rightarrow \Delta, x:^{\alpha,!\varphi}\chi}{\Gamma \Rightarrow \Delta, x:^{\alpha}[!\varphi]\chi} \ (R[!])$$

$$\frac{x:^{\alpha,\circ\varphi}\chi, \Gamma \Rightarrow \Delta}{x:^{\alpha}[\circ\varphi]\chi, \Gamma \Rightarrow \Delta} \ (L[\circ]) \quad \frac{\Gamma \Rightarrow \Delta, x:^{\alpha,\circ\varphi}\chi}{\Gamma \Rightarrow \Delta, x:^{\alpha}[\circ\varphi]\chi} \ (R[\circ])$$

where $\circ \in \{\flat, \sharp\}$

(Rules for relation atoms)

$$\frac{x:^{\alpha}\varphi, x:^{\alpha}\varphi, x\mathsf{R}_a^{\alpha}y, \Gamma \Rightarrow \Delta}{x\mathsf{R}_a^{\alpha,!\varphi}y, \Gamma \Rightarrow \Delta} \ (LR_a!) \quad \frac{\Gamma \Rightarrow \Delta, x:^{\alpha}\varphi \quad \Gamma \Rightarrow \Delta, y:^{\alpha}\varphi \quad \Gamma \Rightarrow \Delta, x\mathsf{R}_a^{\alpha}y}{\Gamma \Rightarrow \Delta, x\mathsf{R}_a^{\alpha,!\varphi}y} \ (RR_a!)$$

$$\frac{x\mathsf{R}_a^{\alpha}y, \Gamma \Rightarrow \Delta}{x\mathsf{R}_a^{\alpha,\circ\varphi}y, \Gamma \Rightarrow \Delta} \ (LR_a\circ) \quad \frac{\Gamma \Rightarrow \Delta, x\mathsf{R}_a^{\alpha}y}{\Gamma \Rightarrow \Delta, x\mathsf{R}_a^{\alpha,\circ\varphi}y} \ (RR_a\circ)$$

where $\circ \in \{\flat, \sharp\}$

$$\frac{y:^{\alpha}\varphi, x\mathsf{Q}_a^{\alpha}y, \Gamma \Rightarrow \Delta}{x\mathsf{Q}_a^{\alpha,\flat\varphi}y, \Gamma \Rightarrow \Delta} \ (LQ_a\flat) \quad \frac{\Gamma \Rightarrow \Delta, y:^{\alpha}\varphi \quad \Gamma \Rightarrow \Delta, x\mathsf{Q}_a^{\alpha}y}{\Gamma \Rightarrow \Delta, x\mathsf{Q}_a^{\alpha,\flat\varphi}y} \ (RQ_a\flat)$$

$$\frac{x\mathsf{R}_a^{\alpha}y, y:^{\alpha}\varphi, \Gamma \Rightarrow \Delta \quad x\mathsf{Q}_a^{\alpha}y, \Gamma \Rightarrow \Delta}{x\mathsf{Q}_a^{\alpha,\sharp\varphi}y, \Gamma \Rightarrow \Delta} \ (LQ_a\sharp) \quad \frac{\Gamma \Rightarrow \Delta, x\mathsf{R}_a^{\alpha}y, x\mathsf{Q}_a^{\alpha}y \quad \Gamma \Rightarrow \Delta, y:^{\alpha}\varphi, x\mathsf{Q}_a^{\alpha}y}{\Gamma \Rightarrow \Delta, x\mathsf{Q}_a^{\alpha,\sharp\varphi}y} \ (RQ_a\sharp)$$

$$\frac{x:^{\alpha}\varphi, x:^{\alpha}\varphi, x\mathsf{Q}_a^{\alpha}y, \Gamma \Rightarrow \Delta}{x\mathsf{Q}_a^{\alpha,!\varphi}y, \Gamma \Rightarrow \Delta} \ (LQ_a!) \quad \frac{\Gamma \Rightarrow \Delta, x:^{\alpha}\varphi \quad \Gamma \Rightarrow \Delta, y:^{\alpha}\varphi \quad \Gamma \Rightarrow \Delta, x\mathsf{Q}_a^{\alpha}y}{\Gamma \Rightarrow \Delta, x\mathsf{Q}_a^{\alpha,!\varphi}y} \ (RQ_a!)$$

(Rules for frame properties)

$$\frac{x\mathsf{R}_a^{\varepsilon}y, \Gamma \Rightarrow \Delta}{\Gamma \Rightarrow \Delta} \ (ref_a) \quad \frac{\Gamma \Rightarrow \Delta, x\mathsf{R}_a^{\varepsilon}y \quad \Gamma \Rightarrow \Delta, x\mathsf{R}_a^{\varepsilon}z \quad y\mathsf{R}_a^{\varepsilon}z, \Gamma \Rightarrow \Delta}{\Gamma \Rightarrow \Delta} \ (euc_a)$$

Proof. By induction on the height of the derivation. We go through almost the same procedure in the proof as in Negri *et al.* [15, p. 194].   □

We now show that every provable formula in H_{LON} is also provable in G^+_{LON}.

Theorem 4. *For any formula* φ, *if* $\vdash_{H_{LON}} A$, *then* $\vdash_{G^+_{LON}} \Rightarrow x{:}^\varepsilon A$ (*for any* $x \in \mathsf{Var}$).

Proof. The proof is carried out by the height of the derivation in G_{LON}. Let us take one direction of $(RA\flat 5)$ and $(RA\sharp 5)$ to prove as significant base cases (the derivation height of G_{LON} is equal to 0).

The case of $(RA\flat 5)$ *right to left*

$$
\dfrac{
\dfrac{
\dfrac{Init}{xQ_ay, y{:}\psi \Rightarrow y{:}^\flat\psi\varphi, xQ_ay}(LQ_a\flat)
}{xQ_a^{\flat\psi}y \Rightarrow y{:}^\flat\psi\varphi, xQ_ay}
\quad
\dfrac{
\dfrac{
\dfrac{Init}{xQ_ay, y{:}\psi \Rightarrow y{:}^\flat\psi\varphi, y{:}\psi}(LQ_a\flat)
}{xQ_a^{\flat\psi}y \Rightarrow y{:}^\flat\psi\varphi, y{:}\psi}
\quad
\dfrac{
\dfrac{Init}{y{:}^\flat\psi\varphi, xQ_a^{\flat\psi}y \Rightarrow y{:}^\flat\psi\varphi}(L[\flat])
}{y{:}[\flat\psi]\varphi, xQ_a^{\flat\psi}y \Rightarrow y{:}^\flat\psi\varphi}
}{y{:}\psi \to [\flat\psi]\varphi, xQ_a^{\flat\psi}y \Rightarrow y{:}^\flat\psi\varphi}(L\to)
}{
\dfrac{
\dfrac{
\dfrac{x{:}N_a(\psi \to [\flat\psi]\varphi), xQ_a^{\flat\psi}y \Rightarrow y{:}^\flat\psi\varphi}{x{:}N_a(\psi \to [\flat\psi]\varphi) \Rightarrow x{:}^\flat\psi N_a\varphi}(RN_a)
}{x{:}N_a(\psi \to [\flat\psi]\varphi) \Rightarrow x{:}[\flat\psi]N_a\varphi}(R[\flat])
}{\Rightarrow x{:}N_a(\psi \to [\flat\psi]\varphi) \to [\flat\psi]N_a\varphi}(R\to)
}(LN_a)
$$

The case of $(RA\sharp 5)$ *left to right*

$$
\dfrac{
\dfrac{
\dfrac{\mathcal{D}_1}{1x{:}[\sharp\psi]N_a\varphi \Rightarrow x{:}N_a[\sharp\psi]\varphi}
\quad
\dfrac{\mathcal{D}_2}{x{:}[\sharp\psi]N_a\varphi \Rightarrow x{:}K_a(\psi \to [\sharp\psi]\varphi)}
}{x{:}[\sharp\psi]N_a\varphi \Rightarrow x{:}N_a[\sharp\psi]\varphi \wedge K_a(\psi \to [\sharp\psi]\varphi)}(R\wedge)
}{\Rightarrow x{:}[\sharp\psi]N_a\varphi \to N_a[\sharp\psi]\varphi \wedge K_a(\psi \to [\sharp\psi]\varphi)}(R\to)
$$

- $\mathcal{D}_1$ is as follows.

$$
\dfrac{
\dfrac{
\dfrac{
\dfrac{Init}{xQ_ay \Rightarrow x{:}^{\sharp\psi}\varphi, xQ_ay, xR_ay}
\quad
\dfrac{Init}{xQ_ay \Rightarrow x{:}^{\sharp\psi}\varphi, xQ_ay, y{:}\psi}
}{xQ_ay \Rightarrow x{:}^{\sharp\psi}\varphi, xQ_a^{\sharp\psi}y}(RQ_a\sharp)
\quad
\dfrac{Init}{y{:}^{\sharp\psi}\varphi, xQ_ay \Rightarrow y{:}^{\sharp\psi}\varphi}(LN_a)
}{
\dfrac{
\dfrac{
\dfrac{x{:}^{\sharp\psi}N_a\varphi, xQ_ay \Rightarrow y{:}^{\sharp\psi}\varphi}{x{:}^{\sharp\psi}N_a\varphi, xQ_ay \Rightarrow y{:}[\sharp\psi]\varphi}(R[\sharp])
}{x{:}^{\sharp\psi}N_a\varphi \Rightarrow x{:}N_a[\sharp\psi]\varphi}(RN_a)
}{x{:}[\sharp\psi]N_a\varphi \Rightarrow x{:}N_a[\sharp\psi]\varphi}(L[\sharp])
}
}
$$

- $\mathcal{D}_2$ is as follows.

$$
\dfrac{
\dfrac{
\dfrac{
\dfrac{Init}{y{:}\psi, xR_ay, \Rightarrow xQ_ay, xR_ay}
\quad
\dfrac{Init}{y{:}\psi, xR_ay, \Rightarrow xQ_ay, y{:}\psi}
}{xR_ay, y{:}\psi \Rightarrow xQ_a^{\sharp\psi}y}(RQ_a\sharp)
}{xR_ay, y{:}\psi \Rightarrow y{:}^{\sharp\psi}\varphi, xQ_a^{\sharp\psi}y}(Rw)
\quad
\dfrac{Init}{y{:}^{\sharp\psi}\varphi, xR_ay, y{:}\psi \Rightarrow y{:}^{\sharp\psi}\varphi}(LN_a)
}{
\dfrac{
\dfrac{
\dfrac{
\dfrac{x{:}^{\sharp\psi}N_a\varphi, xR_ay, y{:}\psi \Rightarrow y{:}^{\sharp\psi}\varphi}{x{:}[\sharp\psi]N_a\varphi, xR_ay, y{:}\psi \Rightarrow y{:}^{\sharp\psi}\varphi}(L[\sharp])
}{x{:}[\sharp\psi]N_a\varphi, xR_ay, y{:}\psi \Rightarrow y{:}[\sharp\psi]\varphi}(R[\sharp])
}{x{:}[\sharp\psi]N_a\varphi, xR_ay \Rightarrow y{:}\psi \to [\sharp\psi]\varphi}(R\to)
}{x{:}[\sharp\psi]N_a\varphi \Rightarrow x{:}K_a(\psi \to [\sharp\psi]\varphi)}(RK_a)
}
}
$$

In the inductive step, we show the admissibility of G_{LON}'s inference rules, (MP), $(NecK_a)$ and $(Nec[!])$, by G_{LON}^+.

The case of (MP): It is shown with (Cut).

The case of $(NecK_a)$: It is shown by (RK_a), (Lw) and Lemma 3.

The case of $(Nec[!])$: In this case, we show the admissibility of the following rule:

$$\frac{\Rightarrow x:^{\varepsilon}\varphi}{\Rightarrow x:^{\varepsilon}[!\chi]\varphi} \ (Nec[!])$$

Suppose $\vdash_{G_{LON}} \Rightarrow x:^{\varepsilon}\varphi$. It is obvious that $\vdash_{G_{LON}} \Rightarrow x:^{\varepsilon}\varphi$ implies $\vdash_{G_{LON}} \Rightarrow x:^{!\chi}\varphi$ since if there is a derivation of $\Rightarrow x:^{\varepsilon}\varphi$, there can also be a derivation of $\Rightarrow x:^{!\chi}\varphi$ where $!\chi$ is added to the most left side of restricting formulas of each labelled expression appeared in the derivation. Therefore, we obtain $\vdash_{G_{LON}} \Rightarrow x:^{!\chi}\varphi$, and by the application of (Lw) and $(R[!])$, we conclude $\vdash_{G_{LON}} \Rightarrow x:^{\varepsilon}[!\chi]\varphi$.

The case of $(Nec[\flat])$ and $(Nec[\sharp])$: These cases can be shown with a similar method to the case of $(Nec[!])$ without the application of (Lw).

$\square$

5.2 Cut Elimination of G_{LON}^+

Now, we show the cut-elimination for G_{LON}^+.

Theorem 5 (Cut elimination of G_{LON}^+). *For any sequent $\Gamma \Rightarrow \Delta$, if $\vdash_{G_{LON}^+} \Gamma \Rightarrow \Delta$, then $\vdash_{G_{LON}} \Gamma \Rightarrow \Delta$.*

Proof. The proof is carried out in Ono and Komori's method [18] of an extended version of cut where we employ the following rule $(Ecut)$. We denote the n-copies of the same labelled expression $\mathfrak{A}$ by $\mathfrak{A}^n$, and $(Ecut)$ is defined as follows:

$$\frac{\Gamma \Rightarrow \Delta, \mathfrak{A}^n \quad \mathfrak{A}^m, \Gamma' \Rightarrow \Delta'}{\Gamma, \Gamma' \Rightarrow \Delta, \Delta'} \ (Ecut)$$

where $0 \leq n, m < \omega$. The theorem is shown by double induction on the height of the derivation and the length of the cut expression $\mathfrak{A}$ of $(Ecut)$. The proof is divided into four cases:

(1) at least one of uppersequents of $(Ecut)$ is an initial sequent;
(2) the last inference rule of either uppersequents of $(Ecut)$ is a structural rule;
(3) the last inference rule of either uppersequents of $(Ecut)$ is a non-structural rule, and the principal expression introduced by the rule is not a cut expression;
(4) the last inference rules of two uppersequents of $(Ecut)$ are both non-structural rules, and the principal expressions introduced by the rules used on the uppersequents of $(Ecut)$ are both cut expressions.

We look at one of base cases and one of significant subcases of (4) in which principal expressions introduced by non-structural rules are both cut expressions.

A case of (4): principal expressions are $xQ_a^{\alpha,\sharp\varphi}y$:

Let us consider the case where both sides of $\mathfrak{A}$ are $xQ_a^{\alpha,\sharp\varphi}y$ and principal expressions. When we obtain the derivation:

$$
\dfrac{
\dfrac{\vdots\ \mathcal{D}_1}{\Gamma \Rightarrow \Delta, (xQ_a^{\alpha,\sharp\varphi}y)^n}\ (LQ_a\sharp)
\quad
\dfrac{\vdots\ \mathcal{D}_2}{(xQ_a^{\alpha,\sharp\varphi}y)^m, \Gamma' \Rightarrow \Delta'}\ (RQ_a\sharp)
}{\Gamma, \Gamma' \Rightarrow \Delta, \Delta'}\ (Ecut)
\quad,
$$

- $\mathcal{D}_1$ is as follows:

$$
\dfrac{
\dfrac{\vdots\ \mathcal{D}_{1\text{-}1}}{\Gamma \Rightarrow \Delta, (xQ_a^{\alpha,\sharp\varphi}y)^{n-1}, xR_a^\alpha y, xQ_a^\alpha y}
\quad
\dfrac{\vdots\ \mathcal{D}_{1\text{-}2}}{\Gamma \Rightarrow \Delta, (xQ_a^{\alpha,\sharp\varphi}y)^{n-1}, y:^\alpha\varphi, xQ_a^\alpha y}
}{\Gamma \Rightarrow \Delta, (xQ_a^{\alpha,\sharp\varphi}y)^n}\ (RQ_a\sharp)
$$

- $\mathcal{D}_2$ is as follows:

$$
\dfrac{
\dfrac{\vdots\ \mathcal{D}_{2\text{-}1}}{xR_a^\alpha y, y:^\alpha\varphi, (xQ_a^{\alpha,\sharp\varphi}y)^{m-1}, \Gamma' \Rightarrow \Delta'}
\quad
\dfrac{\vdots\ \mathcal{D}_{2\text{-}3}}{xQ_a^\alpha y, (xQ_a^{\alpha,\sharp\varphi}y)^{m-1}, \Gamma' \Rightarrow \Delta'}
}{(xQ_a^{\alpha,\sharp\varphi}y)^m, \Gamma' \Rightarrow \Delta'}\ (LQ_a\sharp)
$$

Then this derivation is transformed into the following derivation. First, let us apply $(Ecut)$ to the bottom labelled sequents of ($\mathcal{D}_1$ and $\mathcal{D}_{2\text{-}1}$), and ($\mathcal{D}_1$ and $\mathcal{D}_{2\text{-}3}$), and ($\mathcal{D}_2$ and $\mathcal{D}_{1\text{-}1}$), and ($\mathcal{D}_2$ and $\mathcal{D}_{1\text{-}2}$); each application is feasible because the height of the derivation is reduced. As a result of that, we obtain $\mathcal{D}'_{2\text{-}1}$, and $\mathcal{D}'_{2\text{-}3}$, and $\mathcal{D}'_{1\text{-}1}$, and $\mathcal{D}'_{1\text{-}2}$, where $(xQ_a^{\alpha,\sharp\varphi}y)^k$ is removed from the bottom labelled sequent and Γ and Δ (or Γ' and Δ') are added to it. Then we continue to apply $(Ecut)$ to construct a derivation as follows.

$$
\dfrac{
\dfrac{
\dfrac{\vdots\ \mathcal{D}'_{1\text{-}1}}{\Gamma, \Gamma' \Rightarrow \Delta, \Delta', xR_a^\alpha y, xQ_a^\alpha y}
\quad
\dfrac{\vdots\ \mathcal{D}'_{2\text{-}3}}{xQ_a^\alpha y, \Gamma, \Gamma' \Rightarrow \Delta, \Delta'}
}{\Gamma, \Gamma, \Gamma', \Gamma' \Rightarrow \Delta, \Delta, \Delta', \Delta', xR_a^\alpha y}\ (Ecut)
}{\Gamma, \Gamma' \Rightarrow \Delta, \Delta', xR_a^\alpha y}\ (Lc), (Rc)
$$

$$
\dfrac{
\dfrac{
\dfrac{
\dfrac{\vdots\ \mathcal{D}'_{1\text{-}2}}{\Gamma, \Gamma' \Rightarrow \Delta, \Delta', y:^\alpha\varphi, xQ_a^\alpha y}
\quad
\dfrac{\vdots\ \mathcal{D}'_{2\text{-}3}}{xQ_a^\alpha y, \Gamma, \Gamma' \Rightarrow \Delta, \Delta'}
}{\Gamma, \Gamma, \Gamma', \Gamma' \Rightarrow \Delta, \Delta, \Delta', \Delta', y:^\alpha\varphi}\ (Ecut)
}{\Gamma, \Gamma' \Rightarrow \Delta, \Delta', y:^\alpha\varphi,}\ (Lc), (Rc)
\quad
\dfrac{\vdots\ \mathcal{D}'_{2\text{-}1}}{xR_a^\alpha y, y:^\alpha\varphi, , \Gamma, \Gamma' \Rightarrow \Delta, \Delta'}
}{
\dfrac{xR_a^\alpha y, \Gamma, \Gamma, \Gamma', \Gamma' \Rightarrow \Delta, \Delta, \Delta', \Delta'}{xR_a^\alpha y, \Gamma, \Gamma' \Rightarrow \Delta, \Delta'}\ (Lc), (Rc)
}\ (Ecut)
$$

The applications of $(Ecut)$ in the above two fragments of a derivation are allowed because the length of every cut expression is reduced. Again, applying $(Ecut)$ to the bottom labelled sequents of above two derivations, and then apply $(Lc), (Rc)$ finite times, we obtain the goal $\vdash_{\mathsf{G_{LON}}} \Gamma, \Gamma' \Rightarrow \Delta, \Delta'$.

$\square$

5.3 Soundness of $\mathsf{G_{LON}}$

Now, we switch the subject to the soundness theorem of $\mathsf{G_{LON}}$. At first, we define the notion of the satisfaction relation for the labelled expressions, i.e., lift the satisfaction relation for the non-labelled formulas to that of the labelled expressions. Let us say that $f : \mathsf{Var} \to \mathcal{D}(\mathcal{M})$ is an *assignment*.

Definition 8. *Let* $\mathcal{M} = (S, (\mathcal{R}_a)_{a \in \mathbb{A}}, (\mathcal{Q}_a)_{a \in \mathbb{A}}, V)$ *be an en-model and* $f : \mathsf{Var} \to \mathcal{D}(\mathcal{M})$ *an assignment.*

$$\mathcal{M}, f \models x{:}^\alpha \varphi \quad \text{iff } \mathcal{M}^\alpha, f(x) \models \varphi \text{ and } f(x) \in \mathcal{D}(\mathfrak{M}^\alpha)$$
$$\mathcal{M}, f \models x\mathsf{R}_a^\varepsilon y \quad \text{iff } (f(x), f(y)) \in \mathcal{R}_a$$
$$\mathcal{M}, f \models x\mathsf{R}_a^{\alpha, !\varphi} y \text{ iff } (f(x), f(y)) \in \mathcal{R}_a^\alpha \text{ and } \mathcal{M}^\alpha, f(x) \models \varphi \text{ and } \mathcal{M}^\alpha, f(y) \models \varphi$$
$$\mathcal{M}, f \models x\mathsf{R}_a^{\alpha, *\varphi} y \text{ iff } \mathcal{M}, f \models x\mathsf{R}_a^\alpha y \quad (* \in \{\flat, \sharp\})$$
$$\mathcal{M}, f \models x\mathsf{Q}_a^\varepsilon y \quad \text{iff } (f(x), f(y)) \in \mathcal{Q}_a$$
$$\mathcal{M}, f \models x\mathsf{Q}_a^{\alpha, !\varphi} y \text{ iff } (f(x), f(y)) \in \mathcal{Q}_a^\alpha \text{ and } \mathcal{M}^\alpha, f(x) \models \varphi \text{ and } \mathcal{M}^\alpha, f(y) \models \varphi$$
$$\mathcal{M}, f \models x\mathsf{Q}_a^{\alpha, \sharp\varphi} y \text{ iff } (f(x), f(y)) \in \mathcal{Q}_a^\alpha \text{ or } ((f(x), f(y)) \in \mathcal{R}_a \text{ and } \mathcal{M}^\alpha, f(y) \models \varphi)$$
$$\mathcal{M}, f \models x\mathsf{Q}_a^{\alpha, \flat\varphi} y \text{ iff } (f(x), f(y)) \in \mathcal{Q}_a^\alpha \text{ and } \mathcal{M}^\alpha, f(y) \models \varphi$$

In this definition, we have to be careful of the notion of *surviveness* as suggested in [17]. In brief, $f(x)$ and $f(y)$ above must be defined in $\mathcal{D}(\mathcal{M}^\alpha)$ which may be smaller than $\mathcal{D}(\mathcal{M})$ (e.g, consider the case of $\mathcal{D}(\mathcal{M}^{!\varphi})$). It is possible that $f : \mathsf{Var} \to \mathcal{D}(\mathcal{M})$ assigns a state which is not include in such a restricted model (e.g., $f(x) \notin \mathcal{D}(\mathcal{M}^{!\varphi})$), and so we should carefully define the notion of validity (which is called t-validity) of a labelled expression through a peculiar negation for a labelled expression.

Definition 9. *Let* $\mathcal{M}$ *be an en-model and* $f : \mathsf{Var} \to \mathcal{D}(\mathcal{M})$ *an assignment. The satisfaction relation for the negation of labelled expression* $\mathcal{M}, f \models \overline{\mathfrak{A}}$ *is defined as follows.*

$$\mathcal{M}, f \models \overline{x{:}^\alpha \varphi} \quad \text{iff } \mathcal{M}^\alpha, f(x) \not\models \varphi \text{ and } f(x) \in \mathcal{D}(\mathfrak{M}^\alpha),$$
$$\mathcal{M}, f \models \overline{x\mathsf{R}_a^\varepsilon y} \quad \text{iff } (f(x), f(y)) \notin \mathcal{R}_a,$$
$$\mathcal{M}, f \models \overline{x\mathsf{R}_a^{\alpha, !\varphi} y} \text{ iff } \mathcal{M}, f \models \overline{x\mathsf{R}_a^\alpha y} \text{ or } \mathcal{M}, f \models \overline{x{:}^\alpha A} \text{ or } \mathcal{M}, f \models \overline{y{:}^\alpha A},$$
$$\mathcal{M}, f \models \overline{x\mathsf{R}_a^{\alpha, *\varphi} y} \text{ iff } \mathcal{M}, f \models \overline{x\mathsf{R}_a^\alpha y} \quad (* \in \{\flat, \sharp\})$$
$$\mathcal{M}, f \models \overline{x\mathsf{Q}_a^\varepsilon y} \quad \text{iff } (f(x), f(y)) \notin \mathcal{Q}_a$$
$$\mathcal{M}, f \models \overline{x\mathsf{Q}_a^{\alpha, !\varphi} y} \text{ iff } \mathcal{M}, f \models \overline{x\mathsf{Q}_a^\alpha y} \text{ or } \mathcal{M}, f \models \overline{x{:}^\alpha \varphi} \text{ or } \mathcal{M}, f \models \overline{y{:}^\alpha \varphi}$$
$$\mathcal{M}, f \models \overline{x\mathsf{Q}_a^{\alpha, \sharp\varphi} y} \text{ iff } \mathcal{M}, f \models \overline{x\mathsf{Q}_a^\alpha y} \text{ and } (\mathcal{M}, f \models \overline{x\mathsf{R}_a^\alpha y} \text{ or } \mathcal{M}, f \models \overline{y{:}^\alpha \varphi})$$
$$\mathcal{M}, f \models \overline{x\mathsf{Q}_a^{\alpha, \flat\varphi} y} \text{ iff } \mathcal{M}, f \models \overline{x\mathsf{Q}_a^\alpha y} \text{ or } \mathcal{M}, f \models \overline{y{:}^\alpha \varphi}$$

Note that the first item means that $f(x)$ exists at the domain of the restricted model $\mathfrak{M}^\alpha$ and φ is false at the survived world $f(x)$ in $\mathfrak{M}^\alpha$.

Definition 10 (*t*-validity). $\Gamma \Rightarrow \Delta$ *is t-valid in* $\mathcal{M}$ *if there is no assignment* $f : \mathsf{Var} \to \mathcal{D}(\mathcal{M})$ *such that* $\mathcal{M}, f \models \mathfrak{A}$ *for all* $\mathfrak{A} \in \Gamma$, *and* $\mathcal{M}, f \models \overline{\mathfrak{B}}$ *for all* $\mathfrak{B} \in \Delta$.

Following these, settings, we may show the soundness theorem of $\mathsf{G_{LON}}$ straight-forwardly.

Theorem 6 (Soundness of $\mathsf{G_{LON}}$). *Given any sequent* $\Gamma \Rightarrow \Delta$ *in* $\mathsf{G_{LON}}$, *if* $\vdash_{\mathsf{G_{LON}}} \Gamma \Rightarrow \Delta$, *then* $\Gamma \Rightarrow \Delta$ *is t-valid in every en-model* $\mathcal{M}$.

Proof. The proof is carried out by induction of the height of the derivation of $\Gamma \Rightarrow \Delta$ in $\mathsf{G_{LON}}$. We only confirm one of base cases of relational atoms and some cases in the inductive step.

The Case Where the Last Applied Rule is $(Rat\flat)$**:** we show the contra-position. Suppose there is some $f : \mathsf{Var} \to \mathcal{D}(\mathcal{M})$ such that, $\mathcal{M}, f \Vdash \mathfrak{A}$ for all $\mathfrak{A} \in \Gamma$, and $\mathcal{M}, f \Vdash \overline{\mathfrak{B}}$ for all $\mathfrak{B} \in \Delta$, and $\mathcal{M}, f \Vdash \overline{x{:}^{\alpha,\flat\varphi}p}$. Fix such f. It suffices to show $\mathcal{M}, f \Vdash \overline{x{:}^{\alpha}p}$. By Definition 9, $\mathcal{M}, f \Vdash \overline{x{:}^{\alpha,\flat\varphi}p}$ is equivalent to $\mathcal{M}^{\alpha,\flat\varphi}, f(x) \not\Vdash p$ and $f(x) \in \mathcal{D}(\mathcal{M}^{\alpha,\flat\varphi})$. Because $\flat\varphi$ in $\mathcal{M}^{\alpha,\flat\varphi}$ has an affect only on the $(\mathsf{Q}_a)_{a\in\mathbb{A}}$ in this en-model, these two items are respectively equivalent to $\mathcal{M}^{\alpha}, f(x) \not\Vdash p$ and $f(x) \in \mathcal{D}(\mathcal{M}^{\alpha})$. These two are also equivalent to $\mathcal{M}, f \Vdash \overline{x{:}^{\alpha}p}$ by Definition 9. Therefore, the contraposition has been shown.

The Case Where the Last Applied Rule is $(RQ_a\sharp)$**:** We show the con-traposition. Suppose there is some $f : \mathsf{Var} \to \mathcal{D}(\mathcal{M})$ such that, $\mathcal{M}, f \Vdash \mathfrak{A}$ for all $\mathfrak{A} \in \Gamma$, and $\mathcal{M}, f \Vdash \overline{\mathfrak{B}}$ for all $\mathfrak{B} \in \Delta$, and $\mathcal{M}, f \Vdash \overline{x\mathsf{Q}_a^{\alpha,\sharp\varphi}y}$. Fix such f. By Definition 9 and the distribution of 'or', $\overline{x\mathsf{Q}_a^{\alpha,\sharp\varphi}y}$ is equivalent to $(\mathcal{M}, f \Vdash \overline{x\mathsf{Q}_a^{\alpha}y}$ or $\mathcal{M}, f \Vdash \overline{x\mathsf{R}_a^{\alpha}y})$ and $(\mathcal{M}, f \Vdash \overline{y{:}^{\alpha}\varphi}$ or $\mathcal{M}, f \Vdash \overline{x\mathsf{R}_a^{\alpha}y})$. This is what we want to show, and the contraposition has been shown. $\square$

Finally, we establish the completeness theorem as follows.

Corollary 1 (Completeness of $\mathsf{G_{LON}}$). *Given any formula* φ *and label* $x \in \mathsf{Var}$, *the following are equivalent:* (i) $\models \varphi$, (ii) $\vdash_{\mathsf{H'_{LON}}} \varphi$, (iii) $\vdash_{\mathsf{H_{LON}}} \varphi$, (iv) $\vdash_{\mathsf{G_{LON}^+}} \Rightarrow x{:}^{\varepsilon}\varphi$, *and* (v) $\vdash_{\mathsf{G_{LON}}} \Rightarrow x{:}^{\varepsilon}\varphi$.

Proof. The equivalence of (i), (ii) and (iii) are already established Theorems 1, 2 and 3. The direction from (iii) to (iv) is shown by Theorem 4. The direction from (iv) to (v) is established by Theorem 5. Finally, the direction from (v) to (i) is shown by Theorem 6. $\square$

6   Related Works

In this section, we introduce some related epistemic/doxastic logics. An epistemic logic for implicit and explicit belief by [20] is perhaps the closest concept we can find to that of LON. This logic is based on the logic of awareness logic [6], and it distinguishes the sense of belief into two, implicit and explicit belief, to avoid the logical omniscience in epistemic logic. A traditional approach to mix knowledge and belief operators, sometimes called epistemic-doxastic logic (e.g., see [21]), is another system similar to ours since K_a and N_a of LON may be interpreted as a mixture of these two different human tendencies.

One of differences between LON and the above existing works may relate to the definition of the satisfaction relation of LON:

$$\mathcal{M}, s \models [\sharp\varphi]\chi \quad \textit{iff} \quad \mathcal{M}^{\sharp\varphi}, s \models \chi,$$

where $\mathcal{M} = (S, (\mathcal{R}_a)_{a \in \mathbb{A}}, (\mathcal{Q}_a^{\sharp\varphi})_{a \in \mathbb{A}}, V)$ and $\mathcal{Q}_a^{\sharp\varphi} := \mathcal{Q}_a \cup \{(s, t) \in \mathcal{R}_a \mid t \in [\![\varphi]\!]_{\mathcal{M}}\}$.

Here, we include a mechanism of adding arrows i.e., a mechanism in which some of the information may confuse the agent.

In addition, there are some other attempts to introduce a distinction in our belief/knowledge from a different point of view. Intuitionistic epistemic logic [1,22] is one of them; this epistemic logic is based on intuitionistic logic, which distinguishes knowledge into two: standard knowledge, which normal epistemic logics treat and knowledge in the strict sense. In other words, this aims at introducing a distinction in knowledge, more strict and rational knowledge and not strict knowledge, which is an opposite perspective to our attempt, which introduced a distinction between belief with passion and knowledge.

Moreover, [12] combines DEL and probability theory, and this technique might be utilized for improving our dynamics, i.e., $\sharp$ and $\flat$ operators, since whether an announcement strengthen or weaken the agent's narrow-minded belief is likely to depend on how probable the announcement is. Similarly, it might be possible to incorporate with [3] which focuses on an evidence and justification in support of an agent's beliefs and knowledge. As you can see from our example of *Othello*, [11] is a really interesting work, which attempts to maintain beliefs of a dramatis personae in a logically consistent way. There are also some logics which deal with human emotion; for example [14] and [8]. We may, for the further development, need to consider relevance to these existing logics about emotion.

7   Conclusion and Further Directions

We introduced Logic Of Narrow-minded belief (LON), a variant of dynamic epistemic logic. This aims to formally express a human's passionate and narrow-minded belief, and as an example of the application of LON, we formalized Shakespeare's play *Othello*. Moreover, we also provide two proof systems which are semantically complete, such as a Hilbert-style proof system and a labelled sequent calculus, and a syntactic cut-elimination has been shown for the latter system. Philosophers and neuropsychologists believe that passion, or belief affected by passion, is an indispensable factor and even a basis for our reason. Without passion or emotions, human intelligence may be never realized. Therefore, we hope that our attempt in the present work will contribute to formal expressions of the human mind.

It may be possible to further develop our attempt in various directions. For example, we did not regard the problem of the logical omniscience; the logic of awareness is one of the candidates to be added to LON, as it is difficult to interpret the meaning of awareness in the context of passion. Another interesting feature that should be considered and added to LON is 'a lie' as it pertains to dynamic epistemic logic by van Ditmarsch [9]. Actually, Iago's rumor should be regarded as a lie, as our passion or narrow-mindedness is easily affected by such dubious information. Therefore, it might be interesting to consider these aspects in future researches regarding the logic of passion.

References

1. Artemov, S., Protopopescu, T.: Intuitionistic epistemic logic. Computer Science Technical Reports Paper 401 (2014)
2. Aucher, G.: A Combination System for Update Logic and Belief Revision. Master's thesis, University of Amsterdam (2003)
3. Baltag, A., Fiutek, V., Smets, S.: Beliefs and evidence in justification models. In: Beklemishev, L., Demri, S., Máté, A. (eds.) Advances in Modal Logic, vol. 11, pp. 156–176. CSLI Publications (2016)
4. van Benthem, J.: Logical Dynamic of Information and Interaction. Cambridge University Press, Cambridge (2011)
5. van Benthem, J., van Eijck, J., Kooi, B.: Logic of communications and change. Inf. Comput. **204**(11), 1620–1662 (2006)
6. van Benthem, J., Velázquez-Quesada, F.R.: The dynamics of awareness. Synthese **177**(5), 5–27 (2010)
7. Damasio, A.: Descartes' Error: Emotion, Reason, and the Human Brain. Avon books, New York (1994)
8. Dastani, M., Lorini, E.: A logic of emotions: from appraisal to coping. In: Proceedings of the 11th International Conference on Autonomous Agents and Multiagent Systems, vol. 2, pp. 1133–1140 (2012)
9. van Ditmarsch, H.: The Ditmarsch tale of wonders-the dynamics of lying. In: Reasoning About Other Minds: Logical and Cognitive Perspectives, vol. 65 (2011)
10. van Ditmarsch, H., Hoek, W., Kooi, B.: Dynamic Epistemic Logic. Springer, Dordrecht (2008). https://doi.org/10.1007/978-1-4020-5839-4
11. Eger, M., Martens, C.: Character beliefs in story generation (2017). https://aaai.org/ocs/index.php/AIIDE/AIIDE17/paper/view/15852
12. van Eijck, J., Renne, B.: Update, probability, knowledge and belief. In: Beklemishev, L., Demri, S., Máté, A. (eds.) Advances in Modal Logic, vol. 11, pp. 551–570. CSLI Publications (2016)
13. Hume, D.: A Treatise of Human Nature. Oxford University Press, New York (1739)
14. Lorini, E., Schwarzentruber, F.: A logic for reasoning about counterfactual emotions. Artif. Intell. **175**(3–4), 814–847 (2011)
15. Negri, S., von Plato, J.: Proof Analysis. Cambridge University Press, New York (2011)
16. Nomura, S., Arai, N., Tojo, S.: The dynamics of narrow-minded belief. In: Proceedings of the 11th International Conference on Agents and Artificial Intelligence, ICAART, vol. 2, pp. 247–255. INSTICC, SciTePress (2019). https://doi.org/10.5220/0007394502470255

17. Nomura, S., Sano, K., Tojo, S.: Revising a labelled sequent calculus for public announcement logic. In: Yang, S.C.-M., Deng, D.-M., Lin, H. (eds.) Structural Analysis of Non-Classical Logics. LASLL, pp. 131–157. Springer, Heidelberg (2016). https://doi.org/10.1007/978-3-662-48357-2_7

18. Ono, H., Komori, Y.: Logics without contraction Rule. J. Symbolic Logic **50**(1), 169–201 (1985)

19. Plaza, J.: Logic of public communications. In: Proceedings of the 4th International Symposium on Methodologies for Intelligent Systems: Poster Session Program, pp. 201–216 (1989)

20. Velázquez-Quesada, F.R.: Dynamic epistemic logic for implicit and explicit beliefs. J. Logic Lang. Inf. **23**(2), 107–140 (2014)

21. Voorbraak, F.: As far as I know–epistemic logic and uncertainty. Ph.D. thesis, Utrecht University (1993)

22. Williamson, T.: On intuitionistic modal epistemic logic. J. Philos. Logic **21**(1), 63–89 (1992)

Application of PSO-Based Constrained Combinatorial Optimization to Segment Assignment in Shield Tunneling

Koya Ihara[1,2]([envelope]) [ID], Shohei Kato[1,2] [ID], Takehiko Nakaya[3], Tomoaki Ogi[3], and Hiroichi Masuda[3]

[1] Department of Computer Science and Engineering, Graduate School of Engineering, Nagoya Institute of Technology, Gokiso-cho, Showa-ku, Nagoya 466-8555, Japan
{ihara,shohey}@katolab.nitech.ac.jp
[2] Frontier Research Institute for Information Science,
Nagoya Institute of Technology, Gokiso-cho, Showa-ku, Nagoya 466-8555, Japan
[3] Shimizu Corporation, 2-16-1 Kyobashi, Chuo-ku, Tokyo 104-8370, Japan
https://www.katolab.nitech.ac.jp

Abstract. This paper presents the application of particle swarm optimization (PSO) based constrained combinatorial optimization technique to assign tunnel segments and to improve the productivity in shield tunneling, a widely used tunnel construction method. This study considers the amount of soil excavated along a tunnel composed of the segments as an objective, and the deviation limit as constraints. In this problem, a feasible solution can be easily found by greedy search, though the constraints are very severe. The proposed method utilizes the found feasible solution to start to search near the feasible region. A two-dimensional simulation experiment using real-world construction data was performed to evaluate the effectiveness of the proposed method. The results demonstrate that the proposed method statistically outperforms the work of skilled engineers and other comparative methods in all test problems.

Keywords: Constrained combinatorial optimization · Particle swarm optimization · Shield tunneling

1 Introduction

Labor shortage is a serious problem in the construction industry worldwide. The United States' construction industry, which employs more than seven million workers, has experienced a severe shortage of skilled labor since the early 1980s, and this shortage is expected to continue [22]. In Hong Kong, the scope and extent of public and private sector infrastructure is rapidly growing; however, currently, labor supply cannot keep pace with the demand as 12% of the construction workers in Hong Kong have reached retirement age (60 years) and another 44% are over 50 years of age, *i.e.*, close to retirement [21].

© Springer Nature Switzerland AG 2019
J. van den Herik et al. (Eds.): ICAART 2019, LNAI 11978, pp. 166–182, 2019.
https://doi.org/10.1007/978-3-030-37494-5_9

The Japanese construction industry is facing problems such as manpower shortages, aging workers, and reduced international competitiveness. Since November 2015, the Japanese Ministry of Land, Infrastructure, Transport and Tourism has promoted *i-Construction* [29], an initiative to optimize and upgrade the entire construction process—from investigation and design to construction and inspection, including maintenance. i-Construction's primary concepts are utilization of information and communication technology and the introduction of innovative technology, such as artificial intelligence (AI) through cooperation between industries, governments, and academia. In this study, a practical construction support system based on i-Construction principles and focused on shield tunneling is developed.

The *shield tunneling* [13,19] is a common tunnel construction method. In the planning process, tunnel segments are assigned to a predetermined planning line (curved line along which a tunnel should be constructed), and, conventionally, to minimize the gaps between segments and the planning line, skilled engineers assign segments manually. Nevertheless, we have only to reduce each gap less than a tolerance, and there are assignments that satisfy the gap constraints and whose construction cost is lower than assignments that minimizes gaps. Automation and segment assignment optimization will address the problem of skilled labor shortage and improve productivity. In this study, the amount of soil excavated according to the segments is taken as construction cost and considered as an objective. We addressed segment assignment problem as a constrained combinatorial optimization problem.

This problem has severe constraints, and its feasible region is extremely narrow compared with its large search space. Takahama and Sakai proposed the ε constrained method [32] for optimization problems with such severe constraints. The ε constrained method adds constraint handling to algorithms that were originally designed for unconstrained optimization problems. Although this method has been adapted to several continuous optimizations [1,33,35], to the best of our knowledge, there has been no report of adapting it to discrete optimizations. By adapting the ε constrained method to a discrete version of particle swarm optimization (PSO), which is integer categorical PSO (ICPSO) [27], we propose an ε constrained ICPSO (εICPSO) method for constrained combinatorial optimization problems. In segment assignment, a feasible solution per a problem can be easily found by a greedy search. We also present initialization method for PSO to utilize a heuristic solution such as the feasible solution. Herein, we have attempted to experimentally verify the effectiveness of the proposed method by two-dimensional simulations using real-world construction data.

2   Related Work

Shield tunneling techniques have been intensively studied [17] in the civil and mechanical engineering domains. In addition, previous studies [9,28] have examined shield tunneling in the AI domain. However, to the best of our knowledge, no studies have focused on shield tunneling planning processes.

Previous studies have adapted the ε constrained method to metaheuristics algorithms, such as PSO [14], differential evolution (DE) [26], multiobjective evolutionary algorithm based on decomposition (MOEA/D) [36]. Takahama and Sakai proposed an ε constrained differential evolution (εDE) [31], and its extended version using an archive [33]. Takahama and Sakai proposed an ε constrained particle swarm optimizer (εPSO) [32]. Bonyadi, Li, and Michalewicz proposed the hybrid method of εPSO and an other constraint handling method [1]. Yang, Cai, and Fan introduced the ε constrained method for extending MOEA/D to constrained multiobjective optimization [35]. Note that these methods are only applicable to continuous optimization problems. Few studies have reported discrete constrained optimization methods that adapt the ε constrained method.

3 Segment Assignment

In this section, we explain the segment assignment and its formulation as constrained combinatorial optimization problem.

3.1 Shield Tunneling

Shield tunneling is a tunnel construction method that uses excavation machines (*shield machines*) shown in Fig. 1. The front surface of the shield machine has cutters (called the *cutter head*) for ground excavation. The *over cut i.e.*, the external cutter equipped outside the front surface, is controlled such that the machine body can pass without contacting the ground wall. A shield machines is divided to *front* and *rear drums*, and the angle between the front drum and the rear drum (referred to as the *joint angle*) is controlled to allow the shield machine to move around curves. Segments are assembled at the rear of the shield machine, and the shield machine is propelled by the reaction force given from its jack pushing the located segment.

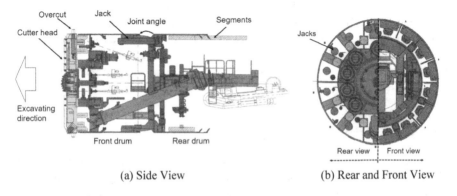

(a) Side View   (b) Rear and Front View

Fig. 1. An example of construction diagrams of a shield machine [12].

3.2 Segment Assignment Problem

In the planning process, multiple types of segments are provided for each construction project that are assigned along a planning line comprising straight lines and curves such that gaps between each segment and the planning line fall within a given tolerance, as shown in Fig. 2. Conventionally, skilled engineers manually assign segments to minimize these gaps without considering construction costs; however, this assignment roughly determines the shield machine's excavation route. Thus, optimization of this assignment will reduce shield construction costs.

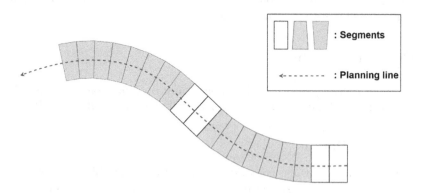

Fig. 2. An example of segment assignment.

There are two primary demands in segment assignment: (1) gaps between each segment and the planning line should be within the given tolerance, and (2) the amount of soil excavated by the shield machine along the segments should be reduced. In this study, the former is treated as an inequality constraint, and the latter is treated as an objective function. We define segment assignment as the following constrained combinatorial optimization problem: where $x_i \in \{1, \cdots, k\}$ corresponds to the type of the segment assigned to i-th position, and k is the number of segment types. A decision variable vector $\boldsymbol{x} = (x_1, x_2, \cdots x_n)$ expresses the assigned segments. The objective function $f(\boldsymbol{x})$ is the amount of soil excavated along to segments $\boldsymbol{x}$ by the shield machine; $g_i(\boldsymbol{x})$ as the gap between the i-th segment and the planning line; and g_t is the gap tolerance. Segments are assigned such that a center point of the i-th segment's backward surface correspond to a center point of the $(i-1)$-th segment's forward surface. Gap $g_i(\boldsymbol{x})$ are defined as Euclidean distance between a planning line and the center point of x_i's forward surface when segments $\boldsymbol{x}$ is assigned.

This problem involves an n-dimensional decision variable vector, where n is generally over several hundreds. Consequently, this problem has an extremely large search space; however, it is required to earn a solution must be quickly obtained because the segment assignment plan should be revised when the actual construction deviates from the plan. Population-based metaheuristics, such as swarm intelligence (SI), are frequently used for real-world optimization problems as they provide easy parallelization and demonstrate good multi-point search efficiency [5, 10, 25, 37]. Although many discrete optimization algorithms are based on SI, they often only consider integer problems [15, 23]. However, segment assignment involves variables whose values are categorical and unordered rather than purely numerical. PSO is one of the most widely used SI algorithms, and integer categorical PSO (ICPSO) [27], outperforms other discrete versions of PSO in unordered discrete optimization. In addition, gap tolerance g_t is typically about 50 mm, whereas the diameter of segments is around 10 m. Segment assignment has n severe constraints. The ε constrained method [32] was proposed to handle such severe constraints: thus, we adapt it to ICPSO to handle constrained combinatorial optimization.

4   Proposed Method

This section describes constrained combinatorial optimization problems, the ε constrained method, εICPSO, and a new initialization method for εICPSO.

4.1   Problem Domain

We consider the following constrained optimization problem. where $x = (x_1, \cdots, x_n)$ is an n-dimensional decision variable vector, $f(x)$ is an objective function, $g_j(x) \leq 0$ are q inequality constraints, and $h_j(x) = 0$ are r equality constraints. $f(x)$, $g_j(x)$, and $h_j(x)$ are real-valued functions. Integer values l_i, and u_i are the lower and upper bounds of x_i respectively, and the search space is defined by the lower and upper bounds. Note that the feasible region is defined by the inequality and equality constraints.

4.2 ε Constrained Method

The ε constrained method [32] adds a constraint handling ability to various algorithms originally designed for unconstrained optimization. This method introduces ε *level comparison*, which is a comparison operator that considers both constraints and objective values when ranking candidate solutions. In the ε constrained method, constraint violation $\phi(x)$ is defined as a measure of how much constraints are violated by a given solution. Constraint violation can be given by the maximum of all constraints or the sum of all constraints as follows.

$$\phi(x) = \max\{\max_j\{0, g_j(x)\}, \max_j |h_j(x)|\},$$

$$\phi(x) = \sum_j \max\{0, g_j(x)\}^p + \sum_j |h_j(x)|^p,$$

where p is a positive number. In this paper, constrain violation is given by the sum of all constraints in Sect. 4.2.

The ε level comparison ($<_\varepsilon, \leq_\varepsilon$) is defined as an order relation on the set of $(f(\boldsymbol{x}), \phi(\boldsymbol{x}))$. If $f_1(f_2)$ and $\phi_1(\phi_2)$ are the objective values and constraint violation, respectively, of solution point $x_1(x_2)$ then the comparison operators $<_\varepsilon$ and $\leq_\varepsilon$ are defined as follows.

$$(f_1, \phi_1) <_\varepsilon (f_2, \phi_2) \Leftrightarrow \begin{cases} f_1 < f_2, & (\phi_1, \phi_2 \leq \varepsilon) \\ f_1 < f_2, & (\phi_1 = \phi_2) \\ \phi_1 < \phi_2, & \text{otherwise} \end{cases}$$

$$(f_1, \phi_1) \leq_\varepsilon (f_2, \phi_2) \Leftrightarrow \begin{cases} f_1 \leq f_2, & (\phi_1, \phi_2 \leq \varepsilon) \\ f_1 \leq f_2, & (\phi_1 = \phi_2) \\ \phi_1 < \phi_2, & \text{otherwise} \end{cases}$$

According to this definition, ε level comparison first compares two solutions by constraint violation value. If both solutions have a violation value that is less than a given small threshold ε the two solutions are then compared by the objective function value only.

4.3 εICPSO

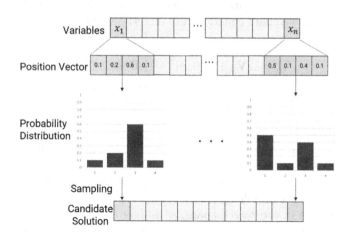

Fig. 3. Representation of a particle's position of ICPSO.

The εICPSO is a constrained combinatorial optimization algorithm based on ICPSO with candidate solutions ranked by the ε level comparison. The ICPSO is a novel PSO algorithm that has been shown to surpass other discrete PSO algorithms [27]. In PSO, particles search for the best position of the search space. Note that particles have a position and a velocity, and the position corresponds to a candidate solution. The original PSO assumes continuous state variables. In contrast, in ICPSO, the representation of the particle's position is changed such that so that each attribute in a particle is a distribution over its possible values rather than a single value as shown in Fig. 3. A particle is evaluated by sampling a candidate solution from these distributions and calculating its fitness. εICPSO is described in further detail as follows.

In εICPSO, particle p's position $\mathbf{X}_p$ is represented as follows:

$$\mathbf{X}_p = [\mathcal{D}_{p,1}, \mathcal{D}_{p,2}, \cdots, \mathcal{D}_{p,n}],$$

where each $\mathcal{D}_{p,i}$ is the probability distribution for variable X_i. In other words, each component of the position vector is a set of probabilities expressed as follows:

$$\mathcal{D}_{p,i} = [d^a_{p,i}, d^b_{p,i}, \cdots, d^k_{p,i}],$$

where $d^j_{p,i}$ denotes the probability by which variable X_i takes on value j for particle p. Particle p's velocity, $\mathbf{V}_p$, is a vector of n vector φ, which control the particle's probability distributions:

$$\mathbf{V}_p = [\varphi_{p,1}, \varphi_{p,2}, \cdots, \varphi_{p,n}],$$
$$\varphi_{p,1} = [\psi^a_{p,i}, \psi^a_{p,i}, \cdots, \psi^a_{p,n}],$$

where $\psi^j_{p,i}$ corresponds to particle p's velocity for variable i in state j. The velocity and position update equations are directly applied to values in the distribution as follows:

$$\mathbf{V}_p = \omega \mathbf{V}_p + U(0, \phi_1) \otimes (\mathbf{pBest} - \mathbf{X}_p)$$
$$+ U(0, \phi_2) \otimes (\mathbf{gBest} - \mathbf{X}_p),$$
$$\mathbf{X}_p = \mathbf{X}_p + \mathbf{V}_p,$$

where each operator is performed in a component-wise manner over each variable in the vector, and $U(0, \phi_1)$ and $U(0, \phi_2)$ are uniformly distributed random numbers between 0 and ϕ_1 and 0 and ϕ_2, respectively. The vector $\mathbf{pBest}$ is the best position in the search space that this particle has reached, and $\mathbf{gBest}$ is the best position in the search space any particle in the swarm has ever reached. The particle moves in the search space by adding the updated velocity to the particle's position vector in the current iteration. The particle's behavior is controlled by adjusting parameters ω, ϕ_1, and ϕ_2 (*i.e.*, inertia, cognitive component and social component, respectively).

After the velocity and position update, any value outside $[0,1]$ is mapped to the nearest boundary to maintain a valid probability. In addition, the distribution is normalized to ensure that its values sum to 1.

To evaluate a particle p, its distributions are sampled to create a candidate solution $\mathbf{S}_p = [s_{p,1}, s_{p,2}, \cdots, s_{p,n}]$, where $s_{p,j}$ denotes the state of variable X_j. The samples are evaluated by the fitness function. Then, the distributions are evaluated by their own sample's fitness value.

When a sample produced by a particle exceed the global or local best values in the ε level comparison, the best values are updated using both the distribution from the particle position P_p and sample S_p. Formally, for all states $j \in Vals(X_i)$, the global best's probability is updated as follows:

$$d^j_{gB,i} = \begin{cases} \epsilon_s \times d^j_{p,i} & (j \neq s_{p,i}) \\ d^j_{p,i} + \sum\limits_{k \in Vals(X_i) \wedge k \neq j} (1 - \epsilon_s) \times d^k_{p,i} & (j = s_{p,i}) \end{cases}$$

where ϵ_s (the *scaling factor*) is a user-controlled parameter that determines the magnitude of the shift in the distribution restricted to $[0, 1)$, and $d^j_{gB,i}$ is the global best position's probability signifying that variable X_i takes value j. This update increases the probability of the distribution producing samples that are similar to the best sample while maintaining a valid probability distribution. Thus, the update ensures that the best position's probability of producing a variable identical to the best sample's greater than $1 - \epsilon_s$, which can be shown as follows:

$$d^k_{gB,i} = d^k_{p,i} + \sum_{j \in S_v(X_i,k)} (1 - \epsilon_s) \times d^j_{p,i}$$

$$= \epsilon_s \times d^k_{p,i} + (1 - \epsilon_s) \times d^k_{p,i} + \sum_{j \in S_v(X_i,k)} (1 - \epsilon_s) \times d^j_{p,i}$$

$$= \epsilon_s \times d^k_{p,i} + (1 - \epsilon_s),$$

where $S_v(X_i, k) = \{j | j \in Vals(X_i) \wedge j \neq k\}$ and $k = s_{p,i}$. The scaling factor should be controlled according to the dimension of the decision variable because a large dimension increases the difference between the best sample and a sample expected to be produced by the updated distribution. The local best is updated in exactly the same way. At the end of the algorithm, the global best sample is returned as the solution.

Algorithm 1 shows the pseudo code of εICPSO, where step 11 and 15 update best positions according to Sect. 4.3, and step 21 and 22 update velocity and position vectors according to Sects. 4.3 and 4.3 respectively.

4.4   Greedy Initialization

In segment assignment problems, a feasible solution per a problem can be easily found via a greedy search where segments are assigned to minimize gaps. Algorithm 2 shows a pseudo code of the greedy algorithm to find a feasible solution for segment assignment, where $\mathbf{x} = \{x_1, \cdots, x_n\}$ is a decision variable vector, x_i is a segment assigned to the i-th position, n is the number of segments, and k is the number of segment types. P_i is a center point of segment x_i's forward surface, and corresponds to a point at which segment x_{i+1} should be assigned and a point used to calculate gap $g_i(\mathbf{x})$. Step 1 sets point P_0 to the start point of the given planning line. Step 4 calculates the next point when segment j is

Algorithm 1. εICPSO.

1: **for** $i = 1$ **to** $n\_particle$
2:     $initialize\_particle(p_i)$
3: **end for**
4: **while** (termination condition not met)
5:     $\varepsilon \leftarrow control\_epsilon\_level()$
6:     **for** $i = 1$ **to** $n\_particle$
7:         $S_{p_i} \leftarrow sample(X_{p_i})$
8:         $f \leftarrow evaluate\_fitness(S_{p_i})$
9:         $\phi \leftarrow constraint\_violation(S_{p_i})$
10:         **if** $(f, \phi) <_\varepsilon (f_{pB_i}, \phi_{pB_i})$ **then**
11:             $\text{pBest}_i \leftarrow update\_best(X_{p_i}, S_{p_i}, \text{pBest}_i)$
12:             $(f_{pB_i}, \phi_{pB_i}) \leftarrow (f, \phi)$
13:         **end if**
14:         **if** $(f, \phi) <_\varepsilon (f_{gB_i}, \phi_{gB_i})$ **then**
15:             $\text{gBest} \leftarrow update\_best(X_{p_i}, S_{p_i}, \text{gBest})$
16:             $(f_{gB}, \phi_{gB}) \leftarrow (f, \phi)$
17:             $S_{gB} \leftarrow S_{p_i}$
18:         **end if**
19:     **end for**
20:     **for** $i = 1$ **to** $n\_particle$
21:         $V_{p_i} \leftarrow update\_velocity(X_{p_i}, V_{p_i}, \text{pBest}_i, \text{gBest})$
22:         $X_{p_i} \leftarrow update\_position(X_{p_i}, V_{p_i})$
23:     **end for**
24: **end while**
25: **return** S_{gB}

Algorithm 2. Greedy Search for Segment Assignment.

1: $initialize\_position(P_0)$
2: **for** $i = 1$ **to** n
3:     **for** $j = 1$ **to** k
4:         $P_i^j \leftarrow next\_position(P_{i-1}, Segment_j)$
5:         $g_j \leftarrow gap(P_i^j)$
6:     **end for**
7:     $x_i \leftarrow \arg\min_{j \in \{1, \ldots, k\}} g_j$
8:     $P_i \leftarrow P_i^{x_i}$
9: **end for**
10: **return** x

assigned to point P_{i-1}. Step 5 calculates Euclidean distance between P_i^j and the planning line. Step 7 selects a segment whose next point's gap is minimum.

Initialization of population plays an important role in any optimization algorithms. Classical PSO works [2,16] consider an initial randomly generated population. It has proven that initialization by random selection of solutions from a given solution space can result in exploiting the fruitless areas of the search space [24]. Intelligent initialization techniques have been intensively developed [8,18,34], which mainly aim to improve the diversity of initial swarm.

In constrained optimization problems, however, algorithms should explore in or near the feasible region rather than all over the search space, particularly when the feasible region is narrow. Thus, we propose greedy initialization method utilizing the feasible solution discovered by the greedy method (Algorithm 2) to narrow search area down to near the feasible region. In our greedy initialization, position and velocity vectors are randomly initialized in the same way as classical PSOs. Then, a particle p is randomly chosen from initial swarm, and p's local best and global best were updated according to Sect. 4.3) under the assumption that the greedy feasible solution was earned by sampling p's position. Since this procedure does not change position and velocity of any other particles, the diversity of initial swarm is maintained, and future particles get to explore near the feasible region as drawn toward the global best.

5 Experimental Studies

We attempted to verify the effectiveness of εICPSO to segment assignment through the two-dimensional simulation experiment using real construction data. At first, experiments are conducted to empirically understand the influence of the scaling factor ϵ_s. Then, εICPSO is compared with the skilled engineer's conventional method and the ε constrained genetic algorithm (εDGA) [11].

A set of experiments was conducted on six segment assignment problems [12], which is made from real construction sites. The six problems involves three planning line p101, p102, and p103, and two set of segments sg01 and sg02 for each planning line. The planning lines are shown in Fig. 4a, b, and c, where R and L denotes a radius and length, respectively, of a curve. Figure 4d shows five segments, and segment sets sg01 and sg02 include segments whose type numbers are one to three, and one to five, respectively. Here, the shield machine shown in Fig. 4e was used and the gap tolerance g_t was set to 50 mm for each problem.

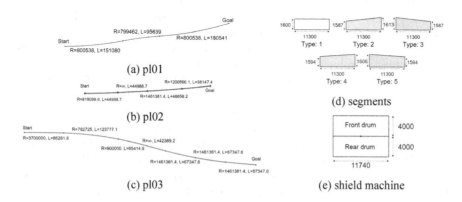

Fig. 4. Dimensions [mm] of the planning lines, segments, and shield machine used in the experiments, which is same setting with [12].

Candidate solutions (assigned segments) were evaluated by the two-dimensional simulator we developed. The simulator evaluated segments based on the area of the region where a shield machine passed when constructing the segments under the assumption that the amount of excavated soil is proportional to the area. Here, the area of the region through which the front of the shield machine passes was determined by the product of the shield machine's width and the planning line's total length. Thus, we define the area of the excavated field excluding this field as the fitness because this field does not depend on segment assignment. This fitness is equivalent to the amount of soil excavated by the overcut.

All statistical results are based on 50 independent runs. For each independent run, the maximum number of fitness evaluations is set to 500,000. In the comparisons between different statistical result, two-tailed Student t-test are conducted at a significance level of $\alpha = 0.01$

εICPSO used a swarm of size 50, and the swarm is evolved for $10,000$ iterations owing to the recommendation of [4], which demonstrated that a large swarm may, counterintuitively, have difficulty exploring the search space. The cognitive component ϕ_1 and social component ϕ_2 were both set to 1.49618, and the inertia ω was 0.729, which has been found to encourage convergent trajectories [3]. The ε level is set to 0 through the evolution.

The experiments have been run on a computer with an Intel Core i7-6950X @3.00 GHz CPU, 64 GB RAM and a Linux Ubuntu 14.04.5 LTS 64-bit operating system. The simulator and algorithms was implemented in Java language.

5.1   Parameter Settings

We investigate the influence of the scaling factor ϵ_s by varying it. Simulations have been conducted on the six problem with ϵ_s varying in $\{1.0 \times 10^{-1}, 1.0 \times 10^{-2}, 1.0 \times 10^{-3}, 5.0 \times 10^{-4}, 1.0 \times 10^{-4}, 5.0 \times 10^{-5}, 1.0 \times 10^{-5}, 1.0 \times 10^{-6}, 1.0 \times 10^{-7}\}$.

Figure 5 summarizes the experimental results as box plots, where boxes represent the 25th to 75th percentiles, lines within the boxes represent the median, and lines outside the boxes represent the minimum and maximum values. We found that the scaling factor should be set to smaller to achieve good performance in a target problem involving larger dimensions, as εICPSO performs the best with $\epsilon_s = 5.0 \times 10^{-4}$, 1.0×10^{-3}, and 1.0×10^{-4} on p101, p102, and p103 problems, respectively. Additionally, we can see that smaller ϵ_s works slightly worse than the best one, and that bigger ϵ_s make it almost impossible to find a good solution. The reason might be that with a small ϵ_s a sampling procedure tends to generate a exactly similar solution to the current best solution, thus leading to premature convergence; however, with a big ϵ_s the sampling procedure tends to generate completely different solutions, particularly in large dimension problems, which prevents to explore the feasible region.

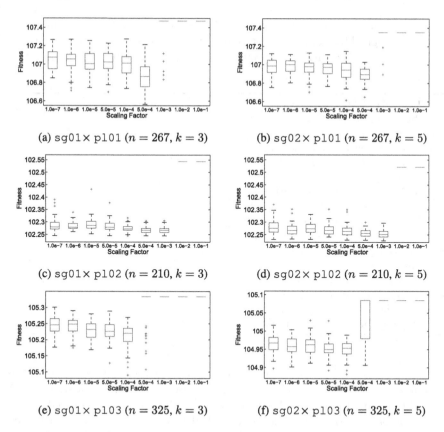

(a) sg01× pl01 ($n = 267, k = 3$)

(b) sg02× pl01 ($n = 267, k = 5$)

(c) sg01× pl02 ($n = 210, k = 3$)

(d) sg02× pl02 ($n = 210, k = 5$)

(e) sg01× pl03 ($n = 325, k = 3$)

(f) sg02× pl03 ($n = 325, k = 5$)

Fig. 5. Box plots of fitness scores obtained εICPSO on six problems with different scaling factors ϵ_s varying in $\{1.0\times10^{-7}, 1.0\times10^{-6}, 1.0\times10^{-5}, 5.0\times10^{-5}, 1.0\times10^{-4}, 5.0\times10^{-4}, 1.0\times10^{-3}, 1.0\times10^{-2}, 1.0\times10^{-1}\}$ for each problem with 50 trials. Note that n denotes the number of segments (dimension number) and k denotes the number os segment types in each problem.

5.2   Comparisons with Previous Works

In order to verify the effectiveness of εICPSOfor segment assignment, εICPSOhas been compared with existing methods on the six problems. The scaling factor is set based on the previous empirical analysis . In problems that use pl01, pl02, and pl03, scaling   factor $\epsilon_s = 5.0\times10^{-4}$, 1.0×10^{-3}, and 1.0×10^{-4} respectively. The comparative methods are described in the following.

Conventional Method. In a construction site, segments are manually assigned by skilled engineers; however, comparing the proposed methods with real skilled engineers' assignments is difficult because engineers spend significant time assigning segments in each problem. Skilled engineers assign segments to minimize gaps without considering the amount of excavated soil; thus, their methods are approximately equivalent to the greedy method (Algorithm 2), where segments are assigned to minimize gaps. Hence, we compared the proposed methods to the greedy method rather than assignments made by skilled engineers.

Algorithm 3. εDGA.

 1: *initialize_population*(P)
 2: *evaluate_population*(P)
 3: **while** (termination condition not met)
 4:    $\varepsilon \leftarrow control\_epsilon\_level()$
 5:    $P_{mating} \leftarrow selection(P_t, \varepsilon)$
 6:    **while** (P_{mating} is not empty)
 7:       $parents \leftarrow pop(P_{mating})$
 8:       $offspring \leftarrow crossover(parents)$
 9:       $offspring \leftarrow mutate(offspring)$
10:       add $offspring$ to $P_{offspring}$
11:    **end while**
12:    $P_{offspring} \leftarrow evaluate(P_{offspring})$
13:    $P \leftarrow replacement(P, P_{offspring}, \varepsilon)$
14: **end while**
15: **return** the best individual ranked by $<_0$

ε**DGA** Ihara *et al.* proposed the εDGA [11] for segment assignment. εDGA is a combination of the ε constraint method and discrete genetic algorithm. εDGA is based on standard genetic algorithms in which individuals are ranked by the ε level comparison with the ε level controlled in each generation. Parents are selected using selection methods based on the comparison of individuals, such as tournament selection [20] and ranking selection [7], using ε level comparison rather than a general comparison. Elite individuals are also selected by ε level comparison to carry over to the next generation. Algorithm 3 summarizes the flow of this method. Initial individuals are created by applying uniform mutation to the feasible solution found by a greedy search (Algorithm 2). In this experiments, populations were evolved for 500 generations, with a population of size 1,000. Uniform crossover [30] is applied 95% of the time offspring are produced, and each offspring performed uniform mutation [6] wherein each gene has a 5% chance of changing to a random value. The ε level is set to 0 through the evolution.

5.3   Results

The experimental results demonstrate that the proposed method has the potential to find a segment assignment that reduces the amount of excavated soil as compared to the conventional method (assignment by skilled engineer) while keeping the all gaps between segments and the planning line falling within the given tolerance. The experimental results for the six problems (Fig. 4) are shown in Table 1, where only fitness scores are summarized because every algorithm obtained feasible solutions on every trial of every problem. In the table, "Mean", "Std dev", "Best", "Worst" indicate the mean values, standard deviations, best values, and worst values, respectively, obtained over 50 trials of each problem. Bold values indicate algorithms that, statistically, significantly outperformed all other methods (two-tailed Student t-Test, $\alpha = 0.01$). Figure 6 shows the performance of the εICPSO and εDGA. Their fitness scores are shown as box plots and the conventional method's scores are represented by the horizontal dashed lines.

Clearly, εICPSO is advantageous over εDGA. In all problems, εICPSO statistically performed the best. Note that the worst εICPSO scores exceeded both, the εDGA's best scores and the skilled engineer's score. In complex problems with large n or k, the difference in performance is particularly remarkable. Although the εDGA has potential to find the solution superior to the skilled engineer in

Table 1. Statistical results (Mean, Best, and Worst Values and Standard Deviations) of Fitness Scores [m^2].

Problem		Skilled engineer	εICPSO			εDGA		
Segment set	Planning line	(greedy method)	Mean(Std dev)	Best	Worst	Mean(Std dev)	Best	Worst
sg01 ($k = 3$)	pl01 ($n = 267$)	107.48	**106.86(1.54e−1)**	106.56	107.21	107.42(4.33e−2)	107.30	107.47
	pl02 ($n = 210$)	102.54	**102.27(1.41e−2)**	102.24	102.31	102.47(1.82e−2)	102.39	102.48
	pl03 ($n = 325$)	105.33	**105.21(3.77e−2)**	105.09	105.27	105.33(1.64e−2)	105.30	105.39
sg02 ($k = 5$)	pl01 ($n = 267$)	107.35	**106.89(7.30e−2)**	106.65	107.03	107.32(3.05e−2)	107.24	107.35
	pl02 ($n = 210$)	102.52	**102.25(1.72e−2)**	102.23	102.30	102.46(2.55e−2)	102.38	102.52
	pl03 ($n = 325$)	105.08	**104.95(2.46e−2)**	104.88	104.99	105.08(1.60e−2)	105.04	105.11

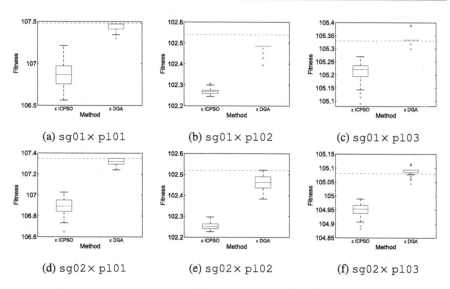

(a) sg01× pl01   (b) sg01× pl02   (c) sg01× pl03

(d) sg02× pl01   (e) sg02× pl02   (f) sg02× pl03

Fig. 6. Box plots of fitness scores of the εDGA and εICPSO for each problem with 50 trials, with horizontal dashed lines representing the conventional method's evaluations.

terms of the best score, its score averagely almost equivalent and at worst inferior in the p103 problems.

6   Conclusion

In this study, we have addressed segment assignment in shield tunneling as a constrained combinatorial optimization problem. We have proposed εICPSO method, which is the combination of a discrete version of PSO and ε constrained method, and intelligent initialization method utilizing a feasible solution found via a greedy search. Two-dimensional simulation experiments were conducted to investigate influence of scaling factor, and demonstrate our method's effectiveness for segment assignment problems. The experimental results have shown εICPSO's potential to reduce construction costs as compared to the conventional method. In all test problems, the proposed method exhibited the best performance. In the future, we plan to conduct additional experiments using a three-dimensional simulator for more accurate evaluation of the proposed method.

Acknowledgements. This work was supported in part by the Ministry of Education, Science, Sports and Culture, Grant–in–Aid for Scientific Research under grant #JP19H01137 and #JP19H04025.

References

1. Bonyadi, M., Li, X., Michalewicz, Z.: A hybrid particle swarm with velocity mutation for constraint optimization problems. In: Proceedings of the 15th Annual Conference on Genetic and Evolutionary Computation (GECCO), pp. 1–8. ACM (2013)
2. Eberhart, R., Kennedy, J.: Particle swarm optimization. In: Proceedings of the IEEE International Conference on Neural Networks, vol. 4, pp. 1942–1948. Citeseer (1995)
3. Eberhart, R.C., Shi, Y.: Comparing inertia weights and constriction factors in particle swarm optimization. In: Proceedings of IEEE Congress on Evolutionary Computation (CEC), vol. 1, pp. 84–88. IEEE (2000)
4. Engelbrecht, A.P.: Fitness function evaluations: a fair stopping condition? In: Proceedings of 2014 IEEE Symposium on Swarm Intelligence (SIS), pp. 1–8. IEEE (2014)
5. Glover, F.W., Kochenberger, G.A. (eds.): Handbook of Metaheuristics, vol. 57. Springer, Heidelberg (2006). https://doi.org/10.1007/b101874
6. Goldberg, D.E.: Genetic Algorithms in Search, Optimization and Machine Learning. Addison-Wesley, Reading (1989)
7. Goldberg, D.E., Deb, K.: A comparative analysis of selection schemes used in genetic algorithms. Found. Genet. Algorithms (FOGA) 1, 69–93 (1991)
8. Gutiérrez, A., et al.: Comparison of different PSO initialization techniques for high dimensional search space problems: a test with FSS and antenna arrays. In: Proceedings of the 5th European Conference on Antennas and Propagation (EUCAP), pp. 965–969. IEEE (2011)

9. Hasanipanah, M., Noorian-Bidgoli, M., Armaghani, D.J., Khamesi, H.: Feasibility of PSO-ANN model for predicting surface settlement caused by tunneling. Eng. Comput. **32**(4), 705–715 (2016)
10. Hassanien, A.E., Emary, E.: Swarm Intelligence: Principles, Advances, and Applications. CRC Press, Boca Raton (2018)
11. Ihara, K., Kato, S., Nakaya, T., Ogi, T.: Constrained GA based segment assignment in shield tunneling to minimize the amount of excavated soil. In: Proceedings of 2018 IEEE 7th Global Conference on Consumer Electronics, pp. 229–230 (2018)
12. Ihara, K., Kato, S., Nakaya, T., Ogi, T., Masuda, H.: A PSO based approach to assign segments for reducing excavated soil in shield tunneling. In: Proceedings of the 11th International Conference on Agents and Artificial Intelligence, vol. 2, pp. 328–336 (2019)
13. Japan Society of Civil Engineers: Standard specifications for tunneling-2006: shield tunnels. Tunnel Engineering Committee, August 2007
14. Kennedy, J.: Particle swarm optimization. In: Encyclopedia of Machine Learning, pp. 760–766. Springer, New York (2011)
15. Kennedy, J., Eberhart, R.: Particle swarm optimization. In: Proceedings of IEEE International Conference on Neural Networks, pp. 1942–1948. IEEE (1995)
16. Kennedy, J., Eberhart, R.C.: A discrete binary version of the particle swarm algorithm. In: Proceedings of the IEEE International Conference on Systems, Man, and Cybernetics. Computational Cybernetics and Simulation, vol. 5, pp. 4104–4108. IEEE (1997)
17. Koyama, Y.: Present status and technology of shield tunneling method in Japan. Tunn. Undergr. Space Technol. **18**(2–3), 145–159 (2003)
18. Liu, B., Wang, L., Jin, Y.H., Tang, F., Huang, D.X.: Improved particle swarm optimization combined with chaos. Chaos, Solitons Fractals **25**(5), 1261–1271 (2005)
19. Maidl, B., Herrenknecht, M., Maidl, U., Wehrmeyer, G.: Mechanised Shield Tunnelling. Wiley, New York (2013)
20. Miller, B.L., Goldberg, D.E., et al.: Genetic algorithms, tournament selection, and the effects of noise. Complex Syst. **9**(3), 193–212 (1995)
21. Ng, J.Y., Chan, A.H.: The ageing construction workforce in Hong Kong: a review. In: Proceedings of International MultiConference of Engineers and Computer Scientists 2015 (IMECS). Newswood Limited (2015)
22. Olsen, D., Tatum, M., Defnall, C.: How industrial contractors are handling skilled labor shortages in the United States. In: 48th ASC Annual International Conference Proceedings (2012)
23. Pampara, G., Franken, N., Engelbrecht, A.P.: Combining particle swarm optimisation with angle modulation to solve binary problems. In: Proceedings of IEEE Congress on Evolutionary Computation (CEC), vol. 1, pp. 89–96. IEEE (2005)
24. Rahnamayan, S., Tizhoosh, H.R., Salama, M.M.A.: Opposition-based differential evolution. IEEE Trans. Evol. Comput. **12**(1), 64–79 (2008)
25. Soares, J., Ghazvini, M.A.F., Silva, M., Vale, Z.: Multi-dimensional signaling method for population-based metaheuristics: solving the large-scale scheduling problem in smart grids. Swarm Evol. Comput. **29**, 13–32 (2016)
26. Storn, R., Price, K.: Differential evolution-a simple and efficient heuristic for global optimization over continuous spaces. J. Global Optim. **11**(4), 341–359 (1997)
27. Strasser, S., Goodman, R., Sheppard, J., Butcher, S.: A new discrete particle swarm optimization algorithm. In: Proceedings of the Genetic and Evolutionary Computation Conference (GECCO), pp. 53–60. ACM (2016)

28. Suwansawat, S., Einstein, H.H.: Artificial neural networks for predicting the maximum surface settlement caused by EPB shield tunneling. Tunn. Undergr. Space Technol. **21**(2), 133–150 (2006)
29. Suzuki, A.: 2016 annual report of NILIM: productivity improvement in infrastrucure development process using i-construction (2016). http://www.nilim.go.jp/english/annual/annual2016/ar2016e.html. Accessed 23 Oct 2018
30. Syswerda, G.: Uniform crossover in genetic algorithms. In: Proceedings of the 3rd International Conference on Genetic Algorithms, pp. 2–9. Morgan Kaufmann Publishers (1989)
31. Takahama, T., Sakai, S.: Constrained optimization by the ε constrained differential evolution with gradient-based mutation and feasible elites. In: Proceedings of IEEE Congress on Evolutionary Computation (CEC), pp. 1–8. IEEE (2006)
32. Takahama, T., Sakai, S.: Constrained optimization by ε constrained particle swarm optimizer with ε-level control. In: Abraham, A., Dote, Y., Furuhashi, T., Köppen, M., Ohuchi, A., Ohsawa, Y. (eds.) Soft Computing as Transdisciplinary Science and Technology. Advances in Soft Computing, vol. 29, pp. 1019–1029. Springer, Heidelberg (2005). https://doi.org/10.1007/3-540-32391-0_105
33. Takahama, T., Sakai, S.: Constrained optimization by the ε constrained differential evolution with an archive and gradient-based mutation. In: Proceedings of IEEE Congress on Evolutionary Computation (CEC), pp. 1–9. IEEE (2010)
34. Weng, W.C., Yang, F., Elsherbeni, A.: Electromagnetics and antenna optimization using Taguchi's method. Synth. Lect. Comput. Electromagnet. **2**(1), 1–94 (2007)
35. Yang, Z., Cai, X., Fan, Z.: Epsilon constrained method for constrained multiobjective optimization problems: some preliminary results. In: Proceedings of the Companion Publication of the 2014 Annual Conference on Genetic and Evolutionary Computation, pp. 1181–1186. ACM (2014). https://doi.org/10.1145/2598394.2610012
36. Zhang, Q., Li, H.: MOEA/D: a multiobjective evolutionary algorithm based on decomposition. IEEE Trans. Evol. Comput. **11**(6), 712–731 (2007)
37. Zhang, Z., Long, K., Wang, J., Dressler, F.: On swarm intelligence inspired self-organized networking: its bionic mechanisms, designing principles and optimization approaches. IEEE Commun. Surv. Tutorials **16**(1), 513–537 (2014)

Boosting Local Search Using Machine Learning: A Study on Improving Local Search by Graph Classification in Determining Capacity of Shunting Yards

Arno van de Ven[1], Yingqian Zhang[1(✉)], and Wan-Jui Lee[2]

[1] Eindhoven University of Technology, Eindhoven, The Netherlands
yqzhang@tue.nl
[2] Maintenance Development, NS (Dutch Railways), Utrecht, The Netherlands
wan-jui.lee@ns.nl

Abstract. Determining the maximum capacities of shunting yards is an important problem at Dutch Railways (NS). Solving this capacity determination problem is computational expensive as it requires to solve an NP-hard shunting planning problem. Currently, NS uses a shunt plan simulator where a local search heuristic is implemented to determine such capacities.

In this paper, we study how to combine machine learning with local search in order to speed up finding shunting plans in the capacity determination problem. We investigate this in the following two ways. In the first approach, we propose to use the Deep Graph Convolutional Neural Network (DGCNN) to predict whether local search will find a feasible shunt plan given an initial solution. Using instances generated from the simulator, we build a classification model and show our approach can significantly reduce the simulation time in determining the capacity of a given shunting yard.

In the second approach, we investigate whether we can use machine learning to help local search decide which promising areas to explore during search. Therefore, DGCNN is applied to predict the order of search operators in which the local search heuristic should evaluate. We show that accurately predicting the evaluation order could find improved solutions faster, and may lead to more consistent plans.

Keywords: Planning and scheduling · Machine learning - Convolutional neural networks · Classification · Local search

1 Introduction

The Dutch Railways (NS) operates 4,800 domestic trains every day. Trains are maintained at specific shunting yards for shunting activities [1] when they are not needed temporarily. Figure 1 shows an example of a shunting yard.

© Springer Nature Switzerland AG 2019
J. van den Herik et al. (Eds.): ICAART 2019, LNAI 11978, pp. 183–203, 2019.
https://doi.org/10.1007/978-3-030-37494-5_10

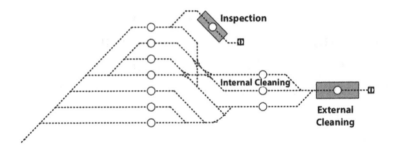

Fig. 1. Shunting yard with specific tracks for inspection and cleaning activities *Source:* www.sporenplan.nl.

To cope with the expanding plan of fleet of train units, a shunt plan simulator has been developed to help solve the *capacity determination problem*, which studies whether the capacity of existing shunting yards is sufficient to handle the increased train units. The simulator is used to both determine the capacity of shunting yards as well as analyze different scenarios on each shunting yard. In the simulator, a local search heuristic (or LS) [2] is implemented. LS takes an initial solution generated by a simple algorithm and searches for the feasible solution. After a predefined running time, LS either returns a feasible plan, or cannot find any feasible plan. Essential to any local search algorithm is a solution representation that properly captures all important aspects of the solution. The local search heuristic by [2] models the activities that take place on the shunting yards as nodes in an activity graph. Representing shunt plans as activity graphs enables us to use graph classification. Recent research on graph classification has proven to achieve high accuracy in predicting the class labels of an arbitrary graph, see e.g., [13,18] and [8].

Compared to the mathematical optimization approach [9], LS can solve the determination problem much faster. However, given that there are over 30 shunting yards in The Netherlands, and more than 50 possible scenarios to be evaluated for each shunting yard, there is a need for new solutions to speeding up capacity determination. One promising direction is on using machine learning to boost local search. In recent years, many studies have investigated boosting optimization using machine learning, see e.g. [6,10,11,17]. In planning and scheduling, [14] develops a Deep Reinforcement Learning (DRL) solution to decide the best strategy of parking trains. In their work, the existing optimization model is completely replaced by a machine learning model.

In this paper, we propose to use machine learning techniques to learn the relation between the input instances and the corresponding outcomes of local search. In our first line of approach, given any initial solution, we use the constructed classification model to predict whether LS can find a feasible solution before actually applying LS. In this way, LS does not have to evaluate every generated initial solution, and hence its computation time on determining the maximum capacity of a given shunting yard is greatly reduced. The initial results have been reported in [16], where we use a Deep Graph Convolutional Neural Network (DGCNN) to train a classification model that predicts whether a schedule instance is expected to be feasible or infeasible. In [4], we improved the approach of [16] by investigating how to use DGCNN to predict the feasibility of solutions during the run of the LS heuristic, and then to decide whether to continue or abort the search process. In our second approach, we investigate the use of DGCNN on helping local search decide which promising areas to explore next during search. The LS heuristic attempts to find a feasible shunt plan by applying search operators in iterations to move through the search space. In every iteration, the search operators are shuffled in random order. This will be the order in which the operators will be evaluated. We replace random ordering by predicting in which order search operators should be evaluated to speed up the search of LS. The output of DGCNN is a vector of probabilities for each search operator. These probabilities determine the order in which search operators are evaluated. The operator with the highest probability will be evaluated first. We show using proposed method, LS can find improvements faster.

The rest of our paper is organized as follows. In Sect. 2, we describe background information that helps to understand the capacity determination problem. Section 3 shows the use of DGCNN on predicting the feasibility of solutions of the local search heuristic, and describes the experiment setup and results in terms of prediction accuracy and decreased computation time. Section 4 shows how to use DGCNN to guide the operator selection for local search during its search process. Finally, we conclude in Sect. 5.

2   Background

2.1   Shunt Plan Simulator

The shunt plan simulator at NS consists of three sequential stages: (1) generating an instance of a given shunting yard, (2) generating an initial solution, and (3) finding a feasible solution using a local search heuristic. The maximum capacity of a given shunting yard is determined by repeatedly running the local search heuristic with different instances of different scenarios. After a sufficient number of runs, the simulation converges towards a number of train units for which the heuristic can solve at least 95% of the instances. This number is used to determine the capacity of the given shunting yard. The capacity is defined as the number of train units a shunting yard can serve during a 24-h time period.

Figure 2 shows a diagram explaining the software structure of the simulator. The instance generator is a parameterizable program, which derives instances for the Train Unit Shunting Problem automatically. Instances can be generated for each shunting yard individually with parameters specifically based on a day-to-day schedule at that shunting yard. Examples of parameters are number of train units, arrival/departure distribution and the set of service tasks that can be performed. Parameters can be changed to test different scenarios.

The output of the instance generator is a set of arriving trains (AT), a set of departing trains (DT) and a set of service tasks for each train unit that has

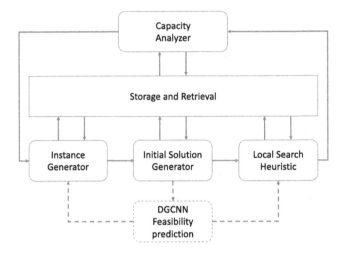

Fig. 2. Diagram software structure simulator [16].

to be performed. For both (AT) and (DT), train composition, train units and arrival/departure time are specified. The set of service tasks contains a list of service tasks for each train unit that has to be done in the time that the train unit is present on the service site. Trains can be composed of one or more train units of the same type, which are a set of carriages that form a self-propelling vehicle that can drive in both directions. Of the same train unit type, there exist multiple subtypes, where the subtype indicates how many carriages the train unit consists of. Figure 3 shows a train unit type and corresponding subtypes. Train composition, train units and arrival/departure time are specified for both AT and DT. The set of service tasks contains a list of service tasks for each train unit that has to be done in the time that the train unit is present on the shunting yard.

Fig. 3. Train unit type VIRM with 6 and 4 carriages.

The output of the instance generator serves as input for the initial solution generator. The Hopcroft-Karp algorithm [7] is used to produce a matching between arriving and departing train units. Next, a service task schedule is constructed in a greedy way, which forms an initial solution of the given instance. Note that initial solutions are typically not feasible, that is, an initial solution may violate the temporal or routing constraints. The purpose of an initial solution is that it contains all important features to serve as a starting point for the

local search heuristic to find a feasible solution. In earlier work [2,3], 11 operators in LS have been defined to move through the search space. LS ends when a
feasible solutions has been found or when the predefined maximum runtime has
been reached. In the latter case, no feasible solutions are found. Experiments
in [3] show that LS is capable to find feasible shunt plans in both artificial and
real-world scenarios. The performance of LS has been compared to a mathematical optimization model developed at NS that tries to find the optimal solution,
and LS is capable of planning more train units in most experiments. As it is
computationally expensive to use LS to evaluate every instance, in this work, we
evaluate instances using a machine learning model before applying LS.

The position of our work in the shunt plan simulator is between the initial
solution generation and applying initial solutions to local search (Fig. 2). For
the first approach, after generating an initial solution, a trained classification
model (DGCNN) predicts whether LS can find a feasible solution. If the outcome
is positive, LS is applied to find a feasible solution. Otherwise, the negative
outcome leads to discarding the initial solution and drawing a new instance
from the instance generator. Therefore, accurately predicting feasibility leads
to a decrease in computation time since less time is wasted on instances that
may turn out to be infeasible (see Sect. 3). In our second approach, after an
initial solution is generated, a DGCNN model predicts which operators the LS
heuristic should evaluate during each iteration. LS terminates when it finds a
feasible solution, or the maximum running time has been reached (see Sect. 4).

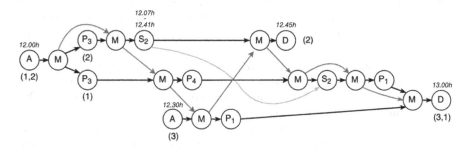

Fig. 4. The activity graph of a shunt plan. The activity nodes in an shunt graph are
encoded with starting and/or ending times. For clarity, only a few starting and ending
times are visualized [16].

3   Boosting LS Using DGCNN

3.1   DGCNN

A shunt plan can be modelled as an activity graph. Figure 4 shows an example of
an activity graph. The activities nodes, including arrival (A), service (S), parking
(P), movement (M) and departure (D), are connected by edges indicating the
precedence relations. The solid, black arcs represent the order of operations of

one or more train units. The corresponding train units of the nodes are between parentheses. The blue edges determine the order of the movements, and the green edge indicates which service task is completed first. The assigned track for each parking node is shown in subscript. The specific service task for each service node is shown in subscript.

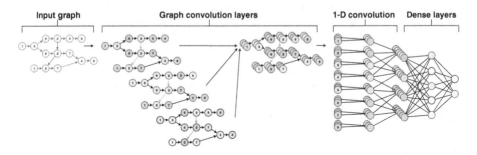

Fig. 5. The overall structure of DGCNN used in our problem. An input graph of arbitrary structure is first passed through multiple graph convolution layers where node labels are propagated between neighbors, visualized as different colors. Then the node features are passed to traditional CNN structures to learn a predictive model. The figure is slightly modified from [18].

We predict whether an initial solution that is represented by a given activity graph can lead to a feasible solution. To this end, we treat the prediction problem as a graph classification problem. Given a graph $G = (V, E)$ where V is a finite set of nodes and E is a finite set of edges. Node features encode information about tracks, train units, duration and activities. Each graph $G_i \in G$ has a corresponding class $y_i \in C$ where C is the set of class labels given as $C = 0$ (infeasible), 1 (feasible). The accuracy of the derived model is assessed by comparing the predicted label y_i' with the actual label y_i.

There are many successful machine learning algorithms that could be used to predict feasibility of initial solutions. However, most algorithms involve heavy feature engineering on problem instances. Recently, a Deep Graph Convolutional Neural Network (DGCNN) has been proposed in [18] for graph classification, which accepts graphs of arbitrary structure. The proposed architecture addresses two main challenges: (1) how to extract useful features characterizing the rich information encoded in graph classification and (2) how to sequentially read a graph in a meaningful and consistent order.

To tackle the first challenge, graph convolution layers are used to extract local substructure features from nodes and define a consistent node ordering. Their graph convolution model effectively mimics two popular kernels, the Weisfeiler-Lehman Subtree Kernel [15] and the Propagation Kernel [12], explaining its graph-level classification performance. To address the second challenge, a Sort-Pooling layer is introduced, which sorts the node features under the previously defined order and unifies input sizes. This is done because in contrast to images graphs lack a tensor representation with fixed ordering, which limits the applicability of neural networks on graphs. Finally, traditional convolutional and dense layers are added to read the sort graph representations and make predictions. The authors of [18] show DGCNN can achieve good performance on several graphs such as social networks. In this paper, we apply a modified DGCNN, which is described as follows.

The second localized graph convolution step involves appending node labels of neighbouring nodes to original node labels. The variety of original node labels defines how many new node labels will be created after appending neighbouring node labels. Local search specifies eight different activities in shunt graphs. This original representation can be modified to include more information in the graphs. The amount of original node labels can be increased by including specific types of activities to effectively exploit the graph structure for a classification task.

In our problem, shunt graphs contain, among others, Parking (P) and Service (S) activity nodes. Instead of just using P and S as original node labels, both can be encoded with more information. The specific parking track can be appended to get P_i, where $i = 1, ..., T$ and T is the number of parking tracks on a shunting yard. The specific service task can be appended to get S_i, where $i = 1, ..., ST$ and ST is the number of service tasks that can be performed on a shunting yard. Experiments showed that including both P_i and S_i is beneficial.

As the train unit shunting problem is a scheduling problem, the activity nodes in an shunt graph are encoded with starting and ending times. Therefore, the nodes in an activity graph are implicitly sorted based on the starting time. Thus, the sorting function of Sortpooling in DGCNN is redundant, and therefore is removed from our model. Figure 5 shows the network structure that we use in our problem. It is slightly modified from DGCNN in [18].

3.2 Experiments and Results

We evaluate how much running time can be reduced in determining capacity in shunting yards with our approach. To this end, we first generate and analyze data from the simulator. Then we report the performance of the DGCNN model on predicting whether initial plans would lead to feasible plans. From the performance of DGCNN, we can finally estimate the difference of running time with or without using DGCNN feasibility prediction in the simulator (illustrated in Fig. 2).

Data Instances. In order to evaluate our method, we generate data instances from the instance generator in the shunt plan simulator. The instance generator can be specified according to a set of input parameters based on the day-to-day schedule at the given service site. The most important parameters include: (1) number of train units, (2) different train unit types and subtypes, (3) probability distributions of arrivals per train unit type, and (4) set of service tasks including duration.

We generated 10,000 instances with 21 train units based on one of the service sites operated by NS. The amount of 21 train units has been purposely chosen. An increasing number of train unit increases the difficulty in finding feasible solutions. The preliminary experiments have shown that the instances with fewer train units are rather easy for the local search algorithm to find feasible solutions and hence, less insightful and valuable to the business. For the shunting yard that we used in the experiments, the instances with 20 to 22 train units are most interesting for NS, as they are neither easy nor too difficult for LS. Among them, initial solutions generated for 21 train units are the hardest to be correctly classified, and therefore they are considered the most suitable data to explore the usefulness of our approach to NS.

Initial solutions were created for all instances and LS was applied to solve them. The maximum running time for LS to solve each instance is set to 300 s. Among 10,000 instances, LS was not able to find feasible solutions for 2,750 instances. The outcomes (feasible, infeasible) were recorded as classification labels, where feasible instances (class 1) are initial solutions leading to feasible plans using LS within 300 s, while infeasible ones (class 0) are those LS could not find feasible plans within the time limit.

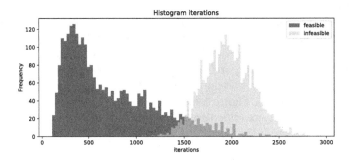

Fig. 6. Distribution of iterations for feasible and infeasible solutions [16].

Figure 6 visualizes the distribution of iterations for both feasible and infeasible instances. Regarding feasible solutions, the minimum and maximum numbers of iterations in local search are 108 and 2599 respectively with an average of 733 iterations. The minimum and maximum number of iterations for infeasible solutions are 1057 and 2939 with an average of 1962 iterations. Clearly, the number of iterations for infeasible solutions are much higher because local search ran for the maximum time of 300 s and was not able to find a feasible solution. Figure 7 shows a scatterplot with the number of iterations on the x-axis and runtime on the y-axis. The runtime of feasible instances increases as the number of iterations increases. The spread in the beginning is small, meaning that the time per iteration is quite similar. As the runtime increases, the spread becomes larger. Figure 8 shows a histogram of the runtime for all feasible instances. Infeasible instances are omitted for clarity because their runtime is always around 300 s.

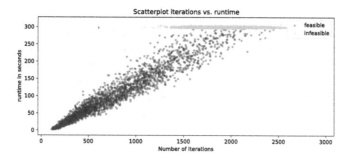

Fig. 7. Scatter plot of iterations versus runtime [16].

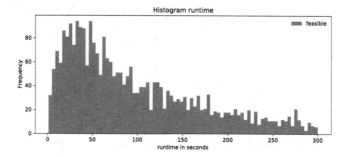

Fig. 8. Histogram of the runtime (in seconds) for feasible solutions [16].

Considering feasible instances, the minimum runtime is 1 s, while the maximum runtime is 300 s. The average runtime is 96 s. ±80% of all feasible instances has been found within 150 s.

Results on Predicting Feasibility. The PyTorch (0.4.0) implementation of DGCNN is used with Python (3.6.4) for the experiments. Training was done on an 1.7 GHz Intel Core i7 MacBook Air. The DGCNN implementation is not parallelized, thus only 1 CPU core is used. Every time a new epoch begins, training data is randomly shuffled and processed in batches of several graphs to enable faster learning.

When applying DGCNN, we need to determine the level of details, or node representation, on the node labels in the graph. We apply the Weisfeiler-Lehman subtree kernel [15] to append node labels of the neighbouring nodes to the original node labels. The appended labels are sorted alphabetically and compressed into new, shorter labels. At the end of an iteration, the counts of the original node labels and the counts of the compressed node labels are represented as a feature vector. Neural networks are trained on these feature vectors. The original node labels define how many new node labels will be created after appending neighbouring node labels. The length of the feature vector depends on the amount of different node labels in the initial solution. Figure 9 visualizes how the length of the feature vector changes if node labels differ for the same graphs. In the left graph, originally, all nodes have the same node label. The right graph originally contains three different node labels. The appended and compressed labels after one iteration of the Weisfeiler-Lehman subtree kernel are visualized below both graphs. The feature vectors of both graphs contain the counts of the compressed node labels after one iteration. As can be seen, the length of the feature vector gets bigger when the level of detail (variety of node labels in the original graph) increases.

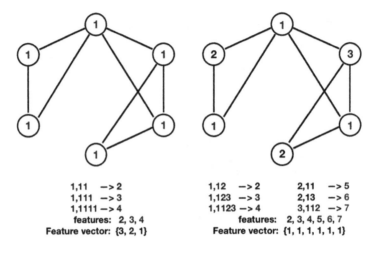

Fig. 9. Different feature vectors for different amounts of node labels [16].

Too many node labels may result in very dissimilar feature vectors. In both cases, neural networks may not be able to distinguish between feasible and infeasible instances. Hence it is important to select the best amount of the original node labels. Based on the data associated to the nodes (Fig. 4) the level of detail can be determined in the following three ways: (1) regular labels, (2) regular labels and service tasks, (3) regular labels, service tasks, and parking locations. Regular labels are the labels of the 8 node types (7 illustrated in Fig. 4 and one additional activity called "Saw Move"). This level of detail would result in the smallest feature vectors. One step further is to specify the service task as a node type. On the chosen service site, five different service tasks are available: internal cleaning, soap external cleaning, oxalic external cleaning, technical checkup A, and technical checkup B. Either one would replace the regular service task node (S) resulting in 12 different node labels. The most detailed representation specifies both parking locations and service tasks, which results in 24 different node labels given 13 different tracks in the service site.

Sampling. The generated instances are not balanced, with 7205 samples in class 1, and 2795 in class 0. Undersampling and oversampling are two commonly used

Table 1. Accuracy, standard deviation and runtime DGCNN on test sets of 9 datasets [16].

DGCNN RESULTS	Undersampling			Oversampling			Undersampling and Oversampling		
# node labels	8	12	24	8	12	24	8	12	24
Accuracy (%)	59.89	60.80	62.10	60.15	60.85	61.28	60.15	60.19	60.89
Standard deviation (%)	±1.28	±0.92	±0.88	±0.47	±0.74	±0.16	±0.56	±1.06	±0.50
runtime (h)	3.6	3.6	3.6	13.1	13.1	13.1	10.4	10.4	10.4

methods dealing with class imbalance problems. The risk of undersampling is loss of information due to removing potentially important instances. Whereas oversampling increases the possibility of overfitting. We create three datasets with different balancing strategies: (1) only undersampling, with 2795 samples for both classes, (2) only oversampling, with 7205 samples for both classes, (3) both under- and oversampling, with 5000 samples for both classes.

Together with the three different node representation strategies, we end up with nine datasets. DGCNN is applied on all nine datasets to find the best combination of methods dealing with class imbalance and the level of detail of node labels. We use 5-fold cross validation. Table 1 shows the classification performance. It shows that the performance increases as we add more detailed information about the planning instances on the nodes in the graph. The three datasets with the highest level of detail are highlighted in the table. In addition, the results show that using undersampling is the best of the methods dealing with class imbalance. The runtime for undersampled datasets is also significantly lower than when (a combination with) oversampling is used, which is logical as the undersampled dataset is smaller.

Hyperparameter Tuning. We use the best performing dataset to tune the hyperparameters of DGCNN using grid search. The following combination of parameter values has achieved the best performance and is used to generate the final prediction model: (1) unifying nodes in graph: 0.7; (2) learning rate: 1×10^{-5}; (3) number of convolution layers: 3; (4) number of nodes in convolution layers: 64; (5) number of training epochs: 120; (6) batch size: 100.

Table 2 shows the confusion matrix of the final classification model. Each column of the matrix represents the instances in a predicted class while each row represents the instances in an actual class. Each cell counts the number of instances that corresponds to the row and column value. Correctly predicted classes are true negatives (TN; top left cell) and true positives (TP; bottom right cell). Incorrectly predicted classes are false negatives (FN; bottom left cell) and false positives (FP; top right cell). The final classification model of DGCNN is able to predict feasibility of an initial solution with 65.1% accuracy. It has been shown to be a difficult classification problem. A previous study [5] applied heavy feature engineering and tested various classifiers for this classification task, which resulted in a highest accuracy of 66.3%. However, to derive features, that approach assumes extensive domain knowledge on the shunting services planning problem. In comparison, DGCNN takes initial solutions directly as inputs.

Despite the difficulty of the classification problem, in the next section, We show the value of our approach in speeding up finding feasible solutions for capacity determination.

Table 2. Confusion matrix of the final classification model DGCNN [16].

		Predicted labels		
		0	1	Correct Incorrect
	0	372 33.3%	185 16.5%	67% 33%
Actual labels	1	205 18.3%	356 31.9%	63% 37%
	Correct Incorrect	64% 36%	66% 34%	65.1% 34.9%

3.3 Evaluation on Accelerating Simulations to Determine Capacities

Being able to predict feasibility of an initial solution before applying local search may lead to a decrease in computation time when determining the maximum capacity of a service site. We measure the effect of our approach by calculating the expected difference in running time with and without using DGCNN. As every instance was solved by the local search heuristic and its running time was recorded, we derive in Table 3 the running time of LS without DGCNN for all four types of instances (TN, FP, FN, and TP), as well as the average running time of feasible and infeasible instances.

Table 3. Runtime per quadrant and average runtimes [16].

Quadrant	Time (sec)
True negatives	110,877
False positives	56,037
False negatives	24,362
True positives	30,434

Averages	Time (sec)
Average feasible	97.7
Average infeasible	299.7

The total running time on the testing data without applying DGCNN in Table 3 is 221,710 s, roughly 62 h. This is the existing situation, where the local search algorithm has to evaluate every generated instance. We call our approach where DGCNN is applied to predict the feasibility of instances before applying LS "the new situation".

We use the following process to estimate the running time in the new situation. For each instance in the test set, DGCNN is used to predict whether it is feasible or infeasible. If feasible, the local search heuristic is applied to find a feasible solution (or terminate if it turns out to be infeasible given the predefined time limit). If, however, the predicted outcome is infeasible, this instance is discarded immediately and a new instance is drawn from the instance generator. This new instance is again fed to DGCNN, and the prediction of feasibility leads to either applying LS, or discarding this instance. This process continues until all instances have been classified as feasible. Figure 10 shows a Markov Transition Diagram to visualize this process, where the probabilities of transitions are obtained from Table 2.

Figure 10 shows that if an instance is classified as feasible, it will never leave that state. Note that being classified as feasible can either be correct (true) or incorrect (false). Since no new instances will be generated for instances classified as FP or TP, those runtimes remain the same in the new situation. If an instance is classified as infeasible, a new instance is drawn. This new instance can be transferred to any other state based on the probabilities. The runtime for TN and FN will change in the new situation.

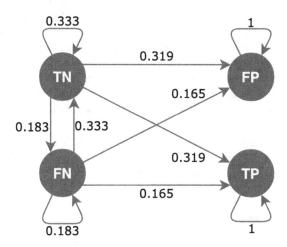

Fig. 10. Markov Transition Diagram transfer probabilities [16].

The total runtime for the TN instances without DGCNN is 110,877 s. The total runtime decreases to 62,123 s when using DGCNN. A decrease of 44.0%. The runtime for FN without DGCNN is 24,362 s. The total runtime increases to 34,259 s when using DGCNN. This is because the instances are actually feasible, but incorrectly classified as infeasible. Therefore, new instances will be generated and some of those will turn out to be infeasible, causing a longer running time.

While the runtime for FN instances increased with 40.6%, the total runtime of all instances decreased with 38,857 s to a total of 182,853 s. This decrease in runtime will save 17.5% when determining the capacity of a service site.

We have shown that using our approach, roughly 51 h can be saved in determining whether one given shunting yard has sufficient capacity in handling 21 train units with one particular scenario. Such tests have to be done for more than 50 scenarios. Hence, our approach will save about 100 days on determining whether 21 train units can be handled in the testing yard. Furthermore, if it is concluded that the site has sufficient capacity for 21 trains units, the scenarios with 22 or more train units will be generated and tested in order to find out the maximum number of the units that the given shunting yard can deal with. With 35 service sites in the Netherlands, the time reduction using our approach has a great impact.

4   Guiding Local Search Using DGCNN

4.1   Modeling the Operator Selection Problem

The local search heuristic attempts to find a feasible shunt plan by applying search operators in iterations to move through the search space. The heuristic uses 11 search operators to move through the search space. In every iteration, the search operators are shuffled in random order. This will be the order in which the operators will be evaluated. Starting with the first search operator, the heuristic evaluates the set of candidate solutions that can be reached through that search operator. A candidate solution is immediately accepted as the new solution for the next iteration if it is an improvement over the current solution. If the candidate solution is worse, it is selected with a certain probability depending on the difference in solution quality and the progress of the search process. This probabilistic technique is called simulated annealing. DGCNN can replace the random selection of operators by predicting in which order search operators should be evaluated. Figure 11 shows one iteration for both simulated annealing and DGCNN within the local search heuristic.

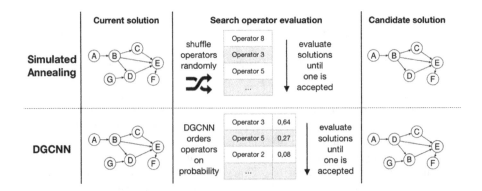

Fig. 11. From random local search to guided local search.

Similar to predicting feasibility, DGCNN will be trained on graphs and corresponding labels. The difference is that the dataset not only contains graphs from initial solutions, but also contains graphs of intermediate ones, from initial to final solutions. Furthermore, 11 different labels are used to represent 11 different operators. The label for a particular solution is the search operator that has been applied to that solution to get to the next iteration with an improved solution. The output of DGCNN will be a vector of probabilities for each search operator. These probabilities determine the order in which search operators are evaluated. The operator with the highest probability will be evaluated first. Using DGCNN to guide search could be beneficial for two reasons: (1) finding improvements faster, and (2) generating more consistent plans. With regard to the first reason, if DGCNN is able to accurately predict the order, the local search heuristic is more likely to find an improvement in the first search operator that it evaluates. As for the potential of more consistent plans, compared to a random selection, the prediction model DGCNN is more likely to choose the same operators for similar initial and immediate solutions that are represented by similar features, resulting in similar final solutions for similar scheduling instances. This consistency property on schedules is what the human planners prefer in daily operations.

4.2   Search Operators

We first describe how we generated the instances. The local search heuristic was slightly adapted such that it outputted all solutions from initial solution to final solution in a JSON file. The key/value pair about feasibility was changed into one representing the search operator. The instances were generated for the service site "the Kleine Binckhorst" with the default parameters and 21 train units. The local search heuristic was set up to run 1500 times and every time a new instance was drawn from the instance generator. This amount of runs minimally led to 150,000 graphs. The local search heuristic solved 859 out of 1500 instances. The remaining instances were not solvable within the maximum runtime of 300 s. We disregarded infeasible instances and included only feasible ones to train the DGCNN model. The reason is that for the infeasible instances, the heuristic may not apply the correct search operators during solving, which led to infeasible solutions in the end. Therefore, we decided not use the instances in which wrong decisions have been made.

Regarding the feasible instances, over 600,000 search operators have been applied on those 859 instances. On average, 740 operators have been applied with a minimum amount of 122 operators and a maximum amount of 2527 operators. Figure 12 shows a plot that has been made to check whether there is a pattern between the number of iterations and the times a search operator has been applied. The number of times an operator is applied increases linearly as the number of iterations increases. No unusual patterns can be observed. Box plots have been made to find out if there are major differences in the application of search operators between feasible instances with a low and high number of iterations. No major differences were observed. This could indicate that the major cause affecting the number of iterations is the initial solution and not the applied search operators. Figure 13 shows the distribution of search operators that have been applied in all feasible instances. Out of 11 operators, three are responsible for almost 90% of all applied operators.

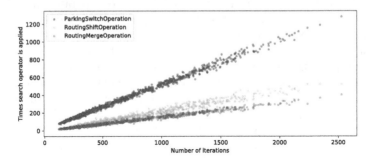

Fig. 12. Scatter plot three biggest operators against number of iterations.

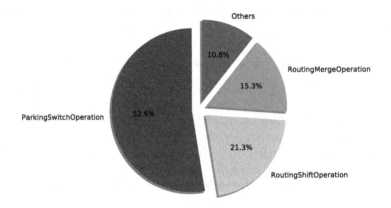

Fig. 13. Distribution of the search operators applied in the feasible instances by LS.

4.3   Predictive Modelling

We model the problem of learning which operators to select as a classification problem. This distribution in Fig. 13 indicates that it might be beneficial to focus on the top three operators. Hence, we take the following two different modelling strategies:

– Single-classifier approach: in this modelling approach, we train one classifier that predicts all 11 search operators, i.e., there are 11 classes to predict.
– Sequential-classifier approach: in this approach, we train multiple, sequential classifiers. The first classifier is a binary classifier, which predicts whether one of the three largest operators should be selected or one of the eight others should be chosen. Dependent on the output of the first classifier, either the

second or third classifier will be applied. If the first classifier predicts that one of the three largest operators should be applied, the second classifier will be used to predict which of the three. If the first classifier predicts otherwise, the third classifier will be used to predict which of the other eight operators will be applied. The idea of this modelling approach is that it may yield good prediction results if the first classifier performs well.

4.4 Experiments of Using DGCNN to Determine Operator Order

We discuss the results of two modelling approaches.

Single-classifier. We first create a balanced dataset. The least applied search operator has been applied just over 1100 times in all 859 runs. To create a balanced dataset, all search operators are undersampled to 1100 samples. Undersampling is done randomly, but in such a way that all graphs in the dataset are unique. Consequently, the dataset contains 12,100 unique graphs. The performance is validated by applying cross validation. Training the model on this amount of graphs took ± 25 h. Figure 14 shows the performance of training DGCNN directly on 11 search operators.

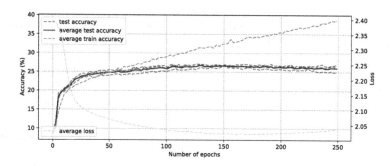

Fig. 14. Performance of the single-classifier approach.

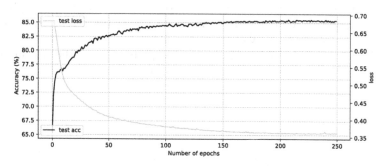

Fig. 15. Performance of the first classifier in the sequential-classifier approach.

We plot the development of loss since loss starts increasing after around 145 epochs, which indicates that the model starts overfitting. The accuracy at that point is around 26.9%. This percentage means that in 26.9% of the instances, DGCNN places the search operator, that the heuristic applied, on top of the list. Meaning that if DGCNN would be implemented, the heuristic only needs to evaluate one search operator in 26.9% of the instances to find an improvement over the current solution. Even though this percentage does not seem very high, consider the fact that immediately picking the *best* search operator by randomly shuffling the order results in a probability of 9.1%. Because the heuristic accepts the first candidate solution that is an improvement over the current solution, it could be that there were better search operators to apply. The chosen operator could even be one that worsened the current solution. 26.9% accuracy is achieved by comparing the operator that got the highest probability by DGCNN with the operator that the heuristic choose. When also looking at the operator with the second highest probability given by DGCNN, the accuracy would increase to 41.5%.

Sequential-classifier. Similar to the single-classifier approach, we create a balanced dataset. 4000 graphs are randomly sampled from the three largest search operators. Another 4000 graphs are randomly sampled from the other eight search operators. As a result, the dataset contains 8000 unique graphs. Figure 15 shows the performance of the first classifier.

The first classier shows a good performance with an classification accuracy of 86.5%. Clearly, DGCNN is able to find patterns in the data such that it can accurately distinguish between applying one of the three largest search operators and one of the eight others. Figure 16 shows the performance of both the second and third classifier. Note that the number of classes are three and eight respectively. Meaning that randomly predicting the correct classes would be 33.3% and 12.5%.

The second classifier is trained on a balanced dataset with 12,000 randomly sampled, unique graphs. The third classifier is trained on a balanced dataset with 8000 randomly sampled, unique graphs. The performance of the second classifier before overfitting is 75%, while the performance of the third classifier is 35.9%. These percentages have to be multiplied by the accuracy of the first classifier to be able to compare this approach with the basic approach, i.e. single-classifier. The average accuracy of the sequential-classifier approach is computed as: $(0.865 \times 0.75 + 0.865 \times 0.359)/2 = 48\%$. The performance of both approaches seems quite fair, especially the results of the second approach.

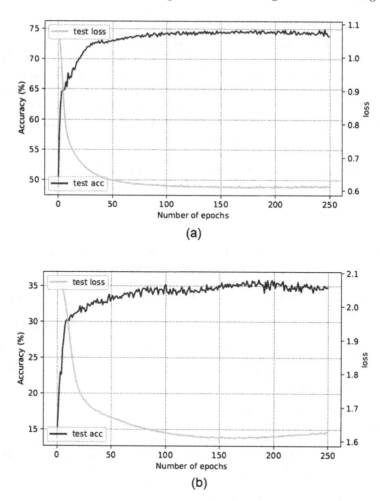

Fig. 16. Performance of the (a) second and (b) third classifier in the sequential-classifier approach.

5   Conclusion

In this work we have demonstrated how existing research in machine learning can be used to boost optimization algorithms in several ways in an industrial application.

First, we have shown the value of using machine learning models as approximation functions of optimization algorithms in finding solutions. The results demonstrate that combining a Deep Graph Convolutional Neural Network with local search leads to a decrease in computation time in determining capacities in shunting yards. The computation time was decreased by 17.5% determining the capacity of one shunting yard if DGCNN is used to predict whether an initial solution will become feasible after applying local search.

Second, we have shown that we can use machine learning to help local search decide which promising areas to explore during the search process. The experiment results illustrate that using DGCNN to evaluate and determine the search operators leads to faster improvements on solutions and less randomness. Furthermore, DGCNN is able to accurately predict the search operator that improves a solution with 48%. We show using proposed method, LS can find improvements faster. In the future, we plan to investigate the consistency of the generated plans, and validate it with the human planners at NS.

Acknowledgements. The work is partially supported by the NWO funded project Real-time data-driven maintenance logistics (project number: 628.009.012).

References

1. Boysen, N., Fliedner, M., Jaehn, F., Pesch, E.: Shunting yard operations: theoretical aspects and applications. Eur. J. Oper. Res. **220**(1), 1–14 (2012)
2. van den Broek, R., Hoogeveen, H., van den Akker, M., Huisman, B.: A local search algorithm for train unit shunting with service scheduling. Transportation Science (2018, submitted)
3. van den Broek, R.: Train Shunting and Service Scheduling: an integrated local search approach. Master's thesis, Utrecht University (2016)
4. de Oliveira da Costa, P.R., Rhuggenaath, J., Zhang, Y., Akcay, A., Lee, W.J., Kaymak, U.: Data driven policy on feasibility determination for train shunting problem. In: ECML PKDD 2019 (2019)
5. Dai, L.: A machine learning approach for optimization in railway planning. Master's thesis, Delft University of Technology, March 2018
6. Defourny, B., Ernst, D., Wehenkel, L.: Scenario trees and policy selection for multistage stochastic programming using machine learning. J. Comput. (2012)
7. Hopcroft, J., Karp, R.: An algorithm for maximum matchings in bipartite graphs. Ann. Symp. Switching and Automata Theory **2**(4), 225–231 (1973)
8. Kipf, T., Welling, M.: Semi-supervised classification with graph convolutional networks. CoRR abs/1609.02907 (2016)
9. Kroon, L.G., Lentink, R.M., Schrijver, A.: Shunting of passenger train units: an integrated approach. Transp. Sci. **42**(4), 436–449 (2008)
10. Lombardi, M., Milano, M.: Boosting combinatorial problem modeling with machine learning. In: Proceedings of the 27th International Joint Conference on Artificial Intelligence (IJCAI-18), pp. 5472–5478 (2018)
11. Meisel, S., Mattfeld, D.: Synergies of operations research and data mining. Eur. J. Oper. Res. **206**(1), 1–10 (2010)
12. Neumann, M., Garnett, R., Bauckhage, C., Kersting, K.: Propagation kernels: efficient graph kernels from propagated information. Mach. Learn. **102**(2), 209–245 (2016)
13. Niepert, M., Ahmed, M., Kutzkov, K.: Learning convolutional neural networks for graphs. CoRR abs/1605.05273 (2016)
14. Peer, E., Menkovski, V., Zhang, Y., Lee, W.J.: Shunting trains with deep reinforcement learning. In: Proceeding of 2018 IEEE International Conference on Systems, Man, and Cybernetics. IEEE (2018)
15. Shervashidze, N., Schweitzer, P., van Leeuwen, E., Mehlhorn, K., Borgwardt, K.: Weisfeiler-lehman graph kernels. J. Mach. Learn. Res. **12**, 2539–2561 (2011)

16. van de Ven, A., Zhang, Y., Lee, W.J., Eshuis, H., Wilbik, A.: Determining capacity of shunting yards by combining graph classification with local search. In: Steels, L., Rocha, A., van den Herik, J. (eds.) 11th International Conference on Agents and Artificial Intelligence (ICAART 2019), vol. 2, pp. 285–293. SCITEPRESS-Science and Technology Publications, Lda. (2019)

17. Verwer, S., Zhang, Y., Ye, Q.C.: Auction optimization using regression trees and linear models as integer programs. Artif. Intell. **244**, 368–395 (2017). https://doi.org/10.1016/j.artint.2015.05.004

18. Zhang, M., Cui, Z., Neumann, M., Chen, Y.: An end-to-end deep learning architecture for graph classification. In: AAAI, pp. 4438–4445 (2018)

Bipartite Split-Merge Evolutionary Clustering

Veselka Boeva[1], Milena Angelova[2(✉)], Vishnu Manasa Devagiri[1],
and Elena Tsiporkova[3]

[1] Blekinge Institute of Technology, Karlskrona, Sweden
{veselka.boeva,vishnu.manasa.devagiri}@bth.se
[2] Technical University of Sofia, Plovdiv, Bulgaria
mangelova@tu-plovdiv.bg
[3] EluciDATA Lab, Sirris, Brussels, Belgium
elena.tsiporkova@sirris.be

Abstract. We propose a split-merge framework for evolutionary clustering. The proposed clustering technique, entitled *Split-Merge Evolutionary Clustering* is supposed to be more robust to concept drift scenarios by providing the flexibility to consider at each step a portion of the data and derive clusters from it to be used subsequently to update the existing clustering solution. The proposed framework is built around the idea to model two clustering solutions as a bipartite graph, which guides the update of the existing clustering solution by merging some clusters with ones from the newly constructed clustering while others are transformed by splitting their elements among several new clusters. We have evaluated and compared the discussed evolutionary clustering technique with two other state of the art algorithms: a bipartite correlation clustering (PivotBiCluster) and an incremental evolving clustering (Dynamic split-and-merge).

Keywords: Data mining · Dynamic clustering · Evolutionary clustering · Bipartite clustering · Split-merge framework · Unsupervised learning

1 Introduction

The problem addressed in this article deals with the development of evolutionary clustering algorithm that can be used to (continuously) adjust existing clustering solution to match newly arrived data. For example, in many real-world applications such as personalizing customer recommendations, the information available in the system database is periodically updated by collecting new data. The available data elements, e.g., customers of a retailing company, are usually partitioned into a number of segments (clusters of customers with similar product preferences). As the data increases we need to re-group existing data and also accommodate new customers in the existing customer segments. However, the existing original segments (clusters) can become outdated due to shifts in preferences and characteristics of the newly attracted customers. Another example is profiling of users with wearable applications with the purpose to provide

This work is part of the research project "Scalable resource efficient systems for big data analytics" funded by the Knowledge Foundation (grant: 20140032) in Sweden.

© Springer Nature Switzerland AG 2019
J. van den Herik et al. (Eds.): ICAART 2019, LNAI 11978, pp. 204–223, 2019.
https://doi.org/10.1007/978-3-030-37494-5_11

personalized recommendations. As more users get involved one needs to update the division of the initial set of users into groups of characteristic profiles and also assign new incoming users to these groups.

In the context of profiling of machines (industrial assets) for the purpose of condition (health) monitoring the existing original clusters can become outdated caused by aging of the machines and degradation of performance due to influence of changing external factors. This gradual or abrupt (e.g. due to software update) model invalidation is in fact known as a concept drift and requires that the clustering techniques, used for deriving the original machine profiles, can deal with such a concept drift and enable reliable and scalable model update.

Evolving clustering models are good candidate to tackle concept drift scenarios as discussed above. They have been designed to mine very large datasets or online continuous data streams [8] in an unsupervised learning context by grouping and summarizing data in a fast incremental manner. Evolving clustering models are also referenced as incremental or evolving (dynamic) clustering methods, because they can process data step-wise and update and evolve cluster partitions in incremental learning steps [12]. Incremental clustering methods process one data element at a time and maintain a good solution by either adding each new element to an existing cluster or placing it in a new singleton cluster while two existing clusters are merged into one [1,15,38]. Incremental algorithms also bear a resemblance to one-pass stream clustering algorithms [33]. Although, one-pass stream clustering methods address the scalability issues of the clustering problem, they are not sensitive to the evolution of the data, because they assume that the clusters are to be computed over the entire data stream. This implies that changes in the characteristic of newly arriving data are not well reflected while building the clustering solution.

Dynamic clustering is also a form of online/incremental unsupervised learning. However, it considers not only the incremental fashion of building the clustering model, but also self-adaptation of the built model. In that way, the incremental model construction deals with the problem of model re-training over time and memory constrains, while dynamic aspects (e.g., data behavior, clustering structure) of the model to be built can be captured via adaptation of the current model. Notice that the dynamic (evolving) clustering paradigm is also close to the ideas of stream reasoning [17]. Stream reasoning studies the application of inference techniques to data streams to perform continuous reasoning tasks. The access to the stream is managed by creating time-dependent finite views over the streams (windows) over which the tasks are performed. Window contains a portion of the input streams, i.e. a set of timestamped data items, that represents the data needed to solve the task at the current time instant.

The clustering scenario discussed in this work is different from the one treated by incremental clustering methods. Namely, we are interested in clustering techniques that enable to compute clusters on a new portion of data collected over a defined time period (window) and to update the existing clustering solution by the computed new one. Such an updating clustering should better reflect the current characteristics of the data by being able to examine clusters occurring in the considered time period and eventually capture interesting trends in the area. In [10], we have studied two different clustering algorithms to be suited for the discussed scenario: *PivotBiCluster* [2] and *Split-Merge Evolutionary Clustering*. Both algorithms are bipartite correlation clustering algorithms that do not need prior knowledge about the optimal number of clusters in order to produce a good clustering solution. Notice that in our considerations the input graph nodes of PivotBiCluster algorithm are clusters. In the final clustering generated by the PivotBiCluster algorithm some clusters are obtained by merging clusters from both side of the graph, i.e. some of existing clusters will be updated by some of the computed new ones. However, existing clusters cannot be split by the PivotBiCluster algorithm even the corresponding correlations with clusters from the newly extracted data elements reveal that these clusters are not homogeneous. This has motivated us to develop our *Split-Merge Evolutionary Clustering* algorithm that overcomes this disadvantage. Namely, our algorithm is able to analyze the correlations between two clustering solutions and based on the discovered patterns it treats the existing clusters in different ways. Thus some clusters will be updated by merging with ones from newly constructed clustering while others will be transformed by splitting their elements among several new clusters.

An interesting dynamic clustering algorithm which is also equipped with dynamic split-and-merge operations and which is dedicated to incremental clustering of data streams is proposed by Lughofer in [30]. We have found a resemble between this algorithm, entitled *Dynamic split-and-merge algorithm*, and our Split-Merge Evolutionary Clustering. Hence, in this study the Split-Merge Evolutionary Clustering and the PivotBiCluster are further evaluated and compared against the Dynamic split-and-merge algorithm in two different experiment scenarios. Compared to the previous paper [10], the bibliography and related work section have also been extended with more recent works on the studied problem. We have also added a discussion on the computational complexity of our Split-Merge Evolutionary Clustering algorithm.

The rest of the paper is organized as follows. Section 2 reviews related works. Section 3 states the problem and briefly describes the PivotBiCluster and Dynamic split-and-merge algorithms. In addition, it introduces the proposed Bipartite Split-Merge Evolutionary Clustering technique. Section 4 gives an overview of the experimental setup. Section 5 discusses the results from the evaluation of the three clustering algorithms. Section 6 is devoted to conclusions and future work.

2   Related Work

The model of incremental algorithms for data clustering is motivated by practical applications where the demand sequence is unknown in advance and a hierarchical clustering is required. Incremental clustering methods process one data element at a time and maintain a good solution by either adding each new element to an existing cluster or placing it in a new singleton cluster while two existing clusters are merged into one [15]. Incremental algorithms also bear a resemblance to one-pass clustering algorithms for data stream problems [33]. Several incremental clustering techniques have been proposed in the past [3,13,18,20]. Such algorithms need to maintain a substantial amount of information so that important details are not lost. For example, the algorithm in [33] is implemented as a continuous version of k-means algorithm which continues to maintain a number of cluster centers which change or merge as necessary throughout the execution of the algorithm.

To qualify the type of cluster structure present in data, Balcan introduced the notion of clusterability [5]. It requires that every element be closer to data in its own cluster than to other points. In addition, Balcan showed that the clusterings that adhere to this requirement are readily detected offline by classical batch algorithms. On the other hand, it was proven by Ackerman [1] that no incremental method can discover these partitions. Thus, batch algorithms are significantly stronger than incremental methods in their ability to detect cluster structure. This is mainly due to the fact that the latter methods consider incrementality by dealing with the problem of model re-training over time and memory constrains, but they are not robust to the model dynamics.

Dynamic clustering is also a form of incremental unsupervised learning. However, it considers not only incrementality of the methods to build the clustering model, but also self-adaptation of the built model. Lughofer has proposed an interesting dynamic clustering algorithm which is equipped with dynamic split-and-merge operations and which is also dedicated to incremental clustering of data streams [30]. In [19] similarly to the approach of Lughofer a set of splitting and merging action conditions are defined, where optional splitting and merging actions are only triggered during the iterative process when the conditions are met. Wang et al. also propose a split-merge-evolve algorithm for clustering data into k number of clusters [36]. This algorithm has the ability to optimize the clustering result in scenarios where new data samples may be added in to existing clusters. However, a k cluster output is always provided by the algorithm, i.e. it is also not sensitive to the evolution of the data. In general, incremental and one-pass stream clustering methods address the scalability issues of the clustering problem, but they are not sensitive to the evolution of the data because they assume that the clusters are to be computed over the entire data stream.

In [14] an adaptive clustering approach that can apply to re-cluster a set of previously clustered objects when the feature set characterizing the objects increases has been proposed. The authors have developed adaptive extensions for k-means and hierarchical agglomerative clustering algorithms. Further it has been shown how these extensions can be used for adjusting a clustering, that was established by applying the corresponding non-adaptive clustering algorithm before the feature set changed [14]. Such adaptive clustering techniques could be necessary in some applied scenarios, e.g., in the expertise mining context when the recently gathered information reveals that some of the known experts have expanded their competence. However, in this case the clustering scenario will be different from one considered in [14], because usually the expert expertise profiles are not presented by fixed-length feature vectors. Moreover, not all expert profiles will be affected by this expansion.

Gionis et al. proposed an approach to clustering that is based on the concept of aggregation [22]. They are interested in a problem in which a number of different clusterings are given on some data set of elements. The objective is to produce a single clustering of the elements that agrees as much as possible with the given clusterings. Clustering aggregation provides a framework for dealing with a variety of clustering problems. For instance, it can handle categorical or heterogeneous data by producing a clustering on each available attribute and then aggregating the produced clusterings into a single result. Another possibility is to combine the results of several clustering algorithms applied on the same dataset etc. Clustering aggregation can be thought as a more general model of multi-view clustering proposed in [7]. The multi-view approach considers clustering problems in which the available attributes can be split into two independent subsets. A clustering is produced on each subset and then the two clusterings are combined into a single result. Consensus clustering algorithms deal with similar problems to those treated by clustering aggregation techniques. Namely, such algorithms try to reconcile clustering information about the same data set coming from different sources [11] or from different runs of the same algorithm [23]. The both clustering techniques are not suited for our scenario, since they are used to integrate a number of clustering results generated on one and the same data set.

The idea for the proposed *Split-Merge Evolutionary Clustering* algorithm is inspired by the work of Xiang et al. [37]. They have proposed a split-merge framework that can be tailored to different applications. The framework models two clusterings as a bipartite graph which is decomposed into connected components, and each component is further decomposed into subcomponents. Pairs of related subcomponents are then taken into consideration in designing a clustering similarity measure within the framework.

3   Methods and the Proposed Solution

3.1   Problem Description

Let us formalize the cluster updating problem we are interested in. We assume that X is the available set of data points and each data point is represented by a vector of attributes (features). In addition, the data points are partitioned into k groups, i.e. $C = \{C_1, C_2, \ldots, C_k\}$ is an existing clustering solution of X and each C_i ($i = 1, 2, \ldots, k$) can be considered as a disjoint cluster. In addition, a new set X' of recently collected data elements (instances) is created, i.e. $X \cap X'$ is an empty set. Each data point in X' is again represented by a list of attributes and $C' = \{C'_1, C'_2, \ldots, C'_{k'}\}$ is a clustering solution of X'. The objective is to produce a single clustering of $X \cup X'$ by combining C and C' in such a way that the obtained clustering realistically reflects the current distribution in the domain under interest.

3.2   Pivot Bi-Clustering Algorithm

Two existing correlation clustering techniques are suitable for the considered context: correlation clustering [6] and bipartite correlation clustering [2]. The latter algorithm seems to be better aligned to our clustering scenario. In Bipartite Correlation Clustering (BCC) a bipartite graph is given as input, and a set of disjoint clusters covering the graph nodes is output. Clusters may contain nodes from either side of the graph, but they may possibly contain nodes from only one side. A cluster is thought as a bi-clique connecting all the objects from its left and right counterparts. Consequently, a final clustering is a union of bi-cliques covering the input node set. We compare our Split-Merge Evolutionary Clustering algorithm described in Sect. 3.4 with *PivotBiCluster* realization of the BCC algorithm [2]. The PivotBiCluster algorithm is implemented according to the original description given in [2].

Notice that in our considerations the input graph nodes of the PivotBiCluster algorithm are clusters and in the final clustering some clusters are obtained by merging clusters (nodes) from both sides of the graph, i.e. some of the existing clusters will be updated by some of the computed new ones. However, existing clusters cannot be split by the PivotBiCluster algorithm even when the corresponding correlations with clusters from the new data elements reveal that these clusters are not homogeneous.

3.3 Dynamic Split-and-Merge Clustering Algorithm

The proposed algorithm, described in Sect. 3.4, is also compared with the Dynamic split-and-merge clustering algorithm proposed by Lughofer in [30]. The Dynamic split-and-merge algorithm of Lughofer can be used as an extension to any existing incremental and evolutionary clustering algorithm provided it stores details regarding cluster centers, spread, elements of a cluster [30]. Once the newly arriving data points are assigned to existing clusters by applying some incremental clustering algorithm, all the modified clusters are then examined in order to identify whether they need to be split or merged. Optional splitting and merging actions are only triggered during the iterative process if predefined action conditions are met. For example, a cluster is merged with another existing cluster if both of them are homogeneous and the clusters touch or overlap with each other. Whereas a cluster is split into two if the quality criterion of the clustering solution after the split is better than that of before it.

Although, the dynamic split-and-merge algorithm addresses the clustering dynamics, it is not very sensitive to concept drift phenomenon, because it assigns the newly arriving data points to the existing clusters in an incremental way and then improves the clustering solution by either splitting or merging the modified clusters. In comparison our split-merge clustering technique provides the flexibility to compute clusters on a new portion of data collected over a defined time period and to update the existing clustering solution by the computed new one [10]. Such an updating clustering should better reflect the current characteristics of the data by being able to examine clusters occurring in the considered time period and eventually capture interesting trends in the area.

3.4 Bipartite Split-Merge Evolutionary Clustering Algorithm

In this paper, we propose an evolutionary clustering algorithm that overcomes the above mentioned disadvantage of the two discussed state of the art algorithms. Namely, our algorithm is able to analyze the correlations between two clustering solutions C and C' and based on the discovered patterns it treats the existing clusters ($C = \{C_1, C_2, \ldots, C_k\}$) in different ways. Thus, some clusters will be updated by merging with ones from newly constructed clustering (C') while others will be transformed by splitting their elements among several new clusters. One can find some similarity between our idea and an interactive clustering model proposed in [4]. In this model, the algorithm starts with some initial clustering of data and the user may request a certain cluster to be split if it is *overclustered* (intersects two or more clusters in the target clustering). The user may also request to merge two given clusters if they are *underclustered* (both intersect the same target cluster).

As it was already mentioned in Sect. 2 our evolutionary clustering algorithm is inspired by a split-merge framework proposed by Xiang et al. in [37]. By modeling

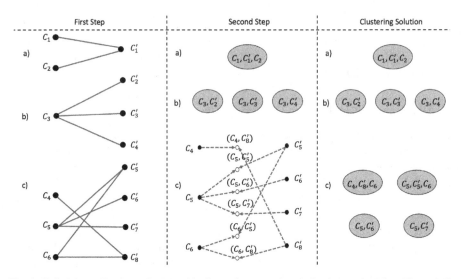

Fig. 1. Split-Merge Framework: (a) a bi-clique that contains underclustered nodes (C_1 and C_2 intersect C_1'); (b) a bi-clique that contains an overclustered node (C_3 intersects C_2', C_3' and C_4'); (c) a bi-clique that has to be decomposed into subcomponents in the second step of the algorithm. It is transformed into a tripartite graph that has split (left) and merge (right) subcomponents.

the intrinsic relation between two clusterings as a bipartite graph, they have designed a split-merge framework that can be used to obtain similarity measures to compare clusterings on different data sets. The problem addressed in this article is different from the one considered by Xiang et al. [37]. Namely, we concern with the development of split-merge framework that can be used to adjust the existing clustering solution to newly arrived data. Our framework also models two clusterings (the existing and the newly constructed one) as a bipartite graph which is decomposed into connected components (bi-cliques) (see Fig. 1(a), (b) and (c)). Each component is further analysed and if it is necessary it is decomposed into subcomponents (see Fig. 1(c)). The subcomponents are then taken into consideration in producing the final clustering solution. For example, if an existing cluster is *overclustered* (Fig. 1(b)), i.e. it intersects two or more clusters in the new clustering, it is split between those. If several existing clusters intersect the same new cluster, i.e. they are *underclustered* (Fig. 1(a)), they are merged with that cluster. Notice that in comparison with the dynamic split-and-merge algorithm of Lughofer [30], the splitting and merging operations of our algorithm can be conducted on more than two clusters.

Let us formally describe the proposed Split-Merge Evolutionary Clustering algorithm. The input bipartite graph is $G = (C, C', E)$, where C and C' are sets of clusters of left and right nodes and E is a subset of $C \times C'$ that represents correlations between the nodes of two sets. The two main steps of the algorithm are as follows:

1. At the first step, all bi-cliques of G are found. Then we consider and treat three different scenarios:

(i) If a bi-clique is an unreachable node it is made a singleton in the final clustering solution.

(ii) If a bi-clique connects a node from the left side of G with several nodes from C' the elements of this node are split among the corresponding nodes from C' (see Fig. 1(b)).

(iii) In the opposite case, i.e., when we have a bi-clique that connects a node from the right side of G with several nodes from left those nodes have to be merged with that node (cluster) (see Fig. 1(a)).

All clustered nodes are removed from the graph.

2. At the second step, the remained bi-cliques are decomposed into split/merge sub-components. Each bi-clique, which is a bipartite graph, is transformed into a tripartite graph constructed by two (split and merge) bipartite graphs. Suppose $G_i = (C_i, C_i', E_i)$ is the considered bi-clique. Then the corresponding tripartite graph is built by the following two bipartite graphs: $G_{iL} = (C_i, E_i, E_{iL})$ and $G_{iR} = (E_i, C_i', E_{iR})$, where C_i, C_i' and E_i are ones from G_i, E_{iL} is a subset of $C_i \times E_i$ that represents correlations between the nodes of C_i and E_i, and E_{iR} is a subset of $E_i \times C_i'$ representing correlations between the nodes of E_i and C_i' (see Fig. 1(c)). For example, $c_i \in C_i$ will be correlated with all pairs $(c_j, c_k') \in E_i$ such that $c_i \equiv c_j$, and $c_i' \in C_i'$ will be correlated with all pairs $(c_j, c_k') \in E_i$ such that $c_i' \equiv c_k'$. Then splitting and merging sub-steps are sequentially conducted:

(i) First all *overclustered* nodes of G_{iL} are *split* and new temporary clusters are formed as a result. This can be implemented, e.g., by calculating the distance between each data point of the overclustered node from C and the centroids of its adjacent nodes (cluster) from C'. Then the data point in question is assigned to the closest cluster.

(ii) Then we perform the corresponding *merging* for all *underclustered* nodes in G_{iR}.

For example, in Fig. 1(c) cluster C_5 will first be split among clusters C_5', C_6' and C_7', i.e. three new clusters, denoted by (C_5, C_5'), (C_5, C_6') and (C_5, C_7'), will be obtained. Then at the next step of the algorithm clusters (C_5, C_5') and (C_6, C_5') will be merged together.

The pseudocode of the proposed *Split-Merge Evolutionary Clustering* algorithm is given in Algorithm 1. In addition, the algorithm is illustrated with an example in Fig. 2. The clustering solution generated by the Split-Merge Clustering is compared to one produced by the PivotBiCluster. It is interesting to notice that the two algorithms will produce very different clustering solutions on the same input graph. For example, the Split-Merge Clustering will generate a 4-cluster solution while one obtained by the PivotBiCluster will have only 2 clusters. The latter number is quite low taking into account the number of clusters in the two input clusterings. Moreover, as it was mentioned in the previous section the PivotBiCluster algorithm cannot produce a clustering solution in which existing clusters are split among new clusters.

We now discuss the computational complexity of the Split-Merge Evolutionary Clustering. Suppose that n is the number of instances in the existing data set and n' ($n' < n$) is the number of instances in the new data set. In addition, we assume that the instances of the existing data set have already been grouped in k ($k << n$) categories. Initially, the new data elements have to be clustered into k' ($k' << n'$) clusters. The computational complexity of this part depends on the used clustering algorithm.

Algorithm 1. Split-Merge Evolutionary Clustering Algorithm.

```
 1: function SPLIT-MERGE(G = (C, C', E))
 2:     for all nodes c ∈ C ∪ C' do (*First step*)
 3:         if c is an unreachable node then
 4:             Turn c into a singleton and remove it from G (*First step (i)*)
 5:         end if
 6:     end for
 7:     for all nodes c ∈ C ∪ C' do
 8:         if c₁ is the only node from C that takes part in a bi-clique connecting it with one or several nodes
            from C' then
 9:             Split c₁ among the corresponding nodes from C' (*First step (ii)*)
10:             Remove the clustered nodes from G
11:         end if
12:     end for
13:     for all nodes c ∈ C ∪ C' do
14:         if c'₁ is the only node from C' that takes part in a bi-clique connecting it with one or several
            nodes from C then
15:             Merge c'₁ with the corresponding nodes from C (*First step (iii)*)
16:             Remove the clustered nodes from G
17:         end if
18:     end for
19:     for all nodes c ∈ C do (*Second step*)
20:         Split c₁ among its adjacent nodes from C' and form new temporary clusters (*Second step (i)*)
21:     end for
22:     for all nodes c' ∈ C' do
23:         Merge c'₁ with its adjacent nodes from the built set of temporary clusters (*Second step (ii)*)
24:         Remove the clustered nodes from G
25:     end for
26:     return all connected components (bi-cliques) as clusters of X ∪ X'
27: end function
```

It will be $O(n'k'mi)$ in case of k-means clustering algorithm [27], where m and i are the dimensionality of the learning problem and the number of iterations, respectively. According to Gan et al. [21], k-means usually converges quickly, i.e. the number of iterations is usually low and the algorithm complexity can be reduced to $O(n'k'm)$. In order to build the bipartite graph we calculate the similarity between the centroids of each pair of clusters belonging to $C \times C'$. Any pair of clusters which centroids' similarity is above a given threshold are considered connected by an edge. Hence, the computational complexity of building the bipartite graph is equal to $O(kk')$. We further focus our discussion on the computational complexity of the main steps of our algorithm, given in Algorithm 1. The first part of the algorithm (steps 2 to 18) requires execution time that is proportional to $k + k'$. The computational complexity of the remainder part of the algorithm (from step 19 downwards) depends on the average size of clusters that have to be split. Suppose that l ($l \ll n$) is the average number of instances in those clusters. Then the computational complexity of this part can be approximated to $O((k + k')l)$. Finally, the total computational complexity of the Split-Merge Evolutionary Clustering is $O(n'k'm + kk' + (k + k') + (k + k')l)$ and $n' \gg (k + k')$, i.e. it can be simplified to $O(n'k'm + kk' + (k + k')l)$. In addition, $l \gg k'$, i.e. we can further simplify to $O(n'k'm + (k + k')l)$ and finally reduce to $O(n'(k + k')m)$, as $n' \gg l$. The latter expression is very close to the computational complexity of the Dynamic split-and-merge algorithm evaluated to $O(n'km)$ in [30]. The complexity of PivotBiCluster, commented in [2], cannot be directly compared to the complexity of our algorithm, since the former algorithm is not originally defined to work with clusters.

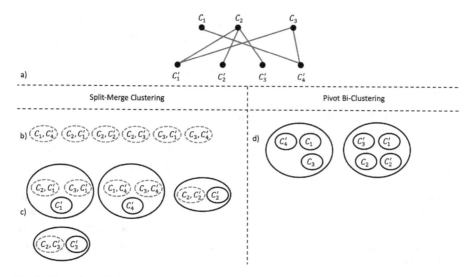

Fig. 2. Clustering solutions generated by Split-Merge Clustering (left) and PivotBiCluster (right), respectively: (a) the input bipartite graph; (b) temporary clusters formed by Split-Merge Clustering after splitting overclustered nodes from the left set (above) ($\{C_1, C_2, C_3 \}$) of the graph among corresponding nodes from the right set (below) ($\{C'_1, C'_2, C'_3, C'_4\}$); (c) the final clustering solution produced by Split-Merge Clustering, (d) the final clustering solution produced by PivotBiCluster.

4   Experimental Setup

In [10], we have evaluated the Split-Merge Evolutionary Clustering and PivotBiCluster algorithms in two different case studies. We have compared the performance of the algorithms in expertise retrieval domain by applying them on data extracted from PubMed repository. In addition, a case study in profiling patients in healthcare domain has been conducted. The Split-Merge Clustering algorithm has shown better performance than the PivotBiCluster in most of the studied experimental scenarios.

In the current work we further study and compare the two clustering algorithms with the Dynamic split-and-merge algorithm, proposed in [30], on four different data sets (explained in the following section) under two different experiment scenarios (see Sect. 4.3).

4.1   Data

Anthropometric Data Set. This dataset is publicly available and published in [24]. The data contains 400 undergraduate students aged between 16 and 63 years old, where a 56.3% are women. The following features describe the data: age, obesity, BMI, WC, HC, WHR, Systolic Blood Pressure (SBP), Diastolic Blood Pressure (DBP), *preh* for women and *hyper* for men, where the *preh* and *hyper* are classification labels that show what kind of blood pressure the individual has (e.g., regular or hyper). According to the results published in [29] people can be grouped into six clusters depending on their blood pressure. This grouping is considered as the ground truth to benchmark the results generated by the three studied clustering algorithms.

Yeast Data Set. The yeast data set obtained from the UCI machine learning repository is used to predict the cellular localization site of protein [32]. Data set consists of 1484 instances of data with 8 attributes, divided into 10 classes.

Wine Quality Data Set. The wine quality-data set obtained from the UCI machine learning repository includes two data sets, related to red and white vinho verde wine samples, from the north of Portugal. The goal is to model wine quality based on physicochemical tests [16]. These data sets are labelled and can be used for classification tasks.

Cover-Type Data Set. The cover-type data set obtained from the UCI machine learning repository is created to predict the forest cover type [9]. The data set contains cartographic values of a forest. It is a labeled data set primarily designed to validate classification algorithms. Data set consists of 581012 instances of data with 54 attributes, divided into 7 classes.

Notice that anthropometric data set has been used in [10] for our case study in healthcare domain, while cover-type data set has been used by Lughofer in [30]. The selected data sets are labelled and their characteristics are summarized in Table 1. One of the advantages of using labeled data is that the available class labels could be used as a benchmark while validating the obtained clustering solution.

Table 1. Characteristics of the used test data sets.

Data sets	#Instances	#Attributes	#Clusters
Antropometric	400	9	6
Yeast	1484	8	10
Wine quality	6498	12	7
Cover-type	581,012	54	7

4.2 Metrics

The data mining literature provides a range of different cluster validation measures, which are broadly divided into two major categories: *external* and *internal* [27]. External validation measures have the benefit of providing an independent assessment of clustering quality, since they validate a clustering result by comparing it to a given external standard. However, an external standard is rarely available. Internal validation techniques, on the other hand, avoid the need for using such additional knowledge, but have the alternative problem to base their validation on the same information used to derive the clusters themselves. Furthermore, internal measures can be split with respect to the specific clustering property they reflect and assess to find an optimal clustering scheme: *compactness*, *separation*, *connectedness*, and *stability* of the cluster partitions.

External validation measures can be two types: *unary* and *binary* [25]. Unary external evaluation measures take a single clustering result as the input, and compare it with a known set of class labels to assess the degree of consensus between the two. Comprehensive measures like the F-measure provide a general way to evaluate this [34]. In addition to unary measures, the data-mining literature also provides a number of indices, which assess the consensus between a produced partitioning and the existing one based on the contingency table of the pairwise assignment of data items. Most of these indices are symmetric, and are therefore equally well-suited for the use as binary measures, i.e., for assessing the similarity of two different clustering results.

In this work, we have implemented three different validation measures for estimating the quality of clusters, produced by the three studied clustering algorithms: F-measure, Jaccard Index and Silhouette Index.

We have used the F-measure as an external (unary) validation metric [28]. The *F-measure* is the harmonic mean of the precision and recall values for each cluster. Let us consider two clustering solutions $C = \{C_1, C_2, \ldots, C_k\}$ and $C' = \{C'_1, C'_2, \ldots, C'_l\}$ of the same data set. The first solution C is a known partition of the considered data set while the second one C' is a partition generated by the applied clustering algorithm. The F-measure for a cluster C'_j is then given as

$$F(C'_j) = \frac{2\left|C_i \cap C'_j\right|}{|C_i| + |C'_j|},$$

where C_i is the cluster that contains the maximum number of objects from C'_j. The overall F-measure for clustering solution C' is defined as the mean of cluster-wise F-measure values, i.e.

$$F(C') = \frac{1}{l}\sum_{j=1}^{l} F_j. \tag{1}$$

For a perfect clustering, when $l = k$, the maximum value of the F-measure is 1.

In addition, we have applied Jaccard Index (Jaccard similarity coefficient) [26] to evaluate the stability of the clustering algorithms. Given a pair of clustering solutions of the same data set, C and C', we define a as the number of data point pairs that belong to the same cluster in C as well as in C'. Let b be the number of data point pairs that belong to the same cluster in C but not in C'. Further, c is defined to be the number of data point pairs that belong to the same cluster in C' but not in C. The *Jaccard Index* (JI) between C and C' is then defined as:

$$J(C, C') = \frac{a}{a+b+c}. \tag{2}$$

The Jaccard Index ranges from 0 to 1, where a higher value indicates a higher similarity between cluster solutions. Jaccard Index has been used to measure the similarity between the generated clustering solutions and the corresponding benchmark partitionings of the used test data sets.

Furthermore, *Silhouette Index* (SI) has been applied as an internal measure to assess compactness and separation properties of the generated clustering solutions [35]. It is a cluster validation index that can be used to judge the quality of any clustering solution

C. Suppose a_i represents the average distance of object i from the other objects of its assigned cluster, and b_i represents the minimum of the average distances of object i from objects of the other clusters. The Silhouette Index for clustering solution C of m objects is defined as:

$$s(C) = \frac{1}{m} \sum_{i=1}^{m} \frac{(b_i - a_i)}{\max\{a_i, b_i\}}. \tag{3}$$

The values of Silhouette Index vary from -1 to 1 and higher values indicate better clustering results.

4.3 Experiments

We have studied two different experiment scenarios. In the first scenario we compare the three clustering algorithms on cover-type and wine quality data sets described in Sect. 4.1. Each data set is used to generated 10 test data set couples by randomly separating the data points in two sets. One set (containing 70% of data) of each couple presents the available data set and the other one (30% of data) is the set of newly collected data objects. In that way 10 test clustering couples are created for each data set.

In the second scenario we examine whether the three studied algorithms are sensitive to the size of the new portion of data. For this purpose we use the other two data sets (anthropometric and yeast) described in Sect. 4.1. For each data set we produce 4 times 10 test data set couples by randomly separating its data points in two sets in a ratio 50/50, 60/40, 70/30 and 80/20, respectively.

4.4 Implementation and Availability

The three studied clustering algorithms (Split-Merge Evolutionary Clustering, PivotBi-Cluster and Dynamic split-and-merge) are implemented in Python. We have selected the MiniBatchKMeans algorithm available in scikit-learn library[1] as an incremental clustering used in the implementation of the Dynamic split-and-merge. F-measure, Jaccard Index and Silhouette Index (see Sect. 4.2) used to validate the clustering solutions generated in our experiments are also implemented in scikit-learn library.

Notice that in the experiments conducted on cover-type data set we have used only the 14 non-binary attributes from all 54 attributes of this data. We have not considered the soil type data, since they are very sparse. In addition, we have used a sample set of 50 000 instances.

Supplementary information is available at GitLab[2].

5 Results and Discussion

The results produced by the three studied clustering algorithms in the first experiment scenario are given in Tables 2 and 3. The performance of the algorithms is studied with

---

[1] Scikit-learn is a Python library for data mining and data analysis.
[2] https://gitlab.com/machine_learning_vm/clustering_techniques.

respect to three different cluster validation measures: Silhouette Index (SI), F-measure and Jaccard Index. The results from the evaluation of the algorithms on cover-type data set are given in Table 2. As one can see, the PivotBiCluster and Split-Merge Clustering have generated significantly higher F-measure scores than the Dynamic split-and-merge. However, the latter algorithm slightly outperforms the other two with respect to SI. Notice that the PivotBiCluster behaviors significantly better then the other two algorithms with respect to F-measure and Jaccard Index. In general, the PivotBiCluster can be considered as the best performing algorithm on cover-type data set. It is further interesting to discuss that although, the incremental algorithm (MiniBatchKMeans) used by the Dynamic split-and-merge has modified all the 7 initial clusters in each test data couple no split and merge actions have been performed. For example, if we compare it with the other two algorithms on one and the same data set couple the PivotBiCluster has performed 2 merges while the Split-Merge Clustering has done 4 merges and 7 splits. In addition, the PivotBiCluster has generated a cluster solution with 5 cluster while the clustering solution produced by the Split-Merge Clustering has 7 cluster. This supports our discussion in Sect. 3.3 that the Dynamic split-and-merge algorithm is not very sensitive to concept drift scenarios compared to the other two algorithms, which update the existing clustering solution by considering the clustering extracted from the new portion of data.

Table 2. Experiment 1: Average cluster validation metrics scores generated on the clustering solutions of the 10 cover-type test data set couples.

Metrics	PivotBiCluster	Split-merge clustering	Dynamic split-and-merge
SI	0.194	0.034	0.196
F-measure	0.903	0.759	0.376
Jaccard Index	0.231	0.021	0.161

Table 3 contains the results obtained from the evaluation of the three clustering algorithms on wine quality data set with respect to the three used cluster validation criteria. The PivotBiCluster is again the best performing algorithm according to the results produced by F-measure and Jaccard Index. However, this is not supported by the generated SI scores. Namely, the Dynamic split-and-merge has the highest average SI score. However, it is outperformed by the Split-Merge Clustering with respect to Jaccard Index and F-measure. It is also interesting to observe that the number of clusters of the clustering solutions generated on the wine quality test data set couples varies from 5 to 8 for the PivotBiCluster, and between 1 and 7 (seven data set couples have generated clustering solutions with 4 or less clusters) for the Dynamic split-and-merge. This might be the main reason for the higher SI scores generated by the Dynamic split-and-merge algorithm, since the SI score generated on the benchmark clustering of wine quality data set is -0.06. In the case of the Split-Merge Clustering the data points are grouped into 7 or 8 clusters, i.e. much closer to the benchmark clustering of wine quality data set. The latter one has 7 clusters (see Table 1). This trend has been noticed also for the other three data sets (see the discussion below about the results generated on antropometric data set).

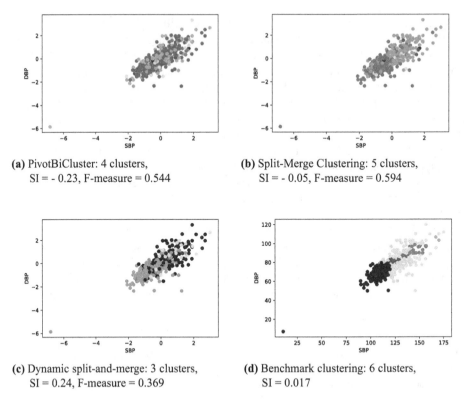

(a) PivotBiCluster: 4 clusters,
SI = - 0.23, F-measure = 0.544

(b) Split-Merge Clustering: 5 clusters,
SI = - 0.05, F-measure = 0.594

(c) Dynamic split-and-merge: 3 clusters,
SI = 0.24, F-measure = 0.369

(d) Benchmark clustering: 6 clusters,
SI = 0.017

Fig. 3. Clustering solutions generated by the three studied clustering algorithms on an antropo-metric 70/30 test data set couple versus the benchmark clustering.

Table 3. Experiment 1: Average cluster validation metrics scores generated on the clustering solutions of the 10 wine quality test data set couples.

Metrics	PivotBiCluster	Split-merge clustering	Dynamic split-and-merge
SI	−0.111	−0.129	0.143
F-measure	0.676	0.461	0.311
Jaccard Index	0.269	0.143	0.137

The results obtained in the second experiment scenario are given in Tables 4, 5 and 6. For example, Table 4 presents the evaluations of the clustering solutions generated by the three algorithms on antropometric and yeast data sets with respect to F-measure. The obtained results support the better performance of PivotBiCluster and Split-Merge Clustering compared to the Dynamic split-and-merge. The PivotBiCluster even slightly outperforms the Split-Merge Clustering with respect to this evaluation criterion (F-measure).

Table 4. Experiment 2: Average F-measure scores generated on the clustering solutions of the 4×10 antropometric data set couples (above) and 4×10 yeast test data set couples (below).

Antropometric	50/50	60/40	70/30	80/20
PivotBiCluster	0.677	0.624	0.544	0.676
Split-merge clustering	0.546	0.504	0.519	0.481
Dynamic split-and-merge	0.374	0.389	0.442	0.482
Yeast				
PivotBiCluster	0.700	0.710	0.821	0.858
Split-merge clustering	0.576	0.522	0.496	0.489
Dynamic split-and-merge	0.419	0.423	0.426	0.410

In line with the results obtained on cover-type and wine quality data sets the Dynamic split-and-merge outperforms the other two algorithms with respect to the SI evaluation criteria (see Table 5). As it was already discussed above we believe that this is due to the fact that it generates the clustering solutions with less number of clusters compared to the other two algorithms. For example, we have compared the three algorithms on the ten 60/40 test couples of antropometric data set. The number of clusters of the clustering solutions generated by the Dynamic split-and-merge varies from 1 to 3, in the case of the PivotBiCluster all ten clustering solutions have 4 clusters, while the Split-Merge Clustering has grouped the data points into 6, 7 or 8 clusters. Evidently, the three clustering algorithms have generated clustering solutions with very different number of clusters. However, the clustering solutions of the Split-Merge Clustering are most close to the benchmark clustering of antropometric data set (Sect. 4.1), which has 6 clusters. This trend has been noticed also for the other three data sets (see the discussion on wine quality data set). Figure 3 further illustrates this by plotting clustering solutions generated by the three algorithms on an antropometric 70/30 test data set couple. The corresponding benchmark clustering and its SI score are given in Fig. 3d. As one can see the three algorithms have generated clustering solutions that have different number of clusters. In addition, they have produced different SI and F-measure scores. The clustering solutions produced by the Split-Merge Clustering (Fig. 3b) and Dynamic split-and-merge (Fig. 3c) seem close to each other and they are visually more similar to the benchmark clustering than the PivotBiCluster solution (Fig. 3a). This is also supported by the calculated SI scores. We further observe that the PivotBiCluster is the worst performing algorithm according to SI on antropometric data set while its performance on yeast data set is almost comparable to that of the Dynamic split-and-merge algorithm. It is interesting to notice that the performance of the Split-Merge Clustering is influenced by the size of the new data set, while this is not clearly demonstrated by the other two algorithms, even in some experiments they have been improving their performance.

The evaluations of the clustering solutions produced by the three algorithms on antropometric and yeast data sets with respect to Jaccard Index are given in Table 6. The Dynamic split-and-merge is the best performing algorithm with respect to this

Table 5. Experiment 2: Average SI scores generated on the clustering solutions of the 4×10 antropometric test data set couples (above) and 4×10 yeast test data set couples (below).

Antropometric	50/50	60/40	70/30	80/20
PivotBiCluster	−0.344	−0.327	−0.231	−0.178
Split-merge clustering	−0.212	−0.189	−0.108	−0.096
Dynamic split-and-merge	0.2	0.238	0.188	0.170
Yeast				
PivotBiCluster	0.142	0.068	0.044	0.076
Split-merge clustering	−0.061	−0.061	−0.048	−0.036
Dynamic split-and-merge	0.164	0.157	0.158	0.150

Table 6. Experiment 2: Average Jaccard Index scores generated on the clustering solutions of the 4×10 antropometric data set couples (above) and 4×10 yeast test data set couples (below).

Antropometric	50/50	60/40	70/30	80/20
PivotBiCluster	0.021	0.015	0.068	0.058
Split-merge clustering	0.077	0.164	0.107	0.074
Dynamic split-and-merge	0.156	0.199	0.119	0.094
Yeast				
PivotBiCluster	0.014	0.022	0.034	0.020
Split-merge clustering	0.086	0.089	0.090	0.086
Dynamic split-and-merge	0.099	0.136	0.105	0.118

evaluation criterion. However, the generated values are very close to ones of the Split-Merge Clustering, particularly for the 70/30 data test couples. It is also interesting to notice that in contradiction to the behaviour of PivotBiCluster on cover-type and wine quality data sets, it is the worst performing algorithm under Jaccard Index on antropometric and yeast data sets.

In [31], Luxburg et al. argue that clustering should not be treated as an application independent mathematical problem, but should always be studied in the context of its end-use. The authors further discuss that the cluster evaluation methods can produce contradictory results and often do not serve their purpose. The main point of the authors is that clustering algorithms cannot be evaluated in a problem independent way, i.e. the known cluster validation measures cannot be used to evaluate the usefulness of the linebreak clustering. However, it is still not clear how we can measure the usefulness of a newly developed clustering algorithm.

The results obtained in this study support the above mentioned arguments of Luxburg et al. [31]. Namely, the conducted experiments have not clearly pointed out an algorithm that we can consider and recommend as the best performing one compared to the other two algorithms with respect to the used cluster validation criteria. For example, SI has favoured the Dynamic split-and-merge algorithm in most of the performed experiments. On the other hand, the PivotBiCluster and Split-Merge Evolutionary Clustering have generated higher values for F-measure than the Dynamic split-and-merge algorithm. Moreover, the Split-Merge Clustering and Dynamic split-and-merge algorithms have performed better compared to the PivotBiCluster algorithm with respect to Jaccard Index on two of the used data sets. However, on the other two data sets the PivotBiCluster algorithm is the best performing one under this evaluation criterion. The PivotBiCluster has slightly outperformed the Split-Merge Evolutionary Clustering with respect to F-measure. However, the Split-Merge Evolutionary Clustering algorithm has shown to be more robust than the other two algorithms in producing clustering solutions with cluster number close to that of the benchmark clustering solutions. Evidently, the three clustering algorithms need to be further studied and validated on different applied scenarios in order to get better understanding of their specific characteristics, behaviour and further evaluate the usefulness.

6   Conclusion and Future Work

In this work, we have studied and evaluated a novel evolutionary clustering technique, entitled Split-Merge (Evolutionary) Clustering. The proposed algorithm is supposed to be more robust to concept drift scenarios by providing the flexibility to update the existing clustering solution by considering the clusters derived from a new portion of data. The proposed technique has been compared with other two state of the art clustering algorithms: PivotBiCluster and Dynamic split-and-merge. The three algorithms have been evaluated and demonstrated in two experiment scenarios on four different data sets using three cluster validation indices: Silhouette Index (SI), F-measure and Jaccard Index. The obtained results have not clearly prioritized any of the three studied clustering algorithms. The Dynamic split-and-merge algorithm has been favoured by SI in the most of conducted experiments. The PivotBiCluster and Split-Merge Evolutionary Clustering have produced higher F-measure scores than the Dynamic split-and-merge algorithm in all the experiments. The PivotBiCluster algorithm has demonstrated a slightly better performance than the Split-Merge Evolutionary Clustering under this evaluation criterion. Jaccard Index has not clearly pointed out an algorithm that can be considered as the best performing one. The Split-Merge Evolutionary Clustering algorithm has shown to be more robust to producing clustering solutions that have number of clusters close to that of the benchmark clustering solutions.

Our future plans are to pursue further study and evaluation of our Split-Merge Evolutionary Clustering technique by comparing it with the other two state of the art algorithms on richer data sets and in case studies from different application domains. For example, we are currently interested in evaluating the algorithms on household electricity consumption data. We study whether they can be applied for modelling and monitoring evolving user behavior.

In a long-term perspective, we are interested in building upon the proposed split-merge evolutionary algorithm and develop measures for monitoring clusters evolution and mining changes. This might be treated as time-series forecasting problem where we need to forecast the changes in the clustering solution that might occur. Other interesting future direction is to use the proposed split-merge framework for developing a continual and shared learning technique that enable to learn from multiple data sources by continual updating and evolving of the model.

References

1. Ackerman, M., Dasgupta, S.: Incremental clustering: the case for extra clusters. In: Proceedings of the 27th International Conference on Neural Information Processing Systems - Volume 1, NIPS 2014, pp. 307–315 (2014)
2. Ailon, N., Avigdor-Elgrabli, N., Liberty, E., van Zuylen, A.: Improved approximation algorithms for bipartite correlation clustering. In: Demetrescu, C., Halldórsson, M.M. (eds.) ESA 2011. LNCS, vol. 6942, pp. 25–36. Springer, Heidelberg (2011). https://doi.org/10.1007/978-3-642-23719-5_3
3. Angelov, P.: An approach for fuzzy rule-base adaptation using on-line clustering. Int. J. Approximate Reasoning **35**, 275–289 (2004)
4. Awasthi, P., Balcan, M.F., Voevodski, K.: Local algorithms for interactive clustering. J. Mach. Learn. Res. **18**(3), 1–35 (2017)
5. Balcan, M.F., Blum, A., Vempala, S.: A discriminative framework for clustering via similarity functions. In: Proceedings of the Fortieth Annual ACM Symposium on Theory of Computing, STOC 2008, pp. 671–680 (2008)
6. Bansal, N., Blum, A., Chawla, S.: Correlation clustering. Mach. Learn. **56**(1–3), 89–113 (2004)
7. Bickel, S., Scheffer, T.: Multi-view clustering. In: Proceedings of the Fourth IEEE International Conference on Data Mining, ICDM 2004, pp. 19–26 (2004)
8. Bifet, A., Holmes, G., Kirkby, R., Pfahringer, B.: MOA: massive online analysis. J. Mach. Learn. Res. **11**, 1601–1604 (2010)
9. Blackard, J.A., Dean, D.J., Anderson, C.W.: UCI machine learning repository (1998). http://archive.ics.uci.edu/ml
10. Boeva, V., Angelova, M., Tsiporkova, E.: A split-merge evolutionary clustering algorithm. In: Proceedings of ICAART 2019, pp. 337–346 (2019)
11. Boeva, V., Tsiporkova, E., Kostadinova, E.: Analysis of multiple DNA microarray datasets. In: Kasabov, N. (ed.) Springer Handbook of Bio-/Neuroinformatics, pp. 223–234. Springer, Heidelberg (2014). https://doi.org/10.1007/978-3-642-30574-0_14
12. Bouchachia, A.: Evolving clustering: an asset for evolving systems. IEEE SMC News Lett. **36**, 1–6 (2011)
13. Bouchachia, A., Vanaret, C.: Incremental learning based on growing Gaussian mixture models. In: Proceedings of 10th International Conference on Machine Learning and Applications (ICMLA 2011), Honululu, Haweii (2011)
14. Câmpan, A., Şerban, G.: Adaptive clustering algorithms. In: Lamontagne, L., Marchand, M. (eds.) AI 2006. LNCS (LNAI), vol. 4013, pp. 407–418. Springer, Heidelberg (2006). https://doi.org/10.1007/11766247_35
15. Charikar, M., Chekuri, C., Feder, T., Motwani, R.: Incremental clustering and dynamic information retrieval. In: Proceedings of the 29th Annual ACM Symposium on Theory of Computing, STOC 1997, pp. 626–635 (1997)
16. Cortez, P., Cerdeira, A., Almeida, F., Matos, T., Reisa, J.: Modeling wine preferences by data mining from physicochemical properties. Decis. Support Syst. **47**(4), 547–553 (2009)
17. Dell'Aglio, D., Valle, E.D., van Harmelen, F., Bernstein, A.: Stream reasoning: a survey and outlook. Data Sci. **1**, 59–83 (2017)
18. Dovzan, D., Skrjanc, I.: Recursive clustering based on a Gustafson-Kessel algorithm. Evolving Syst. **2**, 15–24 (2011)

19. Fa, R., Nandi, A.K.: Smart: Novel self splitting-merging clustering algorithm. In: European Signal Processing Conference, Bucharest, Romania, 27–32 August 2012. IEEE (2012)
20. Farnstrom, F., Lewis, J., Elkan, C.: Scalability for clustering algorithms revisited. In: SIGKDD Explorations, London, vol. 2, pp. 51–57 (2000)
21. Gan, G., Ma, C., Wu, J.: Data clustering: Theory, Algorithms, and Applications. (Asa-Siam Series on Statistics and Applied Probability). Society for Industrial & Applied Mathematics, USA (2007)
22. Gionis, A., Mannila, H., Tsaparas, P.: Clustering aggregation. ACM Trans. Knowl. Disc. Data **1**(1), 4 (2007)
23. Goder, A., Filkov, V.: Consensus clustering algorithms: comparison and refinement. In: ALENEX, pp. 109–234 (2008)
24. Golino, H.F., de Amaral, L.S.B., Duarte, S.F.P., et al.: Predicting increased blood pressure using machine learning. J. Obes. **2014**, 12 (2014)
25. Handl, J., Knowles, J., Kell, D.: Computational cluster validation in post-genomic data analysis. Bioinformatics **21**(15), 3201–3212 (2005)
26. Jaccard, P.: The distribution of flora in the alpine zone. New Phytol. **11**, 37–50 (1912)
27. Jain, K.A., Dubes, C.R.: Algorithms for Clustering Data. Prentice-Hall, Inc., Upper Saddle River (1988)
28. Larsen, B., Aone, C.: Fast and effective text mining using linear-time document clustering. In: Proceedings of the 5th ACM SIGKDD International Conference on Knowledge Discovery and Data Mining, KDD 1999, pp. 16–22. ACM (1999)
29. Li, Y., Feng, X., Zhang, M., Zhou, M., Wang, N., Wangb, L.: Clustering of cardiovascular behavioral risk factors and blood pressure among people diagnosed with hypertension: a nationally representative survey in China. Sci. Rep. **6**, 27627 (2016)
30. Lughofer, E.: A dynamic split-and-merge approach for evolving cluster models. Evolving Syst. **3**, 135–151 (2012)
31. von Luxburg, U., Williamson, R.C., Guyon, I.: Clustering: science or art? In: Proceedings of ICML Workshop on Unsupervised and Transfer Learning. Proceedings of Machine Learning Research, vol. 27, pp. 65–79 (2012)
32. Nakai, K., Kanehisa, M.: Expert system for predicting protein localization sites in gram-negative bacteria. Proteins Struct. Funct. Genet. **11**, 95–110 (1991)
33. O'Callaghan, L., Mishra, N., Meyerson, A., Guha, S., Motwani, R.: Streaming-data algorithms for high-quality clustering. In: Proceedings of IEEE International Conference on Data Engineering, pp. 685–694 (2001)
34. van Rijsbergen, C.: Information Retrieval. Butterworth-Heinemann Newton, Oxford (1979)
35. Rousseeuw, P.J.: Silhouettes: a graphical aid to the interpretation and validation of cluster analysis. J. Comput. Appl. Math. **20**, 53–65 (1987)
36. Wang, M., Huang, V., Bosneag, A.M.C.: A novel Split-merge-evolve k clustering algorithm. In: IEEE 4th International Conference on Big Data Computing Service and Applications (BigDataService), Bamberg, Germany, 26–29 March 2018 (2018)
37. Xiang, Q., Mao, Q., Chai, K.M.A., Chieu, H.L., Tsang, I.W., Zhao, Z.: A split-merge framework for comparing clusterings. In: Proceedings of ICML 2012 (2012)
38. Zopf, M., et al.: Sequential clustering and contextual importance measures for incremental update summarization. In: Proceedings of COLING 2016, pp. 1071–1082 (2016)

Wide and Deep Reinforcement Learning Extended for Grid-Based Action Games

Juan M. Montoya[1(✉)], Christoph Doell[1], and Christian Borgelt[2]

[1] University of Konstanz, 78464 Konstanz, Germany
{juan.montoya-bayardo,christoph.doell}@uni-konstanz.de
[2] University of Salzburg, 5020 Salzburg, Austria
christian.borgelt@sbg.ac.at

Abstract. For the last decade, Deep Reinforcement Learning (DRL) has undergone very rapid development. However, less has been done to integrate linear methods into it. Our research aims at a simple and practical Wide and Deep Reinforcement Learning framework to extend DRL algorithms by combining linear (wide) and non-linear (deep) methods. This framework can help to integrate expert knowledge or to fuse sensor information while at the same time improving the performance of existing DRL algorithms. To test this framework we have developed an extension of the popular Deep Q-Networks Algorithm, which we call Wide Deep Q-Networks. We analyze its performance compared to Deep Q-Networks and Linear Agents, as well as human agents by applying our new algorithm to Berkeley's Pac-Man environment. Our algorithm considerably outperforms Deep Q-Networks both in terms of learning speed and ultimate performance, showing its potential for boosting existing algorithms. Furthermore, it is robust to the failure of one of its components.

Keywords: Wide and deep reinforcement learning · Wide deep Q-networks · Value function approximation · Reinforcement learning agents · Model fusion reinforcement learning

1 Introduction

A prominent objective of Artificial Intelligence is to create rational agents which "act so as to achieve the best outcome or, when there is uncertainty, the best-expected outcome" [14, p. 6]. In the subarea of Reinforcement Learning (RL), the aim is to develop rational agents that learn from their environment by seeking to maximize their outcomes w.r.t. a reward system. RL agents, especially if based on a functional approximation of the (action) valuations, have been able to accomplish different kinds of tasks such as autonomous driving [8], playing games [11], and directing robots [7]. In the last decade, RL has been developing very rapidly, especially in the area of Deep Reinforcement Learning (DRL) [6].

Some RL agents incorporated linear and non-linear functions to improve and extend the RL framework. Noteworthy examples include Stanford University's early work on an autonomous helicopter [8], where the agent learns to hover in place and to fly several maneuvers by applying RL via linear function approximation. This implementation

© Springer Nature Switzerland AG 2019
J. van den Herik et al. (Eds.): ICAART 2019, LNAI 11978, pp. 224–245, 2019.
https://doi.org/10.1007/978-3-030-37494-5_12

exhibits efficient training and solves as well as generalizes the problem of flying and hovering. However, it also assumes implicitly that the problem is linearly solvable and thus has limited use for real-world problems, which are often non-linear. In 2015, Deep Mind's algorithm enabled RL agents to successfully play 49 Atari games using a single algorithm, fixed hyperparameters, and deep learning [11]. Most recently, RL agents controlling robotic arms learned by applying similar principles to generalize from their grasping strategies so as to respond dynamically to perturbations [7]. The used network architectures are robust and can adapt to many real-world problems. However, they inherit the already well-studied difficulties of structuring, parameterizing and training neural networks that require a lot of computation power [4].

To the best of our knowledge, up to now researchers have mainly developed linear function approximation and deep learning approaches separately. However: Why not combine linear function approximation and non-linear deep learning to improve the performance of RL algorithms? Such a combination may be referred to as a wide and deep approach. Here "wide" refers to the linear component, which is improved by adding more features. The computations of this component remain "shallow," though, namely linear combinations. On the other hand, "deep" refers to the non-linear component represented by an artificial neural network. The depth of this component is the number of layers and it can be made more powerful by adding layers. Fortunately, a wide and deep machine learning framework has already been developed in the field of recommendation systems [2]. Our research aims to transfer this approach to RL and thus to develop a framework that will make it easier for researchers to extend already existing DRL algorithms. It may also be used for sensor fusion tasks, rendering the system more robust w.r.t. sensor failures or collapse of one of the components.

To evaluate our framework we developed an extension of the popular Deep Q-Networks (DQN) algorithm, which we call Wide Deep Q-Networks (WDQN). We tested WDQN using a grid-based action game: Berkeley's Pac-Man environment. We chose this environment because it is highly scalable and computationally efficient. Furthermore, playing Pac-Man is more difficult than may be expected at first sight and far from trivial. Actually, the DQN results for this game are some of the worst among the 49 ATARI games and worse than the performance of professional human players [11], even though they already manage to outperform amateur human players as our own results indicate (see Sect. 5).

Using the simple idea of combining linear and non-linear learning approaches, we demonstrate that our WDQN trained agent has a significantly higher winning rate and produces much better results compared to solely linear or non-linear agents, and learns faster compared to a pure DQN. In comparison to our past work [12], we now demonstrate that combining both functions makes the non-linear model more efficient, as if trained independently. In addition, the agent becomes tolerant to a failure of one of the two functions.

The remainder of this paper is structured as follows: Sect. 2 briefly reviews linear function approximation and standard Deep Q-Networks. In Sect. 3 we present our theoretical framework for wide and deep reinforcement learning, in which we develop the core WDQN algorithm. In Sect. 4, we show how WDQN performs compared to pure DQN, pure linear function approximation, and humans. For this, we explain how our test suite—Berkeley's Pac-Man environment—works and present our experimental setup for WDQN. Furthermore, we discuss extended experiments aimed at demonstrating that our agent is robust to the failure of one of its components. In Sect. 5 we report the results of our experiments and finally we draw conclusions in Sect. 6.

2   Background

Our research builds on Reinforcement Learning (RL), especially Q-learning, which is briefly reviewed in Sect. 2.1. In order to make it applicable to real-world problems, functional policy map approximations are needed (Sect. 2.2), which can take a linear form (Sect. 2.3) or the form of a deep neural network (Deep Q-Network), allowing for non-linear functions (Sect. 2.4).

2.1   Reinforcement Learning and Q-Learning

RL agents receive feedback from their actions in the form of rewards that result from their interaction with the environment. The agents aim to solve a sequential decision problem by optimizing their (expected) cumulative future rewards [15]. One of the most popular methods for this is Q-learning [6, 16].

In Q-learning, a so-called *quality map* is created, which assigns to each pair of state and action possible a so-called q-value. This value measures the quality (hence q-value) of executing an action in a state. The q-values are denoted by $Q(S, A)$, where S is a state and A is an action. In a given state S, the agent chooses the action A^* with the highest q-value, i.e. $A^* = \text{argmax}_{A \in \mathcal{A}(S)} Q(S, A)$, where $\mathcal{A}(S)$ is the set of actions possible in state S. In many cases, the set of actions is the same for all states and may then simply be denoted as $\mathcal{A}$.

Initially, the quality policy is unknown (usually represented by all q-values being 0). The goal is to learn its values from experience, that is, by (randomly) trying out actions (or sequences of actions) in various states, observing the reward, and updating the q-values in the policy map accordingly. Instead of always choosing the action with the highest q-value (which is how a fully trained agent behaves), here, this usually requires a random element being introduced in order to ensure a proper exploration of the state space. This random element is usually reduced over time as more information is gathered.

Although very successful for small problems, a core challenge of tackling any real-world problem with such an approach is the size of the state space. Thus, also the size of the quality map, which is the number of states times the number of actions. Hence, standard Q-learning alone cannot solve such problems [14], because the quality map is simply too large to make learning feasible.

2.2   Functional Quality Map Approximations

A very popular way of tackling the challenge of the size of a quality map is to approximate the q-values $Q(S, A)$ by a function $\hat{Q}(S, A; \theta)$, where θ is the set of parameters of this function. That is, instead of looking up q-values in a quality table ("material-ized" quality map), which stores the (learned) q-values of all state/action combinations explicitly, they are computed with a (parameterized) function from the properties of a given state S and a considered action A. As a consequence, only the parameters $\boldsymbol{\theta}$ need to be stored and updated to account for reward information gathered from explorations. This may also simplify the task of training (or estimating) the quality map (function) considerably.

In such an approach, one has to specify how the state S and the action A enter into the computation of the q-value $\hat{Q}(S, A; \boldsymbol{\theta})$. Two schemes are typical: in the first, the function $\hat{Q}$ is composed of multiple sub-functions $\hat{Q}_A(S; \boldsymbol{\theta}_A)$, one for each action $A \in \mathcal{A}$, each of which has its own set $\boldsymbol{\theta}_A$ of parameters, with $\boldsymbol{\theta} = \bigcup_{A \in \mathcal{A}} \boldsymbol{\theta}_A$. These functions take (numerical) features $\boldsymbol{f}(S) = [f_1(S), \ldots, f_n(S)]$ as arguments, which are generated from a given state S. These features are combined with the param-eters $\boldsymbol{\theta}$, so that we have $\hat{Q}_A(S; \boldsymbol{\theta}_A, \boldsymbol{f})$ in this case.

In the second scheme, which is sometimes referred to as a "reflective" agent, the considered action A is hypothetically executed in the given state S to obtain (an approx-imation of) an expected successor state $s(S, A)$. This is in line with the characteri-zation of thinking on a basic level as trial acting in a conceptional space in order to evaluate the consequences of different possible paths of action. In this case, features $\boldsymbol{f}(s(S, A)) = [f_1(s(S, A)), \ldots, f_1(s(S, A))]$ are generated, from which the q-values are computed by a single function $\hat{Q}(s(S, A); \boldsymbol{\theta}, \boldsymbol{f})$.

Note that in the first scheme the generated features depend only on the current state, while the action enters the computation of the q-values via multiple functions, one for each action. In the second scheme, however, there is only one function that computes the q-values, while the action enters by hypothetical "trial acting", thus obtaining multiple states from which features are generated. In our application, we will make use of both schemes (see Sect. 4).

Note also that employing differentiable functions for $\hat{Q}$, such as linear combinations of features or artificial neural networks (which allow for non-linear functions), offers us the additional possibility of using Stochastic Gradient Descent (SGD) as an intu-itive method to optimize the action value function $\hat{Q}$. Then a Q-learning update after executing action A_t in state S_t observing the immediate rewards R_{t+1} and subsequent state S_{t+1} is given by

$$\boldsymbol{\theta}_{t+1} = \boldsymbol{\theta}_t + \alpha(y_t - \hat{Q}(S_t, A_t; \boldsymbol{\theta}_t)) \nabla_{\boldsymbol{\theta}_t} \hat{Q}(S_t, A_t; \boldsymbol{\theta}_t), \tag{1}$$

where α is a scalar step size ("learning rate"), $\boldsymbol{\theta}_t$ are the values that the param-eters $\boldsymbol{\theta}$ of the function $\hat{Q}$ have at time t, and the target function y_t is defined as $R_{t+1} + \gamma \max_A \hat{Q}(S_{t+1}, A; \boldsymbol{\theta}_t)$ [15]. A gradient descent scheme is applied to a loss function derived from the difference of y_t and $\hat{Q}(S_t, A_t; \boldsymbol{\theta}_t)$.

It should be noted, though, that convergence is a problem of a functional represen-tation of the quality map: it is no longer guarantee that the learning process converges to the optimal solution, even if enough time is available to explore the whole state space (which, in case of large state spaces, is a fundamental problem as well). With a func-tional approximation the danger arises that learning converges only to a local optimum. For example, due to limited capacity or flexibility of the chosen functional representa-tion of the quality map.

2.3   Linear Function Approximation

The simplest approach to functional quality map approximation is via a linear combination of features $\boldsymbol{f} = [f_1, \ldots, f_n]$. The q-value function is then constructed, according to the two schemes outlined in the preceding section: Either as $Q_A^{\text{lin}}(S; \boldsymbol{\theta}_A^{\text{lin}}, \boldsymbol{f}) = \boldsymbol{f}(S)^\top \boldsymbol{\theta}_A^{\text{lin}}$, using a separate linear function for each action A. Or as a single function $Q^{\text{lin}}(s(S, A); \boldsymbol{\theta}^{\text{lin}}, \boldsymbol{f}) = \boldsymbol{f}(s(S, A))^\top \boldsymbol{\theta}^{\text{lin}}$, where the features are generated from hypothetical successor states $s(S, A)$, which are reached by executing action A in state S. In both cases, we have [15]

$$y_t^{\text{lin}} = R_{t+1} + \gamma \max_A \hat{Q}^{\text{lin}}(S_{t+1}, A; \hat{\boldsymbol{\theta}}_t^{\text{lin}}). \tag{2}$$

Specifically for the second scheme ("trial acting"), we thus obtain

$$\boldsymbol{\theta}_{t+1}^{\text{lin}} = \boldsymbol{\theta}_t^{\text{lin}} + \alpha(y_t^{\text{lin}} - Q^{\text{lin}}(S_t, A_t; \boldsymbol{\theta}_t^{\text{lin}})) \boldsymbol{f}(s(S_t, A_t)).$$

Therefore it is a very simple matter to compute the update rule in this case. For the first scheme the update rule is analogous but refers separately to the parameters $\boldsymbol{\theta}_A$ of the different linear functions, one per action A.

In practice, linear methods can be very efficient in terms of both data and computation. Nevertheless, prior domain knowledge is usually needed to create useful features, representing interactions between features can be difficult, and convergence guarantees are limited to linear problems [15].

2.4   Deep Q-Networks

A straightforward approach allowing q-values to depend in a non-linear way on state features is to substitute a linear approximation function $\hat{Q}^{\text{lin}}$ by a non-linear function. This may be represented, for example, by an artificial neural network. However, this first "naive" approach under-performed because of problems with non-stationary, non-independent, and non-identically distributed data [11].

The Deep Q-Network (DQN) tackles these problems by using an *experience replay memory* and *target networks*. A DQN relies on an Artificial Neural Network (ANN) to map a state S_t to a vector of action values, again using either separate functions for each action A (first scheme outlined in Sect. 2.2) or using "trial acting" (second scheme outlined in Sect. 2.2). The value function is $Q^{\text{dqn}}(S, A; \boldsymbol{\theta}^{\text{dqn}})$, where $\boldsymbol{\theta}^{\text{dqn}}$ are the parameters (e.g. weights and bias values) of the ANN. The experience replay memory [10] saves observed state transitions for some time in a dequeue. These transitions are later uniformly sampled and used to update the parameters $\boldsymbol{\theta}^{\text{dqn}}$. The parameters $\hat{\boldsymbol{\theta}}^{\text{dqn}}$ of the target network $\hat{Q}^{\text{dqn}}$ are copied from the online network every τ steps, setting $\hat{\boldsymbol{\theta}}^{\text{dqn}} = \boldsymbol{\theta}^{\text{dqn}}$, while fixing $\hat{\boldsymbol{\theta}}^{\text{dqn}}$ on all other steps. The target function of a DQN is [11]

$$y_t^{\text{dqn}} = R_{t+1} + \gamma \max_A \hat{Q}^{\text{dqn}}(S_{t+1}, A; \hat{\boldsymbol{\theta}}^{\text{dqn}}). \tag{3}$$

The most important advantage of using Deep Q-Networks instead of linear functions is, of course, their ability to represent or at least approximate a wide variety of non-linear functions. Thus, the capacity and flexibility of functional quality map representations is considerably enhanced. These algorithms have been successfully extended in various ways since their creation [6].

However, DQN and its variants inherit all the problems of artificial neural networks, such as the difficulty of interpreting the decision making of the networks, the necessity to tune multiple hyperparameters [4], and the complexity of the computation with no guarantees of convergence [15].

3   Wide and Deep Reinforcement Learning

The core idea of our approach is to combine linear function approximation with Deep Q-Networks. The former allows for simple incorporation of background knowledge through expert-designed features. The latter accommodate non-linear functions and have the added benefit that based on more basic properties of states, they may be able to learn useful features in their internal structure. This can enhance the performance of the agent considerably. In this section, we consider the structure (Sect. 3.1) and the training procedure (Sect. 3.2) of such a combined approach, which we call Wide Deep Q-Networks.

3.1   Structure of Wide Deep Q-Networks

Figure 1 shows the general structure of our Wide and Deep Reinforcement Learning (WDRL) framework, which can be used for already existing DRL algorithms. This framework consists of combining a "wide" component (left side) and a "deep" component (right side). The "wide" component consists of a linear combination of features and may be improved by increasing its width, that is, by adding features. The "deep" component is an artificial neural network (ANN) and may be improved by adding layers and thus increasing its depth. Both components together compute the action values $a = [a_1, ..., a_m]$.

Initially, the state S (or states $s(S, A)$, one for each action A) is preprocessed to obtain the features for the wide and the deep component. Since the needed features may be different for each of these components, the preprocessing function ϕ may have to be able to map the state S (or $s(S, A)$) differently for these components. Whether only the current state S or several hypothetical successor states $s(S, A)$ are evaluated, depends on whether the first scheme (one function for each action A) or the second scheme ("trial acting" and thus only a single mapping function to outputs) is used. Note that the wide and the deep component may or may not use the same computation scheme. For example, the wide component may use the second scheme ("trial acting"), while the deep component may use the first scheme (separate function for each action).

For the first scheme, only the current state S is evaluated, which yields a feature vector $f(S) = [f_1(S), \ldots, f_n(S)]$ or two separate feature vectors f^{lin} and f^{dqn}, one for each component. In the wide component this feature vector is used directly, while in the deep component it is first processed by the deep neural network, producing values $x = [x_1, \ldots, x_k]$ as the outputs of the output neurons $u_{r1}, \ldots, u_{rk}$, which enter the computation of the action values $a = [a_1, ..., a_m]$. In this case the parameters θ^{lin} as well as the weights w^{dqn} are matrices, that is, $\theta^{\text{lin}} = \Theta = (\theta_{ij})_{\substack{i=1,\ldots,n \\ j=1,\ldots,m}}$ and

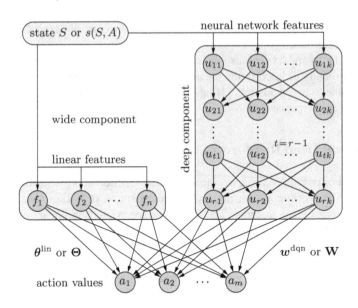

Fig. 1. Wide and Deep Reinforcement Learning Framework showing the connections from the outputs of the wide and deep components to action value a_i, $i = 1, \ldots, m$. These connections are weighted with different parameter vectors $\boldsymbol{\theta}_i^{\text{lin}}$ and $\boldsymbol{w}_i^{\text{dqn}}$ for each output a_i if the first scheme described in Sect. 2.2 (and hence only the current state S) is used, and with single parameter vectors $\boldsymbol{\theta}^{\text{lin}}$ and $\boldsymbol{w}^{\text{dqn}}$ for the second scheme (where computations are separated for each action A and therefore state $s(S, A)$).

$\boldsymbol{w}^{\text{dqn}} = \mathbf{W} = (w_{ij})_{\substack{i=1,\ldots,n \\ j=1,\ldots,m}}$. If both components use this scheme, the action values are computed as $\boldsymbol{a} = \boldsymbol{f}^\top \boldsymbol{\Theta} + \boldsymbol{x}^\top \mathbf{W}$.

For the second scheme, the hypothetical successor state $s(S, A)$ is constructed for each action A and evaluated by computing features, which yields a feature matrix $\mathbf{F}(S, \mathcal{A}) = (f_{ij})_{\substack{i=1,\ldots,n \\ j=1,\ldots,m}}$ with $f_{ij} = f_i(s(S, A_j))$ (or two separate feature matrices $\mathbf{F}^{\text{lin}}$ and $\mathbf{F}^{\text{dqn}}$, one for each component). For the wide component, this feature matrix is used directly, while for the deep component it is processed row by row by the deep neural network, yielding an output matrix $\mathbf{X} = (x_{ij})_{\substack{i=1,\ldots,n \\ j=1,\ldots,m}}$. In this case, the parameters $\boldsymbol{\theta}^{\text{lin}}$ as well as the weights $\boldsymbol{w}^{\text{dqn}}$ are simple vectors ("shared" weights): $\boldsymbol{\theta}^{\text{lin}} = [\theta_1, \ldots, \theta_n]$ and $\boldsymbol{w}^{\text{dqn}} = [w_1, \ldots, w_n]$. If both components use this scheme, the action values are computed as $\boldsymbol{a} = \mathbf{F}^\top \boldsymbol{\theta}^{\text{lin}} + \mathbf{X}^\top \boldsymbol{w}^{\text{dqn}}$. Note again that it is not required for both components to use the same scheme. If the wide component uses the second and the deep component uses the first scheme, the action values may be computed as $\boldsymbol{a} = \mathbf{F}^\top \boldsymbol{\theta}^{\text{lin}} + \boldsymbol{x}^\top \mathbf{W}$. In the experiments reported in Sect. 4 we actually use this mixed approach.

The advantage of this framework is that it flexibly combines both linear and nonlinear methods in order to obtain better, faster and more comprehensive results using DQN algorithms. Cheng *et al.* [2] already showed that such a wide and deep learning model is viable and significantly improves the results for recommendation systems.

Table 1. Semi-ensemble training algorithm for WDQN [12].

Initialize: replay memory D to size N;
        action-value functions Q^{wd}, Q^{lin}, Q^{dqn}
           with random weights $\theta^{wd}, \theta^{lin}, \theta^{dqn}$, respectively;
           target action-value functions $\hat{Q}^{wd}, \hat{Q}^{lin}, \hat{Q}^{dqn}$ with weights
              $\hat{\theta}^{wd} = \theta^{wd}, \hat{\theta}^{lin} = \theta^{lin}, \hat{\theta}^{dqn} = \theta^{dqn}$, respectively;
for episode $= 1$ to M
    initialize sequence $S_1 = [x_1]$;
    preprocess sequence $\phi_1 = \phi(s_1)$
    for $t = 1$ to T
        with probability ϵ select a random action $a_t \in A_t$
           otherwise select $a_t = \text{argmax}_a Q^{wd}(\phi(s_1), a; \theta^{wd})$;
        execute action a_t, observe reward R_t and image x_{t+1};
        set $S_{t+1} = S_t, a_t, x_{t+1}$ and preprocess $\phi_{t+1} = \phi(S_{t+1})$;
        store transition $(\phi_t, a_t, R_t, \phi_{t+1})$ in D;
        sample random mini-batch of transitions $(\phi_t, a_t, R_t, \phi_{t+1})$ from D;
        set $y_j^{dqn}, y^{lin} = r_j$ for terminal $\phi(S_{j+1})$ and non terminal $\phi(S_{j+1})$:
           $y_j^{dqn} = R_{t+1} + \gamma \max_A \hat{Q}^{dqn}(S_{t+1}, A; \hat{\theta}^{wd})$,
           $y_j^{lin} = R_{t+1} + \gamma \max_A \hat{Q}^{lin}(S_{t+1}, A; \hat{\theta}^{lin})$;
        perform gradient descent on $(y_j^{dqn} - Q(S_{t+1}, a; \theta^{dqn}))^2$ and
           $(y_j^{lin} - Q(S_{t+1}, a; \theta^{lin}))^2$ with respect to θ^{lin} and θ^{dqn};
        every C steps reset $\hat{\theta}^{lin} = \theta^{lin}, \hat{\theta}^{wd} = \theta^{wd}$ and $\hat{\theta}^{dqn} = \theta^{dqn}$;
    end for
end for

As a consequence, an analogous approach could yield improvements in this domain as well.

Note that this structure may also be used for approximating simple state valuations instead of a quality map. Formally, this results from a combination of a state S with a simple parameter vector θ and w, or by using a single dummy null action A. Here, however, we focus on approximating quality maps.

3.2 Training Wide Deep Q-Networks

In order to train a combined functional representation, two approaches can be implemented. The first approach is called *joint ensemble training* and executes stochastic gradient descent (SGD) jointly for the linear and non-linear functions. That is, the gradient directing the parameter changes is computed from the joint influence that the wide and deep component have on the error.

The second approach may be called *semi-ensemble training*. Here SGD is executed separately for the two component functions. That is, the wide and the deep component produce separate errors and their parameters are then adapted using separate SGD processes. However, this does *not* lead to independent training of the two components (which is why it is still a form of ensemble training), because predictions of the wide and the deep component influence each other [2]. The reason is that the outputs of the wide and the deep component are combined for generating the actions of the agent, creating experiences that are influenced by both components and subsequently considered during the training for both components. Therefore errors made by one component also influence the other component, namely through the generated training examples.

What both approaches, joint ensemble training and semi-ensemble training, have in common, however, is that both use the combined suggestions of the linear and non-linear function to determine the action to execute.

In our case, DQN algorithms are extended by integrating the wide component Q^{lin} with the deep component Q^{dqn} creating the combined function Q^{wd}, needed for our Wide Deep Q-Networks (WDQN) algorithm. For our WDQN, the wide component uses the target function for the linear combination of features shown in Eq. (2). Meanwhile, the deep component uses the target function of Eq. (3). Therefore, the combined function is $Q^{\text{wd}}(S_t, A_t; \boldsymbol{\theta}^{\text{wd}}) = Q^{\text{lin}}(S_t, A_t; \boldsymbol{\theta}^{\text{lin}}) + Q^{\text{dqn}}(S_t, A_t; \boldsymbol{\theta}^{\text{dqn}})$, where $\boldsymbol{\theta}^{\text{wd}}$ comprises the parameters of the wide and the deep component: $\boldsymbol{\theta}^{\text{wd}} = \boldsymbol{\theta}^{\text{lin}} \cup \boldsymbol{\theta}^{\text{dqn}}$.

The update step can easily be inferred from Eq. (1). Each layer of the artificial neural network (see the box labeled "deep component" in Fig. 1) performs a standard neuron activation computation $\boldsymbol{x}^{(l)} = f_{\text{act}}(\mathbf{W}^{(l)}\boldsymbol{x}^{(l-1)} + \boldsymbol{b}^{(l)})$, where $l \in \{2, \ldots, r\}$ is the layer index, f_{act} is a neuron activation function (e.g. a sigmoid or a ramp function), and $\boldsymbol{x}^{(l)}$, $\boldsymbol{b}^{(l)}$, and $\mathbf{W}^{(l)}$ are the activations, bias values, and connection weights, respectively, of the l-th layer. The output of the deep neural network are the activations $\boldsymbol{x}^{(r)}$ of its last (r-th) layer.

For the computation of (the contribution to) the action values (connections from the neurons $u_{r1}, \ldots, u_{rk}$ to the action values $a_1, \ldots, a_m$), however, a simple linear computation is used: $\boldsymbol{a} = \mathbf{W}\boldsymbol{x}^{(r)} + \boldsymbol{b}^{(r)}$. That is, there is no activation function. A concrete example of a WDQN is discussed in Sect. 4.4.

For the joint training, the algorithm remains almost identical to the original DQN algorithm. Only the online Q^{dqn} and target network $\hat{Q}^{\text{dqn}}$ need to be replaced by Q^{wd} and $\hat{Q}^{\text{wd}}$, respectively. The target is defined as

$$y_t^{\text{wd}} = R_{t+1} + \gamma \max_A \hat{Q}^{\text{wd}}(S_{t+1}, A; \hat{\boldsymbol{\theta}}^{\text{wd}}), \tag{4}$$

where $\hat{\boldsymbol{\theta}}^{\text{wd}}$ are the target parameters of the combined function [12]. Stochastic gradient descent (SGD) is then executed directly on this joint function.

For semi-ensemble training, the algorithm needs to save the resulting action values, but also the separate outputs of the wide and the deep component (see the algorithm in Table 1). Although actions are chosen by the combined function Q^{wd}, SGD training is executed in this case separately on Q^{lin} and Q^{dqn} by implementing both targets from Eqs. (2) and (3).

4   Experiments

In order to evaluate our framework and to compare different agents and training procedures, we chose to train agents for grid-based actions games. As a specific example we used the well-known Pac-Man game, even though the approach is easily transferable to other grid-based action games. We first recall the basic gameplay of Pac-Man (Sect. 4.1) and then describe UC Berkeley's Pac-Man environment [3] (Sect. 4.2).

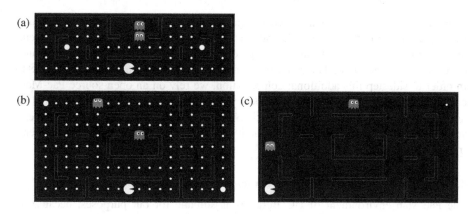

Fig. 2. Initial states of the small (a) and medium (b) maps of Berkeley's Pac-Man environment. Map (c) shows shows a last dot that has to be eaten in order to finish the game [12]. (Color figure online)

Section 4.3 briefly reviews basics of convolutional neural networks, which we use for the deep component of our WDQN approach. Section 4.4 describes the setup of our concrete experiments. In Sect. 4.5, we discuss the problem of learning to eat ghosts and in Sect. 4.6 we describe extended experiments that we added compared to [12].

4.1 The Pac-Man Game

Pac-Man is a classic computer game that was originally released by the Japanese company Namco in 1980. A human player controls an agent, the Pac-Man, by steering it through a grid-based maze, moving it horizontally or vertically to neighboring grid cells, unless such a cell is occupied by a wall of the maze. Example maps of such a maze (smaller than that used in the original game, but employed in our experiments) are shown in Fig. 2. Pac-Man is the yellow agent.

Initially, the maze is largely filled with many small dots, known as Pac-Dots, and a few larger dots called Power-Pellets (e.g. in the corners of the maze in Fig. 2(b)). Both serve as "food" and are collected by Pac-Man if it moves over them. Additionally, ghosts rove the maze, shown in red and blue.

The goal of Pac-Man is to score as many points as possible by eating Pac-Dots and Power-Pellets. When a Pac-Man meets with ghost on the same square, the game is lost. Therefore, one goal is to avoid collisions with ghosts. This situation changes when Pac-Man eats a Power-Pellet; at this moment all ghosts are rendered edible for a limited period of time, which is indicated by a color change. During this time, colliding with a ghost does not lose the game but gives extra scores instead and removes the ghost. Eaten ghosts reappear at their initial position as inedible ghosts (that must again be avoided). An episode is finished when Pac-Man has eaten all Pac-Dots (see Fig. 2(c), in which only one dot is left to be eaten to finish the game) or gets killed by an inedible ghost.

In the original version of the game, additional fruit appears at random, granting bonus score when eaten. Further, it features a bigger map and four ghosts. A fully realistic Pac-Man environment based on the original game is Atari's Ms. Pac-Man, which was used in Mnih *et al.* [11] and Hasselt *et al.* [5]. However, this environment requires image processing to analyze a pixel-based image of the maze as input and to derive the locations of Pac-Man, the ghosts, the Pac-Dots and the Power-Pellets. In order to sidestep this additional complication, we rely on an open source Pac-Man environment made available by UC Berkeley. We made this choice, since our goal is not to use a fully realistic simulator to achieve superhuman results, but rather to have a scalable and computer efficient environment to test our Deep and Wide Reinforcement framework.

4.2   UC Berkeley's Pac-Man Environment

The Pac-Man environment of UC Berkeley is suitable for our purposes, because it guarantees scalability providing customizable map sizes. Moreover, the preprocessing of the game states is more efficient than using raw pixel images as input, because it allows reading the state of the grid cells directly. We test our approach only on small and medium maps (see Fig. 2) due to limitations of computing power for the time-consuming training.

In both of the maps shown in Fig. 2(a) and (b), Pac-Man starts in the bottom middle part of the map. The map also contains two ghosts, many Pac-Dots, and two Power-Pellets. The room where the ghosts start and reappear if they get eaten, is in the middle of the maze for the medium map and at the top of the maze for the small map. Eating a Power-Pellet disables the ghosts for 40 units of time, where one unit of time (or one time step) is the time needed by Pac-Man to move from one grid cell to a neighboring one.

We employ the original reward system of UC Berkeley's environment for scoring. The initial score is zero and resets after each episode. Eating a Pac-Dot or a Power-Pellet scores 10 points. For each ghost that is eaten during the time they are disabled after a Power-Pellet has been eaten, the agent scores 50 points. In order to avoid stagnation, 1 point is deducted for each time step spent in the game. At the end of an episode, Pac-Man either wins by eating the last Pac-Dot, scoring 100 points, or loses by getting killed by a ghost, forfeiting 500 points.

Apart from providing access to grid cell content, UC Berkeley's Pac-Man environment also provides certain features, which are suitable for use in an agent based on linear function approximation. We use a bias and three features:

1. ***#-of-ghosts-1-step-away*** (**g**): states the number of ghosts one step away (i.e. on a neighboring square); this feature does not differentiate between active (dangerous) and disabled ("edible") ghosts, though.
2. ***eats-food*** (**f**): true if the square, to which an action moves the Pac-Man, contains food and there is no ghost on a neighboring square (i.e., g is 0).
3. ***closest-food*** (**c**): states the distance to the closest food (measured as the Manhattan distance between Pac-Man's position and the food), which often coincides with the number of steps Pac-Man needs to reach the food.

Note that the third feature, in a "trial acting" approach (see Sect. 2.2), indirectly provides information about the direction in which Pac-Man may have to move in order to reach the closest food.

4.3 Convolutional Neural Networks

In order to easily process grid-based action game states as input, we chose a convolutional neural network (CNN) for the Deep Q-Network as well as for the deep component of our Wide Deep Q-Network. CNNs were originally developed for processing images, which is very similar to processing a game screen.

In a CNN, the input as well as each layer is a three-dimensional neuron array, with two dimensions referring to the image dimensions and a third dimension referring to different pieces of information per pixel. This third dimension is usually referred to as *channels* for the input (e.g. color channels for images) and as *filters* for the subsequent layers. In a CNN each neuron receives input *not* from all neurons of the preceding layer, but only from a limited subset of neurons that are spatially co-located, called the *receptive field* of the neuron. Furthermore, the connection weights are shared for all neurons in the same filter. In this way a layer of a CNN implements several convolutions (with the receptive field specifying the convolution kernel size), namely one per filter.

Such a network can more easily learn the occurrence of localized features that, however, may appear anywhere in the input. This is an advantage compared to fully connected neural networks having the same amount of layers [4]. A CNN also has the advantage that it accelerates training due to the reduced number of parameters (compared to fully connected layers). Reassuringly, the use of CNNs has been a standard tool for DRL research for some time [5, 6, 11].

Figure 3 shows the WDRL framework for our specific use case—that is, playing grid-based action games like Pac-Man—that uses a CNN architecture for its deep component (as well as for the pure DQN agent). In order to save computational power, we do not use a raw pixel image as input for the DQN and the deep component of our WDQN.[1] Rather, we use the maze grid directly and construct the input as a tensor that stacks six binary matrices, indicating for each grid cell whether it contains (1) ghost, (2) wall, (3) Pac-Dot, (4) Power-Pellet, (5) Pac-Man and (6) "edible" ghost [13]. These matrices are easily retrievable for each state and are a distinctive feature of UC Berkeley's Pac-Man environment.

This direct access allows us to bypass the interpretation of a raw pixel image of the game screen and therefore avoids all image analysis and processing problems. The input tensor, therefore, has the dimensions $w \times h \times 6$ (see Fig. 3) and permits a fast identification of important game elements.

The CNN we use as the deep component of our WDQN has two convolutional layers and one fully connected layer that finally connects to the four outputs. The first layer applies 16 filters with kernel size 3×3 with full padding of the input and stride 1 (in order to maintain the grid dimensions w and h), while the second applies 32 filters with kernel size 3×3, also with full padding and stride 1. The fully connected layer has $k = 256$ neurons.

This architecture permits us to keep the network small but with the capacity of making complex decisions. By using convolution kernels of size 3×3 in two layers, which results in a 5×5 field of view in the input, the agent can "see" at least two steps away from its current cell. This is important to avoid being killed by a ghost. The two

---

[1] For agents that learn directly from pixel images, see [5, 11].

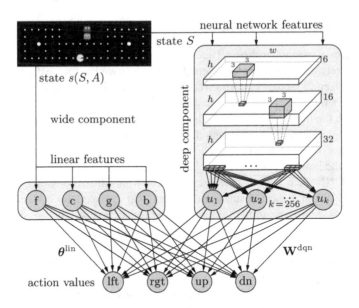

Fig. 3. Wide Deep Q-Network for the Pac-Man experiments with wide (linear) and deep (CNN) components. The connection parameters are shared for the wide component (vector $\boldsymbol{\theta}^{\text{lin}}$), while the output neurons are fully connected to the action values (matrix $\mathbf{W}^{\text{dqn}}$). The linear features are those described in Sect. 4.2 (i.e. *eats-food* f, *closest-food* c and *#-of-ghosts-1-step-away* g) plus a simple constant bias b.

layers with a depth of 16 and 32 dimensions, respectively, allow the agent to be able to abstract from a combination of 32 different base maze patterns. A similar architecture was implemented for a DQN in [13] and was confirmed to be effective during our preliminary experiments.

4.4 Experimental Setup

In our experiments, we compare agents based on a linear function approximation, a pure Deep Q-Network (DQN), and our Wide Deep Q-Network. All of these agents produce values for the same set of four actions, i.e. the four possible directions in which Pac-Man can move: left, right, up, down (see Fig. 3).

To tune the hyperparameters of the agents and their training process, we performed around 100 preliminary experiments for the linear and DQN agent in different maps. Among the hyperparameters we adjusted are the size of the experience replay memory, the learning rates, the update rate of the target function, the network structure, and the exploration value ϵ with its final exploration frame. We consistently maintained the final hyperparameters shared between the linear and DQN agent. Afterward, we used these hyperparameters for the WDQN. However, our pure DQN agent does not use the same hyperparameters but rather the algorithm structure as described in [11].

The linear function approximation agent chooses, in state S_t, the action that likely yields (according to the current approximation of the quality map) the highest q-value in the next state S_{t+1} (using "trial acting", see Sect. 2.2). The training of this linear function approximation follows the DQN's algorithmic structure (i.e. target function, memory replay etc.).

Figure 3 shows our Pac-Man WDQN structure: The wide component (left) processes the features for the linear function approximation (obtained via "trial acting", that is, from hypothetical states $s(S, A)$), while the deep component (right) is provided with the image-like representation of the map (in tensor form as described above), which is to be processed by the CNN.

The WDQN is trained using semi-ensemble training based on the knowledge about learning rates obtained for linear function and CNN from the preliminary experiments. The linear features described in Sect. 4.2 are used for the wide component in different combinations. We test our WDQN with different wide components, using only one, two, or all three feature(s), respectively:

1. An agent denoted by WDQN[f,c,g] combines all three available features with the CNN-based DQN. This is the fully-fledged WDQN agent.
2. An agent denoted WDQN[g] that uses only the feature *#-of-ghosts-1-step-away* (g), which helps to avoid ghosts and thus to survive the game.
3. An agent denoted by WDQN[f,c] that omits the feature *#-of-ghosts-1-step-away* (g). Although this features helps to avoid ghosts, we conjectured that it may also prevent the agent from learning to eat ghosts (see below). The other two features *closest-food* (c) and *eats-food* (f) are maintained.

The deep component uses the ADAM optimizer [9] and a learning rate of 0.001. In the wide component, we apply standard SGD with a learning rate of 0.1.

In order to guarantee transparency and reproducibility, our Python code using TensorFlow, is available on GitHub.[2] Following the recommendations of Henderson *et al.* [6], this also includes the exact description of the used hyperparameters and random seeds.

The actual training was done on a server with an NVIDIA Titan GPU, which allows for high parallelism and speedy training. Nevertheless, we confined our experiments to the small and medium maps (see Fig. 2) in order to limit the computational overhead of processing the input and the back-propagation training of the deep component. Even with these restrictions the training takes considerable time. One training run, with 11,000 episodes, took about two hours for the small map and four hours for the medium map.

We found that the learning curve (score) started to stagnate after around 11000 training episodes. Therefore, we chose this value as the training limit for the final experiments. In order to compare the agent's performance, we use the averaged score and the win rate of each agent from 100 episodes. Finally, we repeat multiple randomly seeded experiments with the same hyperparameters for each selected agent to guarantee consistency.

---

[2] https://github.com/JuanMMontoya/WDRL-ext.

4.5   The Problem of Learning to Eat Ghosts

When observing the linear agent, we noticed that it does not eat ghosts. One reason for this behavior could be the inability of *#-of-ghosts-1-step-away* to distinguish the ghost type. This creates a dichotomy: either learning to eat ghosts or to avoid them. Since the reward incentives are higher to survive, the agent evades them. However, eating ghosts is highly desirable, because it allows the agent to achieve higher scores due to the comparatively high rewards received from eating ghosts. However, the original DQN algorithm also did not learn to eat them [11], which explains to some extent the poor scores of DQN in this game. Furthermore, the DQN agent received a clipped reward of either $+1$ or -1 at each state S_t. For example, the agent gets 1 point for eating either a ghost or a Pac-Dot, and a negative score (-1 point) for dying. The agent, therefore, did not learn the significance of eating ghosts because of the indistinctive reward [5]. However, the agent did learn to eat disabled ghosts in two other approaches: Hasselt *et al.* [5] tackled this problem by adaptively normalizing the targets of the network, making it possible to process all types of rewards. Meanwhile, van der Ouderaa [13] used the incoming reward of Berkeley's environment at each state S_t to train the DQN algorithm. For our approach, we use van der Ouderaa's method, because it keeps our implementation as small as possible and because it was successfully tested using the same reward system.

Whether Pac-Man eats ghosts or not may strongly influence the score. Hence, we measure this in our experiments by observing at least 10 games for each of the selected agents. We consider that an agent has learned to eat ghosts when it actively hunts the edible ghosts and not only eats them purely by chance.

4.6   Extended Experiments

The agent's actions are memorized as replays, which are buffered and used later to change the agent's actions again. Hence there is a mutual dependency of the actions the agent takes and the available training data. Unfortunately, in the preliminary results, it cannot be distinguished whether a good (or bad) performance of an agent is caused by good (or bad) replays. Further, replays of another source might be special examples, which might help to overcome a situation where an agent is stuck and unable to significantly improve its performance.

As we use two components within our agent, we developed the idea to try to turn the wide component off and on again. This creates replays for both a pure DQN and a WDQN and thus forces the deep component to work independently (namely when the wide component is switched off). This approach has both similarities with as well as differences to the work of Bohez *et al.* [1] on fusing sensors in DRL: On the one hand both approaches should result in models that are more robust towards sensor or even model failures. On the other hand Bohez *et al.* apply two non-linear models and test it in a robotic setup, while we apply one linear and one non-linear model in a simulation.

In our extended experimental setup, the wide component is first active for 3000 episodes and then alternatingly switched off and on again for 1000 episodes each. More precisely, the training starts with a random exploration phase of 800 episodes, then uses more and more replays created by the movements of the agent. At episode 2000,

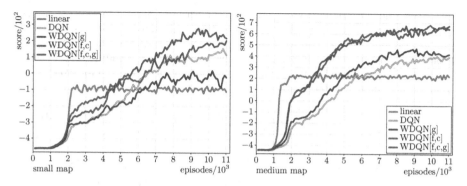

Fig. 4. Each agent is evaluated during training on the small (left side) and medium map (right side). Five randomly seeded training sessions are conducted for each agent with the same hyperparameters for 11,000 episodes and averaged pointwise [12].

the replay buffer does not contain any random exploration instances anymore. After another 1000 episodes we switch off the wide component for the first time, lasting 1000 episodes. During this time, the WDQN agent relies exclusively on the deep component, but uses the buffered replays created by the actions of the full WDQN agent. At 4000 episodes, the wide component is switched on again, after 5000 episodes switched off etc. Thus, we force the models be able to work independently as well as jointly, hoping that in this way the components benefit from both experiences and are trained better. In the end, we evaluate all of our WDQN models twice: once with an activated wide component (WDQN[g], WDQN[f,c], and WDQN[f,c,g]) and once with a deactivated wide component (DQN[g], DQN[f,c] and DQN[f,c,g]). The latter are DQN models (deep components) which used wide components and their replays during training, but were evaluated as stand-alone DQN models.

5   Results

For reliability, we have repeated all of our experiments at least eight times. The visualizations in Figs. 4 and 5 average over these repetitions. Figure 4 shows the scores for each agent on the small (left side) and medium map (right side) during training. The linear agent learns faster than all other agents but stabilizes once a certain threshold is reached. For the small map, this threshold is at a score of about −100 points and is reached after only 2200 episodes. For the medium map, training is completed even faster: The score converges at 200 points after only 1900 episodes. All other agents use a neural network, which takes longer to train but then they exceed the score threshold of the linear agent.

The DQN and WDQN[g] agents are the slowest learning agents in our experiments. On the medium map, they behave similarly: They reach the quality of the linear agent after 4900 to 5700 episodes but afterward can only increase their score slowly. On the small map, similar training results are attained for 5000 episodes. But DQN surpasses the score threshold earlier and in further training extends its lead, gaining scores above 100, while WDQN[g] stays around zero. We conjecture that the feature [g] makes Pac-Man too scared of ghosts.

Table 2. Win rate, average total score, average score when the agent won (score$_+$), average score when the agent lost (score$_-$) for the small and the medium map, as well as whether the agents learned to eat ghosts. The agents presented are the linear function approximation, the random agent, a human amateur player, as well as the DQN and WDQN with 3, 2 and 1 features respectively. For each algorithm, the best training run is chosen and evaluated for 100 episodes. The human amateur played 100 games.

	Small map				Medium map				Eats ghost
	Wins	Score	Score$_+$	Score$_-$	Wins	Score	Score$_+$	Score$_-$	
Linear	17	−114.6	572.3	−255.3	54	481.6	933.1	−48.5	No
DQN	32	105.0	608.8	−132.0	47	625.3	1005.4	288.2	Yes
WDQN[g]	50	211.6	550.7	−127.5	61	618.6	879.9	210.1	No
WDQN[f,c]	60	350.6	639.5	−82.7	66	733.5	973.9	266.8	Yes
WDQN[f,c,g]	59	293.2	567.9	−102.1	64	669.9	910.4	242.3	No
Human	11	−99.3	601.1	−185.9	12	125.1	957.8	11.5	Yes
Random	0	−462.8	n/a	−462.8	0	−443.8	n/a	−443.8	No

The agents with two and three features (green and blue) learn faster than the other neural network based agents. On the medium map, their scores always differ less than 100 points. On the small map, these agents reach the threshold of the linear agent's performance after around 4500 episodes. WDQN[f,c] performs better than the agent with three features in the early episodes but is outperformed afterward. WDQN[f,c] is only able to narrow the performance gap toward the end, scoring more than 200 while WDQN[f,c,g] fluctuates around 240.

At episode 4000, WDQN[f,c,g] scores about 100 points less than WDQN[f,c]. However, between episode 4000 and 8000, WDQN[f,c,g] trains clearly faster than WDQN[f,c]. One may speculate that this is caused by certain replays which help to overcome the slow training between episodes 2000 and 4000. This effect continues, even after WDQN[f,c,g] exceeds the performance attained by WDQN[f,c].

The scores for the medium map are generally higher compared to those for the small map. This is not surprising as the bigger map uses a larger grid that contains more Pac-Dots allowing a higher maximal score. Furthermore, Pac-Man has more space to evade ghosts, as the map also uses (only) two ghosts. Overall, the agents with a wide component using the features [f,c] outperform the DQN in both maps. This performance gap is bigger in the medium map.

Table 2 shows the winning rate and averaged score for WDQN, DQN, random and linear agents, and human players on the small and medium map for 100 episodes. We refrain from showing the standard deviation of the score, as this would implicitly assume a single mode distribution. However, since 100 points are scored for winning and 500 points forfeited for losing, the distribution is clearly bimodal. Thus, the dispersion is better captured by showing the average scores for episodes won (score$_+$) and episodes lost (score$_-$). In contrast to Figs. 4 and 5, Table 2 shows results from the best training run of each agent, not the average. The score is computed as the average over 100 episodes.

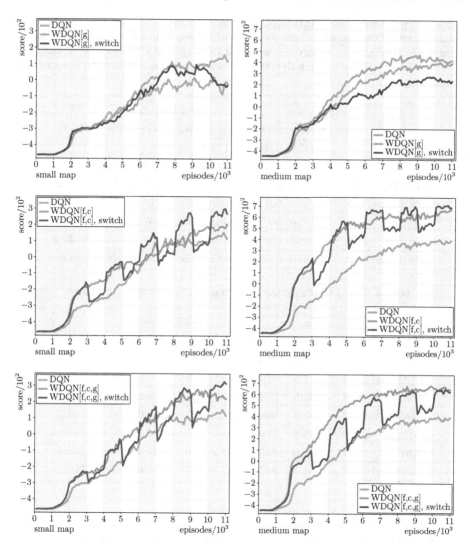

Fig. 5. Results of normal and switch training, on the left side for the small map, on the right side for the medium map. The pure DQN is shown in all plots as a comparison. Each row contains the curves measured for one version of the WDQN agents and for the corresponding agent, when the wide component is switched on and off. A white background indicates episodes during which the wide component was deactivated in the switch training approach. The top row shows WDQN[g], middle row WDQN[f,c] and bottom row WDQN[f,c,g]. (Color figure online)

The ability to eat ghosts does not depend on the map. The linear agent, the human as well as all agents without the feature [g] eat ghosts, while the others do not. As expected, the random agent performs badly on both maps and only establishes a baseline. For the human row, we selected the best player of a round-robin tournament with 9 volunteers (see our GitHub repository for the recorded human's games). This demonstrates that

Table 3. Results on the small map comparing normal and switch training. WDQN models are evaluated twice. Once, as before, with the active wide component and once when it is deactivated during testing. When deactivated, we call it DQN[x], with x being the set of wide features used during training. For each algorithm, the best training run is chosen and averaged over 100 episodes.

	Normal training				Switch training			
	Wins	Score	Score+	Score−	Wins	Score	Score+	Score−
DQN	32	105.0	608.8	−132.0				
WDQN[g]	50	211.6	550.7	−127.5	41	149.9	558.3	−133.8
WDQN[f,c]	60	350.6	639.5	−82.7	65	408.6	643.8	−28.4
WDQN[f,c,g]	59	293.2	567.9	−102.1	65	319.1	557.7	−124.1
DQN[g]	0	−333.4	n/a	−333.4	36	197.7	660.1	−62.4
DQN[f,c]	6	−258.3	560.0	−310.5	38	233.1	658.0	−27.2
DQN[f,c,g]	2	−130.6	617.5	−145.8	30	91.0	598.1	−126.4

Table 4. Results for normal and switch training, here for the medium map.

	Normal training				Switch training			
	Wins	Score	Score+	Score−	Wins	Score	Score+	Score−
DQN	47	625.3	1005.4	288.2				
WDQN[g]	61	618.6	879.9	210.1	36	376.2	831.6	120.0
WDQN[f,c]	66	733.5	973.9	266.8	63	670.2	974.3	152.5
WDQN[f,c,g]	64	669.9	910.4	242.3	71	684.0	909.1	132.7
DQN[g]	51	626.8	976.2	263.1	45	534.7	907.6	229.6
DQN[f,c]	22	375.6	930.1	219.2	55	645.9	992.5	222.4
DQN[f,c,g]	13	162.5	846.7	60.2	47	596.6	968.9	266.4

the problem is not trivial for humans. However, the human amateur plays better than a random agent and wins 11 times on the small and 12 times on the medium map. When winning, the scores are high. However, the remaining 88 and 89 losing episodes cause a low average score. The linear agent is about as bad as the human on the small map winning only 17 of 100 games. On the medium map, on the other hand, it wins 54 episodes, scoring 933 points on average. Unfortunately, when losing, it scores −48 points on average—resulting in an overall average score of 481. WDQN[f,c], WDQN[f,c,g] and WDQN[g] show the highest win rate and excellent average scores for both maps. DQN wins less often, but achieves the best score+ of more than 1000 and also the highest score− of 288 on the medium map. With only 32 wins, the win rate on the small map is too low to enter the top ranks. Best ranked here are again the WDQN agents, achieving 50 to 60 wins. DQN's score+ is second highest with 608. So if winning, the DQN agent gets a high average score that may also be caused by its ability to eat ghosts.

The influence of feature [g] can be seen in two comparisons: (1) In DQN vs. WDQN[g] we see that [g] increases the win rate but lowers the average scores. It further removes the ability to eat ghosts. (2) WDQN[f,c] outperforms WDQN[f,c,g] in all measures, even in win rate. Here, [g] reduces the quality in the long run. Overall, the wide and deep model beats the purely deep one.

Figure 4 and Table 2 present almost equivalent outcomes. Yet, the most notable difference is that when averaging over the repetitions WDQN[f,c,g] in Fig. 4 (left side) is the best. When taking the model with the highest win rate (Table 2), the best scores in are produced by WDQN[f,c].

Tables 3 and 4 compare the results of normal and switch training for the WDQN models. The top left (normal training) parts are shown again to simplify the comparison with the switch training on the right. The bottom three rows contain the evaluation results when the wide component is inactive.

Starting with the small map, the switch training of WDQN[g] has a lower win rate— reduced from 50 to 41 wins—and similar values for score$_+$ and score$_-$. Thus, the overall score is reduced from 212 to 150. The other two wide and deep models improve their win rates. Although WDQN[f,c,g] has reduced score$_-$ and score$_+$, the overall score improves by 26 points. The switch training on WDQN[f,c] boosts its score$_-$, while score$_+$ stays roughly the same. This results in an overall score of 408 points—the best performance on the small map.

Testing the WDQN models without their wide component, when they were never trained this way, may seem unfair, but builds a baseline for the question as to which of the two parts of the model is more important. On the small map, the deep component is lost without the wide part, winning only zero to six of 100 games and when losing, forfeiting up to 333 points per match.

With switch training, the comparison is fair, as the models were at least trained for some episodes on the identical task. This pushes the win rate to values between 30 and 38 and high scores for score$_+$ around 660. Compared with the pure DQN model at normal training, this shows extraordinary performance and indicates that the DQN model alone cannot reach its peak performance without the examples created by the WDQN model.

On the medium map (Table 4), there are some differences: The switch training for the WDQN models decreases their score$_-$ by approximately 100 points, keeps the score$_+$ constant for the two and three feature model and reduces the score$_+$ by nearly 50 for WDQN[g]. The latter's win rate decreases from 61 to only 36 making its score even worse than that of the linear model.

The DQN models with normal training show surprisingly good results, although they were trained with an active wide component and tested without. While on the small map the win rates were below 10 out of 100, here they are 13 (for [f,c,g]), 22 (for [f,c]) and even as high as 51 (for [g]) out of 100 episodes. The latter is even on a similar level as plain DQN, which seems to be caused by its wide component using only one feature.

Switch training improves the two and three feature DQN models to win rates of 47 and 55 out of 100, while DQN[g] loses 6. Score$_-$ is very good with values over 220, especially when compared with WDQN, whose scores are always below 160. Here, deactivating the wide component seems to make the agents play more cautiously, being caught by the ghosts later in the match, after more Pac-Dots are already eaten. The average score when winning is also increased between 18 and 76 points. Only the win rates tend to be smaller.

Just like for the small map, the DQN can reach a higher quality when trained with additional wide features, and performs best when those features are [f,c]. Models with active wide components show higher win rates with and without switch training. The results are inconclusive w.r.t. the question whether switch training or normal training is better—it seems to depend on the wide features as well as on the map size.

Figure 5 compares the performance of the models when the wide component is always off (DQN), when the wide component is always on (WDQN), and when the wide component is switched on and off (switch). In contrast to the Tables 3 and 4, the *average* models are depicted here and the focus lies on the quality during training as opposed to at the end of training. Plots on the left show the small map, those on the right show the medium map. The WDQN[g] model and DQN (shown in the upper two plots) only differ in one feature and are therefore expected to perform similarly. The corresponding similar curves are shown on the right for the medium map, less similar, with more fluctuation also for the small map. WDQN[g] is outperformed by the other WDQN models. Also, the WDQN switch model is not promising in this case. We expected a spike in the performance whenever the switch is toggled, but this is shown in the results. For the medium map, switch training starts to perform similarly to the others, but after 4000 episodes cannot keep up. On the small map, it performs well until around episode 9200, then the performance drops from an average score of 150 to −30. We think this is a random fluctuation.

In the other four plots, we can see the expected spike. Whenever the wide component is switched off (at episodes 3000, 5000, 7000 and 9000), performance drops by some points. When switched back on (episodes 4000, 6000, 8000, 10000) the corresponding spike occurs and increases the score. This increase is bigger than the previous decrease, though, meaning that the pure training of the deep component positively influences the combined model. One strong example is the WDQN[f,c] on the medium map between episodes 3000 and 4000, where the score increases by 200 points. When the switch models are turned on for the medium map they perform similarly to their WDQN counterpart and even converge to nearly identical scores. On the small map, they even beat the pure WDQN models by 60 to 100 points. With average scores of 270 (WDQN[f,c], switch) and 320 points (WDQN[f,c,g] switch), they show best scores.

6   Conclusion

Summing up the results, we see that switch training decreases the performance of WDQN[g]. Our conjecture that WDQN[g] would learn faster is thus proven wrong. This feature has the opposite effect on performance as it prevents the agent from learning to eat ghosts. The *#-of-ghosts-1-step-away* feature helps to develop the capacity to survive in the short-term but restricts the capacity to achieve high scores in the long term. Features [f,c] on the other hand improve the learning speed and the quality of the final model. Although this result was not clear in the tables, the figures show that switch training leads not to worse, but sometimes (in our case on the small map) even to better final results. Models trained with active and tested with inactive wide component perform similar or better than the pure DQN. This indicates that the pure DQN alone is unable to reach the best possible model. Thus, we recommend using wide and deep models instead of only deep models and to use switch training in both cases: when the final model has to be a deep model, and when it may be wide and deep.

References

1. Bohez, S., Verbelen, T., De Coninck, E., Vankeirsbilck, B., Simoens, P., Dhoedt, B.: Sensor fusion for robot control through deep reinforcement learning. In: 2017 IEEE/RSJ International Conference on Intelligent Robots and Systems (IROS), pp. 2365–2370. IEEE, September 2017
2. Cheng, H.T., et al.: Wide & deep learning for recommender systems. In: Proceedings of the 1st Workshop on Deep Learning for Recommender Systems, DLRS 2016, pp. 7–10. ACM, New York (2016)
3. DeNero, J., Klein, D.: Teaching introductory artificial intelligence with pac-man. In: Proceedings of the Symposium on Educational Advances in Artificial Intelligence, pp. 1885–1889 (2010)
4. Goodfellow, I., Bengio, Y., Courville, A.: Deep Learning. MIT Press, Cambridge (2016)
5. van Hasselt, H.P., Guez, A., Hessel, M., Mnih, V., Silver, D.: Learning values across many orders of magnitude. In: Advances in Neural Information Processing Systems 29: Annual Conference on Neural Information Processing Systems 2016, Barcelona, Spain, 5–10 December 2016, pp. 4287–4295 (2016)
6. Henderson, P., Islam, R., Bachman, P., Pineau, J., Precup, D., Meger, D.: Deep reinforcement learning that matters. In: Proceedings of the Thirtieth-Second AAAI Conference on Artificial Intelligence, AAAI 2018. AAAI Press (2018)
7. Kalashnikov, D., et al.: QT-Opt: scalable deep reinforcement learning for vision-based robotic. CoRR abs/1806.10293 (2018)
8. Kim, H.J., Jordan, M.I., Sastry, S., Ng, A.Y.: Autonomous helicopter flight via reinforcement learning. In: Thrun, S., Saul, L.K., Schölkopf, B. (eds.) Advances in Neural Information Processing Systems 16, pp. 799–806. MIT Press (2004)
9. Kingma, D.P., Ba, J.: Adam: A method for stochastic optimization. arXiv preprint arXiv:1412.6980 (2014)
10. Lin, L.J.: Self-improving reactive agents based on reinforcement learning, Plann. Teach. Machine Learning 8(3), 293–321 (1992). https://doi.org/10.1007/BF00992699
11. Mnih, V., et al.: Human-level control through deep reinforcement learning. Nature 518(7540), 529–533 (2015)
12. Montoya., J.M., Borgelt., C.: Wide and deep reinforcement learning for grid-based action games. In: Proceedings of the 11th International Conference on Agents and Artificial Intelligence - Volume 2: ICAART, pp. 50–59. INSTICC, SciTePress (2019). https://doi.org/10.5220/0007313200500059
13. van der Ouderaa, T.: Deep Reinforcement Learning in Pac-Man (2016). Bachelor thesis, University of Amsterdam
14. Russell, S.J., Norvig, P.: Artificial Intelligence: A Modern Approach. Pearson Education, 3 edn. (2003)
15. Sutton, R.S., Barto, A.G.: Introduction to Reinforcement Learning (71 2018), working Second Edition
16. Watkins, C.J.C.H.: Learning from Delayed Rewards. Ph.D. thesis, King's College, Cambridge, UK (1989). http://www.cs.rhul.ac.uk/~chrisw/new_thesis.pdf

Adaptive-Aggressive Traders Don't Dominate

Daniel Snashall[ID] and Dave Cliff[✉][ID]

Department of Computer Science, University of Bristol, Bristol BS8 1UB, UK
ds15012.2015@my.bristol.ac.uk, csdtc@bristol.ac.uk

Abstract. For more than a decade Vytelingum's *Adaptive-Aggressive* (AA) algorithm has been recognized as the best-performing automated auction-market trading-agent strategy currently known in the AI/Agents literature; in this paper, we demonstrate that it is in fact routinely outperformed by another algorithm when exhaustively tested across a sufficiently wide range of market scenarios. The novel step taken here is to use large-scale compute facilities to brute-force exhaustively evaluate AA in a variety of market environments based on those used for testing it in the original publications. Our results show that even in these simple environments AA is consistently outperformed by IBM's *GDX* algorithm, first published in 2002. We summarize here results from more than one million market simulation experiments, orders of magnitude more testing than was reported in the original publications that first introduced AA. A 2019 ICAART paper by Cliff claimed that AA's failings were revealed by testing it in more realistic experiments, with conditions closer to those found in real financial markets, but here we demonstrate that even in the simple experiment conditions that were used in the original AA papers, exhaustive testing shows AA to be outperformed by GDX. We close this paper with a discussion of the methodological implications of our work: any results from previous papers where any one trading algorithm is claimed to be superior to others on the basis of only a few thousand trials are probably best treated with some suspicion now. The rise of cloud computing means that the compute-power necessary to subject trading algorithms to millions of trials over a wide range of conditions is readily available at reasonable cost: we should make use of this; exhaustive testing such as is shown here should be the norm in future evaluations and comparisons of new trading algorithms.

Keywords: Automated trading · Auction markets · Adaptive bidding agents

1 Introduction

For hundreds of years regional, national, and international financial markets involved human traders interacting with one another to negotiate and agree details of transactions. In the past 15 years the number of human traders in financial markets has fallen very sharply, as humans have been systematically replaced by automated trading systems. These automated systems, known in the industry as "algorithmic traders" (often abbreviated simply to "algos") or "robot traders", can employ artificial intelligence (AI) and machine learning (ML) techniques to adapt their responses over multiple timescales ranging from milliseconds to years. In a large investment bank, a single robot trader

© Springer Nature Switzerland AG 2019
J. van den Herik et al. (Eds.): ICAART 2019, LNAI 11978, pp. 246–269, 2019.
https://doi.org/10.1007/978-3-030-37494-5_13

might routinely handle daily order flows of US$20Bn or more. This is manifestly a big business, and the replacement of highly-paid humans (whom, it seems reasonable to assume, were also highly intelligent) with more cost-efficient robot traders is potentially a notable success story for AI/ML. Major investment banks and fund-management companies no longer compete to hire only the best traders; now they compete to hire the best trading-algorithm designers too. See [16] for an entertaining first-hand account of these changes.

Because of the large sums of money at stake, precise details of the specific robot traders used in industry are closely guarded commercial secrets. If a robot is making millions of dollars for a bank, the last thing the bank wants is for someone to publish an academic paper describing how that robot works: any commercial advantage would be immediately lost. Nevertheless, there is a body of work in the academic AI/ML literature stretching back to the late 1990s that describes a sequence of adaptive automated trading algorithms which have stood the test of time and remain influential to this day.

Although a few significant publications contributing to the development of robot-trading systems came from academic economists, the landmark papers largely appeared in AI and autonomous-agent publication venues such as the *International Joint Conference on Artificial Intelligence* (IJCAI), the *International Conference on Autonomous Agents and Multi-Agent Systems* (AAMAS), the *International Conference on Agents and Artificial Intelligence* (ICAART), and the prestigious *Artificial Intelligence* journal (AIJ): Sect. 2 reviews in more detail eight major publications in the development of this field. The review in Sect. 2 is important, because there we trace the way in which the methodology of initial experiments published in 1962 by a young economist, Vernon Smith (who 40 years later would be awarded the Nobel Prize for his empirical research work) have since come to be fixed, or fixated upon, in the AI/agents literature on robot traders. Motivated by what it seems fair to assume was a wholly well-intentioned desire to show each set of the latest results in the context of what had gone before, papers subsequent to Smith's replicated much or all of his 1962 experiment design and analysis. And this, it seems, may have led down something of a dead end.

More details are given in Sect. 2 but for the purposes of this introduction it is sufficient to summarize the key events as follows: at the 2001 IJCAI a team of researchers at IBM published results [7] which showed that two robot trading algorithms, known as *MGD* [23] and *ZIP* [3], could consistently out-perform human traders when tested in rigorous laboratory-style experiments; in the years after this, several other trading algorithms were published, each being claimed as the best-performing algorithm in the public domain at the time of its publication; and the most recent of these is Vytelingum's *AA* algorithm [26] which was described in a 2006 paper in the AIJ [27], and was later shown to outperform human traders in a 2011 IJCAI paper [9]. Put simply, AA is widely believed to be the best-performing trading algorithm in the published literature.

In this paper we demonstrate that belief to be wrong: we show here that AA is not the best. Our demonstration builds on recently-published work by Vach [25] and by Cliff [6]. As far as we are aware, Vach's 2015 MSc thesis [25] was the first to publicly question whether AA is indeed dominant: Vach reported results in which he populated markets with a variety of different robot traders (i.e., some traders running AA and other traders running different strategies, such as MGD or ZIP), that then interacted with one another;

Vach found that whether AA was the best-performing algorithm or not in any particular trial depended on the relative proportions of the different trading agents present in the market for that trial. But if AA was truly dominant then it should have outperformed other robot traders regardless of what the mix of strategies is in the market at any one time. Inspired by Vach, and seeking to independently replicate his results, Cliff's 2019 ICAART paper [6] presented results from exhaustive brute-force testing in which, for a market with N traders active in it, and with a selection of T robot-trader algorithms (including AA) available, the performance of AA in every possible permutation of the T different trader types was studied over a variety of values of N. Cliff's results, gathered from more than 3 million individual market simulation trials, confirmed and extended Vach's observation: for each value of N that Cliff studied, there was some permutation of the T different robot-trader strategies in which AA is outperformed by one or more of the other strategies. Cliff assumed that this result was attributable to his use of test environments that were more realistic (i.e., closer to real-world financial markets) than those that had been used by Vytelingum in his 2006 [26] and 2008 [27] publications introducing AA. In this paper we present results demonstrating that Cliff's assumption in [6] was incorrect. Here we go back to the original test-cases used by Vytelingum [26, 27], but we follow Cliff's [6] method of running brute-force exhaustive testing of all possible permutations of AA and other strategies: whereas Vytelingum published results from fewer than 30,000 simulation trials, in this paper we show results from more than 1,000,000 market sessions: a 30-fold increase over the original publications. Our results here are consistent with those reported by Vach [25] and by Cliff [6]: AA can be routinely outperformed by other strategies, depending on the relative proportions of the different strategies in the market; thus the claims of AA's dominance in earlier publications seem now to be due entirely to an insufficient number of trials having been conducted, even in the original test-cases used in the initial publications on AA. If the exhaustive testing we used here had been conducted at the time of the original publications, AA would not have been mistakenly described as the best-known strategy.

The testing we use is not complicated: it just requires some nested loops to iterate through all possible permutations of the various trader-types, but its combinatorics are truly explosive and hence performing all the necessary trials is highly computationally expensive, and would have taken an awful long time on a single desktop computer. Possibly these high computational costs are why such exhaustive testing has not previously been commonplace in the evaluation of trading algorithms. For computing the brute-force simulation studies described here we used our University's in-house *Blue Crystal* supercomputer, to which we have free access; but all of our experiments could just as easily have been run instead on commercial cloud computing services such as those available from Amazon, Google, Microsoft, or Oracle, incurring only modest fees (a few hundred dollars at most, at today's prices). And so, while the results from our experiments constitute the *empirical* contribution in this paper, we also offer the style of testing used here as a *methodological* contribution: given the present-day ready availability of cheap large-scale computing via cloud service providers, we argue later in this paper that the kind of brute-force studies reported here should from now on be adopted as the norm in any work that evaluates and compares trading algorithms.

The rest of this paper is structured as follows. Section 2 covers the necessary background material, and Sect. 3 describes how AA can be modified to work in contemporary market simulators. The text in those two sections is taken verbatim from [6], and readers familiar with that paper can safely skip straight to Sect. 4, which is where we describe our methods and results for exhaustive testing of AA. Section 5 then discusses methodological implications, and conclusions are drawn in Sect. 6.

2 Traders, Markets, and Eight Key Papers

The 2002 Nobel Prize in Economics was awarded to Vernon Smith, in recognition of Smith's work in establishing and thereafter growing the field of *Experimental Economics* (abbreviated hereafter to "ExpEcon"). Smith showed that the microeconomic behavior of human traders interacting within the rules of some specified market, known technically as an *auction mechanism*, could be studied empirically, under controlled and repeatable laboratory conditions, rather than in the noisy messy confusing circumstances of real-world markets. The minimal laboratory studies could act as useful proxies for studying real-world markets of any type, but one particular auction mechanism has received the majority of attention: the *Continuous Double Auction* (CDA), in which any buyer can announce a bid-price at any time and any seller can announce an offer-price at any time, and in which at any time any trader in the market can accept an offer or bid from a counterparty, and thereby engage in a transaction. The CDA is the basis of most major financial markets worldwide.

Smith's initial set of experiments were run in the late 1950's, and the results and associated discussion were presented in his first paper on ExpEcon, published in the highly prestigious *Journal of Political Economy* (JPE) in 1962 [18]. It seems plausible to speculate that when his JPE paper was published, Smith had no idea that it would mark the start of a line of research that would eventually result in him being appointed as a Nobel laureate. And it seems even less likely that he would have foreseen the extent to which the experimental methods laid out in that 1962 paper would subsequently come to dominate the methodology of researchers working to build adaptive autonomous trading agents by combining tools and techniques from AI, ML, agent-based modelling (ABM), and agent-based computational economics (ACE). Although not a goal stated at the outset, this strand of AI/ML/ABM/ACE research converged toward a common aim: specifying an artificial agent, an autonomous adaptive trading strategy, that could automatically tune its behavior to different market environments, and that could reliably beat all other known automated trading strategies, thereby taking the crown of being the current best trading strategy known in the public domain, i.e., the "dominant strategy". Over the past 20 years the dominant strategy crown has passed from one algorithm to another. Here, we demonstrate that the current holder of the title, Vytelingum's [26, 27] *AA* strategy, does not perform nearly so well as was previously believed from earlier successes in small numbers of trials.

Given that humans who are reliably good at trading are generally thought of as being "intelligent" in some reasonable sense of the word, the aim to develop ever more sophisticated artificial trading systems is clearly within the scope of AI research, although some very important early ideas came from the economics literature: a comprehensive review of relevant early research was given in [3]. Below in Sect. 2.1 we first briefly introduce eight key publications leading to the development of AA; then describe key aspects of ExpEcon market models in Sect. 2.2; and then discuss each of the eight key publications in more detail in Sect. 2.3. After that, Sect. 2.4 summarizes the results of Vach [25] and Cliff [6], which together cast doubts on the hitherto apparently resolved issue of which trading agent is the best.

2.1 A Brief History of Trading Agents

If our story starts with Smith's 1962 JPE paper, then the next major step came 30 years later, with a surprising result published in the JPE by Gode and Sunder in 1993 [14]: this popularized a minimally simple automated trading algorithm now commonly referred to as *ZIC*. A few years later two closely related research papers were published independently and at roughly the same time, each written without knowledge of the other: the first was a Hewlett-Packard Labs technical report [3] describing the adaptive AI/ML trading-agent strategy known as the *ZIP* algorithm; the second summarized the PhD thesis work of Gjerstad, in a paper [11] co-authored with his PhD advisor Dickhaut, describing an adaptive trading algorithm now widely known simply as *GD*. After graduating his PhD, Gjerstad worked at IBM's TJ Watson Labs where he helped set up an ExpEcon laboratory that his IBM colleagues used in a study that generated world-wide media coverage when the results were published by Das *et al.* at IJCAI-2001 [7]. This paper presented results from studies exploring the behavior of human traders interacting with GD and ZIP robot traders, in a CDA with a Limit Order Book (LOB: explained in more detail in Sect. 2.2, below), and demonstrated that both GD and ZIP reliably outperformed human traders. Neither GD nor ZIP had been designed to work with the LOB, so the IBM team modified both strategies for their study. A follow-on 2001 paper [23] by Tesauro and Das (two co-authors of [7]) described a more extensively *Modified GD* (MGD) strategy, and later Tesauro and Bredin [23] described the *GD eXtended* (GDX) strategy. Both MGD and GDX were each claimed to be the strongest-known public-domain trading strategies at the times of their publication.

Subsequently, Vytelingum's 2006 thesis [26] introduced the *Adaptive Aggressive* (AA) strategy which, in an AIJ paper [27], and in later *ICAART* and *IJCAI* papers [8, 9], was shown to be dominant over ZIP, GDX, and also human traders. Thus far then, AA holds the title.

However Vach [25] presented results from experiments with the *OpEx* market simulator [10], in which AA, GDX, and ZIP were set to compete against one another, and in which the dominance of AA is questioned: Vach's results indicate that whether AA dominates or not can be dependent on the ratio of AA:GDX:ZIP in the experiment: for some ratios, Vach found AA to dominate; for other ratios, it was GDX. Vach studied only a relatively small sample from the space of possible ratios, but his results prompted Cliff [6] to exhaustively step through a wide range of differing ratios of four trading strategies (AA, ZIC, ZIP, and the minimally simple SHVR strategy described in Sect. 2.2), doing a brute-force search for situations in which AA is outperformed by the other strategies. The combinatorics of such a search are quite explosive: Cliff reported on results from over 3.4 million individual simulations of market sessions. Cliff's findings indicated that Vach's observation was correct: AA's dominance does indeed depend on how many other AA traders are in the market; and, in aggregate, AA was routinely outperformed by ZIP and by SHVR.

2.2 On Laboratory Models of Markets

Smith's early experiments were laboratory models of so called *open-outcry trading pits*, a common sight in any real financial exchange before the arrival of electronic trader-terminals in the 1970s. In a trading pit, human traders huddle together and shout out their bids and offers, and also announce their willingness to accept a counterparty's most recent shout. It was a chaotic scene, now largely consigned to the history books. In the closing quarter of the 20th Century, traders moved *en masse* to interacting with each other instead via electronic means: traders "shouted" their quote-prices (offer or bid) or acceptances by typing orders on keyboards and then sending those orders to a central server that would display an aggregate summary of all orders currently "shouted" (i.e., quoted) onto the market. That aggregate summary is very often in the form of a *Limit Order Book* or LOB: the LOB summarizes all bids and offers currently live in the market. At its simplest, the LOB is a table of numbers, divided into the *bid side* and the *ask side* (also known as the *offer side*). Both sides of the LOB show the best price at the top, with less good prices arranged below in numeric order of price: for the bid side this means the highest-priced bid at the top with the remaining bid prices displayed in descending order below; and for the ask side the lowest-priced offer is at the top, with the remaining offers arranged in ascending order below. The arithmetic mean of the best bid and best ask prices is known as the *mid-price*, and their difference is the *spread*. For each side of the LOB, at each price on the LOB, the quantity available on that side at that price is also indicated, but with no indication of who the relevant orders came from: in this sense the LOB serves not only to aggregate all currently live orders, but also to anonymize them.

Traders in LOB-based markets can usually cancel existing orders to delete them from the LOB. In a common simple implementation of a LOB, traders can accept the current best bid or best offer by issuing a quote that *crosses the spread*: i.e., by issuing an order that, if added to the LOB, would result in the best bid being at a higher price than the best ask. Rather than be added to the LOB, if a bid order crosses the spread then it is matched with the best offer on the ask side (known as *lifting the ask*), whereas an ask that crosses the spread is matched with the best bid (*hitting the bid*); and in either case a transaction then occurs between the trader that had posted the best price on the relevant side of the LOB, and the trader that crossed the spread. The price of the resulting transaction is whatever price was hit or lifted from the top of the LOB.

Smith's earliest experiments pre-dated the arrival of electronic trading in real financial markets, and so they can be thought of as laboratory models of open-outcry trading pits. Even though the much later work by Gode and Sunder [14], Cliff [3], Gjerstad and Dickhaut [11], and Vytelingum [26] all came long after the introduction of electronic LOBs in real markets, these academic studies all stuck with Smith's original methodology, of modelling open-outcry markets (often by essentially operating a LOB with the depth fixed at 1, so the *only* information available to traders is the current best, or most recent, bid and ask prices).

Nevertheless, the studies by IBM researchers [7, 23, 24], and also the replication and confirmation of AA results by De Luca and Cliff [8–10] and by Stotter *et al.* [21,

22], all used LOB-based market simulators. The IBM simulator *Magenta* seems to have been proprietary to IBM; developed at TJ Watson Labs and not available for third-party use, but De Luca made an open-source release of his *OpEx* simulator [10] which was subsequently used by Vach [25] in the studies that prompted our work reported here. Also of relevance here is the *ExPo* simulator described by Stotter *et al.* [21, 22]: in the work by De Luca [8–10], by Vach [25], and by Stotter *et al.* [21, 22], Vytelingum's original AA needed modifications to make it work in a LOB-based market environment: this is discussed further in Sect. 3.

In the work reported here we used neither OpEx nor ExPo, but instead *BSE* [1, 5] which is another open-source ExpEcon market simulator, initially developed as a teaching aid but subsequently used as a platform for research (see, e.g. [15]). BSE has the advantage of being relatively lightweight (a single Python script of c.2500 lines) and hence readily deployable over large numbers of virtual machines in the cloud. BSE maintains a dynamically updated LOB and also publishes a *tape*, a time-ordered record of all orders that have been executed, and other significant events such as the cancellation of earlier orders (which are deleted from the LOB). BSE comes with pre-defined versions of ZIC and ZIP, and also some additionally minimally-simple non-adaptive trading strategies that can be used for benchmarking against other more complex strategies added by the user. One of these, the *Shaver* strategy (referred to in BSE by the "ticker symbol" SHVR) simply reads the best prices on the LOB and, if it is able to do so without risking a loss-making deal, then issues an order that improves the current best bid or best ask by 0.01 units of currency (i.e., one penny/cent), which is BSE's *tick size*, i.e. the minimum change in price that the system allows.

2.3 Eight Key Papers, One Methodology

Smith [18]. Although precedents can be pointed to, Smith's 1962 JPE paper [18] is widely regarded as the seminal study in ExpEcon. In it he reported on experiments in which a group of c.12-25 human subjects were each randomly assigned to be either a *buyer* or a *seller* in the market experiment. Buyers were given a supply of artificial money, and sellers were given one or more identical items, of no intrinsic value, to sell. Each trader in the market was assigned a private valuation, a secret *limit price*: for a buyer this was the price above which he or she should not pay when purchasing an item; for a seller this was the price below which he or she should not sell an item. These limit-price assignments model the client orders executed by sales traders in real financial markets; we'll refer to them just as *assignments* in the rest of this paper. After the allocation of assignments to all traders, the traders then interacted via an open-outcry CDA while Smith and his assistants made notes on the sequence of events that unfolded during the experiment: typically, buyers would gradually increase their bid-prices, and sellers would gradually lower their offer-prices (also known as ask-prices) until transactions started to occur. Eventually, usually within a few minutes, the experimental market reached a position in which no more trades could take place, which marked the end of a *trading period* or "trading day" in the experiment; any one experiment typically ran for $n = 5$–10 periods, with all the traders being resupplied with fresh assignments of limit prices and money-to-buy-with and items-for-sale at the start of each trading period. The sequence of n contiguous trading periods (or an equivalently long single-period experiment with continuous replenishment, as discussed further in Sects. 2.4 and 4.4) is referred to here as one *market session*. Smith could induce specific supply and demand curves in these experimental markets by appropriate choices of the various limit-prices he assigned to the traders. As any high-school student of microeconomics knows, the market's theoretical *equilibrium price* (denoted hereafter by $P0$) is given by the point where the supply curve and the demand curve intersect. Smith found that, in these laboratory CDA markets populated with only remarkably small groups of human traders, transaction prices could reliably and rapidly converge on the theoretical $P0$ value despite the fact that each human trader was acting purely out of self-interest and knew only the limit price that he or she had been assigned. Smith's analysis of his results focused on a statistic that he referred to as α, the root mean square deviation of actual transaction prices from the $P0$ value over the course of an experiment. In his early experiments, $P0$ was fixed for the duration of any one experiment; in later work Smith explored the ability of the market to respond to "price shocks" where, in an experiment of N trading days, on a specific day $S < N$ the allocation of limit prices would be changed, altering $P0$ from the value that had been in place over trading periods *1, 2, ..., S*, to a different value of $P0$ that would then remain constant for the rest of the experiment, i.e. in trading periods $S + 1, S + 2, ..., N$. For brevity, in the rest of this paper Smith's initial style of experiments will be referred to as *S'62* experiments.

ZIC: Gode and Sunder [14]. Gode and Sunder's JPE paper [14] used the S'62 methodology, albeit with the CDA markets being electronic (a move Smith himself had made in his experiments many years earlier), so each trader was sat at a personal terminal, a computer screen and keyboard, from which they received all information about the market and via which they announced their orders, their bids or offers, to the rest of the traders in the experiment. Gode and Sunder first conducted a set of experiments in which all the traders were human, to establish baseline statistics. Then, all the human traders were replaced with automated trading systems, absolute-zero minimally-simple algo traders which Gode and Sunder referred to as *Zero Intelligence* (ZI) traders. Gode and Sunder studied markets populated with two type of ZI trader: *ZI-Unconstrained* (ZIU), which simply generated random prices for their bids or offers, regardless of whether those prices would lead to profitable transactions or to losses; and *ZI-Constrained* (ZIC), which also generated random order prices but were constrained by their private limit prices to never announce prices that would lead them to loss-making deals. Gode and Sunder used fixed supply and demand schedules in each experiment, i.e. there were no price-shocks in their experiments.

Not surprisingly, the market dynamics of ZIU traders were nothing more than noise. But the surprising result in Gode and Sunder's paper was the revelation that a commonly used metric of market price dynamics known as *allocative efficiency* (AE, hereafter) was essentially indistinguishable between the human markets and the ZIC markets. Because AE had previously been seen as a marker of the degree to which the traders in a market were behaving intelligently, the fact that ZIC traders scored AE values largely the same as humans was a shock. Gode and Sunder proposed that a different metric should instead be used as a marker of the intelligence of traders in the market. This metric was *profit dispersion* (PD, hereafter) which measures the difference between the profit each trader accrued in an experiment, compared to the profit that would be expected for that trader if every transaction in the market had taken place at the market's theoretical equilibrium price $P0$: humans typically showed very low values of PD (which is assumed to be good) while ZIC traders did not. On this basis, Gode and Sunder argued that PD should be used in preference to AE in future.

Other researchers were quick to cite Gode and Sunder's ZIC result, and often used it to support the claim that, given the ZIC traders have no intelligence, then for transaction prices to converge toward the theoretical equilibrium price and/or for a group of traders to score highly on AE, somehow the "intelligence" required to do this must reside within the rules of the CDA market system rather than within the heads of the traders. Strangely, Gode & Sunder's 1993 paper [14] provides no concrete causal mechanistic explanation of how their striking ZIC results arise; they describe their methods, and the results observed, but the internal mechanisms that give rise to those results are left as something of a mystery, as if the CDA market was an impenetrable black-box.

A causal mechanistic analysis of markets populated by ZIC traders was subsequently developed by Cliff [3], who considered the probability mass functions (PMFs) of prices generated by ZIC buyers and sellers, and the joint PMF of transaction prices in ZIP markets, which is given by the intersection of the bid-price and offer-price PMFs: the shape of the transaction-price PMF is determined by the nature of the supply and demand curves in the market, and Cliff demonstrated that the supply and demand curves in a ZIC market experiment could be arranged so that the expected value of the transaction prices (computable as an integral over the PMF) is identical to the theoretical equilibrium price given by the intersection point of the supply and demand curves. This was why the five ZIC experiments reported in Gode and Sunder's [14] paper showed transaction prices that were centered on the theoretical equilibrium price in each case: the supply and demand curves were arranged in such a way that this was the expected outcome. Cliff showed that with different arrangements of supply and demand curves, such as situations where one or both curves were flat (as had been used in Smith's original 1962 JPE paper [18]), the expected price of transactions in ZIP markets could differ considerably from the theoretical equilibrium price, and so transaction prices in those ZIC markets would fail to exhibit human-like convergence toward the theoretical equilibrium value. In these differently-designed experiments, ZIC traders would be revealed for exactly what they are: simple stochastic processes that only coincidentally exhibit human-like market dynamics when the experimenters happen to have chosen to impose just the right kind of supply and demand curves. Cliff's analysis showed that the level of intelligence in the ZIC traders was insufficient to recreate human-like market dynamics more broadly, and so a more intelligent automated trading strategy was required.[1]

ZIP: Cliff [3]. Taking direct inspiration both from Smith's work and from the ZI paper by Gode and Sunder, Cliff [3] developed a ZI trading strategy that used simple machine-learning techniques to continuously adapt the randomly-generated prices quoted by the

---

[1] Independently, and via a wholly different line of attack, Gjerstad and Shachat [13] also demolished the argument that Gode and Sunder's [14] ZIC results indicate that the efficiency or intelligence in the market system lies solely within the CDA mechanism. Nevertheless, Gode and Sunder's results continue to be cited uncritically by various authors in the economics literature: we can only assume that such authors prefer a nice fairy story, rather than hard facts.

traders: this strategy, known as ZI-Plus (ZIP) was demonstrated to show human-like market dynamics in experiments with flat supply and/or demand curves: Cliff also showed theoretical analyses and empirical results which demonstrated that transaction prices in markets populated only by ZIC traders would not converge to the theoretical equilibrium price when the supply and/or demand curves are flat (or, in the language of microeconomics, "perfectly elastic"). ExpEcon studies in which the supply and/or demand curve was flat had previously been reported by Smith and others, but Gode and Sunder had not explored the response of their ZIC traders to this style of market. Cliff's work involved no human traders: all the focus was on markets populated entirely by autonomous agents, by ZIP traders. In total Cliff [3] reported on fewer than 1,000 simulated market sessions. The focus on *homogenous* markets can fairly be interpreted as continuing the tradition established by Gode and Sunder (who studied markets homogeneously populated with either human, ZIU, or ZIC traders) and by Smith (who studied all-human markets). In all other regards Cliff continued the S'62 tradition: key metrics were Smith's α, AE, and PD.

GD: Gjerstad and Dickhaut [11]. Gjerstad's PhD studies of price formation in CDA markets also involved creating an algorithm that could trade profitably by adapting its behavior over time, in response to market events [11]. In contrast to the ZI work, Gjerstad's trading algorithm uses frequentist statistics, gradually constructing and refining a *belief function* that estimates the likelihood for a bid or offer to be accepted in the market at any particular time, mapping from price of the order to its probability of success. Gjerstad did not explicitly name his strategy, but it has since become known as the GD strategy. In all other regards, as with Cliff's work [3] and Gode and Sunder's [14], Gjerstad's [11] work was firmly in the S'62 tradition: homogenous markets of GD traders interacting in a CDA, buying and selling single items, with the metrics being Smith's α, AE, and PD. In a later paper [12], Gjerstad made some refinements to the GD algorithm, adding a time-sensitivity or *pace* parameter, and named it *HBL* (for Heuristic Belief Learning), although the original GD form remains by far the most cited.

MGD: Das *et al.* [7]. In their landmark 2001 IJCAI paper [7], IBM researchers Das, Hanson, Kephart, and Tesauro studied the performance of GD and ZIP in a series of ExpEcon market experiments where, for the first time ever in the same market, some of the traders were robots while others were human (recall that the earlier work of Smith, of Gode and Sunder, of Cliff, and of Gjerstad and Dickhaut had all studied homogeneous markets: either all-human or all-robot). Das *et al.* used a LOB-based market simulator called *Magenta*, developed by Gjerstad, and ran a total of six experiments, six market sessions, in which humans and robots interacted and where there were three shock-changes to *P0*, i.e. four phases in any one experiment, each phase with a different *P0* value that was held static over that phase. The surprising result in this paper was that robot trading strategies could consistently outperform human traders, by significant margins: a result that attracted worldwide media attention. Both GD and ZIP outperformed human traders, and in the six experiments reported by Das *et al.* the results from the two robot strategies are so similar as to not obviously be statistically significant. A subsequent paper by IBM's Tesauro and Das [23], reported on additional studies in which a *Modified GD* (MGD) strategy was exhibited what the authors described in the abstract of their paper as *"...the strongest known performance of any published bidding strategy"*.

GDX: Tesauro and Bredin [24]. Extensions to MGD were reported by IBM researchers Tesauro and Bredin at AAMAS 2002 [24]. This paper described extensions to MGD, using dynamic programming methods: the extended version was named *GDX* and its performance was evaluated when competing in heterogenous markets with ZIP and other strategies. Tesauro and Bredin reported that GDX outperformed the other strategies and claimed in the abstract of their paper that GDX *"...may offer the best performance of any published CDA bidding strategy."*

AA: Vytelingum [26]. Vytelingum developed AA and documented it in full in his PhD thesis [26] and in a major paper in the *AIJ* [27]. The internal mechanisms of AA are described in greater detail in Sect. 3 of this paper. Although Vytelingum's work came a few years after the IBM publications, the discussion within Vytelingum's publications is phrased very much in terms of the S'62 methodology: the $P0$ value in his AA experiments was either fixed for the duration of each market session, or was subjected to a single "price shock" partway through the session (as described in Sect. 2.3); and again the primary metrics studied are Smith's α, AE, and PD. Vytelingum presented results from heterogeneous market experiments where AA, GDX, and ZIP traders were in competition, and the published results indicated that AA outperformed both GDX and ZIP by small margins. In total, results from c.25,000 market sessions are presented in [27].

AA Dominates: De Luca and Cliff [8, 9]. As part of the research leading to his 2015 PhD thesis [10], De Luca used his LOB-based *OpEx* market simulator system to study the performance of AA in heterogeneous market experiments where some of the traders were AA, some were other robot strategies such as ZIP, and some were human traders sat at terminals interacting with the other traders (human and robot) in the market via the OpEx GUI, in the style introduced by the IBM team in their IJCAI 2001 paper. De Luca and Cliff [8] had previously published results from comparing GDX and AA in OpEx, at ICAART-2011; and the first results from AA in human-agent studies were then published in a 2011 IJCAI paper [9], in which AA was demonstrated to dominate not only humans but also GDX and ZIP. For consistency with what was by then a well-established methodology, in De Luca's experiments the $P0$ value was static for sustained periods with occasional "shock" step-changes to different values. Continuing the tradition established by the IBM authors, the abstract of [9] claimed supremacy for AA: *"We... demonstrate that AA's performance against human traders is superior to that of ZIP, GD, and GDX. We therefore claim that... AA may offer the best performance of any published bidding strategy"*. And, until the publication of Vach's 2015 MSc thesis [25], that claim appeared to be plausibly true.

2.4 Actually, AA Doesn't Dominate: Vach [25]; Cliff [6]

Vach's Master's Thesis [25] tells the story of his design of a new trading strategy based on ZIP and called ZIPOJA, which he then tested against AA, GDX, and ZIP. The testing revealed that ZIPOJA did not consistently outperform any of the three pre-existing strategies. But, in the course of that testing, as Vach checked and calibrated his implementations of the three pre-existing strategies, he found that AA could fail to dominate ZIP or GDX, depending on the proportions of the two strategies in the market: this runs counter to the established story that AA is the best-performing strategy. Tables 6.2 and 6.3 on p. 47 of Vach's thesis show results from tests in which the performance of two trading strategies were tested in trials with proportions of the two trader strategies set at 6:0, 5:1, 4:2, 3:3, 2:4, 5:1, and 0:6. The ratios 6:0 and 0:6 are homogenously populated by one strategy or the other and hence are of little interest, because that single strategy necessarily dominates in those markets. In Vach's Table 6.2, AA is outperformed by ZIP when the ZIP:AA ratio is 1:5 – i.e., if one in six of the traders in the market are ZIP with the rest AA, then the ZIP traders will outperform the AAs: the efficiency of the ZIP traders was 99.5% while the efficiency of the AAs was 88.5%. In Vach's Table 6.3, AA is outperformed by GDX when the GDX:AA ratio is 3:3, 2:4, and 1:5.

Vach then performed three-way simulations systematically varying the ratios of AA:GDX:ZIP over all possible permutations and, in his Fig. 6 1i [25, p. 53] he shows a 2D simplex diagram which summarizes those results: a 28-node regular isometric mesh is drawn over the surface of the simplex as a co-ordinate frame, and AA is the dominant strategy in only 11 of those 28 nodes. Each of the three strategies is by definition dominant at the node representing a homogeneous ratio (i.e., either 1:0:0 or 0:1:0 or 0:0:1), so AA actually only dominates at 10 of the 25 nodes where it is actually contesting with the other two strategies: ZIP dominates one of the remaining nodes; and GDX dominates the remaining 14.

In a final four-way study, with AA, GDX, ZIP, and ZIPOJA competing against each other, Vach [25, Table 6.7, p. 60] declares GDX the overall winner although in that experiment the scores of GDX and AA are sufficiently close that, in our opinion, the difference between the two may not be statistically significant. Nevertheless, it is undeniable that in Vach's four-way study AA again fails to clearly dominate. To the best of our knowledge, Vach's results are the first such exhaustive study of AA's performance as the number and proportion of competitor strategies is systematically varied, and he was the first to demonstrate that AA is in fact not the best-performing strategy.

Subsequently Cliff [6] set out to replicate and extend Vach's results, using a finer-grained analysis, varying the proportions of AA, SHVR, ZIP, and ZIC, and also studying the effects of altering other aspects of the experiment design such as whether the replenishment of assignments to the traders is periodic or continuous-stochastic (as in [4]); and whether the equilibrium price P_0 is largely constant with occasional shock-jumps, or continuously varying according to price-movements taken from real-world markets. Cliff's results from conventional S'62-style experiments, with periodic replenishment and with P_0 largely constant, confirmed the established view: when AA was tested in the kind of simple market environment as has traditionally been used in the previous literature, AA scored just as well as well-known other trading strategies and was not dominated by them.

But, merely by altering the nature of the market environment to have continuous stochastic replenishment (which is surely what happens in real markets) and to have the equilibrium price P_0 continuously varying over time (which is also surely what happens in real markets), Cliff's results from AA became very poor indeed. Cliff [6] wrote:

"It seems very hard to avoid the conclusion that AA's success as reported in previous papers is largely due to the extent to which its internal mechanisms are designed to fit exactly the kind of experiment settings first introduced by Vernon

Smith: AA is very well suited to situations in which all assignments are issued to all traders simultaneously, and in which the equilibrium price remains constant for sustained periods of time, with only occasional step-change "shocks". Real markets are not like this, and when AA is deployed in the more realistic market setting provided by BSE, its dominance disappears."

Cliff did not test AA against GDX, but we do here. The results that we present in Sect. 4 demonstrate that actually, even in the S'62 style of experiment that AA was first tested in, if it actually is tested exhaustively across a wide range of proportions, then AA can be outperformed by trading algorithms that predated it, specifically by GDX. Before that, in Sect. 3 we briefly discuss the issue of modifying AA to operate in realistic LOB-based markets.

3   Modifying AA for LOB Markets

Taking the AA algorithm and attempting to run it in a LOB-based market reveals the extent to which AA seems designed to fit very well in the Smith'62 style of experiments with periodic replenishment, and is less well suited to a continuously varying market dynamic. In brief, AA's internal mechanisms revolve around three questions that each AA trader attempts to answer: (1) What is my best estimate of the current equilibrium price $P0$? (2) What is my best estimate of the current volatility of transaction prices around $P0$? And (3) is the limit price on my current assignment intramarginal (i.e., could be sold/bought at $P0$ and still make a profit) or extramarginal? For its estimate of $P0$, the original AA trader computes a moving average of recent transaction prices. For its volatility estimate, it computes Smith's α metric, taking the difference between recent transaction prices and the trader's current estimate of $P0$ (i.e., ignoring any trend in $P0$, which is safe to do if, as in the S'62 experiments, $P0$ changes rarely or never). Deciding on whether the current assignment is intra/extra marginal is done by comparing its limit price to its $P0$ estimate.

In MAA, our modified implementation of AA, these questions can instead each be answered by reference to information that is routinely available from an exchange: the LOB and the exchange's "tape" (the record of timestamped transactions). $P0$ can be better estimated by using the volume-weighted mid-price at the top of the book (known as the *microprice*: see e.g. [2, 20]): this is a better metric because it can be sensitive to shifts in the $P0$ value *before* any transactions go through that reflect the shift. Volatility can be estimated by reference not to only the current estimate of $P0$ but also to BSE's tape data: a time-series of transaction-price values correlated with a time series of microprice values is better to use in situations where the $P0$ value is continuously changing: for each transaction on the tape, the microprice at the time of that transaction (or immediately before) is the better reference value for calculating Smith's α. Extra-/intra-marginality is still decided by reference to the trader's $P0$ estimate, but in MAA that estimate can come from the microprice.

Previous authors have also needed to adapt AA for LOB-based markets: De Luca [8–10] and Vach [25] each used AA in the *OpEx* simulator, and Stotter *et al.* [20, 21] used AA in the *ExPo* simulator. However, the modified AA proposed here is novel insofar as prior authors don't report using the exchange's tape data or the microprice.

There is a tension between modifying AA in an attempt to better fit it to a LOB-based market, and making claims about AA's poor performance in those markets: the more heavily AA is modified, the more one is open to accusations that the modifications themselves are the cause of the poor performance, rather than that poor performance being a reflection of the original AA being badly-suited to LOB markets. For that reason, in this paper, we keep AA very close to the original, using only the microprice modification in generating the results presented here.

The Python source-code used to generate the results in this paper has been made publicly available on the main BSE GitHub site [1].

4   Exhaustive Testing of AA

4.1   Market Supply and Demand Schedules

Vytelingum [26, 27] tested AA using the methods first established by Smith [18] and then followed by all of the key papers reviewed in Sect. 2: he did some studies with markets in which the supply and demand schedules (SDSs) were constant for the duration of each experiment, which we will refer to as *static markets*; and he did other studies in which part-way through the experiment there was a sudden "market-shock" change from the initial static SDS to some other static SDS that remained in place from the point of the shock to the end of the experiment – we will refer to those experiments as *market shocks*. Vytelingum studied AA's response in four static SDSs, which he referred to as M1, M2, M3, and M4; and his market shock studies involved switching from one of these four to one of the three other SDSs. The market shock studies were referred to using multi-character codes of the form MSnm where n is the single-digit identifier of the initial static SDS, and m is the single-digit identifier of the static SDS that is switched to at the time of the shock. For example, MS31 denotes an experiment in which the traders are initially given allocations according to M3, which switches to M1 at the point of the shock-change. Each of the experiments were conducted over 20 trading periods or "days", and when shocks were imposed they occurred at the start of Day 11 (i.e., halfway through the session). After carrying out preliminary tests on the SDSs used by Vytelingum, we decided that the Vytelingum's market-shock scenarios were not sufficient to completely test the algorithms: each trading algorithm adapted relatively quickly to a single shock, and hence to fully compare the trading strategies we decided to introduce more challenging markets, some containing more shocks, and also some with a continuously changing equilibrium price.

Static Markets. First we tested the trading agents using static SDSs based on M1 to M4 as used by Vytelingum [26, 27]: the supply and demand curves for each market are shown in Fig. 1.

Complex Markets. We tested market shocks introduced in the manner described by Vytelingum [26, 27], specifically MS14, MS21, MS31, MS23, and MS1231. We then also explored the responses of the traders in situations where all prices on assignments came from M1 with a time-varying offset function $F(t)$ added to them over the course of the experiment. We refer to these as follows:

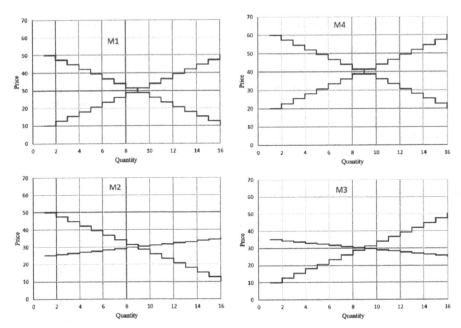

Fig. 1. Supply and Demand curves for M1, M2, M3, and M4. The expected equilibrium price is marked: for M1, M2, and M3 it is 30; for M4 it is 40.

- M6: $F(t) = c \sin(t/30)$ (a sinusoid of constant amplitude and frequency).
- M7: $F(t) = ct(1 + \sin(wt))$ (a sinusoid of increasing amplitude and frequency).
- M8: $F(t) = (t \% 75)/2$ (a sawtooth wave of constant amplitude and frequency).
- M9: $F(t) = c \, \text{sgn}(\sin(t/30))$ (a square wave of constant amplitude and frequency).

4.2 Verification

Although the source-code for ZIP was published as an appendix to the technical report that introduced that algorithm [3], no standard reference implementations exist for either GDX or AA: in both cases, the papers that introduced the algorithm gave verbal descriptions of how the algorithm works, along with associated equations. To verify that the implementations of the algorithms used in this paper are correct, we conducted experiments whose purpose was to replicate results achieved in the algorithms' original papers. Full details of these verification experiments are given in [19], to which the reader is referred for further details. It is sufficient to note here that our results from GDX and AA were in both cases very close but not identically equal to the results published in the relevant original paper. We believe that the differences in results are more likely to be due to differences in test environment than due to any problems with our implementation of the algorithms. The original papers for GDX and for AA say very little about the nature of the market simulator that was used to generate the results. We use the public-domain BSE simulator, but GDX was tested on IBM's in-house Magenta market simulator, about which nothing was ever published; and Vytelingum [26, 27] discusses his own market simulator only in very scant terms. Thus, to the best of our ability, we believe the implementations of GDX and AA used here to be faithful to the original specification. The source-code used to generate the results in this section (which summarizes the results presented in [19]) has been made publicly available in the BSE GitHub repository [1]: see the script snashall2019.py.

4.3 Experiment Design

As each market scenario has a different expected profit, and we used allocative efficiency as the measure of performance, for ease of comparison across all experiments. As described in above, this is the percentage of the maximum expected profit the algorithm has been able to extract from the market.

Each trial involves 16 traders on each side (32 in total). It is known that the different trader ratios can have a profound and significant effect on their respective performance. For example, a single ZIP agent in a market populated by ZIC agents will do exceedingly well, however a single ZIP agent in a market otherwise saturated with GDX agents will not do as well. To eliminate this effect, the experiments here are conducted with every possible permutation of trader ratios, and the results are averaged over every experiment. We conducted 100 i.i.d trials per ratio, which equates to around 2 million trading days in total. We then compute summary statistics, such as average efficiency, across all trials, and present those in tabular form; for ease of identification we use a bold-face font to highlight the highest (best) value in each row.

4.4 Results

Static Markets.

Tables 1, 2, 3 and 4 show various results from simple static market experiments. Tables 1 and 2 are from S'62-style experiments in which the assignments to buy and sell are refreshed periodically, with all traders receiving their updates simultaneously. Tables 3 and 4 are from experiments in which the assignments are instead stochastically drip-fed into the population of traders in a continuous-replenishment approach as described by [4].

Table 1 shows results from markets populated by mixes of AA, ASAD, GDX, and ZIP traders, with periodic allocation: the overall average has AA scoring a shade higher than GDX, but GDX scores slightly higher than AA in markets M1 and M3. Because ASAD and ZIP are very closely related, and AA is arguably also an extension of the basic ZIP algorithm (i.e., it shares the same heuristic decision tree, but adds sophistication in how the trader's profit margin is altered over time), it might be argued that the experiments summarized in Table 1 are essentially GDX *versus* three variants of ZIP-style algorithms. Indeed, if (as we believe) it is fair to characterize ASAD as ZIP with extensions to detect shock-changes in market prices and act appropriately, the absence of any market shocks in these simple experiments mean that ZIP and ASAD are essentially functionally identical. To increase the heterogeneity, we ran the same experiments again but replaced ZIP with the simpler, more noisy, ZIC strategy: results from that are shown in Table 2. Now only in M5 does AA still dominate: GDX wins in M1, M2, and M3.

Table 1. Efficiencies in AA/ASAD/GDX/ZIP experiments with periodic replenishment.

Market	AA	ASAD	GDX	ZIP
M1	97.03	79.97	**98.85**	80.95
M2	**103.21**	54.57	100.01	55.92
M3	99.13	85.80	**99.41**	85.23
M5	**99.52**	60.32	97.13	58.67
Average	**99.73**	70.16	98.85	70.19

Table 2. Efficiencies in AA/ASAD/GDX/ZIC experiments with periodic replenishment.

Market	AA	ASAD	GDX	ZIC
M1	94.47	87.90	**96.78**	59.82
M2	96.51	75.98	**100.2**	77.49
M3	94.39	84.69	**94.77**	43.06
M5	**95.18**	72.53	91.58	50.12
Average	95.14	80.27	**95.82**	57.64

When we switch from periodic to continuous replenishment, the summary data show broadly the same pattern: Table 3 shows that when GDX is pitted against three ZIP-style strategies, it is out-scored by AA in half of the markets studied, and AA scores best overall; but Table 4 shows that when we replace ZIP with ZIC, this alters the market dynamics and GDX now dominates in three of the four markets and also in aggregate score.

Table 3. Efficiencies in AA/ASAD/GDX/ZIP experiments with continuous replenishment.

Market	AA	ASAD	GDX	ZIP
M1	92.70	80.34	**98.43**	80.26
M2	**105.27**	60.71	105.24	60.53
M3	100.66	87.17	**103.80**	87.43
M5	**97.40**	52.54	92.01	52.53
Average	99.01	70.19	**99.87**	70.19

Table 4. Efficiencies in AA/ASAD/GDX/ZIC experiments with continuous replenishment.

Market	AA	ASAD	GDX	ZIC
M1	88.58	89.33	**94.60**	59.82
M2	99.71	82.41	**102.07**	77.49
M3	97.87	97.99	**102.91**	43.05
M5	**94.94**	83.44	93.18	50.18
Average	95.28	88.29	**98.19**	57.64

Complex Markets. Tables 5 and 6 respectively summarize our results from testing in the complex markets introduced in Sect. 4.1, with ZIP and ZIC. Here there are no subtleties in the outcomes: GDX is clearly dominant in all markets reported on in Table 5, and again in Table 6.

The nonparametric Wilcoxon-Mann-Whitney U-Test was used to evaluate the statistical significance of the differences in scores between AA and GDX in Tables 5 and 6. This indicated that the difference is significant in all cases except for M2 in Table 6, and for M7 in Table 7. In all cases where a significant difference was detected, GDX had the better score: for further details see [19, pp. 29–30].

Table 5. Efficiencies in complex markets, with ZIP.

Market	AA	ASAD	GDX	ZIP
MS14	93.40	75.36	**96.22**	73.30
MS21	91.18	73.17	**94.43**	73.24
MS31	93.06	83.55	**98.10**	83.63
MS23	104.46	50.72	**105.79**	50.69
MS1231	102.18	87.76	**104.37**	84.51
M6 Sin	70.53	55.62	**72.87**	55.56
M7	99.21	92.09	**102.18**	91.12
M8 Saw	86.52	91.79	**95.80**	91.71
M9 Sqr	69.30	63.46	**74.61**	63.70
Average	89.98	74.84	**93.82**	75.92

To summarize, the results presented here show that GDX routinely and reliably dominates AA. That reinforces the message from Vach [25] and Cliff [6]: AA does not dominate.

Table 6. Efficiencies in complex markets, with ZIC.

Market	AA	ASAD	GDX	ZIC
MS14	85.08	87.14	**91.12**	42.05
MS21	92.68	89.04	**96.76**	68.45
MS31	89.64	91.16	**95.83**	51.50
MS23	100.62	97.74	**104.57**	61.76
MS1231	94.34	95.52	**101.52**	60.56
M6 Sin	69.93	65.98	**72.89**	44.58
M7	75.86	69.58	**77.71**	50.68
M8 Saw	86.77	91.59	**95.02**	64.69
M9 Sqr	70.93	64.35	**72.56**	53.03
Average	85.10	83.57	**89.78**	55.25

5   Methodological Issues

Having demonstrated that AA does not always dominate other trading strategies, it is worth reflecting on the methods that have been used here, how they compare to current real-world financial markets, and how they compare to the S'62 methods that were described in Sect. 2.

5.1   Real-World Relevance

BSE, the open-source public-domain CDA market simulator that we have used as the platform for our studies, was introduced in Sect. 2.2. There are numerous differences between BSE and real financial markets: BSE is not intended to be a perfect imitation of a real stock exchange; indeed it was initially created to support graduate-level teaching, conducting experiments in the same vein as S'62. It is designed to provide an environment in which experiments can be reliably repeated and controlled, rather than providing an environment which is as close as possible to real-world market scenarios.

BSE does not simulate communications latency: it assumes all traders receive information updates from the exchange instantaneously, and similarly it assumes that any message sent by a trader to the exchange takes zero time to arrive. In the real world, things are not so simple: it takes finite time for the market information published by an exchange to reach any given trader, and it takes finite time for a trader's order to reach the exchange. Communications latency of this form can play a large part in the performance of an algorithm. For example, if a trader is designed to execute an arbitrage strategy (that is to take advantage of price difference between markets, e.g. buying something on Exchange A and then immediately selling it on Exchange B for a higher price), the trader may have only milliseconds to act before parity is restored.

Another form of real-world latency that BSE fails to simulate is the processing latencies of the trading algorithms themselves, i.e. their *reaction-time*. The reaction time of an algorithm can play just as an important role in its performance as the communications delay. In real markets, the traders must respond as quickly as possible to the market. If, for example, ZIP is able to respond more quickly than GDX and therefore put an ask/bid in earlier, it will steal the opportunity for GDX to make a trade. In the currently available version of BSE, this is not captured, because each algorithm is allowed to take as long as it wants to respond (the simulation is single-threaded, and simulates parallel activity by allowing all traders to settle on a response to any change in the market before processing the responses of each trader). Each algorithm implemented in BSE was written with the assumption that the state of the market will not change while the algorithm is 'thinking'. In the real world this is absolutely not the case. The market is changing constantly, and any trader can submit a fresh ask or bid at any time. In the case of both GDX and AA, their designs mean that each time a new ask/bid is submitted, they must start their processing again from the beginning. GDX must re-compute its belief function, and AA must re-compute all of its various calculations. Due to the frequency of submission of quotes in CDAs dominated by 'high frequency' traders, it could be argued that neither AA nor GDX would ever be quick enough to submit an ask/bid before the market has significantly changed again, forcing them to re-start their calculations. This lack of any modelling of reaction-times runs the risk of incorrect conclusions about dominance relationships being drawn when trading agents are evaluated only in the simple S'62 style scenarios used here.

It could be argued that the aim of algorithms such as AA is not necessarily to perform well in the real world, but instead just to beat their competitor algorithms in the kind of comparative studies described here (on in actual international trading-agent contests, popular with academics around the world, as described in e.g. [28]). We don't agree with that view: our opinion is that if a trading agent does well in academic research contests but is not applicable in real-world deployments, it is of little interest to us.

To test the extent to which actual reaction-times could affect our results, we conducted an experiment where, for the various trading strategies used here, we measured how long it takes for our implementation of that strategy in BSE to respond with an order after it is sent updated market information. We conducted this in four of the markets used previously, over 500 trials each, and with a fixed ratio of 5 buyers and 5 sellers using each strategy: the results are shown in Table 7.

Table 7. Efficiencies in complex markets, with ZIP.

Market	AA	ASAD	GDX	ZIP
M7 czy	6.20 µs	5.00 µs	80.83 µs	5.27 µs
M6 sin	5.14 µs	5.69 µs	87.56 µs	4.73 µs
M1	6.27 µs	5.33 µs	57.18 µs	4.94 µs
MS23	5.96 µs	5.44 µs	87.43 µs	5.44 µs
Average	5.89 µs	5.37 µs	78.25 µs	4.96 µs

Clearly, the implementation of GDX used here is consistently an order of magnitude slower than the other strategies when deciding on its next ask/bid price. In the experiments in this paper, of course this is of no significance. However, in a real market, this could very easily cause the GDX strategy to fail to generate a profit because AA, ZIP, and ASAD all have at least 10 opportunities to trade while GDX is calculating a single ask/bid price. BSE does not yet include functionality for multi-threading which makes it a poor platform for studying time-sensitive responses. We should also note here that in our implementation of these algorithms very little thought was given to run-time efficiency. GDX requires the creation of a 2D data structure containing expected values, and also computes the argmax of a relatively complicated function, which is understandably slow as the program must traverse every possible input. Our implementation of this is simplistic and written to be easy to follow, rather than to be quick. A more time-efficient implementation might reduce the disparity between GDX and its competitor strategies, e.g. by using precomputed look-up-tables.

5.2   Perpetuation of Smith'62-Style Norms

We find it hard to avoid the conclusion that AA's success as reported in previous papers is largely due to the extent to which its internal mechanisms are designed to fit exactly the kind of experiment settings first introduced by Vernon Smith: AA is very well suited to situations in which all assignments are issued to all traders simultaneously, and in which the theoretical equilibrium price remains constant for sustained periods of time, with only occasional step-change "shocks". Real markets are not like this, and as Cliff showed in [6], when AA is deployed in the more realistic market setting provided by BSE, its dominance disappears. The novel aspect of the results we present here is that we have now demonstrated that even in the simple style of experiments that AA was first tested in, AA can be shown not to dominate if sufficiently many tests are run.

Surely then the broader methodological lesson here is that we should not allow ourselves to be seduced by results from small-scale studies in minimally simple approximations to real-world markets. Smith developed his experimental methods in the late 1950's when there were no realistic alternative ways of doing things. Running experiments with human subjects is laborious and slow, but experiments in electronic markets populated entirely by robot traders can proceed in appropriate simulators at speeds much faster than real-time, and are "embarrassingly parallelizable": the more computational cores or virtual machines dedicated to the task, the faster the exhaustive experiments complete.

At this point in time, 20% of our way into the 21st Century, surely trading-agent researchers should collectively abandon the simple minimal test-environments that worked well for Vernon Smith in the middle of the 20th Century and instead start to tolerate the minor inconvenience of running very large numbers of trials on reasonably accurate simulations of realistic market situations: the methods used here should be the norm, not the exception. The availability of open-source public-domain exchange simulators such as BSE as a common platform for experiments and as a source of reference implementations, coupled with readily available cheap cloud-computing for doing the necessary processing, means that there are now really no excuses for not doing so.

6 Conclusions

The design of trading agents has been a research topic within AI/ML for over two decades, with the initial work taking place in the research labs of major technology companies such as IBM and HP, and at peak involved 20 or more teams of researchers around the world, some of whom would compete in the various trading agent competitions (TAC) held at AAAI and AAMAS conferences (see e.g. [28] for a summary of TAC research). Anyone reading the published literature might reasonably come to the conclusion that Vytelingum's AA strategy [26, 27] has remained unchallenged for more than a decade as the best-known public domain strategy for trading in continuous double auctions (CDAs) such as those found in the global financial markets; and in that sense CDA trading-agent design may have been thought by many to have been consigned to AI's list of "solved problems".

In this paper we have demonstrated that the apparent success of AA was in fact due to it not having been tested sufficiently. Our experiments were inspired by, and extend, those of Vach [25] and Cliff [6] but the AA source-code we used to generate the results presented here was developed independently of those two authors' work. That is, there are now three independent studies that each indicate AA to not be a dominant strategy.

We do not intend this paper to cast any doubts on the scientific or engineering merits of the previous work that we here call into question. In the decade that has passed since Vytelingum first published his AA work, the continuing Moore's Law fall in the real cost of computing hardware, combined with the rise of cheap and readily scalable remotely accessed cloud computing, gives today's researchers access to compute-power that would arguably have been unimaginable, or at least prohibitively expensive, over a decade ago when the first tests were being run on AA. As our brute-force exhaustive evaluation of AA competing with other strategies across all possible permutations shows, we are now in the lucky position to be able to ask, and to answer, questions that would not have been practicable to attempt to explore 10 or 15 years ago.

And the conclusion that we have arrived at is this: AA is clearly not the dominant, best-performing CDA trading strategy; in the experiments reported here, it is outperformed by GDX (as in [25]), and in [6] it is outperformed by ZIP. This reverses the solidly-stated conclusions of previous papers, asserting AA's dominance.[2]

Methodologically, all of the studies reviewed here (including our own experiments) are firmly in the same minimally simple frame of reference first established by Vernon Smith in his 1962 experiments: agents are assigned a right to buy or sell only a small number of items (typically only one) at any one time; and none of AA or ZIP or ASAD or GDX or ZIC have any sense of size-sensitivity (larger-sized orders being more significant than smaller ones) nor of time-sensitivity (some orders being more urgent to get executed than others). The strategies that have been studied in the CDA trading-agent literature are (with the notable exceptions of the famous *Kaplan Sniper* algorithm described in [17]; and Gjerstad's *HBL* strategy [12]) almost exclusively focused solely on price. Yet traders in real-world markets need to reason about price, and quantity, and time, making dynamic tradeoffs as the market moves over time. There is a clear need for further research

---

[2] At least two of those papers were co-authored by one of us, Dave Cliff. So this present paper is offered as something of a *mea culpa* from Cliff.

directed at creating such more sophisticated, and hence more real-world-relevant, trading strategies, and then comparing and evaluating them appropriately.

But, as we have argued here, there is also a clear need for future research to be conducted in such a way that erroneous conclusions are less likely to be drawn and promulgated. One way of doing that is to burn through very large numbers of compute-cycles, working exhaustively through all permutations of different strategies that might reasonably be found in a CDA market somewhere sometime. A CDA trading strategy should only be described as dominant, or the best-performing, if it really is; and some-times, more often than not, the only way of determining that is to run an awful lot of experiments. If all those experiments take a lot of money to run on a lot of machines, we just need to bear that cost; and if they take a long time to run, we just need to be patient. But, thankfully, the availability of low-cost cloud computing services means that we don't need to spend as much money on supercomputers, and nor do we need to wait as long as if we only had a few cores available. Now that the results we've presented here have overturned long-held beliefs about which is the best-performing public-domain trading strategy, running large-scale exhaustive experiments on contemporary scalable cloud services (or equivalent locally-available hardware) seems like the only reasonable way forward in future.

References

1. BSE: Bristol Stock Exchange. GitHub public source-code repository (2012). https://github.com/davecliff/BristolStockExchange
2. Cartea, Á., Jaimungal, S., Penalva, J.: Algorithmic and High-Frequency Trading. Cambridge University Press, Cambridge (2015)
3. Cliff, D.: Minimal-intelligence agents for bargaining behaviours in market-based environ-ments. Hewlett-packard labs technical report HPL-97-91 (1997)
4. Cliff, D., Preist, C.: Days without end: on the stability of experimental single-period continuous double auction markets. Hewlett-packard labs technical report HPL-2001-325 (2001)
5. Cliff, D.: An open-source limit-order-book exchange for teaching and research. In: Proceed-ings of the IEEE Symposium on Computational Intelligence in Financial Engineering (CIFEr), Bengaluru, India, vol. SS-1296, pp. 1853–1860 (2018)
6. Cliff, D.: Exhaustive testing of trader-agents in realistically dynamic continuous double auction markets: AA does not dominate. In: Proceedings ICAART (2019)
7. Das, R., Hanson, J., Kephart, J., Tesauro, G.: Agent-human interactions in the continuous double auction. In: Proceedings IJCAI-2001, pp. 1169–1176 (2001)
8. De Luca, M., Cliff, D.: Agent-human interactions in the CDA, Redux. In: Proceedings ICAART 2011 (2011a)
9. De Luca, M., Cliff, D.: Human-agent auction interactions: adaptive-aggressive agents dominate. In: Proceedings IJCAI-2011, pp. 178–185 (2011b)
10. De Luca, M.: Adaptive algorithmic trading systems. Ph.D. thesis, University of Bristol, UK (2015)
11. Gjerstad, S., Dickhaut, J.: Price formation in double auctions. Games Econ. Behav. **22**(1), 1–29 (1997)
12. Gjerstad, S.: The impact of pace in double auction bargaining. Working Paper, Department of Economics, University of Arizona (2003)

13. Gjerstad, S., Shachat, J.: Individual rationality and market efficiency. Working Paper, Department of Economics, Purdue University (2007)
14. Gode, D., Sunder, S.: Allocative efficiency of markets with zero-intelligence traders. J. Polit. Econ. **101**(1), 119–137 (1993)
15. le Calvez, A., Cliff, D.: Deep learning can replicate adaptive traders in a LOB financial market. In: Proceedings of the IEEE Symposium on Computational Intelligence in Financial Engineering (CIFEr), vol. S1070, pp. 1876–1883 (2018)
16. Rodgers, K.: Why Aren't they Shouting? A Banker's Tale of Change, Computers, and Perpetual Crisis. RH Business Books/Cornerstone Digital, New York (2016)
17. Rust, J., Miller, J., Palmer, R.: Behavior of trading automata in a computerized double auction market. In: Friedman, D., Rust, J. (eds.) The Double Auction Market: Institutions, Theories, & Evidence, pp. 155–198. Addison-Wesley, Boston (1992)
18. Smith, V.: An experimental study of competitive market behavior. J. Polit. Econ. **70**(2), 111–137 (1962)
19. Snashall, D.: An exhaustive comparison of algorithmic trading strategies: AA does not dominate. Master's thesis, Department of Computer Science, University of Bristol (2019)
20. Stoikov, S.: The micro-price: a high-frequency estimator of future prices (2017). https://papers.ssrn.com/sol3/papers.cfm?abstract_id=2970694
21. Stotter, S., Cartlidge, J., Cliff, D.: Exploring assignment-adaptive (ASAD) trading agents in financial market experiments. In: Proceedings ICAART, vol. 1, pp. 77–88 (2013)
22. Stotter, S., Cartlidge, J., Cliff, D.: Behavioural investigations of financial trading agents using exchange portal (ExPo). In: Nguyen, N.T., Kowalczyk, R., Fred, A., Joaquim, F. (eds.) Transactions on Computational Collective Intelligence XVII. LNCS, vol. 8790, pp. 22–45. Springer, Heidelberg (2014). https://doi.org/10.1007/978-3-662-44994-3_2
23. Tesauro, G., Das, R.: High-performance bidding agents for the continuous double auction. In: Proceedings of the 3rd ACM Conference on Electronic Commerce, pp. 206–209 (2001)
24. Tesauro, G., Bredin, J.: Sequential strategic bidding in auctions using dynamic programming. In: Proceedings AAMAS 2002 (2002)
25. Vach, D.: Comparison of double auction bidding strategies for automated trading agents. MSc thesis, Charles University in Prague (2015)
26. Vytelingum, P.: The structure and behaviour of the continuous double auction. Ph.D. thesis, School of Electronics and Computer Science, University of Southampton, UK (2006)
27. Vytelingum, P., Cliff, D., Jennings, N.: Strategic Bidding in CDAs. Artif. Intell. **172**(14), 1700–1729 (2008)
28. Wellman, M., Greenwald, A., Stone, P.: Autonomous Bidding Agents: Strategies and Lessons from the Trading Agent Competition. MIT Press, Cambridge (2007)

Improvement of Multi-agent Continuous Cooperative Patrolling with Learning of Activity Length

Ayumi Sugiyama[✉], Lingying Wu, and Toshiharu Sugawara

Department Computer Science and Communications Engineering,
Waseda University, Tokyo 1698555, Japan
sugi.ayumi@ruri.waseda.jp

Abstract. We propose a learning method that decides the period of activity according to environmental characteristics and the behavioral strategies in the multi-agent continuous cooperative patrol problem. With recent advances in computer and sensor technologies, agents, which are intelligent control programs running on computers and robots, obtain high autonomy so that they can operate in various fields without pre-defined knowledge. However, cooperation/coordination between agents is sophisticated and complicated to implement. We focus on the activity cycle length (ACL) which is the time length from when an agent starts a patrol to when the agent returns to a charging base in the context of a cooperative patrol where agents, like robots, have batteries with limited capacity. A long ACL will enable an agent to visit distant locations, but the agent will require a long rest time to recharge. The basic idea of our method is that if agents have long-life batteries, they can appropriately shorten the ACL, and thus can visit important locations with a short interval of time by recharging frequently. However, appropriate ACL must depend on many elements such as environmental size, number of agents, workload in an environment, and other agents' behavior and ACLs. Therefore, we propose a method in which agents autonomously learn the appropriate ACL on the basis of the number of events detected per cycle. We experimentally indicate that our agents are able to learn appropriate ACL depending on established spatial divisional cooperation. We also report the details of the analysis of the experimental results to understand the behaviors of agents with different ACLs.

Keywords: Continuous cooperative patrol problem · Cycle learning · Multi-agent · Division of labor · Battery limitation

1 Introduction

Coordination in a shared environment is one major issue in the research on multi-agent systems because it heavily affects the entire performance of cooperative activities. However, identifying what coordination regime and behavior

---

T. Sugawara—This work was partly supported by JSPS KAKENHI (17KT0044).

J. van den Herik et al. (Eds.): ICAART 2019, LNAI 11978, pp. 270–292, 2019.
https://doi.org/10.1007/978-3-030-37494-5_14

are appropriate is quite complicated because it depends on the nature of the environment and the structure of the tasks that multiple agents have to work on. In addition, agents are often required for better coordination to infer others' plans and goals because agents are autonomous, having their own behavioral strategies and different computational skills and costs. Therefore, creating methods for establishing cooperation among multiple agents is challenging due to the difficulty of realizing advanced autonomy and various complex interaction patterns between agents with limited communication opportunity. To tackle these issues, the *multi-agent patrol problem* (MAPP) has attracted attention as a good case study on many multi-agent systems because it has essential issues, such as autonomy, dispersibility, communication restriction, and scalability, all of which are required to realize intelligent autonomous distributed systems [6].

We extend this problem to the *multi-agent continuous cooperative patrol problem* (MACCPP) in which multiple autonomous agents with limited battery capacities continuously move around in an environment where events occur at a certain probability [17]. In the MAPP, all nodes (locations) are visited with the same priority/frequency because the purpose of the conventional MAPP is to minimize *idleness* which is the interval of two visits for every node. In comparison, agents in the MACCPP are required to visit individual nodes with different visitation requirements, which reflect that events that should be monitored or observed in the nodes occur with different probabilities or reflect the importance of nodes. Thus, high visitation requirements indicate, for example, locations that require a high-security level at which no events must be missed in security patrolling applications. Thus, the objective of agents in the MACCPP is to minimize the *duration of unawareness* which is the length of time for which agents remain unaware of occurred events by not visiting the locations of these events.

There are a number of studies that have tackled MAPPs and MACCPPs in multi-agent system contexts because of their applicability to many real-world problems. For example, Cheva [5] classified various classes of patrolling strategies and compared these strategies. David and Rui [6] summarized developments of patrolling methods and indicated issues that must extensively be studied regarding the MAPPs. Sugiyama et al. [16] proposed a learning method, in which agents individually decide where they should work by using lightweight communications and by learning which locations they should visit more frequently than others. They found that the agents with their methods could effectively move around the environment by identifying their responsible areas, i.e., the agents finally formed a certain cooperation structure based on the division of labor by autonomous area segmentation.

Although this method [16] could improve efficiency in patrolling the given environment to detect/observe events occurring there, we found that agents have to consider the temporal aspect, i.e., the interval of visits to some important locations in their coordinated behaviors to minimize the duration of unawareness of events, if we assume that agents are (the control programs of) robots and often stop operation for battery charging and/or periodic inspections. This interruption in operation usually negatively affects patrolling, such as security surveillance and cleaning tasks. Because temporarily stopping for charging is frequent and inevitable in actual operation, strategic behavior is required to minimize the influence of stopping by taking into account a robots' capability and the characteristics of the areas in which they move around. Although a few studies discussed the battery capacity of agents (robots) [2,8,10,14], the appropriate timing for when to return to charge and when to resume operation for autonomous agents was not clarified in their methods.

The cyclic behavior of agents, in which agents move around until their batteries become empty and then charge to make the batteries full in different periodic phases is one of the simplest ways of coordination, but it is somewhat doubtful whether this behavior contributes to reducing the duration of unawareness in the MACCPP. In this paper, a sequence of actions from the agent leaving the charging base with a full battery, moving around the environment, returning to the base, and completing the charge is called a *round* and the time length to complete a round is called an *activity cycle length* (ACL). The system's performance seems to be affected by cyclic strategies based on the battery capacity. For example, agents with a small battery capacity cannot cover distant tasks/events, and the cumulative return cost for recharging is high in a large environment due to frequent charging. In contrast, agents with long-life batteries can be expected to move more effectively and cover distant events, but they must stop operations for a long time for recharging, resulting in a long duration of unawareness. In addition, because appropriate ACL may depend on the environmental characteristics they will be deployed in, and the behaviors of other cooperative agents, as well as the agent's own behavioral strategies, it is almost impossible to decide the ACL in the design phase of the systems. Therefore, agents are required to autonomously learn which ACL will lead to better results through actual cooperative behavior from the viewpoint of the entire performance.

In this paper, we extend the method proposed in [16] to learn appropriate ACL in the MACCPP model to adapt other agents' cooperative strategies and ACLs as well as the characteristics of the areas in which individual agents mainly move around. In this method, we assume that agents have long-life batteries and they can adaptively decide their ACL by returning/restarting regardless of their remaining battery capacities because it is easy to shorten ACL. Of course, they must not run out of battery during operations. The features of our method is that, like the method in [16], it does not require tight communication and deep inference for cooperation, meaning that frequent message exchange and the sophisticated reasoning of others' internal intentions are not used; this makes our method efficient and lightweight. For this reason, our method is applicable to dynamic environments. We experimentally indicate that agents with our method are able to identify appropriate ACL. Furthermore, we found that agents established a division of labor by spatial segmentation, as in [16]; thus, agents individually identify where they should move around according to the nodes they are responsible for. This enables agents to decide ACL differently and appropriately for their own specific situations. We have already reported some results along this line about the learning of ACLs elsewhere [18], but in this study, we added more detailed experimental results with reasonable assumptions and we extensively analyzed the benefits and features of the proposed method.

2   Related Work

Cooperation in a distributed manner by multiple agents has received increasing demands for continuous and sustainable real-world systems. Cao et al. [3] summarized some main results of distributed multi-agent coordination techniques in control systems and robotics. They mentioned that many benefits can be obtained when a single complicated robot is equivalently replaced by simpler multi-robots. They also mentioned that distributed approaches are more useful to cope with many constraints such as limited resources and available energy in real-world applications. In many social insects and animals including humans, individuals must adjust the consumption of limited energy for continuous behavior of the group. For example, Hasegawa et al. [7] observed ant behavior and obtained the results which suggested that lazy ant workers that consumed less energy than other ants were indispensable for long-term sustainability of the ant group. This kind of coordination and cooperation by multiple agents also seem to be required in artificial systems. However, common theories for cooperation are not clarified due to diversity of real-world environments and the complexity of interactive relationships between many agents. Therefore, studies using one of simplified and analyzable problems, like the MACCPP, will help clarify how we realize a sustainable artificial system.

Various approaches, especially approaches based on reinforcement learning for the MAPP and MACCPP, have been examined so far. David and Rui [6] summarized the development of patrolling methods. They stated that non-adaptive solutions such as methods based on the traveling salesman problem often outperform other solutions in many cases except in large or dynamic environments. To adapt to these environments, they insisted that agents must have high autonomy. Machado et al. [9] evaluated reactive agents and cognitive agents that have different depths to analyze patrol graphs and investigated the characteristics of these agents. In actual patrol problems, because cognitive agents have greater perception, they can do more sophisticated operations due to recent developments in technology. Santana et al. [13] modeled a patrolling task as a reinforcement learning problem and proposed adaptive strategies for autonomous agents. Then, they showed that their strategies were not always the best but were superior in most of the experiments.

The MACCPP assumes a dynamic environment in which events occur with certain probabilities and the duration of unawareness is considered instead of idleness as in the MAPP. According to Ahmadi and Stone [1], by assuming that events to be found were generated stochastically, the proposed agents learned the probability of events and adjusted their area of responsibility to minimize the average required time to detect events. Chen and Yum [4] modeled a patrolling environment with a non-linear security level function in the context of a security problem. In this model, agents have to visit each node with a different frequency according to the values of the function. Pasqualetti et al. [11] studied a patrol problem in which all nodes have different priorities, but their model was a simple cyclic graph with a small number of nodes. Popescu et al. [12] proposed a patrolling method for a wireless sensor network in which agents independently collect saved data from sensors with limited storage. Agents in this model decide the priorities of nodes to visit on the basis of the accumulated amount of data and data generation rate. Stump and Michael [15] considered a persistent surveillance problem where six quad-rotor robots patrol around buildings through some points in three-dimensional space that have different priorities. In this problem, robots have to repeatedly visit each point for continuous surveillance, so we can regard this problem as a kind of MACCPP.

Sugiyama et al. [16] proposed a method called the *adaptive meta-target decision strategy with learning of dirt accumulation probabilities* (AMTDS/LD) by combining the learning of a target decision strategy in the planning process and the learning of the importance of each location for cleaning tasks. Agents with AMTDS/LD indirectly cooperate with other agents by learning the importance of nodes, which is partly taken into account and reflects the visiting frequencies of other agents. The researchers also extended their method by introducing simple negotiation to enhance the division of labor in a bottom-up manner [17]. However, they did not discuss the intervals of visits, which is another key issue of the MACCPP. In the MACCPP, agents with limited capacity batteries have to stop their operation to recharge, so agents have to coordinate with each other by adjusting timings of starting and recharging for appropriate visiting patterns.

Other researchers also take into account battery capacity in the multi-robot patrol problem. Jensen et al. [8] presented strategies for replacing robots that have almost empty batteries with other robots that have fully charged ones to keep coverage and minimize interruptions for sustainable patrol. Bentz and Panagou [2] proposed an energy-aware global coverage technique that shifts distributions of effort networks according to the degree of an agent's energy constraints. Sipahioglu et al. [14] proposed a path planning method that covers an environment by considering energy capacity in multi-robot applications. This method partitions a complete coverage route into sub-routes and assigns them to robots by considering the energy capacities of the robots. Mersheeva and Friedrich [10] proposed a negotiation mechanism between aerial vehicles in a monitoring problem with limited energy resources and different priorities of locations. In many multi-robot problems, limited energy resources of robots was considered, but the number of robots was not so many because they assumed strict limitation of robotics such as processing capability and communication bandwidth/noise. However, we can expect that many more agents will work in a shared environment in the near future. Additionally, these methods are mainly focused on how to divide work areas for cooperative activities. However, they do not focus on controlling the phases of ACL on the basis of an agent's battery capacity. Therefore, we propose a learning method with which each agent decides the appropriate duration of activity (so appropriate charging time) depending on the characteristics of the tasks of agents for more effective cooperation. We have already reported some results by taking into account the learning ACLs elsewhere [18], but we added more detailed experimental results and analysis on the benefits and features of the proposed method.

3   Model

3.1   Environment

We introduce discrete time with units called *ticks*. The environment in which agents patrol is described by graph $G = (V, E)$, which can be embedded into a two-dimensional plane with a metric, where $V = \{v_1, \ldots v_m\}$ is a set of nodes. An agent, an event, and an obstacle can exist on node v. E is a set of edges. An edge connecting v_i and v_j is expressed by $e_{i,j} \in E$. By adding dummy nodes if necessary, we assume that agents can move one of their neighbor nodes along an edge in one tick. An environment may have obstacles, R_o ($\subset V$). Agents cannot move to and events do not occur on the nodes in R_o. Therefore, nodes with obstacles and edges that contain obstacles are removed from V and E.

Node $v \in V$ has the *event occurrence probability value* $p(v)$, where $0 \leq p(v) \leq 1$, and it indicates that an event occurs on v with probability $p(v)$. The number of unaware events without processing on v at time t is expressed by $L_t(v)$, where $L_t(v)$ is a non-negative integer. $L_t(v)$ is updated on the basis of $p(v)$ every tick by

$$L_t(v) \leftarrow \begin{cases} L_{t-1}(v) + 1 & \text{(if an event occurs)} \\ L_{t-1}(v) & \text{(otherwise).} \end{cases} \tag{1}$$

$L_t(v)$ becomes 0 when an agent visits v. In one tick, events occur on nodes, agents decide their target nodes, agents move to neighbor nodes, and agents process events on the move destination.

3.2   Agent

Before we describe the agent model, we explain one assumption which we introduce to simplify our problem. In this study, we assume that agents always get their own and others' locations. An environment with this assumption can be realized, for example, by equipping agents with indicators, such as infrared emission and reflection devices and detecting them using cameras. We believe that this is a reasonable assumption because technology for sensors and positioning systems are being rapidly developed. However, we do not assume that agents can get others' internal information such as the adopted strategies and the target nodes selected with planning processes in individual agents because inference and reasoning by using/estimating others' internal information seems complicated. Because we want to focus on the period of cyclic behavior for better cooperative work, we do not consider such costly reasoning.

Let $A = \{1, \ldots, n\}$ be a set of agents. When agents obtain $p(v)$ in advance, they can use $p(v)$ for their patrol. However, in actual patrol problems, $p(v)$ may be unknown. Moreover, the appropriate frequency to visit depends not only on $p(v)$ but also on the frequencies of other agents' visits.

Therefore, agents have to learn priorities to visit nodes from their local viewpoints through their actual patrols. Agent i has the *degree of importance* (simply, *importance* after this) $p^i(v)$ for all nodes in an environment, and it reflects both $p(v)$ and other agents' behaviors. When i visits node v at t and detects events $L_t(v)$, i updates $p^i(v)$, as

$$p^i(v) \leftarrow (1 - \beta)p^i(v) + \beta \frac{L_t(v)}{I_t^i(v)}, \qquad (2)$$

where $I_t^i(v)$ is the elapsed time from t_{visit}^v which is the time of the last visit to v and calculated as

$$I_t^i(v) = t - t_{visit}^v. \qquad (3)$$

β $(0 < \beta \leq 1)$ is the learning rate. If the initial value of $p^i(v)$ is in interval $[0, 1]$, $p^i(v)$ is always in $[0, 1]$, because $L_t(v) \leq I_t^i(v)$ from the definition of $L_t(v)$.

3.3 Target Decision and Path Generation Strategy

Agents repeatedly generate paths to follow through a *planning process*. The planning usually consists of two subprocesses: *target decision* and *path generation* (e.g., [19]). Agent i first decides the next target node $v_{tar}^i \in V$ by using the target decision process and then generates the appropriate path from the current node to v_{tar}^i by using the path generation process. Because our purpose is to extend the AMTDS/LD and to compare our proposed method with AMTDS/LD, we will briefly explain it. Agent i with AMTDS/LD simultaneously learns the appropriate strategy s in S_{plan} and $p^i(v)$ with Formula (2), where S_{plan} is the set of target decision strategies described below. The policy for selecting the target decision strategy from S_{plan} is adjusted based on Q-learning with the ε-greedy learning strategy. Thus, i updates the Q-value for selecting $s \in S_{plan}$ on the basis of the sum of detected events until i arrives at v_{tar}^i, which is the target decided by s. The details of Q-learning for this policy and AMTDS/LD are outside the scope of this paper; please refer to [16].

We will explain the elements of S_{plan}, i.e., the target decision strategies used in the experiments below.

- **Random Selection (R)**
  Agent i randomly selects v_{tar}^i among all nodes V.
- **Probabilistic Greedy Selection (PGS)**
  Agent i selects v_{tar}^i in which i estimates the value of unaware events $EL_t^i(v)$ at time t using $p^i(v)$ and elapsed time from last visit $I_t^i(v)$ by

$$EL_t^i(v) = p^i(v) \cdot I_t^i(v). \qquad (4)$$

Then, i selects v_{tar}^i randomly from the N_g highest nodes in V according to the values of $EL_t^i(v)$, where N_g is a positive integer.

- **Prioritizing Unvisited Interval Selection (PI)**
  Agent i selects v_{tar}^i randomly from the N_i highest nodes according to the value of interval $I_t^i(v)$ for $v \in V$, where N_i is a positive integer. Agents with this strategy are likely to prioritize nodes that have not been visited recently.
- **Balanced Neighbor-Preferential Selection (BNPS)**
  Agent i estimates if many unaware events may exist near nodes by using the learned threshold value, and i selects v_{tar}^i from such nodes. Otherwise, i selects v_{tar}^i by using the PGS. The details are described elsewhere [20].

Note that we can also regard AMTDS, AMTDS/LD, and our proposed method as target decision strategies.

We use the *gradual path generation* (GPG) method as the path generation strategy in this research [20]. Agent i with the GPG first calculates the shortest path from current node to v_{tar}^i and then regenerates a path to v_{tar}^i by adding nodes nearby the shortest path and whose values of $EL_t^i(v)$ are identified as high. We do not explain the GPG method in detail because it is beyond the scope of this paper, but it is also described elsewhere [20].

Battery Setting. Agent i has a battery with a limited capacity, so it must periodically return to its charging base $v_{base}^i \in V$ to charge its battery for continuous patrolling. The battery specifications of agent i are denoted by $(B_{max}^i, B_{drain}^i, k_{charge}^i)$, where $B_{max}^i(> 0)$ is the maximal capacity of the battery, $B_{drain}^i(> 0)$ is the amount of battery consumption per one tick, and $k_{charge}^i(> 0)$ is the time taken to charge one battery at charging base v_{base}^i. The remaining amount of the battery of agent i at time t is expressed in $b_t^i(0 \leq b_t^i \leq B_{max}^i)$; therefore, it takes $k_{charge}^i(B_{max}^i - b_t^i)$ to charge to full, when i starts to charge at time t.

Agents in this model must go back to v_{base}^i before $b^i(t)$ becomes 0 as shown below. Agent i calculates the *potential*, $\mathcal{P}(v)$, for all nodes in advance. $\mathcal{P}(v)$ is the minimal amount of battery consumption necessary to return from node v to v_{base}^i and is calculated as

$$\mathcal{P}(v) = d(v, v_{base}^i) \times B_{drain}^i, \tag{5}$$

where $d(v_k, v_l)$ is the shortest path length from node v_k to node v_l. After agent i decides v_{tar}^i on the basis of the target decision strategy, i judges whether i can arrive at v_{tar}^i before i moves to v_{tar}^i using

$$b_t^i \geq \mathcal{P}(v_{tar}^i) + len_{GPG}(v_t^i, v_{tar}^i) \times B_{drain}^i, \tag{6}$$

where $v_t^i \in V$ is current node of agent i at time t and $len_{GPG}(v_t^i, v_{tar}^i)$ is the length of the path generated by the GPG (so it takes $len_{GPG}(v_t^i, v_{tar}^i)$ ticks for i to follow the path to the target). If this inequation does not hold, i changes v_{tar}^i as

$$v_{tar}^i \leftarrow v_{base}^i, \tag{7}$$

and immediately returns to v_{base}^i. Agents recharge batteries at charging bases until they are full and then restart patrol.

Our purpose is to appropriately decide ACL depending on the characteristics of their working environments, the recognition of the importances of all locations, and the behavior of other agents. Because agents can return to the charging base earlier, it is easy to shorten ACL if they have long-life batteries.

3.4   Performance Measure and Requirement of MACCPP

The requirement of the MACCPP is to minimize the duration of unaware events, $L_t(v)$, by visiting important nodes without being aware of event occurrences. For example, in cleaning tasks, agents should vacuum accumulated dirt as soon as possible without leaving it and keep the amount of dirt low. Therefore, we define a performance measure when agents adopted strategy $s \in S_{plan}$, $D_{t_s,t_e}(s)$, for the interval from t_s to t_e to evaluate our method.

$$D_{t_s,t_e}(s) = \sum_{v \in V} \sum_{t=t_s+1}^{t_e} L_t(v), \tag{8}$$

where $t_s < t_e$. $D_{t_s,t_e}(s)$ is the cumulative unaware duration in $(t_s, t_e]$, so a smaller D_{t_s,t_e} indicates better system performance.

We can also consider another performance measure. For example, in security patrol applications, agents should keep the maximal number of events $L_t(v)$ as low as possible, because a high value for $L_t(v)$ indicates significant danger. This measure is defined by

$$U_{t_s,t_e}(s) = \max_{v \in V, t_s < t \leq t_e} L_t(v). \tag{9}$$

Therefore, agents in the MACCPP are required to lower one or both of the performance measures, $D_{t_s,t_e}(s)$ or $U_{t_s,t_e}(s)$, depending on the type of application.

4   Proposed Method

We explain our method with which agents learn the appropriate ACL to improve their own performance [18]. We named our method, which is an extension of AMTDS/LD [16], *AMTDS with cycle learning* (AMTDS/CL). Agent i has ACL as s_c^i ($0 < s_c^i \leq \lfloor B_{max}^i / B_{drain}^i \rfloor$) (we normalize the value in (B_{max}^i, B_{drain}^i) so that $B_{drain}^i = 1$ hereafter). Agent i with AMTDS/CL regards its battery capacity B_{max}^i as s_c^i and then uses the battery control algorithm in Sect. 3.3. The length of ACL is a trade-off because a longer ACL enables agents to act for a long time, but agents also require a long charging time. In our method, agent i selects s_c^i from a set of possible ACLs, $S_c^i = \{s_{c1}, s_{c2}, \dots\}$, where $\max_{s \in S_c^i}(s) = B_{max}^i$. For simplicity, $s \in S_c^i$ is a divisor of B_{max}^i in this paper, but we can select any number between 0 and B_{max}^i.

The learning process of deciding the ACL consists of two learning subprocesses. The purpose of the first subprocess is to decide the initial Q-values for all possible ACLs in S_c^i because the initial Q-values offset the performance of

Q-learning and, in general, their appropriate values are dependent on the characteristics of the working areas in the environment. In this subprocess, agents calculate the average number of detected events per one tick while active as follows. First, i selects an ACL from S_c^i at random and starts patrol. Then, when i returns to the base to charge, it calculates e_1^i by using

$$e_1^i = E_1^i / l_1^i, \tag{10}$$

where E_1^i is the number of detected events in the first round and l_1^i is time length when agent i moved in the first round.

Agents repeat this pair of the patrol and the computation; i.e., they randomly select an ACL in each round and calculate the average of the detected events per tick in the k-th round, $e_k^i = E_k^i / l_k^i$, where E_k^i is the number of detected events in the k-th round and l_k^i is the time length of the k-th round. Agent i continues this process for the initial T_{init} ticks, where T_{init} is a positive integer. Then, at the end of the first subprocess, i calculates e^i, which is the average of the values of $e_1^i, e_2^i, \ldots$ obtained by Formula (10) during the first subprocess. The e^i will be set to the initial Q-value $Q^i(s_c)$ of $s_c \in S_c^i)$ in the second subprocess. Note that $p^i(v)$ is calculated by using Eq. (2).

If agent i finds that the current time t is larger than T_{init}, it enters the second learning subprocess. Before i starts to patrol from its charging base, i decides s_c with probability $1 - \varepsilon$ as

$$s_c \leftarrow \arg\max_{s_c' \in S_c} Q^i(s_c'), \tag{11}$$

where $0 < \varepsilon \ll 1$ is the greedy parameter for the e-greedy strategy; otherwise, i randomly selects s_c from S_c. When there is a tie break in Eq. (11), agents select one of the candidates at random.

In the proposed method, i will continuously use the selected s_c for several times without updating Q-value to balance the weights of $Q(s_c)$ for $\forall s_c \in S_c$. In the MACCPP, it is better for agents to visit individual nodes, especially important nodes, in shorter intervals when their battery levels are high. However, when agents visit nodes so frequently, they may find a smaller number of events; therefore, the Q-values of the short ACLs tend to be small, even if i visits the important nodes where i must find as many events as possible and keep the number of unaware events low. This means that if agents update $Q^i(s_c)$ every short round, they cannot correctly evaluate the ACL. Therefore, we introduce the parameter $C_{s_c}^i$ to make the weights of their activity time identical regardless of the value of s_c; this achieves fair learning results. When agent i decides its ACL with Formula (11), i calculates $C_{s_c}^i$ by

$$C_{s_c}^i = B_{max}^i / s_c. \tag{12}$$

After that, i selects the s_c in $C_{s_c}^i$ rounds continuously without updating the Q-value.

After i finishes $C^i_{s_c}$ rounds of patrol using the selected s_c, i updates $Q^i(s_c)$;

$$Q^i(s_c) \leftarrow (1-\gamma)Q^i(s_c) + \gamma\frac{\sum_{k=k_0-C^i_{s_c}+1}^{k_0} E^i_k}{C^i_{s_c}}, \tag{13}$$

where k_0 indicates the number of the most recent round. We have assumed that s_c is is a divisor of B^i_{max} but if not, we use $C^i_{s_c} = \lceil B^i_{max}/s_c \rceil$. Note that the first learning subprocess is dedicated to calculating the initial Q-values and i never updates $Q^i(s_c)$. The calculation of initial Q-values is mandatory for the fast convergence of Q-learning.

5   Experiments and Discussion

We evaluated our method with two experiments. First, we investigated whether agents with our method will learn the appropriate ACL, by comparing the results of our learning method with those of the AMTDS/LD with a fixed ACL. Note that in this experiment, all agents had a charging base in the same location. In the second experiment, we investigated the difference in learned ACLs when the agents' charging bases were located at different locations. Therefore, they were likely to be affected by the characteristics of the local areas near the charging bases.

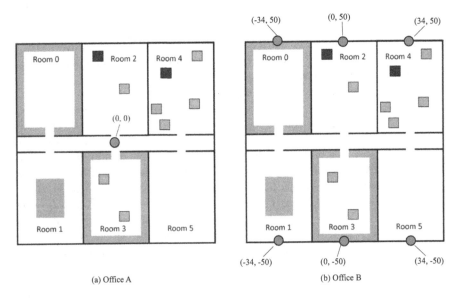

(a) Office A   (b) Office B

Fig. 1. Environments in experiments [18]. (Color figure online)

Table 1. Parameters and values [18].

Model	Parameter	Value
PGS	N_g	5
PI	N_i	5
AMTDS/LD	β	0.05
	ε	0.05
AMTDS/CL	γ	0.05
	ε	0.05
	T_{init}	100,000

5.1 Experimental Setting

We constructed two simulated large environments, called "Office A" and "Office B," for agents to patrol as shown in Fig. 1. These environments consisted of six rooms (labeled *Rooms 0–5*), a corridor, and a number of nodes where events occurred frequently. We set $p(v)$ for $v \in V$ as

$$p(v) = \begin{cases} 10^{-3} \text{ if v was in a red region,} \\ 10^{-4} \text{ if v was in an orange region, and} \\ 10^{-6} \text{ otherwise,} \end{cases} \quad (14)$$

and the colored regions are shown in Fig. 1. The green circles in these environments are charging bases. In Office A, all agents had charging bases in the same location. In Office B, we divided agents into six groups, and the charging bases of each group were assigned to one of six rooms differently. Each room had charging bases in Office B, but agents had to return to their own assigned charging bases. The environments can be embedded into a 101×101 2-dimensional grid graph whose center is $(0,0)$ and nodes are represented by coordinates (x, y), where $-50 \leq x, y \leq 50$. They may have several obstacles (walls). We set the length of edges between nodes to one. We introduced the Manhattan distance between two nodes; this was used to calculate the lengths of path generated by agents.

We deployed 20 agents into each environment. We assumed that agents did not know $p^i(v)$ in advance, so we initially set $p^i(v)$ for $\forall v \in V$ as 0 and each agent adjusted their $p^i(v)$ using Formula (2). Agents started their patrols from the assigned v^i_{base} and periodically returned to v^i_{base} to recharge before their batteries became empty. We set the actual battery specifications of all agents as $(B^i_{max}, B^i_{drain}, k^i_{charge}) = (2700, 1, 3)$ and set S_c to $S_c = \{300, 900, 2700\}$. When agents selected s_c to be 2700, the patrol cycle length was at maximum (10,800 ticks), whose breakdown consists of the active time (2700 ticks) and the charging time (8100 ticks). Therefore, for the target decision strategy s, we measured $D_{t_s,t_e}(s)$ and $U_{t_s,t_e}(s)$ every 10800 ticks, which was the length of maximum cycle length (and the least common multiple) of the recharge and movements. In the experiments below, we set AMTDS/LD or AMTDS/CL to s.

The parameter values used in the model are listed in Table 1. The experimental results shown below are the average values of ten independent experimental runs.

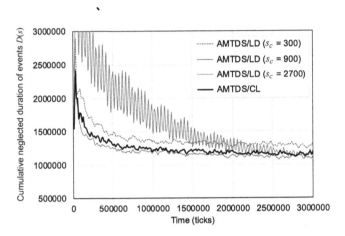

Fig. 2. Improvement in $D(s)$ over time in Office A.

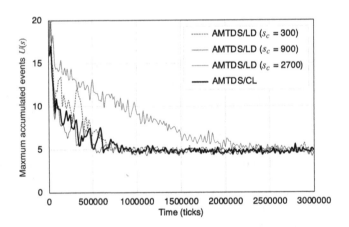

Fig. 3. Improvement in $U(s)$ over time in Office A.

5.2   Experiment 1—Office A

Performance Evaluation. In the first experiment, we compared the performance results of four types of agents that used AMTDS/LD with one of the fixed ACLs, $s_c = 300$, 900, or 2700 with those by the agents with AMTDS/CL in Office A as shown in Fig. 1(a). Hereinafter, AMTDS/LD with fixed ACL s_c

is denoted as AMTDS/LD(s_c). Figure 2 plots the performance, $D(s)$, and Fig. 3 plots the performance of $U(s)$ over time. Note that the smaller $D(s)$ and $U(s)$ are better. We also note that these figures are similar to but different from those in [18], since we fully conducted the new experiments.

Both figures indicate that agents with AMTDS/LD(900) were the most efficient, and the agents with AMTDS/CL exhibited almost the same efficiency as that with AMTDS/LD(900). The efficiency of the agents with AMTDS/LD(2700) was the worst and seemed unstable at first, but it gradually improved over time. Because AMTDS/LD(2700) requires quite a long time to recharge, the number of patrolling agents and thereby the number of unaware events were unstably fluctuated. However, the phases of their periodic cycles gradually shifted automatically and finally disappeared. In contrast, the converged performance of the agents with AMTDS/LD(300) was always worse than the others. This is because the ACL was too short to cover the entire environment, especially areas distant from the charging bases, and the agents in charge of distant area had to return very frequently to the charging bases. We can say that in this particular experimental environment, the ACL of 900 seemed the best. However, this depends on the environmental characteristics and we cannot decide the appropriate ACL in advance. In comparison, the agents with the proposed AMTDS/CL can adaptively select ACLs by themselves without such a prior decision.

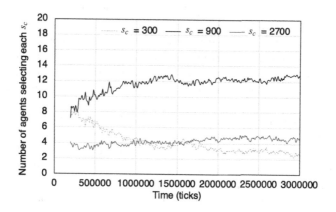

Fig. 4. Number of agents selecting each s_c over time in Office A [18].

Breakdown of the Selected ACLs. Figure 4 indicates the number of agents that selected $\forall s_c \in S_c^i$ with AMTDS/CL over time. Note that we plotted in this figure the values of every 10,000 ticks from 200,000 to 3,000,000 ticks. Because agents started from deciding the initial Q-values until 100,000 ticks and then entered the learning of ACL, the learning results in the first 200,000 were unstable. We can see from this figure that many agents selected 900 ticks for s_c since

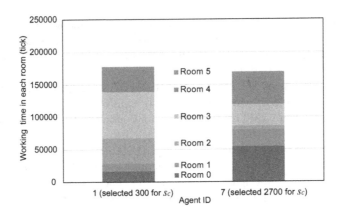

Fig. 5. Working time of Agents 1 and 7 in individual rooms of Office A [18].

AMTDS/LD(900) exhibited the best performance in this environment, and this was consistent with the results when agents have the fixed ACL.

Additionally, we investigated the characteristics of agents that selected 300 and 2700 as their ACL. Figure 5 shows the working time of agents whose IDs were 1 and 7, i.e., how long they spent in each room during the last 1,000,000 ticks. Note that Agent 1 selected 300 and Agent 7 selected 2700 for their ACLs at the end, though 900 was usually the best as the ACL in the environment. We also note that the data shown in Fig. 5 is one result selected from multiple experimental trials, but we found that a similar tendency could be observed in other trials. Agent 1 patrolled Room 2 and Room 3 more often than Agent 7. Room 2 and Room 3 were near the charging base. Room 2 had specific regions in which events frequently occurred, and many nodes in Room 3 also had a higher $p^i(v)$. Therefore, Agent 1 could find many events in Room 2 and Room 3; thus, patrolling with a short ACL was better from the viewpoint of Agent 1 to keep the number of unaware events low.

Meanwhile, Agent 7 frequently patrolled many rooms, some of which were distant from the charging base. We confirmed that, unlike Agent 1, Agent 7 had a high value of $p^i(v)$ in more and farther nodes, so Agent 7 selected a long ACL to move around in a large area. This analysis indicates that, from a global viewpoint, agents with a short s_c and long s_c covered different areas in a complementary manner. That is because some agents with AMTDS/CL did not select 900 for s_c and deterioration of efficiency did not occur, although AMTDS/LD(900) was best in terms of efficiency. These results showed that agents with our method learned the appropriate ACL s_c without prior knowledge of the environments. Instead, agents decided ACLs on the basis of their learned $p^i(v)$ and working area. We believe that such diversity in agent strategies also enhances the response capabilities to environmental changes as well as the improvement in efficiency.

Table 2. Converged performance on different numbers of agents in Office A.

		Number of agents $|A|(= n)$			
		5	10	15	20
Performance $D(s)$	AMTDS/LD(900)	4600101	2154396	1451049	1116220
	AMTDS/CL	4558343	2218133	1486534	1157499
Performance $U(s)$	(AMTDS/LD(900))	60.15	13.36	6.56	5.06
	(AMTDS/CL)	54.58	12.22	6.56	5.18

Effect of Number of Agents on Performance. To show that the proposed method can effectively determine the ACL even if the number of agents is different, we conducted the same experiment using different numbers of agents and compared the results with those under the condition in which all agents had the fixed ACL. Table 2 lists the average performance $D(s)$ and $U(s)$ of ATMDS/LD(900) and AMTDS/CL between 2,500,000 and 3,000,000 ticks when the number of agents, $|A|$, is 5, 10, 15 or 20. This table indicates that the agents with the AMTDS/CL could exhibit comparable performance in all cases by deciding their own ACL values. Note that we only conducted the experiment using AMTDS/LD(900) because the performance with ACL = 900 was better than those with other ACL values.

We can also see from Table 2 that when the number of agents was small ($|A|$ = 5 or 10), the performance of AMTDS/CL was better than that of AMTDS/LD(900). When $|A|$ was not small, agents with the fixed ACL had the same activity duration, but the phase of their cycle had gradually shifted; thus, they could patrol in the environment with the different phases of activity cycles. However, conditions were different when the number of agents was small. First, it was not possible for agents to compensate for each other by shifting the phase of the activity cycle. Second, they could find sufficient number of events just moving around the nodes whose $p(v)$ was higher; thus, they were likely to identify these nodes as important nodes. Additionally, they have the same ACL. Under this situation, agents' explorations were limited and biased, and then their convergence became slow. In contrast, agents with the AMTDS/CL had a variety of ACLs; and then, agents with the smaller ACL visited the areas not so far, and those with the larger ACL visited the distant areas. Agents with the AMTDS/CL seem better at compensating for each other when there are only a few agents.

Selected Strategies and ACL Values. Next, we investigated the relationships between the ACL values and the selected target decision strategies because the activity time seemed to affect agents' behaviors. The results were indicated in Fig. 6. This figure shows that almost all agents selected the PGS or BNPS as the target decision strategies and this result is consistent with that in AMTDS/LD [16].

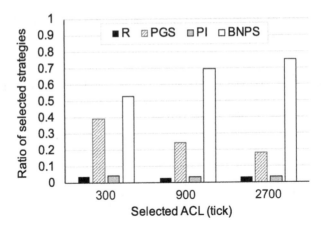

Fig. 6. Selected Target Decision Strategies.

If we look at this figure more carefully, we can notice that agents with the larger ACL tended to select BNPS. So relatively, the agents selecting PGS decreased according to the length of the activity cycle. This is because the agents with a short activity cycle had to eagerly visit the locations (near the charging bases) that were important and had been left unvisited for a long time based on the values of $EL_t^i(v)$. Of course, such agents have the important locations near the charging base, and thus, selecting the greedy strategy was advantageous to observe more events. In contrast, agents with the longer cycle length visited the locations while observing the neighborhood firmly. This strategy might delay the visits of distant important locations somewhat, but they could afford to behave that way. In particular, firm visits by this method was clearly better for

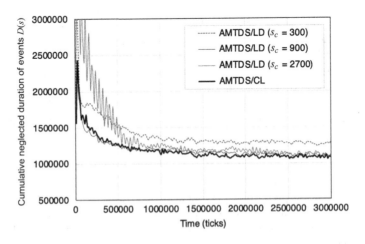

Fig. 7. Improvement in $D(s)$ over time in Office B.

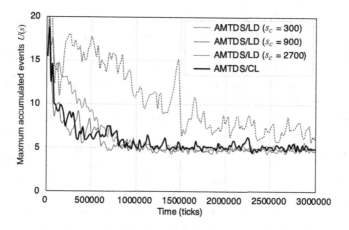

Fig. 8. Improvement in $U(s)$ over time in Office B.

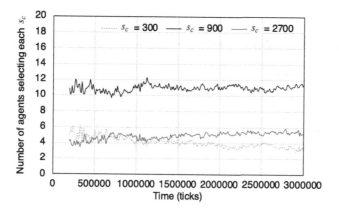

Fig. 9. Number of agents selecting each s_c over time in Office B [18].

patrolling far from the charging base because it was costly to visit far locations. This analysis suggested that agents could decide the target decision strategies according to the ACL values.

5.3 Experiment 2—Effect of Base Locations

Adaptation to Environmental Characteristics. In the second experiment, we evaluated the four types of agents in a slightly different environment where there were six charging bases for each room named "Office B," as shown in Fig. 1(b) because the ACLs may be affected by the distance between the charging bases and the working areas. A charging base in Room n ($n = 0, \ldots, 5$) is denoted by v_{base-n}. We set Agents 0, 1, 2, and 3 to v_{base-0}, Agents 4, 5, and 6 to v_{base-1}, Agents 7, 8, and 9 to v_{base-2}, Agents 10, 11, 12, and 13 to v_{base-3}, Agents 14, 15, and 16 to $v_{base\text{-}4}$, and Agents 17, 18, and 19 to $v_{base\text{-}5}$. The improvement $D(s)$ is plotted in Fig. 7, and $U(s)$ over time in Office B is plotted in Fig. 8.

We can confirm that the efficiency of AMTDS/CL and AMTDS/LD(900) was almost identical from these figures. If we carefully compare Fig. 7 with Fig. 2, the converged performances of $D(s)$ for all methods were almost identical for both performances. However, the convergence of the AMTDS/LD(2700) in Fig. 7 seemed faster, and the performance also seemed stabler than those of AMTDS/LD(2700) in Fig. 2. In Office B, the charging bases were distributed, so the patrol patterns of individual agents differed even if agents had the same length of ACL. Meanwhile, Fig. 8 indicates that agents with AMTDS/LD(300) were the worst and the performance converged very slowly, which differed from the results of the first experiment (see Fig. 3). This indicates that the performance, $U(s)$, also depended on the distance between the charging bases and the work locations. In the second experiment, the areas individual agents visited were distinct, so nodes were covered by a smaller number of agents than in Office A.

Table 3. Number of agents selecting an ACL s_c in Office B [18].

| | Room of charging base | | | | | |
	Room 0	Room 1	Room 2	Room 3	Room 4	Room 5
$s_c = 300$	1.2	0.3	0.2	1.7	0.0	0.0
$s_c = 900$	2.1	1.7	2.3	2.2	2.1	1.0
$s_c = 2700$	0.7	1.0	0.5	0.1	0.9	2.0

Analysis of the Learned ACLs. The number of agents that selected each s_c for AMTDS/CL as shown in Fig. 9, was similar characteristic to Fig. 4. In this experiment, we were interested in the differences in ACL learned on the basis of the locations of agents' charging bases. Table 3 lists the average number of agents that selected $s_c \in S_c^i$ for AMTDS/CL for each charging base location between 2,000,000 and 3,000,000 ticks in Office B. This table shows that 900 was mainly selected as the value of s_c by many agents, but we can observe different characteristics according to agents' base locations. We already knew that 900 was appropriate for this environment; thereby, we focused on and analyzed the agents that selected other ACLs. Table 3 indicates that agents whose charging bases are Room 1, Room 2, and Room 4 were likely to select 900 as ACLs. On the other hand, agents whose charging base was in Room 5 obviously learned that the long ACLs were better. Because they could find only a few events near their base (Room 5 did not have a node with a high $p(v)$), they had to explore nodes farther away to help other agents. Relatively more agents whose bases were in Rooms 0 and 3 selected 300 as their ACL. In these rooms, there were many nodes near the walls with a high $p(v)$ as shown in Fig. 1. Thus, these agents

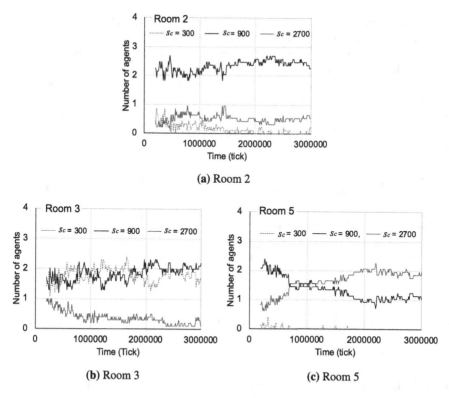

Fig. 10. Number of selected ACLs by agents in Room 2, Room 3 and Room 5.

could find many events near their bases. They could reduce the cost of moving to other rooms and focused on specific nodes in the local rooms by selecting the shorter ACLs. In addition, they could visit nearby nodes at an appropriate and shorter frequency by improving the accuracy of the estimated $p^i(v)$ for the specific nodes.

We also plot in Fig. 10 the selected ACLs by agents whose charging bases were Room 2, Room 3, and Room 5 to identify the differences in the selected ACLs in more detail. First, we could see that agents whose base was in Room 5 selected 900 as their ACL at first, but after that, they gradually changed to 2700. We can explain this change as follows. At first, all agents were likely to select 900 as the ACL since it seemed more appropriate than others. Then, agents whose bases were not in Room 5 focused on nodes near their base and improved their patrol performance. In contrast, agents whose base was Room 5 could find no nodes with high importance values $p^i(v)$ nearby and had to visit more of the other distant rooms to find events. Therefore, it is disadvantageous to select the small ACL ($s_c = 300$) to find more unaware events. This suggests indirect communication through learning of the importance value; therefore, agents could perform the learning of the ACLs for the entire system's performance in a real-time manner thanks to the simultaneous learning of importance $p^i(v)$.

Another finding from Table 3 is that agents whose charging bases were in the centrally located rooms (i.e., Rooms 2 and 3) tended not to choose the longer ACLs, presumably because they do not need a longer cycle to reach the edges of the environment, and the longer ACL was disadvantageous due to the longer charging time. Agents in other rooms have longer ACLs to visit other edges of the environment, and thus, only a few agents chose 2700 as their ACLs.

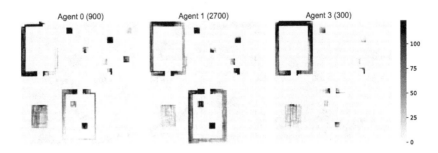

Fig. 11. Heatmap for Visited Locations.

Visited Locations. From our intuition and also from the experimental results, agents with the longer activity cycle length tended to patrol distant locations. To confirm this consideration, we counted the number of the detected events by individual agents. As an example, we show the results of Agents 0, 1, and 3 whose charging base was in Room 0 and their ACLs were 900, 2700, and 300, respectively in Fig. 11, which is the heatmap showing where they found events between 2,000,000 and 3,000,000. Note that agents' behaviors were likely to be affected by the size of areas with high values of $p(v)$. Therefore, their main locations to work were Room 0 because there were many nodes near the walls there.

Figure 11 indicates that agents decided the lengths of ACLs on the basis of their working locations. Agent 3 whose ACL was 300 usually was moving around and found events in Room 0. On the other hand, Agent 1 visited other rooms, especially Room 3 and moved around the area near the walls. Agent 0 also visited Room 3 but moved around near its entrance. Note that the size of the environment was 101 × 101, so Agent 3 could reach any locations in this environment.

6   Conclusion

We proposed an autonomous method for deciding the activity cycle length (ACL), which is how long individual agents act to work in collaborative environments by using reinforcement learning. This method reflects the activities of other collaborative agents, which are also learning mutually to contribute to the entire performance. Although we already reported the preliminary results of the proposed method [18], we have totally recaptured the experimental results for evaluations and have added the detailed analysis and consideration to clarify its effects on the agents' behaviors.

The proposed method to decide their ACLs consists of two learning subprocesses. The first subprocess is dedicated to decide the initial Q-values for possible ACLs because appropriate Q-values are affected by the environmental characteristics and their initial values affect the convergence speed of learning. The second subprocess is to identify their own ACL values with the simultaneous learning of the target decision strategies and the importance of each node, $p_t^i(v)$.

Then, we found that agents with our method, AMTDS/CL, performed effectively comparable with the same efficiency as the best case with a fixed ACL, without giving any prior knowledge on the best ACL and the environmental characteristics in advance. We also analyzed the relationships between the selected ACL and agents' behaviors such as the selected target decision strategies and the locations of working areas. Nodes were covered with a number of agents with different visiting cycles. These results indicated effective covering of the environments without direct communications with each other.

Our future work is to find an activity control strategy in which agents estimate a workload with high accuracy and flexibility to control their activities while taking into account their remaining energy.

References

1. Ahmadi, M., Stone, P.: A multi-robot system for continuous area sweeping tasks. In: Proceedings of the 2006 IEEE International Conference on Robotics and Automation, pp. 1724–1729 (2006)
2. Bentz, W., Panagou, D.: An energy-aware redistribution method for multi-agent dynamic coverage networks. In: 2016 IEEE 55th Conference on Decision and Control (CDC), pp. 2644–2651 (2016). https://doi.org/10.1109/CDC.2016.7798661
3. Cao, Y., Yu, W., Ren, W., Chen, G.: An overview of recent progress in the study of distributed multi-agent coordination. IEEE Trans. Industr. Inf. 9(1), 427–438 (2013). https://doi.org/10.1109/TII.2012.2219061
4. Chen, X., Yum, T.P.: Patrol districting and routing with security level functions. In: 2010 IEEE International Conference on Systems, Man and Cybernetics, pp. 3555–3562, October 2010. https://doi.org/10.1109/ICSMC.2010.5642353
5. Chevaleyre, Y.: Theoretical analysis of the multi-agent patrolling problem. In: Proceedings of Intelligent Agent Technology, pp. 302–308 (2005)
6. Portugal, D., Rocha, R.: A survey on multi-robot patrolling algorithms. In: Camarinha-Matos, L.M. (ed.) DoCEIS 2011. IAICT, vol. 349, pp. 139–146. Springer, Heidelberg (2011). https://doi.org/10.1007/978-3-642-19170-1_15
7. Hasegawa, E., Ishii, Y., Tada, K., Kobayashi, K., Yoshimura, J.: Lazy workers are necessary for long-term sustainability in insect societies. Sci. Rep. 6, 20846 (2016)
8. Jensen, E., Franklin, M., Lahr, S., Gini, M.: Sustainable multi-robot patrol of an open polyline. In: 2011 IEEE International Conference on Robotics and Automation, pp. 4792–4797, May 2011. https://doi.org/10.1109/ICRA.2011.5980279

292 A. Sugiyama et al.

9. Machado, A., Ramalho, G., Zucker, J.-D., Drogoul, A.: Multi-agent patrolling: an empirical analysis of alternative architectures. In: Simão Sichman, J., Bousquet, F., Davidsson, P. (eds.) MABS 2002. LNCS (LNAI), vol. 2581, pp. 155–170. Springer, Heidelberg (2003). https://doi.org/10.1007/3-540-36483-8_11

10. Mersheeva, V., Friedrich, G.: Multi-UAV monitoring with priorities and limited energy resources. In: International Conference on Automated Planning and Scheduling (2015)

11. Pasqualetti, F., Durham, J.W., Bullo, F.: Cooperative patrolling via weighted tours: performance analysis and distributed algorithms. IEEE Trans. Rob. **28**(5), 1181–1188 (2012). https://doi.org/10.1109/TRO.2012.2201293

12. Popescu, M.I., Rivano, H., Simonin, O.: Multi-robot patrolling in wireless sensor networks using bounded cycle coverage. In: 2016 IEEE 28th International Conference on Tools with Artificial Intelligence (ICTAI), pp. 169–176, November 2016. https://doi.org/10.1109/ICTAI.2016.0035

13. Santana, H., Ramalho, G., Corruble, V., Ratitch, B.: Multi-agent patrolling with reinforcement learning. In: Proceedings of the Third International Joint Conference on Autonomous Agents and Multiagent Systems - Volume 3, pp. 1122–1129 AAMAS 2004. IEEE Computer Society, Washington, DC, USA (2004). https://doi.org/10.1109/AAMAS.2004.180

14. Sipahioglu, A., Kirlik, G., Parlaktuna, O., Yazici, A.: Energy constrained multi-robot sensor-based coverage path planning using capacitated arc routing approach. Robot. Auton. Syst. **58**(5), 529–538 (2010). https://doi.org/10.1016/j.robot.2010.01.005

15. Stump, E., Michael, N.: Multi-robot persistent surveillance planning as a vehicle routing problem. In: 2011 IEEE International Conference on Automation Science and Engineering, pp. 569–575 (2011). https://doi.org/10.1109/CASE.2011.6042503

16. Sugiyama, A., Sea, V., Sugawara, T.: Effective task allocation by enhancing divisional cooperation in multi-agent continuous patrolling tasks. In: 2016 IEEE 28th International Conference on Tools with Artificial Intelligence (ICTAI), pp. 33–40, November 2016. https://doi.org/10.1109/ICTAI.2016.0016

17. Sugiyama, A., Sugawara, T.: Improvement of robustness to environmental changes by autonomous divisional cooperation in multi-agent cooperative patrol problem. In: Demazeau, Y., Davidsson, P., Bajo, J., Vale, Z. (eds.) PAAMS 2017. LNCS (LNAI), vol. 10349, pp. 259–271. Springer, Cham (2017). https://doi.org/10.1007/978-3-319-59930-4_21

18. Sugiyama, A., Wu, L., Sugawara, T.: Learning of activity cycle length based on battery limitation in multi-agent continuous cooperative patrol problems. In: Proceedings of the 11th International Conference on Agents and Artificial Intelligence - Volume 1: ICAART, pp. 62–71. INSTICC, SciTePress (2019). https://doi.org/10.5220/0007567400620071

19. Wooldridge, M.: An Introduction to MultiAgent Systems, 2nd edn. Wiley, Hoboken (2009)

20. Yoneda, K., Kato, C., Sugawara, T.: Autonomous learning of target decision strategies without communications for continuous coordinated cleaning tasks. In: 2013 IEEE/WIC/ACM International Joint Conferences on Web Intelligence (WI) and Intelligent Agent Technologies (IAT), vol. 2, pp. 216–223, November 2013. https://doi.org/10.1109/WI-IAT.2013.112

Symmetry Breaking in Evacuation Exit Choice: Impacts of Cognitive Bias and Physical Factor on Evacuation Decision

Akira Tsurushima[✉]

Intelligent Systems Laboratory, SECOM CO., LTD.,
8-10-16 Shimorenjaku, Mitaka, Tokyo, Japan
a-tsurushima@secom.co.jp

Abstract. When people evacuate from a room with two identical exits, it is known that these exits are often unequally used, with evacuees gathering at one of them. This inappropriate and irrational behavior sometimes results in serious loss of life. In this paper, this symmetry breaking in exit choice is discussed from the viewpoint of herding, a cognitive bias in humans during disaster evacuations. The aim of this paper is to show that simple herd behavior is sufficient to reproduce symmetry breaking in exit choice, whereas many models in the literature adopt predefined rules, scenarios, or some models representing rational decision making processes such as utility functions or payoff matrices. The evacuation decision model, based on the response threshold model in biology, is presented to reproduce human herd behavior. Simulation with the evacuation decision model shows that almost all agents gather at one exit at some frequency, despite individual agents choosing the exit randomly. Moreover, the social force model is employed in conjunction with the evacuation decision model to take physical factors such as clogging and collisions into account. The effects of physical factors on both evacuation decisions and evacuation times are analyzed.

Keywords: Response threshold model · Exit choice · Evacuation behavior · Social force model · Emergency decision making

1 Introduction

One of the most critical issue in emergency evacuations is the choice of the right exit. The wrong choice will cause inefficient evacuations which are possible to result in serious loss of life. Much work have been done investigating human exit choice in evacuations. Some of these works point to symmetry breaking in exit choice [10, 16].

Symmetry breaking in exit choice is a phenomenon observed when people evacuate from a room with two identical exits, in which the exits are often unequally used and evacuees gather at one of them. These behaviors result in

© Springer Nature Switzerland AG 2019
J. van den Herik et al. (Eds.): ICAART 2019, LNAI 11978, pp. 293–316, 2019.
https://doi.org/10.1007/978-3-030-37494-5_15

the inefficient use of exits, increasing the total evacuation time. This inefficient use of exits is not necessarily limited to panic situations. It was observed that, even in an evacuation drill conducted at the New National Theater in Tokyo [30], with incorrect routing of the people at the front, all subsequent people followed, resulted in inappropriate evacuation.

Many researchers consider herd behavior, one of the most representative and important cognitive biases in disaster evacuations, to be an underlying mechanism of symmetry breaking in exit choice [2,15,25,31]. Herd behavior, which is caused by the mental tendency to decide one's behavior based on the behavior of others, has been observed in many evacuations including the Three Mile Island nuclear power plan accident [7] and football stadium disasters in the United Kingdom [10]. It has been studied extensively in numerous fields such as economics, sociology, psychology, and biology, and is also known as crowd behavior, conformity bias, peer effect, bandwagon effect and majority syncing bias [9,18,34].

Numerous models have been proposed to represent exit choice in evacuations. However, many of these models consider the major cause of symmetry breaking in exit choice to be either panic [15] or rational behaviors [28]. The aim of this paper is twofold. First, in contrast to the previous works, we show that it can be reproduced by simple herd behaviors without assuming any rational decision making processes or predefined rules or scenarios. Second, we also investigate the effects of physical factors such as collisions, clogging, and disturbances on this phenomenon.

A method is proposed to reproduce symmetry breaking in evacuation through two exits with the use of the evacuation decision model which represents herd behavior in humans [39]. The evacuation decision model is based on the response threshold model in biology. Furthermore, the model does not incorporate predefined rules or scenarios nor assumes the ratio of individualistic and herd behaviors in advance. The model is totally distributed and can automatically coordinates the dynamics of the interaction between leader agents and follower agents.

This paper extends the recent study [40] by taking physical factors surrounding agents into account and analyzed the impact of these physical factors on evacuation decisions and evacuation times. The social force model [15,16] is employed in conjunction with the evacuation decision model to deal with these physical factors. In order to examine the effect of physical factors on symmetry breaking in exit choice, the results are analyzed by comparison with those without the social force model. With varying the population size, the effects of physical factors on evacuation times, another important factors in evacuation, are also analyzed.

The remainder of this paper is organized as follows. Section 2 shows the models of exit choice in the literature. Section 3 discusses herd behavior from the viewpoint of leaders and followers. Section 4 introduces the response threshold model and Sect. 5 presents the evacuation decision model. The simulation model of exit choice is stated in Sect. 6 and the simulation results are analyzed in Sect. 7. In order to take physical factors into account, the new model which incorporates the social force model with the evacuation decision model is proposed in Sect. 8. The results using the new model are presented and analyzed in Sect. 9. The discussion and the conclusion are given in Sects. 10 and 11, respectively.

2   Related Works

Symmetry breaking in exit choice is first introduced by Helbing et al. [15], followed by numerous studies in several fields. Evacuation experiments with human subjects were conducted to investigate several features of human exit choice behaviors [11,22] and a database containing evacuation data including exit choice was developed [37]. It was also found that symmetry breaking in emergency exit choice is not peculiar to human beings, as observed in non-intelligent animals such as ants [2,20] and mice [35].

Multi-agent simulations and cell automaton models have been used to study efficient evacuations in disaster situations. Many models to reproduce human exit choice in evacuations have been proposed by several authors and these models can be categorized into the following five classes.

Rule Based Model

Agents in this class have predefined rules, scenarios, or sequences of actions, and their choice of exits is made by these rules. One example of such a rule is "if an agent detects two exits and its uncertainty level is high, then the agent pursues the exit that has the most crowds" [32]. These rules are built by surveys conducted at target sites and some literature [3], or based on theories such as Cialdini's social proof theory [31], the OCC (Ortony, Clore and Collins) model [36,42], etc. The choice of rules are arbitrary made by designers though there is no widely accepted general way of choosing these rules.

Cell Automaton Model

The cell automaton (CA) model represents collective behaviors of evacuees using a two dimensional matrix with simple rules. This model can efficiently reproduce dynamics of self-organization phenomena such as jamming, clogging, oscillation and so on. The relation between evacuation time and exit width or door separation was studied using the CA model [33]. The floor field model was also used to analyze herd behaviors by varying the length between two exits [21] and in environments with multiple exits and obstacles [19]. One of the strengths of the CA model is its high computational efficiency since the model itself is simple and abstract. However, none of the above was able to reproduce the symmetry breaking in exit choice.

Social Force Model

Helbing et al. introduced the phenomenon of inefficient use of alternative exits in evacuations. They conducted simulations of evacuation from a room with multiple exits filled with smoke using the social force model [15,16]. They showed that some mixture of individualistic and herd behaviors is more efficient than purely individualistic or herd behaviors. However, in their simulations, the relation between exit choice and evacuation efficiency is unclear. What they have shown is the efficiency of *finding* unknown exits in invisible environments, not the evacuation efficiency of *choosing* alternative exits. The agents in their model do not choose exits in any meaningful way since, in the social force model, the desired direction of an agent is predetermined via input to the model.

Game Theory Based Model

Some models assume the existence of a utility function in an agent, with the agent behaving to maximize its utility. In the game theory based model, agents interact with each other and try to achieve Nash equilibrium for the game in order to maximize mutual utilities. In [24] the choice of exits was formulated as a noncooperative game, and the mixed strategy solution of the game was analyzed. In exit choice experiments using ants, the number of ants escaping from different exits was found to be equal to the ratio between the widths of the exits; and this finding was analyzed from the viewpoint of Nash equilibrium [20].

Discrete Choice Model

The discrete choice model assumes that agents make exit choices decisions based on a finite set of attributes associated with the exit alternatives. The utility function of an agent consists of two terms: the first part is the expected value of the perceived utility derived from the attributes, and the second term is its random residual from the real value. A mixed logit model or multinomial logit model is often used to formulate the utility function, and data collected from human subjects are applied to estimate its coefficients. For example, the following factors are used as attributes to formulate the utility function [27].

- Number of evacuees close to the exits
- Flow of evacuees through the exits
- Number of evacuees close to the decision maker towards one of the exits
- Smoke near the exits
- Evacuation lights above the exits
- Distance of the decision maker from the exit

The relation between evacuation time and exit choice strategies (e.g, least distance, least travel time, hive, vision field) was studied using multinomial logit models and an internet survey [8]. Paper-based surveys and face-to-face interviews have been conducted using the SP-off-RP method to formulate the exit choice behaviors using multinomial logit models and mixed logit models [12]. The difference between behavioral features of emergency and non-emergency egress was analyzed using a mixed logit model and face-to-face interviews [13]. Online surveys using video simulations were conducted to formulate a mixed logit model [25,26]. In [27] the effect of the presence of smoke and emergency lighting was analyzed using online surveys with virtual reality and a mixed logit model.

Utility-based models (e.g. game theory-based models and discrete choice models) consider the exit choice decisions as rational behaviors, whereas other models consider them as the result of panic or irrational behaviors [28]. The major limitation of utility based approaches is the assumption that decisions in emergency evacuations can be obtained through surveys and interviews. This is because it is difficult to reproduce the imminent situation of real evacuations, and subjects are only able to respond to questionnaires based on conscious decisions.

In this paper, we propose a novel approach to reproduce the symmetry breakage in exit choice. Our approach, which is able to reproduce herd behaviors in evacuations, is based on the response threshold model in biology. It shows that symmetry breaking in exit choice can be reproduced without assuming any decision making process including rules, scenarios, or utilities. In this approach, the symmetry breaking in exit choice emerges as the result of herd behaviors, even though agents choose the exit randomly.

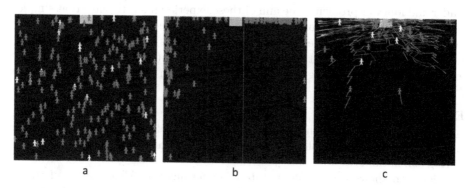

Fig. 1. The leader and follower simulations. (a) Experiment 1 or 2 - initial state, (b) Experiment 1 - terminal state, (c) Experiment 2 - state near the end of the experiment (thin lines following agents indicate their trails) [40].

3   Leaders and Followers in Herding

Raafat et al. [34] defined herding as "the alignment of thoughts or behaviors of individuals in a group (herd) through local interactions rather than centralized coordination." According to this definition, when determining its own behavior, every individual is affected by other surrounding individuals in some way. Meanwhile, no one would be able to act, without assuming that there must at least be one individual that can behave by its own intentions and affects others.

Thus it is reasonable to assume that a herd consists of leaders and followers, where the leaders determine their behaviors through their own intentions and the followers determine their behaviors through the behavior of other leaders or followers. In addition, no individual shall affect or be affected by all the members of the group.

This leads to several questions. How is a leader or follower determined? Is there an appropriate ratio of leaders to followers? Are the roles of the leaders and followers fixed, or do they change dynamically? If they change, what rules affect those changes? To answer to these questions is difficult unless assuming privileged and centralized control mechanisms. This can be called the leader and follower problem.

If the leader and follower problem is focused on evacuation, where a room with a single exit is filled with randomly distributed agents, the goal would be to evacuate all the agents from the room. A leader will be intent on leaving the room and be able to adjust its behaviors accordingly, so clearly it is able to leave the room. On the other hand, a follower determines its own behavior through the behavior of others, regardless of its own intention. In this case, a follower will move toward the exit if many agents move, but will stay put if they do not. Thus, it is unclear whether a follower will be able to leave the room.

Two simulation experiments[1] were conducted to investigate the nature of the leader and follower problem. The aim of these experiments is to show that simple rules of assigning the role of leaders and followers are inadequate to reproduce evacuation behaviors. In these experiments, 200 agents are distributed in a room (33 × 33 units) with an exit (Fig. 1a). A leader agent (white) moves toward the exit but a follower agent (gray) randomly chooses an agent in its vicinity and mimics its movement.

Experiment 1
In experiment 1, 10% of the agents are randomly selected as the leaders and the remaining agents are followers. The roles of the leader and follower are fixed during simulation.

Figure 1b shows the terminal state of experiment 1. All leaders and some followers have evacuated but most of the followers are still in the room. Since they are all followers, they cannot move through their own intention, and thus all of them are unable to move. This is because most followers choose to follow other followers, but only some follow leaders. Chains of followers who do not have a leader will not be able to exit under these conditions. Only followers following a leader will be able to exit.

It is obvious that the assumptions of experiment 1 are not suitable as a solution to the leader and follower problem.

Experiment 2
In experiment 2, 10% of agents are chosen as leaders as in experiment 1, but the roles of the leaders and followers dynamically change during the simulation. Therefore, an agent acts as a leader at certain moments, but acts as a follower at other times. Only the ratio of the leaders and followers is constant.

At the end of the simulation, all agents have left the room. Thus experiment 2 may be a candidate solution of the leader and follower problem. However, as shown in Fig. 1c, some unnatural and wasteful movements (e.g. oscillating back and forth between the two walls) of the followers are observed just before the end of the simulation. Such unnatural movements can be avoided by increasing the ratio of leaders, but it is not obvious what ratio is appropriate. Also, the assumption that the ratio of the leaders and followers is always constant is unrealistic.

---

[1] NetLogo 6.0.2 [41] is used to implement the models presented in this paper.

Derek Sivers pointed out the importance of the first follower in his famous talk at TED2010 and said "the first follower is what transforms a lone nut into a leader"[2]. This implies that there is no leader without any follower, and vice versa. Therefore, leader and follower is a mutual dependence relation since the existence of one can only be supported by the existence of the other.

From the above, we conclude that

- the roles of leaders and followers should change over time
- the assumption that the ratio of leaders to followers is constant is unrealistic.
- leaders and followers is a mutual dependence relation

Hasegawa et al. showed a similar kind of mutual relation between hardworking ants and lazy ants using the response threshold model. There was a negative correlation between hardworking and lazy workers. Lazy workers automatically replaced hardworking but resting workers in processing tasks when the number of hardworking workers decreased [14]. Therefore, the existence of inactive workers is only supported by the existence of active workers, and vice versa. To take these points into account, the response threshold model, which is an ideal model to represent this kind of mutual relationship, is adopted as a model for human herd behaviors in evacuation situations.

4   The Response Threshold Model

The response threshold model [5] is well known in biology and ecology as a model for division of labor in eusocial organisms. It is also known as an efficient distributed algorithm to solve task allocation problems [4] and has a variety of applications in engineering including the coordination of multiple robots [6,23], efficient coverage of distributed mobile sensor networks [29], and distributed allocation of multi-agent systems [1].

The response threshold model consists of agents with response thresholds θ and an environment with task-related stimuli s. An agent responds to the stimuli and engages in a task if s exceeds its θ. The intensity of s will increase if the task is not performed sufficiently and will decrease if a sufficient number of agents are engaged in the task. An agent i has a random variable X representing its mental state. The agent is active if $X = 1$, and inactive if $X = 0$. The probability P_i that an agent will be active per unit time is:

$$P_i(X = 0 \rightarrow X = 1) = \frac{s^2}{s^2 + \theta_i^2}, \tag{1}$$

and inactive per unit time is:

$$P_i(X = 1 \rightarrow X = 0) = \varepsilon, \tag{2}$$

---

[2] https://www.ted.com/talks/derek_sivers_how_to_start_a_movement.

where ε is a constant probability with which an active agent gives up task performance [40]. The intensity of s per unit time is given by:

$$s(t+1) = s(t) + \delta - \alpha\frac{c}{C},\qquad(3)$$

where δ is the increase of the stimulus per unit time, α is a scale factor of the efficiency of task performance, c is the number of agents engaging in the task, and C is the total number of agents [40].

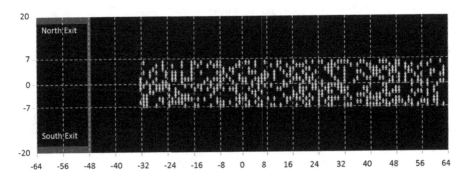

Fig. 2. The initial screen of the simulation [40].

5   The Evacuation Decision Model

In this paper, the evacuation decision model [39], based on the response threshold model, which reproduced the evacuation behaviors observed at the Great East Japan Earthquake [38], is adopted to study symmetry breaking in exit choice in evacuations.

By designating the task to be performed as removing all agents from the room, the evacuation decision model can be applied for solving the leader and follower problem in order to represent human herd behaviors. The environment (the room) has a risk value r which represents the level of objective risks in the environment, and an agent has risk perception parameter μ which represents an individual's risk sensitivity.

In contrast to the model (Eq. 3) discussed in Sect. 4, each agent in this model has its own stimulus s_i which is the local estimate of the stimulus s instead of the global stimulus of the environment. The stimulus of the agent i is defined as:

$$s_i(t+1) = max\{s_i(t) + \hat{\delta} - \alpha(1-R)F, \, 0\},\qquad(4)$$

where $\hat{\delta}$ is the increase of the stimulus per unit of time

$$\hat{\delta} = \begin{cases} \delta & \text{if } r > 0 \\ 0 & \text{otherwise,} \end{cases}\qquad(5)$$

α is a scale factor of the stimulus [40]. R is the risk perception which is the function of r:

$$R(r) = \frac{1}{1 + e^{-g(r-\mu_i)}},\tag{6}$$

where g is the activation gain which determines the slope of the sigmoid function [40]. F is the task progress function, the local estimate of task performance:

$$F(n) = \begin{cases} 1 - n/N_{max} & n < N_{max} \\ 0 & \text{otherwise,} \end{cases}\tag{7}$$

where n is the number of agents in the vicinity, and N_{max} is the maximum number of agents in the vicinity [40]. Each agent has a visibility of 120° and a sight distance of five units toward the west direction. This range is considered the vicinity of an agent.

Algorithm 1. Follower's action ($X = 0$).

1: $V \leftarrow$ the set of agents in the vicinity
2: $v_0 \leftarrow$ the number of agents not moving in V
3: $v_1 \leftarrow$ the number of agents moving in V
4: **if** $v_1 > v_0$ **then**
5:     $M \leftarrow$ a set of the moving agents in the vicinity
6:     $e_N \leftarrow$ the number of agents with $d = north$ in M
7:     $e_S \leftarrow$ the number of agents with $d = south$ in M
8:     $e_W \leftarrow$ the number of agents with $d = undecided$ in M
9:     **if** e_N is the maximum **then**
10:         $d \leftarrow north$
11:         Solve **problem(Find Step North)** with respect to $\Delta x(t)$ and $\Delta y(t)$
12:     **else if** e_S is the maximum **then**
13:         $d \leftarrow south$
14:         Solve **problem(Find Step South)** with respect to $\Delta x(t)$ and $\Delta y(t)$
15:     **else if** e_W is the maximum **then**
16:         $d \leftarrow undecided$
17:         Solve **problem(Find Step West)** with respect to $\Delta x(t)$ and $\Delta y(t)$
18:     **end if**
19:     $x(t + 1) \leftarrow x(t) + \Delta x(t)$, $y(t + 1) \leftarrow y_i(t) + \Delta y(t)$
20: **else**
21:     do nothing
22: **end if**

---

6   The Exit Choice Simulation

We assumed a rectangular room (40×128 units) with four walls in the directions north, east, south, and west clockwise from the top, with two exits at the west end of the room, where the north and south exits are located at the top left

---

Algorithm 2. Leader's action $(X = 1)$.

1: $cx \leftarrow$ the X-coordinate of the current position
2: $gx \leftarrow$ the X-coordinate of G-line
3: **if** $cx \leq gx$ **and** $d = undecided$ **then**
4:    $randValue \leftarrow$ randomly select a value $\in [0, 1]$
5:    **if** $randValue < 0.5$ **then**
6:       $d \leftarrow north$
7:       Solve **problem(Find Step North)** with respect to $\Delta x(t)$ and $\Delta y(t)$
8:    **else**
9:       $d \leftarrow south$
10:       Solve **problem(Find Step South)** with respect to $\Delta x(t)$ and $\Delta y(t)$
11:    **end if**
12: **else**
13:    Solve **problem(Find Step West)** with respect to $\Delta x(t)$ and $\Delta y(t)$
14: **end if**
15: $x(t + 1) \leftarrow x(t) + \Delta x(t)$, $y(t + 1) \leftarrow y_i(t) + \Delta y(t)$

---

and bottom left, respectively (Fig. 2). As shown in Fig. 2, there are 600 agents initially distributed in the middle of the room in a rectangular shape (14×96 units) and start moving to the west according to the risk level r.

The initial coordinates of an agent at time 0 are given by $x(0) \sim U(-32, 64)$ and $y(0) \sim U(-7, 7)$. Assuming $\Delta x(0) = -1$ and $\Delta y(0) = 0$, the difference vector to the new coordinates at time t $(\Delta x(t), \Delta y(t))$ will be given by solving any one of **Problem(Find Step North)**, **Problem(Find Step South)**, or **Problem(Find Step West)** where $x(t)$ and $y(t)$ are the x- and y- coordinates of the agent at time t; GN_x and GN_y are the x- and y- coordinates of the north exit; and GS_x and GS_y are the x- and y- coordinates of the south exit.

Problem (Find Step North)

$$minimize \quad (x(t) + \Delta x(t) - GN_x)^2 \; + \; (y(t) + \Delta y(t) - GN_y)^2 \qquad (8)$$
$$subject\ to \quad \Delta x(t)^2 \; + \; \Delta y(t)^2 \; = \; 1.0 \qquad (9)$$

Problem (Find Step South)

$$minimize \quad (x(t) + \Delta x(t) - GS_x)^2 \; + \; (y(t) + \Delta y(t) - GS_y)^2 \qquad (10)$$
$$subject\ to \quad \Delta x(t)^2 \; + \; \Delta y(t)^2 \; = \; 1.0 \qquad (11)$$

Problem (Find Step West)

$$\Delta x(t) \; = \; \Delta x(t - 1), \quad \Delta y(t) \; = \; \Delta y(t - 1) \qquad (12)$$

The northern and southern sections of the room are initially left empty at the beginning of the simulation because each agent will choose either *north* or *south* direction later (the initial choice of the direction is set to *undecided*). The gray vertical line at -48 (G-line) indicates the position where an agent must decide to go to the northern or southern exit, if its direction is not determined by herd behavior ($X = 0$). This decision is only made if the mental state of the agent is a leader ($X = 1$); and the choice of north or south is made at random (choose north with probability 0.5). Assuming $d = undecided$ and $X = 0$ as initial settings, an agent will perform Algorithm 1 if it is a follower ($X = 0$) or Algorithm 2 if it is a leader ($X = 1$). An agent executes Algorithm 1 or Algorithm 2 every unit of time [40].

Thus the follower may determine its direction even though it has not yet crossed G-line. The parameters of the evacuation decision model are assumed to be $\varepsilon = 0.8$, $\delta = 0.5$, $\alpha = 1.2$, $N_{max} = 10$, and $g = 1.0$.

7 Results and Analysis 1

We conducted the same experiments as in [40] with a few changes. Initial coordinates of agents are in real numbers instead of integers to prevent multiple agents from being assigned to the same location. Algorithm 2 is performed every time unit whenever the agent is a leader, whereas it was executed with a probability of 0.5 in [40].

As shown in Fig. 3, in many cases, the agents are equally divided between north and south exits. Despite the fact that each agent randomly chooses north or south, most agents will automatically head toward the closer exit.

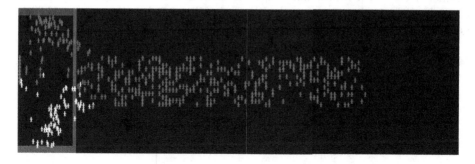

Fig. 3. The exit choice simulation [40].

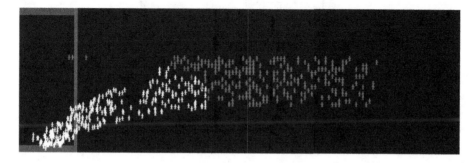

Fig. 4. Symmetry breaking in the exit choice simulation. Notice the arc when agents choose the same exit [40].

Sometimes almost all agents happen to choose the same direction and gather at one exit (Fig. 4). In this figure, the decisions of the white agents, which move to the south direction, propagate far to the east from G-line (the arc in the figure). This kind of behavior is commonly observed when many agents choose the same direction.

The entropy of the agents that select north or south can be expressed by the following equation:

$$H = -r_n log(r_n) - r_s log(r_s), \qquad (13)$$

where r_n is the ratio of the agents heading north and r_s is the ratio of the agents heading south at the end of the simulation [40]. The range of H is $H \in [0.0, 1.0]$. The ratios of the agents moving north and south are equal if $H = 1.0$, and all the agents moving toward the same direction if $H = 0.0$. The frequency of H over 300 simulations is shown in Fig. 5. Although the frequency is small, the phenomenon where most of the agents gathered at a single exit was observed.

Figure 6 shows how the difference between the number of agents choosing north and south (D) varies with the probability to choose the north exit. For example, $D = 600$ means all agents evacuated from the north and $D = -600$ means all agents evacuated from the south. The figure shows that most agents may happen to gather at the opposite (south) exit even though leaders chose the north exit with a probability greater than 0.5. For instance, there was a case where the leaders chose north with probability 0.8, but 456 agents (76.0%) gathered at the south exit.

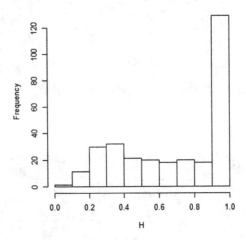

Fig. 5. The frequency of H.

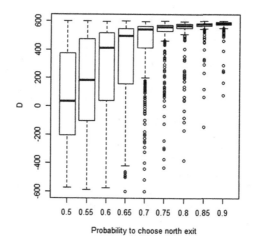

Fig. 6. The distribution of D with different probabilities.

The value of ε and the position of G-line are major factors that affect the value of H. Figure 7 shows the results of simulations varying the value of ε from 0.1 to 0.9. The values of H in each simulation are shown in Fig. 7 (small circles on dotted lines). The means of 100 simulations with different ε are shown by the broken line and the standard deviations are shown by the dotted line. In Fig. 7, the symmetry breakings are observed when ε is greater than 0.2 and the means of H tends to decrease as the values of ε increase. This implies that the greater chances of herd behavior results in the symmetry breakings.

Figure 8 shows the results of simulations where the position of G-line was moved from -48 to $+48$. In Fig. 8, the X-axis shows the position of G-line. The G-lines in Figs. 3 and 4 are located at -48, and the center of the room is at 0. The values of H in each simulation are shown in Fig. 8 (small circles on dotted lines). The means of 100 simulations with different G-line positions are shown by the broken line and the standard deviations are shown by the dotted line. This shows that the mean of H tends to decrease as the position of G-line shifts to east, meaning that an earlier decision results in the uneven use of two exits. An earlier decision implies that the agents have more chances to be affected by others because all agents move in the same direction and the traveling time of an agent moving along with others who have already chosen their direction increases.

The long arc of white agents in Fig. 4 shows that when symmetry breaking happens, many agents have already made decisions well before G-line. The results of 200 simulations in which the position of G-line is set to -48 are given in Fig. 9. This shows the correlation of the values of H and the maximum distances between G-line and the positions of decisions made by the agents (X-axis). The correlation coefficient of -0.3402 suggests that a longer arc will result in a smaller H.

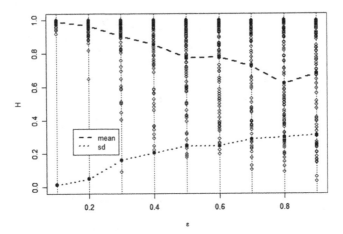

Fig. 7. Relationship between ε and H over 50 simulations.

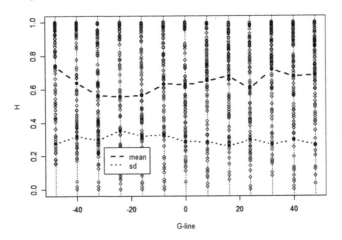

Fig. 8. Relationship between position of G-line and H over 50 simulations.

In Fig. 9, some samples with long arcs and large H values are observed, whereas no samples with short arcs and small H value is observed. This suggest that the long arc of agents may be an important factor in symmetry breaking in the exit choice problem.

Figure 10 shows the values of H in 50 simulations each with varying the number of agents to 200, 300, 400, 500, 600, 700, and 800. The means of H is close to 1.0 in most cases, meaning that the choices of the exits are nearly symmetrical besides with a few symmetry breaking cases. This indicates that the difference in the number of agents has little effect on the value of H (Fig. 10).

Furthermore, we also investigate the evacuation time, one of the most critical issues in disaster evacuation. Figure 11 shows the evacuation times of the agents in 50 simulations each with varying the number of agents to 200, 300, 400, 500,

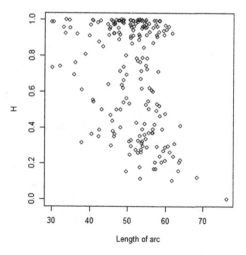

Fig. 9. Correlation of arc length of agents and H.

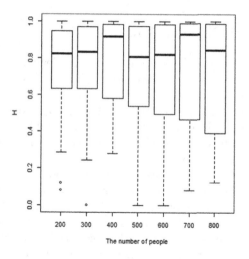

Fig. 10. The values of H in different population size.

600, 700, and 800. The upper items are the times that the 90% of the agents have completed the evacuation and the lower times shows the evacuation times of the firts 10% of the agents. This means that most agents (80%) have evacuated between these two periods. The figure shows that the higher the population density, the shorter the time to complete evacuation.

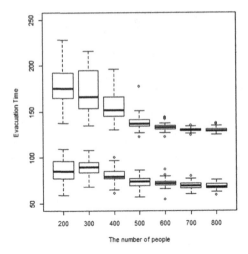

Fig. 11. Evacuation Time in different population size.

8   Incorporated Physical Factors

The evacuation decision model discussed so far only deals with cognitive or psychological factors such as decision, perception, and bias; physical factors such as collision, clogging, and disturbance are not considered at all. An agent can simply pass through other agents, even though they are positioned in front of it. In this sense, the results of the evacuation decision model differ from the real evacuation. In order to address this problem, other models that can deal with these physical factors can be employed in conjunction with the evacuation decision model. The simplicity of the evacuation decision model facilitates integration with other models. The social force model is adopted for this purpose.

The social force model is developed by Helbing et al. to represent behaviors of pedestrians [17], and it has been used in a wide variety of pedestrian simulation models including several commercial packages. The social force model was later extended to represent human behavior in disaster evacuation, and some evacuation-specific behaviors were analyzed and demonstrated including freezing by heating, arch-like blocking of an exit, faster-is-slower effect, phantom panics, and symmetry breaking in exit choice [15,16]. The social force model refers to Newton's second low of motion; it uses virtual forces, called the social force, acting between people and other objects. The simple form of the social force model is given as:

$$m_i \frac{dv_i}{dt} = m_i \frac{v_i^0(t)e_i^0(t) - v_i(t)}{\tau_i} + \sum_{j(\neq i)} f_{ij} + \sum_W f_{iW} \qquad (14)$$

where m_i is the mass of an agent i, dv_i/dt is the change of velocity at time t, v_i^0 is the desired speed, v_i^0 is the desired speed, e_i^0 is the desired direction, f_{ij}

is the interaction force acting between the agent i and agent j, and f_{iW} is the interaction force between the agent i and the walls. In the social force model, the desired speed $v_i^0(t)$ and the desired direction $e_i^0(t)$ are given as an input. Thus, assuming that all agents have a constant velocity, the desired vector $v_i^0(t)e_i^0(t)$ of the social force model is given by $(\Delta x(t), \Delta y(t))$ which is the difference vector to the new coordinates in the evacuation decision model (Fig. 12). The new coordinates of the agents can be calculated by the social force model base on $(\Delta x(t), \Delta y(t))$, whereas they are calculated in the step 19 in Algorithm 1 and the step 15 in Algorithm 2.

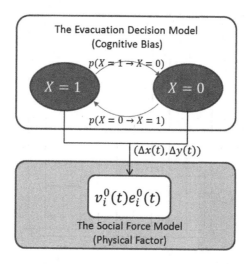

Fig. 12. Connecting the evacuation decision model with the social force model.

Since the time step of the social force model is usually smaller than that of the evacuation decision model, it is necessary to adjust these two in some way. In our simulation, the time step of the evacuation decision model is set to 1.0 time unit, while that of the social force model is 0.05. Therefore, the basic time unit of the simulation is set to 0.05, and the evacuation decision model is executed with updating the desired vector of the social force model $v_i^0(t)e_i^0(t)$ once in every 20 times the social force model is called.

The same simulations stated in Sect. 6 are conducted to examine the effects of physical factors, the results are given in Sect. 9.

9   Results and Analysis 2

Figure 13 is a simulation result when the social force model is incorporated. As shown in this figure, almost all agents select the same (south) exit even if the social force model is employed in conjunction with the evacuation decision model.

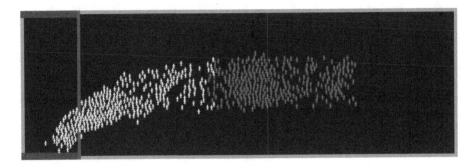

Fig. 13. Symmetry breaking when the social force model is incorporated.

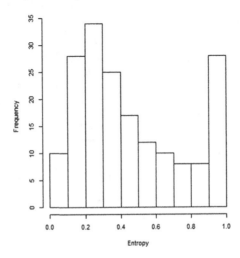

Fig. 14. The frequency of H when the social force model is incorporated.

This figure demonstrates that physical factors do not prevent the occurrence of symmetry breaking in exit choice.

Figure 14 shows the frequency of the values of H, which indicate symmetry or asymmetry of the exit choices, over 180 simulations when adopting the social force model. In contrast to Fig. 5, this figure reveals that rather than symmetrical exit choice, asymmetrical exit choice occurs significantly more frequently if physical factors are taken into account.

Figure 15 shows that the values of H over 50 simulations each when the number of agents is changed to 200, 300, 400, 500, 600, 700, and 800. Compared with Fig. 10, the values of H in Fig. 15 are much smaller, symmetry breaking occurs more frequently, especially in the higher population ranges, and the means of H decrease as population increase. This implies that physical factor has a significant effect on exit choice decision in evacuation.

Figure 16 shows the evacuation completion times in 50 simulations varying the number of agents to 200, 300, 400, 500, 600, 700, and 800. The upper items are

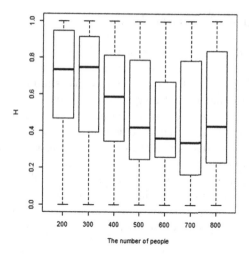

Fig. 15. The values of H in different population size when the social force model is incorporated.

Table 1. The mean evacuation time and H with varying V.

V	10%	90%	100%	H
0.5	75.86	136.92	268.80	0.5202
1.0	84.92	166.94	259.14	0.5084
1.5	93.68	233.40	280.98	0.4911
2.0	107.60	264.60	340.22	0.5261

the evacuation completion times of the first 90% of the agents and the lower items are those of the first 10% of the agents. Compared with Fig. 11, the evacuation completion times increase significantly in the higher population ranges, while they are almost equivalent in the lower population ranges, if physical factors are taken into account.

Note that the parameter sensitivity of the social force model may result in different results. In our implementations of the social force model, there is a parameter V which controls the distance from which an agent will take other agents into account when computing interaction forces. In the simulations discussed so far, the parameter V was set to 1.0 unit. Table 1 shows the mean evacuation times of the first 10%, 90%, and 100% of the agents and the values of H in 50 simulations with different V values. Table 1 shows that evacuation times increase as the value of V increase, however the means of H are indifferent even if the parameter V is changed. Figure 16 might be changed depending on the parameter V. In contrast, the results of Fig. 15, the effects of physical factors on evacuation decisions, are unchanged because they are independent of the parameter V.

10   Discussion and Future Work

Lovreglio et al. stated that the evacuation decision of choosing the most crowded exit can be the result of a rational decision making process instead of an "irrational-panic" decision [28]. In our exit choice simulation, the evacuation decision model shows that even though an agent selects exits randomly, with some frequency we can observe almost all agents gathering at one exit. This shows that symmetry breaking in exit choice during evacuation can be the result of simple herd behavior, disregarding any rational decision making processes. The fact that the same phenomenon can be observed in experiments using organisms without intelligence such as ants and mice [2, 20, 35] also supports our result. Furthermore, our results also show that herd behavior is a major factor of this phenomenon and that the parameter ε and the arc length of agents, indicating early decision making, especially affect the occurrence of symmetry breaking in the exit choice.

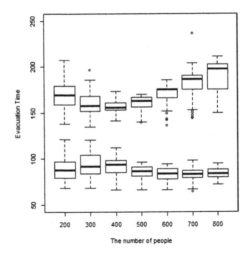

Fig. 16. The evacuation times in different population size when the social force model is incorporated.

Physical factors surrounding an agent such as collisions, clogging, and disturbances are taken into account by incorporating the social force model with the evacuation decision model. Figures 10 and 15 show that physical factors increase the value of H, meaning that uneven exit choice occurs more frequently, especially when population density increases. Figures 11 and 16 show that physical factors also increase evacuation times in the higher population ranges, whereas evacuation times in the lower population ranges are indifferent. Thus, the effect of physical factors on evacuation time is considered to be somewhat moderate. It is intriguing that physical factor have a greater impact on evacuation decision than evacuation time, since the fact that physical factors such as collision and clogging increase evacuation time is obvious, while the correlation between physical factor and evacuation decision is unknown. Table 1 suggests that the results of evacuation time might be parameter dependent, while the results of evacuation decision do not. The fact that physical factors have major impact on evacuation decisions remains unchanged.

The evacuation decision model is a bio-inspired distributed task allocation algorithm based on the response threshold model. The model itself is simple, simply switching between two mental states, $X = 0$ and $X = 1$, in some probabilistic manner. What to do in these states is not stated and is open to the user, giving broad generality to the model. In the case of the exit choice simulation, we chose Algorithms 1 and 2 for $X = 0$ and $X = 1$, respectively. The evacuation decision model only represents the cognitive bias in evacuation, but for actual evacuation scenarios, the consideration of physical factors is necessary; and, especially in the case of human evacuation, higher cognitive functions such as choosing the shortest route are also very important to consider.

The generality of the evacuation decision model allows these factors to be easily incorporated. By assuming the output as a movement vector, the evacuation decision model can be employed easily in conjunction with a physical pedestrian dynamics model such as Helbing's social force model, as shown in this paper. The higher cognitive model which represents intentional decision making can be incorporated in the state $X = 1$. This can be done easily by replacing the Algorithm 2, the leader's action by this model. The following models may be able to used to represent human higher cognitions: the utility theory based model, the game theory based model, or the BDI (Belief-Desire-Intension) model. The analysis of the effects of the higher cognitive model will be an important issue for future research.

In this paper, we do not claim that rational decisions are irrelevant to evacuation decision making. It is rather natural for evacuees to choose the closest exit when choosing an emergency exit. What we mean here is that herding is a sufficient condition to reproduce symmetry breaking in emergency exit choice. Rational decision making processes can easily be incorporated in the leader's action ($X = 1$) of the evacuation decision model, if it is necessary.

The evacuation decision model can be viewed as a platform that separates a higher cognitive model and a physical model, and then naturally connects these two by introducing the layer of cognitive bias.

11 Conclusion

The evacuation decision model, based on the response threshold model in biology, represents human herd behavior in evacuation situations. The exit choice simulation with the evacuation decision model shows that almost all evacuees gather at one exit at a non-negligible frequency even though they choose exits randomly. The results show that exit choice decision can be the result of simple herd behaviors disregarding any rational decision. The simulation also showed the relation between these inappropriate uses of exits and earlier decision making. Furthermore, in order to examine the effects of physical factors, the social force model is incorporated with the evacuation decision model. Physical factors such as collision, clogging, and disturbance increase both the frequency of asymmetrical exit choices and evacuation times. The effect of physical factors on evacuation decision making is stronger than evacuation times.

Acknowledgements. The author is grateful to Robert Ramirez, Yoshikazu Shinoda, and Kei Marukawa for their helpful comments and suggestions.

References

1. Agassounon, W., Martinoli, A.: Efficiency and robustness of threshold-based distributed allocation algorithms in multi-agent systems. In: Proceedings of the First International Joint Conference on Autonomous Agents and Multiagent Systems, AAMAS 2002, vol. 3, pp. 1090–1097 (2002)
2. Altshuler, E., Ramos, O., Nuñez, Y., Fernández, J., Batista-Leyva, A.J., Noda, C.: Symmetry breaking in escaping ants. Am. Nat. **166**(6), 643–649 (2005)
3. Augustijn-Beckers, E.W., Flacke, J., Retsios, B.: Investigating the effect of different pre-evacuation behavior and exit choice strategies using agent-based modeling. Proc. Eng. **3**, 23–35 (2010)
4. Bonabeau, E., Sobkowski, A., Theraulaz, G., Deneubourg, J.L.: Adaptive task allocation inspired by a model of division of labor in social insects. In: Proceeding of Biocomputing and Emergent Computation, pp. 36–45 (1997)
5. Bonabeau, E., Theraulaz, G., Deneubourg, J.L.: Quantitative study of the fixed threshold model for the regulation of division of labour in insect societies. Proc. Roy. Soc. B **263**(1376), 1565–1569 (1996)
6. Castello, E., et al.: Adaptive foraging for simulated and real robotic swarms: the dynamical response threshold approach. Swarm Intell. **10**(1), 1–31 (2016)
7. Cutter, S., Barnes, K.: Evacuation behavior and three mile island. Disasters **6**(2), 116–124 (1982)
8. Duives, D.C., Mahmassani, H.S.: Exit choice decisions during pedestrian evacuations of buildings. Transp. Res. Rec. J. Transp. Res. Board **2316**, 84–94 (2012)
9. Dyer, J.R.G., et al.: Consensus decision making in human crowds. Anim. Behav. **75**, 461–470 (2008)
10. Elliott, D., Smith, D.: Football stadia disasters in the United Kingdom: learning from tragedy? Ind. Environ. Cris. Q. **7**(3), 205–229 (1993)
11. Fridolf, K., Ronchi, E., Nilsson, D., Frantzich, H.: Movement speed and exit choice in smoke-filled rail tunnels. Fire Saf. J. **59**, 8–21 (2013)
12. Haghani, M., Ejtemai, O., Sarvi, M., Sobhani, A., Burd, M., Aghabayk, K.: Random utility models of pedestrian crowd exit selection based on SP-off-RP experiments. Trans. Res. Proc. **2**, 524–532 (2014)
13. Haghani, M., Sarvi, M.: Human exit choice in crowd built environments: investigating underlying behavioural differences between normal egress and emergency evacuations. Fire Saf. J. **85**, 1–9 (2016)
14. Hasegawa, E., Ishii, Y., Tada, K., Kobayashi, K., Yoshimura, J.: Lazy workers are necessary for long-term sustainability in insect societies. Sci. Rep. **6** (2016). Article number: 20846. https://doi.org/10.1038/srep20846
15. Helbing, D., Farkas, I., Vicsek, T.: Simulating dynamical features of escape panic. Nature **407**(28), 487–490 (2000). http://angel.elte.hu/panic/

16. Helbing, D., Farkas, I.J., Molnar, P., Vicsek, T.: Simulation of pedestrian crowds in normal and evacuation situations. Pedestr. Evacuation Dyn. **21**(2), 21–58 (2002)

17. Helbing, D., Molnár, P.: Social force model for pedestrian dynamics. Phys. Rev. E **51**(5), 4282–4289 (1995)

18. Henrich, J., Boyd, R.: The evolution of conformist transmission and the emergence of between-group differences. Evol. Hum. Behav. **19**, 215–241 (1998)

19. Huang, H.J., Guo, R.Y.: Static floor field and exit choice for pedestrian evacuation in rooms with internal obstacles and multiple exits. Phys. Rev. E **78**, 021131 (2008)

20. Ji, Q., Xin, C., Tang, S., Huang, J.: Symmetry associated with symmetry break: revisiting ants and humans escaping from multiple-exit rooms. Phys. A (2017). https://doi.org/10.1016/j.physa.2017.11.024

21. Kirchner, A., Schadschneider, A.: Simulation of evacuation processes using a bionics-inspired cellular automaton model for pedestrian dynamics. Phys. A **312**, 260–276 (2002)

22. Kobes, M., Helsloot, I., de Vries, B., Post, J.: Exit choice, (pre-)movement time and (pre-)evacuation behavior in hotel fire evacuation - Behavioural analysis and validation of the use of serious gaming in experimental research. Proc. Eng. **3**, 37–51 (2010)

23. Krieger, M.J.B., Billeter, J.B., Keller, L.: Ant-like task allocation and recruitment in cooperative robots. Nature **406**, 992–995 (2000)

24. Lo, S., Huang, H., Wang, P., Yuen, K.: A game theory based exit selection model for evacuation. Fire Saf. J. **41**, 364–369 (2006)

25. Lovreglio, R., Fonzone, A., dell'Olio, L., Ibeas, A.: The role of herding behaviour in exit choice during evacuation. Proc. Soc. Behav. Sci. **160**, 390–399 (2014)

26. Lovreglio, R., Borri, D., dell'Olio, L., Ibeas, A.: A discrete choice model based on random utilities for exit choice in emergency evacuations. Saf. Sci. **62**, 418–426 (2014)

27. Lovreglio, R., Fonzone, A., dell'Olio, L.: A mixed logit model for predicting exit choice during building evacuations. Transaportation Res. Part A Policy Pract. **92**, 59–75 (2016)

28. Lovreglio, R., Fonzone, A., dell'Olio, L., Borri, D.: A study of herding behaviour in exit choice during emergencies based on random utility theory. Saf. Sci. **82**, 421–431 (2016)

29. Low, K.H., Leow, W.K., Ang Jr., M.H.: Task allocation via self-organizing swarm coalitions in distributed mobile sensor network. In: AAAI 2004 Proceedings of the 19th National Conference on Artificial Intelligence, pp. 28–33 (2004)

30. Onishi, M., Yamashita, T., Hoshikawa, T., Sato, K.: Transmission of knowledge for evacuation drill using pedestrian tracking and simulation - example of opera concert with evacuation drill in new national theater, Tokyo. In: Handouts in SIGCONF 2015. The Japanese Society for Artificial Intelligence SIG-KST-026-06 (2015)

31. Pan, X.: Computational modeling of human and social behaviour for emergency egress analysis. Ph.D. thesis, Stanford University (2006)

32. Pan, X., Han, C.S., Law, K.H.: A multi-agent based simulation framework for the study of human and social behaviour in egress analysis. In: 2005 International Conference on Computing in Civil Engineering, pp. 1–12 (2005)

33. Perez, G.J., Tapang, G., Lim, M., Saloma, C.: Streaming, disruptive interference and power-law behavior in the exit dynamics of confined pedestrians. Phys. A **312**, 609–618 (2002)

34. Raafat, R.M., Chater, N., Frith, C.: Herding in humans. Trends Cogn. Sci. **13**(10), 420–428 (2009)

35. Saloma, C., Perez, G.J., Tapang, G., Lim, M., Palmes-Saloma, C.: Self-organized queuing and scale-free behavior in real escape panic. PNAS **100**(21), 11947–11952 (2003)

36. Sharpanskykh, A., Treur, J.: Adaptive modelling of social decision making by agents integrating simulated behaviour and perception chains. In: Pan, J.-S., Chen, S.-M., Nguyen, N.T. (eds.) ICCCI 2010. LNCS (LNAI), vol. 6421, pp. 284–295. Springer, Heidelberg (2010). https://doi.org/10.1007/978-3-642-16693-8_31

37. Shi, L., Xie, Q., Cheng, X., Chen, L., Zhou, Y., Zhang, R.: Developing a database for emergency evacuation model. Build. Environ. **44**, 1724–1729 (2009)

38. Tsurushima, A.: Simulating earthquake evacuation decisions based on herd behavior. In: Proceedings of the 35th Annual Meeting of the Japanese Cognitive Science Society (2018)

39. Tsurushima, A.: Modeling herd behavior caused by evacuation decision making using response threshold. In: Davidsson, P., Verhagen, H. (eds.) MABS 2018. LNCS (LNAI), vol. 11463, pp. 138–152. Springer, Cham (2019). https://doi.org/10.1007/978-3-030-22270-3_11

40. Tsurushima, A.: Reproducing symmetry breaking in exit choice under emergency evacuation situation using response threshold model. In: Proceedings of the 11th International Conference on Agents and Artificial Intelligence, ICAART, vol. 1, pp. 31–41. INSTICC, SciTePress (2019). https://doi.org/10.5220/0007256000310041

41. Wilensky, U.: NetLogo. Center for Connected Learning and Computer-Based Modeling, Northwestern University, Evanston, IL (1999). http://ccl.northwestern.edu/netlogo/

42. Zia, K., Riener, A., Ferscha, A., Sharpanskykh, A.: Evacuation simulation based on cognitive decision making model in a socio-technical system. In: 15th IEEE/ACM International Symposium on Distributed Simulation and Real Time Applications, pp. 98–107 (2011)

The Effect of Laziness on Agents for Large Scale Global Optimization

Jörg Bremer$^{(\boxtimes)}$ and Sebastian Lehnhoff

University of Oldenburg, 26129 Oldenburg, Germany
{joerg.bremer,sebastian.lehnhoff}@uni-oldenburg.de

Abstract. Practical optimization problems from engineering often suffer from non-convexity and rugged, multi-modal fitness or error landscapes and are thus hard to solve. Especially in the high-dimensional case, a lack of derivatives entails additional challenges to heuristics. High-dimensionality leads to an exponential increase in search space size and tightens the problem of premature convergence. Parallelization for acceleration often involves domain-specific knowledge for data domain partition or functional or algorithmic decomposition. On the other hand, fully decentralized agent-based procedures for global optimization based on coordinate descent and gossiping have no specific decomposition needs and can thus be applied to arbitrary optimization problems. Premature convergence can be mitigated by introducing laziness. We scrutinized the effectiveness of different levels of laziness on different types of optimization problems and for the first time applied the approach to a real-world optimization problem: to predictive scheduling in virtual power plant orchestration. The lazy agent approach turns out to be competitive and often superior to the non-lazy one and to standard heuristics in many cases including the real world problem.

Keywords: Global optimization · Distributed optimization ·
Multi-agent systems Lazy agents · Coordinate descent optimization ·
Predictive scheduling

1 Introduction

Many real-world optimization problems from engineering are hard to solve and can be formulated as global optimization problem [65], i.e. as a problem with non-convex objective functions and multiple (local) minima where the task is to find the global minimum. Global optimization comprises many problems in practice as well as in the scientific community. These problems are often hallmarked by presence of a rugged fitness landscape, high dimensionality and non-linearity. Thus optimization algorithms are likely to become stuck in local optima and guaranteeing the exact optimum is often intractable.

Some global optimization problems have so far been successfully solved by exact solvers and a number of software packages can be found that reliably

© Springer Nature Switzerland AG 2019
J. van den Herik et al. (Eds.): ICAART 2019, LNAI 11978, pp. 317–337, 2019.
https://doi.org/10.1007/978-3-030-37494-5_16

solve many global optimization problems in small (and sometimes larger) dimensions [44]. Complete methods reach a global optimum with certainty, assuming exact computations and indefinitely long run time, but are in general not efficient enough for industrial size, high-dimensions problems when applied to online problem solving [65].

Global optimization of non-convex, non-linear problems has long been subject to research [4,33]. Approaches can roughly be classified into deterministic and probabilistic methods. Deterministic approaches like interval methods [21], Cutting Plane methods [67], or Lipschitzian methods [25] often suffer from intractability of the problem or getting stuck in some local optimum [60]. In case of a rugged fitness landscape of multi-modal, non-linear functions, probabilistic heuristics are often indispensable. For many problems, derivative free methods are needed, too [56].

Many optimization approaches have so far been proposed for solving these problems; among them are evolutionary methods or swarm-based methods [4, 19,22,35,60,63]. Sometimes model-based or response surface methods are used where a model of the objective function is concurrently learned and improved in case no closed form of the objective is available [42]. Such problems for example occur in Smart Grid management [72].

In order to accelerate execution, parallel implementations based on a distribution model on an algorithmic level, iteration level, or solution level can be harnessed [64] to parallelize meta-heuristics. The iteration level model is used to generate and evaluate different off-spring solutions in parallel, but does not ease the actual problem. The solution level parallel model always needs a problem specific decomposition of the data domain or a functional decomposition based on expert knowledge. In [7], an agent-based method has been proposed with the advantaged of good scaling properties as with each new objective dimension an agent is added locally searching along the respective dimension [7]. In this approach, the agents perform a decentralized block coordinate descent [73] and self-organized aggregate locally found optima to an overall solution. The approach is based on the protocol of the combinatorial optimization heuristics for distributed agents (COHDA) [31].

Agents in the COHDA protocol act after the receive-decide-act metaphor [31]. When applied to local optimization, the decide process decides locally on the best parameter position with regard to just one respective dimension of the objective function. Thus, each agent performs a 1-dimensional optimization along an intersection of the objective function and takes the other dimensions (his belief on the other agent's local optimizations) as fixed for the moment. This approach has been further improved by a mechanism that postpones the decision process in [11]. With this extension, each agent gathers more information from other agents (including transient ones with more communication hops) and may decide on a more solid basis. In this way, in [11] a concept of laziness has been introduced in this agent concept. Lazy agents postpone some decision with a given likelihood. Depsite this simple mechanism, the observed effect on solution quality was significant and is further scrutinized and applied to Smart Grid problems in this contribution.

The rest of the paper is organized as follows. We start with a description of the base algorithms and on other related work. After a recap and discussion of the most important results from [11] we extend the evaluation by scrutinizing the sensitivity of the convergence process to different laziness factors. Practical applicability is finally studied by applying the extended algorithm to a use case from the Smart Grid domain: namely predictive scheduling in virtual power plant coordination.

2 Related Work

Global optimization comprises many problems in practice as well as in the scientific community. These problems are often hallmarked by presence of a rugged fitness landscape with many local optima and non-linearity. Thus optimization algorithms are likely to become stuck in local optima and guaranteeing the exact optimum is often intractable; leading to the use of heuristics.

Evolution Strategies [54] for example have shown excellent performance in global optimization especially when it comes to complex multi-modal, high-dimensional, real valued problems [36,68]. Each of these strategies has its own characteristics, strengths and weaknesses. A common characteristic is the generation of an offspring solution set by exploring the characteristics of the objective function in the immediate neighborhood of an existing set of solutions. When the solution space is hard to explore or objective evaluations are costly, computational effort is a common drawback for all population-based schemes. Real world problems often face additional computational efforts for fitness evaluations; e.g. in Smart Grid load planning scenarios, fitness evaluation involves simulating a large number of energy resources and their behaviour [5].

Especially in high-dimensional problems, premature convergence [37,58,66] entails additional challenges onto the used optimization method. Heuristics often converge too early towards a sub-optimal solution and then get stuck in this local optimum. This might for instance happen if an adaption strategy decreases the mutation range and thus the range of the currently searched surrounding sub-region and possible ways out of a current trough are no longer scrutinized.

On the other hand, much effort has been spent to accelerate convergence of these methods. Example techniques are: improved population initialization [53], adaptive populations sizes [2] or exploiting sub-populations [55]. Sometimes a surrogate model is used in case of computational expensive objective functions [41] to substitute a share of objective function evaluations with cheap surrogate model evaluations. The surrogate model represents a learned model of the original objective function. Recent approaches use Radial Basis Functions, Polynomial Regression, Support Vector Regression, Artificial Neural Network or Kriging [20]; each approach with individual advantages and drawbacks.

Recently, the number of large scale global optimizations problems grows as technology advances [38]. Large scale problems are difficult to solve for several reasons [71]. The main reasons are the exponentially growing search space and a potential change of an objective function's properties [38,59,71]. Moreover, evaluating large scale objectives is expensive, especially in real world problems [61]. Growing non-separability or variable interaction sometimes entail further challenges [38].

For faster execution, different approaches for parallel problem solving have been scrutinized in the past; partly with a need for problem specific adaption for distribution. Four main questions define the design decisions for distributing a heuristic: which information to exchange, when to communicate, who communicates, and how to integrate received information [45, 64]. Examples for traditional meta-heuristics that are available as distributed version are: Particle swarm [69], ant colony [16], or parallel tempering [39]. Distribution for gaining higher solution accuracy is a rather rare use case. An example is given in [6].

Algorithm 1. Basic scheme of an agent's decision on local optima in the extension of COHDA to global optimization; cf. [7, 12].

1: // let $x \in \mathbb{R}^d$ an intermediate solution

2: $x_k \leftarrow \begin{cases} x_k & \text{if } x_k \in K_{a_j} \\ x \sim U(x_{\min}, x_{\max}) & \text{else} \end{cases} \quad \forall k \neq j$

3: // solve with Brent optimizer:

4: $x_j \leftarrow \arg \min f_j(x) = f(x, x) = f(x_1, \ldots, x_{j-1}, x, x_{j+1}, \ldots, x_d)$

5: **if** $f(x) < f(x_{\text{old}})$ **then**

6:     update workspace K_j

7: **end if**

Another class of algorithms for global optimization that has been popular for many years by practitioners rather than scientists [73] is that of coordinate descent algorithms [49]. Coordinate descent algorithms iteratively search for the optimum in high dimensional problems by fixing most of the parameters (components of variable vector x) and doing a line search along a single free coordinate axis. Usually, all components of x a cyclically chosen for approximating the objective with respect to the (fixed) other components [73]. In each iteration, only a lower dimensional or even scalar sub-problem has to be solved. The multi-variable objective $f(x)$ is solved by looking for the minimum in one direction at a time. There are several approaches for choosing the step size for the step towards the local minimum, but as long as the sequence $f(x^0), f(x^1), \ldots, f(x^n)$ is monotonically decreasing the method converges to an at least local optimum. Like any other gradient based method this approach gets easily stuck in case of a non-convex objective function.

In [31] an agent based approach has been proposed as an algorithmic level decomposition scheme for decentralized problem solving [32, 64], making it especially suitable for large scale problems.

Each agent is responsible for one dimension of the objective function. The intermediate solutions for other dimensions (represented by decisions published by other agents) are regarded as temporarily fixed. Thus, each agent only searches along a 1-dimensional cross-section of the objective and thus has to solve merely a simplified sub-problem. Nevertheless, for evaluation of the solution, the full objective function is used. In this way, the approach achieves an asynchronous coordinate descent with the ability to escape local minima by parallel searching different regions of the search space. The approach uses as basis a protocol from [31].

In [31] a fully decentralized agent-based approach for combinatorial optimization problems has been introduced. Originally, the combinatorial optimization heuristics for distributed agents (COHDA) had been invented to solve the problem of predictive scheduling [62] in the Smart Grid.

The key concept of COHDA is an asynchronous iterative approximate best-response behavior, where each participating agent – originally representing a decentralized energy unit – reacts to updated information from other agents by adapting its own action (select an energy production scheme that enables group of energy generators to fulfil an energy product from market as good as possible). All agents $a_i \in \mathfrak{A}$ initially only know their own respective search space S_i of feasible energy schedules that can be operated by the own energy resource. From an algorithmic point of view, the difficulty of the problem is given by the distributed nature of the system in contrast to the task of finding a common allocation of schedules for a global target power profile.

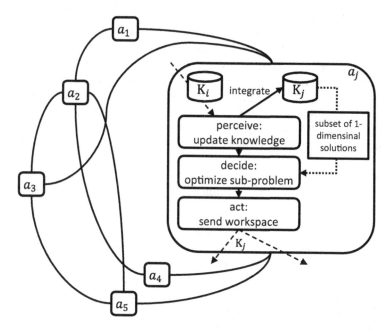

Fig. 1. Internal receive-decide-act architecture of an agent with decision process. The agent receives a set of optimum coordinates from another agent, decides on the best coordinate for the dimensions the agent accounts for and sends the updated information to all neighbors; cf. [7].

Thus, the agents coordinate by updating and exchanging information about each other. For privacy and communication overhead reasons, the potential flexibility (alternative actions) is not communicated as a whole by an agent. Instead, the agents communicate single selected local solutions (energy production schedules in the Smart Grid case) within the approach as described in the following.

First of all, the agents are placed in an artificial communication topology based on the small-world scheme, (e.g. a *small world* topology [70], such that each agent is connected to a non-empty subset of other agents. This overlay topology might be a ring in the least connected variant.

Each agent collects two distinct sets of information: on the one hand the believed current configuration γ_i of the system (that is, the most up to date information a_i has about currently selected schedules of all agents), and on the other hand the best known combination γ_i^* of schedules with respect to the global objective function it has encountered so far.

Beginning with an arbitrarily chosen agent by passing it a message containing only the global objective (i.e. the target power profile), each agent repeatedly executes the three steps *perceive, decide, act* (cf. [46]):

1. `perceive`: When an agent a_i receives a message κ_p from one of its neighbors (say, a_p), it imports the contents of this message into its own memory.
2. `decide`: The agent then searches $\mathcal{S}_i$ for the best own local solution regarding the updated system state γ_i and the global objective function. Local constraints are taken into account in advance if applicable. Details regarding this procedure have been presented in [47]. If a local solution can be found that satisfies the objective, a new solution selection is created. For the following comparison, only the global objective function must be taken into account: If the resulting modified system state γ_i yields a better rating than the current solution candidate γ_i^*, a new solution candidate is created based on γ_i. Otherwise the old solution candidate still reflects the best combination regarding the global objective, so the agent reverts to its old selection stored in γ_i^*.
3. `act`: If γ_i or γ_i^* has been modified in one of the previous steps, the agent finally broadcasts these to its immediate neighbors in the communication topology.

During this process, for each agent a_i, its observed system configuration γ_i as well as solution candidate γ_i^* are filled successively. After producing some intermediate solutions, the heuristic eventually terminates in a state where for all agents γ_i as well as γ_i^* are identical, and no more messages are produced by the agents. At this point, γ_i^* is the final solution of the heuristic and contains exactly one schedule selection for each agent.

The COHDA protocol has meanwhile been applied to many different optimization problems [8,9]. In [7] COHDA has also been applied to the continuous problem of global optimization.

In [3,28], the effect of communication delays in message sending and the degree of variation in such agent systems on the solution quality has been scrutinized. Increasing variation (agents with different knowledge interact) leads to better results. An increase in inter-agent variation can also be achieved by letting agents delay individual decisions. Hence, we combine the ideas from [7] and [28] and extend the agent approach to global optimization by integrating a decision delay into the agents. In this way, the agents sort of behave lazy with regard to their decision duty. The effectiveness has already been shown in [11].

3   Lazy COHDAgo

In [7] the COHDA protocol has been applied to global optimization (COHDAgo) for the first time. Each agent is responsible for solving one dimension x_i of a high-dimensional function $f(x)$ as global objective. Each time an agent receives a message from one of its neighbors, the own knowledgebase with assumptions about optimal coordinates x^* of the optimum of f (with $x^* = \arg\min f(x)$) is updated. Let a_j be the agent that just has received a message from agent a_i. Then, the workspace K_j of agent a_j is merged with information from the received workspace K_i. Each workspace K of an agent contains a set of coordinates x_k such that x_k reflects the kth coordinate of the current solution x so far found from agent a_k. Additionally, information about other coordinates

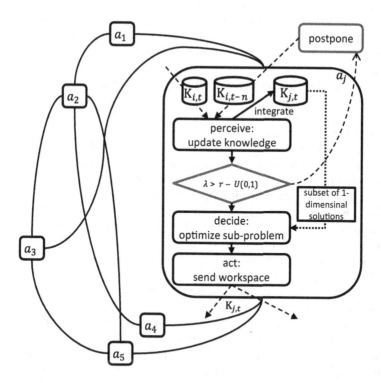

Fig. 2. Extended agent protocol for integrating laziness into the protocol from Fig. 1; cf. [11].

$x_{k_1}, \ldots, x_{k_n}$ reflecting local decisions of $a_{k_1}, \ldots, a_{k_n}$ that a_i has received messages from is also integrated into K_j if the information is newer or outdates the already known. Thus each agent gathers also transient information; finally about all local decisions.

In general, each coordinate x_ℓ that is not yet in K_j is temporarily set to a random value $x_\ell \sim U(x_{\min}, x_{\max})$ for objective evaluation. W.l.o.g. all unknown values could also be set to zero. But, as many of the standard benchmark objective function have their optimum at zero, this would result in an unfair comparison as such behavior would unintentionally induce some priori knowledge. Thus, we have chosen to initialize unknown values with a random value.

After the update procedure, agent a_j takes all elements $x_k \in \boldsymbol{x}$ with $k \neq j$ as temporarily fixed and starts solving a 1-dimensional sub-problem: $x_j = \arg \min f(x, \boldsymbol{x})$; where f is the objective function with all values except element x_j fixed. This problem with only x as the single degree of freedom is solved using Brent's method [14]. Algorithm 1 summarizes this approach.

Brent's method originally is a root finding procedure that combines the previously known bisection method and the secant method with an inverse quadratic interpolation. Whereas the latter are known for fast convergence, bisection provides more reliability. By combining these methods – a first step was already undertaken by [17] – convergence can be guaranteed with at most $\mathcal{O}(n^2)$ iterations (with n iterations for the bisection method). In case of a well-behaved function the method converges even superlinearly [14]. We used an evaluated implementation from Apache Commons Math after a reference implementation from [15].

After x_j has been determined with Brent's method, x_j is communicated (along with all x_ℓ previously received from agent a_i) to all neighbors if $f(\boldsymbol{x}^*)$ with x_j gains a better result than the previous solution candidate. Figure 1 summarizes this procedure.

Into this agent process, the concept of laziness has been integrated [11]. Figure 2 shows the basic idea. As an additional stage within the receive-decide-act protocol, a random decision is made whether to postpone a decision on local optimality based on aggregated information. In contrast to the approach of [3], aggregation is nevertheless done with this additional stage. Only after information aggregation and thus after belief update it is randomly decided whether to continue with the decision process of the current belief (local optimization of the respective objective dimension) or with postponing this process. By doing so, additional information – either update information from the same agent, or additional information from other agents – may meanwhile arrive and aggregate. The delay is realized by putting the trigger message in a holding stack and resubmitting it later. Figure 3 shows the relative frequencies of delay (additional aggregation steps) that occur when a uniform distribution $U(0, 1)$ is used for deciding on postponement. The likelihood of being postponed is denoted by λ. In this way, information may also take over newer information and thus may trigger a resumption at an older search branch that led to a dead-end. In general, the disturbance within the system increases, and thus premature convergence is better prevented. This extension has been denoted lazyCOHDAgo [11].

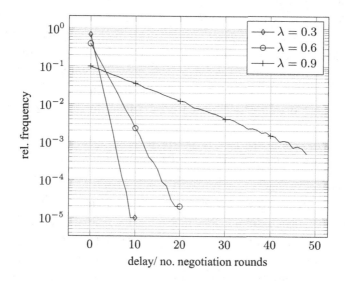

Fig. 3. Probability density of postponement delay for different laziness factors λ denoting the probability of postponing an agent's decision process; modified after [11].

4 Results

For evaluation, a set of well-known test functions that have been developed for benchmarking optimization methods has initially been used: Elliptic, Ackley [68], Egg Holder [34], Rastrigin [1], Griewank [40], Quadric [34], and examples from the CEC '13 Workshop on Large Scale Optimization [38]. We added Alpine [52]

In this field, many well tested implementation are readily available [51].

In a first experiment, the effect of lazy agents has been tested. To achieve this, a set of test functions with agents of different laziness λ has been solved. Tables 1 and 2 shows the result for 50-dimensional versions of the test functions. In this rather low dimensional cases the effect is visible, but not that prominent. In most cases a slight improvement can be seen with growing laziness factor ($\lambda = 0$ denotes no laziness at all and thus responds to the original COHDAgo). The Elliptic function for example shows no improvement. In some cases, e.g. for the Quadric function the result quality deteriorates. But, also an overshoot can be observed with the Griewank function where the best result is obtained with a laziness of $\lambda = 0.3$.

When applied to more complex and higher-dimensional objective functions the effect is way more prominent as can be seen in Table 3. The CEC f_1 function [38] is a shifted elliptic function which is ill-conditioned with condition number

Table 1. Performance of the lazy agent approach on different 50-dimensional test functions for laziness factors $\lambda = 0$ and $\lambda = 0.3$.

Function	$\lambda = 0.0$	$\lambda = 0.3$
Elliptic	$1.527 \times 10^{-21} \pm 2.876 \times 10^{-28}$	$1.527 \times 10^{-21} \pm 1.976 \times 10^{-28}$
Ackley	$1.306 \times 10^1 \pm 2.988 \times 10^{-1}$	$1.217 \times 10^1 \pm 1.665 \times 10^{-1}$
EggHolder	$1.453 \times 10^4 \pm 8.639 \times 10^2$	$1.423 \times 10^4 \pm 8.81 \times 10^2$
Rastrigin	$2.868 \times 10^2 \pm 2.493 \times 10^0$	$2.87 \times 10^2 \pm 1.569 \times 10^0$
Griewank	$2.95 \times 10^{-3} \pm 9.328 \times 10^{-3}$	$1.478 \times 10^{-3} \pm 4.674 \times 10^{-3}$
Quadric	$6.51 \times 10^{-26} \pm 6.525 \times 10^{-26}$	$1.196 \times 10^{-25} \pm 8.128 \times 10^{-26}$

Table 2. Performance of the lazy agent approach on different 50-dimensional test functions continued for laziness factors $\lambda = 0.6$ and $\lambda = 0.9$.

Function	$\lambda = 0.6$	$\lambda = 0.9$
Elliptic	$1.527 \times 10^{-1} \pm 2.594 \times 10^{-29}$	$1.527 \times 10^{-21} \pm 7.48 \times 10^{-28}$
Ackley	$1.205 \times 10^1 \pm 1.86 \times 10^{-1}$	$1.124 \times 10^1 \pm 2.088 \times 10^{-1}$
EggHolder	$1.384 \times 10^4 \pm 9.119 \times 10^2$	$1.345 \times 10^4 \pm 9.441 \times 10^2$
Rastrigin	$2.868 \times 10^2 \pm 2.427 \times 10^0$	$2.858 \times 10^2 \pm 3.088 \times 10^0$
Griewank	$1.59 \times 10^{-3} \pm 3.219 \times 10^{-2}$	$3.07 \times 10^{-2} \pm 4.132 \times 10^{-2}$
Quadric	$3.65 \times 10^{-5} \pm 5.141 \times 10^{-25}$	$4.43 \times 10^{-15} \pm 1.40 \times 10^{-14}$

$\approx 10^6$ in the 1000-dimensional case. Due to dimensionality best results have been obtained with a laziness of $\lambda = 0.99$. From the wide range of solution qualities for $\lambda = 0.9$ – the achieved minimum result out of 20 runs was (200-dimensional case) 3.40×10^{-19}, which is almost as good as the result for $\lambda = 0.9$ – it can be concluded that the lazy agent system is less susceptible to premature convergence and thus yields better mean results. The used Rosenbrock function in Table 4 is a asymmetrically, non-linearly shifted version of the original test function [57] multiplied by the Alpine function (Table 4).

Next, the results of the lazy agent approach have been compared with other established meta-heuristics for functions where the agent approach was successful. Please note that for some function (e.g. the result in Tables 1 and 2) were not that promising. For comparison we used the co-variance matrix adaption evolution strategy (CMA-ES) from [24] with a parametrization after [23], Differ-

Table 3. Performance of the lazy agent approach on different high-dimensional, ill-conditioned test functions for different laziness factors λ.

Function	$\lambda = 0.0$	$\lambda = 0.9$	$\lambda = 0.99$
CEC f_1, $d = 200$	$1.81 \times 10^{10} \pm 5.78 \times 10^9$	$2.20 \times 10^8 \pm 4.11 \times 10^8$	$3.40 \times 10^{-19} \pm 1.54 \times 10^{-23}$
CEC f_1, $d = 500$	$4.28 \times 10^9 \pm 8.28 \times 10^9$	$6.55 \times 10^4 \pm 1.85 \times 10^5$	$3.76 \times 10^{-19} \pm 1.31 \times 10^{-21}$
Rosenbrock* $d = 250$	$1.01 \times 10^{-5} \pm 1.71 \times 10^{-5}$	$2.41 \times 10^{-7} \pm 5.37 \times 10^{-7}$	$5.68 \times 10^{-8} \pm 1.60 \times 10^{-7}$

Table 4. Comparison of the lazy agent approach with different established meta-heuristics.

f	CMA-ES	DE	PSO
Elliptic	$3.41 \times 10^{-5} \pm 7.47 \times 10^{-5}$	$4.48 \times 10^{-9} \pm 2.24 \times 10^{-9}$	$2.65 \times 10^5 \pm 8.37 \times 10^5$
Ackley	$1.02 \times 10^1 \pm 7.07 \times 10^0$	$4.73 \times 10^{-2} \pm 7.06 \times 10^{-5}$	$2.0 \times 10^1 \pm 0.0 \times 10^0$
Alpine	$4.2 \times 10^0 \pm 3.96 \times 10^0$	$2.82 \times 10^{-3} \pm 9.18 \times 10^{-5}$	$6.61 \times 10^{-9} \pm 1.29 \times 10^{-8}$
Griewank	$9.99 \times 10^{-4} \pm 3.11 \times 10^{-3}$	$4.41 \times 10^{-4} \pm 1.51 \times 10^{-5}$	$8.92 \times 10^{-3} \pm 4.54 \times 10^{-3}$

Table 5. Results for lazyCOHDAgo for the comparison from Table 4.

f	Lazy COHDAgo
Elliptic	$1.14 \times 10^{-21} \pm 2.64 \times 10^{-27}$
Ackley	$1.54 \times 10^1 \pm 1.01 \times 10^{-1}$
Alpine	$4.51 \times 10^{-12} \pm 1.32 \times 10^{-13}$
Griewank	$5.11 \times 10^{-16} \pm 9.2 \times 10^{-16}$

Table 6. Respective best results (residual error) out of 20 runs each for the comparison from Table 4.

f	CMA-ES	DE	PSO	lazy COHDAgo
Elliptic	9.28×10^{-7}	1.89×10^{-9}	1.04×10^{-4}	1.14×10^{-21}
Ackley	6.02×10^{-6}	4.73×10^{-2}	2.0×10^1	1.52×10^1
Alpine	1.28×10^{-1}	2.7×10^{-3}	1.2×10^{-15}	4.3×10^{-12}
Griewank	3.57×10^{-6}	4.23×10^{-4}	1.51×10^{-5}	0.0×10^0

ential Evolution [63] and Particle Swarm Optimization [35]. The lazy COHDAgo approach has been parametrized with a laziness of $\lambda = 0.9$. Table 4 shows the result.

As the agent approach terminates by itself if no further solution improvement can be made by any agent and no further stopping criterion is meaningful in an asynchronously working decentralized system, we simply logged the number of used function evaluations and gave this number as evaluation budget to the other heuristics. In this way we ensured that every heuristics uses the same budget of maximum objective evaluations. As CMA-ES was not able to succeed for some high-dimensional functions with this limited budget, this evolution strategy was given the 100 fold budget.

The agent approach is competitive for the Ackley function. In most of the cases lazyCOHDAgo succeeds in terms of residual error, but also, when looking at the absolute best solution out of 20 run each (Table 6), the lazy agent-approach is successful.

The experimental results in Fig. 4 give a first impression on the convergence process. The whole agent optimization process usually runs with asynchronously

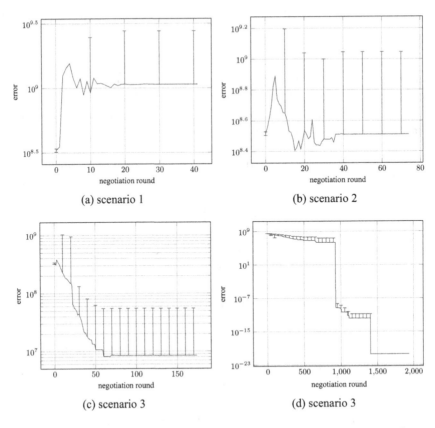

Fig. 4. Results for the 150-dimensional CEC function for laziness $\lambda \in \{0.0, 0.5, 0.9, 0.99\}$ (scenario 1–4).

acting agents. Thus, in order to be able to measure the course of convergence, we run the process in a quasi-asynchronous manner with discrete synchronization points at which the intermediate result from each agent is requested from the agents and logged. Although, a single agent does not represent a complete solution, each agent has a specific belief about what schedule other agents are going to select for their energy unit. This belief is the basis for an agent's decision and also used for local solution evaluation. The result of this local solution evaluation is logged together with the time tick at which the decision for a schedule that led to this solution was made.

Figure 4 shows the convergence of the 150 dimensional CEC f_1 function for different laziness factors. For the low laziness factors the improvement is rather low and is achieved basically due to the fact that the process is kept alive for some longer time. For the laziness factor $\lambda = 0.99$ another effect of the laziness can be observed. Several times, a significant jump in error degradation is noteworthy. At these incidents, obviously a postponed and so far abandoned search path comes back into play, leading with the meanwhile done decisions of other

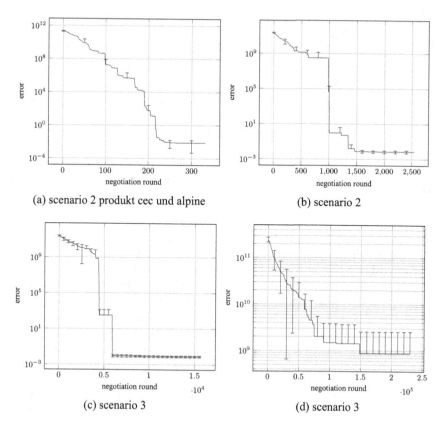

(a) scenario 2 produkt cec und alpine

(b) scenario 2

(c) scenario 3

(d) scenario 3

Fig. 5. Results for the combined CEC and Alpine function for laziness $\lambda \in \{0.9, 0.99, 0.999, 0.9999\}$ (scenario 1–4).

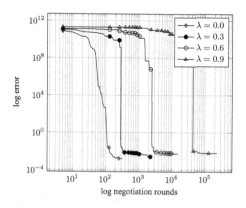

Fig. 6. Best (out of 20) found solutions for the 200-dimensional Alpine function for different laziness factors.

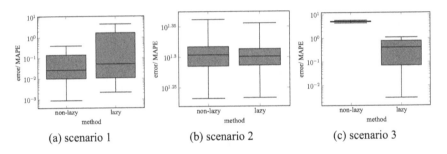

Fig. 7. Results of the non-lazi and the lazy algorithm from three scenarios of the virtual power plant use case. The residual error is given as mean absolute percentage error (MAPE).

agents to a sudden improvement. Due to these jumps and the followed (standard) improvements, the process converges to a significantly better solution.

On the other hand, this is not always the case and depends presumably on the structure of the fitness- or error landscape. Figure 5 shows another example. Here the objective was constructed by multiplying the CEC f_1 function with the Alpine function. Again, with increasing laziness, jumps can be observed; but this time they are not leading to better result than the earlier convergence with less laziness. Thus the invest of a higher evaluation budget is not rewarding here. Moreover, with a too high laziness of $\lambda = 0.9999$ the solution quality massively degrades. Thus, one can overshoot the mark with too lazy agents.

Figure 6 shows the best (out of 20) results for the 200-dimensional Alpine function. Again, increasing the laziness does not work out, but this time without overshoot.

Finally, we applied the lazy algorithm to a practical problem from engineering, namely from the Smart Grid domain. For many use cases in the Smart Grid domain, it is advantageous to bundle energy resources within a local region. A single energy resource like a renewable generator or a battery storage usually has neither the size nor the flexibility to take on responsibility for control tasks within the electricity grid. One way to cope with volatility and small size is bundling of different energy resources and orchestrating them via communication and common control. This concept is known as virtual power plant (VPP) [50].

Predictive scheduling terms the problem of finding an operation schedule (determining the individual course of generated power) for each energy resource within a VPP for a given future time horizon, e.g. the next day. This constitutes a distributed combinatorial optimization problem [27]. For solving this problem within VPPs solutions for appropriate orchestration of generation (and sometime also consumption) are already known [18, 29, 50]. Due to the problem size that results from the huge number of controllable energy resources in some VPP, decentralized algorithms are seen as a promising approach. Gossiping-based, decentralized algorithms like the COHDA can easily cope with this problem [30], and in fact COHDA had originally been designed for this specific problem. Here, we extend the lazy agent approach to the original COHDA and test it on predictive scheduling.

It is the goal of the predictive scheduling problem to find exactly one schedule for each energy unit such that

1. each assigned schedule can be operated by the respective energy unit without violating any hard technical constraint, and
2. the difference between the sum of all targets and a desired given target schedule is minimized.

A schedule in this context is simply a real-valued vector with each element denoting the mean generated (or consumed) power during the respective time interval. The target schedule usually comprises 96 time intervals of 15 min each with a given amount of energy (or equivalently mean active power) for each time interval, but might also be constituted for a shorter time frame by a given energy product that the coalition has to deliver.

A basic formulation of the scheduling problem is given by

$$\delta \left(\sum_{i=1}^{m} s_i, \zeta \right) \to min \tag{1}$$

such that

$$s_i \in \mathcal{F}^{(U_i)} \ \forall U_i \in \mathcal{U}. \tag{2}$$

In Eq. (1) δ denotes an (in general) arbitrary distance measure for evaluating the difference between the aggregated schedule of the group (sum $\sum_{s_i}$ of individual schedules) and the desired target schedule ζ. W.l.o.g., in this contribution we use the Euclidean distance $\| \cdot \|_2$. To each energy unit U_i exactly one schedule s_i has to be assigned. The desired target schedule is given by ζ. $\mathcal{F}^{(U_i)}$ denotes the individual set of feasible schedules that are operable for unit U_i without violating any (technical) constraint.

The objective function is quite simple. The crucial part of this problem is constraint handling. Schedules may be chosen only from a very specific feasible region $\mathcal{F}^{(U_i)}$ of the individual phase spaces of the energy units [10]. Each unit has individual technical (and other) operation constraints. Usually so called decoders are used for constraint handling [13]. A decoder is trained e.g. by a machine learning approach to learn a function that maps any (probably infeasible) schedule to the feasible region. Due to such space mapping, the optimization algorithm might operate in an unconstrained search space. On the other hand, ruggedness and non-linearity are induced into the objective due to mapping the search space [48].

For our simulations we used the model of a co-generation power plant that has already been used and evaluated in different projects, e.g. [9,12,26,43].

Figure 7 presents the results for the Smart Grid use case. The approach has been tested on three different scenarios. In scenario 1 and scenario 2 to we simulated a virtual power plant with 5 co-generation plants each and a planning horizon of 96 15-min intervals covering a whole day. This results in a $5 \cdot 96 = 480$

dimensional planning problem. In scenario 1 we selected the wanted target schedule in a way that the plants could operate it without violating any technical constraints. Thus, the optimum is known to be zero. In scenario 2 the target schedule was selected such that it cannot be operated exactly. Here, the real optimum is unknown. For scenario 3 we simulated a virtual power plant consisting of 25 plants resulting in a problem dimension of $25 \cdot 96 = 2400$! All scenarios are solved 20 times with and without laziness ($\lambda = 0.9$). Improvements can be observed for the harder cases where the target schedule cannot be reached exactly by the energy units. Especially for the larger case scenario 3 a significant improvement can be observed when laziness is introduced.

5   Conclusion

Global optimization is a crucial task for many real world applications in industry and engineering and many practical problems are of a high-dimensional structure. Most meta-heuristics deteriorate rapidly with growing problem dimensionality. Exact methods can often not be applied due to the ruggedness of the objective function. But also statistical heuristics need mechanisms to escape local minima and prevent premature convergence.

We scrutinized a laziness extension to an agent-based algorithm for global optimization that achieves a way better performance compared with the non-lazy base algorithm when applied to large scale problems. Randomly postponing the agent's decision on local optimization leads to less vulnerability to premature convergence, obviously due to an increasing inter-agent variation [3] and thus to the incorporation of past (outdated) information. This re-stimulates a search in already abandoned paths. Delaying the reaction of the agents in Gossiping algorithms is known to increase the diversity in the population [28]. On the one hand, this diversity leads to better results – especially in large scale problems, but the number of necessary negotiation rounds increases on the other. For a better understanding of the convergence process and its sensitivity to different degrees of laziness and type of objective, we studied and compared the convergence processes.

The lazy COHDAgo approach has shown good and sometimes superior performance especially regarding solution quality for standard testbed objectives from the computational intelligence community as well as for a practical problem from the Smart Grid domain. In future work, it may also be promising to further scrutinize the impact of the communication topology asa further design parameter.

References

1. Aggarwal, S., Goswami, P.: Implementation of Dejong function by various selection method and analyze their performance. IJRCCT **3**(6) (2014). http://www.ijrcct. org/index.php/ojs/article/view/755

2. Ahrari, A., Shariat-Panahi, M.: An improved evolution strategy with adaptive population size. Optimization **64**(12), 2567–2586 (2015). https://doi.org/10.1080/02331934.2013.836651

3. Anders, G., Hinrichs, C., Siefert, F., Behrmann, P., Reif, W., Sonnenschein, M.: On the influence of inter-agent variation on multi-agent algorithms solving a dynamic task allocation problem under uncertainty. In: Sixth IEEE International Conference on Self-Adaptive and Self-Organizing Systems (SASO 2012), pp. 29–38. IEEE Computer Society, Lyon (2012). https://doi.org/10.1109/SASO.2012.16, (Best Paper Award)

4. Bäck, T., Fogel, D.B., Michalewicz, Z. (eds.): Handbook of Evolutionary Computation, 1st edn. IOP Publishing Ltd., Bristol (1997)

5. Bremer, J., Sonnenschein, M.: Parallel tempering for constrained many criteria optimization in dynamic virtual power plants. In: 2014 IEEE Symposium on Computational Intelligence Applications in Smart Grid (CIASG), pp. 1–8, December 2014. https://doi.org/10.1109/CIASG.2014.7011551

6. Bremer, J., Lehnhoff, S.: A decentralized PSO with decoder for scheduling distributed electricity generation. In: Squillero, G., Burelli, P. (eds.) EvoApplications 2016. LNCS, vol. 9597, pp. 427–442. Springer, Cham (2016). https://doi.org/10.1007/978-3-319-31204-0_28

7. Bremer, J., Lehnhoff, S.: An agent-based approach to decentralized global optimization: adapting cohda to coordinate descent. In: van den Herik, J., Rocha, A., Filipe, J. (eds.) ICAART 2017 - Proceedings of the 9th International Conference on Agents and Artificial Intelligence, vol. 1, pp. 129–136. SciTePress, Science and Technology Publications, Lda., Porto (2017)

8. Bremer, J., Lehnhoff, S.: Decentralized coalition formation with agent-based combinatorial heuristics. ADCAIJ: Adv. Distrib. Comput. Artif. Intell. J. **6**(3) (2017). http://revistas.usal.es/index.php/2255-2863/article/view/ADCAIJ2017632944

9. Bremer, J., Lehnhoff, S.: Hybrid multi-ensemble scheduling. In: Squillero, G., Sim, K. (eds.) EvoApplications 2017. LNCS, vol. 10199, pp. 342–358. Springer, Cham (2017). https://doi.org/10.1007/978-3-319-55849-3_23

10. Bremer, J., Lehnhoff, S.: Phase-space sampling of energy ensembles with CMA-ES. In: Sim, K., Kaufmann, P. (eds.) EvoApplications 2018. LNCS, vol. 10784, pp. 222–230. Springer, Cham (2018). https://doi.org/10.1007/978-3-319-77538-8_16

11. Bremer, J., Lehnhoff, S.: Lazy agents for large scale global optimization. In: Proceedings of the 11th International Conference on Agents and Artificial Intelligence. SciTePress, January 2019

12. Bremer, J., Sonnenschein, M.: Automatic reconstruction of performance indicators from support vector based search space models in distributed real power planning scenarios. In: Horbach, M. (ed.) Informatik 2013, 43. Jahrestagung der Gesellschaft für Informatik e.V. (GI), Informatik angepasst an Mensch, Organisation und Umwelt. LNI, Koblenz, 16–20 September 2013, vol. 220, pp. 1441–1454. GI (2013)

13. Bremer, J., Sonnenschein, M.: Constraint-handling with support vector decoders. In: Filipe, J., Fred, A. (eds.) ICAART 2013. CCIS, vol. 449, pp. 228–244. Springer, Heidelberg (2014). https://doi.org/10.1007/978-3-662-44440-5_14

14. Brent, R.P.: An algorithm with guaranteed convergence for finding a zero of a function. Comput. J. **14**(4), 422–425 (1971)

15. Brent, R.: Algorithms for Minimization Without Derivatives: Dover Books on Mathematics. Dover Publications, Mineola (1973). https://books.google.de/books?id=6Ay2biHG-GEC

16. Colorni, A., Dorigo, M., Maniezzo, V., et al.: Distributed optimization by ant colonies. In: Proceedings of the First European Conference on Artificial Life, Paris, France, vol. 142, pp. 134–142 (1991)

17. Dekker, T.: Finding a zero by means of successive linear interpolation. In: Constructive Aspects of the Fundamental Theorem of Algebra, pp. 37–51 (1969)

18. Dethlefs, T., Beewen, D., Preisler, T., Renz, W.: A consumer-orientated architecture for distributed demand-side-optimization. In: EnviroInfo, pp. 349–356. BIS-Verlag (2014)

19. Dorigo, M., Stützle, T.: Ant Colony Optimization. Bradford Company, Scituate (2004)

20. Gano, S.E., Kim, H., Brown II, D.E.: Comparison of three surrogate modeling techniques: datascape, kriging, and second order regression. In: Proceedings of the 11th AIAA/ISSMO Multidisciplinary Analysis and Optimization Conference, AIAA 2006, Portsmouth, Virginia, p. 7048 (2006)

21. Hansen, E.: Global optimization using interval analysis - the multi-dimensional case. Numer. Math. **34**(3), 247–270 (1980). https://doi.org/10.1007/BF01396702

22. Hansen, N.: The CMA evolution strategy: a comparing review. In: Lozano, J.A., Larranaga, P., Inza, I., Bengoetxea, E. (eds.) Towards a New Evolutionary Computation. STUDFUZZ, vol. 192, pp. 75–102. Springer, Heidelberg (2006). https://doi.org/10.1007/3-540-32494-1_4

23. Hansen, N.: The CMA evolution strategy: a tutorial. Technical report (2011). www.lri.fr/~hansen/cmatutorial.pdf

24. Hansen, N., Ostermeier, A.: Completely derandomized self-adaptation in evolution strategies. Evol. Comput. **9**(2), 159–195 (2001). https://doi.org/10.1162/106365601750190398

25. Hansen, P., Jaumard, B., Lu, S.H.: Global optimization of univariate lipschitz functions II: new algorithms and computational comparison. Math. Program. **55**(3), 273–292 (1992). https://doi.org/10.1007/BF01581203

26. Hinrichs, C., Bremer, J., Martens, S., Sonnenschein, M.: Partitioning the data domain of combinatorial problems for sequential optimization. In: Ganzha, M., Maciaszek, L., Paprzycki, M. (eds.) 9th International Workshop on Computational Optimization, Proceedings of the 2016 Federated Conference on Computer Science and Information Systems, Gdansk (2016)

27. Hinrichs, C., Lehnhoff, S., Sonnenschein, M.: A decentralized heuristic for multiple-choice combinatorial optimization problems. In: Helber, S., et al. (eds.) Operations Research Proceedings 2012. ORP, pp. 297–302. Springer, Cham (2014). https://doi.org/10.1007/978-3-319-00795-3_43

28. Hinrichs, C., Sonnenschein, M.: The effects of variation on solving a combinatorial optimization problem in collaborative multi-agent systems. In: Müller, J.P., Weyrich, M., Bazzan, A.L.C. (eds.) MATES 2014. LNCS (LNAI), vol. 8732, pp. 170–187. Springer, Cham (2014). https://doi.org/10.1007/978-3-319-11584-9_12

29. Hinrichs, C., Sonnenschein, M.: Design, analysis and evaluation of control algorithms for applications in smart grids. In: Gómez, J.M., Sonnenschein, M., Vogel, U., Winter, A., Rapp, B., Giesen, N. (eds.) Advances and New Trends in Environmental and Energy Informatics. PI, pp. 135–155. Springer, Cham (2016). https://doi.org/10.1007/978-3-319-23455-7_8

30. Hinrichs, C., Sonnenschein, M.: A distributed combinatorial optimisation heuristic for the scheduling of energy resources represented by self-interested agents. Int. J. Bio-Inspired Comput. **10**, 69 (2017). https://doi.org/10.1504/IJBIC.2017.085895

31. Hinrichs, C., Sonnenschein, M., Lehnhoff, S.: Evaluation of a self-organizing heuristic for interdependent distributed search spaces. In: Filipe, J., Fred, A.L.N. (eds.) International Conference on Agents and Artificial Intelligence (ICAART 2013), vol. Volume 1 - Agents, pp. 25–34. SciTePress (2013). https://doi.org/10.5220/0004227000250034

32. Hinrichs, C., Vogel, U., Sonnenschein, M.: Approaching decentralized demand side management via self-organizing agents. In: ATES Workshop (2011)

33. Horst, R., Pardalos, P.M. (eds.): Handbook of Global Optimization. Kluwer Academic Publishers, Dordrecht (1995)

34. Jamil, M., Yang, X.: A literature survey of benchmark functions for global optimization problems. CoRR abs/1308.4008 (2013)

35. Kennedy, J., Eberhart, R.: Particle swarm optimization. In: 1995 Proceedings of the IEEE International Conference on Neural Networks, vol. 4, pp. 1942–1948. IEEE, November 1995. https://doi.org/10.1109/ICNN.1995.488968

36. Kramer, O.: A review of constraint-handling techniques for evolution strategies. Appl. Comp. Intell. Soft Comput. **2010**, 1–19 (2010). https://doi.org/10.1155/2010/185063

37. Leung, Y., Gao, Y., Xu, Z.B.: Degree of population diversity - a perspective on premature convergence in genetic algorithms and its Markov chain analysis. IEEE Trans. Neural Netw. **8**(5), 1165–1176 (1997). https://doi.org/10.1109/72.623217

38. Li, X., Tang, K., Omidvar, M.N., Yang, Z., Qin, K.: Benchmark functions for the CEC 2013 special session and competition on large-scale global optimization. Techical report (2013)

39. Li, Y., Mascagni, M., Gorin, A.: A decentralized parallel implementation for parallel tempering algorithm. Parallel Comput. **35**(5), 269–283 (2009)

40. Locatelli, M.: A note on the Griewank test function. J. Glob. Optim. **25**(2), 169–174 (2003). https://doi.org/10.1023/A:1021956306041

41. Loshchilov, I., Schoenauer, M., Sebag, M.: Self-adaptive surrogate-assisted covariance matrix adaptation evolution strategy. CoRR abs/1204.2356 (2012)

42. Myers, R.H., Montgomery, D.C., Anderson-Cook, C.M.: Response Surface Methodology: Process and Product Optimization Using Designed Experiments. Wiley, Hoboken (2016)

43. Neugebauer, J., Kramer, O., Sonnenschein, M.: Classification cascades of overlapping feature ensembles for energy time series data. In: Woon, W.L., Aung, Z., Madnick, S. (eds.) DARE 2015. LNCS (LNAI), vol. 9518, pp. 76–93. Springer, Cham (2015). https://doi.org/10.1007/978-3-319-27430-0_6

44. Neumaier, A.: Complete search in continuous global optimization and constraint satisfaction. Acta Numer. **13**, 271–369 (2004). https://doi.org/10.1017/S0962492904000194

45. Nieße, A.: Verteilte kontinuierliche Einsatzplanung in Dynamischen Virtuellen Kraftwerken. Ph.D. thesis (2015)

46. Nieße, A., Beer, S., Bremer, J., Hinrichs, C., Lünsdorf, O., Sonnenschein, M.: Conjoint dynamic aggregation and scheduling methods for dynamic virtual power plants. In: Ganzha, M., Maciaszek, L.A., Paprzycki, M. (eds.) Proceedings of the 2014 Federated Conference on Computer Science and Information Systems. Annals of Computer Science and Information Systems, vol. 2, pp. 1505–1514. IEEE (2014). https://doi.org/10.15439/2014F76

47. Nieße, A., Bremer, J., Hinrichs, C., Sonnenschein, M.: Local soft constraints in distributed energy scheduling. In: Proceedings of the 2016 Federated Conference on Computer Science and Information Systems (FEDCSIS), pp. 1517–1525. IEEE (2016). https://doi.org/10.15439/2016F76

48. Nieße, A., Bremer, J., Lehnhoff, S.: On local minima in distributed energy scheduling. In: Ganzha, M., Maciaszek, L.A., Paprzycki, M. (eds.) Position Papers of the 2017 Federated Conference on Computer Science and Information Systems, FedCSIS 2017, Prague, Czech Republic, 3–6 September 2017. Annals of Computer Science and Information Systems, vol. 12 (2017)

49. Ortega, J.M., Rheinboldt, W.C.: Iterative solution of nonlinear equations in several variables (1970)

50. Othman, M., Hegazy, Y., Abdelaziz, A.: A review of virtual power plant definitions, components, framework and optimization. Int. Electr. Eng. J. (IEEJ) 6, 2010–2024 (2015)

51. Pampara, G., Engelbrecht, A.P., Cloete, T.: Cilib: a collaborative framework for computational intelligence algorithms - part I. In: 2008 IEEE International Joint Conference on Neural Networks. IEEE World Congress on Computational Intelligence, pp. 1750–1757, June 2008. https://doi.org/10.1109/IJCNN.2008.4634035

52. Rahnamayan, S., Tizhoosh, H., Salama, M.: A novel population initialization method for accelerating evolutionary algorithms. Comput. Math. Appl. 53, 1605–1614 (2007). https://doi.org/10.1016/j.camwa.2006.07.013

53. Rahnamayan, S., Tizhoosh, H.R., Salama, M.M.: A novel population initialization method for accelerating evolutionary algorithms. Comput. Math. Appl. 53(10), 1605–1614 (2007). https://doi.org/10.1016/j.camwa.2006.07.013. http://www.sciencedirect.com/science/article/pii/S0898122107001344

54. Rechenberg, I.: Cybernetic solution path of an experimental problem. Technical report, Royal Air Force Establishment (1965)

55. Rigling, B.D., Moore, F.W.: Exploitation of sub-populations in evolution strategies for improved numerical optimization, vol. 1001, p. 48105, Ann Arbor (1999)

56. Rios, L.M., Sahinidis, N.V.: Derivative-free optimization: a review of algorithms and comparison of software implementations. J. Glob. Optim. 56(3), 1247–1293 (2013). https://doi.org/10.1007/s10898-012-9951-y

57. Rosenbrock, H.H.: An automatic method for finding the greatest or least value of a function. Comput. J. 3(3), 175–184 (1960). https://doi.org/10.1093/comjnl/3.3.175

58. Rudolph, G.: Self-adaptive mutations may lead to premature convergence. IEEE Trans. Evol. Comput. 5(4), 410–414 (2001). https://doi.org/10.1109/4235.942534

59. Shang, Y.W., Qiu, Y.H.: A note on the extended rosenbrock function. Evol. Comput. 14(1), 119–126 (2006). https://doi.org/10.1162/106365606776022733

60. Simon, D.: Evolutionary Optimization Algorithms. Wiley, Hoboken (2013)

61. Sobieszczanski-Sobieski, J., Haftka, R.T.: Multidisciplinary aerospace design optimization: survey of recent developments. Struct. Optim. 14(1), 1–23 (1997). https://doi.org/10.1007/BF01197554

62. Sonnenschein, M., Lünsdorf, O., Bremer, J., Tröschel, M.: Decentralized control of units in smart grids for the support of renewable energy supply. Environ. Impact Assess. Rev. 52, 40–52 (2015)

63. Storn, R., Price, K.: Differential evolution - a simple and efficient heuristic for global optimization over continuous spaces. J. Glob. Optim. 11(4), 341–359 (1997). https://doi.org/10.1023/A:1008202821328

64. Talbi, E.: Metaheuristics: From Design to Implementation. Wiley Series on Parallel and Distributed Computing. Wiley, Hoboken (2009). https://books.google.de/books?id=SIsa6zi5XV8C

65. Törn, A., Žilinskas, A.: Introduction. In: Törn, A., Žilinskas, A. (eds.) Global Optimization. LNCS, vol. 350, pp. 1–24. Springer, Heidelberg (1989). https://doi.org/10.1007/3-540-50871-6_1

66. Trelea, I.C.: The particle swarm optimization algorithm: convergence analysis and parameter selection. Inf. Process. Lett. **85**(6), 317–325 (2003). https://doi.org/10.1016/S0020-0190(02)00447-7

67. Tuy, H., Thieu, T., Thai, N.: A conical algorithm for globally minimizing a concave function over a closed convex set. Math. Oper. Res. **10**(3), 498–514 (1985). https://doi.org/10.1287/moor.10.3.498

68. Ulmer, H., Streichert, F., Zell, A.: Evolution strategies assisted by Gaussian processes with improved pre-selection criterion. In: IEEE Congress on Evolutionary Computation, CEC 2003, pp. 692–699 (2003)

69. Vanneschi, L., Codecasa, D., Mauri, G.: A comparative study of four parallel and distributed pso methods. New Gener. Comput. **29**(2), 129–161 (2011)

70. Watts, D., Strogatz, S.: Collective dynamics of 'small-world' networks. Nature **393**, 440–442 (1998)

71. Weise, T., Chiong, R., Tang, K.: Evolutionary optimization: Pitfalls and booby traps. J. Comput. Sci. Technol. **27**(5), 907–936 (2012). https://doi.org/10.1007/s11390-012-1274-4

72. Wipke, K., Markel, T., Nelson, D.: Optimizing energy management strategy and degree of hybridization for a hydrogen fuel cell SUV. In: Proceedings of 18th Electric Vehicle Symposium, pp. 1–12 (2001)

73. Wright, S.J.: Coordinate descent algorithms. Math. Program. **151**(1), 3–34 (2015). https://doi.org/10.1007/s10107-015-0892-3

Conversational Agents for Insurance Companies: From Theory to Practice

Falko Koetter[1], Matthias Blohm[1(✉)], Jens Drawehn[1], Monika Kochanowski[1], Joscha Goetzer[2], Daniel Graziotin[2], and Stefan Wagner[2]

[1] Fraunhofer Institute for Industrial Engineering,
Nobelstr. 12, 70569 Stuttgart, Germany
{falko.koetter,matthias.blohm,jens.drawehn,
monika.kochanowski}@iao.fraunhofer.de
[2] University of Stuttgart, Universitätsstr. 38, 70569 Stuttgart, Germany
joscha.goetzer@gmail.com, {daniel.graziotin,
Stefan.Wagner}@iste.uni-stuttgart.de

Abstract. Advances in artificial intelligence have renewed interest in conversational agents. Additionally to software developers, today all kinds of employees show interest in new technologies and their possible applications for customers. German insurance companies generally are interested in improving their customer service and digitizing their business processes. In this work we investigate the potential use of conversational agents in insurance companies theoretically by determining which classes of agents exist which are of interest to insurance companies, finding relevant use cases and requirements. We add two practical parts: First we develop a showcase prototype for an exemplary insurance scenario in claim management. Additionally in a second step, we create a prototype focusing on customer service in a chatbot hackathon, fostering innovation in interdisciplinary teams. In this work, we describe the results of both prototypes in detail. We evaluate both chatbots defining criteria for both settings in detail and compare the results and draw conclusions for the maturity of chatbot technology for practical use, describing the opportunities and challenges companies, especially small and medium enterprises, face.

Keywords: Conversational agents · Intelligent user interfaces · Hackathon · NLP chatbot · Insurance

1 Introduction

With the digital transformation changing usage patterns and consumer expectations, many industries need to adapt to new realities. The insurance sector is next in line to grapple with the risks and opportunities of emerging technologies, in particular *Artificial Intelligence* [31]. Additionally, innovation methods like design thinking and open innovation are on the rise. In unsecure market times innovation is crucial, and all organizations and also traditional companies need to keep up to date by using new technologies for innovative business processes [27].

© Springer Nature Switzerland AG 2019
J. van den Herik et al. (Eds.): ICAART 2019, LNAI 11978, pp. 338–362, 2019.
https://doi.org/10.1007/978-3-030-37494-5_17

Fraunhofer IAO as an applied research institution supports digital transformation processes in an ongoing project with multiple insurance companies [35]. The goal of this project is to scout new technologies, investigate them, rate their relevance and evaluate them (e.g. in a model trial or by implementing a prototype). While insurance has traditionally been an industry with very low customer engagement, insurers now face a young generation of consumers with changing attitudes regarding insurance products and services [32]. Another goal of the project is the establishment of innovation methods within the companies and enable them to develop new products and services themselves.

Traditionally, customer engagement uses channels like mail, telephone and local agents. In 2016, chatbots emerged as a new trend [16], making it a topic of interest for Fraunhofer IAO and insurance companies. With the rise of the smartphone, many insurers started offering apps, but success was limited [33], which may stem from app fatigue [38]. App use has plateaued, as users have too many apps and are reluctant to add more [13]. In contrast, conversational agents require no separate installation, as they are accessible via messaging apps, which are likely to be already installed on a user's smartphone. Conversational agents are an alternative to improve customer support and digitize processes like claim handling or managing customer data.

The objective of this work is to describe the creation of conversational agents in theory and practice and show the outcomes of both views. We facilitate the creation of conversational agents by defining the traits of an agent more clearly using a (1) classification framework, which is based on current literature and research topics, and systematically analyzing (2) use cases and requirements in an industry, shown in the example insurance scenario. We frame two application scenarios with this theoretical foundation. Prototype 1 is a claim-handling scenario, which shows technological progress for a conversational agent. In this extended version of our former paper [23], we present prototype 2. This new prototype has been created for the scenario of customer service and cross selling. It is created in the setting of a chatbot hackathon event that Fraunhofer IAO organized in 2018. The goal is to gain more insights about conversational agent creation while examining the practicability of chatbot implementation for small insurance scenarios. Furthermore, we enriched the evaluation chapter of both prototypes and compare the results of both activities. We derive possible applications, knowledge about challenges and success factors as learnings from both activities. We apply this knowledge in a new project for supporting small and medium enterprises in adoption of new technologies.

2   Related Work

In this section we investigate work in the area of conversational agents, dialog management, and research applications in insurance. In extension to the previous paper [23], we add theory on hackathons at the end of the section.

[26] offer detailed explanations about background and history of conversational interfaces as well as techniques to build and evaluate own agent applications. Another literature review about chatbots was provided by [4], where common approaches and

design choices are summarized followed by a case study about the functioning of IBM's chatbot Watson, which became famous for winning the popular quiz game *Jeopardy!* against humans.

Many chatbot applications have already been built nowadays with the goal to solve actual problems. One example is PriBot, a conversational agent, which can be asked questions about an application's privacy policy, because users tended to skip reading the often long and difficult to understand privacy notices. Also, the chatbot accepts queries of the user which aim to change his privacy settings or app permissions [17].

In the past there have already been several studies with the goal to evaluate how a conversational agent should behave for being considered as human-like as possible. In one of them, conducted by [22], fourteen participants were asked to talk to an existing chatbot and to collect key points of convincing and unconvincing characteristics. It turned out that the bot's ability to hold a theme over a longer dialog made it more realistic. On the other hand, not being able to answer to a user's questions was regarded as an unsatisfying characteristic of the artificial conversational partner [22].

In another experiment, which was done by [40], eight users had to talk to two different kinds of chatbots, one behaving more human-like and one behaving more robotic. In this context, they had to fulfill certain tasks like ordering an insurance policy or demanding an insurance certification. All of the participants instinctively started to chat by using natural human language. In cases in which the bot did not respond to their queries in a satisfying way, the users' sentences continuously got shorter until they ended up with writing key words only. Thus, according to the results of this survey, conversational agents preferably should be created human-like, because users seem to be more comfortable when feeling like talking to another human being, especially in cases in which the concerns are crucial topics like their insurance policies [40].

Dialog management strategies (DM) define the conversational behaviors of a system in response to user message and system state [26].

In industry applications, DM often consists of a handcrafted set of rules and heuristics, which are tightly coupled to the application domain [26] and improved iteratively. One problem with handcrafted approaches to DM is that it is challenging to anticipate every possible user input and react appropriately, making development resource-intensive and error-prone. But if few or no recordings of conversations are available, these *rule-oriented* strategies may be the only option.

As opposed to the rule-oriented strategies, data-oriented architectures work by using machine learning algorithms that are trained with samples of dialogs in order to reproduce the interactions that are observed in the training data. These statistical or heuristical approaches to DM can be classified into three main categories: Dialog modeling based on *reinforcement learning*, *corpus-based* statistical dialog management, and *example-based* dialog management (simply extracting rules from data instead of manually coding them) [26,41]. [41] highlights neural networks, Hidden-Markov Models, and Partially Observable Markov Decision Processes as possible implementation technologies.

The following are common strategies for rule-based dialog management:

- Finite-state-based DM uses a finite state machine with handcrafted rules, and performs well for highly structured, system-directed tasks [26].

- Frame-based DM follows no predefined dialog path, but instead allows to gather pieces of information in a frame structure and no specific order. This is done by adding an additional entity-value slot for every piece of information to be collected and by annotating the intents in which they might occur. Using frames, a less restricted, user-directed conversation flow is possible, as data is captured as it comes to the mind of the user [37].
- Information State Update represents the information known at a given state in a dialog and updates the internal model each time a participant performs a *dialog move*, (e.g. asking or answering). The state includes information about the mental states of the participants (beliefs, desires, intentions, etc.) and about the dialog (utterances, shared information, etc.) in abstract representations. Using so-called update moves, applicable moves are chosen based on the state [43].
- Agent-based DM uses an agent that fulfills conversation goals by dynamically using plans for tasks like intent detection and answer generation. The agent has a set of beliefs and goals as well as an information base which is updated throughout the conversation. Within this information framework the agent continuously prioritizes goals and autonomously selects plans that maximize the likelihood of goal fulfillment [29].

[6] describes how multiple DM approaches can be combined to use the best strategy for specific circumstances.

A virtual insurance conversational agent is described by [46], utilizing *TEATIME*, an architecture for agent-based DM. TEATIME uses emotional state as a driver for actions, e.g. when the bot is perceived unhelpful, that emotion leads the bot to apologize. The shown example bot is a proof of concept for TEATIME capable of answering questions regarding insurance and react to customer emotions, but does not implement a full business process.

[25] describe a text-based healthcare chatbot that acts as a companion for weightloss but also connects a patient with healthcare professionals. The chat interface supports non-textual inputs like scales and pictorials to gather patient feedback. Study results showed a high engagement with the chatbot as a peer and a higher percentage of automated conversation the longer the chatbot is used.

Overall, these examples show potential for conversational agents in the insurance area, but lack support for complete business processes.

Considering *hackathons* previous research has been done on (examples include [27] and [3]). Important for hackathons are *goals* of a hackathon as well as *success factors*. Hackathons are problem-focused computer programming events in which teams of programmers and other stakeholders prototype a software solution within a limited timeframe [3]. Hackathons usually are characterized by three features: (1) intensive collaborative work experience (2) solution of a concrete problem with a demonstrable solution (3) and a short time span. Depending on the focus and target group several specific formats are possible, like internal or external or application or technology specific hackathons [3]. Much work apart from the work cited here on hackathons has been published. To the best of our knowledge, an internal but company-spanning conversational agent hackathon in the insurance industry has not been described yet. We will compare the resulting prototypes based on the same technology of the hackathon with the prototype developed within a traditional project setting for deriving potentials and success factors for conversational agent creation. Furthermore, we will compare technological progress of the resulting prototypes.

3 Theory on Conversational Agents and Insurance Industry

3.1 Application Scenarios and Types of Agents

The idea of conversational agents that are able to communicate with human beings is not new: In 1966, Joseph Weizenbaum introduced *Eliza*, a virtual psychotherapist, which was able to respond to user queries using natural language and which could be considered as the first *chatbot* [45]. However, Eliza used quite simple structures by just picking up keywords and asking more questions, not serving a purpose itself. Nowadays, the idea of speaking machines has experienced a revival with the emergence of new technologies, especially in the area of artificial intelligence. Novel machine learning algorithms allow developers to create software agents in a much more sophisticated way and in many cases they already outperform previous statistical NLP methods [26]. Additionally, the importance of messaging apps such as WhatsApp or Telegram has increased over the last years. In 2015, the total number of people using these messaging services outran the total number of active users in social networks for the first time. Today, each of these app has about between 200 million and 1.5 billion users [19]. Currently the topic voice is on the rise - not only Gartner considers the breakthrough of voice applications in the next years.

Conversational agents can be basically employed in these settings:

- **Customer Service.** In 2016 [16] the topic of customer service chatbots lead to a great variety with a wide range of terminology.
- **Recruitment.** Recruitment chatbots become more popular, also the insurance company Allianz launched a recruitment bot recently.
- **Marketing.** Chatbots can be used for giving a company an innovative and up-to-date view without really serving a business process.
- **Internal Support.** Before chatbots became so popular, many companies already used chatbots for internal purposes. One example is IBM with its' "Whatis Bot"[1], which answered questions by instant messaging about acronyms already many years ago. The requirements for internal chatbots tend to be lower than for external ones, as customers usually have the choice of a communication channel or provider.

This paper focuses on *customer service* only for demonstration purposes and simple explainability. However, in the insurance project mentioned beforehand, the second category of internal support by NLP chatbots or voice systems has gathered even more interest.

For being able to draw a big picture of the current trends in the area of conversational agents, we divide them into the following four common categories:

---

[1] https://www.academia.edu/35150361/IBM_whatis.

- **(Virtual, Intelligent, Cognitive, Digital, Personal) assistants (VPAs).** Agents fulfilling tasks intelligently based on spoken or written user input and with the help of data bases and personalized user preferences [7] (e.g. Apple's Siri or Amazon's Alexa [8]).
- **Specialized Digital Assistants (SDAs).** Focused on a specific domain of expertise, goal-oriented behavior [8]. SDAs can be used in customer service as well as for internal support tasks.
- **Embodied Conversational Agents (ECAs).** Visually animated agents, e.g. in form of avatars or robots [34], where speech is combined with gestures and facial expressions.
- **Chatterbots.** Bots with focus on small talk and realistic conversations, not task-oriented, e.g. Cleverbot [5].

Figure 1 shows the results of evaluating these four classes in terms of different characteristics such as *realism* or *task orientation* based on own literature research. Chatterbots provide a high degree of entertainment since they try to imitate the behavior of human beings while chatting, but there is no specific goal to be reached within the scope of these conversations. In contrast, general assistants like Siri or Alexa are usually called by voice in order to fulfill a specific task. Specialized assistants concentrate even more on achieving a specific goal, which often comes at the expense of realism and user amusement because their ability to respond to not goal-oriented conversational inputs like small talk is mostly limited. The best feeling of companionship can be experienced by talking to an embodied agent, since the reactions of these bots are closest to human-like behavior.

Taking a look at the insurance project, it was decided to create prototypes for customer service in the type of *specialized digital assistants*. In the next paragraph, the processes in the insurance domain which might be chosen for this implementation are described. As shown in Fig. 1, it has shown that although the goal was to created a specialized digital assistant, humans have their own goals in prototype creation. Adding small talk in a limited scope affected the prototype creation and led to a more realistic and human-like user experience and more entertainment for the prototype in the hackathon as well.

3.2 Insurance Processes and Requirements for Prototypes

Insurance is an important industry sector in Germany, with 560 companies that manage about 460 million policies [39]. However, the insurance sector is under a high cost pressure, which shows in a declining employee count and low margins [42]. The insurance market is saturated and has transitioned from a growth market to a displacement market [1]. For the greater part, German insurance companies have used conservative strategies, caused by risk aversion, long-lived products, hierarchical structures, and profitable capital markets [47]. As these conditions change, so must insurance companies. One effort is the insurance project [35] with the goal of innovation and new technologies performed by Fraunhofer IAO since several years as described in Sect. 1. The two touch points of interest in the insurance industry are *selling a product* and *the claims process*. A study found that consumers interact less with insurers than with any other

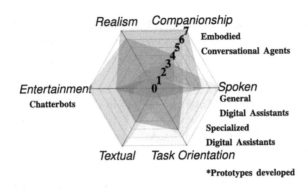

Fig. 1. Classification of conversational agents with their characteristics (based on own presentation from [23]). Values between 0 and 7 indicate how strong a characteristic applies for the given type of agent. Additionally to the classification, the prototype implementations are shown by the black box.

industry [30]. This is the reason why although chatbots become more popular in other use cases like recruitment, the focus of this paper is the application in customer service.

Many insurance companies have heterogeneous IT infrastructures incorporating legacy systems (sometimes from two or more companies as the result of a merger) [44]. These grown architectures pose challenges when implementing new data-driven or AI solutions, due to issues like data quality, availability and privacy. Nonetheless, the high amount of available data and complex processes make insurance a prime candidate for machine learning and data mining. The adoption of AI in the insurance sector is in early stages, but accelerating, as insurance companies strive to improve service and remain competitive [31].

Conversational agents are one AI technology at the verge of adoption. In 2017, ARAG launched a travel insurance chatbot, quickly followed by bots from other insurance companies [15]. Examples are a chatbot on moped insurance by wgv[2] and a chatbot on car insurance by Allianz[3].

To identify areas of possible chatbot support, we surveyed the core business processes of insurance companies as described in [1] and [18]. Three core areas of insurance companies are customer-facing: *marketing/sales*, *contract management* and *claim management*. Figure 2 shows the main identified processes related to this area.

We identified all these processes as possible use cases for conversational agent support, in particular support by SDAs. As two prototypes are planned, the criteria are analyzed for both settings. The chosen scenario for prototype 1 is a special case of the damage claim process: *The user has a damaged smartphone or tablet and wants to make an insurance claim.* The scenario for prototype 2 in the hackathon is: *The user has received an annual bill. Answer frequently asked questions concerning the annual bill for car insurance and combine with change of personal data and cross selling activities* (see also Fig. 2).

---

[2] https://www.wgv.de/versicherungen/kfz/moped/.
[3] https://www.facebook.com/AllianzCarlo/.

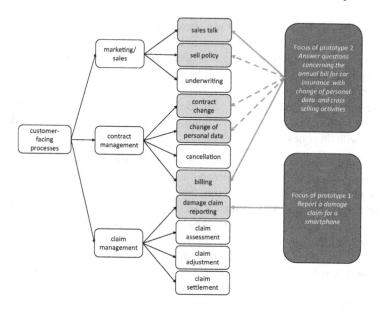

Fig. 2. Customer-facing insurance processes (original in [23] based on [1] and [18]) with additional information on the prototypes as described in this paper shown in grey.

Furthermore, we investigated general requirements for conversational agents in these processes:

Availability and Ease-of-use. Conversational agents are an alternative to both conventional customer support (e.g. phone, mail) as well as conventional applications (e.g. apps and websites). Compared to these conventional solutions, chatbots offer more availability than human agents and have less barriers of use than conventional applications, requiring neither an installation nor the ability to learn a new user interface, as conventional messaging services are used [10]. This includes the requirement of understanding and answering to human language, which applies to both prototypes developed.

Guided Information Flow. Compared to websites, which offer users a large amount of information they must filter and prioritize themselves, conversational agents offer information gradually and only after the intent of the user is known. Thus, the search space is narrowed at the beginning of the conversation without the user needing to be aware of all existing options. This is done for both prototypes by narrowing the scope.

Smartphone Integration. Using messaging services, conversational agents can integrate with other smartphone capabilities, e.g. making a picture, sending a calendar event, setting a reminder or calling a phone number. This applies for both prototypes.

Customer Call Reduction. Customer service functions can be measured by reduction of customer calls and average handling time [16]. SDAs can help here by automating conversations, handling standard customer requests and performing parts of conversations (e.g. authentication). This is relevant for projects, but out of scope for the prototype. However, questions about the annual bill arise very frequently.

Human Handover. Customers often use social media channels to escalate an issue in the expectation of a *human* response, instead of an *automated* one. A conversational agent thus must be able to differentiate between standard use cases it can handle and more complicated issues, which need to be handed over to human agents [28]. One possible approach is to use sentiment detection, so customer who are already stressed are not further aggravated by a bot [16]. Being out of scope for the prototype, this has only be investigated for some technology providers that have different levels of experience with this question.

Digitize Claim Handling. Damage claim handling in insurance companies is a complex process involving multiple departments and stakeholders [24]. Claim handling processes are more and more digitized within the insurance companies [18], but paper still dominates communication with claimants, workshops and experts. [12] defines maturity levels of insurance processes, defining *virtual handling* as a process where claims are assessed fully digitally based on digital data from the claimant (e.g. a video, a filled digital form), and *touchless handling* as a fully digital process with no human intervention on the insurance side. SDAs help moving towards these maturity levels by providing a guided way to make a claim digitally and communicate with the claimant (e.g. in case additional data is needed). Prototype 1 covers this area.

Conversational Commerce. Is the use of Conversational Agents for marketing and sales related purposes [11]. Conversational Agents can perform multiple tasks using a single interface. Examples are using opportunities to sell additional products (*cross-sell*) or better versions of the product the customer already has (*up-sell*) by chiming in with personalized product recommendations in the most appropriate situations. One example would be to note that a person's last name has changed during an address update customer service case and offer appropriate products if the customer has just married. Prototype 2 covers this area.

Internationalization. Is an important topic for large international insurance companies. However, most frameworks for implementing conversational agents are available in more than one language. To the best of our knowledge, the applied conversational agents in German insurance today are optimized only for one language. So this topic is future work in respect to both prototypes, but will become more important in the future.

Compliance. to privacy (GDPR) is usually guaranteed by the login mechanisms on the insurance sites, therefore the topic is out of scope for our research prototype. For broader scenarios not requiring identification on the insurance site and the usage of the data for non-costumers, this is an area of ongoing research on compliant technical solutions or workarounds.

4   Practice in Two Prototypes in Insurance Industry

4.1   Technical Requirements and Framework Options for the Prototypes

For dialog design within prototype 1, experimenting with machine learning algorithms was the preferred implementation strategy. For this purpose, discussions with insurance companies were held to assess the feasibility of receiving existing dialogs with customers, for example for online chats, phone logs or similar. However, such logs generally seem to be not available at German insurers, as the industry has self-regulated to only store data needed for claim processing [14]. As a research institute represents a third party not directly involved in claims processing, data protection laws forbid sharing of data this way without steps to secure personal data. During our talks we have identified a need for automated or assisted anonymization of written texts as a precondition for most customer-facing machine learning use cases, at least when operating in Europe [20]. However, these issues go beyond the scope of our current project, but provide many opportunities for future research.

To still build a demonstrator in face of these challenges as outlined in [2], dialogs for both prototypes were manually designed without using real-life customer conversations and fine-tuned by user testing with fictional issues. As this approach entails higher manual effort for dialog design, a narrower scenario was chosen for both prototypes to still allow for the full realization of a customer-facing process.

Based on the work presented in the last sections and our talks with insurance companies, we arrived at the following non-functional requirements that the chatbot prototype 1 ideally should fulfill:

- **Interoperability:** The agent should be able to keep track of the conversational context over several message steps and messengers.
- **Portability:** The agent can be run on different devices and platforms (e.g. Facebook Messenger, Telegram). Therefore it should use a unified, platform-independent messaging format.
- **Extensibility:** The agent should provide a high level of abstraction that allows designers to add new conversational content without having to deal with complicated data structures or code.

For natural language understanding, we compared four possible frameworks (Microsoft's LUIS, Google's Dialogflow, Facebook's wit.ai and IBM's Watson) regarding important criteria for prototype implementation in a first step just for prototype 1. The comparison was extended for the frameworks moni.ai and Kauz.net for prototype 2 in the hackathon. All six frameworks support textual input and output, this was amongst others a basic requirement, but not all support complex conversation flows for advanced use cases. A comparison table for these criteria is shown in Table 1. As a result of the comparison, Google Dialogflow was chosen as a basic framework for prototype 1 based on the fulfillment of all requirements of prototype 1, one of which was the free availability. For prototype 2 and the hackathon, Google Dialogflow and IBM Watson Assistant were chosen, as an important factor next to the available user interface to enable non-programmers to work with the software was the fact that the providers agreed to accompany the hackathon event by sending experts for local support.

4.2 Prototype 1: Claim Management with Technological Extensions

Prototype 1 fulfills the following scenario: *The user has a damaged smartphone or tablet and wants to make an insurance claim.* The goal here is to focus on technology and build a demonstratable prototype in a 'traditional' project setting. We describe

Table 1. Comparison of Microsoft's LUIS, Google's Dialogflow, Facebook's wit.ai, and IBM's Watson (from the requirements for the technical prototype (1) as in the original paper [23], based on [9]) and extended for prototype 2 by additional hackathon requirements and two new providers nameley moni.ai and Kauz.net (n.c. stands for Not Considered anymore or not yet for the prototype 1 or 2 as of early in 2018).

Requirement		LUIS	Dialogflow	Wit.ai	Watson	moni.ai	Kauz.net
Overall (1,2)	Textual in-/output	yes	yes	yes	yes	yes	yes
Overall (1,2)	German language	yes	yes	in Beta	yes	yes	yes
Technical (1)	Python bindings	no	yes	yes	yes	n.c.	n.c.
Technical (1)	Free service	no	yes	yes	partly^a	n.c.	n.c.
Technical (1)	Remember state	yes	yes	yes	yes	n.c.	n.c.
Technical (1)	Service bound	yes	yes	yes	yes	n.c.	n.c.
Technical (1)	Simple training	partly	yes	yes	yes	n.c.	n.c.
Hackathon (2)	Complex conversation flows	no	yes	n.c.	yes	n.c.	n.c.
Hackathon (2)	Provider support	n.c.	yes	n.c.	yes	no	yes
Hackathon (2)	User Interface	yes	yes	n.c.	yes	yes	no

^{a} 10 000 free messages per month

the results technically in the following. Figure 6 shows the main components of the prototype and their operating sequence when processing a user message. To provide extensibility prototype architecture strictly separates service integration, internal logic and domain logic.

The user can interact with the bot over different communication channels which are integrated with different *bot API clients*. To integrate a different messaging service, a new bot API client needs to be written. The remainder of the prototype can be reused. See Fig. 3 for an example of the prototype on different communication channels.

Once a user has written a message, a lookup of *user context* is performed to determine if a conversation with that user is already in progress. User context is stored in a database so no state is kept within external messaging services. Afterwards, a *typing* notification is given to the user, indicating the bot has received the message and is working on it. This prevents multiple messages by a user who thinks the bot is not responsive.

In the next step, the message has to be understood by the bot. In case of a voice message, it is transcribed to text using a *Google* speech recognition web service. Dialogflow is used for intent identification, which determines the function of a message and based on that a set of possible parameters [26]. For example, the intent of the message "the display of my smartphone broke" may have the intent phone_broken with the parameter damage_type as display_damage, while the parameter phone_type is not given. Together, this information given by Dialogflow is a MessageUnderstanding.

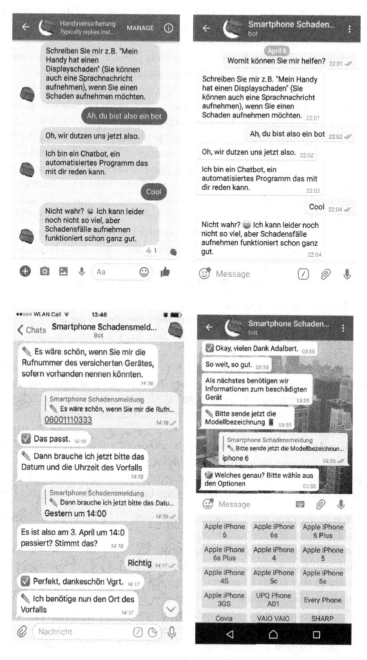

Fig. 3. Top: The system is mirrored on both the Facebook and Telegram Messengers. Bottom left: Additional view with customer data input and intelligent recognition of words like *yesterday*. Bottom right: Dialog excerpt of the prototype, showing the possibility to clarify the phone model via multiple-choice input. Extended version of figures in [23].

As soon as the message is understood, the user context is updated. Afterwards, a response needs to be generated. This process, which was labeled with *Plan and Realize Response* in Fig. 6, is shown in detail in Fig. 7.

In the prototype, an agent-based strategy was chosen in order to combine the capabilities of the frame-based entities and parameters in Dialogflow with a custom dialog controller based on predefined rules in a finite state machine. This machine allows to define rules that trigger *handlers* and *state transitions* when a specific intent or entity-parameter combination is encountered. That way, both intent and frame processing happen in the same logically encapsulated unit, enabling better maintainability and extensibility. The rules are instances of a set of `*Handler` classes such as an `IntentHandler` for the aforementioned intent and parameter matching, supplemented by other handlers, e.g. an `AffirmationHandler`, which consolidates different intents that all express a confirmation along the lines of "yes", "okay", "good" and "correct", as well as a `NegationHandler`, a `MediaHandler` and an `EmojiSentimentHandler` (to analyze positive, neutral, or negative sentiment of a message with emojis). Each implements their own `matches (Message Understanding)` method.

The following types of rules (handlers) are used within the dialog state machine:

1. *Stateless* handlers are checked independently of the current state. For example, a `RegexHandler` rule determines whether the formality of the address towards the user should be changed (German differentiates the informal "du" and the formal "Sie")

2. *Dialog States* map each possible state to a list of handlers that are applicable in that state. For instance, when the user has given an answer and the system asks for *explicit confirmation* in a state `USER_CONFIRMING_ANSWER`, then an `AffirmationHandler` and a `NegationHandler` capture "yes" and "no" answers.

3. *Fallback* handlers are checked if none of the applicable state handlers have yielded a match for an incoming `MessageUnderstanding`. These `fallbacks` include static, predefined responses with lowest priority (e.g. small talk), as well as handlers to repair the conversation by bringing the user back on track or changing the topic.

At first, the system had only allowed a single state to be declared at the same time in the router. However, this had quickly proven to be insufficient as users are likely to want to respond or refer not only to the most recent message, but also to previous ones in the chat. With only a single contemporaneous state, the user's next utterance is always interpreted only in that state. In order to make this model resilient, every state would need to incorporate every utterance that the user is likely to say in that context. As this is not feasible, the prototype has state handlers that allow layering transitions on top of each other, allowing multiple simultaneous states which may advance individually.

To avoid an explosion of active states, the system has *state lifetimes*: new states returned by callbacks may have a lifetime that determines the number of dialog moves this state is valid for. On receiving a new message, the planning agent decreases the lifetimes of all current dialog states by one, except for the case of utter non-understanding ("fallback" intent). If a state has exceeded its lifetime, it is removed from the priority queue of current dialog states.

Figure 7 contains details about how the system creates responses to user queries. Based on the applicable rule, the conversational agent performs chat actions (e.g. sending a message), which are generated from response templates, taking into account dialog state, intent parameters, and information like a user's name, mood and preferred level of formality.

RuleHandlers, states and other dialog specific implementations are encapsulated, so a new type of dialog can be implemented without needing to change the other parts of the system.

Generated chat actions are stored in the user context and performed for the user's specific messenger using the *bot API*. As the user context has been updated, the next message by the user continues the conversation.

The prototype explains its functionality and offers limited small talk. As soon as the user wants to make a damage claim, a predetermined questionnaire is used about type of damage, damaged phone, phone number, IMEI, damage time, damage event details, etc. Interpretation results of answers have to be confirmed by the user. For specific questions domain specific actions for clarification are implemented (see bottom right in Fig. 3). In a real-life application, claim management systems would be integrated to automatically trigger subsequent processes.

4.3 Prototype 2: Customer Service and Cross-selling in Hackathon

For receiving more insights about the practicability of introducing chatbots to the insurance domain and for gaining experience with the usage of conversational frameworks, Fraunhofer IAO organized a four-day hackathon with five German insurance companies participating [21]. This results in prototype 2 for the given task: *Create a chatbot using IBM Watson Assistant or Google Dialogflow for answering questions about the annual bill of car insurance and leveraging cross-selling opportunities.*

In the scope of the event four minimal products were created by four interdisciplinary teams of IT specialists, sales experts and other employees of the insurance companies. Doing so, in contrast to posing the challenge to external developers, our insurance partners were directly involved and could profit from the lessons learned from this *internal hackathon* [36]. One impression from the resulting video is shown in Fig. 4 and also described in a blog article [21].

Following four prototypes can be characterized as the teams worked independently:

Prototype A Voice Focus. One more technically oriented team started by adding voice technology to the chatbot for output purposes. Analogously, voice input could be used - although findings in the insurance project show that the input direction is more difficult to handle than the output direction. It showed that the focus is very entertaining in presentation and that the presentation especially of voice technology has to be performed carefully. In addition, the chatbot has been made more human-like by adding personal opinions on sports.

Prototype B Multimedia Focus. Team B integrated several resources for better multimedia presentation, like images, videos, and the like. This already started with using an QR-code for accessing the prototype. The idea of using sophisticated multimedia content for explaining the annual bill like clickable graphics with videos has

Hack with Fraunhofer IAO: Innovate Insurance

Fig. 4. Hackathon impressions (www.youtube.com/watch?v=yHRLYJ_olZ8, [21]).

impressed the jury. The team focused therefore on customer experience and fine-tuned their interaction patterns by introducing delay in the response times.

Prototype C Stability and Scope Focus. The C-team focused on building a stable prototype for the complete task, achieving a large coverage of topics. The team spent most time in designing entities and intents as well as dialogue flow. This led to a comprehensive design and the most resilient result. The team was successful in maintaining background knowledge in a database and integrate it into the conversation flow.

Prototype D Customer Identification Focus. The team D focused on solving the customer identification issue. Using this information, they could give very detailed information on the current contract of the customer and the bill and use customer specific information for guiding the conversation itself. Another demonstration was the change of customer data. Additionally, some small talk was introduced for entertainment purposes.

Concerning the results, it is worth mentioning that all four groups succeeded in creating a usable product within the given timeframe that was able to handle the required use case of answering questions about annual bills for a small set of predefined queries. However, when letting a chatbot talk to people of other groups who were not involved in its development and thus not aware of the underlying dialog structure, the solutions proved to be error prone since they could not handle these unexpected inputs. This stems from *hardcoding* parts of the scenario due to time constraints. In some cases, more expertise in dialog design would have helped anticipate typical user inputs. All teams worked with the *entities* and *intents* as are defined in most chatbot technologies, adding no programmable extensions (as compared to prototype 1). Therefore, the dialogue structure is static and creating the chatbot is done by adding intents and entities as well was *if-then* like programming of the dialogue. The teams got only the plain frameworks of the providers and no specific extensions as for example for thorough testing. Working in teams on a chatbot proved to be helpful, but added organizational complexity, since resource access had to be shared and organized. Additionally, it turned out that professional content designers that build appropriate conversation models may be even more important than programmers, at least in case the used technology is enhanced enough. A final survey among the participants showed that they enjoyed working in the chosen hackathon format and could benefit a lot from its results and lessons learned.

5 Evaluation

Both prototypes were evaluated using appropriate methods. For prototype one, a questionnaire-based approach with 14 participants was chosen. For prototype two, an expert commission had to choose and rate all four prototypes based on a very short questionnaire and come up with a point rating in a very short time span, as is typical for hackathons. We will first describe the results of both evaluation processes and then compare the results in the overall conclusion of this paper (see Sect. 6).

5.1 Evaluation of Prototype 1 Claim Management

To evaluate the produced prototype's quality and performance, we conducted a model trial with the goal to report a claim by using the chatbot without having any further instructions available.

Of the 14 participants (who all had some technical background), 35.7% claimed to regularly use chatbots, 57.1% to use them occasionally, and only 7.1% stated that they had never talked to a chatbot before. However, all participants were able to report a claim within a range of about four minutes, resulting in an overall task completion rate of 100%.

Additionally, the users had to rate the quality of their experiences with the conversational agent by filling out a questionnaire. For each question they could assign points between 0 (did not apply at all) and 10 (did apply to the full extent). The most important quality criteria, whose choice was oriented on the work of [34], are listed with their average ratings in Fig. 5 and are discussed in detail.

Ease of Use. With an average of 8 points for *Ease of Use*, the users had no problems with using the bot to solve the task, since none of them gave less than 5 points. However, a variance of 2.46 still indicates a strong gap among the participants' experienced degree of usability.

Appropriate Formality. 8.3 points on average for *Appropriate Formality* indicate that the participants were comfortable with the formal and informal language the bot talked to them. Nonetheless, this criteria was also rated with points of only one and two. One of these users stated that he felt worried about permanently being called by his first name after he told it. Therefore, development of a more fine-grained detection mechanism for formal and informal language sould be considered in future versions of the chatbot, since for now we only rely on simple regular expressions.

Natural Interaction. The rating for convincing *Natural Interaction* with 7.9 points may be due to the fact that the conversation was designed in a strongly questionnaire-oriented way, which might have restricted the feeling of having a free user conversation. Therefore, improving the flexibility of the conversational flow and granting more freedom for user-centric dialog control might strengthen the authentic feeling during interaction with the agent.

Response Quality. The satisfaction with given answers to users' domain specific questions was considered quite (but not totally) convincing with 7.6 points. Note that the high number of points might not be justified entirely, because the chatbot's implemented ability to answer questions is still very basic and restricted to concerns of claim handling. But, since the whole conversation is strongly driven by the agent itself, the users probably didn't find the time to ask many questions that went beyond the current limits of understanding. Connecting any kinds of knowledge bases might serve as a first future step towards extending the agent's response qualities.

Personality. The least convincing experience was that chatbot's *Personality*, which was rated with only 5.2 points on average. This is not surprising, since during this work we put comparatively less efforts in strengthening the agent's personal skills as it does not even introduce itself with a name, but instead mainly acts on a professional level, always concentrating on the fulfillment of its task. Facing these facts, a professional copywriter should have no problems developing a more convincing character for the chatbot.

Funny and Interesting. With 7.2 points, talking to the chatbot was experienced as quite *Funny & Interesting*, but still with a lot of room for further improvement. Again, the key here stays to loosen the strict procedure of forcing the user to finish the process and to allow more room for smalltalk and off topic contents.

Entertainment. The agent's *Entertainment* capabilities, which are at 7.7 points on average, could be upgraded by extending the conversational contents with additional enjoyable features not related to the questionnaire. At the moment, the chatbot is only able to tell some jokes from the insurance domain, but does not provide a holistic concept for customer entertainment.

No Deception Feeling. The agent's *lack of deceptiveness*, i.e. the degree to which users know it is not human, which at 9.6 points show that the bot's statements made its nature clear to users.

5.2 Evaluation of Prototype 2 as in the Hackathon

Typically, the evaluation in hackathons is done by a very short demo and questions from the audience by an expert committee. After four days, the resulting prototypes were examined by a jury considering the following predefined criteria. These differ strongly from the criteria in the first evaluation due to the time-constrained focused question. Most of the questions tackle the aforementioned *response quality*, with a second thought on *natural interaction*. They clarify what is actually a focus of the hackathon and what is not, putting emphasis on getting done. The *formality* is just a subcriterion if the language style is adapted. All further going criteria like personality, fun, entertainment etc. have explicitly not been stated, but it is interesting that all groups put a strong focus on this during their presentation, trying to stand out from the field and enjoying to add human-like behavior.

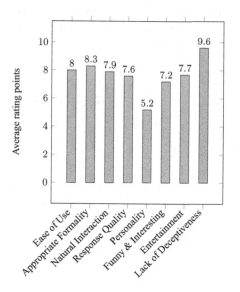

Fig. 5. Survey results for prototype 1: average user experience ratings (fourteen participants, 0..10 points) from [23].

Language Support
- Is the chatbot able to recognize the user input?
- Are the outputs of the chatbot adequate and understandable?
- Is the language style used by the bot adequate and consistent?
- Is the language style used by the bot adapted individually to user properties?

Flexibility
- Is the chatbot able to correctly recognize input even in unusual phrases?
- Is the chatbot able to respond appropriately to unexpected input?

Scope of Functions
- How well has the scenario *Annual fee bill* been covered by the prototype?
- How well are extensions and transitions implemented leading to other topics such as cross selling?

Presentation
- Is the presentation convincing? Are there any differences to the other groups?
- Did the team manage to explain the chatbot in a timely manner?

The expert committee had difficulties finding a winner in the given time span, as all of the four prototypes fulfilled certain aspects that were identified as interesting to the jury. Altogether the participants and experts learned a lot about chatbot design and technologies and were satisfied with the results. Both technologies led to good results in the hackathon, but most of the participants felt they needed provider support and expert knowledge on dialogue design for creating a real product for customers. More overall conclusions follow in the next section.

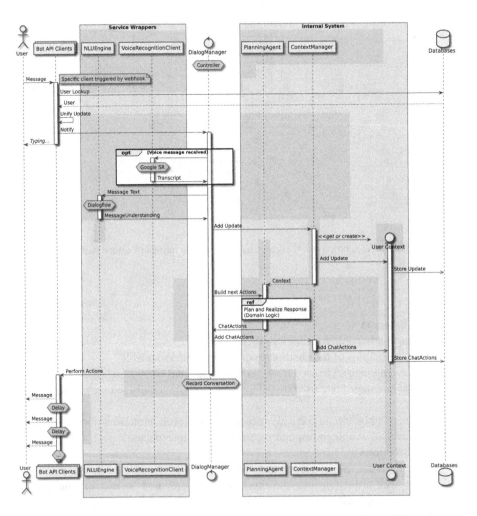

Fig. 6. Sequence diagram of the conversational agent prototype from [23].

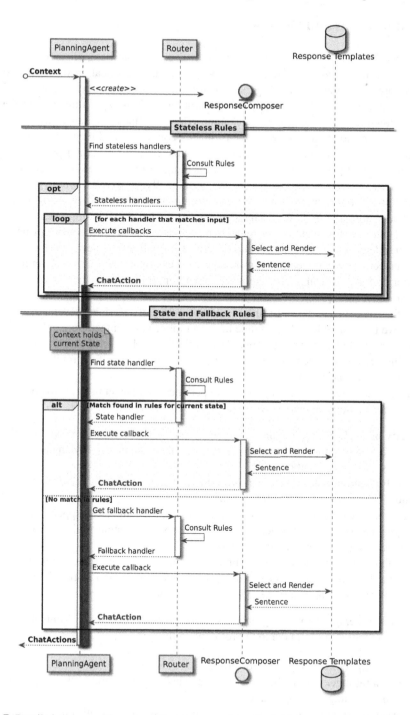

Fig. 7. Detailed sequence diagram of the response generation in the conversational agent prototype from [23].

6   Conclusions and Outlook

In this work we have shown how conversational agents can be applied for different use cases in theory and practice. We showed how our classification of conversation agents applies for the prototypes generated for our two scenarios: (1) claim management process support in traditional project setting as well as (2) customer service and cross selling in an interdisciplinary hackathon. The potential processes to employ chatbots have been shown in general for the insurance companies and focused on customer service processes. One key result of our former paper [23] containing prototype 1 is a system of multiple conversational states enabling more flexible conversations. We extended the evaluation with real users and additionally showed the prototype to various customer groups, small businesses and more insurance companies. Altogether, the prototype is able to handle the scenario satisfactory. One possible improvement is the point of *realism*, for example by more human-like behavior in a consistent persona and better determination of the desired degree of formality. The newly performed and described activity is the creation of prototype 2 for customer service consisting of actually four prototypes in an interdisciplinary hackathon. It has shown that the results here differ strongly form prototype 1 due to different goals, different time span and different skills. No extensions to the entity-intent concept were performed, but several innovative ideas have been included like multimedia integration, voice integration, several entertaining aspects and especially persona design. Prototype 1 did not have a name in the beginning, whereas all teams came up with innovative names for prototype 2 at the beginning of the hackathon.

Altogether, after two years of chatbot experience, we can summarize the potentials for the conversational agent technology:

Maturity of Technology. Technology matures and is more often perceived in all day activities, most people know chatbots and how they can be used. Many people have already tried out a chatbot.

Service Enhandement. Agents can be used for better availability (24/7/365) and to reduce the workload of the service staff.

Tools. Tools are available especially for good English language support. More languages and features are added as time passes. New technological frameworks are available, the existing ones are improved.

Simple Tasks. Easy application for simple tasks and simple prototype creation is possible in a short time span. Transfer from prototype to live system is still more difficult.

Applicability. Many application scenarios are possible.

We have identified following challenges for new conversational agents and especially for transitioning from demo to prototype to live service:

Testing. Is time-consuming and error-prone

Domain Language. Has to be usually hardcoded or added manually supported by machine learning in an optimal case

Handovers. Designing handovers is a challenging tasks that not all frameworks fulfill perfectly

Maintenance. Of the chatbot and further development is a challenging tasks and the process has to be defined

Self-learning. Is not available in the expected scope as lots of people have very high and unrealistic expectations to machine learning

High Expectations. To chatbot technology in general which might not be fulfilled in the begining

Security and Integration. Issues as with most technologies

As a result of our two prototypes, the evaluations and the hackathon participant surveys, we came up with the following success factors that we believe need to be respected when planning to introduce conversational agents to companies:

Clear Scope Definition. Use cases and functionality of the conversational agent should be predefined as detailed as possible.

Customer-oriented development. Tests with intended audience and changing test participants to prevent them getting used to the dialog structure.

Careful Improvements and Testing. Sufficient time and care should be invested in testing and improving the agent. A nonfunctional or only partly functional bot deployed to the public too early might cause a negative reception that cannot be corrected with future improvements.

Perform Regression Tests. Especially for self-learning agents it is crucial to ensure that the bot does not "unlearn" skills that once worked successfully.

Facilitate Maintenance. Provide high-level (graphical) dialog customization options for the employees of the related department for supporting easy extension and improvement of the agent.

Choice of Technology Provider. Technology providers should be compared and chosen according to the company environment and its conditions. One partner should be selected for longer cooperation.

The model trial covering two prototypes has shown that conversational agents are ready for productive use. However, the effort in creating and maintaining a conversational agent is not to be underestimated. While a successful conversation with a chatbot provides a satisfying customer experience, errors and gaps in dialog flow let user satisfaction drop rather quickly. While users do not expect a human like conversation and phrase their statements accordingly, they expect clearly formulated requests and answers to be readily understood. Currently we are working on supporting small and medium enterprises with evaluation of the technology and potential use cases for their businesses. In future research, we would like to implement a real-life conversational agent as well as perform a real-life evaluation with an insurance partner to quantify the benefits of agent use, e.g. call reduction, success rate, and customer satisfaction as well as support small and medium businesses with agent creation.

Acknowledgements. The work is partially based on work carried out in the project 'Business Innovation Engineering Center', which is funded by the Ministry of Economic Affairs, Labour and Housing Baden-Wuerttemberg under the reference number 3-4332.62-IAO/56. The hackathon itself was conducted within the 'Innovationsnetzwerk Digitalisierung fuer Versicherungen' [35]. The authors want to thank all participants for their contributions and feedback.

References

1. Aschenbrenner, M., Dicke, R., Karnarski, B., Schweiggert, F.: Informationsverarbeitung in Versicherungsunternehmen. Springer, Heidelberg (2010). https://doi.org/10.1007/978-3-642-04321-5
2. Blohm, M., Dukino, C., Kintz, M., Kochanowski, M., Koetter, F., Renner, T.: Towards a privacy compliant cloud architecture for natural language processing platforms. In: Proceedings of the 21st International Conference on Enterprise Information Systems, ICEIS, vol. 1, pp. 454–461. INSTICC. SciTePress (2019). https://doi.org/10.5220/0007746204540461
3. Briscoe, G., Mulligan, C.: Digital innovation: the Hackathon phenomenon (2014). http://www.creativeworkslondon.org.uk/wp-content/uploads/2013/11/Digital-Innovation-The-Hackathon-Phenomenon1.pdf
4. Cahn, J.: CHATBOT: Architecture, Design, & Development (2017)
5. Carpenter, R.: Cleverbot (2018). https://www.cleverbot.com/
6. Chu, S.W., O'Neill, I., Hanna, P., McTear, M.: An approach to multi-strategy dialogue management. In: Ninth European Conference on Speech Communication and Technology, pp. 865–868 (2005)
7. Cooper, R.S., McElroy, J.F., Rolandi, W., Sanders, D., Ulmer, R.M., Peebles, E.: Personal virtual assistant. US Patent 7,415,100, 19 August 2008
8. Dale, R.: Industry watch: the return of the Chatbots. Nat. Lang. Eng. **22**(5), 811–817 (2016)
9. Davydova, O.: 25 Chatbot platforms: a comparative table (2017). https://chatbotsjournal.com/25-chatbot-platforms-a-comparative-table-aeefc932eaff
10. Derler, R.: Chatbot vs. app vs. website - chatbots magazine, December 2017. https://chatbotsmagazine.com/chatbot-vs-app-vs-website-en-e0027e46c983
11. Eeuwen, M.: Mobile conversational commerce: messenger Chatbots as the next interface between businesses and consumers. Master's thesis, University of Twente (2017)
12. Fannin, T., Brower, B.: 2017 future of claims study. Tech. rep. LexisNexis (2017)
13. Gartner: Market trends: mobile app adoption matures as usage mellows (2015). https://www.gartner.com/newsroom/id/3018618
14. GDV: Verhaltensregeln für den Umgang mit personenbezogenen Daten durch die deutsche Versicherungswirtschaft (2012). http://www.gdv.de/wp-content/uploads/2013/03/GDV_Code-of-Conduct_Datenschutz_2012.pdf. datum des Aufrufes des Dokumentes: 11.02.2015
15. Gorr, D.: Ein Versicherungsroboter für gewisse Stunden. Versicherungswirtschaft Heute (2018). http://versicherungswirtschaft-heute.de/schlaglicht/ein-versicherungsroboter-fur-gewisse-stunden/
16. Guzmán, I., Pathania, A.: Chatbots in customer service. Tech. rep. Accenture (2016)
17. Harkous, H., Fawaz, K., Shin, K.G., Aberer, K.: Pribots: conversational privacy with Chatbots. In: Twelth Symposium on Usable Privacy and Security (SOUPS 2016). USENIX Association, Denver, CO (2016). https://www.usenix.org/conference/soups2016/workshop-program/wfpn/presentation/harkous
18. Horch, A., Kintz, M., Koetter, F., Renner, T., Weidmann, M., Ziegler, C.: Projekt openXchange: Servicenetzwerk zur effizienten Abwicklung und Optimierung von Regulierungsprozessen bei Sachschäden. Fraunhofer Verlag, Stuttgart (2012)
19. Inc, S.: Most popular messaging apps (2018). https://www.statista.com/statistics/258749/most-popular-global-mobile-messenger-apps/
20. Kamarinou, D., Millard, C., Singh, J.: Machine learning with personal data. Queen Mary School of Law Legal Studies Research Paper, no. 247 (2016)
21. Kasper, H.: Hack deine versicherungs-innovation: 4 Chatbots in 4 tagen (2018). https://blog.iao.fraunhofer.de/hack-deine-versicherungs-innovation-4-chatbots-in-4-tagen/

22. Kirakowski, J., O'Donnell, P., Yiu, A.: Establishing the hallmarks of a convincing chatbot-human dialogue. In: Maurtua, I. (ed.) Human-Computer Interaction. InTech, Rijeka (2009). https://doi.org/10.5772/7741

23. Koetter, F., Blohm, M., Kochanowski, M., Goetzer, J., Graziotin, D., Wagner, S.: Motivations, classification and model trial of conversational agents for insurance companies. In: Rocha, A.P., Steels, L., van den Herik, J. (eds.) Proceedings of the 11th International Conference on Agents and Artificial Intelligence, ICAART 2019, Volume 1, Prague, Czech Republic, 19–21 February 2019, pp. 19–30. SciTePress (2019). https://doi.org/10.5220/0007252100190030

24. Koetter, F., Weisbecker, A., Renner, T.: Business process optimization in cross-company service networks: architecture and maturity model. In: 2012 Annual SRII Global Conference (SRII), pp. 715–724. IEEE (2012)

25. Kowatsch, T., et al.: Text-based healthcare Chatbots supporting patient and health professional teams: preliminary results of a randomized controlled trial on childhood obesity. In: Persuasive Embodied Agents for Behavior Change (PEACH2017). ETH Zurich (2017)

26. McTear, M., Callejas, Z., Griol, D.: The Conversational Interface. Springer, Cham (2016). https://doi.org/10.1007/978-3-319-32967-3

27. Mohajer Soltani, P., Pessi, K., Ahlin, K., Wernered, I.: Hackathon - a method for digital innovative success: a comparative descriptive study. In: Proceedings of the 8th European Conference on Information Management and Evaluation, ECIME 2014, September 2014

28. Newlands, M.: 10 ways AI and Chatbots reduce business risks. https://www.entrepreneur.com/article/305073(2017)

29. Nguyen, A., Wobcke, W.: An agent-based approach to dialogue management in personal assistants. In: Proceedings of the 10th International Conference on Intelligent User Interfaces, pp. 137–144. ACM (2005)

30. Niddam, M., Barsley, N., Gard, J.C., Cotroneo, U.: Evolution and revolution: how insurers stay relevant in a digital future (2014). https://www.bcg.com/publications/2014/insurance-technology-strategy-evolution-revolution-how-insurers-stay-relevant-digital-world.aspx

31. Nordman, E., DeFrain, K., Hall, S.N., Karapiperis, D., Obersteadt, A.: How artificial intelligence is changing the insurance industry (2017)

32. Pohl, V., Kasper, H., Kochanowski, M., Renner, T.: Zukunftsstudie 2027 #ichinzehnjahren (2017). http://s.fhg.de/zukunft2027. (in german)

33. Power, J.D.: 2017 U.S. auto claims satisfaction study (2017). http://www.jdpower.com/resource/jd-power-us-auto-claims-satisfaction-study

34. Radziwill, N., Benton, M.: Evaluating quality of Chatbots and intelligent conversational agents. arXiv preprint arXiv:1704.04579 (2017)

35. Renner, T., Kochanowski, M.: Innovationsnetzwerk digitalisierung für versicherungen (2018). http://s.fhg.de/innonetz. (in German)

36. Rosell, B., Kumar, S., Shepherd, J.: Unleashing innovation through internal hackathons, pp. 1–8, May 2014. https://doi.org/10.1109/InnoTek.2014.6877369

37. Rudnicky, A., Xu, W.: An agenda-based dialog management architecture for spoken language systems. In: IEEE Automatic Speech Recognition and Understanding Workshop, vol. 13 (1999)

38. Schippers, B.: App fatigue (2016). https://techcrunch.com/2016/02/03/app-fatigue/

39. Schwark, P., Theis, A.: Statistisches Taschenbuch der Versicherungswirtschaft. Gesamtverband der Deutschen Versicherungswirtschaft (GDV), Berlin (2014)

40. Sörensen, I.: Expectations on Chatbots among novice users during the onboarding process (2017). http://urn.kb.se/resolve?urn=urn:nbn:se:kth:diva-202710

41. Spierling, U.: Interactive digital storytelling: towards a hybrid conceptual approach. In: Worlds in Play: International Perspectives on Digital Games Research (2005)

42. Stange, A., Reich, N.: Die Zukunft der deutschen Assekuranz: chancenreich und doch ungewiss. In: Zimmermann, G. (ed.) Change Management in Versicherungsunternehmen, pp. 3–9. Springer, Wiesbaden (2015). https://doi.org/10.1007/978-3-658-05974-3_1

43. Traum, D.R., Larsson, S.: The information state approach to dialogue management. In: van Kuppevelt, J., Smith, R.W. (eds.) Current and new directions in discourse and dialogue, pp. 325–353. Springer, Dordrecht (2003). https://doi.org/10.1007/978-94-010-0019-2_15

44. Weindelt, B.: Digital transformation of industries. Tech. rep. World Economic Forum and Accenture (2016)

45. Weizenbaum, J.: Eliza - a computer program for the study of natural language communication between man and machine. Commun. ACM **9**(1), 36–45 (1966). https://doi.org/10.1145/365153.365168

46. Yacoubi, A., Sabouret, N.: Teatime: a formal model of action tendencies in conversational agents. ICAART **2**, 143–153 (2018)

47. Zimmermann, G., Richter, S.-L.: Gründe für die Veränderungsaversion deutscher Versicherungsunternehmen. In: Zimmermann, G. (ed.) Change Management in Versicherungsunternehmen, pp. 11–35. Springer, Wiesbaden (2015). https://doi.org/10.1007/978-3-658-05974-3_2

Author Index

Printed in the United States
By Bookmasters